New Myth, New World

Bernice Glatzer Rosenthal

NEW MYTH, NEW WORLD

FROM NIETZSCHE TO STALINISM

THE PENNSYLVANIA STATE UNIVERSITY PRESS   UNIVERSITY PARK, PENNSYLVANIA

Library of Congress Cataloging-in-Publication Data

Rosenthal, Bernice Glatzer.
    New myth, new world : from Nietzsche to Stalinism /
    Bernice Glatzer Rosenthal.
        p.   cm.
    Includes bibliographical references and index.
    ISBN 0-271-02218-3 (cloth : alk. paper)
    1. Soviet Union—Intellectual life—1917–1970.
    2. Nietzsche, Friedrich Wilhelm, 1844–1900—influence.
    I. Title.

DK266.4 .R67 2002
947.084—dc21   2002005452

The paper used in this publication is both acid-free and totally
chlorine-free (TCF). It meets the minimum requirements of
American National Standard for Information Sciences—Permanence
of Paper for Printed Library Materials,
ANSI Z39.48-1992.

to George L. Kline
Inspiration and Guide

Contents

Illustrations

Acknowledgments

I wish to thank my colleagues for their helpful comments and suggestions. Peter Bergmann, Jeffrey Brooks, Edith Clowes, John Burt Foster, George L. Kline, Robert Maguire, Nina Melechen, Susan Ray, James P. Scanlan, Andrzej Walicki, Richard Wortman, and Reginald Zelnik read the entire manuscript at different stages in its gestation. John Biggart, Abbott Gleason, Louise Loe, and Nina Gurianova read parts of it. Errors of fact or interpretation are, of course, my own. I would also like to thank Edward Kasinec and the staff of the New York Public Library, Slavonic and Baltic Division; Charlotte Labbe and the staff of Fordham University's interlibrary loan office; and Fordham University, for a faculty fellowship. I express my appreciation to the University Seminars at Columbia University for their help in publication. Material in this work was presented to the University Seminars.

Works Frequently Cited

Nietzsche

All references to Nietzsche's works are by page number, not section.

AC   *The Antichrist,* trans. R. J. Hollingdale (Harmondsworth and Baltimore, 1969).

BGE   *Beyond Good and Evil,* trans. W. Kaufmann (New York, 1966).

BT   *The Birth of Tragedy,* trans. W. Kaufmann (New York, 1967).

CW   *The Case of Wagner,* trans. W. Kaufmann (New York, 1967).

D   *Daybreak,* trans. R. J. Hollingdale, (Cambridge, 1982).

EH   *Ecce Homo,* trans. W. Kaufmann (New York, 1967).

GM   *On the Genealogy of Morals,* trans. W. Kaufmann (New York, 1967).

GS   *The Gay Science,* trans. W. Kaufmann (New York, 1974).

H   *On the Advantage and Disadvantage of History for Life,* trans. Peter Preuss (Indianapolis, 1980).

HH   *Human, All Too Human,* 2 vols., trans. R. J. Hollingdale (Cambridge, 1996).

KSA   *Friedrich Nietzsche. Sämtliche Werke. Kritische Studienausgabe,* 15 vols., ed. Giorgio Colli and Mazzino Montinari (Berlin, 1967–77).

PN   *The Portable Nietzsche,* ed. and trans. Walter Kaufmann (New York, 1954).

TI   *Twilight of the Idols,* trans. W. Kaufmann and R. J. Hollingdale (Harmondsworth and Baltimore, 1969).

UT   *Untimely Meditations,* trans. R. J. Hollingdale (Cambridge, 1983).

WP   *The Will to Power,* trans. W. Kaufmann and R. J. Hollingdale (New York, 1968).

Z   *Thus Spoke Zarathustra,* trans. R. J. Hollingdale (Harmondsworth, 1961).

Other

BSS	Aleksandr Blok, *Sobranie sochinenii,* 8 vols. (Moscow-Leningrad, 1960–63).
CM	*Communist Manifesto,* in *The Marx Engels Reader,* ed. Robert C. Tucker (New York, 1978). Quotations from other works in this anthology cited as *MER.*
GSS	Maksim Gor'kii, *Sobranie sochinenii v tridtsati tomakh* (Moscow, 1960).
HM	Nikolai Bukharin, *Historical Materialism* (Ann Arbor, 1969).
IR	N. Ia. Marr, *Izbrannye raboty,* 5 vols. (Moscow, 1933–37).
ISS	*Viacheslav Ivanov: Sobranie sochinenii,* 4 vols. to date, ed. D. V. Ivanov and I. O. Deschartes (Brussels, 1971–79).
KhCW	*Velimir Khlebnikov, Collected Works,* 3 vols., vol. 1, trans. Paul Schmidt, ed. Charlotte Douglas, vols. 2 and 3, trans. Paul Schmidt, ed. Ronald Vroon (Cambridge, Mass., 1987–97).
LCW	*Lenin. Collected Works,* 47 vols. (Moscow-Leningrad, 1960–70).
Literature	Leon Trotsky, *Literature and Revolution* (Ann Arbor, 1971).
LA	*The Lenin Anthology,* ed. Robert C. Tucker (New York, 1975).
LSS	A. V. Lunacharskii, *Sobranie sochinenii v vos'mi tomakh* (Moscow, 1963–1967).
MER	*See CM.*
NR	Bernice Glatzer Rosenthal, ed., *Nietzsche in Russia* (Princeton, 1986).
NSC	Bernice Glatzer Rosenthal, ed., *Nietzsche and Soviet Culture: Ally and Adversary* (Cambridge, Eng., 1994).
MPSS	Dmitrii Merezhkovskii, *Polnoe sobranie sochinenii* (Moscow, 1914).
PSL	H. Scott, ed., *Problems of Soviet Literature* (London, [1935]).
Pervyi	*Pervyi Vsesoiznyi s"ezd sovetskikh pisatelei, 1934. Stenograficheskii otchet,* ed. Ivan Luppol et al. (Moscow, 1934; reprinted 1990).
SW	*J. Stalin. Works.* Vols. 1–13 in English translation (Moscow, 1952–55). This edition is based on the Russian edition of 1946–49. Vols. 14–16 in Russian were reprinted by the Hoover Institute (Stanford, 1966).
RF	Anna Lawton, *Russian Futurism Through Its Manifestoes* (Ithaca, 1988).
VOS	Velimir Khlebnikov, Aleksei Kruchenykh, Mikhail Matiushin, and Kazimir Malevich, *Pobeda nad solntsem* (Petersburg, 1913). Translated into English under the title *Victory Over the Sun* by Ewa Bartos and Victoria Nes Birby, it appeared in *Drama*

Review 15, no. 4 (1971): 107–24. The quotations are from this translation. The introduction (pp. 93–106) includes excerpts from Futurist writings about the production and is cited as *VOS Intro.*

VOS Intro   *See VOS.*

Transliteration follows the Library of Congress system, except that names ending in -ii are transliterated as ending in -y, and the familiar English spellings of the names of such well-known figures as Mayakovsky, Meyerhold, Sinyavsky, and Tolstoy are used.

Introduction

The worst readers. The worst readers are those who
behave like plundering troops; they take away a few
things they can use, dirty and confound the remain-
der, and revile the whole.   —*HH,* 2:245

All the aphorisms of Zarathustra
And the virgin soil of paradoxes.
Elegantly subtle sophistries—
All turned into blood.   —Nikolai Bukharin,
        "The Mad Prophet (Nietzsche)" (1937)

Some of the most powerful ideas are those that are hidden.
This book excavates the long-obscured trail of ideas influenced by Nietzsche that entered into and helped shape
Bolshevism and Stalinism. The excavation begins in late
Imperial Russia, goes through the thickets of the revolutionary and early Soviet periods, and culminates in Stalin's
time.[1] Throughout, Nietzsche's thought was mediated by

1. This books builds on Bernice Glatzer Rosenthal, ed., *Nietzsche
in Russia* (Princeton, 1986), henceforth *NR,* and idem, *Nietzsche and
Soviet Culture: Ally and Adversary* (Cambridge, 1994), henceforth NSC.
See also Edith Clowes, *The Revolution of Moral Consciousness* (DeKalb,
Ill., 1988); Ann Lane, "Nietzsche in Russian Thought" (Ph.D. diss.,
University of Wisconsin, 1976); George L. Kline, "'Nietzschean Marxism'
in Russia," in *Demythologizing Marxism,* ed. Frederich J. Adelmann,
Boston College Studies in Philosophy, vol. 2 (Boston, 1968), 166–83;
and Hans Günther, *Der sozialistische Übermensch: Maksim Gor'kij und
der sowjetische Heldenmythos* (Stuttgart, 1994).

1

Russians who picked up the aspects of it that appealed to them and reconfigured them for their own purposes until they were transformed in ways that obscured their provenance. Without knowledge of Nietzsche's thought, and Russian appropriations, modifications, and embellishments of it before the Bolshevik Revolution, the trail of Nietzschean ideas we will be following is virtually invisible, because for most of the Soviet period, either his name was unmentionable or it could be used only as a pejorative. By Nietzschean ideas, I mean ideas indebted to Nietzsche directly or at one or more removes. One did not have to read Nietzsche to be influenced by him. The pollen of his ideas hung in the atmosphere for decades, fertilizing many Russian and Soviet minds.

Nietzsche's brilliant style and compelling images appealed to people everywhere, Russians included. His quotable aphorisms could be detached from their context and deployed in a variety of ways. "Tell me what you need," Kurt Tucholsky, a German writer, quipped, "and I will supply you with a Nietzsche citation."[2] The bi-polar and complex nature of Nietzsche's thought accommodated contradictory ideas and changing circumstances. Its open-endedness and ambiguity enabled people to read their own meanings into such concepts as the Superman, the "will to power," and "great cultural projects." Nietzsche's works provided intellectual ammunition for a prolonged conflict that was conducted in all areas of Russian life—culture, society, politics—a conflict over *whose* will, values, and ideals would prevail, in *whose* image the society of the future would be shaped.

The works of the "philosopher with a hammer" touched deep cultural chords, reverberating with, reinforcing, and reactivating ideas indigenous to Russia. His striking slogans and memorable images stayed with people long after they read him. Nietzsche was the spark that fused discrete, seemingly contradictory, elements into new amalgams, such as Nietzschean Marxism and Nietzschean Christianity. Some of these were unstable and transitory. Others endured and evolved, but one idea remained constant: art can create a new consciousness, a new human being, a new culture, and a new world. Nietzsche imbued radicals of various persuasions with visions of total transformation against which liberalism and evolutionary Marxism seemed pallid. Nietzsche enthusiasts seized on the eschatological and voluntarist aspects of Marxism to commandeer the existing Russian apocalypticism and to revitalize the voluntaristic and "heroic" aspects of the intelligentsia ethos.

Bolshevik intellectuals did not confine their reading to Marxist works. They knew Russian and European literature and philosophy and kept up with current trends in art and thought. Aspects of Nietzsche's thought were either surprisingly compatible with Marxism or treated issues that Marx and

---

2. Quoted in Steven Aschheim, *The Nietzsche Legacy in Germany* (Berkeley and Los Angeles, 1992), 274.

Engels had neglected. Nietzsche sensitized Bolsheviks committed to reason and science to the importance of the nonrational aspects of the human psyche and to the psychopolitical utility of symbol, myth, and cult. His visions of "great politics" (*grosse Politik*) colored their imaginations. *Politik*, like the Russian word *politika*, means both "politics" and "policy"; *grosse* has also been translated as "grand" or "large scale." The Soviet obsession with creating a new culture stemmed primarily from Nietzsche, Wagner, and their Russian popularizers. Marx and Engels never developed a detailed theory of culture because they considered it part of the superstructure that would change to follow changes in the economic base.

Nietzsche's influence operated below the surface of events, accelerating the repudiation of established authorities and values, nourishing a panoply of utopian doctrines, reinforcing the Promethean aspects of Marxism, and contributing (along with other factors), to an eschatological mood and a free-floating radicalism that worked to the Bolsheviks' advantage in 1917. Nietzsche's thought affected aspects of Stalinism that explanations based on class conflict, rationally calculating "economic man," or modernization theory cannot account for.

Focusing on culture, rather than political events or social structure, I highlight a set of issues that I call the Nietzschean agenda. This agenda was established by his Russian admirers between 1890 and 1917, when Nietzsche could be discussed openly and his thought was russified and absorbed into the culture. Responding to the changes transforming their country, Nietzsche enthusiasts espoused new values and sought a new ideal (in Nietzschean terms, a new myth) by which to live and on which to base their work and transform their world. The other items on the agenda—a quest for a "new word," a new art form, a new ideal of man (and woman), a new morality, a new politics, and a new science—were related to the quest for a new myth. Nietzsche's popularizers shaped the wider culture, disseminating their renditions of his ideas, and raising issues that were debated by Bolsheviks and non-Bolsheviks, and among the Bolsheviks, until the mid 1930s when the Communist Party resolved these issues. For close to half a century, then, the Nietzschean agenda thus passed from one generation to another, each generation offering new answers to the same questions and issues.

Excavating Nietzsche's "buried influence" in the Soviet period presents special problems. It is not just that Nietzsche's influence operated below the surface of events, on the level of values, attitudes, and expectations; there was a good deal of deliberate burying as well. As early as 1908–9, some of his popularizers repudiated him, or claimed to have done so, while continuing to draw on his thought. During World War I, Nietzsche was linked with German militarism. In the early Soviet period, the Bolsheviks ordered his books removed from public libraries and coupled him with "bourgeois decadence" and "bourgeois individualism." In the 1930s, Soviet propagandists labeled Nietzsche the "philosopher of fascism," even while covertly appropriating his ideas. For a person to refer to Nietzsche positively in these years would have been foolhardy, but ideas indebted to Nietzsche were discussed and they affected Bolshevik policy.

Nietzsche's first admirers associated him with authors they deemed his precursors or kindred spirits, forging associative links with such authors as Pushkin or Goethe that were so tenacious and durable that from the 1890s on, discussion of one of these evoked Nietzsche, positively or negatively, depending on the speaker and the situation. Sometimes the linkage encompassed a constellation of authors. Associative linkage was a facet of Nietzsche's reception everywhere, but it was particularly important in Russia, where literature was the primary vehicle for discussing ideas. In the Soviet period, authors formerly paired with Nietzsche were sometimes used as stand-ins for him.

Before World War I, Nietzsche appealed to individuals who were radical by temperament, not just political radicals, but poets, painters, and philosophers who viewed him as a liberator. Many of them regarded Darwin, Marx, and Nietzsche as pilot stars in a constellation of oppositional thinkers. Conservatives, on the other hand, were scandalized by Nietzsche's attack on Christianity. After the war, however, in Western and Central Europe, he was appropriated by the radical right, which stressed the hierarchical and repressive aspects of his thought. A similar transposition occurred in Soviet Russia in the 1930s. Throughout, cultural and historical factors specific to Russia affected how Russians understood Nietzsche and determined which aspects of his thought they emphasized, and which they ignored or rejected, at any particular time.

Nietzschean ideas kept reappearing in Russian and Soviet discussions on literature, art, psychology, social questions, and politics. Their cumulative effect was enormous. If we isolate the Nietzschean components of these discussions, mark each one with a red dot, and connect the dots, we will have delineated the Nietzschean substratum of twentieth-century Russian culture. Russian appropriations of Nietzsche were not simply borrowings or misreadings. They illustrate the creative invention that lies at the heart of the reception process. Russian intellectuals read Nietzsche intensively,[3] making certain texts into bibles, deriving from them principles by which to live and pushing these principles to their ultimate limits. Some Nietzsche enthusiasts assumed that "the new man, the *Übermensch*, would be created in Russia."[4]

---

3. See Matei Calinescu, *Rereadings* (New Haven, 1993), 59–90, for a discussion of the difference between intensive and extensive reading.

4. Alexander Etkind, *The Eros of the Impossible: The History of Psychoanalysis in Russia*, trans. Noah Rubins and Maria Rubins (Boulder, Colo., 1997), 2.

Sverkhchelovek, the Russian word for Superman, has a qualitative connotation, "higher"

Before embarking on the trail of Nietzschean ideas that led from the Silver Age (1890–1917) to Stalin's time, let us first describe the aspects of Nietzsche's thought that his Russian admirers made into an agenda, then limn the culture-specific factors that gave his thought a special relevance for them.

The Nietzschean Agenda

Established by poets, philosophers, and political activists some two decades before the Bolshevik Revolution, the Nietzschean agenda was inspired mainly by *The Birth of Tragedy from the Spirit of Music* (1872), the book in which Nietzsche's aesthetic was most fully developed and other aspects of his thought anticipated. The agenda was cultural but it had political implications, for its central tenet was that art and myth could be used to mobilize the masses or to construct a new culture, a goal of almost all of Nietzsche's Russian admirers. Most of them were also admirers of Wagner (as Nietzsche himself was when he wrote the *Birth of Tragedy*), so they assimilated the *Gesamtkunstwerk* ideal into a Nietzschean framework.[5]

A New Myth

Russian writers and artists learned about Nietzsche when their society was in the first stage of the all-pervasive cultural, political, and social crisis that was to explode in the revolutions of 1905 and 1917. Nietzsche's association of myth with aesthetic creativity and his statement that myth is essential to the health of a culture spoke directly to individuals dissatisfied with positivism and rationalism and seeking a new identity (personal and national) and a new "ruling idea" by which to live.

Nietzsche maintained that rationalism was sapping the vital sources of creativity, that the endless quest for knowledge had annihilated myth and driven poetry "like a homeless being from her natural ideal soil" (*BT*, 106). He predicted the rebirth of tragedy from the (Dionysian) spirit of music, having Beethoven's and Wagner's music in mind, and claimed that myth would restore the German spirit and revitalize German culture. Romantics had been drawing on folk myth and legends for decades, but *The Birth of*

---

or "better," absent from the German word. A Russian scholar, Julia Sineokaya, claims that the Superman was the main problem of Russian philosophy between 1890 and 1917. Iuliia Sineokaia, "Problema sverkhcheloveka u V. Solov'ieva i F. Nitsshe," forthcoming in the proceedings of the conference on Nietzsche and Soloviev, Trier, Germany, March 2001.

5. For Wagner's influence, see Bernice Glatzer Rosenthal, "Wagner and Wagnerian Ideas in Russia," in *Wagnerism in European Culture and Politics*, ed. David Large and William Weber (Ithaca, 1984), 198–245, and Rosamund Bartlett, *Wagner and Russia* (Cambridge, 1995).

Tragedy provided a philosophic rationale for myth at a time when positivism and scientism (the belief that science can answer all questions) dominated European thought, and when both positions assumed that myth is something prescientific and in a sense primitive. In addition to insisting on the centrality of myth for every culture, Nietzsche furnished several compelling new myths: that of the Dionysian and the Apollonian, and in subsequent writings—especially *Thus Spoke Zarathustra*—that of the general myth of the remote historical future as the locus of creativity and value, and the specific myth of the Superman as the creator of cultural values in that future. Nietzsche did not borrow the distinction between Dionysian and Apollonian from the Greeks, for they did not counterpose Dionysus and Apollo. Rather, he derived it from the "agonal principle," which underlies his thought and which was based on the festive *agon* (contest) of ancient Greece, in which only equals competed.[6] Nietzsche's concern for German culture, the German soul, and the German spirit stimulated similar concerns in readers of other nationalities, Russians included.[7]

To be emotionally compelling, a myth needs a visual image, a cult figure, or an icon, as well as heroes and villains. It also needs bold metaphors and emotionally charged symbols and rituals. Nietzsche's appropriators tried to furnish these for their own myths, drawing on Orthodoxy, folklore, and the traditional cults of saints, tsars, and writers.

A New Word

Nietzsche's Russian admirers assumed that the new myth would be expressed in a new language—a "new word" (*novoe slovo*) as symbolist writers put it, basing this assumption, in part, on Nietzsche's connection of word, music, and myth. The ancients, Nietzsche wrote, "took for granted, the *union*, indeed the identity, of the *lyrist* [lyric poet] *with the musician*" (*BT*, 49), because the word, the image, the concept, seeks a musical expression and is imbued with the spirit of music. The language of Greek tragedy changed over time, Nietzsche observed. Once Dionysus enters onto the stage the language becomes Apollonian. Dionysus "no longer speaks through forces, but as an epic hero, almost in the language of Homer" (*BT*, 67). When Dionysus and Apollo finally speak the same language, the "highest goal of tragedy and of all art is attained" (*BT*, 130).

Nietzsche's subsequent pronouncements on the inadequacy of language are foreshadowed in *The Birth of Tragedy*: "The myth does not at all obtain

6. Peter Bergmann, *Nietzsche, "the Last Antipolitical German"* (Bloomington, 1987), 60–64, 75–76, 87.

7. Bernice Glatzer Rosenthal, "Nietzsche, Nationality, Nationalism," in *East Europe Reads Nietzsche*, ed. Alice Freifeld, Peter Bergmann, and Bernice Glatzer Rosenthal (Boulder, Colo., 1998), 181–206.

adequate objectification in the spoken word" (*BT,* 105). Language can never adequately render the cosmic significance of music. The poet "can express nothing that did not already lie hidden in that vast universality and absoluteness in the music that compelled him to figurative speech" (*BT,* 55). In his "Attempt at a Self-Criticism," the preface to the 1886 edition of *The Birth of Tragedy,* Nietzsche wrote, "It should have sung, this 'new soul,' and not spoken!" His target was dry, rational philosophy. He did not necessarily intend to disparage the spoken word, but the statement could be understood that way.

In *On the Genealogy of Morals,* Nietzsche asked: "*What light does linguistics, and especially the study of etymology, throw on the history of the evolution of moral concepts?*" (*GM,* 55). He answered his own question by an archaeology of words—"good," "bad," "debt," "guilt," "noble," "base"— each containing an entire world of hidden or buried meanings. In the same essay, he emphasized the linguistic sources of morality, distinguishing between a "noble" or a "master" morality of "good and bad" and a "slave morality" of "good and evil." Showing how words gain and lose meaning, *On the Genealogy of Morals* exemplifies Nietzsche's view of the malleability of language and myth and their interrelatedness. Here and in other works, Nietzsche connected language with power, mentioning Adam's "God-given" right to name the animals and the power of the "master" to assign values by calling things "good" and "bad" and to give names to his slaves. In *Zarathustra,* Nietzsche expressed contempt for "old words" learned from fools and liars (*Z,* 119).

The expression "new word" has obvious biblical overtones. "In the beginning was the Word" (John 1:1) and "the Word was made flesh and dwelt among us" (John 1:14). To the apocalyptically oriented Russian symbolists, the term "new word" meant a new world, a new dispensation, the Second Coming of Christ. "The word" also had an incantational or magical connotation, for the symbolists were drawn to occult doctrines, as were the Nietzschean Marxists Anatoly Lunacharsky and Maksim Gorky. The biblical and occult connotations do not contradict the Nietzschean: rather, they intertwine with and mutually reinforce them. Nietzsche himself used biblical language, albeit to subvert the Bible. He exalted the "magic transformation" of the chorus effected by the Dionysian dithyrambs (*BT,* 64) and credited magicians, alchemists, astrologers, and witches for creating a thirst "for hidden and forbidden powers" without which the sciences would not have originated and grown (*GS,* 240). The symbolists believed that "the word" had theurgic properties; a "new word" could generate a new world. The "new word" can also have a political implication; it can be a "directing" or "order-bringing word" pronounced by a higher authority.[8]

8.   I am indebted to Halju Bennett for this observation; letter to author, May 19, 2000.

A New Art Form

Russians were impressed by Nietzsche's distinction between two types of aesthetic energies or impulses, dream and intoxication, symbolized by Apollo and Dionysus. Apollo connotes clarity, harmony, measure, the form-giving power that engenders illusions, images, and visions and, on different levels, reason, structure, organization, individuation, self-discipline, and sublimation. Sculpture is the quintessentially Apollonian art, but the Apollonian impulse is also expressed in words. Conversely, Dionysus connotes dissolution, formlessness, chaos, ceaseless creativity, and destruction and, on different levels, ecstasy, excitement, boundless energy, liberation of the passions, loss of self-consciousness, and the trespassing of limits and norms. Its artistic expression is music (even though Apollo was the Greek god of music) and dance—the frenzied Dionysian dithyrambs which transform the chorus into "timeless servants of their god who live outside the spheres of society . . . a community of unconscious actors who consider themselves and one another transformed" (*BT*, 64). Nietzsche distinguished between the continuous and piercing Dionysian sound of the aulos, a kind of flute,[9] and the Apollonian sound of the kithara, a kind of harp, which produces pleasant, distinct notes. He also distinguished between the Bacchantes, who forgot their very identities in their ecstasies, and the virgins in the procession to the Temple of Apollo, who "remain what they are and retain their civic names" (*BT*, 64). Most of Nietzsche's first admirers considered the Dionysian aspects of his thought liberating.

Like male and female, the Apollonian and Dionysian impulses unite and in their unions give birth to new and more powerful forms. One of the first was lyric poetry. A later union produced Attic tragedy, Aeschylus' and Sophocles' dramatizations of the Greek myths, which Nietzsche traced to the cult of Dionysus. In fully developed Attic tragedy, he explained, Dionysus appeared on the stage; the actors wore masks to represent Apollonian visions; and the myths of the Homeric world were reborn. Music invested them with a new and more powerful significance, and the characters expanded into eternal (mythic) types. Precise delineation of individual traits and psychological refinement, as in the plays of Euripides, represented the triumph of realism in drama and the end of myth. Nietzsche considered music and tragic myth expressions of the Dionysian (creative) capacity of a people and maintained that myth and creativity are inseparable. The degeneration of one entails the deterioration of the other. When Nietzsche wrote *The Birth of Tragedy,* he believed, following Wagner, that the disintegration of Greek tragedy into separate art forms presaged the decline of classical Greece. He

9. There may have also been a reed aulos. Musicians are usually depicted as playing two *auloi* simultaneously. One aulos was probably used as a drone, and the other as a chanter, or melody pipe. It is ancestral to the bagpipe.

expected future unions of Apollo and Dionysus to engender new art forms. Russian modernists (the symbolists and their successors) agreed. The Nietzschean Marxist Aleksandr Bogdanov insisted that the proletariat must create its own art form in order to liberate itself psychologically from the bourgeoisie.

A New Man (and Woman)

The creation of "new people" (*novye liudi*) or a "new man" (*novyi chelovek*) was a goal of Russian radicals since the 1860s. The word *chelovek* is gender neutral, and can also be translated "person" or "human being," but Nietzsche's Russian admirers (with some notable exceptions), were talking mostly about men. They endowed their "new man" with traits that Nietzsche admired—beauty, autonomy, daring, creativity, and in some cases, hardness, and they shared Nietzsche's contempt for "ultimate man" (*der letzte Mensch*, literally the "last man"), one who seeks security, comfort, and happiness (Z, 45–47).

Nietzsche was disgusted with the men of his day. In *The Birth of Tragedy*, he called for a purification of the German character and invoked, among other things, romantic notions of German knights. In *Zarathustra*, written a decade after his break with Wagner, he predicted the emergence in the distant future of a Superman, a being that would regard man as man now regards the ape, a painful embarrassment and a laughingstock (Z, 42). The Superman's antipode is not the sub-man (*Übermensch*) but the "most contemptible ultimate man." Nietzsche considered himself and Wagner (in his pro-Wagner period) free spirits (*freie Geister*), not Supermen. The "higher man" is a kind of "free spirit" and a prelude to the Superman. In the section "Of the Higher Man" in *Thus Spoke Zarathustra* (Z, 299–306), Nietzsche described him as "stout-hearted," "open-hearted," "evil," "selfish," autonomous, possessed of great will, and able to endure great suffering, but also able to laugh and to dance. Zarathustra also extols hardness: "All creators are hard" (Z, 231). *Mensch*, the German word for "man" or "person," is gender neutral, but Nietzsche meant men even though he did not use "man" in the gendered sense (*Mann*). He said little about women, but what he did say was mostly negative. He never speaks of a "higher woman" or *Überfrau*.

Nietzsche was not a proponent of individualism as we understand it. On the contrary. For him, the rebirth of Dionysus augured a welcome *end* to individualism, to "a world torn asunder and shattered into individuation." He extolled the "*mystery doctrine of tragedy,* the fundamental knowledge of the oneness of everything existent, the conception of individuation as the primal cause of evil, and of art as the joyous hope that the spell of individuation may be broken in augury of a restored oneness" (*BT,* 74). In the

Dionysian rites, the union between man and man is reaffirmed, and the mysterious primeval unity of man and nature is restored. "In song and in dance man expresses himself as a member of a higher community; he has forgotten how to walk and speak and is on the way toward flying into the air, dancing ... he feels himself a god, he himself now walks about enchanted, in ecstasy, like the gods he saw walking in his dreams. He is no longer an artist; he has become a work of art" (*BT*, 37). Nietzsche later repudiated these romantic notions of a mysterious oneness, but not his apotheosis of art. In *Zarathustra*, he expanded the idea of man as a work of art to denote a man who creates himself, defines his own values, affirms himself against the vulgar herd.

Although Nietzsche recognized that the high culture that he prized is created by strong individuals, he did not believe that individuals have intrinsic value as such. His emphasis is on the species "man," not on individual well-being or happiness. "Man is a bridge and not a goal" (*Z*, 215). "Man is something that should be overcome" (*Z*, 41; "must be overcome," 216 and 279). Nietzsche's concern was not "the degree of freedom that is granted to the one or to the other or to all, but the degree of *power* that the one or the other should exercise over others or over all, and [the extent to which] a sacrifice of freedom, even enslavement, provides the basis for the emergence of a *higher type*" (*WP*, 458).

In *Genealogy of Morals,* he mentioned a work in progress, to be titled *The Will to Power: Attempt at a Revaluation of All Values* (160). After Nietzsche died, his sister rearranged his notes into four "books," each subdivided into chapters, to imply an argument, and published them as *The Will to Power*. Colli and Montinari, and Karl Schlechta before them, excluded *The Will to Power* from their editions of his collected works, but it cannot be excluded from a study of his reception because, rightly or wrongly, it was widely regarded as his last word. Book 3, "Principles of a New Evaluation," is subdivided into "The Will to Power as Knowledge," "The Will to Power in Nature," "The Will to Power as Society and Individual" and "The Will to Power as Art." Boris Groys contends that Stalinism realized the avant-garde's vision of the will to power as art.[10] I find a "will to power" in other figures indebted to Nietzsche, not just with respect to art but in the other three categories as well. Political activists wanted power to implement (or impose) their ideals.

A New Morality

The first Russian discussions of Nietzsche counterposed his amoralism to Christian or Kantian morality, or conflated it with Marx and Engels's contempt for "bourgeois morality." In *The Birth of Tragedy,* Nietzsche criti-

---

10. Boris Groys, *The Total Art of Stalinism,* trans. Charles Rougle (Princeton, 1992).

cized "abstract morality" (morality "untutored by myth," 135) and claimed that the purpose of tragic myth is the aesthetic transformation of life, not instruction in morality (141). In "An Attempt at a Self-Criticism," he asked: "What, seen in the perspective of *life,* is the significance of morality?" He reminded readers that in the preface to the first edition of *The Birth of Tragedy,* he had presented "art and *not* morality [as] the truly *metaphysical* activity of man" (BT, 22). In *Zarathustra,* he said that "creators" are those who smash the "old tables of values" and inscribe "new values on new tables"—values that affirm life on earth (51–52). In *Genealogy of Morals,* he distinguished between the Judeo-Christian "slave morality" of passivity, *ressentiment,* and instinctual repression and the "noble morality" of creativity, self-affirmation, activism, and instinctual release. *Ressentiment* can be creative, however, if it gives birth to new values. "While every noble morality develops from a triumphant affirmation of itself, slave morality from the outset says No to what is 'outside,' what is 'different,' what is 'not itself' and *this* NO is its creative deed" (*GM,* 36).

Like Schopenhauer, Nietzsche assumed an irrational universe in which blind will is the only constant. But Schopenhauer preached a Christian/ Buddhist ethic and taught that man can escape suffering only by asceticism, which deadens the will, or by aestheticism, immersion in art. The "will to power" epitomizes Nietzsche's repudiation of Schopenhauer's quietism, but not of Schopenhauer's irrationalism. Nietzsche stressed self-mastery, sometimes to the point of asceticism, but his asceticism was an affirmation of the will, not its denial. He even called asceticism a "gymnastics of the soul" (*WP,* 483). In *On the Genealogy of Morals, Beyond Good and Evil, Twilight of the Idols,* and *The Will to Power,* Nietzsche connected ethics with ontology and epistemology. There is no absolute morality because there is no objective reality, no eternal truth.

A New Politics

Nietzsche detested democracy, liberalism, socialism, and the "*petty* politics" of European particularism (*EH,* 321), but he never offered a comprehensive political theory or political program. His scattered political pronouncements support extreme positions—anarchism at one end, a repressive superstate at the other. In Russia, as elsewhere in Europe, the libertarian aspects of Nietzsche's thought were stressed before World War I and the statist aspects later on.

In his early writings, Nietzsche praised the revolutionary character of Dionysus, but after 1871, appalled by the Paris Commune, he depoliticized the Dionysian by identifying the political exclusively with the Apollonian. In Peter Bergmann's words: "The Dionysian was no longer to be an eruptive, emancipatory force capable of transforming society, but was instead to be a cult of a select and elite brotherhood."[11] Tracy Strong has a different view: for Nietzsche, the state is "an Apollonian scrim on which dangerous Dionysian understandings are transvalued into culture . . . or exteriorized into warfare." In the *agon,* "the chaos lurking in desire for domination and in domination itself is refracted in a healthy manner, such that political stability and continuity—the prerequisite for culture—be ensured."[12] In Nietzsche's last works, the state has changed from an arena of power to an instrument of power.

In *Zarathustra,* Nietzsche called the nationalistic state "the new idol" and seemed to champion anarchism. "The state is the coldest of all cold monsters. Coldly it lies, too; and this lie creeps from its mouth: 'I, the state, am the people'" (75). Deeming Bismarck's "great politics" antagonistic to culture, Nietzsche noted that Athenian, Renaissance, and classical German culture developed in the absence of a powerful state. Later on, however, Nietzsche predicted an entirely new form of politics, a *"great politics"* of apocalyptic upheavals and convulsions (*EH,* 327), a "fight for dominion of the earth—the *compulsion* to large-scale politics" (*BGE,* 131).

> From now on there will be more favorable preconditions for more comprehensive forms of dominion, whose like has never yet existed. And even this is not the most important thing; the possibility has been established for the production of international racial unions whose task will be to rear a master race, the future "masters of the earth";— a new tremendous aristocracy, based on the severest self-legislation, in which the will of philosophical men of power and artist-tyrants will be made to endure for millennia—a higher kind of man who, thanks to their superiority in will, knowledge, riches, and influence, employ democratic Europe as their most pliant and supple instrument for getting hold of the destinies of the earth, so as to work as artists upon "man" himself. Enough: the time is coming when politics will have a different meaning. (*WP,* 504)

This kind of "great politics" would create the conditions for great cultural projects that would take thousands of years to complete. "Whole portions of the earth can dedicate themselves to conscious experimentation."[13] Nietzsche's view of Russia did not go far beyond the traditional and already commonplace German attitude toward that gigantic and mysterious enigma in the East.[14] He admired and feared the "strength to will" that he discerned

---

11. Bergmann, *Nietzsche,* 86–87.
12. Tracy Strong, *Friedrich Nietzsche and the Politics of Transfiguration* (Berkeley and Los Angeles, 1988), 194.
13. Quoted in ibid., 215.
14. Susan Ray, "Afterword: Nietzsche's View of Russia and the Russians, in *NR,* 393.

in Imperial Russia, which could be discharged as a "will to negate or a will to affirm" (*BGE*, 131), and praised Russia as the "*only* power today . . . which can still promise something—Russia, the antithesis of that pitiable European petty-state politics and nervousness" (*TI*, 93). He might have responded similarly to Soviet Russia.

A New Science

Russians hostile to positivism and rationalism appreciated Nietzsche's prediction of the imminent collapse of science, but they ignored his statements in support of reason and science and his belief that science is a supporter of life. (The German and the Russian words for science, *Wissenschaft* and *nauka*, include the social sciences and humanities, not just the physical sciences.) Nietzsche respected scientists and kept up with developments in chemistry and physics; it was scientism that he opposed (*BT*, 106). For Nietzsche, the scientist's "will to truth" was an attempt to endow life with meaning and purpose (*GM*, 151, 159–63). In *The Birth of Tragedy*, he raised the issue of science as a "*new* problem . . . science considered for the first time as problematic, as questionable" (*BT*, 18). Since it is impossible to know a constantly changing reality, science is limited and at its limits "must turn into art—*which is really the aim of this mechanism*; [its function] is to make existence appear comprehensible and thus justified; and if reasons do not suffice, myth has to come to their aid in the end—myth which I have just called the necessary consequence, indeed the purpose of science" (*BT*, 95–96). In other words, science is a function of myth.

Paradoxically, in *Beyond Good and Evil*, Nietzsche advocated a kind of scientific naturalism. "To translate man back into nature . . . to see to it that man henceforth stands before man as even today, *hardened in the discipline of science* [emphasis added], he stands before the *rest* of nature, with intrepid Oedipus eyes and sealed Odysseus ears, deaf to the siren songs of old metaphysical bird-catchers who have been piping at him too long, 'you are more, you are higher, you are of a different origin!'" (*BGE*, 161). In *The Antichrist*, he praised the scientific method and "*the sense for facts*, the last-developed and most valuable of all the senses" (*AC*, 182).

In *The Will to Power*, Nietzsche attacked the Newtonian worldview, Locke's pain-pleasure psychology, and Darwin's theory of evolution (because it diminishes man by emphasizing mere survival rather than creativity and growth). He also attacked the concepts of causality, logic, and objectivity, declaring that truth is not discovered, but created, and that science is an interpretation which, like all interpretations, depends on one's perspective. The world is a human construct, a simplification that falsifies by reducing "the confusing multiplicity to a purposive and manageable schema" (*WP*, 315). Most Russians passed over the implications of Nietzsche's views on the nature and conduct of science. The Nietzschean Marxist Aleksandr

Bogdanov did not. He advocated a new proletarian science, for unlike Marx and Engels, who considered the physical sciences objective, Bogdanov regarded all the sciences as functions of myth.

Nietzsche's influence was not confined to the foregoing. Russian thought was permeated with images and slogans derived from his works, most notably the "will to power," which Nietzsche called the "strongest, most-life affirming drive" (*GM*, 135). He associated it with creativity and claimed that it is manifested in great works of art and in the creation of new values and a new culture. He also used the term to denote power over people and the enjoyment thereof. "The will of the weaker persuades it to serve the stronger; its will wants to be master of those weaker still: this delight alone it is unwilling to forgo" (*Z*, 138).

Culture-Specific Factors in Nietzsche's Appeal

Nietzsche's challenge to prevailing myths and values, and to all established authorities, struck Russian intellectuals of the fin de siècle with particular force because they were seeking new myths that would revitalize the culture, reintegrate society, and transform their world. Like their predecessors, these intellectuals looked to Germany for the latest philosophical word. Many of them read German; some had lived there. Culture-specific factors enhanced Nietzsche's relevance to Russians. Aspects of his thought were surprisingly compatible with Orthodoxy, the state religion, which was taught in the schools.

Russian intellectuals were questioning the existence of God and justifying transgressions of conventional morality well before anyone had ever heard of Nietzsche. Indeed, several nineteenth-century Russian writers and political activists had so many ideational affinities (in Russian eyes) with Nietzsche that they were later regarded as his precursors. The ethos of the intelligentsia intersected with Nietzsche's thought at key points and predisposed the most radical *intelligenty* to welcome his extremism and his apotheosis of will.

The German authors to whom Nietzsche responded were part of the cultural baggage of Russian intellectuals too. Sturm und Drang writers, German romantics, and Hegel were assimilated into Russian culture in the first half of the nineteenth century. Schiller's plays, with their rebel heroes, his essay *On the Aesthetic Education of Man* (1795), and Goethe's forever-striving, amoral Faust helped prepare the soil in which Nietzsche's ideas took root.

Hegel posited a rational Divine Idea working dialectically through history to reconcile subject and object, being and thought, God and the world. His historicism was essentially a theodicy; unlike Marx, he never tried to predict the future course of history. Rather, he maintained that "what is real is rational and what is rational is real." He defined "freedom" as the recognition of necessity (a definition that passed into Marxism), and called the Prussian state the Divine Idea as it exists on earth.[15] He praised "world-historical individuals"—figures such as Alexander the Great, Julius Caesar, and Napoleon—who move history forward, impelled by "necessity" and the "cunning of reason." They are "devoted, come what may, to one purpose. Therefore, such men may treat other great and even sacred interests inconsiderately—a conduct which indeed subjects them to moral reprehension. But so mighty a figure must trample down many an innocent flower, crush to pieces many things in its path." Similarly: "They stand outside of morality. The litany of the private virtues of modesty, humility, love, and charity must not be raised against them."[16] To some Russians, Hegel epitomized abstract rationalism and remorseless historicism. Nietzsche used and misused Hegel, taking from him the emphasis on historical becoming and transforming the concept of the "world-historical individual" into that of the Superman, except that Hegel's figure has already lived, while the Superman is to appear in the remote world-historical future.[17]

In the early 1840s, Hegelians divided into "right Hegelians," who accepted "reality," and "left Hegelians," who demanded radical change. Ludwig Feuerbach, Max Stirner, and Karl Marx were "left Hegelians." A few years later, Marx "turned Hegel on his head" to emphasize socioeconomic forces rather than ideas. The leading Russian "left Hegelians" were the anarchist Mikhail Bakunin (1814–76), whom Russian intellectuals of the fin de siècle later called a "Nietzschean before Nietzsche"; the radical literary critic Vissarion Belinsky (1811–48), formerly a "right Hegelian"; and Aleksandr Herzen (1812–70), who called Hegel's dialectic "the algebra of revolution." Herzen's fulminations against Western European philistinism (*meshchanstvo*) were quoted by Russian Nietzscheans and may have actually influenced Nietzsche.[18] Herzen is best known for his belief that the Russian peasant commune (the *mir*) could serve as the basis of a libertarian socialism that would enable Russia to avoid capitalism. He championed "individuality" (self-expression or self-realization within a community), as opposed to atomistic

15. Politically, Hegel was an exponent of a *Rechtsstaat* (a state governed by law), and a liberal in the German context. The Prussian state that he extolled was not the Prussia of 1848, still less that of 1914, but a relatively enlightened polity. This synopsis does not do justice to the full range of Hegel's impact on Russia. He was a major influence on Russian liberalism and on the state school of Russian historiography.

16. G.W.F. Hegel, *Reason in History* (Indianapolis, 1953), 43, 83.

17. George L. Kline, "The Use and Abuse of Hegel by Nietzsche and Marx," in *Hegel and His Critics: Philosophy in the Aftermath of Hegel,"* ed. William Desmond (Albany, 1989), 2–3.

18. George L. Kline, "Foreword," in *NR*, xv–xvi.

individualism, and refused to sacrifice living individuals to an idol of progress. Some turn-of-the-century Russian anarchists linked Herzen with Nietzsche, even though Herzen advocated humaneness and Nietzsche did not. Also associated with Nietzsche (not necessarily by the same people) were Feuerbach, who maintained that god is a human construct, and Max Stirner, advocate of egoistic anarchism.

Kant, Marx, and Schopenhauer were assimilated into Russian thought in the second half of the century. Kant's "morality of duty" was propounded by populists (advocates of a Russian form of socialism) and Tolstoy, and adamantly rejected by Nietzsche enthusiasts. Marxism deepened the populists' determination to avoid capitalism. It was two populists who translated *Capital* into Russian in 1872. Schopenhauer influenced Ivan Turgenev, Fedor Sologub, and the poets Innokenty Annensky and Afanasy Fet; the last three were also interested in Nietzsche. Dmitry Merezhkovsky, initiator of Russian symbolism, considered Nietzsche an antidote to the Schopenhauerian pessimism that enveloped the intelligentsia in the 1880s. Nevertheless, Schopenhauer's antirationalism paved the way for Nietzsche's.

Orthodox Christianity, and the values and attitudes derived from it, permeated Russian culture, affecting even nonbelievers who had imbibed it in childhood. And it was Orthodox theologians who had associated rationalism with the "Latin West" (the Roman Catholic West) and then with the West of the Enlightenment, an association that Slavophiles perpetuated. Roman Catholic theology incorporated the Roman concept of "natural law," which John Locke reformulated as "natural rights"—life, liberty, and property—guaranteed by a social contract. Slavophiles rejected both Western "legalism" and the social contract. Some Nietzsche-influenced fin de siècle intellectuals further linked rationalism with the "bourgeois" West. A factor in this linkage was the Orthodox presumption of a universe of dynamic becoming, which is closer to Nietzsche's Heraclitean epistemology than it is to Newton's mechanical universe, the epistemological basis of the Enlightenment. In line with the mystical orientation of Orthodoxy, many of Nietzsche's first admirers perceived him as a mystic and a prophet.

Orthodoxy distinguishes between Divine Essence (*ousia*) and Divine Energies (*energeia*). The Divine Essence is unapproachable, but Divine Energies imbue all God's creation, including man. If Divine Essence is removed, and teleology along with it, we have Nietzsche's Dionysian universe, a world without the Logos. Also crucial in shaping Russian responses to Nietzsche were the doctrines of transfiguration and deification, the kenotic Christ, the Orthodox ontology of wholeness, and its apotheosis of Beauty.

The Orthodox doctrine of transfiguration pertains to the body as well as the soul, and to matter as well as spirit. Transfiguration is associated with radiant beauty, the radiance of the uncreated light of Mount Tabor (Matthew

17:1–4, Mark 9:2–14, Luke 9:28–36), and is closely linked with the Orthodox concept of deification. Just as the flesh of Christ had been transfigured to glory, so too would the flesh of the redeemed. The Greek Fathers "dared to speak of 'deification' (in Greek *theosis*). If man is to share in God's glory, they argued, if he is to be 'perfectly one' with God, this means in effect that man must be 'deified'; he is called to become by grace what God is by nature." Or, as was said at the first Nicene Council, "God became man that we might be made God."[19]

Far from being an esoteric theological construct, the concept that "we may be made God" formed the cornerstone of Orthodox mysticism, sacramental theology, soteriology (the doctrine of salvation through Jesus Christ), and Incarnation theology. Orthodoxy emphasizes the authority inherent in the body of the faithful (the *oikoumene*) by virtue of their participation in and identification with God. By contrast, Catholicism and Protestantism emphasize the subjection of individuals to a concrete authority, an infallible pope or Scripture. The vesting of authority in the *oikoumene* has communitarian, egalitarian, and democratic implications.

Transfiguration and deification were interwoven in hesychasm, a strain of Orthodox monasticism. Hesychasts believed that after the Last Judgment, the entire universe, people and matter, would be transfigured, or transformed into something radiantly beautiful.[20] (*Preobrazhenie*, the Russian word for "transfiguration," also means "transformation.") In the mid-nineteenth century, hesychasm was perpetuated by the Elders of Optina Pustyn Monastery.[21]

Optina Pustyn became a center of pilgrimage, attracting such luminaries of Russian culture as the Slavophiles Aleksei Khomiakov (1804–60) and Ivan Kireevsky (1806–56); the writers Konstanin Leontiev (1831–91), Fedor Dostoevsky (1821–81), and (Leo) Lev Tolstoy (1828–1910); and the philosopher Vladimir Soloviev (1853–1900). Through these authors, aspects of hesychasm filtered into the lay culture, but with an emphasis on beauty rather than on rules. Hesychasts observed the strict rules of monastic life. Without Church discipline, however, the doctrine of deification can nourish visions of an amoral Superman, a free spirit above the law, which it did in certain fin de siècle intellectuals with the help of Nietzsche.

---

19. Timothy Ware, *The Orthodox Church* (Baltimore, 1963), 29. See also John Meyendorff, *St. Gregory Palamas and Orthodox Spirituality* (Crestwood, N.Y., 1974); Jaroslav Pelikan, *The Christian Tradition* (Chicago, 1977), 2:11, 263; and Vladimir Lossky, *The Mystical Theology of the Eastern Church* (Crestwood, N.Y., 1976), 9–10.

20. I discuss hesychasm in more detail in "Orthodox Christianity and Nietzsche: Elective Affinities," forthcoming in the proceedings of the Trier Conference.

21. The Elder (*Starets*, the term connotes spiritual authority, not age) is a characteristic figure in Orthodox monasticism. He receives no special ordination or appointment to this role, but is guided to it by the direct inspiration of the Spirit and advises people on moral or spiritual questions through his special gift or charisma.

Kenosis means "emptying" in Greek, "the 'self-emptying abasement of the Son of God,' the renunciation of His own will in order to accomplish the will of the Father, by his obedience to Him unto death and the Cross."[22] The image of the kenotic Christ (the humiliated and suffering Christ, as distinct from the Pantokrator or victorious Christ) pervades Russian spirituality, culture, and literature.[23] We see it in the canonization of the young Kievan princes Boris and Gleb because they submitted meekly to their murderers, even refusing an opportunity to escape; in St. Seraphim of Sarov (canonized in 1903), who was beaten by robbers, but offered no resistance and refused to testify at their trial; and in Dostoevsky's belief in redemption through suffering. To Dostoevsky, suffering had positive value as part of a Christian morality of humility and love; it was not just something to be endured if necessary. Nietzsche's first admirers rejected the "slavish" kenotic values of humility, self-sacrifice, and asceticism, but some of them rehabilitated self-sacrifice later on in a new framework.

Orthodox ontology presumes organic wholeness, which it conflates with beauty. The Russian word for ugly, *bezobraznyi,* literally means "formless," and implies violation of the divine order in which man is made in the image and likeness of God (Genesis 1:26–27). Self-assertion shatters the wholeness of being. The Orthodox ontology of wholeness made the Slavophiles receptive to German romanticism (which counterposed organic wholeness to Newtonian mechanism and abstract rationalism) and underlines the Slavophile concept of *sobornost',* a Christian community united in love and freedom, which stems from the biblical notion of the unity of all believers in the mystical body of Christ (Ephesians 1:23). The Orthodox apotheosis of beauty is conveyed in Leontiev's aestheticism, in Dostoevsky's conviction that "beauty will save the world"; in Soloviev's assertion that "beauty is saving the world," that is to say, the process of salvation has already begun; and more remotely, in Tolstoy's didactic aesthetic (art must be morally uplifting and inspire brotherly love), and in the philosophy of Nikolai Fedorov (1828–1903). The same ontology underlies Soloviev's concepts of total unity (*vseedinstvo*) and Godmanhood (*Bogochelovechestvo*) (see Chapter 1). All of these authors were later associated with Nietzsche, although for different reasons.

Leontiev was called the "Russian Nietzsche" because of his aestheticism, his unabashed elitism, and his valorization of power, even though he rejected a Nietzschean "love for the most distant" (*Fernstenliebe*) and championed Good Samaritanism. For Leontiev, beauty was romantic disharmony, picturesque contrasts marked by an exuberant variety that cohered in a unity of opposites that he called form. Universal history was a triune process of development: primitive unity, exuberant growth and flowering complexity

22. Lossky, *Mystical Theology,* 144.
23. Natalia Gorodetsky, *The Humiliated Christ in Russian Thought* (New York, 1938).

(feudalism), and "secondary simplification and decay" (the modern age). Liberalism and democracy were symptoms of decay; social mobility should be prevented so that the creative minority could cultivate an aesthetic world-view.[24] All his life, Leontiev struggled between aestheticism and Orthodoxy, opting for Orthodoxy shortly before his death—not the "rosy" Christianity of Dostoevsky and Tolstoy, based on universal love, but a dark version of Christianity, based on a fear of God. His thought appealed to aesthetes and elitists who admired Nietzsche.

Dostoevsky opposed all forms of determinism, including the impersonal laws of nature and historical "necessity." His characters revolt against God, and they refuse to accept the constraints of empirical reality and the human condition. He exposed the dark side of the human psyche and predicted the advent of a demonic "man-god" (later interpreted as an amoral superman). Nietzsche himself said that Dostoevsky was the only psychologist from whom he ever learned anything. More than any other single figure, Dostoevsky prepared Russians for Nietzsche. Some Russians considered these authors spiritual twins; others considered them polar opposites. In either case, each was responding, in his own way, to the fading of institutional Christianity. To describe the parallels and divergences in their views would require a separate book.

Tolstoy's Gospel Christianity of nonviolence and brotherly love, his didactic aesthetic, his preachments of sexual abstinence, even in marriage, led many of his contemporaries to view him as Nietzsche's antipode, especially since he attacked Nietzsche. In *What Is Art?* Tolstoy accused him of unleashing the animal instincts in people.[25] In *The Kreutzer Sonata*, he initiated a debate on Christian attitudes to sex that was soon framed in Nietzschean terms.

Fedorov offered his own version of transfiguration and deification—a vast project of universal salvation that featured resurrection of the dead by means of science, to be initiated and supervised by a tsar-autocrat—which he called the "Common Task." After everyone was resurrected, humankind would pass from the "moral" stage of its development to the "aesthetic" stage, in which all would be united into one harmonious society and, possessing complete control over nature, would create collective works of art on a cosmic scale. Despite Fedorov's strenuous objections to Nietzsche, the "Common Task" is comparable to a Nietzschean great cultural project, and there are other affinities in their thought, such as, for example, contempt for inactivity.[26] Nietzsche believed that only slaves need a sabbath. Fedorov taught that by working together for many generations in developing science

24. George Ivask, ed., *Konstantine Leontiev, Against the Grain. Selections from the Novels, Essays, Notes, and Letters of Konstantine Leontiev* (New York, 1969), x–xi, 116, 148–49, 160, 208, 210.

25. *What Is Art?* trans. Maude Almyer (Indianapolis, 1960), 165–66.

26. Taras Zakydalsky, "Fedorov's Critique of Nietzsche," in *NR*, 113–25. For Fedorov's

and technology, humankind could eventually attain sufficient control over nature to realize paradise on earth. He envisioned changing the climate, cloning, solar energy, and space travel. But to achieve paradise on earth, people would have to stop procreating and devote all their energy to resurrecting the dead; this was a moral obligation based on brotherly love. Everyone would have to participate. Fedorov talked mostly about resurrecting the dead "fathers." He viewed women as temptresses and opposed sex because it would distract people from the "Common Task." His resurrected beings would have no sex organs. Dostoevsky, Tolstoy, and Soloviev esteemed Fedorov as a human being and as a thinker. After he died, Fedorov's disciples collected his reflections and published them as *The Philosophy of the Common Task (Filosofiia obshchego dela,* 2 vols., 1906, 1913). Somehow, for the circulation was miniscule, his ideas became known to symbolists, Nietzschean Marxists, and early Soviet technocrats, inspiring aestheticized or technologized utopias and visions of an immortal Superman.

Equally important in affecting Russian responses to Nietzsche was the ethos of the Russian intelligentsia, a movement born in the mid-nineteenth century that was comprised mainly of sons and daughters of the nobility and sons of priests (Orthodox priests can marry, but must do so before their ordination)[27] who devoted their lives to transforming Russia. Although many *intelligenty* were atheists, they accepted the kenotic values of self-sacrifice, humility, and love, secularizing these values in a distinctive subculture that was passed on, with important modifications, from one generation of young people to the next, and which functioned as a surrogate religion, giving believers an ideal by which to live. They were obsessed with ideas, turning them into ideologies of salvation.

The *intelligenty* encompassed revolutionaries and gradualists, moralists and immoralists, terrorists and do-gooders, would-be dictators and anarchists. Just about all *intelligenty* believed that the human will could override impersonal socioeconomic processes and "historical laws." Proselytizing their beliefs with great intensity, they judged art and literature by moral, political, and social criteria and disdained compromise as a moral failing.

The ideologies of the intelligentsia were nihilism, populism, and Marxism, in that order. Nihilists insisted that the corrupt old society had to be completely destroyed before a new one could be built. Resolutely antiromantic, they espoused materialism, scientism, rationalism, a realist aesthetic, and a

---

philosophy, see George Young, *Nikolai Fedorov* (Belmont, Mass., 1979); Michael Hagemeister, *Nikolaj Fedorov* (Munich, 1989); Svetlana Semenova, *Nikolai Fedorov: Tvorchestvo zhizni* (Moscow, 1990); and Irene Masing-Delic, *Abolishing Death* (Stanford, 1992).

27. The Orthodox clergy is divided into "white clergy," who can marry, and the celibate "black clergy." Only the latter could rise in the church hierarchy to become bishops and eventually patriarchs. Sons of priests tended to marry daughters of priests.

crude utilitarianism epitomized by Dmitri Pisarev's (1840–68) dictum, "a pair of boots is higher than Shakespeare." Their utilitarianism extended to science, which was supposed to serve the people in a practical way. Theoretical science was an indulgence.

Nikolai Chernyshevsky (1828–89), author of the novel *What Is To Be Done?* (1863), depicted "new people" (*novye liudi*) motivated by rational egoism—the realization that the interests of the rational individual and society coincide—who practice gender equality and free love, a tenet of the intelligentsia ethos from then on. The heroine, Vera (the Russian word for faith), organizes a successful sewing cooperative, demonstrating that people can live and work together harmoniously for mutual benefit. The highest exemplar of the "new man," however, is Rakhmetov, a rigorist who eats raw meat and sleeps on a bed of nails to learn to withstand torture. Chernyshevsky modeled him on the eponymous saint portrayed in the popular *Aleksei, a Man of God. What Is To Be Done?* became one of the intelligentsia's bibles. Men and women read it not just for spiritual sustenance but as a literal guide to life. Nikolai Dobroliubov's (1838–61) essay "What Is Oblomovitis?" (1859), made the lazy, passive nobleman depicted in Goncharov's novel *Oblomov* (also 1859) the symbol of what ails Russia, and as such, the antipode of the "new man." Pisarev's references to man's "Promethean" and "Titanic nature," his contempt for "bees," "drones," and the "herd," and his visions of projects that would last thousands of years anticipated Nietzsche, as did Pisarev's dictum, "What can be smashed should be smashed." Zarathustra said, "That which is falling should also be pushed!" (*Z*, 226). Pisaerev's anti-aestheticism was decidedly un-Nietzschean, however. His hero, the nihilist Bazarov, in Turgenev's novel *Fathers and Sons* (1861), considers a decent chemist "twenty times more useful than any poet."

Populism (*narodnichestvo*), the ideology of the 1870s, extolled duty rather than "rational egoism" and idealized the peasants and the peasant commune. The ideologue of populism, Petr Lavrov (1823–1900), taught that educated men and women had a duty or debt (*dolg*) to the people (*narod*) that they had to repay. The stress on "duty" is from Kant. Critically thinking, single-minded individuals could change the course of history and save Russia from capitalism, provided they were organized in a revolutionary party. The populist movement reached a crescendo in the "mad summer" of 1874 when thousands of students went to the countryside to preach the new gospel. The peasants did not trust the interlopers, however, and reported them to the police. Hundreds of populists were imprisoned or exiled to Siberia. Others, including Lavrov, fled Russia to avoid being arrested. In his post-1870 writings, which were deeply influenced by Marxism, Lavrov emphasized economic factors and class struggle, but he remained a voluntarist and an advocate of "individuality," using that term much as Herzen did.

Within Russia, the predominant trend in populism was Nikolai Mik-hailovsky's (1842–1904) "small deeds" version (serving the people as teach-ers, nurses, doctors, veterinarians, etc.). Although Mikhailovsky accepted Marx's critique of capitalism, he opposed Marxist historicism and imper-sonalism and advocated a "subjective sociology" that factored in human feelings and desires. Challenging Western theories of social progress, he pro-claimed a "struggle for individuality" and argued that capitalism and the division of labor destroy "individuality" and the commune in which "individuality" flourishes. After discovering Nietzsche, Mikhailovsky hailed him as a liberator, an idealist, an apostle of personal development and self-realization, but he objected to Nietzsche's pitiless elitism, attributing it to Darwin's baleful influence.[28] Like most Russian radicals, however, Mikhailovsky credited Darwin with emancipating biology from mysticism and metaphysics and believed that the "struggle for survival" pertained to life in a capitalist society.

The "heroic" tradition of populism ("heroic" because the revolutionary risked imprisonment or execution) sanctioned political assassinations, vio-lence, and terror. Bakunin urged revolutionaries to appeal to the masses' instincts and passions, and to ally with bandits and criminals. This stance and his statements, "the passion for destruction is also a creative passion" and "if God exists man is a slave," account, in part, for his reputation as a "Nietzschean before Nietzsche." Sergei Nechaev (1847–82), the notorious author (or coauthor with Bakunin) of *Catechism of a Revolutionary* (1869), instructed the revolutionary to reject the "soft and tender" feelings of fam-ily, friendship, and love, as well as gratitude, pity, and honor, and to study only "the science of destruction." Because of his amoralism and his "hard-ness" he, too, was later regarded as a "Nietzschean before Nietzsche." (His own generation of radicals rejected him.) Petr Tkachev (1844–85) advocated a Jacobin seizure of power, before the capitalist "weeds" could take root and grow, the takeover to be followed by a dictatorship, compulsory level-ing, and mass terror. His Jacobinism appealed to Lenin. Members of a pop-ulist organization called the People's Will (*Narodnaia volia*) believed that the assassination of Tsar Aleksandr II would trigger a mass uprising. Instead, it ushered in decades of reaction.

The first Marxist organization, the League for the Liberation of Labor, was formed by Russian exiles in Geneva in 1883, as a response to the per-ceived failure of populism. Georgy Plekhanov (1857–1918), the "father" of Russian Marxism (and a former populist), transferred his hopes from the peasantry to the proletariat and advocated a two-stage revolution, first a bourgeois revolution (as in France in 1789) and then, after an unspecified

28. For Mikhailovsky and Nietzsche, see Lane, "Nietzsche Comes to Russia: Popularization and Protest in the 1890s," in *NR*, 63–65.

period, the proletarian revolution. Plekhanov believed that all societies were subject to the same laws of development, so Russia could not skip the capitalist stage, even though Marx himself said, in reply to a query on whether the commune could serve as a stepping-stone to socialism, that *Capital* did not contain a universal theory of economic development.[29] Vehemently opposed to Jacobinism, and to revolutionary conspiracies in general, Plekhanov insisted that the emancipation of the workers must be accomplished by the workers themselves. Fearing that a premature proletarian revolution would result in an aborted socialism and a new ruling class, he almost obliterated the voluntaristic and "heroic" aspects of the intelligentsia ethos. The Bolsheviks restored them, in some cases with Nietzsche's help.

Maximalists of the 1890–1917 period, including Bolsheviks, were drawn to Nietzsche's apotheosis of will, his extremism, his warrior ideal, his amoralism, in some cases, his atheism (even though it was not a materialistic atheism), and the Superman ideal. Nietzsche also appealed, very powerfully, to artists and intellectuals who rejected the intelligentsia ethos, because they found its tendentiousness obnoxious, or because they had no interest in "serving the people," or because they rejected a worldview that excluded intuition, introspection, and fantasy; ignored or disdained metaphysical questions; and subordinated art and thought to political and social criteria.

Andrzej Walicki argues that Soviet totalitarianism stemmed from the chiliastic and utopian aspects of classical Marxism and cannot be attributed primarily to the Russian cultural heritage or to socioeconomic or political circumstances.[30] I agree on the importance of the chiliastic and utopian aspects of classical Marxism but diverge from Walicki in my insistence on the pivotal role of Nietzsche. To be sure, Nietzsche was not theoretically necessary for a Marxist totalitarianism, but he was, in fact, a major presence on the Russian cultural scene. Walicki and Martin Malia regard Communism as an ideocracy. Malia also uses the term "partocracy."[31] Mikhail Heller and Aleksandr Nekrich describe the Soviet regime as "Utopia in Power."[32] I do not deny the ideocratic, partocratic, or utopian aspects of Communism, but rather than treat Communism as an alien doctrine imposed from above and maintained only by force, I underscore the ideology's cultural roots and treat it in Nietzschean terms as a myth.

I do not claim that Nietzsche "caused" the Bolshevik Revolution, nor do

29. The query was from Vera Zasulich (1849–1919). Details in Teodor Shanin, *Late Marx and the Russian Road* (London, 1983).

30. Andrzej Walicki, *Marxism and the Leap to the Kingdom of Freedom* (Stanford, 1997).

31. Martin Malia, *The Soviet Tragedy* (New York, 1994), 137.

32. Mikhail Heller and Aleksandr Nekrich, *Utopia in Power: The History of the Soviet Union from 1917 to the Present*, trans. Phyllis B. Carlos (New York, 1986).

I "blame" him for Stalinism, nor do I contend that Nietzscheanism replaced Marxism-Leninism as the primary ideology of Bolsheviks and Stalinists. My point is that Nietzsche reinforced their "hard" interpretation of Marxism, colored their political imagination and policy decisions, and fueled their drive to create new political myths, new cult figures, and a new culture. This book is not about Nietzsche per se, but about selective appropriations and modifications of his thought, by his first popularizers and by Russians influenced by them.

The Plan of the Book

This book is divided into four sections, each of which corresponds to a phase of Nietzsche's reception. Each section is prefaced by a synopsis of the political, socioeconomic, and cultural trends of the period to be discussed.

Section I, "The Seed-Time: The Russification of Nietzsche, 1890–1917," treats the symbolist writers, religious philosophers, Nietzschean Marxists, and futurists who established the Nietzschean agenda that served as the starting point for subsequent generations.

Section II, "Nietzsche in the Bolshevik Revolution and the Civil War, 1917–1921," discusses applications of Nietzsche by Lenin, Bukharin, and Trotsky on the one hand and by proponents of a spiritual revolution on the other.

Section III, "Nietzschean Ideas in the Period of the New Economic Policy (NEP), 1921–1927," reveals the Nietzschean roots of the Lenin Cult, proletarian morality, and the new Soviet man, and limns the Nietzschean elements in the culture wars of that period.

Section IV, "Echoes of Nietzsche in Stalin's Time, 1928–1953" is subdivided into three parts. Part I, "Dionysus Unleashed: The Cultural Revolution and the First Five-Year Plan, 1928–1932," delineates Stalin's version of "great politics," Bukharin's theory of cultural revolution, and the trajectory of cultural revolution in the arts and sciences. Part II, "Art as a Lie: Nietzsche and Socialist Realism," discloses Nietzschean elements in the theory and implementation of the official Soviet aesthetic. Part III, "The Lie Triumphant: Nietzsche and Stalinist Political Culture," treats official pronouncements on Nietzsche, the Stalin Cult and its complements, and some cultural expressions of the "will to power." The Epilogue, "De-Stalinization and the Reemergence of Nietzsche," treats the official Soviet position on Nietzsche, intellectuals' rediscovery of the Silver Age (1890–1914), and the reopening of the Nietzschean agenda.

In following this multigenerational dialogue, we will see that different items on the Nietzschean agenda came to the fore as circumstances changed; different Nietzsche texts were taken as central at different times; readings of the same text varied; each generation responded to the "solutions" of the preceding one(s); and Soviet, Fascist, and Nazi propagandists learned from one another, the common socialist and Nietzschean elements in their ideologies facilitating the exchange. This book is not a history of twentieth-century Russian culture, nor does it cover all aspects of Nietzsche's influence. Its focus is on the trail of Nietzschean ideas that began in the 1890s and ended in the 1930s. I emphasize literature, because it was a major venue for the expressions of ideas, but I approach literature from the perspective of a historian interested in the filiation of ideas. Marginalized or disaffected writers indebted to Nietzsche will not be discussed, except insofar as their views illuminate the main trail.[33] Music will not be discussed, not because I consider it unimportant, but because I not a musicologist. For the convenience of persons who do not read Russian, English translations are cited when available.

33. Some of these figures are treated in *NSC*. See Elaine Rusinko, "Apollonianism and Christian Art: Nietzsche's Influence on Acmeism," 84–105; Clare Cavanaugh, "Mandelstam, Nietzsche, and the Conscious Creation of History," 338–65; Edith Clowes, "From Beyond the Abyss: Nietzschean Myth in Zamiatin's *We* and Pasternak's *Doctor Zhivago*," 313–36; and Boris Groys, "Nietzsche's Influence on the Non-official Culture of the 1930s," 367–89. See also James Curtis, "Michael Bakhtin, Nietzsche, and Russian Pre-Revolutionary Thought," in *NR*, 331–53.

The Seed-Time: The Russification of Nietzsche, 1890–1917

Between 1890 and 1917 Russia was jolted by rapid industrialization, revolution, and war. Industrialization, or more broadly, modernization, undermined social controls and support systems, creating new opportunities and new problems in the countryside and in the burgeoning cities. Agrarian distress, the emergence of a proletariat, and a reactionary new tsar, Nicholas II (1894–1917), reenergized the intelligentsia. Marxists founded the Russian Social Democratic Workers Party (henceforth SDs) in 1898; populists formed the Party of Socialist Revolutionaries (henceforth SRs) in 1901; and gentry liberals and urban professionals organized the Constitutional Democratic Party (Kadets) in 1905. The SDs split into Bolshevik and Menshevik factions in 1903, but officially they were one party until 1912.

The Russo-Japanese War (1904–5) exacerbated urban poverty while military defeats emboldened the Autocracy's opponents. "Bloody Sunday" (January 9, 1905 OS / January 22 NS),[1] the day that government troops massacred unarmed workers peacefully petitioning the tsar (at his palace in St. Petersburg), is considered the beginning of the Revolution of 1905, which lasted until mid-1907. In May 1905, a new force emerged, the soviets, workers' councils that combined economic and political protest. The following October, a general strike paralyzed the capital for ten days, impelling Nicholas II to issue a manifesto which promised a *duma* (parliament) and other major reforms.[2] Some political activists wanted to cooperate with the tsar on the basis of the October Manifesto; others resolved to continue the struggle, but disagreed on strategy and tactics. Reactionaries formed their own party, the Union of the Russian People; its unofficial arm was the pogromist Black

---

1. In January 1918, when the Bolsheviks changed the Russian calendar, it was thirteen days behind the calendar used in the West. OS means old style and NS new style.

2. For the role of the soviets, see Abraham Ascher, *The Revolution of 1905: Russia in Disarray* (Stanford, 1988), 145–55.

Hundreds. The government replied to revolutionary terror and violence with reprisals and executions and by placing entire provinces under martial law. Even so, between 1904 and 1911, thousands of people, including Prime Minister Peter Stolypin (1862–1911), were victims of revolutionary terror, much of it perpetrated by the Combat Organization, the unofficial arm of the SRs.

Rapid industrialization resumed around 1908; the middle class grew in size and importance, and a civil society began to emerge. But many educated people lost interest in politics; there was a tug of war between the tsar and the Duma, and the majority of Russians remained mired in poverty. The number and intensity of strikes increased after 1912. Historians debate whether there would have been a revolution if Russia had not entered World War I, but no one denies that the war was a disaster for Russia. Defeats in battle, enormous casualties, hunger in the cities, scandals (many connected with Rasputin), and a succession of ministers so rapid it was termed "ministerial leapfrog" brought down the tsarist government in February 1917 (OS/March NS).

Culturally, the late Imperial period was marked by an explosion of artistic creativity, philosophic inquiry, and religious revival. Intellectuals disenchanted with populism sought a new faith by which to live. Some found it in symbolism, others in Marxism. The symbolists wanted to create a new, distinctively Russian culture as an equal part of European culture as a whole. New journals—*The World of Art* (*Mir iskusstva*, 1898–1904), *New Path* (*Novyi put'*, 1902–4), *The Scales* (*Vesy*, 1904–9), *Golden Fleece* (*Zolotoe runo*, 1906–9), *Apollo* (*Apollon*, 1909–17)—provided outlets for them and informed readers of the latest trends in Europe. *The World of Art* and *Golden Fleece* sponsored art exhibitions and concerts. The founders of *The World of Art* were Nietzsche enthusiasts (a full-page portrait commemorated his death), but Wagner was more important to their aesthetic sensibility. "Self-expression," "self-fulfillment," and "self-development" became bywords. Confidence in human powers was accompanied by a sense of expanded horizons and, in some cases, by delight in transgressing conventional morality and established literary and artistic norms.[3] Upward mobility became a theme of popular fiction. and new types of heroes emerged—strong-willed autonomous individuals who neither bowed to fate nor deferred to authority.[4] The rapid-

3. The *Golden Fleece* sponsored a competition for the best literary and pictorial depiction of the devil. Mikhail Vrubel (1856–1910) painted Lermontov's Demon, who was in turn based on Milton's Satan, who would rather reign in hell than serve in heaven. On Vrubel and Nietzsche, see Aline Izdebsky-Pritchard, "Art for Philosophy's Sake: Vrubel Against the Herd," in *NR*, 219–48.

4. Details in Jeffrey Brooks, *When Russia Learned to Read: Literacy and Popular Literature, 1861–1917* (Princeton, 1985), and idem, "Russian Popular Fiction: From

ity of change was one of the factors that gave rise to apocalypticism and occultism, often in tandem with an interest in Nietzsche.

Educated Russians could read Nietzsche in the original German or in French translations, and Russian translations began to appear in 1898. By 1911 all his major works were available in Russian, but some translations were seriously flawed, or the censor had mandated excisions. Russian radicals, some of them living abroad, followed the debates of their European counterparts. European Marxists were not uniformly hostile to Nietzsche; some of them were very sympathetic.[5] Anarchists regarded Nietzsche as a kindred soul.[6] Occultists regarded Nietzsche as one of their own.[7] His summons to "live dangerously" had a special appeal to young people. In every country that had a youth movement, Nietzsche was part of a cluster of ideas that provided "a ready-made language of cultural and political combat."[8] In Russia, his extremism fit in with the intelligentsia's maximalism and its contempt for compromise as a moral failing.

Nietzsche appealed to people yearning to cast off old constraints and seeking new identities and new values by which to live. Accentuating the liberational aspects of Nietzsche's thought, they welcomed his attack on positivism, rationalism, and conventional morality and hailed his call for a "revaluation of all values." Most of them exalted a struggle for grand distant goals (which the apocalyptically minded did not regard as distant) while remaining indifferent to immediate, practical reforms. They distinguished between atomistic individualism, which they came to reject, and "individuality," self-expression within the community, which they championed; and they expected the "new man" to be a Superman. Their writings are studded with words such as "ecstasy," "passion" (*pafos*), and "fullness of life" (*pol'nota zhizni,* German *Lebensfülle*), "exuberance," "energy," "joyousness," "enthusiasm" (*entuziazm*, a foreign borrowing), "affirmation of life," "daring," "tragic," "Promethean," and "Titanic" (Prometheus was a Titan)—all so very different from the dry economic terminology of most of *Das Kapital* or the sober

Chapbooks to Socialist Realism, from Pastukhov to Shaginian," in *Il Romanzo populare in Russia: dalle stovie di briganti al realismo socialista*, ed. Franco Moretti, vol. 2 (Turin, 2002), 447–69.

5. William McGrath, *Dionysian Art and Populist Politics* (New Haven, 1974); Ernst Behler, "Zur frühen sozialistischen Rezeption Nietzsches in Deutschland," *Nietzsche Studien* 13 (1984): 503–20; Steven Aschheim, "Nietzschean Socialism Left and Right," in *The Nietzsche Legacy in Germany*, 164–200; Christopher Forth, *Zarathustra in Paris: The Nietzsche Vogue in France, 1891–1918* (DeKalb, Ill., 2001), 100–125.

6. The anarchist Peter Kropotkin listed Nietzsche as a congenial thinker in his entry, "Anarchism," in the *Encyclopedia Britannica* (1910).

7. Maria Carlson, "Armchair Anarchists and Salon Supermen: Russian Occultists Read Nietzsche," in *NSC*, 107–23; Bernice Glatzer Rosenthal, ed., *The Occult in Russian and Soviet Culture* (Ithaca, 1997).

8. Robert Wohl, *The Generation of 1914* (Cambridge, Mass., 1979), 204.

language of John Locke or John Stuart Mill. "Slavish," a word used by critics of Russia as early as the 1840s, took on a Nietzschean surcharge.

Symbolists, philosophers, and Marxists drawn to Nietzsche focused on the aspects of his *oeuvre* that appealed to them, manipulating these aspects in their own ways, for their own purposes, typically as part of a constellation of related ideas. The symbolists' constellation included Dostoevsky, Soloviev, Wagner, apocalypticism, occult doctrines (especially Theosophy), and neo-Slavophilism. Philosophers used Nietzsche to challenge positivism and abstract rationalism, and to modify or reject Kant's "morality of duty." The Marxists' constellation featured Marx and Engels, Feuerbach, Darwin, and anarcho-syndicalism, especially as articulated by Georges Sorel (1847–1922), and Empiriocriticism, a philosophy developed independently by the Swiss philosopher Richard Avenarius (1846–1996) and the Austrian physicist and philosopher Ernst Mach (1838–1916). These three groups, none of which was homogeneous, were linked by friendship and mutual interests. They responded to each other's articles and lectures and reviewed each other's books. Populists drawn to Nietzsche, such as Viktor Chernov (1873–1952), head of the SRs, and Boris Savinkov (1879–1925), head of the SR Combat Organization, also took part in these debates. The Revolution of 1905 was a watershed for symbolists, philosophers, and Marxists alike.

A new stage in Nietzsche's reception began in 1909–10. The symposium *Landmarks* (*Vekhi*, 1909), which lambasted the revolutionary intelligentsia, included denunciations of would-be Supermen and of nihilists impelled by the will to power. Symbolism entered a state of crisis from which it never emerged. Individual symbolists remained creative but went their separate ways. The philosopher Nikolai Berdiaev began to work out a Nietzsche-imbued philosophy that featured creativity, ungrounded freedom (freedom ungrounded in empirical reality), and self-sacrifice. The theologian Pavel Florensky propounded an existential Orthodoxy that incorporated symbolist and Nietzschean themes. The Nietzschean Marxist Aleksandr Bogdanov worked out a program for cultural revolution.

Proponents of two new aesthetic doctrines, futurism and acmeism, emphasized Nietzsche texts that the symbolists ignored or interpreted differently the ones they had not. Early futurism had much in common with primitivism, for both were part of a Europe-wide cultural shift that rejected positivism, rationalism, and liberalism. Intellectuals were fascinated by "savage" and "primitive" cultures—the Arabs, sub-Saharan Africa, precolonial Mexico, and Polynesia—and by the anthropological studies of Sir James Frazer and Edward Tylor. Nietzsche's observation, "the savage (or in moral terms the evil man) is a return to nature—and in a certain sense, his recovery, his 'cure' from culture" (*WP*, 363–64), encapsulates their attitude, except that "over-refined" or "bourgeois" would have to be inserted before the word "culture." Young people bored with peace and prosperity exalted war as an opportunity for adventure and self-sacrifice. Their will to war fed on and fed cultural and political nationalism.

The Russian variant of this Europe-wide shift is called the *sdvig*, which means "displacement" or "fault" as in the fault lines of an earthquake, and was characterized by an apocalyptic intensity, for the old order really was ending. Trying to fashion a new national identity, Russian artists and writers drew on the lore of their own "primitives"—the peasantry, the nomadic peoples of the steppe, Christian sectarians—and reworked folk tales and legends, icons, and popular art forms into new literary and pictorial languages. This process began in artists' colonies in the 1880s, that is, before Russians learned about Nietzsche and Wagner, but Nietzsche and Wagner deepened it. Diaghilev's *Ballets russe* (founded in Paris, in 1909) produced Russian *Gesamtkunstwerke*, some of which stressed the exotic, oriental aspects of the Russian legacy. Stravinsky's *The Rite of Spring* (1912), which premiered in Paris, highlighted the savage aspects of Russia's past (and was booed off the stage). Skriabin experimented with synesthesia and thought that he could bring on the Apocalypse by the force of his music.[9] Prokofiev composed a "Scythian Suite" (1915).

Primitivists and futurists reformulated the old dichotomy of Russia and the West in terms of "barbarian" folk culture versus "decadent" bourgeois civilization, or "Europe" versus "Asia." To some Russians, "Asia" meant India, China, Tibet, or Japan; to others, the nomadic peoples of their own country. The primitivist painter Aleksandr Shevchenko (1881–1948) proclaimed: "We are called barbarians, Asians. Yes, we are Asia, and are proud of this because 'Asia is the cradle of nations,' a good half of our blood is Tartar, and we hail the East to come, the source and cradle of all culture, of all arts." Natalia Goncharova (1881–1962) claimed to be "opening up the East again."[10] The futurists identified with the Scythians, the fierce Asiatic nomads who once ruled what later became Southern Russia. In Nietzschean terms, the Scythians were wild "Dionysian barbarians," not "Greek barbarians" (*BT,* 39).

Popular culture was laced with vulgarized renditions of Nietzsche's thought. The prefix "super" (*sverkh*) was attached to a wide range of entities, even dogs. A vaudeville house in St. Petersburg staged a farce about contemporary philosophy titled "Thus Spoke Zarathustra." Petr Boborykin (a novelist of the 1890s), young Gorky, and Leonid Andreev (1871–1919)

9.   For Scriabin and Nietzsche, see Ann Lane, "Bal'mont and Scriabin: The Artist as Superman," in *NR*, 209–18; for Scriabin and Wagner, see Rosenthal, "Wagner and Wagnerian Ideas in Russia," 221–23, 225.

10.   Aleksandr Shevchenko, "Neoprimitivsm and Cubofuturism" (1913); Natalia Gonacharov, "Preface to Catalogue of One-Man Exhibition" (1913), 49, 56. See also Ilia Zdanevich and Mikhail Larionov, "Why We Paint Ourselves," 81–82. These essays are found in *Russian Art of the Avant-Garde*, ed. John Bowlt (London, 1988).

"democratized" the idea of a brutal, amoral, Superman. Best-selling novels such as Mikhail Artsybashev's *Sanin* (1907), Anastasia Verbitskaia's *The Keys to Happiness* (5 vols., 1908–13), and Evdokhia Nagrodskaia's *The Wrath of Dionysus* (1910) featured promiscuity and sexual deviance as part of a mythos of self-fulfillment.[11] Except for Gorky, these authors were tangential to the dialogue to be described, but they coarsened popular conceptions of the new morality and the new man and woman. Nietzsche had a salutary impact, however, on worker-intellectuals who berated "slavish" behavior and demanded respect for human dignity and an end to suffering.[12]

Plekhanov associated Nietzsche with bourgeois decadence and observed that "there is a not single country in the contemporary civilized world where bourgeois youth does not sympathize with the ideas of Friedrich Nietzsche," but the anarchist Georgy Chulkov viewed young people's interest in Nietzsche positively as part of "our cultural renaissance."[13] The vogue of Nietzsche subsided during World War I because he was associated with German militarism and imperialism. Wagner's operas were banned from the Imperial theaters. Interest in both figures revived in 1916–1917 along with apocalypticism and political radicalism.

11. Edith Clowes, "Literary Reception as Vulgarization: Nietzsche's Idea of the Superman in Neo-Realist Fiction," in *NR*, 315–30. See also, Mikhail Artsybashev, *Sanin*, trans. Percy Pinkerton (New York, 1932); Evdokia Nagradskaia, *The Wrath of Dionysus*, ed. and trans. Louie McReynolds (Bloomington, 1997); Anastasia Verbitskaia, *The Keys to Happiness* (abridged), trans. and ed. Beth Holmgren and Helena Goscilo (Bloomington, 1999); and Laura Engelstein, *The Keys to Happiness: Sex and the Search for Modernity in Fin de Siècle Russia* (Ithaca, 1992).

12. Mark D. Steinberg, "Worker-Authors and the Cult of the Person," in *Cultures in Flux*, ed. Stephen P. Frank and Mark D. Steinberg (Princeton, 1994), 168–84; idem, "Vanguard Workers and the Morality of Labor," in *Making Workers Soviet: Power, Class, and Identity*, ed. Lewis H. Siegelbaum and Ronald Suny (Ithaca, 1994), 68, 75, 77. For a literate worker's responses to Gorky, Andreev, Nietzsche, and Berdiaev, see *A Radical Worker in Tsarist Russia: The Autobiography of Semen Ivanovich Kanatchikov*, trans. and ed. Reginald E. Zelnik (Stanford, 1986), 112–13, 129, 258, 262–63.

13. George Plekhanov, "Art and Social Life" (1912), in *Art and Social Life*, vol. 3, ed. Peter Davison, Rolf Meyerson, Edward Shils (Teaneck, N.J., 1978), 39; Georgii Chulkov, "Iskhod," in *Stat'i 1905–11* (St. Petersburg, 1912), 42–43.

Symbolists

For the sake of the new beauty,
We will break all laws,
We will trespass all limits. —Dmitry Merezhkovsky,
"Deti nochi"

For the symbolists, the key Nietzsche text was *The Birth of Tragedy,* even though much of their imagery stemmed from *Zarathustra.* They were dazzled by Nietzsche's aesthetic justification of the world and human existence, his celebration of the Dionysian, and his belief that myth is essential to the health of a culture. Their primary interests were art, culture, and the "inner man" (the soul or the psyche). Spiritual radicals, they interpreted the "will to power" as creativity, detested the quotidian aspects of life (*byt*), and unlike Nietzsche, held that empirical reality is but a symbol of a higher reality that can be apprehended intuitively. Opposed to positivism, rationalism, and materialism, they imagined "other worlds than ours" and plumbed the depths of the human soul. Rejecting the "slavish" kenotic values of humility, altruism, and asceticism, they hailed Nietzsche as a proponent of self-affirming individualism and enjoyment of life, a trespasser of forbidden boundaries and established moral codes, and highlighted his paeans to laughter and to dancing. Later on, however, they denounced individualism as atomistic or decadent and restored one or more of the kenotic values (which ones depended on the symbolist), defending their turnabout with different quotations from Nietzsche. Their myths featured a leap from necessity to freedom in the cosmic, rather than the Marxist, sense, and the transfiguration of man and the world through art. The symbolist poet would articulate the salvific "new word."

The leading symbolists were Dmitry Merezhkovsky (1865–1941), the initiator of the movement; his wife Zinaida Gippius (1869–1945); Valery Briusov (1873–1924); and Konstantin Bal'mont (1867–1942).[1] A "second generation" emerged around 1902—Viacheslav Ivanov (1866–1949), Andrei Bely (Boris Bugaev, 1880–1934), and Aleksandr Blok (1880–1921). Symbolism began as protest against realism, naturalism, the moral and socio-political didacticism of populists and Tolstoy, and vulgar mass culture. Symbolist works bypass the intellect to address the psyche directly and were crafted to evoke chains of subliminal associations and a mysterious, otherworldly mood. The poetry suggests rather than states, sometimes in arcane or vatic language, and attempts to replicate music. The paintings depict divine and demonic subjects, archetypal events (such as the Apocalypse), and incarnations of the "eternal feminine." Early symbolism was vehemently apolitical and asocial, but the aesthetic was intertwined with issues of philosophy and religion from the start. Most symbolists became Godseekers (*Bogoiskat'eli*) another movement that Merezhkovsky initiated. The Revolution of 1905 politicized the symbolists; they perceived it as the start of the Apocalypse that would culminate in the establishment of the Kingdom of God on Earth.

Symbolism as a Surrogate Religion

Merezhkovsky learned about symbolism and Nietzsche in Paris. French symbolism was more indebted to Wagner than to Nietzsche and invited introspection and a mystical withdrawal from the world. Nietzsche's thought helped Merezhkovsky give Russian symbolism its fighting edge and (with Soloviev and Fedorov) was an inspiration for the later symbolist concept of "life-creation" (*zhiznetvorchestvo*).

Russian symbolism started out as a religion of art. Merezhkovsky mingled romanticism and idealism with a Nietzschean aestheticism and accused populists and positivists of ignoring the "eternal questions" of human existence. Aesthetic creativity gives life meaning, he argued in the early 1890s, and art leads to higher truths (note the plural). Only a "new idealism" could

1. For Bal'mont and Nietzsche, see Ann Lane, "Bal'mont and Skriabin," in *NR*, 195–218.

unite the intelligentsia and the people (*narod*) (a populist goal).[2] Yet only a few years later, Merezhkovsky turned his back on the people and insisted on the autonomy of art. Using Nietzsche as a battering ram to smash the old Christian/populist "tables of values," Merezhkovsky championed an aesthetic individualism in which self-expression and beauty were the highest values. The artist was a hero, a warrior for a new culture, and the people were rabble. The artist was not obligated to serve them.

Merezhkovsky's aesthetic individualism was short-lived, because art alone proved insufficient as a guide to life, and it failed to enable him to overcome his inordinate fear of death. In his essay "Pushkin" (1896), Merezhkovsky asserted that paganism (really Nietzscheanism) and Christianity were two halves of a yet undiscovered greater truth. Paganism sanctioned self-affirmation and worldly pleasures; it was the "truth of the earth" ("remain true to the earth," Z, 42). Christianity preached personal immortality and love; it was the "truth of heaven." Merezhkovsky resolved to reconcile the two truths, so that people could enjoy the worldly pleasures prohibited to Christians and still be assured of eternal life. In the same essay, he exalted Pushkin as the perfect combination of Apollo and Dionysus. This essay became the subtext of discussions about Pushkin from then on.[3] Elsewhere, Merezhkovsky praised Goethe as a pan-European writer, as Nietzsche did (*TI*, 102), and discussed the Apollonian and Dionysian aspects of Goethe's life and work, thereby linking Goethe and Nietzsche.

In 1900, Merezhkovsky embarked on a "revaluation of all [Christian] values," based on the assumption that "historical Christianity" (Christianity as preached by the churches) was obsolete. Jesus Christ Himself would grant humankind a Third Testament (*Zavet*, sometimes translated "revelation") that would reconcile all dualisms: Christianity and paganism, Westernism and Slavophilism, spirit and flesh, Russia and Europe, God-man and Man-God, Christ and Antichrist. From then on, Merezhkovsky cast all problems in terms of an eschatological dualism that only the Second Coming could resolve. The distinction between institutional Christianity and Christ is an old one but, in Merezhkovsky's case, the distinction was informed by Tolstoy and Nietzsche. Tolstoy attacked the state-controlled Orthodox Church and preached a Gospel-based Christianity. Nietzsche wrote: "I shall now relate the *real* history of Christianity—The word 'Christianity' is already a misunderstanding—in reality there has been only one Christian and he died on the Cross" (*AC*, 151). Merezhkovsky did not quote the good things Nietzsche said about Jesus, lest he blur the eschatological dualism. Rather, he challenged

2. D. S. Merezhkovskii, "O prichinakh upadka i o novykh techeniiakh sovremennoi literatury," in *MPSS*, 18:175–275.
3. Irina Paperno, "Nietzscheanism and the Return of Pushkin in Twentieth-Century Russian Culture (1899–1937)," in *NSC*, 211–32.

Nietzsche's anti-Christian statements. Authentic Christianity is not a slave morality, Merezhkovsky proclaimed, but a new and higher supramoral phenomenon beyond good and evil. Christianity is not life-denying; personal immortality is the supreme affirmation of life. God is not dead; He lives and will come again. Jesus Christ is the Superman Nietzsche sought in vain.[4]

Arguing that people need religious faith as much as they need food, Merezhkovsky proselytized his "new religious consciousness" in novels and essays, in the Religious Philosophical Society of St. Petersburg (founded by him and Gippius in 1901), and in their *revue, New Path*. The Society featured debates between clergymen and lay intellectuals on burning issues of the day, including the Holy Synod's excommunication of Tolstoy, Christian attitudes toward sex, and whether or not new Christian dogma was needed, and if so, who would create it. Outraged at Tolstoy's excommunication (even though he disagreed with Tolstoy), Merezhkovsky challenged the subordination of the Orthodox Church to the state and tried to found a new church a few years later. In the debates on sex, Merezhkovsky championed the idea of "holy flesh," not realizing that he was advocating transfiguration. One of the Society's most prominent figures, the writer Vasily Rozanov (1856–1919) extolled the holiness of sex and the family, praised Judaism's positive attitude to sex, and claimed that Christianity was a religion of death because it was fixated on celibacy. Because of his diatribes against Christianity and his unabashed amoralism, Rozanov was called the "Russian Nietzsche."[5] Unlike the other "Russian Nietzsche," Leontiev, Rozanov idealized domesticity. In private life, he was a pillar of the Church, which he regarded as a haven of beauty, warmth, and spiritual succor. He found supreme beauty in the visage of Jesus and in Orthodox rituals.

The unprecedented spectacle of clergymen and lay intellectuals debating one another on equal terms attracted capacity audiences. The government shut down the Society in April 1903, lest it provide a forum for heresy, but repression could not squelch the revaluation of all Christian values that the Society had provoked. It was a major stimulus to the early-twentieth-century religious renaissance. The Society was revived in 1907, and branches were founded in Moscow, Kiev, and other cities. The members of all the religious-philosophical societies were called Godseekers, even though many were already believers, because they were seeking answers to questions raised in the original Society or in the writings and lectures of its leading figures. Most symbolists were Godseekers, but not all Godseekers were symbolists.

---

4. For details on Merezhkovsky and Nietzsche, see Bernice Glatzer Rosenthal, "Stages of Nietzscheanism: Merezhkovsky's Intellectual Evolution," in *NR*, 69–94, and Clowes, *Revolution*, 115–34.

5. For Rozanov and Nietzsche, see Anna Lise Crone, "Nietzschean, All Too Nietzschean," in *NR*, 95–112.

The Moscow branch was called the Religious Philosophical Vladimir Soloviev Society, after Russia's greatest philosopher. Soloviev (1853–1900) preached an activist Christianity that would transfigure the world and establish the Kingdom of God on Earth, a realm of pure joy and love. He considered art a form of inspired prophecy and had a special regard for lyric poetry, which he associated with Sophia (Divine Wisdom) and romantic notions of "the eternal feminine" (Goethe's phrase). He believed that the poet's task was to bring Sophia down from heaven by love and find forms to suit her essence. He considered Beauty to be the carrier of the Idea, not in the Hegelian sense, the reflection of an eternal Idea upon fleeting phenomena, but that which incarnates a spiritual or divine principle in matter. He saw nature as the body of Sophia and the flesh as something that should not be denied but transfigured. In *The Meaning of Love* (1892–94), Soloviev separated pro-creation and sexual pleasure and sanctioned sexual pleasure as a means of overcoming egoism. His ideal human being was androgynous, a tenet that can be interpreted either as recommending bisexuality or as calling for the transcendence of sexual relations in a transfigured world.

Soloviev's most fundamental concept was "Godmanhood" (*Bogoche-lovechestvo*), the incarnation of the divine idea in man (in other words deification) and the salvation and transfiguration of all humankind, not just righteous individuals. The antipode of "Godmanhood" was demonic "Mangodhood." (Dostoevsky also contrasted Godman and man-god.) Although Soloviev disapproved of Nietzsche, he considered the Superman a religiously significant idea, because it expressed a yearning to be more than human. "Godmanhood" was related to Soloviev's concept of "total unity" (*vseedinstvo*), the unity of being central to Orthodox ontology. He rejected abstract Western philosophy, represented in his early works by Hegel, in favor of an integral worldview, an all-encompassing synthesis of philosophy, religion, science, and art. In the 1880s, Soloviev advocated "free theocracy," a variant of the Slavophile ideal of *sobornost'*, to be instituted by the tsar and the pope, for one of his goals was the reunion of the Christian churches. In the 1890s, dismayed by the failure of his theocratic project, Soloviev espoused a kind of liberalism. (The symbolists ignored this aspect of his views.) Throughout, he advocated an activist Christianity, one that would really change the world.

In the last year of his life (1900), Soloviev predicted the imminent advent of the Antichrist in a tale that portrayed him as a composite figure with Nietzschean traits. Indeed, says the narrator, "many called him a Superman."[6] Dazzlingly beautiful, the Antichrist uses science, magic, and technology to control nature (an allusion to Fedorov) and ends the age-old scourges of

6. Soloviev, "A Story of Antichrist," in *Three Conversations: War Progress and the End of History*, trans. S. Bakshy (London, 1915), 187–90, 192–93, 197, 200.

hunger and war. But he abolishes the distinction between good and evil, loves only himself, and presumes to replace Christ, for his real motivation is power. After the political and social problems have been solved, the religious question comes to the fore. The Jews revolt when they learn that he is not the Messiah after all (note the importance of human agency); evil is vanquished; and the Millennium begins. Soloviev's apocalypticism and his prophesy of pan-Mongolism (the rule of the "yellow" races over the "white") influenced symbolist political thought during the Russo-Japanese War, merging with other apocalyptic visions, especially Merezhkovsky's Third Testament, Wagner's *Götterdämmerung,* and Nietzsche's "great noontide": "One day they shall proclaim with tongues of flame: It is coming, it is near, *the great noontide!*" (Z, 192).

Ivanov, Bely, and Blok combined Nietzsche with Soloviev, "correcting" Nietzsche's misogyny with visions of Sophia or the "eternal feminine." All three were Wagnerophiles (Merezhkovsky was not). Ivanov regarded man as a religious animal *(animal religiosum)* and since ecstasy is the "alpha" and "omega" of the religious state, as an ecstatic animal *(animal ecstaticum).* In "The Hellenic Religion of the Suffering God" and "The Religion of Dionysus" (1904–5) Ivanov underscored the interrelated religious and sexual aspects of the cult and the role of the maenads.[7] He believed that "mad" intoxication and oblivion were the outward manifestations of a state of ecstasy that was intimately connected with sacrifice and suffering in an eternally self-renewing cycle of birth, death, and rebirth. Dionysian ecstasy enabled the celebrants to accept the reality of death by providing them with the certainty of mystical unity with the "suffering god," who was both priest and sacrificial victim. Viewing the myths and rituals of the cult as expressions of a primordial mystical idea, Ivanov emphasized the common elements in Christianity and Dionysianism—passion, death, and resurrection—and argued that Dionysus was a precursor of Christ.

Ivanov's Nietzschean Christianity differed from Merezhkovsky's. The latter believed that the reconciliation of paganism and Christianity lay in the future; Ivanov held that they were once one, but then tragically separated. Ivanov's orientation was almost purely Dionysian; he exalted loss of self in mystical ecstasy and assimilated Dionysus to the kenotic Christ. His eschatology was attuned to immanent transfiguration. Merezhkovsky's apocalypticism posited grand historical schemes along the lines of a Hegelian dialectic, which he sometimes he conflated with Nietzsche's idea of eternal

---

7. "Ellinskaia religiia stradaiushchego boga," in *Novyi Put'*, 1904, no. 1:110–34, no. 2:48–78, no. 3:38–61, no. 5:28–40, no. 8:17–26, no. 9:47–70; continued as "Religiia Dionisa," in *Voprosy zhizni*, 1905, no. 6:185–220, no. 7:122–48. For his discussion of man as a "religious animal," see 7:137.

recurrence, misunderstood as historical cycles. Merezhkovsky's Christianity centered on Jesus; Ivanov's was part of an amorphous "new religious synthesis." Merezhkovsky's writing style was clear and simple, as befit his proselytizing orientation; Ivanov's was turgid, esoteric, and replete with neologisms that had Greek or Latin roots. Between 1904 and 1912, Ivanov's salon eclipsed Merezhkovsky's salon as a gathering place for the literary and artistic intelligentsia. Ivanov was more important as a theorist of symbolism, but Merezhkovsky's writings reached a larger audience. Indeed, Merezhkovsky's historical novels were bestsellers.

Bely tried to make symbolism the basis of a integral worldview that encompassed science, philosophy, religion, and art (Soloviev's idea). The Nietzschean aspects of Bely's aesthetics were derived primarily from *The Birth of Tragedy*.[8] Soloviev shaped Bely's concept of the redemptive role of the poet, his conviction that religion, rather than unformulated mystical feeling, must be the basis of art, and his emphasis on ethics, which he merged with a Nietzschean aestheticism. Like Ivanov, Bely reworked Nietzschean images of ascent and descent in Christian terms. Blok tried to integrate Soloviev and Nietzsche intuitively and poetically, wavering between them all his life. At Ivanov's suggestion, he re-read *The Birth of Tragedy* in 1906. From then on, Blok viewed the Dionysian rites as the origin of all drama, and the Dionysian principle as the foundation of all art.[9]

Idealization of human sacrifice is the dark side of symbolism. The Dionysian dithyrambs that accompanied the ritual sacrifice of the god in ancient Greece were not only erotic but frenzied, bloody, and cruel. The original Dionysian rites were not just sexual orgies, they were orgies of cannibalism (which Ivanov recognized). For the celebrants, it was Dionysus himself who was sacrificed. He was literally torn to pieces, pieces which the celebrants ate, thereby becoming god, or god-like, or so they believed. To Ivanov, Dionysus's dismemberment and resurrection symbolized the cycle of birth, death, and rebirth. Eroticization of suffering and fascination with violent death are obvious in his cycle of poems "To Dionysus" (1903).[10] One of Blok's greatest poetic cycles, *The Snow Mask* (1907), ostensibly about a love affair, is ordered around the lines of the Dionysian ritual described in Ivanov's essays. In Edith Clowes's words, "The poet becomes a Christ figure who rebels, affirms his own will, invokes the god, and finally gives himself up to Dionysian androgynous chaos. Out of chaos emerges a new mystical-creative consciousness. This resurrection lasts only a short time." In the end the poet

8.   Virginia Bennett, "Esthetic Theories from *The Birth of Tragedy* in Andrei Bely's Critical Articles, 1904–1908," in *NR*, 161–79.

9.   Evelyn Bristol, "Blok Between Nietzsche and Soloviev," in *NR*, 150.

10.   "K dionisu," in *ISS*, 1:538–51. For the sinister aspects of Ivanov's theory, see Jurij Murašov, *Im Zeichen des Dionysos: zur Mythopoetik in der russischen Moderne am Beispiel von Vjačeslav Ivanov* (Munich, 1999), esp. "Die drastische Opfertat," 93–117.

realizes that he is only human and accepts his final sacrifice on the "snowy pyre."[11] Years later, Nadezhda Mandelstam contended that the symbolist attempt to combine paganism and Christianity implied an apologia for cruelty that conditioned people to accept terror, giving as an example Ivanov's statement, "Cruelty is distinguished by a serene expression while the victim drinks in the radiant energy of the tormenter."[12]

Symbolist reinterpretations of Christianity included visions of a new man— an artist-hero, a creator of a new culture and new values—the polar opposite of rationally calculating, self-interested "economic man." In addition, he was depicted as young, daring, forever striving, and a transgressor of established norms. Merezhkovsky depicted such figures in his trilogy of historical novels, *Christ and Anti-Christ—Death of the Gods (Julian the Apostate)* (1895), *Resurrection of the Gods (Leonardo da Vinci)* (1900), and *Antichrist (Peter and Alexis)* (1904). The protagonists illustrate Merezhkovsky's tendency to make individuals into symbols. Julian, Leonardo, and Peter each have Nietzschean and Christian traits, combined differently as Merezhkovsky's views changed. In his study of Tolstoy and Dostoevsky (1900–1902), Merezhkovsky compared the Russian literary giants to each other and to Nietzsche (to Tolstoy's detriment) and posited a polarity *within* Christianity between "the flesh" and "the spirit." Tolstoy represents "the flesh" (on which he was fixated, according to Merezhkovsky), while the tormented Dostoevsky represents the yearnings of "the spirit."[13] In the new man "flesh" and "spirit" would be harmoniously combined. And he would have wings, literally, because they signify freedom from nature's law. Merezhkovsky took the Wright Brothers' airplane flight to mean that if human beings could ascend to heaven, then heaven could descend to earth. Bely used "new man" and "Superman" interchangeably to denote his ideal of the new human being of the future.[14]

The symbolists' revolt against "necessity" included gender issues and, in some cases, rejection of procreation and the nuclear family. Dionysus was an androgynous god, but Nietzsche did not say so. The symbolists took that idea from Soloviev, who probably took it from Plato, and/or occult doctrines, and the Bible: "There is neither male nor female for ye are all one in Christ Jesus" (Galatians 3:28). Some symbolists interpreted bisexuality in terms of a mystique of the Trinity, which they used to justify triadic sexual arrangements.[15] They spoke of the "feminine" element in man, but except

---

11. Clowes, *Revolution*, 144–50.
12. Nadezhda Mandelstam, *Hope Abandoned*, trans. Max Hayward (New York, 1974), 408.
13. Details in Rosenthal, "Stages of Nietzscheanism."
14. See, for example, Andrei Bely, *Arabeski* (Moscow, 1911), 45.
15. Olga Matich, "The Merezhkovskys' Third Testament and the Russian Utopian

for Gippius, who signed some of her articles "Comrade Herman," they ignored the "masculine" element in woman. Rozanov called homosexuals "people of the moonlight" and argued against persecuting them.

Symbolist revaluations of Christian morality extolled liberation of the passions and instincts repressed by Christianity, made beauty and creativity into virtues, and extolled "Nietzschean" individualism, self-realization, and emotional liberation. Merezhkovsky claimed that Tolstoy's invocations of celibacy, even in marriage, exemplified the hatred of the flesh preached by "historical Christianity." Dostoevsky exemplified the spirit and was Nietzsche's precursor.[16] Pointing out the many parallels in their thought, Merezhkovsky explained them as responses to the exhaustion of "historical Christianity." His treatment of Dostoevsky and Nietzsche as kindred spirits was crucial in shaping the Russian reception of Nietzsche.

Political Myths and a Dionysian Theater

The symbolists interpreted the Revolution of 1905 as primarily a religious and cultural crisis, and as the beginning of the Apocalypse that would inaugurate the Kingdom of God on Earth, a new world of freedom, beauty, and love. Hoping to shape a still-fluid situation, they created new political myths and concentrated their efforts on the theater as the best way to reach the people (*narod*). Once politicized, symbolists inclined to anarchism, utopian socialism, and neo-Slavophilism, for they detested Marxist (and liberal) materialism and claimed that Marxism suppresses "individuality," using that term much as Herzen, Lavrov, and Mikhailovsky did, as opposed to "individualism," which they defined as self-affirmation apart from or against the community. All of them considered Nietzsche an anarchist.

Merezhkovsky's political myth was a "religious revolution" that would culminate in a "religious society" characterized by *sobornost'*, in which the "truth of anarchism" (unlimited personal freedom) and the "truth of socialism" (belonging to a loving community) would be reconciled. He proclaimed that Jesus was a revolutionary and a warrior, who brought humankind "not peace but a sword," and came to turn the whole world upside down. After the revolution, Jesus would be the sole ruler and His only law would be love. Merezhkovsky's revolutionary Christ was an implicit response to Nietzsche's contempt for "slavish" Christianity and Tolstoy's pacifism. He ignored, at

---

Tradition," in *Christianity and the Eastern Slavs*, ed. Robert P. Hughes and Irina Paperno (Berkeley and Los Angeles, 1994), 2:158–71.

16. For Merezhkovsky's deconstruction and reconstruction of Tolstoy, see Bernice Glatzer Rosenthal, "Merezhkovsky's Readings of Tolstoi," in *Russian Thought After Communism: The Recovery of a Philosophical Heritage*, ed. James P. Scanlan (Armonk, N.Y., 1994), 121–46.

least publicly, Nietzsche's view that Jesus was in rebellion against the "Jewish church":

> "Church" taken in precisely the sense in which we take the word today.
> . . . This holy anarchist who roused up the lowly, the outcasts and
> "sinners," the *Chandala* within Judaism to oppose the ruling order—
> in language which, if the Gospels are to be trusted, would even today
> lead to Siberia—was a political criminal in an *absurdly unpolitical*
> society. This is what brought him to the Cross. . . . He died for *his*
> guilt [not] for the guilt of others. (*AC,* 139, 140)

The censor would not have passed such an inflammatory statement. Moreover, Merezhkovsky wanted to found his own church.

In *Griadushchii Kham* (The Ham of the Future, 1906), Merezhkovsky imagined the Beast of the Apocalypse with three faces: Autocracy, Orthodoxy, and *meshchanstvo,* a word that originally pertained to the lower middle class, but came to mean philistinism and vulgarity. Since Autocracy and Orthodoxy were in their death throes, the boorish Ham (son of the biblical Noah) was the real victor of the Revolution. The title of the English translation, *The Menace of the Mob,* captures Merezhkovsky's fear of the rampaging mob, but obscures his aristocratic contempt for the middle class. The same year, he called Dostoevsky "the prophet of the Russian Revolution." In his essay, "Revolution and Religion" (1907), Merezhkovsky "revalued" Dostoevsky, Tolstoy, and other Russian writers for their "religious-revolutionary significance," returning to the didactic tradition of Russian literature he had previously opposed. In *Le Tsar et la revolution* (also 1907), he treated Russia and Europe as two halves of an eschatological dualism— Russians are Dionysian and Europeans Apollonian—invoked Russian messianism, and predicted that Russia and Europe would both go up in flames. In other essays, he praised the revolutionary intelligentsia as "Christians without Christ."

Ivanov supported Mystical Anarchism, a doctrine concocted by Georgy Chulkov (1879–1939) that purported to combine personal freedom with membership in a loving community, for which Ivanov used the Slavophile term *obshchina.* The doctrine was a mish-mash of Nietzsche, Herzen, Bakunin, Merezhkovsky (Chulkov was a former editor of *New Path*), Ibsen, Byron, utopian socialism, Tolstoy's Christian anarchism, and Dostoevsky's rejection of necessity.[17] Ivanov's slogan "nonacceptance of the world" stemmed from Ivan Karamazov's refusal to accept the world God created, as did more

17. Details in Bernice Glatzer Rosenthal, "The Transmutation of the Symbolist Ethos: Mystical Anarchism and the Revolution of 1905," *Slavic Review* 36, no. 4 (December 1977): 608–27.

remotely, Ivanov's concept of "struggling with God" (*Bogoborchestvo*). The latter concept was also informed by Nietzsche's depiction of Prometheus defying the Olympian gods. Turning Nietzsche's aestheticism into a theurgy, Ivanov envisioned a "new organic society" (Saint-Simon's term) characterized by freedom, beauty, and love. He ignored the productionist and technocratic aspects of Saint-Simon's utopian socialism.

Mystical Anarchism was a politicized Dionysianism that emphasized destruction and creativity. To be destroyed were all authorities external to the individual—especially government, law, social custom, and morality. Ivanov and Chulkov based their doctrine on the "mystical person" who seeks union with others, as opposed to the egoistic "empirical person," who asserts his interests and claims his rights. Repudiating "Nietzschean" individualism and the will to power, Ivanov invoked "powerlessness" as his social ideal. In the new society, no human being would rule another and dominance and subordination would cease. The social cement would be the internal and invisible bonds of love, myth, and sacrifice. Ivanov's social ideal was a cultic version of *sobornost'*, in which eros replaced agape; a "new religious synthesis" (the new myth) that was Christian but not exclusively Christian replaced the state religion; a Dionysian theater replaced the state church; and "inner experience" replaced dogma. He and Chulkov never specified who or what would be sacrificed and who or what would be worshiped.

The idea of love replacing law is Christian, but it can also be supported by Nietzsche: "In the entire psychology of the 'Gospel,' the concept of guilt and punishment is lacking; likewise the concept reward. 'Sin,' every kind of distancing relationship between God and man, is abolished—*precisely this is the 'glad tidings.'* Blessedness is not promised, it is not tied to any conditions: it is the *only* reality" (*AC*, 145). The judgmental aspects of Christianity, Nietzsche attributed to Paul's desire for priestly power (*AC*, 155).

The positive aspect of Mystical Anarchism was a Dionysian theater (Ivanov's idea), devoted to "myth-creation" (*mifotvorchestvo*) and characterized by "collective creativity." In such a theater the dormant "mystical person" in everyone would be evoked and developed and a new socially unifying myth would be collectively created or, more accurately, reformulated. Ivanov believed that while myths reflect a timeless reality, they change as circumstances change. The symbolist poet, acting as a high priest, would articulate the "new word," becoming the progenitor of a "new religious synthesis" (= new myth), a new cult, a new culture, and a "new organic society" in that order.[18] The "new religious synthesis" would be Christian, but not exclusively Christian (it would include occult doctrines), and it would not be dogmatic. By contrast, Merezhkovsky believed that new

---

18. Details in Bernice Glatzer Rosenthal, "Theater as Church: The Vision of the Mystical Anarchists," part 2, *Russian History* 4 (1977): 122–41.

Christian dogma was necessary and called for a *sobor* (church council) to formulate it. As far as he was concerned, the Mystical Anarchists were "mystical hooligans"

To Ivanov, the Dionysian rites embodied the essence of the theatrical art—action. He wanted to abolish the stage and have the crowd dance and sing, as in a Dionysian dithyramb, and praise the god with words. In the original Dionysian theater, he explained, there were no spectators; each participant in the rites had a dual role: to participate in the "orgy of action" and the "orgy of purification," to make holy and to become holy, to attract the divine presence and to receive the divine gift. Ivanov's performance theory modified Wagner's *Gesamtkunstwerk* to emphasize the (Dionysian) chorus rather than the orchestra, the theurgic aspects of myth, and the spoken word. The chorus was a mystical entity, an embodiment of *sobornost'*, in which the participants shed their separateness to achieve a "living union," which Ivanov hoped to extend to society at large. The chorus, not the newly created Duma, was the authentic voice of the people (*narod*); constitutions and legal rights were merely "formal freedoms." Note that Ivanov gave the chorus a quasi-political function; Nietzsche explicitly denied such a function. Ivanov's emphasis on the *narod* harks back to Slavophilism and populism except that he and Chulkov added a new element; the *narod* were the "new barbarians" destined to revitalize Russian culture.

Ivanov contended that a theater that played to the unconscious and that included orgiastic rituals that induced self-forgetting in "mystical ecstasy" would foster the non-egoistic, communitarian psyche required in a society without coercion. Although he highlighted Eros (sexual love) rather than Thanatos (death), the idea of ritual sacrifice was embedded in his performance theory, albeit vaguely. As noted above, he did not specify who or what would be sacrificed, or worshiped in the Dionysian theater. Mood creation by techniques that were part of the symbolist theatrical inventory was the corollary of myth-creation. Techniques are neutral; the same technique can be deployed on behalf of a range of ideologies.

The Dionysian theater never materialized for lack of funds, but the Nietzsche/Wagner/Ivanov syndrome (Lars Kleberg's term) was widely discussed and taken up in modified forms. Pavel Gaideburov, director of the Mobile Popular Theater, combined Ivanov's idea of "collective creativity" with his own view of theater as festival. Theater-cafes abolished the stage and experimented with actor-audience dialogue. Nikolai Evreinov (1879–1953), a long-time admirer of Nietzsche, responded to Ivanov with his own theory, "theater for oneself," which dropped the sacerdotal trappings of Ivanov's theory and introduced Freudian ideas. Evreinov talked about a "will to the theater" and "will to theatricality." He believed that human beings are theatrical animals; they act with an audience in mind.

Bely objected to the "orgiasm" (*orgiazm*) and amoralism of Mystical Anarchism, but Blok was sympathetic. Around 1908, he superimposed Nietzsche's categories of Dionysian and Apollonian onto the Wagnerian categories of culture and civilization, as Nietzsche himself did on occasion. Wagner described culture as organic, spontaneous, noncerebral, and residing in the German *Volk*, as distinct from and opposed to abstract, rational civilization, exemplified by the French. Russians could read "Russian" culture and "Western" civilization or, as Blok did, folk culture and intellectual civilization. Blok associated Dionysus with the elemental folk, the carriers of culture in his view, and prophesied the "revenge of the elements," the flaming lava of revolution breaking through the encrusted "Apollonian" layers of bourgeois civilization, destroying the cerebral intelligentsia.

The Apocalypse Deferred

Around 1908, disappointed with the outcome of the Revolution, the symbolists began to reconsider their views. Merezhkovsky and Ivanov blamed the nihilism and amoralism of postrevolutionary Russian society on Nietzsche's influence and repudiated him, or claimed to, but they continued to draw on his thought. Ivanov proclaimed that "Dionysus in Russia is dangerous." He stopped talking about "orgiasm" and "ecstasy," condemned self-affirmation as Luciferan or demonic, and pointed out that Zarathustra was a "lawgiver" as well as a "lawbreaker." Muting his association of Dionysus and Christ, Ivanov criticized Nietzsche (as Soloviev did) for his "naturalism," "biologism," and "physiologism," and for lacking transcendence. Merezhkovsky and Rozanov called Nietzscheanism a childhood sickness, fatal to adults. Merezhkovsky announced that his previous attempts to reconcile paganism and Christianity were dangerous heresies. As he distanced himself from Nietzsche, Merezhkovsky's esteem for Tolstoy grew correspondingly, but it was always qualified. Occasionally, Merezhkovsky discussed Nietzschean ideas under other rubrics. In "Lermontov: Poet of Super-Humanity" (1908, in *MPSS*, 16:157–205), for example, he criticized individualism. (Mikhail Lermontov, 1814–41, was deeply influenced by Byron and later regarded as a precursor of Nietzsche.) Bely depicted the destruction of a naive intellectual by a (Dionysian) religious sect in his novel *The Silver Dove* (1909). Chukholka, a conveyer of evil forces, is a composite of Chulkov and the Theosophist Kobylinsky-Ellis. Having never championed Dionysianism, Bely felt no need to disguise his interest in Nietzsche and continued to refer to him. Nietzschean motifs pervade his novel *Petersburg* (1916).[19]

19. Details in Virginia Bennett, "Echoes of Friedrich Nietzsche's *The Birth of Tragedy*

In 1908, Chulkov organized a symposium on the theater of the future.[20] Ivanov did not participate, but his views were extensively discussed. The speakers included Chulkov, Bely, Briusov, Sologub, the future Soviet director Vsevolod Meyerhold (1874–1970), who had staged symbolist plays, and the Nietzschean Marxist Anatoly Lunacharsky. Chulkov maintained that as long as society remained bourgeois, the attempt to abolish the stage was premature, but the theater could still play a prophetic, countercultural role in the struggle against "bourgeois individualism" and the spirit of property. Lunacharsky envisioned an ideological theater-temple as the center of a "free religious cult" and a locus of collective creativity. Such a theater would be considered barbarian, he said, but "the salvation of civilization is in its barbarians." Soon after the symposium, Lunacharsky retracted his views and stopped calling the people "barbarians," but an ideological theater-temple remained one of his goals.

Briusov, Meyerhold, and Sologub advocated a theater of pure theatricality, that is to say, a theater for theater's sake, as distinct from a theater subordinated to a religious or a social ideal. In 1902, Briusov had called for a "conditional theater" (*uslovnyi teatr*); *uslovnyi* can also be translated "conventional," as in theatrical conventions. He wanted a stylized theater that required the audience to use its imagination, rather than a theater that attempted to replicate every detail of reality, like Stanislavsky's Moscow Art Theater. (One of its productions included a live frog croaking for verisimilitude!) Briusov argued that such "unnecessary truths" clutter the stage and distract from the main thing—the actor's performance. At the Symposium, he advocated simplified staging and an actor-centered, rather than a director-centered, theater.

Meyerhold and Sologub offered their own versions of a "conditional theater" that separated symbolist techniques of mood creation and subliminal communication from attempts to unite art and life, or theater and revolution. Meyerhold wanted the spectators to be constantly reminded of the illusory nature of the production and used masks to underscore the performance aspects of theater. He wanted a theater centered on a director who controlled utterly submissive actor-marionettes from afar.

---

in Andrej Bely's *Petersburg*," *Germano-Slavica* 4 (1980): 243–59; Robert Maguire and John Malmstad, "Petersburg," in *Andrei Belyi: The Spirit of Symbolism*, ed. John Malmstad (Ithaca, 1987), 96–144; Peter Barta, "Nietzschean Masks and the Classical Apollo in Andrei Bely's *Petersburg*," *Studia slavica Hungaricae* 37 (1991–92): 393–403; Carol Anschuetz, "Bely's *Petersburg* and the End of the Russian Novel," in *The Russian Novel*, ed. John Garrard (New Haven, 1983), 125–53; and Robert Mann, "Apollo and Dionysus in Andrei Bely's *Petersburg*," *Russian Review* 57 (October 1998): 507–25.

20. *Teatr, kniga o novom teatre* (Peterburg, 1908). English translations of the presentations of Briusov, Bely, and Sologub are in *Russian Dramatic Theory from Pushkin to the Symbolists*, ed. Laurence Senelick (Austin, Tex., 1981). For the occult elements, see Rosenthal, *Occult*, 385–87.

Among the sources of their versions of "conditional theater" were the Austrian symbolist Maurice Maeterlinck (1862–1949), whose plays were staged in Moscow; the British director Gordon Craig (1872–1966), author of an influential essay "The Actor and the Übermarionette"; Nietzsche; and the Russian symbolists. Nietzsche considered the tragic heroes of ancient Greece masks of Dionysus. Ivanov believed that Don Quixote and the heroes of Shakespeare and Ibsen were "new masks" of the same "suffering god" ("Novye maski," in *ISS*, 2:76–82). Some symbolist plays used comic masks such as the masks of the Commedia dell'arte, which Bely and Blok linked with Nietzsche's idea that masks are illusions that shield the spectators from the harshness of reality. In other symbolist plays, clowns or harlequins represent the alter ego or the unconscious. Meyerhold associated with the symbolists; as noted above he had staged some of their plays.

Sologub championed a "Theater of a Single Will," the will of the poet-playwright. Since drama is the product of a single conception, he argued, "why shouldn't the actor resemble a marionette?" There would be only one hero, both sacrificer and sacrifice. The spectator would become a participant in the mysterium, a liturgical ritual, in which he could "join hands with his brother and his sister and press his lips eternally parched with thirst to the mysteriously filled cup where 'I shall mingle blood with water.' To consummate in a bright public temple what can now be consummated only in catacombs."[21] Sologub wanted the spectators to lose themselves in the hectic rhythms of a dervish dance, his counterpart to the Dionysian dithyrambs. But he also invited them to join in the spectacle as they did in the sports and games of their youth. There was an element of playful "let's pretend" in Sologub's theatrical vision. The political implication of a theater of marionettes is dictatorship, but Sologub and Meyerhold were not trying to unite art and life, or present the illusion on the stage as truth.

Bely wanted to transform life itself into theater and his own life into a work of art. *The Birth of Tragedy* was being overemphasized, he complained. "The virtuous Zarathustra . . . walked off stage into life. The third and fourth parts of Zarathustra are the drama of life in earnest." Instead of freeing modern drama from the "morbid excesses of the mysterium mania," contemporary theorists are perpetuating Nietzsche's errors and "reject[ing] his sane protest against mass Wagneritis."[22] In other words, the struggle for a new life must continue outside the theater. Bely wanted "myth-creation" to be transformed into "life-creation." To Bely, art was the creation of life and life was creativity. He took Nietzsche's metaphor of an "artist-god" (*BT*,

21. Sologub, "Theater of a Single Will," in Senelick, *Russian Dramatic Theory*, 41 and 135.

22. Bely, "Theater and Contemporary Drama," in Senelick, *Russian Dramatic Theory*, 154–55.

22) literally, but dropped Nietzsche's amoralism. In Bely's words: "The ideal of beauty is the ideal of a human being and aesthetic creation, as it expands, it inevitably leads to the transfiguration of human personality: Zarathustra, Buddha, and Christ are as much the artists of life as they are life's lawgivers; their ethics merges with their aesthetic and vice versa."[23] Bely had mingled aesthetics and morality before, but not as drastically.

Other symbolists developed their own versions of "life-creation," making them into great projects of theurgic transfiguration. Challenging Briusov's view that art is autonomous, Ivanov declared, "Symbolism never was and never wanted to be merely art." "Art is not the creation of images [or icons], but the creation of life [*ne ikonotvorchestvo a zhizne tvorchestvo*]." Gippius counterposed the notion of life as creation to quotidian life (*byt*), which she regarded as dead matter.[24] "Life-creation" was a symbolist rendition of what Nietzsche called the "will to power as art." On another level, "life-creation" derived from the Orthodox concept of divine energies permeating the universe, which the symbolists interpreted in the spirit of deification, making man a cocreator with God.

Ivanov's failed attempt to create a Dionysian theater led him to realize that a myth needs a visual image, Apollo descending from the clouds (see *BT*, 143–44), and that a new myth had to be couched in terms familiar to the people. He began to theorize about Apollo and Apollonianism and to treat Christianity, most unconventionally, as a myth. Describing Jesus as an Apollonian figure, Ivanov interpreted Apollo as the principle of unity and reinterpreted Dionysus as the principle of multiplicity or fragmentation. The symbol became the Word with its explicitly Christian associations; the cultic community became a transcendental church or nation (depending on the context); and the passions became the Russian soul. Like Soloviev, Ivanov distinguished between "nationality," a cultural concept, and "nationalism," an expression of the will to power. "Nations" were the "persons" of humankind.

In "The Russian Idea" (1909), a term coined by Dostoevsky and popularized by Soloviev, Ivanov proposed a specifically Christian integrating myth. Every nation has its own "idea," Ivanov maintained. It is a basic fact of history, a product of the psychological substratum of the unconscious spheres of the national soul. "The Russian idea" is a Christian idea because the Russian soul is Christian. Christianity is a form of "primitive culture" (= organic culture) that arose in response to the "critical culture" of Ancient Rome. Christianity prevailed because it was couched in the form of mystery. All new religious truths must be "hidden in mystery, in the form of myth." As

---

23. Andrei Bely, *Simvolizm* (Moscow, 1910), 10.
24. Gippius, *Creating Life*, ed. Joan Grossman and Irina Paperno (Stanford, 1994), 8, 21, 152.

an example, Ivanov gave the religious innovations of Pisistratus, founder of the Orphic mystery religion, which were so in tune with the subliminal yearnings of the people that their novelty was forgotten. Pisistratus was remembered as a tyrant, not as a renegade from the popular faith. By contrast, Socrates, founder of critical rationalism, was perceived as a heretic and a danger to the state. He did not understand the people, nor did they understand him. Implicitly, the secular intelligentsia was repeating Socrates' error. Religious innovations (which Ivanov did not specify) must be expressed in mythic form and incorporated into Christian mystery. He also emphasized the intelligentsia's selflessness, its yearning for "descent" (to the people) and service, thereby restoring the kenotic virtues of self-sacrifice, humility (vis-à-vis the people), and love.[25] Self-sacrifice was morally superior to self-preservation, "the law of Moses and of our culture" (*ISS*, 2:126). Authentic Christianity transcends (or negates) natural law.

In other writings, Ivanov rejected the "pagan" Renaissance, as well as the Enlightenment and "godless" mechanical civilization, subordinated Nietzsche to Orthodoxy, and redefined the Renaissance to include the High Middle Ages. He read Dante as a symbolist poet of the divine Sophia, misinterpreted Dante's *amor* as Dionysian ecstasy, and suppressed the moral element in Dante's works.[26] He saw World War I as the beginning of a new constructive era and Russia as having a messianic task. In chauvinistic articles written against "the German spirit" he used terms such as "superbeast" and compared the German state to Hobbes's Leviathan.[27] At first, Merezhkovsky opposed Russian participation in the war, but as it dragged on he too came to see it in eschatological terms.[28]

In an essay about the Russian poets Fedor Tiutchev (1803–73) and Nikolai Nekrasov (1825–77), Merezhkovsky blamed Tiutchev's "chaotic" epistemology and Tiutchev's poem *Silentium* for driving symbolists to unbearable loneliness and suicidal despair in the 1890s, placing particular emphasis on the lines "Be silent, conceal yourself, and hide both your feelings and your dreams . . . learn how to live within yourself." Fedor Tiutchev was indeed one of symbolists' favorite poets, but Merezhkovsky's real target was Nietzsche's Dionysian epistemology and solipsistic "Nietzschean" individualism.[29] He did

25. Ivanov, "O Russkoi idee," in *ISS*, 3:321–28. For Merezhkovsky's response, see "Zemlia vo rtu," *Bol'naia Rossiia*, in *MPSS*, 15:167–78.

26. Pamela Davidson, *The Poetic Imagination of Vyacheslav Ivanov: A Russian Symbolist's Perception of Dante* (Cambridge, 1989). See also Lena Szilard and Peter Barta, "Dantovskoi khod russkogo simvolizma," *Studia slavica Hungaricae* 35, no. 1–2 (1989): 61–95.

27. Viacheslav Ivanov, "Vselenskoe delo" and "Legion i sobornost'," in *Rodnoe i vselenskoe. Stat'i 1914–1916* (Moscow, 1917), 5–18 and 37–46. See also, Ben Hellman, *Poets of Hope and Despair: The Russian Symbolists in War and Revolution* (Helsinki, 1995), 84–93, 197–201.

28. Hellman, *Poets of Hope and Despair*, 139–67, 217–27.

29. Merezhkovskii, *Dve tainy russkoi poezii: Tiutchev i Nekrasov* (Petrograd, 1915).

not want to admit to having been influenced by a German. Nekrasov, the populists' favorite poet, bewailed the misery of the lower classes. Russia needs Nekrasov now, Merezhkovsky declared, returning once again to the social didacticism he had previously opposed.

Symbolist ideas pervaded poetry, prose, music, painting, and theater, providing a rich store of symbols, images, and slogans, many gleaned from Nietzsche and Wagner, that were adapted by a broad range of artists and writers. The *Gesamtkunstwerk* ideal, symbolist techniques for bypassing the intellect and appealing directly to the unconscious, and Ivanov's call for a Dionysian theater dedicated to "myth-creation" and characterized by collective creativity and the abolition of the stage, had a wide-ranging influence on performance theory and practice and were later adapted to Soviet propaganda. The figures to be discussed in the next three chapters responded to the symbolists as well as to Nietzsche.

The essay tells more about Merezhkovsky's "turn to Christ" than about Tiutchev. Details in Bernice G. Rosenthal, *D. S. Merezhkovsky and the Silver Age* (The Hague, 1975), 73–75.

Philosophers

The world revolves, not around the inventors of new
noises, but around the inventors of new values; it
revolves *inaudibly.*   —*Z,* 153–54

The philosophers to be discussed in this chapter hailed
Nietzsche's critique of rationalism, positivism, and conventional morality. Nikolai Berdiaev (1874–1948) and Semen
Frank (1877–1950) tried to combine Nietzsche and Kant
in a metaphysical liberalism. Nietzsche spurred their search
for new values and inspired hopes of creating a new man,
a new culture, and a new society. Berdiaev later abandoned
liberalism and proclaimed a Nietzsche-imbued religion of
creativity. Lev Shestov (Leib Yehuda Shvartsman, 1866–1938)
used Nietzsche to attack Tolstoy's moralism and abstract
philosophical systems. Pavel Florensky (1882–1937) propounded an existential Orthodoxy that emphasized ecclesiality (*tserkovnost'*) and exalted beauty and creativity as
emanations of love. All these philosophers went through a
Godseeking period.

Nietzsche Versus Kant's "Morality of Duty"

Kant's morality can be summed up in his imperatives: "Act only on that maxim that can be universally applied" and "Treat humanity always at the same time as an end, and never merely as a means." Neo-Kantianism dominated German academic philosophy from the 1860s on. Kant's tenet that the human mind orders experience through a priori categories (time, space, causality) fostered an interest in psychology and led some neo-Kantians to become interested in archetypes and myths and in Nietzsche.[1] This also happened in the Moscow Psychological Society, a bastion of neo-Kantianism, which initiated philosophic discussion of Nietzsche in 1892 in its journal, *Problems of Philosophy and Psychology* (*Voprosy filosofii i psikhologii*).[2]

Ten years later, the Moscow Psychological Society published a symposium titled *Problems of Idealism* (*Problemy idealizma,* 1902), to which Berdiaev and Frank contributed, mingling Kant and Nietzsche in a metaphysical liberalism based on personhood, rather than a social contract, that emphasized freedom and self-realization and excluded eudaemonism and utilitarianism. In the mid-1890s, they had initiated (with Petr Struve, 1870–1944, and Sergei Bulgakov, 1871–1944) a "back to Kant" movement in Marxism, in order to supplement it with an autonomous ethic. A few years later, they repudiated Marxist materialism for a Kantian idealism. In *Problems of Idealism,* they used Nietzsche to supplement Kant. Perceiving Nietzsche as an idealist, an advocate of a "higher morality" that stemmed from free volition and ardent conviction, they interpreted his *"new nobility"* (Z, 220) as a spiritual aristocracy, a creator of new values and a new culture, and the Superman as the symbol of Nietzsche's lofty moral and cultural ideal. Berdiaev went so far as to proclaim that "man has not only the right but even the duty to become a 'Superman,' because the 'Superman' is the path from man to God."[3]

Freedom, moral autonomy, and duty were central to Kant and Nietzsche alike, Berdiaev contended. "Kant provides the philosophic basis for ethical individualism, for the recognition of the person as an end in itself and an unconditional value. Nietzsche overcomes the middle-class [*meshchanskii*] element in Kantian practical morality and prepares the free morality of the

---

1. Examples include Alois Riehl's *Friedrich Nietzsche: Der Kunstler und der Denker* (1897) and George Simmel's *Fridrikh Nitsche: Eine moral-philosophische Silhouette* (1896); both works were translated into Russian and reviewed in Russian journals.

2. Details in Ann Lane, "Nietzsche Comes to Russia," in *NR,* 51–68. For their interpretation of Kant, see Randall Poole, "The Neo-Idealist Reception of Kant in the Moscow Psychological Society," *Journal of the History of Ideas* 60, no. 2 (April 1999): 319–43.

3. Berdiaev, "Eticheskaia problema v svete filosofskogo idealizma," in *Problemy idealizma* (Moscow, 1902), 124.

future, the morality of strong human individuality" (126). Despite Nietzsche's "demonism," his core ideals were essentially Christian: the absolute value of man as the image and likeness of God, the equal worth of people before God, the belief in spiritual perfection, and the conception of freedom as an internal matter. "All of Nietzsche is a passionate tormented protest against reality in the name of a higher ideal," a protest against existing morality in the name of a higher morality, against evil in the name of good (93–94). Nietzsche's philosophy is a corrective to Kant's "practical morality," which stemmed from the "old idea" of original sin.

Berdiaev faulted Kant for denying the "Dionysian principle of life" and for dividing personality into sensory (*chuvstvennyi*) and moral-rational natures, thereby creating an "absurd" opposition of duty and self-realization. "In man there is a mad thirst for life, intensive and vivid, for a strong and powerful life"; this thirst is neither good nor evil. Morality must not deny it, but unite it with the affirmation and development of the "spiritual I" (= individuality) (131). For Nietzsche, the greatest moral crime was the betrayal of one's "inner I." Invocation of the "sacred right of self-determination" was Nietzsche's greatest service to ethical philosophy. Freedom is not a negative conception (freedom from) as bourgeois thinkers hold, but a matter of inner spiritual creativity, Berdiaev asserted.

To Berdiaev, self-determination entailed fidelity to a lofty ideal, symbolized by the Superman, a "religious-metaphysical ideal" that had nothing in common with political or economic oppression or crude physical power. He believed that people need a "supra-empirical ideal world" and a "spiritual aristocracy" to lead them to spiritual self-perfection and beauty, and to enable them to break the chains of "natural necessity" (the laws of nature). He objected to the biological aspects of Nietzsche's Superman, however, and to Nietzsche's "Darwinian" emphasis on struggle. Berdiaev considered the Marxist "ethic of class antagonism" a major obstacle to personal (and social) development, but he was just as hostile to "bourgeois" values. One epigraph to his article was, "I go among this people and keep my eyes open: they have become *smaller* and are becoming ever smaller: and *their doctrine of happiness and virtue is the cause*" (91; Z, 189). Another one was, "Always do what you will—but first be such as *can will!*" (91; Z, 191). Berdiaev's "new man" was a strong-willed individual who set himself great tasks.

Frank based his argument for a metaphysical liberalism on Zarathustra's concept of *Fernstenliebe*, "love of the most distant" (Z, 86–88), as opposed to *Nächstenliebe*, literally "love for the nearest," the standard German term for the biblical injunction to love one's neighbor as oneself. Frank interpreted "love of the most distant" as a creative love that must always be active and that, inevitably, "takes the form of *struggle* with people, creative struggle, creativity in the form of struggle. The warrior and the creator serve the most distant." Such service requires firmness, hardness, courage, and willingness to sacrifice, because "a firstborn is always sacrificed" (Z, 217).[4] Frank seconded Zarathustra's assertion, "Higher *still* than love of one's neighbor, I value love for things and specters" (162)—"causes" and "phantoms" in Hollingdale's translation (Z, 87); "things and ghosts" in Kaufmann's (PN, 173). The German word *Sache* (pl. *Sachen*) means both "things" and "causes." The Russian word *veshchi* only means "things." By this odd choice of words, Frank indicated the reality of such intangible essences as truth, justice, beauty, harmony, and honor. Quoting Zarathustra's injunction to love one's "children's land," Frank pointed out that in Nietzsche's eyes, people were only material for the future, stones for a great edifice that is being constructed.

Oblivious to the sinister implications of viewing people as building blocks, Frank interpreted "love for the most distant" to mean love for one's fellow citizens (although he admitted a certain contempt and hatred for the "humanity that is near"), and an active and heroic struggle for noble "things and specters." He expected "the blissful *self-love* that flows from a powerful soul" (Nietzsche's words), healthy, vital self-love, to inspire people to demand truth and justice, human dignity, the moral rights of the person, and so on (182). These were radical ideas in Russia at the time. Frank regarded each person as a concrete, original essence, whose cultivation and flowering would augment society's spiritual and cultural wealth. Zarathustra alluded to selfishness as one of "three most cursed things" (Z, 206). Frank ignored the other two—"sensual pleasure" and "lust for power." He and Berdiaev joined forces with Merezhkovsky for a few years; they edited *New Path* before its demise and its successor journal *Problems of Life* (*Voprosy zhizni*).

Shestov's interpretation of Nietzsche stressed "that terrible metamorphosis called sickness" as the motivation for Nietzsche's "revaluation of all values," perhaps because Shestov also had an incapacitating illness (in 1895).[5] According to Shestov, *Human, All Too Human,* the first book Nietzsche wrote after his illness, was the key Nietzsche text, because here Nietzsche began to question idealist pieties and to emancipate himself from Schopenhauer and Wagner. All his life, Shestov stressed the inability of positivism, rationalism, or idealism to assuage or explain tragedy and suffering. In his studies of Tolstoy and Dostoevsky, Shestov traced their views to

---

4. Frank, "Fr. Nitsshe i etika 'liubvi k dal'nemu,'" in *Problemy idealizma,* 146–48. See also Phillip Swoboda, "The Philosophical Thought of S. L. Frank, 1902–15: A Study of the Metaphysical Impulse of Early 20th Century Russian Culture" (Ph.D. diss., Columbia University, 1992), 150–295, 359, 371–77, 458–71.

5. Lev Shestov, *The Good in the Teaching of Tolstoi and Nietzsche,* trans. and ed. Bernard Martin and Spencer Roberts (Columbus, 1969), 81. Published in one volume with *Dostoevsky and Nietzsche: The Philosophy of Tragedy* (1902).

a defining personal experience and contrasted the literary giants to each other and to Nietzsche, to Tolstoy's detriment. According to Shestov, great suffering led Nietzsche and Dostoevsky to new truths.

In *The Good in the Teachings of Tolstoy and Nietzsche: Philosophy and Preaching* (1900), Shestov contrasted Nietzsche's passionate search for truth "beyond good and evil" with Tolstoy's "cowardly" submission to idealist pieties. As Shestov tells it, Tolstoy was appalled by the poverty he saw in Moscow, but rather than admit his inability to do anything about it, he retreated to his estate to perfect himself. From then on, Tolstoy preached the identity of goodness and God and tried to impose his self-denying morality on others. *What Is Art?* was the conclusion of a life-long sermon and a cry of pain. By contrast, the sickness that struck Nietzsche after he wrote *The Birth of Tragedy* led the young romantic to realize the futility of lofty ideals. Nietzsche's punishment was unjustified; he had lived a virtuous life, but that was Shestov's point—great suffering is inexplicable, causeless, a bolt from the blue. From personal experience, Nietzsche learned that nature is pitiless, that brotherly love is a lie, and that goodness (God) is dead. Neither an immoralist nor an Antichrist, Nietzsche "understood" that evil was as necessary as good, that as the Gospel says, the sun shines on the good and the wicked alike (Matthew 5:45). "This is the meaning of [Nietzsche's] formula 'beyond good and evil.' There can be no doubt: to Nietzsche was revealed a truth hidden in the words of the gospel which we did indeed recognize, but never dared to introduced into our 'philosophical' conception of the world. This time also a new Golgotha was necessary for a new truth to be born" (133–34; see also 116). Nietzsche's "immoralism" was the result of his unexpected "plunge into the dark abyss of suffering" (135). In the end, however, Nietzsche created a new idol—the Superman—his counterpart to Tolstoy's "goodness." Nevertheless, "Nietzsche has shown us the way [*put*']. We must seek what is *higher* than compassion, what is *higher* than good. We must seek God" (140). Shestov's God-seeking did not lead to Jesus, but he was not a "Jewish Jew" either; he did not identify with Judaism or with the Jewish community.

In *Dostoevsky and Nietzsche: The Philosophy of Tragedy* (1903), Shestov describes these authors as "underground" thinkers and spiritual twins because they dared to acknowledge ugly truths. Dostoevsky's defining experience was hard labor and exile in Siberia, followed by his discovery of his own egoism upon his return to St. Petersburg. The protagonist of *Notes From Underground* (1866) declares that the whole world could "go to pot" as long as he has his regular cup of tea. Such extraordinary egoism, said Shestov, was Dostoevsky's reaction to injured pride, to an accumulation of humiliations, and it continued to grow, asserting its rights in ever-new forms. The most compelling one was Raskolnikov's assertion (in *Crime and Punishment*) that there are two moralities, one for ordinary people, the other for extraordinary people. As an extraordinary person, Raskolnikov was entitled to murder a "useless" old woman because he needed her money. Nietzsche's "underground" was illness, physical pain, and loneliness. Like the protagonist of *Notes From Underground*, Nietzsche openly admitted that he was not interested in the happiness of humanity.

Both he and Dostoevsky were driven from the "path of Wagnerian commonplaceness" by chance. ("Wagnerian" refers to Faust's lackey and to Nietzsche when he was Wagner's lackey.) Circumstances, not their own free will, forced them to rise above ordinary ways of looking at life. Theirs was "no 'revolt of slaves of morality,' as Nietzsche teaches . . . character is irrelevant here and if there are two moralities, it is not a morality of ordinary and extraordinary people, but of a morality of *commonplaceness* and a *morality of tragedy*—this correction must be made in [their] terminology" (300–301). The task of philosophy is "not to teach us humility, submission, or renunciation" but to teach people not "to transfer all the horrors of life into the sphere of the *Ding an sich*" (319–22). These books made Shestov's reputation as a major interpreter of Nietzsche, Dostoevsky, and Tolstoy.

In subsequent works, Shestov continued his attack on philosophic systems that impose a nonexistent unity on the world and gloss over the horrors of life. He rejected Soloviev's idea of "total unity," had no eschatological expectations, and was not a mystic. There is nothing lyrical or cultic, or utopian, in his philosophy, and nothing communal either, no church or synagogue. His focus was on the suffering individual. In *Apofeoz bezpochvennosti* (The Apotheosis of Groundlessness, 1905; published in English under the title *All Things Are Possible*), which was modeled after Nietzsche in its aphoristic structure and basic concepts, Shestov argued that philosophy must cease its search for eternal truth and teach people to live in uncertainty. This book was a succès de scandale. It contained statements such as "the first and essential condition of life is lawlessness. Laws are a refreshing sleep— lawlessness is creative activity," and "science cannot be uprooted except we first destroy morality."[6] Shestov was talking only about metaphysical truths and "objective" moral norms. Politically, he was a liberal or a moderate socialist, but he believed that no amount of reform could banish tragedy and suffering from life. Around 1910, he began to write about religion per se. Eventually, he made a leap into faith, much like Kierkegaard's, whom he discovered in the 1920s. Nietzsche and Dostoevsky remained Shestov's life-long reference points. Some Bolsheviks considered him a revolutionary thinker. After the Bolshevik Revolution they offered to publish his latest book if he would add a Marxist introduction. He refused. He emigrated in 1920. In emigration he denounced Bolshevism as a doctrine of pure destructiveness.[7]

6. Lev Shestov, *All Things Are Possible*, trans. with an introduction by Bernard Martin (Athens, Ohio, 1977), 60–61.
7. Lev Shestov, *Chto takoe bol'shevism?* (What is Bolshevism?) (Berlin, 1920).

A Dashed Hope: The Revolution of 1905

Berdiaev and Frank placed great hopes in the Revolution of 1905, but dismay at escalating violence and terror led them to place even more emphasis on developing a new culture. In 1909, they contributed, along with Struve and Bulgakov, to the symposium *Landmarks* (published as a book in 1909), which lambasted the revolutionary intelligentsia and called for new religious values.[8]

During the Revolution, Berdiaev was sometimes swept away by a millennial enthusiasm similar to Merezhkovsky's and the Mystical Anarchists'. He called Marx and Engels "bourgeois" (because they accepted the laws of nature), denounced Kant as "very dangerous" (because rationalism restricts man's "limitless strivings"), and praised Nietzsche's anarchism and Ivanov's conception of "struggling with God."[9] At other times, Berdiaev supported a moderate Christian socialism that would guarantee everyone the necessities of life. Frank, on the other hand, advocated an "individualist humanism" and supported political and social reform, but he came to see revolution as primarily about power, the "lust for power" he had previously ignored. He placed his hopes for political freedom on cultural development, by which he meant imbuing the masses with new values. Partly with that goal in mind, he and Struve became founders of the Moscow Religious-Philosophic Society. They also founded and edited the journals *Polar Star* (*Poliarnaia zvezda*, 1905–6) and *Freedom and Culture* (*Svoboda i kul'tura*, 1906).

Polar Star had also been the title of one of Herzen's journals, and just as Herzen had opposed Bakunin's maximalism in his *Polar Star*, Berdiaev and Frank opposed the maximalists of their day, who justified bomb-throwing and "expropriations" (bank robberies) with a mish-mash of Bakunin, Nietzsche, Stirner, Nechaev, and Sorel. Max Stirner (1806–56), advocate of individualist anarchism and egoistic immoralism, was rediscovered by Nietzscheans in the 1890s and treated as Nietzsche's precursor. Nechaev's contemporaries rejected him, but a new generation of maximalists perceived him as a Nietzschean amoralist. Georges Sorel, author of *Reflections on Violence* (1906; Russian translation, 1907), tried to revitalize Marxism with the aid of Bergson and Nietzsche.[10] For Sorel, myth was a call to violent action. His mobilizing myth was a general strike that would culminate in a syndicalist society. Violence, the "clear and brutal expression of class war," would transform the workers psychologically from slaves to masters. A

8. *Landmarks*, ed. Boris Shragin and Albert Todd, trans. Marian Schwartz (New York, 1977).
9. Berdiaev, "Tragediia i obydennost'," *Voprosy zhizni*, 1905, no. 3, esp. 274–75, 278–79.
10. Sorel's debt to Nietzsche, as well as to Bergson, is obvious in *Reflections on Violence*, trans. T. E. Hulme (London, 1969); see 78, 92, 217–49. See also Forth, *Zarathustra in Paris*, 123–25.

surprisingly large number of Russian maximalists had only the crudest notions of political theory and were indifferent to socialist ideals.[11]

Landmarks went through five printings in one year and provoked over two hundred newspaper and journal articles in praise or denunciation of views expressed by contributors to the symposium. Berdiaev alleged that the intelligentsia's utilitarian approach to truth as justice and law (*pravda*) rendered it indifferent to philosophical truth (*istina*) and resulted in obscurantism, extreme subjectivism, disparagement of reason, and the "demonic deification of man." Russia's regeneration could be achieved only on the basis of an "objective" philosophy that incorporated the insights of Russia's greatest mystics—Rozanov, Merezhkovsky, and Ivanov—but rejected their hostility to reason. "The Dionysian principle of mysticism must be wed to the Apollonian principle of philosophy. . . . Philosophy is one of the ways of *objectifying* mysticism; the highest and most complete form of such an objectification can only be positive religion" (21). He ridiculed the "herds of Nietzschean individualists" that emerged from the Revolution, but credited Nietzsche for revitalizing Marxism (17).

Frank contended that "moral nihilism," the lack of absolute, objective moral values, was the distinguishing feature of the intelligentsia's worldview. The religious person seeks eternal, absolute principles, while the nihilist "strives to immortalize and absolutize the 'human, all too human' exclusively" (160), accepting no limits on satisfying his needs. The classic Russian *intelligent* is a "*militant monk of the nihilistic religion of earthly contentment*" (179) who wishes to rule the world from his monastery, but he cannot create new cultural values or new wealth because he is impelled by hatred and destructiveness (*ressentiment*). Frank associated nihilism with "vulgarized Nietzscheism (which has nothing to do with Nietzsche of course)" (178).[12]

Struve viewed the Revolution of 1905 as a "thieves' revolt," a recapitulation of the Cossack rebellions of previous eras, characterized by "senseless brutality and organized collective brigandage" (138–40). Nietzsche was not a major influence on Struve, but he knew Nietzsche's thought and was one of the first to point out areas of compatibility between it and Marxism.[13] Struve's picture of thieves' revolts is comparable to Nietzsche's idea of a "slave revolt." In the nineteenth century, Struve maintained, the intelligentsia took the Cossacks' place. Implacable, unreasoning hostility to the state was the supreme expression of the intelligentsia's atheism and nihilism, its refusal

11. Paul Avrich, *The Russian Anarchists* (New York, 1978), 44, 63; Anna Geifman, *Thou Shalt Kill* (Princeton, 1993), 123–80.

12. In 1909 Frank became involved in a project to translate all Nietzsche's works into Russian. Four volumes appeared before World War I interrupted the project. It was never resumed.

13. For Struve on Nietzsche, see *Na raznye temi: 1893–1901* (Peterburg, 1902), 170–86, 279–90, 508–21.

to submit to a higher metaphysical ideal. The crisis and disintegration of Western European socialism into Benthamism and syndicalism would have grave consequences in Russia. The year before, in an essay titled "Great Russia" (1908), Struve called for a Russian Bismarck and advocated a mystique of the state to inspire patriotism and redirect popular energies from revolution to economic development and imperial expansion. In a follow-up essay, he referred to the Eros of nationalism.[14] "Great Russia" was Struve's mobilizing myth. Merezhkovsky accused him of advocating a national "will to power" and using other items from a "Nietzschean inventory" that he himself had jettisoned. For his part, Struve accused Merezhkovsky of "painting religion red."[15]

Bulgakov titled his contribution to *Landmarks* "Geroizm and Podvizhnichestvo." Marian Schwartz translated the title as "Heroism and Asceticism," but *podvizhnichestvo* is not exactly asceticism. Derived from *podvig*, a heroic feat or exploit, *podvizhnichestvo* implies selfless devotion, as opposed to the self-aggrandizement that Bulgakov attributed to the intelligentsia. "To a certain extent the hero is a superman, who adopts with regard to his neighbors the proud and defiant pose of a savior. For all of its striving toward democracy, the intelligentsia is merely a special kind of aristocratic class arrogantly distinguishing itself from the philistine crowd" (38). The revolutionaries are closet Jacobins, would-be dictators and architects of a reign of terror. There "is a little Napoleon in every maximalist, be he socialist or anarchist" (42). Implicitly, the maximalist's real motivation is the will to power. Bulgakov predicted (correctly) that Russian maximalists would turn on one another just as the Jacobins did. To the spurious "heroism" of the intelligentsia, he counterposed the Christian ideals of humility and asceticism, "unremitting self-control, a struggle with the lowest, sinful aspects of one's I, an asceticism of the spirit" (50). In Nietzschean terms this can be described as self-overcoming, but Bulgakov did not make the connection. To him, Nietzsche epitomized Dostoevsky's demonic man-god.

Landmarks turned out to be the high-water mark of Berdiaev's political liberalism. In subsequent writings he expressed an indifference verging on contempt for legal rights and material well-being, and preached a Nietzschean Christianity in which creativity was the first commandment. Frank remained a liberal. In 1912, he converted to Orthodoxy, but he never became a Nietzschean Christian. In the mid-1920s, he rebuked Berdiaev for his "Christian Nietzscheanism."[16]

14. Struve, "Velikaia Rossiia" and "Otkryvki o gosudststve," reprinted in *Patriotica* (Peterburg, 1911).

15. Merezhkovskii, "Krasnaia shapochka" and "Eshche o 'Velikoi Rossii'," in *V tikhom omute*, in *MPSS*, 16:50–56 and 57–65; Struve, "Religiia i obshchestvennost'," *Russkaia mysl'*, 1914, no. 3:117 and 136–40.

16. I am indebted to George Kline for this information.

New Versions of Nietzschean Christianity

Berdiaev's and Florensky's versions of Nietzschean Christianity had much in common, but they were not interchangeable. For example, Berdiaev wanted to go beyond the Superman, while Florensky rejected Nietzsche's concept altogether. Both versions had cultic elements, however, and both featured an exaggerated aestheticism, attempts to channel the Dionysian aspects of the human psyche, and the Christian/utopian illusion that love can replace law. Like the symbolists (after 1909), Berdiaev and Florensky rejected the "pagan" Renaissance and "godless" mechanical civilization and subordinated Nietzsche to Orthodoxy, a process that entailed a partial rehabilitation of kenotic values. Berdiaev extolled suffering, sacrifice, and a form of asceticism; Florensky, humility and love.

Berdiaev's Religion of Creativity

Berdiaev's religion of creativity (his new myth) involved an eschatological leap into a new epoch and included a new morality, new cult figures, and a new man. He expounded his views in *The Meaning of the Creative Act* (1916, written 1911–14).[17] The English translation omits the subtitle: *An Essay in the Justification of Man*. According to Berdiaev:

> *Creativeness is neither permitted nor justified by religion—creativeness is itself religion.* Creative experience is a special kind of experience and a special kind of [path]: the creative ecstasy shatters the whole of man's being—it is an out-breaking into another world. Creative experience is just as religious as is prayer or asceticism. . . . Christianity justified creativeness . . . [but] what matters is not to justify creativeness, *but by creativeness to justify life*. Creativeness is the final revelation of the Holy Trinity—its anthropological revelation. (110)

Humanity was standing on the threshold of a cosmic divide, the leap from necessity to freedom, the higher freedom of the eighth day of creation. *"The third creative revelation in the Spirit will have no holy scripture; it will be no voice from on high: it will be accomplished in man and in humanity—it is an anthropological revelation, an unveiling of the Christology of man"* (107). The third revelation (Merezhkovsky's term) would be the work of man, a free, creative act. Christ will only reveal Himself to free men.

To Berdiaev, individuality meant creativity; creativity was inseparable from freedom; freedom was a religious virtue; and all three were interlaced

---

17. *The Meaning of the Creative Act*, trans. Donald Lowrie (New York, 1954). Original title *Smysl' tvorchestva: Opyt opravdaniie cheloveka*.

with sacrifice and suffering. "Formal freedom," the right to do as one wishes, was "negative" and "empty," the reverse side of despotism and slavery. Individualism is a "convulsion of the freedom of the old Adam, of the old freedom" (152–54). Positive freedom is creative. It entails overcoming "natural necessity" and objectification, and it recognizes the person's ties to the cosmos.[18] Berdiaev's cosmic *sobornost'* had no intermediate levels such as "nationality." His philosophy exudes a radical solitude.

At a time when most Godseekers had distanced themselves from Nietzsche, Berdiaev lauded *Zarathustra* as "the most powerful human book without grace; whatever is superior to Zarathustra is so by grace from on high." Nietzsche was the *"forerunner of a new religious anthropology,"* because he overcame humanism for the sake of the superhuman (*Meaning of the Creative Act,* 90). After Nietzsche, there could be no return to the old humanist anthropology. Man himself must become a creator, a God-man. Berdiaev applauded Nietzsche's "vertical morality," his summons to ever higher creativity, and called him an instinctive prophet whose torment was religious through and through. Only Dostoevsky was his equal. Nevertheless, "whatever Nietzsche says about Christianity we must take and turn inside out" (259). Nietzsche was the "sacrificial forerunner of a new moral epoch." But he himself is "altogether transitory; he is forging no new values" (263). Ignorant of the Logos, Nietzsche lacked transcendence and did not know "the path to the Superman." In response to Nietzsche's charge that Christianity is a slave morality, Berdiaev claimed that sacrifice is noble and Christianity, aristocratic. Christian values represent the triumph of man's highest powers; they enable man to overcome himself and the world. Authentic Christianity is a revolt against this world and all its institutions. The third epoch would be of the Holy Spirit, which breathes where it wishes. Berdiaev's desire to break free of the earth, which he called a prison, was almost gnostic in its intensity.

Apropos of morality, Berdiaev opposed daring to obedience and declared that the world must be conquered aesthetically as well as ascetically. In the new world "living dangerously" would be regarded as a virtue and living in beauty as a commandment. Aesthetic creativity was theurgy, divine-activity, man working together with God (126). "In the artist-theurge the power of man over nature is realized by means of beauty. For beauty is a great *force* [*sila*] and it will save the world" (250). Having corrected Dostoevsky's dictum "beauty will save the world" along more Nietzschean lines (*sila* also means "power"), Berdiaev preached a new morality centered on creativity and divine/human potential. For the City of God to be realized, "all the old social order must burn up, the state, every law, every economy" (294). The

18. For Berdiaev's supra-empirical concept of freedom, see *Filosofiia svobody* (Moscow, 1911).

very idea of a Christian state, a Christian family, and a Christian society is "shameful to speak and embarrassing to hear" (335). Compare Nietzsche: "A 'Christian state,' 'Christian politics' . . . are a piece of impudence" (*WP*, 124). Berdiaev denigrated all institutions as concessions to "natural necessity," and all practical morality as essentially bourgeois. He considered lawlessness a sacred duty.

Despite his incendiary language, Berdiaev did not advocate the immediate abolition of government and law. The "new city" would not be born in revolution, which Berdiaev considered a negative reaction against the old order rather than the creation of something new. Rather, the "new city" involved a leap from necessity to freedom, not in the Marxist sense but the Christian, the overcoming of this world. Peace and contentment were bourgeois values. "Until there is the final victory over evil, until this world has been transfigured into a new heaven and a new earth, the military spirit cannot and should not be destroyed in the human heart. This undying spirit of chivalry, eternally resisting the final victory of the bourgeois, is the spirit of holy wrath against the evil which passes all boundaries. The idea of an eternal bourgeois peace is an evil, distorted, ungodly idea" (291). Berdiaev extolled the Middle Ages as the most military, least bourgeois, period of European history and welcomed Russia's entry into World War I.

He expected the new creative epoch to be "supermoral" and "supercultural," rather than "premoral" and "precultural," a time of ascent to Christian Dionysianism (Dionysianism illuminated by the Logos). Man's passionate nature would not be suppressed, but transfigured in the light of a new morality of creativity and sacrifice. Merely doing no wrong was insufficient; one must be creative. The morality of the "elders," based on fear for one's own salvation, must be replaced by a daring and "new creative morality of youth," exemplified by the Gospels and St. Francis—eternally young, carefree, and indifferent to material concerns (258–61). Nietzsche thought that great suffering led to great knowledge, but he did not idealize suffering. Berdiaev considered willingness to suffer and sacrifice the hallmarks of a true nobility. "Readiness to sacrifice is always noble, always aristocratic. The plebeian spirit is not sacrificial." A "truly radical universal revolution in society will only be realized when the Christian world matures to the point of collective readiness to sacrifice" (285). Altruism, however, is a "bourgeois-democratic" substitution for love; people invoke altruism only when love has grown cold. Authentic Christianity is beyond altruism and egoism. Christianity mandates the renunciation of social theories that protect property, but it does not mandate altruism.

Nietzsche advocated sublimation, but he also celebrated sensual pleasure. "Sensual pleasure: innocent and free to free hearts, the earth's garden-joy, an overflowing of thanks to the present from all the future" (Z, 207). Berdiaev called sexual energy the source of creative ecstasy and prophetic vision and advocated the transfiguration of sexuality into artistic creativity. He disapproved of sexual intercourse. "The religion of Christ obliges us to recognize the 'natural' sex life as abnormal, the 'natural' sexual act as perversion" (*Meaning of the Creative Act,* 199). "The Virgin Birth was a conquest of the old 'natural' order in this world." The religion of redemption denies both species (*rod*) and the sex act and installs "the cult of eternal womanliness, the cult of a Virgin giving birth only through the spirit" (191). Nietzsche called the child "a sacred Yes" (*Z*, 55). Berdiaev ignored Zarathustra's references to his children, because he (Berdiaev) wanted sexual procreation to cease in order to break the endless cycle of birth and death (Fedorov's idea).[19] In *The Destiny of Man* (*O naznachenii cheloveka,* 1931), Berdiaev referred twice to the "horror of sex."[20]

Berdiaev's cult figures were the genius and the androgyne (Soloviev's ideal). The "cult of genius" would complement "the cult of saints," because genius is another kind of sainthood. It, too, demands sacrifice—the sacrifice of an assured position, of assured salvation. Genius, therefore, is "essentially tragic." Moreover, "men are elected and called to the path of genius just as they are to the path of sainthood." The saint creates a new self, a more perfect being (= self-overcoming); the genius creates great works or accomplishes great deeds in this world. Genius is "another ontology of human existence," "another world" in man, the part of his nature that is "not of this world," a revelation of man's calling to creativity (*Meaning of the Creative Act,* 172–74).

The "cult of the androgyne" would replace the "cult of the eternal feminine" and become the prototype of the new man, a "new nobility" of androgynous knight-monks, purely spiritual "youth-maidens," as distinct from physical hermaphrodites. "The new man is above all a man of transfigured sex who has restored in himself the androgynous image and likeness of God" (202; see also, 190–91, 203, 218). In the new era, the womanly principle would be virginity, not motherhood (a major departure from the Orthodox image of Mary, Mother of God). Implicitly, woman would no longer be a wife and mother. Berdiaev considered woman "generative, but not creative, a being of quite another order than man . . . much less human, much more nature" (218). This is an echo of Otto Weininger's book *Sex and Character* (1903), which Berdiaev translated into Russian. Female emancipation was a "symptom of the crisis of the race, the breakdown of sex now evident"; it did not point to the "new man" or the "new life." Even so, female emancipation was preferable to the hypocritical compulsion of the old family (202–3).

19. For Fedorov's influence on Berdiaev, see Dmitry Shlapentokh, "Life/Death—Cosmos—Eschatology: Nikolai Berdiaev and the Influence of the Fedorovian Vision," in *Analecta Husserliana* 50 (1997), ed. A. T. Tymieniecka, 301–52.

20. Berdiaev, *The Destiny of Man,* trans. Natalie Duddington (London, 1954), 64 and 65.

Florensky's Existential Orthodoxy

Florensky's theology was, in part, a response to Merezhkovsky, Nietzsche, and symbolism.[21] He attended meetings of the St. Petersburg Religious-Philosophical Society and was a founding member of the Moscow branch. In 1904–5, he helped organize a short-lived group called the Christian Brotherhood of Struggle. He began studying for the priesthood in 1906, became a professor at the Moscow Theological Academy in 1908, and was ordained in 1911. Between 1911 and 1917, he edited the Academy's journal *Theological Herald* (*Bogoslovskii vestnik*), which published some of his works. Throughout, he followed developments in art and literature, especially symbolism, as well as in mathematics and science. His sensibility remained essentially symbolist. He called himself a man of the (Russian) Middle Ages and hated the Renaissance as the time when people fell away from God.

The Nietzschean elements in Florensky's theological opus, *The Pillar and Ground of the Truth* (1914) are not immediately obvious, because he reworked them along Orthodox lines, occasionally alluding to Nietzsche to prove a point. For example, "The world is tragically beautiful in its fragmentedness. Its harmony is in its disharmony; its unity is in its discord. Such is the paradoxical teaching of Heraclitus, later paradoxically developed by Friedrich Nietzsche in the theory of 'tragic optimism.'"[22] Florensky's point was "in heaven there is only one Truth. But here on earth, we have a multitude of truths, fragments of the Truth, noncongruent to one another" (117). Logical formulas and systems cannot encapsulate truth. Florensky hated abstractions; his theology was rooted in concrete experience. In a different context, Florensky called Nietzsche's tragic optimism the "forced smile of a slave" who does not want to show his master that he is afraid of him (202). Opposed to the scientism of his day, Florensky insisted that all knowledge comes from God. In this context, he alluded to "the holy, hoary mysteriousness of ancient science; the moral, serious rigor of the new science; finally, the joyous, light, winged inspiration of the future 'gay science'" (95), clearly a reference to Nietzsche's book. Florensky expected symbolism to lead to a new nonpositivist science. Berdiaev reviewed *The Pillar and Ground of The Truth* in *Russian Thought* (January 1914); he called Florensky's theology a "stylized Orthodoxy."

21. Details in Bernice G. Rosenthal, "The 'New Religious Consciousness': Pavel Florenskii's Path to a Revitalized Orthodoxy," *Christianity and Its Role in the Culture of the Eastern Slavs*, ed. Robert P. Hughes and Irina Paperno (Berkeley and Los Angeles, 1994), 2:134–57, and idem, "Florensky's Russifications of Nietzsche," in *Pavel Florenskij—Tradition und Moderne*, ed. Norbert Franz, Michael Hagemeister, and Frank Haney (Frankfurt, 2001), 247–58.

22. *The Pillar and Ground of the Truth*, trans. Boris Jakim, intro. Richard Gustafson (Princeton, 1998), 115.

In *The Birth of Tragedy*, Nietzsche faulted rationalism for distorting reality and destroying myth. Florensky hated rationalism as something unnatural and destructive and also because he associated rationalism with "the self-assertive I" (egoistic individualism) and, implicitly, with the will to power. "The rationalist intellectual wishes to see only the artificial everywhere, to see everywhere, not life but formulas and concepts, *his own formulas and concepts*" (*Pillar and Ground*, 215, emphasis added). (Note the similarity to poststructuralist critiques of the Enlightenment.) Florensky extolled humility, personified for him by Elder Isidore.[23] Like Berdiaev, Florensky considered Christianity a religion of love, not of altruism.

Florensky's Orthodoxy emphasized "living experience," by which he meant specifically Orthodox experience, as distinct from eclectic religiousness, or abstract concepts, or generalized mysticism. "One can become a Catholic or a Protestant . . . by reading books in one's study. But to become Orthodox, it is necessary to immerse oneself all at once in the very element of Orthodoxy, to begin living in an Orthodox way" (*Pillar and Ground*, 9). Ecclesiality (*tserkovnost'*) was a prominent, arguably the most prominent, aspect of his theology. As Florensky used the term, ecclesiality had several layers of meaning, all related to the Holy Spirit, the invisible Church and the unity of all believers in the mystic body of Christ (the original meaning of *sobornost'*). On one level, ecclesiality was the spiritual beauty that manifests itself when one is united with all creation by way of love for its creator. The emphasis on love is not from Nietzsche, of course, but the aestheticism is, though not only from Nietzsche. Florensky's mystical aestheticism was imbued with Solovievian and symbolist concepts, including Sophia. He considered secular aestheticism superficial, "a 'skin' to use Nietzsche's expression . . . a beautiful form and only that." And beneath the beautiful forms "Chaos moves" (201–2).

On another level, ecclesiality was an implicit response to Ivanov's vision of a theater temple as the embryo of a cultic community. He and Ivanov followed each other's work. Florensky insisted that loving union is possible only in a church. Moreover, there are different kinds of love. Eros is "a passion that erupts" (288). A Christian community is held together by two bonds, general love (*agape*) and individualized friendship (*philia* and *agape*) (300–302). Florensky's concept of friendship drew on an array of sources, including the Bible, Plato, and Nietzsche (especially the section titled "Of the Friend," in *Z*, 82–84). Florensky prefaced his poem "Starry Friend" (1907) with a long epigraph from *The Gay Science* (the section titled "Star Friendship," in *Z*, 225–26).[24] Florensky was married, but he did not think

23. On Elder Isidore, see Florensky's *Salt of the Earth*, trans. Richard Betts (Platina, Calif., 1987).

24. Florenskii, "Zvezdnaia druzhba," reprinted in *Simvol* 21 (July 1989): 256–61. I am indebted to Robert Bird for this reference.

a woman could be a friend. His Christian community was composed of male dyads who form a third person who becomes a molecule in the body of Christ.

Rather than the orgiastic passions that "erupt" in the Dionysian rites, Florensky emphasized the passion of jealousy, quoting the Bible, the ancient Greeks, and Nietzsche to support his views (*Pillar and Ground,* 335). He connected jealousy with ardent love and pointed out that "jealousy" (*revnost'*) and "zeal" (*rvenie*) are etymologically related. The argument from language, one of Florensky's favorite devices, recalls Nietzsche's methodology in *Genealogy of Morals.* Florensky also maintained that while love is unbounded, it must also be bounded. "Together with a uniting force that takes one outside individual existence, there must be an isolating force which sets a limit to diffuseness and impersonality. Together with a centrifugal force, there must also be a centripetal one. This force is *jealousy* and its function is to isolate, separate, delimit, differentiate" (330). Florensky's categories of integration and differentiation are implicitly Nietzschean, though not only Nietzschean. Apollo sets boundaries; Dionysus dissolves them. In his postrevolutionary writings, the implicit became explicit. He referred to "Dionysian dissolution" (*raztorzhenie*) and described icons as the "Apollonian vision [*videnie*] of the spiritual world."[25] In a different essay, he called the person an Apollonian principle, Christianity's answer to the impersonal "titanic principle" and the unbridled passions of Dionysianism,[26] linking "titanic," "barbaric," and "Dionysian" as Nietzsche did (*BT,* 46).

Beauty superseded morality in Florensky's eyes. "Asceticism," he wrote, "produces not a 'good' or a 'kind' man but a beautiful one and the distinguishing feature of the saintly ascetics is "not their 'kindness' which even people of the flesh and very sinful ones, can possess, but spiritual beauty, the blinding beauty of a radiant light-bearing person, a beauty wholly inaccessible to the man of flesh. 'There is nothing more beautiful than Christ, the only sinless one'" (*Pillar and Ground,* 72). Evil is "spiritual distortion" (*iskrivlenie*); sin is anything that leads to such distortion (192). To Florensky, the opposite of evil was not good, but love, which unites the visible and invisible world (the material and the spiritual worlds). Moralism was outside divine love; the holy was above every "No," and a religion of ethics undermined spiritual life. Kant was "the great deceiver."[27]

To Florensky, beauty, truth, love, and spirituality were intertwined aspects of one absolute essence, a metaphysical triad of truth, love, and beauty (trinitarian structures are typical of Florensky's thought), which is absolute, infinite, eternal, and totally incorporating. His concepts of truth, love, and

---

25. Florensky, *Iconostatis,* trans. Donald Sheehan and Olga Andrejev (Crestwood, N.Y., 19), 45. I changed "dispersion" to "dissolution."

26. Florenskii, "Tainstva i obriady," in "Sviashchennik Pavel Florenskii: Iz Bogoslovskogo naslediia," in *Bogoslovskie trudy* 17 (1977): 139–41. Henceforth cited as "Iz naslediia."

27. Florensky, "Kul't i filosofiia," in "Iz naslediia," 122.

spirituality were dependent directly or indirectly on beauty. Many examples of his aesthetic perception of spirituality can be given. "My spiritual life, my life in the Spirit, the process of 'my likening to God' is beauty, that special beauty of the original creature" (62). And: "Ecclesiality is the beauty of a new life in Absolute Beauty—in the Holy Spirit. That is a fact" (234).

Florensky associated evil with self-centeredness and fragmentation. He rejected the law of identity, A = A, as an expression of the epistemological individualism of Descartes and Kant, I = I, and claimed that linear perspective (which originated in the Renaissance) expressed self-centered subjectivism because painters depicted reality as *they* saw it rather than through heavenly eyes. Nietzsche's perspectivism, especially as articulated in the *Gay Science,* was in the air at the time. Florensky's version (to which we will return subsequently) was a consciously Orthodox perspective.

The philosophers discussed in this chapter would today be called public intellectuals. Their articles, lectures, and books sparked polemics, pro and con, and not just in Christian circles.[28] Focusing on ideas and values, they addressed epistemological, psychological, and religious issues, and they wanted to create a "new man" and a new culture. Politics and economics were less important to them than the "inner man," the soul or the psyche. Cumulatively, they helped discredit rationalism, positivism, Kant's imperatives, and the "morality of duty." Shestov's antirationalism was misconstrued as an attack on liberal political ideals. Berdiaev (especially after 1911) and Florensky fostered a militant spiritual maximalism that paralleled, and in Berdiaev's case, sometimes fused with, the sociopolitical maximalism of the revolutionary intelligentsia.

---

28. For the responses of their contemporaries, see *Berdiaev: pro et contra*, ed. A. A. Emichev and A. A. Burlak (St. Petersburg, 1994), and *Florenskii: pro et contra*, ed. D. K. Burlak and K. G. Isupov (St. Petersburg, 1996). Berdiaev's review of *Pillar,* "Stilizovannoe pravoslavie (o Pavel Florenskii)," is on 266–84.

THREE

Nietzschean Marxists

The will to equality is the will to power—the belief
that something is thus and thus (the essence of *judg-*
ment) is the consequence of a will that as much as
possible *shall* be equal.   —*WP,* 277

George L. Kline coined the term "Nietzschean Marxism"
to encapsulate the beliefs of Aleksandr Bogdanov (born
Aleksandr Malinovsky, 1873–1928); his brother-in-law,
Anatoly Lunacharsky (1875–1933); Maksim Gorky (Aleksei
Peshkov, 1868–1936); V. A. Bazarov (V. Rudnev, 1874–
1939); and Stanislav Volsky (Andrei Sokolov, 1880–1936).[1]
I include Aleksandra Kollontai (1872–1952) as well. These
Marxists emphasized issues that Marx and Engels neg-
lected—ethics, epistemology, aesthetics, psychology, cul-
ture, and values—and they recognized the psychopolitical

---

1. George L. Kline, "'Nietzschean Marxism' in Russia," 166–83.
See also idem, "Changing Attitudes Toward the Individual," *The
Transformation of Russian Society*, ed. C. E. Black (Cambridge, Mass.,
1960), 606–25, and "The Nietzschean Marxism of Stanislav Volsky,"
in *Western Philosophical Systems in Russian Literature*, ed. Anthony
Mlikotin (Los Angeles, 1979), 177–95.

utility of myth. All of them were sensitive to problems of artistic and cultural creativity and stressed free volition and desire, but they disagreed on whether volition and creativity would take individual or collective forms. Their collectivism was not meant to be obligatory. They wanted people to identify with the collective, not subordinate themselves to it out of a sense of duty. Nietzsche helped them bring out the "heroic" and voluntaristic aspects of Marxism that Plekhanov almost obliterated and join them with the ethos of revolutionary populism.

When Nietzsche said that *"the will to equality is the will to power,"* he was talking about logic, but his observation can be applied to politics and society, in which case, the "will to equality" entails dethroning the established authority and enthroning a new one. The Nietzschean Marxists wanted to enthrone the proletariat. They are also known as "the romantic revolutionaries" and "the Bolshevik left," even though Gorky was not officially a Bolshevik and Kollontai was a Menshevik until 1915. Lenin called them "Machians" (sometimes translated as "Machists") after Bogdanov's "Machist" epistemology.

The Nietzschean Marxists debated the symbolists and philosophers discussed in Chapters 1 and 2. Berdiaev's insistence on the volitional importance of ideas (they inspire human action) sparked Bogdanov's interest in epistemology. He and Lunacharsky published some early articles in the neo-Idealist journal *Problems of Philosophy and Psychology*. Bogdanov reviewed *Problems of Idealism* and organized a counter-symposium, *Essays on a Realistic World View* (1904).[2] Gorky and Lunacharsky attended Religious-Philosophical Society meetings and Ivanov's salon. Lunacharsky and Berdiaev had been friends since high school. Many other examples of interchange could be given.

Bogdanov did not refer to Nietzsche as frequently as Lunacharsky and Gorky did, and he used dry "scientific" language, so his debt to Nietzsche is less apparent. It is indicated, however, in Bogdanov's belief in the consciousness-transforming power of art and myth, in his own attempts at myth-creation, and in his call for a cultural revolution that included a "revaluation of all values" from a proletarian perspective. Most tellingly, Bogdanov used the term "ideology" positively, a major departure from Marx and Engels, for whom "ideology" was false consciousness, a mystification or distortion of reality in the interests of the ruling class (*MER*, 154–55). Bogdanov accused them of leaving "unclarified the objective role of ideologies in society, their indispensable social functions . . . [ideologies] are organizing forms, or, what is the same, the organizational means for all social practices."[3] Ideology does

---

2. Aleksandr Bogdanov, ed., *Ocherki realisticheskogo mirovozzreniia. Sbornik stat'ei po filosofii, obshchestvennoi nauki i zhizni* (St. Petersburg, 1904). Bogdanov titled his review "Return to the Middle Ages."

3. Aleksandr Bogdanov, *Bogdanov's Tektology*, bk. 1, foreword by Vadim Sadovsky and Vladimir V. Kelle, edited with an introduction by Peter Dudley (Hull, 1996), 97.

not merely reflect the socioeconomic structure, but plays a crucial role in "organizing" and therefore in creating it. Ideology is not only a form of legitimation; it is a constructive phenomenon. In Bogdanov's writings "ideology" is almost a synonym for myth—a rationally constructed myth. On occasion, Bogdanov used Ivanov's term, "myth-creation,"[4] but Bogdanov stressed the role of the rational consciousness.

Bogdanov's essay "The Gathering of Man" (*Sobiranie cheloveka*, 1904) opens with three epigraphs: "Social existence determines consciousness" (Marx); "God created man in His own image" (Genesis 1:27); and "Man is a bridge and not a goal" (Nietzsche).[5] *Sobiranie* can also be translated "collection" or "assembly," and is etymologically linked to the concept of *sobornost'*. In another possible translation, "integration," *sobiranie* connotes the Slavophile conception of wholeness. To Bogdanov, progress meant "the wholeness and harmony of conscious human life."[6] Individualism destroys personal and social harmony, he believed, as does occupational specialization and the division of labor. He was particularly opposed to the separation of mental and physical labor—a theme of young Marx, Mikhailovsky, Kropotkin, and Fedorov as well. Bogdanov's emphasis on overcoming alienation anticipated Marx's yet-unknown 1844 manuscripts. Among Bogdanov's favorite words were "harmony" (not part of Nietzsche's vocabulary but much used by Fourier and other utopian socialists), "mastery" (*ovladenie*), and "to master" (*ovladet'*), which can also be translated "to seize" or "to take possession." In Bogdanov's usage, "mastery" and related words have multiple connotations: a worker mastering knowledge or a skill, species-man (*chelovechestvo*) mastering nature, the slave become master, and the proletariat as the new lord of the earth. "Organization," his most favorite word, harks back to Lavrov's strategy, but in Bogdanov's usage, it has an Apollonian aspect. Apollo integrates and structures; organization enables man to proceed from (Dionsysian) chaos to cosmos. It would not be an exaggeration to say that Bogdanov was impelled by a "will to organization."

Bogdanov's "Machist" Epistemology

Bogdanov's epistemology was based on Empiriocriticism, which he subordinated to Marxism. Marx envisioned a single science of man that encom-

---

4. For example, Bogdanov observed that even in modern times, people "unconsciously repeat the myth-creating process of thought." *Padenie velikogo fetishizma: Sovremennyi krizis ideologii* (Moscow, 1910), 46; published together with *Vera i Nauka (o knige V. Il'ina "Materializm i empioiokrititsizm."*

5. Aleksandr Bogdanov, "Sobiranie cheloveka," in *Novyi mir: stat'i 1904–1905* (Moscow 1905), 1–54.

6. Aleksandr Bogdanov, "Chto takoe idealizm," in *Iz psikhologii obshchestva*, 2d ed. (Peterburg, 1906), 35.

passed the natural sciences and was based on human sense experience as described by Feuerbach. Mach and Avenarius (who was dead by the time Empiriocriticism became an issue to Bolsheviks) rejected all dualisms (spirit and matter, self and other, the ego and the world) for a psycho-physiological monism based on sense experience, in effect dematerializing matter and dissolving the individual into a complex of sensations and elements. All we can know of reality is our (subjective) experience of it and reality is constantly changing. Science, therefore, does not provide absolute truth, but hypotheses that integrate the knowledge and experience of an era and enable people to function in the world. When conditions change, new hypotheses are formulated. Mach tried to develop a positivist grand scheme as a working model for his own time, based on empirical evidence rather than mathematical proofs or metaphysical concepts.

Nietzsche also opposed metaphysics and hypothesized "truth," and his physiologism was roughly compatible with Mach's emphasis on sense experience. These similarities may not be a coincidence, for Mach read Nietzsche and Nietzsche followed developments in the physical sciences. Mach's Heraclitean universe can be regarded as a scientific version of Dionysian dissolution; in fact he meditated on the theme of the "Dionysian" in the life of the natural scientist.[7] Mach's denial of the existence of objective truth and eternal scientific laws, including Newton's laws, was consonant with a Dionysian interpretation of Nietzsche. In *The Birth of Tragedy,* Nietzsche faulted Socratic rationalism for "actually holding out the prospect of the lawfulness of [the] entire solar system" (96). Also consonant with a Dionysian interpretation of Nietzsche was Mach's rejection of egoism, the Superman, and the will to power.

Marx and Engels believed that an objective reality exists, but perception of it is conditioned by class. Bogdanov argued that while both Mach and Marx connected cognition with the social process of labor, Mach lacked an effective principle of causality, namely labor, which cognitively subordinates the psychic to the physical. The basis of objectivity is *"collective* experience," which is the result of mutual verification, synchronization, "and the collective organizing work of all people—a sort of cognitive socialism." And since any worldview is related to class, "the ideology of the technical process is inevitably the ideology of the producers, in the broad sense of the word."[8] Because society changes, any ideology

> can only have a historically transitory meaning . . . it can be a "truth of the time" (*"objective"* truth), but only within the limits of a given

7. A. L. Tait, "Lunacharsky: A Nietzschean Marxist?" in *NR,* 281.

8. Aleksandr Bogdanov, "Empiriomonism," excerpted in Robert Daniels, *A Documentary History of Communism in Russia,* 3d ed. (Hanover, N.H., 1993), 29. Subsequent citations all refer to this volume.

epoch—but in no case can it be a "truth for all time" ("objective" in the absolute meaning of the word). . . . For me, Marxism includes the denial of the unconditional objectivity of any truth whatsoever, the denial of every eternal truth.

Truth is an ideological form—the organizing form of human experience. (Bogdanov, *Empiriomonism,* 27)

In other words, truth is functional rather than ontological. For Bogdanov, Marxism was an activating ideology (a mobilizing myth) not an unchanging dogma. Dogma of any kind was a fetish or an idol.

In another departure from classical Marxism, Bogdanov treated "class" as an epistemological as well as an economic category. The ruling class had the knowledge and skills necessary to "organize" reality, so the abolition of private property would not, by itself, assure equality. To become the new "organizing class," the proletariat would have to acquire technological and organizational skills. For Bogdanov, technology was a quasi-autonomous force (not just an emanation of the economic base), and humankind's weapon in its unrelenting struggle with nature. Unlike both Marx and Nietzsche, Bogdanov was not at all ambivalent about technology.[9] He expected it to liberate people from brute labor, facilitate self-development, and enable the proletariat to displace the bourgeoisie. He also believed that the sensations produced by working with the new technology were in turn producing a new psychological type: not narrow "bourgeois" specialists, but self-motivated, rational men and women, with wide-ranging interests and the leisure time to pursue them—Renaissance persons without the individualism. Ultimately the harmonious organization of collective experience would "give people a grandiose fullness of life such as we, people of the epoch of contradictions, cannot imagine."[10]

Bogdanov's epistemology was tinged with Energetism, a monistic doctrine developed by Wilhelm Ostwald (1853–1932) that reduced the world to energy in various stages of transmutation and was compatible with Empiriocriticism, so much so that Ostwald dedicated his book *Lectures on Natural Philosophy* to Mach. Both doctrines deny the existence of a material reality independent of human perception, hence of objective truth, and seemed to invalidate

9. For Marx, modern technology makes the worker into a living appendage of the machine, but technology is also the means by which production is increased, scarcity is overcome (eventually making a classless society possible), and humankind attains control over nature. For Nietzsche, technology is creative activity that requires intellect, discipline, and scientific imagination, but machine *kultur* leads to routinization, "impersonal enslavement," and a "despondent boredom of the soul." Robert F. McGinn, "Nietzsche on Technology," *Journal of the History of Ideas* 41, no. 4 (October–December 1980): 679–92.

10. Bogdanov, *Empiriomonizm,* 3 vols. (Peterburg, 1904–6), 1:45.

the laws of Newton and, therefore, according to Plekhanov and Lenin, the materialist worldview of Marxism and the historical laws on which Marxism is based.

The New Morality

The Nietzschean Marxists conflated Marx's contempt for "bourgeois morality" with Nietzsche's contempt for Christian morality. Marx held that in a classless society morality would wither away (since morality is a product of class) along with the state and law. The Nietzschean Marxists believed that the proletariat stood beyond bourgeois/Christian conceptions of good and evil, but they disagreed on what, if anything, would replace these conceptions. Bogdanov argued that norms were necessary; without them, society would collapse like a cask without hoops. He advocated "expediency norms" (*normy tselosoobraznosti*) that changed as society's needs changed, as opposed to "coercive norms" (*normy prinuzhdeniia*) such as the Ten Commandments and Kant's imperatives. Kollontai preached a morality of gender equality, self-expression, and love, while Lunacharsky linked aesthetics, morality, and revolution, and Bazarov championed "hedonistic amoralism." Gorky propounded a vulgarized Nietzschean amoralism and then shifted to a heroic ideal. Volsky advocated a morality of struggle, frequently mingling Nietzsche and Darwin (a major influence on Bogdanov as well). All of them were future-oriented, though not to the same degree. George Kline finds a "voracious will to the future" in both Nietzsche and Marx, which involves a readiness to reduce living individuals to instruments or means to a future goal, and to sacrifice their well-being and even their lives, for the sake of this goal. For Marx, the goal is the communist future; for Nietzsche, the elevated culture of the remote historical future and the Superman who will create it. Kline calls this readiness to sacrifice living individuals "instrumental" cruelty, as distinct from sadism.[11] Paradoxically, most Nietzschean Marxists championed the free expression of "individuality."

Bogdanov believed that in a truly scientific society, people would follow "expediency norms" voluntarily, as an engineer follows certain norms when designing a bridge.[12] He based his "expediency norms" on what he considered proletarian values—labor, egalitarianism, collectivism, and comradely cooperation. The individual was merely a "bourgeois fetish." Fetishism (as in "the fetishism of commodities") is Marx's concept, but Bogdanov's use

11. Kline, "Foreword," in *NR*, xii–xv; idem, "Was Marx an Ethical Humanist?" *Studies in Soviet Thought*, 9 (1969): 96–97.
12. Bogdanov, "Tseli i normy zhizni," in *Novyi mir*, 55–135.

of the term also echoes Nietzsche's contempt for "old words" that have lost their meaning and Sorel's disdain for the "idolatry of words." According to Bogdanov, "bourgeois" individualism had served its purpose, ending feudalism, but authoritarian thought continued under individualistic capitalism, producing hierarchies and dualisms in all areas of life, including separate moralities for masters and for slaves. In a socialist society there would be one morality for everyone and all forms of dominance and subordination would disappear. Asceticism was a product of authoritarian dualism, which privileged the spirit over the body. Like almost all Russian radicals, Bogdanov advocated free love.

Bogdanov posited Ten Expediency Norms for his own time.

1. There shall be no herd instinct.
2. There shall be no slavery (and its complement, authoritarianism).
3. There shall be no subjectivism, neither of a personal nor of a group nature.
4. There shall be no Hottentotism (double standards).
5. There shall be no absolute norms.
6. There shall be no inertia [I altered "inertness" to "inertia].
7. There shall be no violation of the purity of purpose.
8. All-mastery [*vseovladenie*]—the greatest goal.
9. All-understanding—the higher ideal of the new consciousness.
10. Pride of the collective—the supreme stimulus of will and thought of the worker.

Each norm was followed by an explanation. Nietzsche's influence is clear in the first norm and in several others.

Bogdanov opposed "creativity" to "inertia" all his life, because he was haunted by Nietzsche's critique of socialism as a slave morality that dooms society to stagnation and decline. "Herd instinct" was prohibited, he explained, because "a passive submissive attitude has more to do with the petty bourgeois fear of being different than with true collectivisim . . . the collectivist maintain[s] and develop[s] his individuality together with the collective." He repeated the prohibition in his explanation of the sixth norm, this time because it "halts movement forward." "Creativity is not only joyful but also painful, as in birth. The proletariat must learn and relearn [= revalue] to create a new culture." "All-mastery," he explained, means the collective organizing the world, gaining mastery over everything, binding everything into a harmonious whole. "Toward this end, it is necessary to master techniques from past labor as well as to seek new paths, new sources of energy." (He predicted atomic energy.) "All-understanding" means mutual understanding among participants, "a continuous deepening of unity of will, mind, and feelings." "Pride of the collective" excludes "serving the higher will (authoritarianism), or truth and duty (individualism). In the development of the collective everything that requires submission or worship is unmasked. Instead, the worker develops a consciousness of self as a living link of the great all-conquering whole."

Nietzsche saw individualism as a way station, a "modest and still unconscious form of the 'will to power'" (*WP*, 411); it is succeeded by strife and power friction with the assertion of an order of rank. According to Zenovia Sochor, Bogdanov "saw exactly the same scenario."[13] Egalitarianism and desire for harmony, and not just "scientific socialism's" emphasis on objectivity, inspired Bogdanov to prohibit subjectivism. "Personal subjectivism is individualism, group subjectivism is clannishness. . . . All of these orientations lead to a waste of collective energy in anarchistic confrontations."

Bogdanov's egalitarian collectivism was inspired by Marx and Engels, of course, but it also had roots in the populists' apotheosis of the commune and was compatible with, and possibly influenced by, Nietzsche's praise of the Dionysian rites. "Now the slave is a free man, now all the rigid hostile barriers that necessity, caprice, or 'impudent convention' have set between man and man are broken. Now, with the gospel of universal harmony, each one feels himself not only united, reconciled, and fused with his neighbor but also as one with him, as if the veil of *maya* had been torn aside and was now merely fluttering in tatters before the mysterious-primordial unity" (*BT*, 37). The fusion that Nietzsche depicted was short-lived, passionate, and confined to the ritual site. Bogdanov wanted the fusion to be permanent, conscious, and worldwide.

Kollontai was recruited into the Social Democratic Party by Bogdanov in 1903, at Lenin's request. One of her activities was lecturing on Nietzsche to students and young workers.[14] Although she lumped Nietzsche, Berdiaev, and Frank together as "idealists," Kollontai praised Nietzsche as an "original thinker" and called Berdiaev and Frank "reactionaries." She applauded Nietzsche's attack on traditional morality because it opened a "limitless expanse for individual aspirations," for the expression of one's "authentic spiritual 'I' "—(personal authenticity or self-expression)—one of her favorite concepts. Kollontai did not object to the Superman ideal per se, just to its aristocratic aspects. In her words: "The true Superman is possible only as the creation of new approaching living forms, fastened together by widely understood principles of community, imbued with the mighty ideal of socialism."[15] The proletariat must create its own "norms," for "*only* by new norms

13. Zenovia Sochor, "A. A. Bogdanov: In Search of Cultural Liberation," in *NR*, 308. For explanations of all the norms, see 305–7.

14. Barbara Clements, *Bolshevik Feminist* (Indiana, 1979), 131.

15. Aleksandra Kollontai, "Problema nravtsevnnosti s positivnoi tochki zreniia," *Obrazovaniia* 14, no. 9 (September 1905): 77–95, esp. 95; no. 10 (October 1905): 92, 107. See also idem, "Etika i Sotsial'demokratiia," *Obrazovanie* 15, no. 2 (February 1906): 22–32.

and ideals" can it successfully wrest power from its antagonists.[16] She envisioned a "new free type," unfettered by the centuries-old material yoke, who will "create his own history," and regarded "love in and of itself [as] a great creative force." Socialism would increase the human capacity for love. "There is no doubt that love will become the cult of future humanity." For her, the ultimate goal of communism was not so much prosperity as the reeducation of the psyche—overcoming the "will to power" in personal and social life, and teaching people to love—a far cry from Nietzsche's project. Like most of Nietzsche's admirers, Kollontai picked up the aspects of his thought that appealed to her and ignored or rejected the others. Her social ideal was a version of *sobornost'*, cemented by Eros, in which each person retained his or her "spiritual I."

Lunacharsky's grandiloquent prose was sprinkled with references to the "fullness of life" and the joy of creativity and struggle. In his first literary essay, "A Russian Faust" (1902), he associated Faust with the Superman, celebrated "healthy egoism," and interpreted the "will to power" as the "will to creativity."[17] In subsequent essays, Lunacharsky attacked altruism, the "morality of duty," and the Kantian idea that each individual is an end in himself. To the social activist, as to the artist, the people are a "lump of marble" from which he creates a beautiful humankind in accordance with his ideal; he is not interested in their happiness and would sacrifice "not even a fingernail" on their behalf.[18]

In "The Basis of a Positivist Aesthetics" (1904), his contribution to Bogdanov's symposium, Lunacharsky argued that aesthetics is the "science of valuation" and the ideal of a just and harmonious society is an aesthetic ideal. Linking aesthetics with action (a code-word for revolution), he claimed that the "*ideal ahead*" is a powerful stimulus to labor, while the "*ideal above us*" fosters passive mysticism and self-absorption.[19] The task of the political activist is to develop people's confidence in their power to achieve a better future and seek a rational path to it. The task of the artist is to depict that future and to inspire people to struggle for it, to imbue them with the "feeling of tragedy, the joy of struggle and victory, with Promethean aspirations, stubborn pride, implacable courage, to unite hearts in a common rush of feeling for the Superman" (180).

16. Quoted in Clements, *Bolshevik Feminist*, 71.
17. Lunacharskii, "Russkii faust," in *Etiudy kriticheskie i polemicheskie* (Moscow, 1905), 179–90. He wrote it in response to Bulgakov's lecture, "Ivan Karamazov as a Philosophic Type" (1901), which contrasted Ivan's "typically Russian" concern for morality with Faust's amoralism and philistinism.
18. Lunacharskii, "Pered litsom roka; K filosofii tragedii" (1903), in *Etiudy kriticheskie i polemicheskie*, 104–5.
19. Lunacharskii, "Osnovy pozitivnoi estetiki," in Bogdanov, *Ocherki realisticheskogo mirovozzreniia*, 130–31.

Linking art and revolution in another way, Lunacharsky declared that struggling societies and classes produce a "romantic art of storm and stress," a "Promethean art" which depicts and inspires actual striving. "Realistic idealism" (classicism), the art of stable societies and triumphant classes, inspires peaceful progress toward the Superhuman; "mystical idealism" (e.g. symbolism) induces escapism (174–75). Lunacharsky perceived Wagner's operas in Nietzschean terms as Apollonian illusions and asserted that beautiful illusions are necessary now that "God is dead and the universe is without meaning."[20] In his introduction to a Russian translation of Wagner's *Art and Revolution* (1849), Lunacharsky attacked "narrow-minded fanatics" concerned solely with economic and political issues and endorsed Wagner's belief that art and the social movement have the same goal: "the creation of a strong, beautiful [new] man, to whom revolution shall give his strength, and art his beauty!"[21]

Bazarov claimed that Kant's imperatives are meaningless and empty, because in bourgeois society the individual is a mere theoretical idea generated by the institution of private property. Moreover, freedom excludes ethical elements and norms as such. "The free man not only regards his neighbor as a means; he demands that his neighbor should see in him only a means" to his own goals and projects (Stirner's idea).[22] A person who fears his own conscience is not really free. Bazarov based his "hedonistic amoralism" on the "free harmonizing of experience," which was in turn based on his belief that a new collectivist consciousness would arise after private property is abolished. To distinguish "hedonistic amoralism" from the orgiastic "Dionysian imperative" (240), he specified that "hedonist amoralism" is deliberate and rational. The hedonistic amoralist "order[s] his psyche in such a way that new values . . . may be conjoined to the old with minimum friction; the principle of the harmonization of given hedonistic values should at the same time clear the way for a revaluation of all values" (236, 275). Like Stirner and young Marx, Bazarov viewed man as a sexual being. He wanted to eliminate sexual repression, and all other forms of repression, and to minimize coercion and violence. The psychology of free people excludes leaders, he asserted; they "do not want or need another Robespierre" or Bonaparte (267–68).

The most collectivist of the Nietzschean Marxists, Bazarov took his pseudonym from the nihilist Bazarov in Turgenev's novel *Fathers and Sons*, a physiological reductionist who claims that "people are like trees in a forest:

20. Quoted in Tait, "Lunacharsky: A Nietzschean Marxist?" in *NR*, 282.

21. Lunacharskii, "Ob iskusstve i revoliutsii" (1906), reprinted in *Teatr i revoliutsiia* (Moscow, 1924), 167–68.

22. V. A. Bazarov, "Avtoritarnaia metafizika i avtonomnaia lichnost'," in Bogdanov, *Ocherki realistichekogo mirovozzreniia*, 271. See also Max Stirner, *The Ego and Its Own*, ed. John Carroll (New York, 1971), p. 11.

no botanist would dream of studying each individual separately."[23] Our Bazarov was a millennialist in his own way. He thought that humanity was on the verge of the second metamorphosis that Zarathustra described (*Z*, 54–56). In Bazarov's rendition, the camel—symbol of the human spirit patiently bearing the burden of virtue through the desert of history—would become a lion. The lion, who "wants to be free and to be a lord in its own desert," would struggle with the "great dragon," whose name is 'Thou shalt," for the spirit of the lion says, "I want!" Bazarov ignored the third metamorphosis when the lion turns into a child, symbol of new values or a new beginning. For Marxists, according to Bazarov, the "narrow small I" endlessly broadens, enveloping the shoreless horizon, identifying itself with the universal world order, and in this way achieves full self-definition (276).

Gorky, already a celebrity, followed a different trajectory.[24] In the early 1890s, Nietzsche helped Gorky justify his rejection of populist duty. The hobo-protagonists of his first short stories have thrown off all personal and social obligations, exploit the weak, and prefer their dangerous freedom to an orderly existence. In mid-decade, however, Gorky began to seek a Russian Superman who would lead the masses in a struggle for liberation. The hero of his short story "The Old Woman Izergil" (1895) cuts out his flaming heart and uses it as a torch to guide his tribe to safety. In "Song of the Falcon" (also 1895), Gorky celebrated the "madness of the brave," exemplified by a wounded falcon (a royal bird in Russian folklore), who tried to fly and died in the attempt, while a serpent, epitome of the "slave morality" (unlike Zarathustra's "wise serpent"), crawls prudently along the earth. In "The Reader" (1898), Gorky urged writers to inspire the people to become "lords of the earth" rather than slaves of life. He wanted reason and science to displace ignorance and superstition.

Gorky's favorite Nietzsche text, "On War and Warriors" (*Z*, 73–75), includes the lines "Not your pity but your courage has saved the unfortunate up to now" and "man is something that should be overcome." Also important to Gorky was Zarathustra's injunction "*Become hard!*" (because "all creators are hard," *Z*, 231). In "Man" (1903), Gorky set forth his vision of a free, proud, tragically beautiful, and courageous Man (he always capitalized the word) constantly moving "forward and higher."[25] In 1904–5,

---

23. Ivan Turgenev, *Fathers and Sons*, trans. Rosemary Edmonds (Harmondsworth, 1972), 160.

24. Betty Forman, "Nietzsche and Gorky in the 1890s: The Case for an Early Influence," *Western Philosophical Systems in Russian Literature*, ed. A. M. Mlikotin (Los Angeles, 1979), 153–63; Louise Loe, "Gorky and Nietzsche: The Quest for a Russian Superman, in *NR*, 251–74; Clowes, *Revolution*, 176–99; Günther, *Der sozialistische Übermensch*; Konstantin Azadovskii, "M. Gorkii v 'Arkhive Nitsshe," *Literaturnaia Gazeta*, nos. 1–2, January 10, 1996, 6.

25. Gor'kii, "Chelovek," in *GSS*, 4:5–10.

Gorky gravitated to the Bolsheviks, so when Lenin denounced "literary supermen," Gorky followed suit. In "Notes on Philistinism" (1905), he excoriated Nietzsche as a bourgeois thinker whose ideas justified the unscrupulousness and cruelty of the ruling class. Privately, he continued to praise Nietzsche and to appropriate his ideas.

The Nietzschean Marxists believed that in a classless society conflict between individuals would disappear. Volsky was the exception. In *The Philosophy of Struggle: An Essay in Marxist Ethics* (1909), he argued that socialist society would be peopled by creative nonconformists and characterized by "freedom of struggle" and the "joy of struggle" (the Nietzschean *agon*).[26] To achieve socialism, the workers must voluntarily and temporarily subject themselves to the morality of an armed camp. Against the class enemy, "all will be permitted," even actions ordinarily considered criminal (261, 286). Solidarity will become the "obligatory norm." After the revolution, there would be absolute freedom and a wide berth for genius. An "ultimate burst" of the "will to creativity" would fuse "all the passions into a single powerful torrent of creation" (275, 295). Equality would make true friendship possible. Volsky's "new man" (he ignored the "new woman") was a "friend-enemy," Nietzsche's concept. "In your friend you should possess your best enemy. Your heart should feel closest to him when you oppose him" (Z, 83). Struggle would continue in the realm of ideas and values, for "mankind is nourished by the struggle of its sons" (301). Socialist morality will be the cultural *agon* of "friend-enemies" fighting for their respective cultural ideals.

Marxist Myth-Creators and the Revolution of 1905

The Nietzschean Marxists perceived the Revolution of 1905 in terms of a secularized apocalypticism that heralded the end of autocracy and capitalism. Bogdanov described revolution as "social creativity" and "social criticism" climaxing simultaneously (note the sexual undertone), a "gust of ecstasy that will envelop society" (not his usual dry language). "New forms of collective life" would develop. "All existence [would] be harmonized." This would not be "an ordinary harmonization . . . but a harmonization of the most *common* forms and their *common* content."[27] Man would "organize" the chaotic, cruel, conflict-ridden world into a new and higher harmony. Meanwhile, he and Leonid Krasin (1870–1926) organized Bolshevik "expropriations," presumably deriving the term from Marx's statement "the expro-

---

26. Stanislav Volskii, *Filosofiia bor'by: opyt postroeniia etiki marksizma* (Moscow, 1909), 302, 306, 309.

27. Bogdanov, "Revoliutsiia i filosofiia," *Obrazovanie*, no. 2 (1906): 271; see also page 183.

priators are expropriated" (*MER*, 438). The tactic could also be justified by
Nietzsche's amoralism; Bakunin's urging revolutionaries to ally with bandits and criminals (which some "expropriators" did); and Machiavelli's dictum, which many political maximalists accepted: the end justifies the means.
Mach and Ostwald furnished Bogdanov and Krasin with new code words.[28]
"Philosophy" meant "politics," "matter" meant the "proletariat," "motion"
meant "revolution," and "energy" meant revolutionary "violence." Bogdanov
opposed parliamentarianism at all costs and wanted to train fighting squads
(a return to the "heroic" tradition of revolutionary populism). We recall that
Sorel's *Reflections on Violence* was translated into Russian in 1907.[29]

In 1907, Bogdanov advocated revising Marxism along the lines of a "religion of socialism," as Marx's friend Joseph Dietzgen had recommended,
thereby giving the Nietzschean idea of myth-creation a Marxist pedigree.
Gorky and Lunacharsky concocted a Marxist surrogate religion called God-
building (*Bogostroitel'stvo*) that featured worship of the immortal spirit of
collective humanity. Gorky coined the term as a challenge to Godseeking.
Lenin strenuously objected to God-building. To him, the difference between
it and Christianity was of no more importance than the difference between
a blue devil and a yellow one; neither belonged in a scientific doctrine.

God-building had much in common with Mystical Anarchism, for both
were ventures in myth-creation. The Marxist religion was designed to keep
the revolution alive by converting the long-suffering masses into heroes willing to fight and die for socialism.[30] The promise of collective immortality
was supposed to overcome their fear of death. Also basic to God-building
were Zarathustra's dictum that "man is a bridge and not a goal"; Feuerbach's
belief that God is a human construct; and Comte's Religion of Humanity.
Mach's social immortality became collective immortality—individuals die
but the collective lives on—or as Ostwald put it: "Matter decays but energy
is immortal."

Gorky and Lunacharsky denounced "slavish" accommodation to bourgeois society. They did not consider urging the masses to sacrifice themselves

---

28. Robert C. Williams, *The Other Bolsheviks* (Bloomington, 1977), 11.

29. Also translated was Arturo Labriola's *Syndicalism and Reformism;* Lunacharsky was
the translator. For more on syndicalism, see ibid., 84–93. See also, Bazarov, *Anarkhicheskii
kommunizm i marksizm* (Peterburg, 1906); *Teoriia i praktika sindikalizma* (1906) by P.
Iushkevich, a sometime associate of the Nietzschean Marxists; *Teoretiki romanskogo
sindikalizma* (1908), by Viktor Chernov; and *Na obshchestvennye temi* (1909) by the former Godseeker Nikolai Minsky (N. M. Vilenkin, 1855–1937).

30. George L. Kline, "The God-Builders, Gorky and Lunacharsky," in *Religious and
Anti-Religious Thought in Russia* (Chicago, 1968), 103–26; Clowes, *Revolution*, 175–222;
Raimund Sesterhenn, *Das Bogostroitel'stvo bei Gor'kij und Lunacharskij bis 1909* (Munich,
1909); Williams, *Other Bolsheviks*, 81–104; and Aileen Kelly, "A Bolshevik Philosophy?"
Toward Another Shore: Russian Thinkers Between Necessity and Chance (New Haven, 1998),
257–84.

for the revolution "slavish." Gorky wrote: "Two hundred black eyes will not deck Russian history in a brighter color; for that you need blood and lots of blood. . . . Life is built on cruelty, horror, force; for reconstruction a cold, rational cruelty is necessary."[31] In other words, the revolutionary must be "hard." Lunacharsky declared: "Life is struggle, a field of battle: we do not conceal that, we rejoice in it, because we see, beyond the burdens of our labors, beyond perhaps rivers of blood, the victory of more grandiose, beautiful, and humane forms of life . . . away with everything sickly that thirsts for rest, for peace at any price, [away] with everything fermented and flabby! We do not fear a stern truth, the cold mountain wind. . . . We are for life because life is *for us*."[32]

The main tracts of God-building, Lunacharsky's *Religion and Socialism* (2 vols., 1908 and 1911) and Gorky's novel *Confession* (1908), appeared after the revolutionary tide had ebbed. Gorky's novel *Mother* (1906) is not a God-building tract because it "revalued" rather than replaced Christianity by presenting the revolutionaries as the real Christians. God-building is anticipated, however, by one character (Rybin), who says, "We have got to change our God. . . . It is necessary . . . to invent a new faith: it is necessary to create a God for all."[33]

In *Religion and Socialism,* Lunacharsky created a "mythology of labor," for he believed that to construct a new world, the new man needs a new myth.[34] Acknowledging that it was his interest in religion that had led him to socialism (1:7), Lunacharsky viewed religion positively as a "tie" that unites people in their struggle against the powerful forces that surround them (1:39), even though the promised paradise remains an unattainable dream. The new man, however, does not fly "on the fleshless wings of mystical daydreams. His ideal is for him a *plan,* by which he must reconstruct the world. In labor, in technology [the new man] found himself to be a god and decided to dictate his will to the world" (1:104).

Furnishing his myth with an origin, a history, and an ending, Lunacharsky posited five stages of religion: cosmism (or animism), Platonism, Judaism, Christianity, and socialism. Socialism is the "Religion of Labor." Progress, the "creation of cultural values" (an un-Marxist definition), was inherent in the laws of nature, but not guaranteed. Human agency was required. *Religion and Socialism* includes discussion of the "myth of the superman" as a collective archetype (1:197–201) and of the Eucharist as the "basic form" of the "Christian cult." The original Eucharist was rationalistic and

---

31. *Letters of Gorky and Andreev,* 1899–1912, ed. Peter Vershov (New York, 1958), 70.

32. Lunacharskii, "Dialog ob isskustve," in *LSS,* 7:130–31.

33. Maxim Gorky, *Mother,* trans. Isidore Schneider (New York, 1991), 60–61.

34. Anatolii Lunacharskii, *Religiia i sotsializm,* 2 vols. (Peterburg, 1908, 1911), 1:95.

democratic, a supper of love, Lunacharsky claimed. The symbolic eating and drinking of Jesus' body and blood entered the "Christian cult" by way of such Greek mystery religions as the Dionysus cult and Orphism, which practiced ritual sacrifice and cannibalism (2:122–24). This is an implicit response to Ivanov, who is not mentioned by name, even though Berdiaev and Merezhkovsky are (in other sections). *Religion and Socialism* is sprinkled with phrases such as the "beauty of Marxism," the "music of Marxism," and Marxism as the "music of the future" (the last from Wagner's essay, "The Music of the Future," 1849) and references to Nietzsche, for example: "Together with Nietzsche, we say 'Man! Your business is not to find meaning in the world but to give meaning to the world'" (1:46).

In the first volume, Lunacharsky contrasted the power of the collective with the helplessness of the isolated individual, extolled "collective egoism" (proletarian self-affirmation), and explained that in religious enthusiasm the "little I" merges with the "We." His "enthusiasm" was similar to Ivanov's "ecstasy," except that the Mystical Anarchist stands outside himself, while in Edith Clowes's words, "Lunacharsky's new man . . . remains within himself, aware at once of being himself and a part of the greater whole of the people. He, in unison with the people, *is* the god, that is the creator of illusions, of grand existential goals."[35] In the seventeenth century, "enthusiasm" (which stems from the Greek words for "the fact of being possessed by a god") meant religious zealotry or fanaticism. Locke decried "enthusiasm." Lunacharsky restored the older meaning. In the second volume, he asserted the primacy of class goals and demands full personal sacrifice on their behalf, "even the sacrifice of a generation." Willingness to sacrifice was "the soul of the contemporary workers' movement"; therefore, it would be more correct to speak of "class idealism" than "class egoism" (2:340). Note his reversion to the kenotic ideal of self-sacrifice.

Gorky's novel *Confession* depicts the wanderings of Matvei, the illegitimate son of an aristocrat (possibly an allusion to Fedorov), in search of truth. Matvei's experiences cause him to become disenchanted with Christianity. Toward the end of the book, he meets a wanderer named Iegudeil. In this character, Gorky combines Zarathustra (also a wanderer, Z, 173–76) with a Russian type, the *strannik,* a wanderer in search of religious truth. Iegudeil tells Matvei that God is created not by man's weakness, but by man's strength (Feuerbach's idea), and that there are two classes: the people, which continually creates new gods, and their oppressors, forever motivated by the will to power, who try to suppress the people's creativity. Even now, the people are secretly busy creating a new god, a god of beauty, wisdom, justice, and love. "It is the people who create gods—the common herd which no

35. Clowes, *Revolution*, 210.
36. Maxim Gorky, *A Confession* (London, 1910), 231.

man can number . . . that is the god who works miracles."[36] Matvei learns that the "'I' is man's worst enemy," for it is "poor in spirit and incapable of creating anything." It must unite "once more" into a great whole that was split open and broken to pieces" (255–56). Immortality resides in the whole; in isolation there is only slavery and darkness, inconsolable sorrow and death (272). In the last chapter, the focused energies of a crowd heal a paralyzed girl, a feat that inspires Matvei to pray to the new god: "Thou art my god o sovereign people and creator of all gods. . . . I shall have no other god but thee" (320). Here, and elsewhere, Gorky adapted romantic and populist myths of folk creativity to Marxism and fused the populist mystique of the commune with Marxist collectivism and Nietzsche's yearning (in *The Birth of Tragedy*) for a "restored oneness."

Confession includes a "new woman," aptly named Christina. Having recently escaped from a convent, she insists on freedom and gender equality. Matvei accommodates her wish to have a child. What makes Christina a Nietzschean figure is her hope of bearing the Superman. "Let the flash of a star glitter in your love! Let your hope be: 'May I bear the Superman!'" (Z, 92). Matvei admires Christina's absolute freedom from fear and her determination to fight for herself with her entire being, but he was "unable to appreciate that quality in its full greatness and significance" (210–13). Christina represents Gorky's ideal of the new woman: independent, heroic, and rational.

Bogdanov's myth-creation took a different form: the utopian science-fiction novels, *Red Star* (1908) and *Engineer Menni* (1913).[37] In *Red Star,* the class struggle has long been over, but an unrelenting struggle against nature continues. Both novels reflect his naturalist worldview. *Red Star* depicts a perfected communist society on the red planet Mars—an egalitarian utopia of rational, productive, well-fed, cultured, happy, and versatile men and women, who perform a variety of industrial tasks and change jobs, and even occupations, frequently and voluntarily. The economy is a self-regulating system (in today's terms a kind of giant computer) into which people feed information. Science can prolong life indefinitely, but not prevent aging and debility. People chose their moment of death in pleasant suicide rooms, as if heeding Nietzsche's dictum, "Die at the right time . . . I commend to you my sort of death, voluntary death that comes to me because *I* wish it" (Z, 97). *Engineer Menni* describes the social and the scientific revolutions that preceded the earthling Leonid's visit to the Red Star.

In *Red Star,* the women are almost physically indistinguishable from the men and names do not announce gender. Leonid, the male protagonist, is

---

37. *Red Star* and *Engineer Menni* were published in one volume under the title *Red Star*, edited by Loren Graham and Richard Stites and translated by Charles Rougle (Bloomington, 1984).

drawn to Lenni, not realizing that she is a woman, until later. Intelligent, rational, and responsible, Lenni defies the usual stereotypes of women, but she is not a Superwoman, nor is Leonid a Superman, for that would have contradicted Bogdanov's egalitarianism. Gender equality is muted in *Engineer Menni*. The only role of the female protagonist, Nella, is to give birth to Netti and to bring father and son together years later. (Menni leaves her to pursue his work before their son, Netti, is born.)

The most adamant Marxist partisan of a "new woman" was, of course, Kollontai. A vehement opponent of "bourgeois feminism," she considered equal rights meaningless in a class society. While organizing women workers during the Revolution of 1905, she encountered the sexism of her male comrades and concluded that the causes of women's subjugation were psychological as well as economic. Woman must "discard the slave mentality that has clung to her," transform herself "step by step" into an "independent worker, an independent personality, free in love . . . fighting in the ranks of the proletariat."[38] She praised the brave solitude of the new woman who refuses to be a slave or to sacrifice her own individuality. Compare Nietzsche: "Loneliness is one thing, solitude another" (*Z*, 202). She considered egoism a socially induced trait more characteristic of men than women. Socialism would help people unlearn egoism; even so, special attention would have to be paid to "reorganizing" the human psyche, in addition to reorganizing society. Gender equality required "separation of the kitchen from marriage" and communal child-rearing. Women would still be obligated to bear children, however, and to breast-feed them personally (a class issue, wet nurses were poor), because motherhood "*is not a private matter but a social obligation.*"[39] Birth control would be unnecessary, because poverty would no longer exist. Like other women radicals impressed by Nietzsche, Kollontai did not address his misogyny. Presumably, they thought it was directed against the "slavish" bourgeois housewife, not the free woman of the future. Among these radicals were the German Marxist Feminist, Lili Braun, with whom Kollontai corresponded; Helene Stöcker, founder of the League for the Protection of Mothers and Sexual Reform; Emma Goldman ("Red Emma"); and the Swedish feminist Ellen Key. All of them emphasized woman's sexuality and maternal nature.

A conflict between Lenin and Bogdanov that had been simmering for several years reached the boiling point in 1908–9, when they became rivals for leadership of the Bolshevik faction. Bogdanov's strategy included a newspaper, *Vpered* (*Forward*); the formation of a separate faction, also called

38. *Alexandra Kollontai, Selected Writings*, ed. Alix Holt (New York, 1977), 64.
39. Ibid., 145.

Vpered;[40] Party training schools; and two symposia, *Essays On the Philosophy of Marxism* (1908) and *Essays on the Philosophy of Collectivism* (1909). The faction Vpered called for proletarian cultural hegemony (*gegemoniia*). The Russian word *gegemoniia* connotes power and control, not just intellectual domination in the Gramscian sense. Bogdanov's contributions to the symposia, which focused on epistemology, demonstrate his knowledge of German philosophy and linguistics; of British Empiricism, especially Hume; and of Bergson, William James, and contemporary literature and art, including symbolist poetry.

The first Party school was held in Capri, at Gorky's villa, in 1909; and the second one, in Bologna in 1910–11. The students, mostly worker-intellectuals, were taught Marxist theory, conspiratorial techniques, the history of the labor movement, and art and literature. Their teachers—Bogdanov, Gorky, Lunacharsky, Volsky, the Marxist historian Mikhail Pokrovsky, and others—drew upon a wide range of ideas, including those of syndicalism and Nietzsche.[41] (Gorky did not participate in the Bologna school.) Lenin countered Bogdanov with a Party school at Longjumeau, a suburb of Paris, and *Materialism and Empiriocriticism* (1909), published under a pseudonym, V. Il'in. Bogdanov answered *Materialism and Empiriocriticism* with *The Fall of a Great Fetishism* and *Faith and Science* (both 1910). In 1913, Lunacharsky moved to Paris, where he set up his own Circle of Proletarian Culture. In 1915, he reconciled with Lenin. That year, Lunacharsky and his friend Pavel Lebedev-Poliansky (P. I. Lebedev, 1882–1948) revived the newspaper *Vpered;* the first issue announced its commitment to proletarian culture.

Conflict with Lenin intensified Bogdanov's collectivism and hatred of authority. Collectivism and proletarian "energy" (a code word for revolution) were the keys to a socialist future, Bogdanov insisted; "a full, decisive collectivism, practical and theoretical" was the true philosophy of Marxism. The material elements of a socialist system already existed, but in a "disorganized spontaneous form."[42] For the next political revolution to be successful, it would have to be preceded and accompanied by a cultural revolution. The modern world required a different kind of integrating ideology (= myth), one that is scientifically unified and consciously constructed.

---

40. Details in John Biggart, "'Anti-Leninist Bolshevism': The *Forward* Group of the RSDRP," *Canadian Slavonic Papers* 23 (June 1981): 134–53.

41. John Biggart, "The Rehabilitation of Bogdanov," in *Bogdanov and His Work: A Guide to the Published and Unpublished Works of Alexander A. Bogdanov (Malinovsky) 1873–1928*, ed. John Biggart, Georgii Glovei, and Avraham Yassour (Brookfield, Vt., 1998), 7.

42. Bogdanov, "Ot redaktsii," in *Ocherki filosofii kollektivizma* (St. Petersburg, 1909), 5; idem, "Filosofiia sovremmennego estestvoispytatel'ia," ibid., 133. See also Bogdanov, "Strana idolov i filosofii marksizma," in *"Ocherki po filosofii marksizma* (St. Petersburg, 1908), 215–48.

He pointed out that "ideology" comes from two Greek words—*idein,* "to see," and *logos,* "speech" or "word." Thus, according to Bogdanov, the literal meaning of ideology is the "science of ideas."[43] (Bogdanov frequently argued from language.) He concluded from this that the collectivist advocates "the *scientific* solution of questions," not majority rule (*Desiatletie,* 112).

Lunacharsky, Gorky, and Bazarov accused symbolists and philosophers of "philistine individualism" and decadence, linking these concepts and associating both with Nietzsche. Gorky announced that (Nietzschean) self-affirmation borders on hooliganism. He also said that priests deceive the people by using an alien language.[44] Gorky was alluding to symbolists such as Ivanov, who saw themselves as high priests, but the statement also applies to Orthodox priests, who used Church Slavonic in their liturgy, and to Roman Catholic priests, who used Latin in theirs. Implicitly, the people, not the symbolist poet or the Orthodox priest, would articulate the salvific "new word." Lunacharsky declared that "philistine individualism" reflected the bourgeois ideal of self interest, rather than the Christian and socialist ideal of altruism. Bazarov rejected altruism. In a socialist society, he maintained, the very idea of mine and thine would vanish, along with any distinction between the self and the other. Even the sense of the body as one's own property would disappear, so intense would be the feeling of unity. Creativity would be enhanced, however, because socialism would liberate people from the yoke of material need. Art would not be "disorderly individual seeking"; rather artists would work in schools, proceeding by a plan toward their goal.[45] Socialism was "impersonal collective creativity."

Bogdanov's Program for Cultural Revolution

In 1911, having lost his battle with Lenin, Bogdanov withdrew from political activity and worked out a program for cultural revolution. By cultural revolution he meant emancipating the proletariat psychologically (as well as economically and politically) from bourgeois dominance, developing a collectivist psyche, reworking (= revaluing) the cultural legacy from a proletarian perspective, and constructing a distinctively proletarian art and science. He wanted proletarian art to assume the "organizational" role that

43. Bogdanov, *Desiatiletie otlichenii ot marksizma: Iubileinyui sbornik* (1904–14), vol. 3 of *Neizvestnyi Bogdanov,* compiled by N. S. Antonov (Moscow, 1995), 55.

44. Gor'kii, "Razrushenie lichnosti," in *Ocherki filosofii kollektivizma,* 364–65.

45. V. Bazarov, "Lichnost' i liubov' v svete 'novogo religioznogo soznaniia,'" in *Literaturnyi raspad* (Peterburg, 1908), 213–30; idem, "Khristiane Tret'ego Zaveta i stroiteli Bashni Vavilonskoi," in *Literaturnyi raspad, Kniga vtoraia* (St. Petersburg, 1911), 5–38. See also idem, "Bogoiskatel'stvo i 'Bogostroitel'stvo,'" in *Vershiny* (St. Petersburg, 1909), 356, 360, 369, and *Na dva fronta* (St. Petersburg, 1910).

religion played in authoritarian societies: disciplining people to fulfill their social role(s); uniting feeling, thought, and praxis; and inculcating proletarian values (labor, egalitarianism, collectivism, and comradely cooperation). The cultural revolution would be led, in its first stages, by the radical intelligentsia, especially those versed in technology, and skilled industrial workers. Since Bogdanov expected the state to disappear, he did not discuss political structures.

He presented his program in *The Cultural Tasks of Our Time* (1911).[46] The original title was "The Cultural Tasks of the Proletariat"; Bogdanov changed it to accommodate the censor. In subsequent essays, he restated, elaborated, or modified ideas first set forth here. His model was the "bourgeois" cultural revolution (the scientific revolution and the Enlightenment) that preceded and made possible the political revolution of 1789. Bogdanov constantly enjoined the proletariat to overcome its "slave mentality," develop its own culture, and "master" the knowledge required to reorganize reality according to its own needs and values. He expressed great confidence in the proletariat's "creative will," its ability to forge a new culture that would be imbued with its values. To say that workers were not up to this task was to insult them (*Kul'turnye*, 42). The proletariat was the "organizing class" of the future because it was the only class that could "master" both nature and the machine. The peasant was ruled by the forces of nature, while the cerebral intelligentsia was entirely cut off from nature. Refusing to privilege spiritual over material culture, Bogdanov defined "culture" as the sum of material and nonmaterial acquisitions used in the labor process or that raised the quality of life. Among these acquisitions were "the physically perfect body—its strength, dexterity, beauty—attainable by conscientious exercise," language, art, habits, customs, laws, and political institutions (3). Marx and Engels did not stress physical perfection, art, or language. A few years later, Bogdanov related speech (*rech'*), epistemology (*poznanie*), art, and the rules or norms of human relations to ideology (*Desiatiletie*, 55). Marx considered language the nexus where social being and social consciousness joined, but he did not theorize about language itself. For Bogdanov, social being and social consciousness were the same.[47]

Bogdanov emphasized language as the "organizer of social life." Relating language to class, he connected word and myth in a nonmystical way. "Truth" for one class was a lie to another; "freedom," "order," and "justice" have different meanings for the ruling class and the subordinated class. Beauty

46. Bogdanov, *Kul'turnye zadachi nashego vremeni* (Moscow, 1911). See also idem, *O proletarskoi kul'ture* (Petrograd, 1924), a collection of previously published essays.
47. Paul Lafargue, Marx's son-in-law, connected language and class struggle in his book *La langue française avant et après la révolution* (written 1876, published 1894), but Bogdanov does not seem to have been aware of it, or of Lafargue's essay "Le myth de Prometée" (1904). Lafargue's name is absent from discussions of language in the 1920s and 1930s as well.

was a class phenomenon too. Bourgeois conceptions of beauty glorified the soldier (*Kul'turnye,* 5–6). Bogdanov later decried such glorification as an indirect cause of World War I. He associated "the word" with authoritarian causality. " 'In the beginning was the word,' says the ancient wisdom [John 1:1] i.e., in the authoritarian world the organizing *word* is the necessary principle of every social-labor activity . . . its first cause." As the reality that the word described changes, words become fetishes, new forms of abstract necessity ruling over man. These ideational tools of labor ruled over his psyche, while his fragmented labor power was ruled by material tools" (*Padenie,* 60, 141). In *Essays on Tektology* (1921), he described the word as one of three instruments of organization.

> Every conscious collaboration of people is organized by means of words. . . . Gigantic collectives are created by the force of a word; gigantic collectives are governed by it. People of the 20th century have seen how the command of the most insignificant individual has directed millions of people into an unprecedented hell of iron and dynamite, of murder and destruction. It was not for nothing that ancient thought, profound in its naïveté, begat the myth about the creation of the world by the word, and believed in the infinite power of the word over the elements. . . . disease and death had to obey the person who knew and uttered an appropriate word.[48]

The other two instruments were the dominant idea (myth), expressed in art and in science, and social norms (morality). All instruments stemmed from humankind's social and natural experience.

A Proletarian Art

Bogdanov believed that each art form serves, or once served, a practical function. It was not accidental, he said, that in Greek, the language of great philosophy, the same word means to 'organize' and to 'beautify' " (*Kul'turnye,* 22n). Poetry originated in religious myth; epics educated people the way science and philosophy do today. Dance and music organized social life. Sculpture, painting, and architecture concentrated the forms of human experience and transmitted them to the collective. Universal types in sculpture and painting resembled universal types in poetry and summarized human experience; they were just as important for life as the highest conceptions of philosophy or the highest generalizations of science. "The ideal of a full and powerful, harmonious and all-conquering life is expressed in the sculptures of the ancient world, and in the statues of its gods, more clearly and I

48. Bogdanov, *Essays in Tektology,* trans. George Gorelik (Seaside, Calif., 1980), 2.

would suggest more deeply, than in the 'superman' of Nietzsche's philosophy" (*Kul'turnye*, 17). Architecture organized the emotions of the masses and expressed social values. As examples, Bogdanov gave the imposing edifices of Imperial Rome, which conveyed national pride, and the soaring Gothic cathedrals, which expressed priestly power and symbolized the medieval renunciation of the earth. Proletarian art and architecture would communicate the proletariat's collective sensation of the world. A mighty weapon or instrument (*orudie* means both) in the class struggle, the "all-penetrating influence of the new art" would harmonize the feelings and aspirations of the masses into one impulse, making it a powerful mover that accelerates the growth and the victory of the collective" (*Kul'turnye*, 76). In a later essay, Bogdanov proclaimed that "myth is not a lie," but the "praxis" of primitive poetic knowledge, the organization of living experience in words.[49] Myth would function as a religion, that is, as an integrating ideology. Indeed, Bogdanov pointed out that the word "religion" itself stems from the Latin word "tie" (*religare*) (*Padenie*, 13n).

Bogdanov did not specify the new form(s) proletarian art would take, but he expected it to encompass far more than class struggle. The proletariat strives to "seize all society and nature," taking what is useful and progressive from other classes in order to create a harmonious, monistic culture. Its art will represent a "beautiful victory over the old society whose creative force is dried up." Cubism was a product of expiring bourgeois society; proletarian art would present "living images" and coherent visions (as opposed to cubist fragmentation) of the collective's life-experience (*Kul'turnye*, 79–89).

A Proletarian Science

For complete liberation the proletariat had to "master science," Bogdanov insisted. It could not continue to leave scientific decisions to specialists. He expected proletarian scientists to develop new collectivist methodologies and to undertake practical projects such as increasing production, maintaining health, and prolonging life. Social scientists would rework data gathered by their predecessors from a proletarian point of view. Physical scientists would do the same in their laboratories and observatories. "Philistine specialists" (Mach's expression) were cut off from the "living praxis" of humanity. Bogdanov denigrated knowledge for its own sake and the solitary pursuit of "abstract truth." Even such seemingly abstruse sciences as astronomy and

49. Bogdanov, "Iskusstvo i rabochii klass," reprinted in *Bogdanov, A. A. Voprosy sotsializma: Rabotyi raznyukh let*, ed. L. I. Abalkin, et al. (Moscow, 1990), 411–60; this collection (henceforth cited as *A. A. Bogdanov*) also contains "Vozmozhno li proletarkskoe iskusstvo?" "Proletariat i iskusstvo," "O khudozhestvemnon nasledstve," "Kritika proletarskogo iskusstva," and "Prostota ili utonchennost'."

geometry originated in practical demands and helped "organize" the economy of their time. Hunters used the stars to avoid getting lost, farmers to predict the seasons, and priests in ancient Egypt and Mesopotamia to regulate river flooding for irrigation. In the feudal-priestly societies of ancient Egypt and Babylon, geometry was part of religion; in mercantile Greece, geometry became abstract as needed for navigation and commerce, hence serving the needs of the ruling class. Priests have always enveloped their scientific knowledge in an aura of mystery, couching that knowledge in a language inaccessible to the masses; modern scientists do the same. Workers require a unified science (rather than fragmented disciplines, each with its own language) and practical knowledge conveyed clearly and simply.[50] All the sciences must be revalued from a proletarian perspective. Endorsing Dietzgen's idea of a "special proletarian logic," Bogdanov advocated a "proletarian mathematics (*Desiatiletie*, 66–67). Even $2 + 2 = 4$ was not an absolute truth but a convenient metaphor.[51] Bogdanov paid a great deal of attention to what Foucault later called "power/knowledge." According to Bogdanov, "Truth is not a petty and act representation of the facts but an instrument for domination over them."[52]

Nietzsche regarded science not just as a function of myth, but also as a weapon. "It is revenge above all that science has been able to employ—the revenge of the oppressed, those who had been pushed aside, and in fact, oppressed by the *prevailing* truth. Truth, that is to say, the scientific method, was grasped and promoted by those who divined in it a weapon of war—an instrument of destruction" (*WP*, 250–51). Bogdanov viewed science as a weapon of class war. "Bourgeois science" stemmed from Copernicus and Galileo, whose theories contradicted the ruling ideology of the feudal order, appealing to people whose economic interests did not mesh with feudalism. The scientific revolution that Copernicus initiated became the basis for a new unified worldview, the bourgeois ideology of the Enlightenment. Once in power, the bourgeoisie organized the world according to its own ideology based on Newton's laws and market forces. Scientific socialism spoke for the oppressed and provided a basis for a proletarian scientific revolution. Time and again, he stressed that Marx "*changed the point of view*" (*Desiatiletie*, 26).[53] Marx was the "Copernicus of the social sciences," "the model of the new man . . . a worker and a warrior," an incarnation of a new type who merges "creative thought and creative practice in one harmonious whole. And in this he belongs to a new world" (*Desiatiletie*, 26–28).

50. See "Nauka i rabochii klass," "Metody truda i metody roznaniia," and "Taina nauki," reprinted in *A. A Bogdanov*, in the section "Sotsialism nauki," 360–410.

51. Williams, *Other Bolsheviks*, 148.

52. Bogdanov, *Filosofiia zhivogo opyta* (St. Petersburg, 1912), 192.

53. See also *A. A. Bogdanov*, 367.

To accelerate development of a proletarian science, Bogdanov proposed a "Proletarian Encyclopedia," with sections on science and technology, and a "Proletarian University." The encyclopedia would "crystallize the truth of the time," link the various branches of knowledge to one another, and show their interconnectedness, just as the *philosophes* had done for the bourgeoisie. Work on the Proletarian Encyclopedia would proceed in connection with the Proletarian University. The contributors would not simply present knowledge, but consciously and systematically rework (= revalue) it in a "gigantic deed of transformation." The Proletarian University was not intended for bourgeois youth (*mal'chiki*) or "human larva" (*lichinka*), but for mature people with serious experience in the world of labor and social struggle; it would not replicate "bourgeois temples of knowledge" (*Kul'turnye*, 58, 69). In Marxist terms, the students would be a scientific vanguard; in Nietzschean terms, a culture-creating new nobility (but without special privileges).

Engineer Menni includes a description of Menni's canalization of Mars, a "wonder of labor and human will" that took several generations to complete and transformed the climate and geography (147). In other words, it was a Nietzschean and a Fedorovian great project, except that it was "dictated by historical necessity," not freely undertaken. In the course of the novel, Menni, an archetype of the strong (bourgeois) individual, and his son Netti, a collectivist and also an engineer, have several discussions. Netti explains that the historical mission of the bourgeoisie "was to create a human individual, an active being inspired with self confidence who would be distinct from the human herd of the feudal epoch." Now these "active atoms" must be bound together and fused into a single human organism. Menni replies, "So you want to transform human individuals into beings which resemble cells?" "No," Netti replies, "because the cells of an organism are not conscious of the whole to which they belong. . . . We are striving to make man "fully aware of himself as an element of the great laboring whole" (196–97). Their dialogue can be read as an individualist versus a collectivist interpretation of Nietzsche. Elsewhere, Bogdanov called Nietzsche a complex thinker whose thought combined authoritarian with individualistic elements (*Padenie*, 60n).

In a different discussion, Menni argues for the existence and importance of autonomous ideas, while Netti contends that ideas are born and die in a particular social context. For example, the idea of freedom will disappear when oppression disappears. On another occasion, Netti contends that the masses organize their experience in myths and legends. Although absurd on its face, the legend of the vampire expresses a profound truth. "Dead life exists—history is full of it; it surrounds us on all sides and drinks the blood of living life." A vampire, a living corpse, is much more harmful than a dead corpse which must be removed lest it spread disease. "Ideas die just like people, but they cling to life even more stubbornly after their death" (213–14). In other words, outmoded ideas and their carriers are dangerous. Bogdanov did not mention Lenin by name but he probably had Lenin in mind, especially since, in 1910, he had published two short essays, "'The Great Vampire' of Our Time" and "Vampires: A Scientific-Popular Sketch."[54] Marx called Capital "dead labor, that, vampire-like, only lives by sucking living labor" (*MER*, 362–63), but he did not apply the concept to ideas or to a person.

Bogdanov opposed the Bolshevik seizure of power in 1917, not only because he detested Lenin's authoritarianism, but also because he believed the workers were not ready to implement socialism. They needed a "socialism of science," not a socialism of faith or a socialism of feelings. "As long as the working class does not possess its own organizational tools, but on the contrary is possessed by them, it cannot and *must* not [attempt to bring about socialism]. This would be an adventure without the slightest chance of success, an attempt to build a world palace without knowledge of the laws of architecture. It would be a new bloody lesson, probably even more cruel than the one we are experiencing now."[55] Bogdanov did not advocate firing nonproletarian scientists after the Revolution, but his occasionally extreme language ("human larva"), his rejection of occupational specialization on principle, and his view that persons who carry outmoded ideas are vampires lent themselves to extremist interpretations, even though Bogdanov himself was emphasizing organizational theory by then. Stressing constructive activity, he disapproved of appeals to vindictiveness and hate, and distinguished between competence and power. Just about everyone is competent in some area.

In *Tektology, A Universal Science of Organization* (3 vols., 1912, 1917, 1922), Bogdanov tried to create a monistic metascience of nature and society that would unite "the most disparate phenomena" in the organic and inorganic worlds—a planned global organization of things, people, and ideas in one well-structured system. "Tektology" stems from the Greek word *techton,* "builder." Combining structure and dynamism in an overall unity that was constantly evolving, Tektology was an open and highly differentiated system with a moving, dynamic equilibrium (rather than static forms or a dialectical struggle of opposites) and a "bi-regulator," in modern terms, cybernetic feedback. One of its features was an international language (with no grammar) that would enable people to understand one another and reduce conflict.[56] The basic concepts of Tektology were "organization" and "deorganization"—in Nietzschean terms, Apollo and Dionysus. Nietzsche's *agon*

---

54. "Velikii upyr' nashevo vremeni" (1910), in *Neizvestnyi Bogdanov*, 1:68–75, and "Upyri. Nauchno-populiarnyi ocherk" (also 1910), listed in *Bogdanov and His Work*, 227.

55. A. A. Bogdanov, 331–32.

56. *Tektologiia: Vseobshchaia organizationnaia nauka*, vol. 1 (St. Petersburg, 1912), vol. 2 (Moscow, 1917), vol. 3 (Berlin, 1922); reprinted in 2 vols. (Moscow, 1989).

is absent, however, and so is class struggle; even class consciousness is muted in this work (though not in contemporaneous pieces). Bogdanov wanted to replace chaos with cosmos, to bring order and harmony into a strife-torn world. On one level, Tektology was an attempt to realize Marx's concept of a single science of man. On another level, it was a technological version of the symbolist project of "life-creation."

The Nietzschean Marxists' attempts to create a collectivist psyche, their ventures in myth-creation, and Bogdanov's call for a cultural revolution made a permanent impression on Bolshevik thought. Conflict with Bogdanov induced Lenin to address epistemological and cultural issues he might have otherwise ignored. After the Bolshevik Revolution, "Bogdanovism" was second only to "Leninism" as the (unacknowledged) ideology of the Party even though Bogdanov himself was no longer a member.[57]

57. Sergei Utechin, "Bolsheviks and Their Allies After 1917: The Ideological Pattern," *Soviet Studies* 10 (October 1958): 115.

Futurists

Not to carry their generation to the grave, but to
found a new generation—that drives them forward
incessantly: and even if they are born as latecomers
. . . the coming generations will only know them as
first-comers.   —*H,* 49

The futurists propagated a new set of Nietzschean ideas,
some derived from *The Advantage and Disadvantage of
History for Life* and *The Gay Science,* others from fresh
readings of *Zarathustra, The Birth of Tragedy,* and *Twilight
of the Idols.* They called themselves the "new people of a
new life" (*RF,* 54). Their new myth was Victory over the
Sun; their "new word" was a transrational language called
zaum, literally "trans-sense" or "beyond the mind," and their
new art forms were futurism and cubism. Iconoclastic and
pugnacious, they brought the issue of the "new word" to
the vital center of literary debate where, conflated with political issues, it remained through the 1920s and into the 1930s.

There were several strands of futurism. Cubo-futurism
(the most prominent one), included the poets Vladimir
Mayakovsky (1893–1930), Aleksei Kruchenykh (1886–1969),

Velimir Khlebnikov (1885–1942), Vasily Kamensky (1884–1961), and the painter Kazimir Malevich (1878–1935), until 1915, when he founded his own movement, suprematism. Mayakovsky and Khlebnikov were playwrights as well as poets. The cubo-futurists accentuated Russia's pre-Christian and Asian roots, even while trying to create a myth for the machine age. They first called their movement Hylaea, after the home of the ancient Scythians. Another strand, Mezzanine of Poetry, was led by Vadim Shershenovich (1893–1942), admirer of the Italian futurist Filippo Marinetti (1876–1944) and translator, into Russian, of Marinetti's *Mafarka: An African Tale* (1909) and his futurist manifestos. Mafarka, a metallic man with spare parts, conceives and bears a son without a woman in a supreme act of will. His son is a new species, a beautiful winged giant who can master nature and subjugate the sun and the stars. Yet another strand, ego-futurism, was founded by Igor Severianin (1887–1941), who laced his manifestos with Nietzschean ideas. Unless otherwise specified, in this book futurism refers to cubo-futurism. These futurists rarely acknowledged their intellectual debts, but we know that Mayakovsky and Kruchenykh read Nietzsche, that Mayakovsky knew *Zarathustra* well, that Khlebnikov used Nietzschean themes, and that contemporaries regarded futurism as a Nietzschean movement.[1]

The Futurist Aesthetic

The futurist aesthetic solidified in a process of polemics against symbolists and acmeists. The acmeist aesthetic was Apollonian. It featured clarity in language, a visual orientation, concreteness, emphasis on the individual, ethics (Apollo is the ethical deity), and a Christian Hellenism that affirmed life on this earth. This aesthetic contradicted the dominant themes of Soviet politics and culture, so the acmeist poets—Nikolai Gumilev (1886–1921), Osip Mandelstam (1891–1938), and Anna Akhmatova (1889–1966)—will not be treated here.[2]

Although the futurists vociferously rejected symbolist mystification for a poetics of direct perception and scrapped the arcane language of symbolism, they perpetuated (in their own way) the symbolist linkage of word and myth, the search for a "new word," and the notion of a generative word. A

1. Bengt Jangfeldt, "Nietzsche and the Young Mayakovsky," in *NSC* 35–57; Henryk Baran, "Khlebnikov and Nietzsche: Pieces of an Incomplete Mosaic," ibid., 58–83; Bernice Glatzer Rosenthal, "A New Word for a New Myth," in *The Russian Foundations of European Modernism*, ed. Peter Barta (Lewiston, N.Y., 1991), 219–50. According to Nina Gurianova, Kruchenykh was very erudite.

2. Details in Rusinko, "Apollonianism and Christian Art," in *NSC*, 84–106; see also Cavanaugh, "Mandelstam, Nietzsche," in *NSC*, 338–66.

literary critic of the time called futurism the "path to a new symbolism."[3] Both movements emphasized orality. The symbolists wanted to replicate music, while the futurists extolled sound per se, even cacophony, and elevated (Dionysian) chaos to the status of a poetic principle. Their poetry was meant to be read aloud, indeed shouted, in the streets and public squares. To enhance the expressiveness of the written word, to "overcome Gutenberg," as they put it, futurists made striking innovations in typography, layout, and page design. Among their slogans were "art for life and life for art" and "it is time for art to invade life" (both from Mikhail Larionov). They wanted to bring art out of the museums and into the streets. Early futurism had much of the "play principle" about it and was not so much a total theatricalization of life, "theater as such," as a model of the free and spontaneous "game as such."[4] Their delight in shocking respectable society is obvious in the title of their first manifesto, "A Slap in the Face of Public Taste" (1912). They painted their faces, put wooden spoons or radishes in their lapels, threw tea at their audiences, traded insults with them (hardly the audience participation Ivanov had in mind), and staged attention-getting happenings. Intent on liberating literature and art from established authorities and canons, they wanted to throw Pushkin "overboard from the Ship of Modernity" (*RF*, 51) (even though they loved his poetry). A sense of disjuncture pervades their productions and expresses their conviction that an era had ended, that god was dead. Paradoxically, Christian themes and images pervade their work.

The figures discussed in the preceding three chapters were historically minded. The futurists propounded a "ruthless forgetting" of history (Paul de Man's term),[5] taking to an extreme Nietzsche's belief that an excess of historical consciousness is detrimental to life (*H*, 14). Khlebnikov and Kamensky were interested in history as material for myth, not in history for its own sake, or what Nietzsche called antiquarian history. He lauded youth for acting unhistorically and recommended two antidotes for "a historical sense that no longer preserves life, but mummifies it" (*H*, 21). The first antidote was unhistorical (forgetting) and the second was "superhistorical," art and religion (*H*, 62). The futurists' iconoclasm was, in part, an attempt at demummification. Nietzsche called for "superhistorical men" (*H*, 13). Khlebnikov proclaimed: "We believe in ourselves. . . . Are we not gods? Are we not unprecedented in this: our steadfast betrayal of our own past?"

3. Genrykh Tastevan, *Futurizm: na puti k novomu simvolizmu* (Moscow, 1914). Gumilev was executed in 1921; Mandelstam and Akhmatova were marginalized; and Mandelstam died in the Gulag.
4. Nina Gurianova, *Exploring Color: Rozanova and the Early Russian Avant Garde, 1910–1918* (Amsterdam, 2000), 34.
5. In "Literary History and Literary Modernity," Paul De Man argues that "ruthless forgetting" characterized post-1910 modernism; in *Blindness and Insight* (New York, 1971), 145–49, 151.

(*KhCW*, 1:321). Contempt for *passeism* (Marinetti's term for Mallarmé's poetry) was part of the futurists' cult of youth.

The symbolists picked up the Alpine imagery of *Zarathustra*—lofty peaks, dangerous paths, deep valleys—and they yearned for wings. The futurists celebrated constructed heights. "Life wants to raise itself on high with pillars and steps; it wants to gaze into the far distance and out upon joyful splendor—*that* is why it needs height!" (*Z*, 125). They envisioned life on roof-tops, gazing down on the crowd from skyscrapers, and flying in airplanes. Zarathustra referred to his "enemy, the spirit of gravity" (*Z*, 210). The futurists wanted to abolish gravity altogether.

Henry Bergson's (1859–1941) concepts of spontaneity, intuition, direct perception, simultaneity, and a space-time continuum were taken up by futurists, symbolists, and acmeists, each movement in its own way. An academic philosopher, Bergson made very few references to Nietzsche, apparently because he didn't want to undermine his credibility in the philosophic community.[6] He treated some of the same issues that Nietzsche did, without tragedy or *agon*. For Bergson, reality was continuous becoming, incomprehensible to the intellect alone. Imagination, intuition, and a fresh perception were required. Bergson's thought appealed to persons seeking "new modes of artistic perception by which to tap into the élan vital of the Dionysian flux and thus to discover the true essence of life."[7]

The New Myth: Victory over the Sun

The futurist opera *Victory over the Sun* (*Pobeda nad solntsem*, 1913) was a *Gesamtkunstwerk*.[8] Khlebnikov wrote the prologue; Kruchenykh, the script; Mikhail Matiushin (1861–1934), the music; and Malevich designed the decorations, costumes, and sets. The subtext of the opera, and of the futurist aesthetic in general, is Nietzsche's announcement of the death of God and its consequences—a world with no inherent order or meaning.

> The madman jumped into their midst and pierced them with his eyes. "Whither is God?" he cried; "I will tell you. *We have killed him*—you and I. All of us are his murderers. But how did we do this? How could

6. See Forth, *Zarathustra in Paris*, 85, and R. C. Grogin, *The Bergsonian Controversy in France* (Calgary, 1988), 84.

7. Hilary Fink, *Bergson and Russian Modernism, 1900–1903* (Evanston, 1999), 25.

8. *Pobeda nad solntsem* (Peterburg, 1913), translated into English under the title *Victory over the Sun* by Ewa Bartos and Victoria Nes Birby, *Drama Review* 15, no. 4 (1971): 107–24; henceforth cited parenthetically as *VOS*; quotations from the English edition. The introduction (93–106), includes excerpts from Futurist writings about the production; henceforth cited parenthetically as *VOS Intro*.

we drink up the sea? Who gave us the sponge to wipe away the entire horizon? What were we doing when we unchained this earth from its sun? Whither is it moving now? Whither are we moving? Away from all suns? Are we not plunging continually? Backward, sideward, forward, in all directions? Is there still any up or down? Are we not straying as through an infinite nothing? Do we not feel the breath of empty space? Has it not become colder? Is not night continually closing in on us? Do we not need to light lanterns in the morning? Do we hear nothing as yet of the noise of the gravediggers who are burying God? Do we smell nothing as yet of the divine decomposition? Gods, too, decompose. God is dead. God remains dead. And we have killed him. (GS, 181)

The capture of the sun (which occurs offstage) casts the earth into darkness, renders old categories of space and time obsolete, abolishes gravity, and eradicates the horizon defined by previous myths, clearing the way for entirely human constructions. The opera brings together key elements in the futurist myth: a directionless universe, abrogation of the laws of nature (symbolized by gravity), rejection of the past, futurist strongmen, a new language (zaum), and pictorial equivalents (alogical abstractions). The opening statement of the opera, "All's well that begins well. What about the end? There will be no end!" contradicted the old saying "all's well that ends well." Victory over the Sun closes with the words "the world will die but for us there is no end" (VOS, 109, 124). A futurist rendition of "eternal recurrence," the closing words also connote personal immortality—another example of the mixture of Nietzsche and Christianity.

The sun of the opera is Apollo, the god of rationality and clarity, the light of logic, hence the archenemy of utopians and visionaries. Its capture liberates humankind from the constraints of necessity. The chorus sings: "We are free / Broken sun . . . / Long live darkness! / and black gods / and their favorite—pig!" (VOS, 117). The juxtaposition of discordant images underscores the lack of inherent meaning, order, or purpose in the world.

The capture of the sun symbolizes not just the death of the biblical God, but the collapse of all cosmologies based on the sun, ranging from pagan sun worship to Newton's heliocentric universe governed by nature's law (the basis of the Enlightenment). There is a hidden polemic with symbolism here too, a rejection of Bal'mont's dictum, "Let us be like the sun." Zarathustra's frequent references to his "enemy, the spirit of gravity" denote Nietzsche's view that the Enlightenment myth is also dead (reason is insufficient). Gravity also means heaviness. Zarathustra wishes to "baptize the earth anew—as 'the weightless'" (Z, 210) and to "kill the Spirit of Gravity" by laughter (Z, 68). Gravity is the force which keeps man bound to the earth and to traditional ways of seeing things; it is heavy because it is a burden. The futurists used "gravity" as Nietzsche did, to signify physical and emotional heaviness, earth-boundedness, and humorlessness. The characters of *Victory over the Sun* feel an "extraordinary lightness," for they have been "liberated from the weight of the earth's gravitation" (*VOS*, 118). But they are also very confused because the streets are upside down like a mirror, the windows face inside, and time runs in all directions. Ordinary life (*byt*) has become impossible. The futurists' rejection of Newton's laws does not imply their rejection of science per se. They followed the early-twentieth-century revolution in physics and were enthralled by the new technology, especially aviation. It was the accelerated pace of technological innovation that fostered their belief in the transience of all things, in change as a permanent condition. Their espousal of technology (in this period) has been exaggerated. They did not exalt the machine as the Italian futurists did.

Victory over the Sun did not promise paradise. The first strongman announces:

> We are striking the universe
> We are arming the world against ourselves
> We are organizing the slaughter of scarecrows
> Plenty of blood Plenty of sabers.
> (*VOS*, 109)

In hindsight, the "slaughter of scarecrows" is chilling. Random, passionless violence, as in a Punch and Judy show, permeates the opera. Warlike colors and beams of red light dominate the scene. The red light reminded one critic of the fires of hell; another critic referred to "blood-red light."[9] The overwhelming mood is dread, for the emptiness of the new reality is indeed terrifying. The "New Ones" report: "Some tried to drown, the weak ones went mad, saying: 'we might become terrible and strong you see.' That oppressed them" (*VOS*, 118). Presumably, they would rather remain slaves.

The Madman's announcement of the death of God is preceded by a passage titled *"In the Horizon of the Infinite,"* which begins with another quotation from Nietzsche: "We have left the land and have embarked. We have burned our bridges behind us; indeed we have gone farther and destroyed the land behind us" (*GS*, 180). For Nietzsche the loss of the horizon is terrifying but it is also pregnant with possibilities. There is still a horizon, but it is not bounded by land. Meanwhile, the culture is in a state of decadence, that period when the old myth is no longer viable but the new one is not yet established and people are lost. The futurists viewed the expanded horizon as simultaneously terrifying and liberating; they were delighted that

---

9. Kruchenykh, "Pervye v mire spektakli futuristov," in *Iz literaturnogo naslediia Kruchenykh*, ed. Nina Gurianova (Berkeley and Los Angeles, 1999), 82–85.

humankind was no longer earthbound. Khlebnikov spoke in galactic terms. Malevich boasted, "I have destroyed the ring of the horizon and got out of the circle of objects, the horizon ring that has imprisoned the artist and the forms of nature."[10] He sought cosmic freedom, a breakthrough to the fourth dimension (an occult concept), a realm beyond death. Liberated from the spatial constraints imposed by the horizon, humankind was also liberated from time. "The Elocutionist" states, "how extraordinary life is without a past / With danger but without regrets and memories . . . / Forgotten are mistakes and failures boringly squeaking / into / one's ear" (*VOS*, 119). Another character says, "The sun of the iron century has died!" (*VOS*, 117). Implicitly, humankind is embarking on a new era.

Victory over the Sun was advertised with *Vladimir Mayakovsky, a Tragedy*, which also expressed hatred of the sun and of the rationality and order symbolized by daylight. In *The Birth of Tragedy*, Dionysus is madness personified. Mayakovsky deemed madness a characteristic of the Superman, a God gone mad. The mutilated bodies in *Vladimir Mayakovsky* were inspired by the section in *Zarathustra* titled "Of Redemption" (159–60). Mayakovsky structured his tragedy as a Dionysian dithyramb and included calls for violence and sex.[11] Here, and in his lyric poetry, Mayakovsky presented himself as a poet-martyr, fusing avant-garde bravado with a tortured nihilism which was a response to the death of God and to a series of unhappy loves. In Dionysian terms, he was offering himself as a leader and as a sacrifice. In Ancient Greece, a drunken poet usually led the Dionysian dithyrambs. Mayakovsky regarded himself as the leader of the entire performance, not just the chorus. In his postrevolutionary political dithyrambs, he envisioned himself leading the entire country in song.[12]

The futurists often combined Nietzsche with Dostoevsky, who considered the laws of nature despotic because they operate independently of human will. The statement in *Victory over the Sun*—"We tore the sun out by its fresh roots. These fat ones became permeated with arithmetics" (*VOS*, 116)— echoes Dostoevsky's underground man who wants 2 + 2 to equal 5—the ultimate affirmation of freedom of the will. The futurist motif of madness stemmed from Nietzsche and Dostoevsky, but was ultimately indebted to Nietzsche. Dostoevsky did not celebrate madness; he invariably explodes the "Nietzschean ideas" introduced by his characters. Prince Myshkin (*The Idiot*) was a "holy fool" (a "fool for the sake of Christ"), not a Dionysian reveler. The "mad" intoxication invoked by Merezhkovsky in the 1890s and

---

10. "From Cubism to Futurism, to Suprematism (1915), in Bowlt, *Russian Art of the Avant-Garde*, 118.

11. Katherine Marie Lahti, "Vladimir Mayakovsky: A Dithyramb," *SEEJ* 40, no. 2 (1996): 251–77.

12. Katherine Marie Lahti, "Mayakovsky's Dithyrambs" (Ph.D. diss: Yale University, 1991), 30.

by Ivanov until around 1908 was a temporary derangement of the senses, not a permanent state, and they dropped the idea later on. Gorky's panegyric to "the madness of the brave" denigrated prudence but did not celebrate madness as such.

The New Man

The futurists' "new man" was young, strong, healthy, daring, combative, heroic, and mad (they associated madness with creativity), and in some cases, a Jesus surrogate or an apostle, as in "The Thirteenth Apostle," the original title of Mayakovsky's poem, "A Cloud in Trousers." He changed it to accommodate the censor. The strongmen who capture the sun are variants of Nietzsche's "new barbarians" (WP, 478). Of indeterminate sex, male or androgynous, but definitely not female, their most striking characteristics are enormous size, great strength, and robust health. The character "Sportsman" epitomizes the futurists' vision of the heroic man of the future, "powerful, and in perfect control of mind and body."[13] There is also an aviator, seen throughout Europe as a daring sportsman, a Nietzschean Superman, and a human machine.[14] In the last scene, a plane crashes; the aviator emerges unhurt and laughing, but a woman has been crushed and no one cares (VOS, 124). The strongmen are hard, a Nietzschean virtue, and hardness is stressed throughout. "The lake is harder than iron / Do not trust old measurements" (VOS, 110). Former scales cannot be trusted either. The collapse of the old world order has invalidated everything. The theme of hardness recurs in other futurist writings too. Khlebnikov declared that "the fusion of Slavic and Tatar blood yields an alloy of some hardness; the Russians are more than mere Slavs" (KhCW, 1:245).

The strongmen exemplify Nietzsche's view of mythic heroes as deindividualized eternal types; their names are generic ("Sportsman," "Aviator," "New Ones") and their facial features are not delineated, a sharp contrast to Orthodox theology, which regards the human face as the epitome of Christian personhood. The facelessness of the futurist strongmen betokens a new species. Malevich's cubist-like costumes forced the actors to walk slowly and clumsily and implied the transformation of human anatomy as prophesied in a vague sort of way by Dostoevsky and Nietzsche. A character in *The Possessed* (Kirillov) says: "Then there will be a new man, then everything will be new. Then history will be divided into two parts: from the gorilla to the death of God [*unichtozheniia Boga*] and from the death of

---

13. Charlotte Douglas, *Malevich* (New York, 1994), 120.
14. Robert Wohl, *A Passion for Wings: Aviation and the Western Imagination* (New Haven, 1994), 279.

God to the change [*do peremeny*] of the earth and man physically" (quoted by Merezhkovsky, in *MPSS*, 10:119). For Nietzsche, evolution was a biological as well as a cultural and historical process. Some Russians assumed that the Superman would be a "new creature" (*novyi tvar*) with a different physiognomy. Matiushin expected the new man to have circumvision (expanded vision), Fedorov's idea.

In "! Futurian" Khlebnikov hailed a valiant new race, "the heroic Futurians" (*Budetlianie*). "Every line we write breathes victory and challenges, the bad temper of a conqueror, underground explosions, howls. We are a volcano. We vomit forth black smoke" (*KhCW,* 1:260). In "Trumpet of the Martians," he envisioned a superman (*zachelovek,* literally beyond man) "in a carpenter's apron [who] saws time into boards and like a turner of wood can shape his own tomorrow" (*KhCW,* 1:322). Here Khlebnikov combines christological symbolism (Jesus was a carpenter) with his own vision of Jesus as Superman. Mayakovsky announced the birth of a powerful Russian giant who would be the "master of his own life and lawgiver to others, a new role for Russian man, whom blind literature has labeled an idler and a thousand-year-old Oblomov. . . . Everybody can be a giant, increasing his strength a thousand fold by the strength of unity . . . the human foundation of Russia has changed. The mighty people of the future have been born."[15] Malevich's new man was a superpeasant.

The role of women, if any, in the new world is not clear. Despite his linguistic masculinism Kruchenykh was personally and professionally linked with, and influenced by, the painter Olga Rozanova (1886–1918), who illustrated some of his books. Matiushin was married to the poet and painter Elena Guro (1877–1913) and was devastated by her untimely death from tuberculosis.[16] The Russian avant-garde included strong women who had the respect of their male colleagues. There was no Russian counterpart to the Frenchwoman Valentine de Saint Point's "Futurist Manifesto of Lust" (1913), which exalted a futurist superwoman with "masculine" qualities of hardness and unsentimentality, and invoked lust as the basic life force, going so far as to justify rape![17] On the other hand, in *Vladimir Mayakovsky, A Tragedy,*" Mayakovsky's "girlfriend" (*ego znakomaia*) is a gigantic, very ugly, papier-mâché dummy. According to Katherine Lahti, she is not just a parody of Blok's "Stranger" (*Neznakomaia*), or only an expression of primitivism. She is Pandora, who released all sorts of woes on humankind by opening the forbidden box.[18] Mayakovsky's "girlfriend" doesn't talk but, surely, she is a mute testimony to the poet's unhappy love life.

15. Mayakovsky, "Budetliane" (1914), in Vladimir Mayakovsky, *Polnoe sobranie sochinenii* (Moscow, 1955–61) 1: 329–32.

16. For Nietzschean themes in Guro's work, see Nina Gurianova, "Tolstoi i Nitsshe v 'tvorchestve dukha' Eleny Guro," *Europa Orientalis* 13 (1994): 64–76.

17. Valentine de Saint Point, "Futurist Manifesto of Lust," in *Futurist Manifestos,* ed. Umbro Apollonio (New York, 1970), 71.

18. Katherine Lahti, "On Living Statutes and Pandora, *Kamennye baby* and Futurist

The New Word

Nietzsche and symbolism set the framework within which futurists thought about language. As one futurist manifesto put it: "We believe the word to be a creator of myth; in dying the word gives birth to myth and vice-versa" (*RF,* 54). Their theory of language was complex and informed by sources that ranged from Wilhelm von Humboldt, Aleksandr Veselovsky, Aleksandr Potebnia, Ferdinand de Saussure (later on), Edmund Husserl, Bergson, and Nietzsche to new discoveries in physics, biology, and physiology, and from symbolism to the glossolalia (speaking in tongues) of the mystic sectarians.

The *zaum* poets' "new word" was nonrational, powerful, aggressively masculine, and assertively Russian. Their linguistic masculinism did not necessarily imply contempt for women, but it definitely implied rejection of the symbolist tropes of Sophia and the "Beautiful Lady" (Blok's rendition), in favor of a heroic, and very aggressive, poetics. The strongmen who capture the sun speak a new language, *zaum,* for ordinary language has been become meaningless. The shared values, common assumptions, and clearly understood referents that make communication possible no longer exist (because the myth is dead). The new language is a language of power. The "New Ones" speak slowly, pausing between syllables to convey the "strength" in each word and maximize its impact. The song of the coward is all vowels (i.e., soft, round, "feminine"), while the song of the aviator is all consonants, hence virtually unsingable. The futurists associated consonants with the "masculine" traits of harshness, hardness, and daring. Kruchenykh wanted to eliminate feminine word endings, but did not do so consistently. Khlebnikov's prologue alternated between masculine and feminine word endings, but not in a regular pattern. The character "Traveler" remarks, "look / everything became masculine" (*VOS,* 110), even though neutral and feminine word endings were retained. The choral song of the gravediggers who are burying the sun (or God) is intentionally sung off-pitch and contains unexpected intervals and dissonances to jolt people out of old thought patterns.[19]

The futurists wanted to construct new words that would engender new things and to invigorate the language by giving worn-out words fresh and shocking forms. They believed that a "new word" generates a new reality. Their concept of the generative word stemmed, by way of Bely and Ivanov, from the Orthodox concept of the divine energies of The Word (God) pervading and transfiguring the cosmos. Orthodoxy also assumes, following Plato's *Cratylus,* that names have a cosmic meaning and incarnate the essence

---

Aesthetics: The Female Body in *Vladimir Mayakovsky: A Tragedy,*" *Russian Review* 58 (July 1999): 432–55. In some Prometheus myths, Pandora is his wife.

19. For a philological analysis of *zaum,* see Rosemary Ziegler, "Zaum," in *Glossarium der russischen Avantgarde,* ed. A. Flaker (Graz and Vienna, 1989), 512–32, and Aage Hansen-Lowe, *Der russische Formalismus* (Vienna, 1978), chap. 4.

of things. Implicitly, the power to name is the power to create new things. In Russia, fundamental political changes result in wholesale renaming of cities and towns, and language is a marker of national identity and doctrinal orthodoxy. For symbolists, futurists, and acmeists alike, "the word" is a tangible entity.

Bely's influential essay "The Magic of Words" (1909) was permeated with the Orthodox concept of the generative word, with occult ideas on incantation, and with Nietzsche's association of word and myth. To quote Bely: "The word begot myth; myth begot religion; religion begot philosophy; and philosophy begot the term." By "the term," he meant abstract thought. When the myth becomes irrelevant, Bely maintained, "the word" loses its meaning and literally decomposes, giving off a stench as it dies. His description recalls the decomposition of Elder Zossima in *The Brothers Karamazov*. In Bely's view, the death of the word engenders a "healthy barbarism," which will give birth to the new word and the new myth. The poet's mission is to find the salvific new word.[20] Bely's notion of the death of the word was imbued with Nietzsche's contempt for "old words" and his genealogical approach to language. Shershenovich had an analogous concept. For him, each word, or rather, "word-image," has its own "smell," which changes as the word decays, that is to say, as the image behind the word fades to be replaced by rational content (RF, 26–28). He coined the term "word-odor" to indicate that the word was more than a sound.[21]

The futurists were aware of Ivanov's distinction between the "useful" language of everyday life and the "sacred language of poets" (Khlebnikov sometimes attended Ivanov's salon), and with Ivanov's complaint that in contemporary Russia, "the crowd no longer understands the 'language of the gods,' now dead and thus useless."[22] Implicitly, eternal truths would have to be couched in a "new word." The futurists rejected vatic language and the "hieratic discourse of prophecy" (Ivanov's phrase), but they too sought a new generative word. Their concept of deliberate "word-creation" (*slovotvorchestvo*) can be interpreted as an aspect of Deification. Since man has become god, or god-like, he has the power to create new words that express purely human feelings and goals. The futurist poet's "new word" would transform the world.

Kruchenykh and Khlebnikov attempted to create a transrational language (*zaum*). Their attempt is important, not for the relatively few *zaum* poems they produced, but because of the underlying assumption that language

20. Bely, "The Magic of Words," in *Selected Essays of Andrei Bely*, ed. and trans. Steven Cassedy (Berkeley and Los Angeles, 1985), 99–100.

21. Anna Lawton, *Vadim Shershenovich: From Futurism to Imaginism* (Ann Arbor, 1981), 11.

22. Ivanov, "The Precepts of Symbolism" (1910), in *Russian Symbolists*, ed. and trans. Ronald Peterson (Ann Arbor, 1985), 148.

imposes a structure on thought and predetermines its conclusions. In Nietzsche's words: "'Reason' in language: oh what a deceitful old woman! I fear we are not getting rid of God because we still believe in grammar" (*TI*, 38).We are "entangled in error, *necessitated* to error, precisely to the extent that our prejudice in favor of reason compels us to posit unity, identity, duration, substance, cause, materiality, being" (*TI*, 37–38). Subject and predicate, cause and effect, deed and doer, being and thing, enclose our thought in the prison-house of language and determine its form.

Exaggerating Nietzsche's attack on "reason in language," the authors of *Victory over the Sun* announced their "wish to free themselves from this ordering of the world, from these means of thought communication, they wish to transform the world into chaos, to break the established values into pieces and from these pieces to create anew" (*VOS Intro*, 104). Smashing grammar was Kruchenykh's way of smashing the "old tables of values."

Zaum was intended to overcome the constraints imposed by grammar, depict the chaos and dizziness of contemporary life, express the full range of emotions, and generate a new dynamic perception of the world. "To depict the new—the future—one needs *totally new words and a new way of combining them*" (*RF*, 72). Irregular sentence structure "generates *movement and a new perception of the world*" (*RF*, 73). Kruchenykh advocated lack of agreement (between subject and predicate or adjective and noun, for example), unexpected phonetic combinations, incongruent similes, strident elements, discordant sounds, and "purely primitive roughness." Such devices would "teach a new understanding of the world, shattering the impoverished constructions of Plato, Kant, and other 'idealists' where man stood not at the center of the universe, but behind the fence." "We do not need intermediaries—the symbol, the thought—we consider our very own truth and do not serve as the reflection of some sort of sun (or a wood log?)" (*RF*, 75–76). Note the jab at symbolism.

Zarathustra complained, "Down there . . . everything among them speaks, no one knows any longer how to understand" (*Z*, 203–4). There is a Russian precedent here. Tiutchev and Fet had also lamented the inadequacy of language: "Oh, if one could express one's soul without words" (Fet) and "A thought put into words is a lie" (Tiutchev). After quoting these lines, Kruchenykh asked, "Why not get away from rational thought, and write not by means of word-concepts, but of words freely formed?" (*RF*, 71). Common language binds; free language allows for fuller expression. He considered glossolalia a precursor of the wild free language of *zaum*.

Kruchenykh's most famous *zaum* poem "dyr bul shchyl" encapsulates his belief in the ultimate irrationality and absurdity of reality. The words have no apparent meaning, but the poet later told David Burliuk (1882–1967), that they are an acronym for "*Dyroi budet urodnoe litso schastlivykh olukhov*" [the ugly face of the happy dolt will become a hole], and claimed that he prophesied the fate of the Russian bourgeoisie and the aristocracy.[23] In *Explodity* (*Vzvorval*, 1913, 1914), a collection of his poems, Kruchenykh asserted that "explodity" pertained to emotions that cannot be put into words, such as religious and sexual ecstasy, thereby detaching Nietzsche's idea from its context. Nietzsche wanted to explode the "lies of millennia" (*EH*, 327). Kruchenykh's assertion, "We split the object open! we started seeing the world through to the core," conveys his belief that the word is a tangible entity, the atom of thought, and implies that splitting the atom will reveal or even create a new world (*RF*, 76).

Unlike Kruchenykh, Khlebnikov sought some deeper meaning beyond reason, not nonsense but a new sense. He believed that the cosmos was rationally structured, so the relation of all events and processes could be mathematically described. He wanted to revitalize poetry by reaching beyond the intellect to the primeval roots of language. In contrast to Marinetti's myth of originality, an entirely new beginning, Khlebnikov's was a myth of returning to origins, a moving backward into a future untainted by Western civilization. He was interested in the nonrational language of the Siberian shamans. Khlebnikov's neologisms and archaist etymology hark back to proto-Slavic roots, but the primordial word-myth creates a new entity. His discussions of the decomposition and reconstitution of words exemplify a kind of Dionysian disaggregation expressed in chemical terms and applied to language. Letters are the elements; substituting or rearranging them, as in "serf" to "self," "exploiter" to "explorer," "investor" to "inventor," accomplishes a real change.[24] This idea stems from Khlebnikov's fascination with Egyptian and Kabbalistic notions of sacred script.

The futurists associated language with power, anticipating French poststructuralism by over half a century. Burliuk even used the word "deconstruction"! "Modern painting rests on three elements: Disharmony, dissymmetry, and deconstruction" (*diskonstruktsiia*, a neologism in Russian). "Deconstruction can be expressed either in linear, planar, or colorific displacement. But these elements cannot be separated from each another and it would be academic to try to produce each displacement independently."[25]

The bellicosity and harshness of futurist rhetoric echo some of Nietzsche's most sanguinary passages: "Of all writings, I love only that which is written with blood" (*Z*, 67). "It is the good war that hallows every cause" (*Z*, 74). Mayakovsky proclaimed: "Today's poetry is the poetry of struggle. Every

23. David Burliuk, *Fragmenty iz vospominanii futurista* (St. Petersburg, 1994), 43.

24. To give some Russian examples: A *dvorianin* (nobleman) turns into a *tvorianin* (creator), a *pravitel'stvo* (government) turns into a *nravitel'stvo* (from *nravit'sia*, to be pleasing), and a *boets* (warrior) into a *poets* (from *pet'*, to sing, one whose weapon is song). Ronald Vroon, *Velimir Khlebnikov's Shorter Poems: A Key to the Coinages* (Ann Arbor, 1988), 165.

25. Benedikt Livshits, *The One and a Half Eyed Archer*, trans. John Bowlt (Newtonville, Mass., 1977), 85.

word must be, like the soldier in an army, made of healthy meat, of red meat!" (*RF*, 88). Kruchenykh wrote: "Language must be first of all *language*. If it has to remind us of something, then better the saw or the poisoned arrow of the savage" (*RF*, 61). Similarly: "When puny and pale man felt the urge to rejuvenate his soul by getting in touch with the strong-rough African gods, when he fell in love with their wild free language, and with the primitive man's cutting teeth and gaze, animal-like in its sharpness, the seven nannies[26] suddenly started yelling. . . . And all of them offer their advice, their sickly bloodless philosophy" (*RF*, 75). Khlebnikov accused the symbolists of servile thought and reviled them as pathetic eunuchs who have emasculated the word (*KhCW*, 1:260).

The futurists rejected "frozen" language (words whose meaning is forever fixed) as unsuited to a state of inspiration (*RF*, 67). Many of their books were handwritten to capture the "ecstasy of the moment of conception." They underscored their preference for impermanence by publishing their works on crude materials that would not last, a contrast to the luxuriousness of such symbolist journals as *Golden Fleece*. Nietzsche alluded to

> *Apollo's* deception: the *eternity* of beautiful form; the aristocratic legislation: "*thus shall it be forever!*"
> *Dionysus:* sensuality and cruelty. Transitoriness could be interpreted as enjoyment of productive and destructive force, as *continual creation*. (*WP*, 539)

Zaum was a Dionysian language, despite the fact that the futurists' approach to language-creation was analytical. They built on Bely's verbal experiments (especially his "Symphonies") and Briusov's ideas on literary craftsmanship.

Futurist publications had a distinctive "look"—words detached from their sentences, sentences detached from their paragraphs, letters disengaged from or dominating the words. Their treatment of space conveys a sense of disconnectedness, disorder, a free-floating rebelliousness against all forms and structures. They announced the "liberation of the word" (comparable to Marinetti's "*parole in liberta*" and "wireless imagination") and the "autonomy of the letter." These concepts illustrate Nietzsche's description of literary decadence, the "anarchy of atoms" that results when "the whole is no longer a whole" (*CW*, 170). Aesthetically, this "look" was the result of a search for new ways to convey emotion to the mass reader, to "overcome Gutenberg," as the futurists put it, the limitations of the printed page. Philosophically, the "look" depicted the lack of direction and the irrelevance of logic, direction, and causality in the post-solar world. Kruchenykh some-

---

26. This is taken from a Russian proverb: "When there are seven nannies, the child is blind." The English equivalent is "Too many cooks spoil the broth."

times numbered his paragraphs out of order. Kamensky's "ferro-concrete poetry" used diagonal lines to give the poem "strength," but it is difficult to tell where the poem begins and ends.

The lines of futurist poetry go off in all directions, for "we learned how to look at the world backward, we enjoy this reverse motion (with regard to the word, we noticed that it *can be read backward, and that then it acquires a more profound meaning!*" (*RF,* 76). This is a futurist version of Nietzsche's concept of reverse perspective. "Now I know how, have the know-how to *reverse perspectives,* the first reason why a 'revaluation of values' is perhaps possible for me alone" (*EH,* 223). In *The Gay Science,* a key text for futurists, formalists, and Florensky, Nietzsche wrote:

> We cannot look around our own corner: it is a hopeless curiosity that wants to know what other kinds of intellects and perspectives there *might* be; for example, whether some beings might be able to experience time backward, or alternately forward and backward (which would involve another direction of life and another concept of cause and effect). But I should think that today we are at least far from the ridiculous immodesty that would be involved in decreeing from our corner that perspectives are permitted only from this corner. Rather has the world become "infinite" for us all over again, inasmuch as we cannot reject the possibility that *it may include infinite interpretations.* (*GS,* 336)

In other words, not only a reverse perspective, but multiple perspectives are required.

The futurists were linguistic nationalists. Khlebnikov coined the term *Budetlianie* because he refused to use the Italian word *futuristi.* Kruchenykh instructed: "Do not give yourself to imitation of things foreign. Do not use foreign words in your literary works. . . . Invent new native words" (*RF,* 76–77). Mayakovsky ridiculed everything foreign except for technology, distorted foreign words, and seldom used foreign morphemes in his neologisms. Their linguistic nationalism paralleled Ivanov's turn to neo-Slavophilism. Paradoxically, Khlebnikov and Kruchenykh also advocated an international language. Khlebnikov wanted a common system of hieroglyphs for the entire planet. Kruchenykh claimed that *zaum* was universally comprehensible. Malevich declared that "the new cubist body . . . has nothing national, geographic, patriotic, or narrowly popular about it . . . in cubism we reach direct unity with [nature]."[27] This aspect of their views on language combines a Dionysian dissolution of differences, including national differences, with a return to origins, to the period before the Tower of Babel when humankind was "of one language and one speech" (Genesis 11:1).

27. *Malevich: Essays on Art,* ed. Troels Anderson (Copenhagen, 1968), 102.

Futurist Paintings

Futurist paintings were characterized by bright primary colors, bold pat-
terning, and geometric forms. Their first paintings were figurative. The
cubism they embraced later on disaggregated or dematerialized reality, making its primordial forms visible, much as recently discovered x-rays revealed
the human skeleton. Kruchenykh explicitly connected cubism and *zaum*.
Malevich said that cubism freed humankind from the "slavish" imitation of
nature. He wished to create a new world out of new forms. Suprematism,
the movement he founded in 1915, entailed continual creation *ex nihilo*
unbounded by nature, reason, subject matter, or content, in order to depict
a purely spiritual reality beyond the world of nature and objects, a breakthrough to the fourth dimension, a realm beyond death.[28] For Malevich, the
square was not a subconscious form, but the creation of intuitive reason,
the face of the new art, "a living, regal infant" destined to rule. His "Black
Square" (1915) symbolizes formlessness, the abyss; "White on White" (1918)
connotes purity, the dawn of a new world to be constructed by artists.[29] He
criticized admirers of technology for depicting merely transitory forms and
things (which is what he did until 1915), and "the art of the savage" (primitivism) for being naturalistic and imitative. He thought of suprematism as
a "New Gospel" that would liberate the spirit and synthesize painting, poetry,
music, and architecture. As Nina Gourianova observes, "Here we find
expressed with new force the nostalgia of the avant-garde for universalism
and a new 'great' style capable of uniting all forms of art and dominating
over earthly reality."[30] She distinguishes between the uncompromising, even
totalitarian, propensity of suprematism and the *zaum* poets' desire for unlimited creative freedom.[31]

A New Politics

The futurists' linguistic nationalism was accompanied, in some cases, by
political nationalism. Khlebnikov's attempt to find a mathematical order in
history was sparked by the Japanese sinking of Russia's entire Pacific fleet
in 1905. During the first Bosnian crisis (1908), he announced: "Holy war!
Unavoidable, approaching, immediate—war for the trampled rights of the
Slavs, I salute you! Down with the Hapsburgs! Hold back the Hohenzollerns!"
(*KhCW*, 1:227). He considered Asia the center of the future world and proph-

28. Malevich, "From Cubism to Suprematism," in Bowlt, *Russian Art of the Avant-
Garde*, 119, 126, 133–34.
29. Groys, *Total Art*, 15–19.
30. Gurianova, *Exploring Color*, 108.
31. Ibid., 120–21.

esied the end of the "German century" and the beginning of the "Slavic century." "More and more of the great men of the West have Slavic connections: Ostwald, Nietzsche, Bismarck. Both Nietzsche and Bismarck are notably non-German. One of them [Nietzsche] even said 'Praise the Lord' on that account" (*KhCW*, 1:245).[32] Pointing to the thousand-year-old history of Teutonic aggression against the Slavic peoples, Khlebnikov suggested that Russians reply to the ring of European allies "with a ring of Asian allies—a friendly alliance of Moslems, Russians, and Chinese" (*KhCW*, 1:245).[33] In the first months of World War I, the futurists produced patriotic ditties and *lubki* (broadsides) but then turned against the war as senseless slaughter. Conversely, the Italian futurists campaigned to have Italy enter the war, which it did in 1915. Marinetti had been glorifying war as the "world's only hygiene" since 1909.

The futurists were not primarily concerned with domestic politics, but they were left-leaning; and their programmatic iconoclasm, their antibourgeois stance, their rhetoric of blood and violence, and their depersonalized strongmen had political implications. Mayakovsky joined the Social Democratic Party in Moscow and worked with the Bolsheviks from the winter of 1907–1908 to mid-summer 1909. He was arrested and imprisoned three times; the last time he was in solitary confinement for several weeks. After he was released (in January 1910), he decided to be an artist rather than a political revolutionary.[34] Jeffrey Schnapp claimed that Marinetti's "agitprop poetry" collapsed the space of analysis, interpretation, and reading, in order "to clear the way for a theatricalization and then politicization of the act of reading," thereby shifting "from a poetics of privacy to one of propaganda."[35] The same could be said about Mayakovsky. Joan Neuberger saw a parallel between hooliganism and futurism (which critics called "literary hooliganism"), in their public mockery of bourgeois propriety and their deep hostility to established authorities and cultural values.[36] On another level, their aggressive masculinism was an expression of a warlike mood, developing all over Europe, that culminated in World War I.

The futurists' appropriations of Nietzsche—Victory over the Sun (symbol of Apollo and all that Apollo denoted), a futurist strongman, "forgetting"

---

32. Nietzsche claimed that his ancestors were Polish noblemen (*EH*, 225) and sometimes called himself "von Nietzky." Peter Bergmann, "Nietzsche and the Christ Among Nations," in *East Europe Reads Nietzsche*, 21–41.

33. See also "An Indo-Russian Union" and "Asianism," in *KhCW*, 1:341–43.

34. Robert Williams, *Artists in Revolution, 1905–1925: Portraits of the Russian Avant-Garde* (Bloomington, 1977), 132.

35. Jeffrey Schnapp, "Politics and Poetics in Marinetti's Zang Tumb Tuum," *Stanford Italian Review* 5 (1985): 78, 80. "Zang Tumb Tuum" replicates the sound of bullets.

36. Joan Neuberger, "Culture Besieged: Futurism and Hooliganism," *Cultures in Flux*, 185–201.

history, jettisoning the culture of the past, metaphors of blood and violence, a transrational language, and alogical abstractions—became part of the general stock of Nietzschean ideas. The futurists never resolved the contradiction between their desire for a new world of continuous innovation and artistic creativity, and their belief in chaos as a permanent state.

Some of their contemporaries saw only destructiveness; others had mixed responses, and still others were enthusiastic. To Merezhkovsky, futurism was "one more step of the coming Ham." To Bogdanov, it was bourgeois nihilism, and to Berdiaev, a "new barbarism at the pinnacle of culture," a symptom of the "crisis of art, "that was in turn a symptom of the "crisis of life." Futurism had to begin in Italy, he said, because the Renaissance began there and that period of history was ending.[37] Florensky thought that *zaum* broadened the possibilities of expression, but disliked its "drunken" aspects. He regarded futurism as a Storm and Stress movement, an adolescent revolt.[38] Ivanov praised the futurists as "the most sympathetic of youths, irrational tramps, prodigal sons who, after abandoning the paternal home, remained solitary on a tall mountain top, rejecting harmony. We shouldn't poke fun at them, but erect a monument to their madly bold feat . . . they won't find themselves a fatherland or a refuge anywhere; they are the sole true Russian anarchists."[39] The formalist critics Roman Jakobson and Viktor Skhlovsky saw real creativity in futurism, as did Trotsky in the 1920s.

37. Berdiaev, *Krizis iskusstva* (Moscow, 1918), 26, given as a lecture in November 1917.
38. "Mysl' i iazyk," in *FSS*, vol. 3, pt. 1, 160–66, 171–73.
39. As related by Roman Jakobson, letter to Kruchenykh (late January or early February 1914), reprinted in Roman Jakobson, *My Futurist Years*, ed. Bengt Jangfeldt and Stephen Rudy, trans. Stephen Rudy (New York, 1992), 104.

Summary: The Nietzschean Agenda in 1917

By 1917, Nietzsche had been russified and absorbed into symbolism, religious philosophy, "left" Bolshevism, and futurism. Despite important differences among, and within, these movements, their "solutions" to the issues of Nietzschean agenda had much in common, for almost all the figures discussed wanted to engage the Dionysian elements in the human psyche and to create a new culture and a new society imbued with their own values.

The New Myth

Their myths featured an eschatological leap from necessity to freedom and the transfiguration of man and the world. The most important attempts at myth-creation, Mystical Anarchism and God-building, failed to rally the masses, but their formulators learned from the experience: a new myth had to be couched in familiar terms, it had to be clearly construed (a "new religious synthesis" or a "collective humanity" were too amorphous), and it required an Apollonian image, an icon or a cult figure. Bogdanov viewed technology as the main world-transforming force, but he came to appreciate the psychopolitical utility of myth. Berdiaev's religion of creativity included new cult figures. Florensky's myth was a revitalized Orthodoxy that emphasized ecclesiality and concrete experience (rather than abstract concepts). The futurists' myth, Victory over the Sun, entailed an unlimited horizon for human creativity. Their iconoclasm precluded cult figures.

The New Word

Nietzsche's terms—"Apollonian," "Dionysian," "revaluation of all values," "the Superman," "the will to power"—were used frequently, and without quotation marks, not just by intellectuals but in publications addressed to a mass readership. Most Nietzsche-influenced intellectuals assumed that the right words could transform consciousness and galvanize unconscious feelings and drives. Symbolists emphasized subliminal communication. Futurists overwhelmed the intellect with sound, but they also paid great attention to the visual impact of the written word. Kruchenykh and Khlebnikov wanted to jolt people out of old thought patterns. Both futurists and symbolists linked word and myth and believed that a new word could generate a new world. Bogdanov concluded that language does indeed change reality and connected word and myth in a nonmystical way.

The New Art Form

Symbolists believed that art leads to "higher truths" and "from the real to the more real," and they regarded aesthetic creativity as a theurgic activity that could transform (transfigure) the world. Ivanov advocated a Dionysian theater, a cultic theater of myth-creation and "collective creativity," as the way to reintegrate Russian society, end the separation of actors and spectators, make passive spectators into active performers, and unite art and life. Modified versions of Ivanov's theory were taken up by theater directors, and it spawned countertheories of pure theatricality (theater for its sake of theater), such as the "conditional theater" advocated by Briusov, Meyerhold, and Sologub. "Life-creation," the grand theurgic projects that most symbolists came to champion, was, in part, their response to the failure of political revolution (the Revolution of 1905) to create a new world of freedom, beauty, and love. Futurists rejected the Platonic aspects of symbolism for a poetics of direct perception. They wanted to democratize art by taking it out of the theaters and museums and into the streets and public squares, and to liberate creativity by jettisoning the cultural legacy and assuming fresh perspectives, seeing the world backwards, for example. Bogdanov's perspectivism was class-based. To liberate itself psychologically, the proletariat would have to create its own art form and revalue (not jettison) the cultural legacy in the light of its own values and needs. He stressed the *class* nature of art, morality, and science. Florensky rejected the individualistic perspective that had dominated European art and thought since the Renaissance.

The New Man and Woman

That the new man would be beautiful, heroic, daring, creative, striving, and a warrior for a lofty ideal was taken for granted. There was no agreement on the new woman. Kollontai, Bogdanov, and Gorky endowed her with such "masculine" traits as daring, independence, and reason, while acknowledging, or even insisting on, her maternal role. Symbolists exalted Sophia and the "eternal feminine," and challenged conventional notions of family and gender. Their ideal human being, and Berdiaev's, was an androgyne, not a parent. Florensky separated masculine and feminine ontologically and socially; his *ecclesia* was composed of male dyads. Volsky ignored women in his writings. The futurists also challenged conventional notions of family and gender but their public stance was aggressively masculinist.

The New Morality

All four movements rejected the Christian/Kantian/populist "morality of duty," including Kant's imperatives, in favor of emotional liberation, free volition, and ardent conviction. Beauty, creativity, and (in some cases) hardness were deemed virtues; pity was a sign of weakness, and "love for the most distant" outweighed love of neighbor or practical reforms. "Nietzschean" individualism was superseded by paeans to "individuality" that were sometimes accompanied by an ethos of self-transcendence, symbolized by a Christ/Dionysus archetype that idealized sacrifice and suffering. Berdiaev, Florensky, and most symbolists joined Nietzschean amoralism with the Christian/utopian illusion that love can replace law. Political maximalists revived the "heroic" tradition of revolutionary populism (terror) and practiced a revolutionary immoralism in which the end justifies the means. Missing from all the new moralities was an ethic of everyday life. The omission was deliberate. Eschatologists, religious or secular, assumed that the quotidian aspects of life (*byt*) would be transfigured.

The New Politics

Most of the figures discussed hoped to transcend politics. Their ideal was a society cemented by passional bonds and common ideals, as opposed to self-interest and a social contract. They disdained, or came to disdain, rights-based liberalism and parliamentary government (Frank's views were more nuanced). Prosperity was considered a philistine value, so mass prosperity (as distinct from abolishing poverty) was not one of their goals. Symbolists, futurists, and religious philosophers ignored economics, even though Berdiaev and Frank started out as Marxists, Shestov's dissertation was on factory law, and Frank treated wealth as a good in *Landmarks*. Gorky, Lunacharsky, and Kollontai assumed that poverty would disappear under socialism, but they paid little attention to economics per se. Bogdanov, Bazarov, and Volsky did write about economics, but the bulk of their published work was on philosophy. It is noteworthy, however, that Bogdanov authored a popular economics textbook for workers (first edition, 1897) that was used well into the Soviet period, and he retranslated *Capital* (with I. I. Skvortsov-Stepanov), that Bazarov had established a reputation as an economist by 1917, and that Volsky lectured on the agrarian question at the Capri School. Attempts to articulate a new cultural identity shaded into neo-Slavophilism, or cultural nationalism, and then into political nationalism. Most Nietzsche-influenced intellectuals either welcomed the outbreak of World War I or came to see it in eschatological terms.

The New Science

Only Bogdanov explicitly called for a new science. Since "truth," including scientific "truth," served a particular class, the proletariat had to develop its own science with a collectivist methodology and practical goals. Bogdanov's quarrel with Lenin about epistemology had implications for science because the issue was whether objective truth exists and who gets to define it (see Chapter 5). Bely and Florensky expected symbolism to lead to a new non-positivist science, a theme that Florensky developed in the 1920s.

The Nietzschean ideas implanted in the culture during the "seed-time" of his influence were recycled and reworked after the Bolshevik Revolution, by the figures discussed above and by a new cast of characters. The revolutionary scenarios of Lenin, Bukharin, and Trotsky included unacknowledged Nietzschean ideas.

Nietzsche in the Bolshevik Revolution and the Civil War, 1917–1921

Revolution had been expected for months as war losses mounted, suffering on the home front intensified, and one government scandal followed another. The end of the tsarist regime came suddenly, however.[1] The February Revolution (February 26–29 OS / March 8–11, 1917 NS) resulted in a "dual power," a provisional government that would rule until a constituent assembly could be elected and convened, and an unofficial power center, the Petrograd Soviet of Workers' and Soldier's Deputies. By autumn, soldiers were deserting in droves, peasants were seizing gentry land, and workers were taking control of the factories. The Bolshevik Revolution (October 26–27 OS / November 7–8, 1917 NS) established a Dictatorship of the Proletariat, which set about solidifying Bolshevik power and getting out of the war. In March 1918, the Russian government accepted German terms. The Treaty of Brest-Litovsk cost Russia the Baltic States, much of Ukraine (its breadbasket), Bielorussia, Poland, and parts of Transcaucasia, plus an indemnity in gold.[2] German troops withdrew the following November (as mandated by the armistice on the Western front), leaving a power vacuum in which "Red" and "White" armies contended in a civil war. By the time

1. For the February and the October Revolutions and the Civil War, see W. H. Chamberlain, *The Russian Revolution*, 2 vols. (London, 1935); Tsuyoshi Hasegawa, *The February Revolution: Petrograd 1917* (Seattle, 1981); Robert Daniels, *Red October* (New York, 1967); Bruce Lincoln, *Red Victory: A History of the Russian Civil War* (New York, 1989); Richard Pipes, *The Russian Revolution* (New York, 1990); idem, *Russia Under the Bolshevik Regime* (New York, 1993); Sheila Fitzpatrick, *The Russian Revolution* (Oxford, 1994); Christopher Read, *From Tsar to Soviets* (Oxford, 1996); Orlando Figes, *A People's Tragedy* (New York, 1996).

2. The treaty reduced Soviet territory by 1,267,000 square miles and its population by 62 million. The areas lost had 32 percent of the arable land, 26 percent of the railroad mileage, 33 percent of the factories, and 75 percent of the coal mines, and the government had to commit itself to supplying Germany and Austria with large quantities of grain.

it was over, the economy was at a standstill, and thirteen million people were dead, most of them from starvation and epidemics. Another five million died in the famine of 1921–22. Millions of orphaned or abandoned children roamed the countryside, resorting to crime in order to survive.

The policies retroactively called "war communism" were begun piecemeal before the onset of full-scale civil war and continued after it was over. So-called "war communism" prohibited private economic transactions, and it featured terror, forced labor, the fanning of class hatred, class-based food rationing, and forced requisitions of grain. Once "Red" victory was in sight, opposition groups emerged in the Party, peasant revolts erupted all over Russia, and Petrograd workers seemed to be on the verge of rebellion. In March 1921, the sailors of the Kronstadt naval base proclaimed a "third revolution," demanding "soviets without communists" and an end to the "Commissarocracy." The Kronstadt revolt was put down, but it prompted Lenin to announce a New Economic Policy (NEP). The most important measure replaced forced requisitions of grain with a tax-in-kind to encourage production. Any after-tax surplus could be sold at local markets. To justify this turnabout theoretically (Lenin had been contemplating it for several weeks), he labeled the failed policies "war communism." The same Party Congress (the Tenth) that adopted NEP ordered all intra-Party factions to dissolve or be expelled.

Apparently, Bogdanov had coined the term "war communism" as early as November 1917, meaning it as a pejorative.[3] He refused to call the Bolshevik government a Dictatorship of the Proletariat and warned of a new *Arakcheevshchina* (a reference to the notorious military colonies established by Arakcheev during the reign of Aleksandr I). He declined several invitations to rejoin the Party and Lunacharsky's offer of a post in the People's Commissariat of Enlightenment (*Prosveshchenie*), known by the acronym Narkompros, and rebuked his brother-in-law for becoming the commissar. *Prosveshchenie* also means "education," but "enlightenment" better conveys the Bolsheviks' missionary attitude. Lunacharsky had reconciled with Lenin in 1915 and rejoined the Party in August 1917. A week before the Bolshevik Revolution, Lunacharsky called the first Proletkult (proletarian culture) conference in Petrograd. Bogdanov organized a similiar congress in Moscow the following March, and the first all-national Proletkult Congress was held there in September. Proletkult was autonomous vis-à-vis the Party and the government (which were formally separate), but it was funded by Narkompros. Although Lunacharsky was never elected to the Party's Central Committee, so did not have the power that insiders did, within his bailiwick he had considerable discretion in how Narkompros disbursed its funds.

---

3. Bogdanov, "Pismo' Lunacharskomu," November 19th, 1917, in *A. A. Bogdanov*, 352–55. Also, idem, "Voennyi kommunizm i gosudarstvennyi kapitalizm" 335–431, and "Gosudarstvo Kommuny," 352–55.

The reversion of Europe to barbarism in the Great War seemed to prove that critics of the Enlightenment had been right; man is not "naturally" rational and good. In Russia, Germany, and Italy, the collapse of the old order made Nietzsche's challenge to all established values and institutions agonizingly relevant and led to calls for an entirely new order, to be created by daring and ruthless "new men."

Nietzsche colored Bolshevik readings of Marx and Engels, reinforced the Bolsheviks' determination to seize power and retain it, and nourished utopian visions of total transformation, such as "war communism" on the one hand and scenarios of spiritual revolution on the other. Artists and writers adapted techniques gleaned from Nietzsche and Wagner to Bolshevik agitation and propaganda. Andrzej Walicki considers "war communism" "a grandiose social experiment" directly inspired by Engels's belief that the leap from the Kingdom of Necessity to the Kingdom of Freedom could be accomplished by replacing the "anarchy" of the market with the "miraculous power" of centralized planning, thereby making "humanity its own conscious master."[4] Nietzsche helped imbue Bolsheviks with the will to attempt the "leap." "War communism" was not limited to economic matters; it was supposed to engender a new man and a new culture. In Nietzschean terms, it was a "great cultural project," except that the Bolsheviks expected to complete it in a few years, not a few millennia.

Early Soviet educational and cultural institutions were conduits for Nietzschean ideas. Lunacharsky invited artists and writers to work with the government. At first, only Blok, Mayakovsky, Meyerhold, the sculptor Natan Altman (1889–1970), and the poet Riurik Ivnev (Mikhail Kovalev, 1891–1981) accepted. Others came over to the Bolsheviks later on, out of conviction, or because the government was the only employer, or both. Meyerhold headed the Theatrical section (TEO) of the Commissariat of Enlightenment. Ivanov, Bely, and Blok worked there and in LITO, the literary section. The Fine Arts section, IZO, was a futurist bailiwick and had its own newspaper, *Art of the Commune* (*Iskusstvo kommuny*, 1918). The diaries of Nikolai Punin (1888–1953), an editor of *Art of the Commune* and the head of the Petrograd section of IZO, reveal a long-standing "love-hate affair" with Nietzsche.[5] Symbolists and futurists taught in Proletkult schools and studios.

In April 1918, Lenin decreed a "monumental propaganda" campaign that entailed dismantling tsarist monuments, erecting monuments to revolutionary heroes and great men, mass festivals on May Day, and decorating pub-

---

4. Walicki, *Marxism*, 204.

5. Sidney Monas, "Nikolay Punin and Russian Futurism," introduction to *The Diaries of Nikolay Punin, 1904–1953*, ed. Sidney Monas and Jennifer Greene Krupala, trans. Jennifer Green Krupala (Austin, 1999), xxiii.

lic spaces.[6] Lenin told Lunacharsky that he got the idea from Tommaso Campanella's *City of the Sun* (1602). Gorky read the book in Italy and told Lenin and Lunacharsky about it.[7] The first monuments were made of clay or other cheap materials (Lenin's intention was propaganda, not immortalization), but they washed away in the rain. The plan for an "Iron Colossus" called for durable materials and was intended to compel attention by its sheer size.[8] Tatlin's Tower was to be a super-sized monument to the Third International (the Comintern, founded in March 1919) as well as its functioning headquarters. The scale model (the Tower was never built) seemed to throw gravity out the window and was a conscious evocation of the Tower of Babel.[9] Other God-defying towers were also planned. A character in a Proletkult play says, "Whoever wishes to know that the old God is dead has only to climb up our tower."[10]

Ivanov's ideas on theater "returned like a boomerang" in the form of mass festivals and political theater.[11] Other inspirations for the mass festivals include Gaideburov's idea of theater as celebration, futurist street theaters, Evreinov's concept of theater as play, Zarathustra's statement *"new festivals are needed"* (Z, 325), and the mass festivals of the French Revolution, which the Wagnerophiles Romain Rolland and Julien Tiersot wanted to revive as a way of reunifying France after the Dreyfus case.[12] Lunacharsky translated Rolland's book *Theatre du peuple* (1903) and Gorky's firm published it in 1910. It was reissued in 1919 with an introduction by Ivanov. Tiersot's book, *Les Fêtes et les chants de revolution française* (1908), was translated too. Lenin read it in the original French.

6.   The list of persons to be honored was published in *Izvestiia* the following August. It was divided into six categories. *Revolutionaries and social activists:* Spartacus, Tiberius Gracchus, Brutus Babeuf, Marx, Engels, Bebel, Lassalle, Jaures, Lafarge, Valian, Marat, Robespierre, Danton, Garibaldi, Razin, Pestel, Ryleev, Herzen, Bakunin, Lavrov, Khalturin, Plekhanov, Kaliaev, Volodarsky, Fourier, Saint-Simon, Robert Owen, Zheliabov, Sofia Perovskaia, and Kilbak'chich. *Writers and poets:* Tolstoy, Dostoevsky, Lermontov, Pushkin, Gogol, Radishchev, Belinsky, Ogarev, Chernyshevsky, Mikhailovsky, Dobroliubov, Pisarev, Uspensky, Saltykov-Shchedrin, Nekrasov, Shevchenko, Tiutchev, Nikitin, Novikov, and Kol'tsov. *Philosophers and scientists:* Skovoroda, Lomonosov, and Mendeleev. *Painters:* Rublev, Kiprensky, Aleksandr Ivanov, Vrubel, Shubin, Kozlovsky, Kazakov. *Composers:* Musorgsky, Skriabin, Chopin. *Theater People:* Kommissarzhevskaia, Molchalov.

7.   In Campanella's utopia, scientific knowledge is translated into pictures and paintings on both sides of all seven walls of the circular city and on the globe beneath the cupola of the central temple, as part of an emphasis on the visual and concrete rather than on abstract verbalization.

8.   Rene Fülop-Miller, *The Mind and Face of Bolshevism* (New York, 1927), 90.

9.   Larissa Zhadova et al., eds., *Tatlin* (New York, 1988), 28.

10.   P. Bessal'ko, *Kamenshchik* (Petrograd, 1918), 7.

11.   Konstantin Rudnitskii, *Russian and Soviet Theater, 1905–32* (New York, 1988), 9.

12.   See also P. G. Kogan, "Theater as Tribune," in *Bolshevik Visions*, ed. William Rosenberg (Ann Arbor, 1984), 435–44. Note his negative reference to Zarathustra (on page 437).

Pavel Kerzhentsev (P. M. Lebedev, 1881–1940), a Proletkult leader, a theorist of proletarian culture in his own right, and a Bolshevik since 1904, proposed a "creative theater" in his book of the same name (*Tvorcheskii teatr,* 1918), a proletarian version of the Nietzsche/Wagner/Ivanov syndrome that featured "creative self-activity" (*samodeiatel'nost'*) and class consciousness. For militants such as Kerzhentsev, the key Nietzschean idea was the "will to power." Some of them produced plays in which revolutions were propelled by a single strong individual, in which case the operative influence was *Zarathustra.* "Self-activity" became a by-word, but its proponents disagreed on what it meant and how to encourage it. Kerzhentsev wanted proletarian theaters to be limited to plays written by full-time workers and to use only worker-actors, worker-directors, and worker-musicians (no professionals). Claiming that opera and ballet were obsolete, he expected workers to develop new theatrical forms as one facet of a distinctive proletarian art.

Lunacharsky and Ivanov saw mass festivals as unions of the artist and the people and of Apollo and Dionysus.[13] Lunacharsky called mass festivals a powerful agitational tool, defining agitation as that which "excites the feelings of the audience and readers and has a direct influence on their will," bringing the whole content of propaganda "to white heat" and making it "glow in all colors." He urged the Party to "adorn itself" with posters, pictures, statues, the "magic strength of music," and to use the new art forms of cinema and rhythmics.[14] When funds became available, he hoped to build great temples to influence the "social soul." In 1919, he announced a melodrama contest to encourage playwrights to create propagandistic works in a psychologically simple genre.

Evreinov directed the most famous mass festival, "The Storming of the Winter Palace," for the third anniversary of the Revolution; the production had a "cast" of 6,000 and was sponsored by the Political Administration of the Petrograd Military District (PUR). There were other mass festivals titled after what they celebrated: "The Mystery of Liberated Labor," "The Third Internationale," "The Overthrow of the Autocracy," and "The Fire of Prometheus." Some festivals were recorded on newsreels to be shown all over the country. Mass festivals were supposed to be characterized by "self-activity," but the actors' roles were scripted by the director and involved a good deal of regimentation. "Just think," Lunacharsky mused, "what character our festive occasions will take on when, by means of General Military Instruction, we create rhythmically moving masses embracing thousands and

---

13. James von Geldern, "Nietzschean Leaders and Followers in Soviet Mass Theater, 1917–27," in *NSC* 127–48; idem, *Bolshevik Festivals 1917–1920* (Berkeley and Los Angeles, 1993).

14. Lunacharsky, "The Revolution and Art," in Bowlt, *Russian Art of the Avant-Garde,* 192.

tens of thousands of people—and not just a crowd, but a strictly regulated, collective, peaceful army sincerely possessed by one definite idea."[15]

Political theaters and decorated agit-trains and agit-boats carried the revolutionary message throughout the land. The Theater-Dramatic Studio of the Red Army was made a special military unit. Actors were drafted for performances at the front. Theatricalized mock trials or "agit-trials" began in the Red Army. By 1920, they had become a regular political ritual. "Defendants," "prosecutors," and "witnesses" improvised rather than recited their lines. According to Julie Cassiday, the "agit-trials" were an adaptation of Ivanov's ideas on theater.[16] Adrian Piotrovsky (1898–1938), a zealous organizer of Red Army theaters, was the illegitimate son of Tadeuz Zelinski, one of Nietzsche's few academic admirers. (Zelinski was a professor of classical philology at the University of Moscow.) Meyerhold used newspaper clippings and radio bulletins for political education, and masks to designate heroes and villains. Political theater demanded extremes of light and darkness, freedom and slavery, good and evil, saviors and demons.

Political activists talked about a "proletarian Athens" to be created by democratizing the arts and sciences and encouraging worker creativity. Posters, poems, and plays celebrated proletarian supermen, typically eliding Nietzsche's concept, which pertained to figures of great cultural creativity, not enormous size or great strength, with folkloric giants. "The Bolshevik" (1918) (Fig. 1) by Boris Kustodiev, a former *Miriskusnik* (associate of the World of Art movement), is a well-known example.[17] The featureless faces of Vladimir Lebedev's "The Red Army and Fleet in Defense of the Frontiers of Russia" (1920) recall those of the strongmen in *Victory over the Sun*.[18] Lazar el Lissitzky adapted geometric forms to political propaganda in his poster "Beat the Whites with the Red Wedge" (1919).[19]

Instructors in the Red Army schools included intellectuals steeped in the culture of the Silver Age. The curriculum featured political literacy (militant class consciousness), literature, theater, music, and physical culture (athletics). Nikolai Podvoisky (1880–1948), a developer of the curriculum, had close ties with the Commissariat of Enlightenment and Proletkult. An enthusiast of mass festivals and athletics for the masses, Podvoisky also ran a children's colony in which his charges chanted "Death to Speculators!"[20] As

15. Ibid.

16. Julie Cassiday, *The Enemy on Trial: Early Soviet Courts on Stage and Screen* (DeKalb, Ill., 2000), 71.

17. For other folkloric Supermen, see Dmitri Moor, "Long Live the Third International"; Sergei Gerasimov, "Master of the Land"; and Ignaty Nivinsky's "Red Lightning," in Mikhail Guerman, *The Art of the October Revolution* (New York, 1979), plates 70, 94, and 10.

18. Ibid., plate 15. See also Lebedov's paintings of workers (plates 143–46).

19. Ibid., plate 25.

20. Von Geldern, *Bolshevik Festivals*, 215.

Fig. 1 B. M. Kustodiev, *The Bolshevik*. In Vs. Voinov, *B. M. Kustodiev* (Leningrad, 1926). Slavic and Baltic Division, New York Public Library, Astor, Lenox and Tilden Foundations.

sensitive to language as any literary modernist, Podvoisky proclaimed: "Our word is our best weapon. Words blow up and scatter the ranks of the enemy, disintegrate his soul, paralyze his nerves, split him into warring camps and class factions."[21] Members of the Communist Youth League (Komsomol) saw themselves as the vanguard of the vanguard, bold creators of the new culture. Nietzsche's warrior ethos pervaded Komsomol poetry and prose, along with Nietzschean iconoclasm and a cult of youth.[22] The Red Army Schools and Komsomol were important formative influences on young men.

Lenin was a Wagnerophile.[23] In 1920 he presided over a wreath-laying ceremony for the fallen heroes of the Revolution, in which Siegfried's funeral march (from *Götterdämmerung*) was played against the background of a cannon salute from the Peter and Paul fortress. When Lenin announced his plans to electrify Russia at the Eighth Congress of Soviets (December 1920),

21. Mark von Hagen, *Soldiers of the Proletarian Dictatorship: The Red Army and the Soviet State* (Ithaca, 1990), 95, 98.
22. Isabel Tirado, "Nietzschean Motifs in the Konsomol's Vanguardism," in *NSC*, 235–55.
23. Bartlett, *Wagner and Russia*, 235, 237.

he did so theatrically. The Congress met in the cold, weakly lighted Bolshoi theater, drowning in shadows as brilliant light flooded the stage and directed the delegates' gaze to a gigantic map which portrayed the electrified Russia of ten years hence. Moscow's generating capacity was so low that the display produced blackouts elsewhere. Despite the paper shortage, five thousand copies of a fifty-page synopsis of the GOELRO (State Commission for the Electrification of Russia) report were distributed to the delegates. It was on this occasion that Lenin made his often-quoted pronouncement: "Communism equals Soviet power plus the electrification of the entire country." He expected electrification to transform Russia economically, politically, and culturally. So grandiose were GOELRO's plans that opponents referred to "electrofiction" (*elektrofiktsiia*).[24] Meyerhold produced a "Dithyramb of Electrification."

By the end of the "heroic period" of Soviet history (the Revolution and the Civil War), the culture was thoroughly politicized. "Fronts," "commands," and other military terms pervaded the discourse. Writers and artists competed for government funds, access to a nationalized printing press, and rations of paper. Rival art schools all claimed to speak for the proletariat. Futurists demanded an end to government interference in the arts, but wanted a "dictatorship over the arts" run by themselves. Proletkult zealots did the same. Lunacharsky tried to accommodate different groups, for which Kerzhentsev accused him of "rightism." To be apolitical, was unacceptable.

Writers described the Bolshevik Revolution as an elemental force, often associating "elemental" with Dionysian as Blok did in "The Elements and Culture" (1908). Hardness, daring, and will displaced other Nietzschean virtues such as generosity, personal integrity, self-development, and the ability to forget injuries. Cruelty to enemies became a sacred duty. Lenin, Bukharin, and Trotsky created new fusions of Marxism and Nietzsche. Artists and intellectuals hoping to go beyond Bolshevism preached a "spiritual" or a "cultural" revolution, using these words interchangeably.

24. Jonathan Coopersmith, *The Electrification of Russia, 1880–1926* (Ithaca, 1992), 174–76.

Apocalypse Now: Bolshevik Fusions of Marx, Engels, and Nietzsche

The knell of capitalist private property sounds. The
expropriators are expropriated.   *—MER,* 438

The time for petty politics is over: the very next century
will bring the fight for domination of the earth—the
compulsion to large-scale politics.   *—BGE,* 131

Genuine philosophers, however, are commanders
and legislators; they say, *"thus it shall be!"* . . . With
a creative hand they reach for the future, and all that
is and has been becomes a means for them, an
instrument, a hammer. Their "knowing" is *creating,*
their creating is a legislation, their will to truth is—
will to power.   *—BGE,* 136

In the crucible of war and revolution a new ideological alloy
was forged in which the hardest, most violent, and most
authoritarian elements of Marx, Engels, and Nietzsche
bonded and from which the humane elements of Marxism
and the libertarian elements of Nietzsche were expelled.
Contributing to this alloy were the revolutionary intelligentsia's apotheosis of will, the brutalizing effects of war
(World War I and the Civil War), and Darwinian notions
of the survival of the fittest. For both sides, the Civil War
was a struggle for survival.

Bolshevism was a utopian and apocalyptic interpretation
of Marxism that aimed at nothing less than a leap from the
Kingdom of Necessity to the Kingdom of Freedom. This
interpretation entailed an option for heroic, "hard" values
as opposed to the "soft" values of democratic socialism.
The Bolsheviks did not come to Marxism by way of

Nietzsche, of course, but Nietzsche reinforced their "hard" interpretation of Marxism and fortified their will to power. Without power, they could not lead the masses to the promised land of socialism. Nietzsche also reinforced the mythic thrust of Marxism, its vision of history as a drama of salvation, and gave new impetus to the perennial radical dream of remaking man.

Important to the Bolsheviks to be discussed in this chapter—Lenin (Vladimir Ilich Ulianov, 1870–1924), Nikolai Bukharin (1888–1938), and Leon Trotsky (Lev Davidovich Bronshtein, 1879–1940)—were ideas found in the writings of Marx, Engels, and Nietzsche: contempt for bourgeois morality, emphasis on struggle, a rhetoric of blood and violence, Prometheanism, a "future-orientation," and its corollary, "instrumental" cruelty, the latter justified in terms of Hegelian-Marxist historicism. Engels once called history the cruelest of all goddesses: "She leads her triumphal car over heaps of corpses, not only in war, but also in 'peaceful' economic development."[1] These Bolsheviks regarded the Great War as an opportunity to accelerate the "laws of history" and create a socialist society in backward Russia. They believed that the Great War would harden the proletariat and push it into active struggle. Trotsky referred to the war as a "school," which through its "terrible realism formulates a new human type."[2] Lenin and Bukharin expressed similar sentiments.

Lenin was a personification of the will to power and a myth-creator in his own way. Bukharin was familiar with Nietzsche's thought and an admirer of Bogdanov. Trotsky's first published article was "Something About the Superman." All of them read Marx and Engels through lenses that magnified the authoritarian, violent, and cruel passages and erased the gradualist ones. Their favorite words—"slavish," "servile," "mastery," "power," and "will"—resonated with Marxism, Nietzsche, and the ethos of the revolutionary intelligentsia. Lenin expressed his hatred for "our slavish past" (*LA*, 197–98) and recalled that Chernyshevsky had called Russia a "nation of slaves." Bukharin complained that "a slave psychology and slavish habits are still deeply ingrained"; the workers must be reeducated for they are the new masters.[3] "You're not slaves any more," Trotsky declared, "Rise higher, master life, do not wait for orders from above."[4] The pseudonyms that certain Bolsheviks adopted—Stalin (Josef Djugashivili), Molotov (Viacheslav Skriabin), and Kamenev (Lev Rozenfeld)—stem from the Russian words for steel, hammer, and stone, respectively; they connote materials or tools used

---

1. Quoted in Walicki, *Marxism*, 160.
2. Quoted in Philip Pomper, *Lenin, Trotsky and Stalin: The Intelligentsia and Power* (New York, 1990), 243.
3. Nikolai Bukharin and Evgeny Preobrazhensky, *The ABC of Communism*, preface and introduction by Sidney Heitman (Ann Arbor, 1966), 286.
4. Quoted in Frederick I. Kaplan, *Bolshevik Ideology and the Ethics of Soviet Labor* (New York, 1968), 393.

by the proletariat and echo Nietzsche's injunction: "Be hard!" After the Revolution, the Bolsheviks became "commanders and legislators," and the masses became their "instrument."

Lenin: A Closet Nietzschean?

The question mark is deliberate because the evidence for Lenin's "Nietzscheanism" is indirect. His rhetoric certainly sounds Nietzschean; "will," "power," and "discipline" (which goes with an Apollonian interpretation of Nietzsche) were among his favorite words. Lenin detested "sentimentality" in politics and relished struggle almost as a way of life. Given these proclivities, plus his admiration for the "heroic" tradition of revolutionary populism, plus his alliance with Bogdanov from 1904 to 1907, plus his friendship with Gorky, plus the Nietzsche-saturated general culture, it is very likely that Nietzsche informed Lenin's interpretation of Marxism. He mentioned Nietzsche in his notebooks and kept a copy of *Zarathustra* in his Kremlin office.[5] Gorky sought a Russian Superman to lead the masses in a struggle for liberation. Lenin might have seen himself in that role or, at least, as a "world historical individual" (Hegel's concept). He replied to Bukharin's book on imperialism, which had Nietzschean elements, with his own book on the subject, and he countered left-Bolshevik "anarchism" by delineating the proletarian state. Lenin did not get his will to power from reading Nietzsche, of course, but Nietzsche probably reinforced it.

Lenin's complete works are far from complete. Documents likely to embarrass him or his cause were excluded. Lenin himself destroyed some of them or, in the case of letters, instructed recipients to do so.[6] His published writings are full of references to Marx, Engels, Plekhanov, and Kautsky, and to a lesser extent, to Chernyshevsky, Herzen, Belinsky, and the "brilliant galaxy of revolutionaries of the seventies," whom he considered precursors of Marxism (*LA*, 20). He was reticent about non-Marxist influences on his thought. From his notebooks, it is clear that Hegel, Clausewitz, and Aristotle helped Lenin sharpen his interpretation of Marxism and his strategy for revolution. Darwin and Machiavelli did too. Lenin kept a "Darwin" statue on his desk, but he rarely mentioned Machiavelli by name, however, not even in private correspondence.[7] In a letter to Politburo leaders (which they were to destroy after reading), Lenin wrote: "One wise writer on matters of statecraft [Machiavelli] rightly said that if it is necessary to resort to certain brutalities for the same of realizing a certain political goal, they must be carried

---

5. Robert Service, *Lenin: A Biography* (Cambridge, Mass., 2000), 203.
6. Richard Pipes, ed., *The Unknown Lenin* (New Haven, 1996), 4.
7. Service, *Lenin*, 203–4, 376. For the "Darwin" statute, see illustration 34.

out in the most energetic fashion and in the briefest possible time, because the masses will not tolerate prolonged applications of brutality."[8]

Nietzsche, as well as Machiavelli, probably reinforced Lenin's elitism and his revolutionary immoralism. Lenin shared Tkachev's view that the proletariat was incapable of liberating itself, and he described revolution as a "tough business." "You can't make it wearing white gloves and with clean hands. . . . The Party is not a ladies' school . . . a scoundrel might be what we need just because he is a scoundrel." He observed that Nechaev's contemporaries forgot "that he possessed a special talent as an organizer, a conspirator, and a skill which he could wrap up in staggering formulations."[9] Maximalists of Lenin's generation regarded Nechaev as a "Nietzschean before Nietzsche." Perhaps Lenin did too.

In *What Is To Be Done?* (1902), the foundational text of Bolshevism, Lenin propounded a revolutionary elitism that went beyond Marx's concept of a vanguard party. "Class political consciousness can be brought to the workers *only from without,* that is, only from outside the economic struggle" (*LA,* 50). On its own, the proletariat is capable only of trade union consciousness. Implicitly, the proletariat was a herd that could be stampeded in the wrong direction. In this book, Lenin distinguished between "the attempt to seize power, which was prepared by the preaching of Tkachev, and carried out by means of the 'terrifying' terror that did really terrify, which had 'grandeur,' and "the 'excitative' terror of a Tkachev the Little [which was] simply ludicrous, particularly so when it [was] supplemented with the ideas of an organization of average people" (*LA,* 107). Concerned that Marxists not repeat the mistakes of revolutionary populists, Lenin insisted on an organization of professional revolutionaries, a conscious, self-disciplined, revolutionary elite.

Lenin's categories of "consciousness" (*soznatel'nost'*) and "spontaneity" (*stikhinost'*) correspond to Nietzsche's Apollonian and Dionysian impulses. This may not be a coincidence; a 1901 German edition of *The Birth of Tragedy* was in Lenin's personal library.[10] *Stikhinost'* comes from the adjective *stikhinyi,* "elemental," and connotes mindless process. Lenin warned against the dangers of "spontaneity" and associated it with slavishness and primitivism (*LA,* 27, 32, 46, 63). As Lenin used the term, "consciousness" was not just awareness but a strategy for gaining power. Like Bogdanov, Lenin treated Marxism as an activating ideology, a mobilizing myth. Both of them stressed the Apollonian principle of organization.

8. Lenin, "Letter to Molotov for Politburo Members" (19 March 1922), in Pipes, *Unknown Lenin,* 153.

9. Quoted in Dmitri Volkogonov, *Lenin* (New York, 1994), 22.

10. Aldo Venturelli, "Eine Historische Peripetie von Nietzsche's Denken: Lenin als Nietzsche-Leser," *Nietzsche Studien* 22 (1993): 324.

In his polemics with the Nietzschean Marxists, Lenin used Nietzschean language and developed his own mobilizing myths. During the Revolution of 1905, he and Bogdanov lived in the same building (in Finland), where they discussed political theory, culture, philosophy, revolutionary strategy, and tactics.[11] Surely, Nietzsche entered into the discussions. Lenin's mobilizing myth came with new slogans, a new morality, and new political forms: a vanguard Party composed of professional revolutionaries; a disciplined, conscious, conspiratorial elite; and a Dictatorship of the Proletariat that would direct the transition from capitalism to the first phase of communism. Marx wrote that every epoch has its illusion (*MER*, 165) (or myth). Lenin claimed to be scientific, but he was creating a socialist countermyth. "The *only* choice is—either bourgeois or socialist ideology. There is no middle course . . . there can never be a non-class or an above-class ideology" (*LA*, 29).

In "Two Tactics of Social Democracy" (June-July 1905), Lenin proposed a *"revolutionary-democratic dictatorship of the proletariat and the peasantry,"* because the proletariat was not strong enough to seize power alone. To justify his tactical shift, Lenin couched his argument in dialectical form: "All things are relative, all things flow, and all things change. . . . There is no such thing as abstract truth. Truth is always concrete" (*LA,* 135). Bogdanov could have used the same language.

In the same article, Lenin proclaimed that "revolutions are festivals of the oppressed"; Bolsheviks must use "this festive energy of the masses and their revolutionary ardor to wage a ruthless and self-sacrificing struggle for the direct and decisive path" (*LA,* 140–41). The words "ardor" and "energy" were favored by the Nietzschean Marxists. He also said that the Bolsheviks needed new slogans (Lenin's version of a "new word"). "Words are action, too." It is treachery "to confine oneself to 'words' *in the old way,* without advancing the *direct slogan* on the need to pass over to action" (*LA,* 134). Lenin's sensitivity to language was another area of congruence with Nietzsche and his Russian admirers. The Bolshevik leader had a life-long interest in classical philology.

Lenin's staple words for dealing with resistance, real or potential, were "smash," "cripple," "crush," and "break." Such violent language, he said, was "calculated to evoke in the reader hatred, aversion, and contempt . . . not to convince, but to break the ranks of the opponents, not to correct the mistake of the opponent, but to destroy him, to wipe his organization off the face of the earth" (*LCW*, 12:424–25). "Harmony," one of Bogdanov's favorite words, was not part of Lenin's vocabulary. Gorky called Lenin's language "the language of the axe."

11. Service, *Lenin*, 183.

In "Party Organization and Party Literature" (1905), Lenin condemned "literary supermen" and "bourgeois-anarchist individualism" (which was associated with Nietzsche). Party literature must be "*part* of the common cause of the proletariat, 'a cog and a screw' of one single great Social Democratic mechanism set in motion" by the vanguard of the proletariat (*LA*, 148–52). Put differently, the Party writer would be part of a revolutionary chorus that Lenin would conduct.

After 1906, Lenin revamped his myth to spotlight the heroic proletariat (a shift from *What Is To Be Done?*), the soviets (workers councils), and the Paris Commune (*LCW*, 9:141, 8:206–8). These changes gave Lenin's myth a Marxist genealogy untainted by such "spiritual booze" as God-building. For Marx and Engels, revolutionary violence was a midwife (Marx was graphic on the blood and agony of a real birth). For Lenin, violence was a psychologically transforming experience, as it was for Bakunin and Sorel. "The Russian people are not what they were prior to 1905. The Revolution has taught them to fight. The proletariat will bring them to victory" (*LCW*, 16:304). Only armed struggle by the masses themselves could achieve their liberation. The Revolution of 1905 was a proletarian revolution (not a bourgeois-democratic one as gradualist Marxists claimed) because the vanguard of the proletariat led it, using a specifically proletarian "form of struggle"— the strike. Struggle imbued the masses with a new spirit. Henceforth, they would give no quarter and expect none; their choice was victory or death. Gradualist Marxists were craven opportunists, personifications of "stagnation, diffidence, flabbiness and inability to break with the psychology of moribund bourgeois society" (*LCW*, 16:307–9, 311–12). In Nietzschean terms, they were carriers of a slave morality.

In search of intellectual ammunition for his battle with Bogdanov's faction (the "Machians"), Lenin read contemporary Western philosophy in the library of a reading society in Geneva to which he belonged and in the Sorbonne Library in Paris. A French translation of Nietzsche's works was in the noncirculating collection of the Geneva library. Lenin went there every day for about two weeks to read Nietzsche, Maupassant, and others.[12] Why Maupassant? Perhaps Lenin picked up the Schopenhauerian undercurrent that attracted intellectuals who were also attracted to Nietzsche, such as Lunacharsky, August Strindberg, Joseph Conrad, Gabriele D'Annunzio, and Isaac Babel. Lunacharsky specifically associated Maupassant with Nietzsche.

The few cryptic references to Nietzsche in Lenin's *Philosophical Notebooks* indicate that he was already familiar with Nietzsche's thought, superficially

---

12. Venturelli, "Eine Historische Peripetie," 321–24. A list of the books Lenin checked out is on page 322. This list includes Tiersot's book on the festivals of the French Revolution and several histories of the French Revolution itself.

at least. The seventh of ten categories that Lenin listed in his summary of Ludwig Stein's *Philosophische Strömungen der Gegenwart* (1908) was "individualism (Nietzsche)" (*LCW*, 38:54). The second reference was in a section of Lenin's notes titled "The Problem of Morality."

> The new philosophies are, therefore, primarily moral doctrines. And it appears that these doctrines can be defined as a *mysticism of action. This attitude is not new. It was the attitude adopted by the sophists, for whom there was also neither truth nor error, but only success.* . . . The doctrines of the intellectual anarchists like Stirner and Nietzsche rest on these same premises. . . .
>
> *When some modernists like LeRoy derive from pragmatism a justification for Catholicism,* they perhaps do not derive from it what some philosophers—the founders of pragmatism wanted to obtain. *But they drew from it conclusions which legitimately can be drawn.* . . .
>
> *It is characteristic of pragmatism that everything is true that succeeds and, on one way or another, is adapted to the moment: science, religion, morality, tradition, custom, routine.* Everything must be taken seriously, and that which realizes an aim and permits one to act must be taken seriously. (*LCW*, 38:454–55)

In other words, "truth" is a pragmatic concept, an organizing principle. Lenin took copious notes on William James. Most Moscow Godseekers associated James's pragmatism with Nietzsche's amoralism.[13] Lenin may have done so as well. Publicly, however, he associated James with Bogdanov and Mach because all of them hypothesized truth.[14]

In *Materialism and Empiriocriticism* (1909), Lenin claimed that in philosophy, as in politics, there was no neutral ground. Every philosophy serves a class interest. By denying the existence of an objective reality and an objective truth, the "Machians" were clearing the way for Marxism's enemies. Bogdanov's faction was guilty of agnosticism (vis-à-vis reality and Marxism) and of fideism (an allusion to God-building). Marx rebuked Feuerbach for trying to invent a new religion, Lenin noted. Bogdanov's faction were following Dietzgen "the muddleheaded," rather than Dietzgen the materialist (254). Moreover, if "organization" is the only thing that matters, then one "truth" is as valid as another. "If truth is only an organizing form of human experience, then the teaching, say, of Catholicism, is also true. For there is not the slightest doubt that Catholicism is an 'organizing form of human

---

13. Bernice Glatzer Rosenthal, "William James Through a Russian Prism: The Case of the Moscow God-seekers," forthcoming in *The Cultural Gradient: The Transmission of Ideas in Europe, 1785–1991*, ed. Catherine Evtuhov and Stephen Kotkin (Lanham, Md.).
14. Lenin, *Materialism and Empiriocriticism* (New York, 1927), 355n.

experience'" (122). Furthermore, Bogdanov's "cognitive socialism" is "insane twaddle. . . . If socialism is thus regarded, the Jesuits are ardent adherents of 'cognitive socialism,' for the basis of their epistemology is divinity as 'socially organized experience'; only it reflects not objective truth (which Bogdanov denies, but which science reflects), but the exploitation of the ignorance of the masses by definite social classes" (234).

There are no references to Nietzsche in *Materialism and Empiriocriticism,* but if "Nietzsche" is substituted for "Mach" the thrust of Lenin's argument remains remarkably unchanged. Then why did Lenin not say Nietzsche? Presumably because keeping the argument on a "scientific" level would fool the censor and camouflage the power-political issues at stake. For Lenin, "truth" was that which would enable the Bolsheviks to prevail—"*everything is true that succeeds.*" In essence, Lenin was arguing, Marxism was an absolute truth as immutable as the laws of Newton. Psychologically, Lenin was right. An activating ideology requires certainty; people do not risk imprisonment or death for hypothetical truths.

In a follow-up article, Lenin discussed the ideology of "meekness" and "repentance" purveyed by former Marxists in *Landmarks,* as well as the "vogue of mysticism," and "Machism," attributing these phenomena to an unthinking (i.e., spontaneous and therefore irrational and unscientific) response to unusual, forceful, and abrupt changes in the social and political situation. It was "natural and inevitable that there should emerge a 'revaluation of all values,' a new study of fundamental problems, a new interest in theory, in elementals, in the ABC of politics." This is precisely because Marxism is not a "lifeless dogma . . . but a living guide to action." Some Marxists had learned "by rote certain 'slogans'" without understanding the Marxist criteria for them. Their "revaluation of all values" (note Lenin's repetition of the phrase) led to a "revision of the most abstract and philosophical fundamental of Marxism, to "empty-phrase-mongering" and a "Machist epidemic" in the Party (*LCW,* 17:39, 42–43).

In April 1917, Lenin urged the Bolshevik Party to change its name to Communist, (to distinguish itself from "bourgeois" social democracy), which it did the following March (1918). Also in 1917, Lenin coined new slogans— "All power to the soviets," "Expropriate the expropriators"—once again indicating his sensitivity to language. In the midst of the Civil War, when the existence of the Bolshevik government was at stake, Lenin sponsored a new four-volume *Dictionary of the Russian Language,* because he believed that the social changes brought about by the Revolution demanded immediate action on the "language front."[15]

15. Michael G. Smith, *Language and Power in the Creation of the USSR, 1917–1953* (Berlin and New York, 1998), 42.

Lenin wrote *State and Revolution,* in late summer 1917, to provide a legitimating mythology for a Marxist (as distinct from a Jacobin or a Blanquist) seizure of power, not knowing at the time when it would be attempted and whether it would succeed. His model was Marx's book on the Paris Commune, *The Civil Wars in France* (1871), which Marx wrote to provide a "heroic legend" (his words) for the workers. In this book, Marx developed his concept of a proletarian dictatorship to direct the transition from capitalism to communism. He further developed the concept in his "Critique of the Gotha Program" (1875), distinguishing between a lower and a higher phase of communism and referring to a political transition period in which the state can be nothing but the "revolutionary dictatorship of the proletariat" (*MER,* 538). Marx envisioned a fairly long transition period between the revolutionary dictatorship and full communism. "The working class did not expect miracles from the Commune. They have no ready-made utopias to introduce [by decree of the people]. They know . . . that they will have to pass through long struggles, through a series of historic processes, transforming circumstances and men. They have no ideals to realize, but to set free the elements of the new society with which the old collapsing bourgeois society itself is pregnant."[16]

By contrast, Lenin expected the transition period to be short. Capitalism had so simplified "accounting and control" that Bolsheviks need only take over mechanisms already in place, "chopping off" those they did not need. The armed workers would "*control* production and distribution," keep account of labor and products, issue receipts, and so on. Control, of course, is power. Engineers, agronomists, and other specialists work for the capitalists today and they will work "even better tomorrow in obedience to the wishes of the armed workers" (*LA,* 382). *All* citizens become hired employees of the state, which consists of the armed workers. *All* citizens become employees and workers of a *single* country-wide state "syndicate," with equality of work and equality of pay. "There will be no getting away from it, there will be 'nowhere to go.'" When everyone has learned to administer and to observe the "simple fundamental rules of the community" out of habit, then the transition to full communism will begin (*LA,* 383).

Highlighting the brutal and violent passages in the writings of Marx and Engels, and there are plenty, Lenin advocated a Dictatorship of the Proletariat unconstrained by any law, a realm of pure force. "The proletariat needs state power, a centralized organization of force, an organization of violence, to crush the resistance of the exploiters and to *lead* the enormous mass of the population—the peasants, the petty bourgeoisie, and the semi-proletarians— in the work of organizing a socialist economy" (*LA,* 328). The commune

16. *The Civil War in France,* in *Karl Marx: The First International and After. Political Writings,* ed. David Fernbach (London, 1992), 3:213.

failed because it did not crush its enemies. The victorious proletariat must maintain its rule by means of coercion and terror. To believe otherwise was utopian. Arguing against anarchists and "left Bolsheviks," including Bukharin, who wanted to abolish the state immediately after the Revolution, Lenin declared: "We are not utopians, we do not 'dream' of dispensing *at once* with all administration, with all subordination. . . . No, we want the social-ist revolution with people as they are now, with people who cannot dispense with subordination, control, and foremen and accounts" (*LA* p. 344). The entire book is a paean to power combined with a naive faith in what can be achieved by power alone and an amazing ignorance of what running a state, or an economy, entails. At the time the proletariat constituted 3 percent of the population, one more reason for ruling out "bourgeois democracy" and majority rule.

Lenin's conception of the first phase of communism combined a Nietzschean exaltation of will with a program of primitive egalitarianism that had nothing in common with Nietzsche's aristocratic elitism. Egalitarianism and the will to power are not mutually contradictory, how-ever, as Nietzsche observed: "The will to equality is the will to power" (*WP*, 277). Lenin's egalitarianism appealed to the anarchistic and leveling instincts of the masses, and was a concession of sorts to Bukharin and other "left Bolsheviks" such as Kollontai. (From outside the Party, Bogdanov decried a "leveling by the inferior.")[17] In a follow-up article, written to refute Bazarov's contentions that the proletariat was not ready for socialism and the soviets were not effective planning instruments, Lenin lauded the "creative enthu-siasm" of the revolutionary classes which gave rise to the soviets in 1905, and once again emphasized the ease of running the state (*LA*, 399–406).[18]

For most of 1917, Lenin's slogan was "All power to the soviets." Soon after seizing power, he dropped that slogan and talked about "human material" ruined by centuries of slavery that would have to be "reworked," invoking the need for organization, discipline, and revolutionary will. In January 1918, he defended coercion and terror against individuals and entire classes and expressed great contempt for "spineless," "drooping intellectuals" who complained about summary arrests, executions, and closing of non-Bolshevik newspapers and journals (*LA*, 424–26). In March 1918, Lenin proclaimed: "Learn discipline from the Germans; if we do not, we as a people, are doomed; we shall live in eternal slavery" (*LA*, 549). Russia had to accept the Treaty of Brest-Litovsk, he argued, lambasting "intellectual supermen" (543) who opposed it. This is a reference to Bukharin, Kollontai, and other "left

17. Bogdanov, *Bogdanov's Tektology*, 25.
18. Francis King, "The Political and Economic Thought of Vladimir Aleksandrovich Bazarov (1874–1904)" (Ph.D. diss, University of East Anglia, 1994), 104.

Bolsheviks" who wanted to turn a defensive war into a revolutionary war, as the Jacobins did in 1792–93. In another article (also March 1918), Lenin said the treaty would steel and temper "our will to liberation" (*LA,* 434).

In "The Immediate Tasks of the Soviet Government" (April 1918), references to "will" appear four times on the same page: "absolute and strict *unity of will,*" "thousands subordinating their will to the will of one," "*unquestioning subordination* to a single will," "*unquestioningly obey the single will* of the leaders of labor" (*LA,* 455). In "How to Organize Competition" (January 1918, published 1929), he decried the "slovenliness, carelessness, untidiness, unpunctuality, nervous haste, the inclination to substitute discussion for action, talk for work," blaming these slavish habits "on the abnormal separation of mental from manual labor" (a favorite theme of Bogdanov's) and spelled out brutal measures to eliminate "parasites" (*LA,* 426–32).

In "A Great Beginning" (July 1919), Lenin called for heroism and will in everyday life (a new deployment of the warrior ethos). The occasion was the *subbotnik* movement (working Saturdays without pay), begun by some railroad workers the previous May. Their "heroism" was the beginning of a revolution of habits, "a victory over our own conservatism, indiscipline, petty-bourgeois egoism, a victory over the [slavish] habits" of the past. Single acts of heroic fervor would not build socialism; required were "the most prolonged, most persistent and most difficult mass heroism in *plain everyday work*" (*LA,* 480). Building socialism also required sublimation. The "demand for free love is a bourgeois, not a proletarian demand" (*LA,* 685). "The revolution calls for concentration and rallying of every nerve by the masses and by the individual. It does not tolerate orgiastic conditions so common among D'Annunzio's decadent heroes and heroines [D'Annunzio's Nietzscheanism was well known]. . . . What [the proletariat] needs is clarity, clarity, and more clarity. Therefore, I repeat, there must be no weakening, no waste and no dissipation of energy. Self-control and self-discipline are not slavery" (*LA,* 694). In "The Tasks of the Youth Leagues" (October 1920), Lenin said that Communists reject "any morality based on extra-human and extra-class concepts." "Our morality is entirely subordinated to the interests of the proletariat's class struggle. The class struggle is continuing; it has merely changed its forms" (*LA,* 668–69).

In *'Left-Wing' Communism, An Infantile Disorder* (April 1920), Lenin attacked purists who opposed participation in coalition governments in Europe and insisted that the Dictatorship of the Proletariat must remain because, even though the Civil War was almost over, the struggle continued. Within the Party, the "strictest centralization and discipline are required [so that] the *organizational* role of the proletariat (and that is its *principal* role) may be exercised correctly, successfully, and victoriously. The dictatorship of the proletariat means a persistent struggle—bloody and bloodless, violent and peaceful, educational and administrative—against the forces and traditions of the old society" (*LA,* 569). Toward the end of 1920, Lenin reiterated his conception of the Dictatorship of the Proletariat as a realm of pure force (*LCW,* 31:353).

Bukharin's Nietzschean Political Imagination

Nikolai Bukharin, the most erudite of the Bolsheviks, lived in Germany and Austria for many years; was fluent in German, French, and English; and wrote about sociology, economics, politics, literature, language, and art. As a young man, he had considered becoming an artist. He drew political cartoons for *Pravda,* served as its theater critic, and remained passionately interested in art all his life. Bukharin knew Nietzsche's thought well, even quoting from Nietzsche's *Nachlaß* in the original German. He considered Nietzsche "one of the most paradoxical intellects of bourgeois philosophy."[19] Nietzsche and Bogdanov colored Bukharin's political imagination.

In *Imperialism and the World Economy* (1915), Bukharin described a new form of imperialism, propelled by a new entity, the Leviathan state created by finance capital. An excerpt was published in German in 1916 under the dramatic title, "The Imperialist Predator-State" ("Der imperialistische Raubstaat"). Marxists routinely referred to Nietzsche's nobility as predators, so Bukharin's title could easily connote Nietzsche's lawless Lords of the Earth, shamelessly plundering the weak. Similar imagery—parasitic imperialists who extort "tribute" and "booty" from subjugated peoples—was used by J. A. Hobson in his book *Imperialism* (1902), which stimulated Marxist theories of imperialism even though Hobson was not a Marxist. He considered imperialism a distortion of capitalism.

A theory of imperialism is implicit in Marx's emphasis on the expansionist dynamic of capitalism, but he never worked it out. Overall, Marx considered imperialism a progressive phenomenon that opened stagnant societies to dialectical transformation; he even warned against the sentimental idealization of "barbaric" preindustrial societies.[20] Marx did not live to see the full scope of the "new imperialism," but other Marxists tried to explain it. Engels said that "capitalist production cannot stop; it must go on increasing and expanding or must die." Overseas expansion only delayed the final conflict between capitalism and socialism.[21] Karl Kautsky (1858–1938), head

---

19. "Gete i ego istoricheskoe znachenie," in Bukharin, *Etiudy* (Moscow, 1932; reprint, 1988), 165.

20. Shlomo Avineri, ed., *Karl Marx on Colonialism and Modernization* (Garden City, N.Y., 1969), passim.

21. F. Engels, introduction to the English edition (1892) of "The Condition of the Working Class in England," in K. *Marx and F. Engels' On Britain* (Moscow, 1953), 29–321; see also 19–20.

of the German Social Democrats and the "pope" of the Second International, blamed imperialism on dynastic, feudal, militarist, and bureaucratic influences and stressed the expansionary dynamic of the state.[22] The Austrian Marxist Rudolf Hilferding (1876–1944) emphasized the interconnection of politics, economics, and ideology in Germany and the new phenomena of trusts, monopolies, and cartels (*Finance Capitalism*, 1910). Hilferding considered imperialism highly exploitative, but he did not argue that it must lead to war. Rosa Luxemburg (1876–1919) did. In *The Accumulation of Capital* (1913), she associated capitalism with militarism and maintained that capitalist accumulation was impossible in a closed system. When capitalist expansion in preindustrial areas reached its limits, the entire system would collapse.

Drawing on Hilferding, Luxemburg, and his own knowledge of Germany, Bukharin claimed that the locus of the new imperialism was an entirely new phenomenon, the Imperialist State, inherently militaristic, aggressive, and impelled by the policy that led Germany to imperial expansion and war. Surely Bukharin knew that in Germany the extreme right was using *The Will to Power* as a bible. Count Philipp von Eulenberg, confidant of Kaiser Wilhelm II and a major figure at the Foreign Office and Diplomatic Corps, was an ardent Nietzschean, as were Admiral von Tirpitz and Alfred Ballin (founder of the Hamburg-America line). Despite personal rivalries, they and their supporters in the Reichstag quoted Nietzsche in support of their position that a state must expand or die.

> It is part of the concept of the living that it must grow—that it must extend its power and consequently incorporate alien forces. Intoxicated by moral narcotics, one speaks of the right of the individual to *defend* himself; in the same sense one might also speak of his right to attack: for both—and the second even more than the first—are necessities for every living thing:—aggressive and defensive egoism are not matters of choice, to say nothing of "free will," but the fatality of life itself. (*WP*, 386)

Moreover:

> A society that definitely and *instinctively* gives up war and conquest is in decline. . . . The maintenance of the military state is the last means of all of acquiring or maintaining the great tradition with regard to the supreme type of man, the strong type. And all concepts that perpetuate enmity and difference in rank between states (e.g. nationalism, protective tariffs) may appear sanctioned in this light. (*WP*, 386)

22. John H. Kautsky, *Karl Kautsky: Marxism, Revolution and Democracy* (New Brunswick, 1994), 134–39, 156.

Bukharin's picture of the "imperialist predator-state" was based on a real entity—the German war economy—which he described as a machine for the "*maximally protracted and maximally successful exploitation of the enslaved classes* in contemporary society, above all, the proletariat," . . . a monster-state that "*sucks in almost all branches of production* . . . [that] *becomes more and more a direct exploiter, which organizes and directs production as a collective, composite capitalist.*" This monster-state absorbs all organizations (trade, denominational, youth, women's, cultural and political groups) into itself, transforms them into "divisions of a gigantic state mechanism, which descends with crushing force upon the obvious and internal enemy. Thus arises the final type of the contemporary imperialist predator-state, the iron organization which, with its grasping, prehensile paws seizes the living body of society."[23]

Bukharin's metaphor can suggest a vampire or a werewolf sucking the workers' blood—Marx's metaphors for capital, rather than the state (*MER*, 362, 367, 373). The metaphor can also suggest the "paws" of the lion, the "splendid *blond beast*" (*GM*, 40) that has turned into a monster, even though Nietzsche did not associate the "blond beast" with the state. He did, however, call the state a monster, not an ordinary monster, but the "coldest of all cold monsters" devouring people, chewing them up and spitting them out. "'There is nothing greater on earth than I, the regulating finger of God'—thus the monster bellows." And "whatever [the state] has, it has stolen" (*Z*, 75–76). In an alternate reading, the monster could be the Beast of the Apocalypse or the Antichrist himself. Bukharin imagined this super-state and super-monster as "a new Leviathan in the face of which the fantasy of Thomas Hobbes seems like child's play.[24] Hobbes considered the "New Leviathan" the only way to stop the "war of all against all," the human condition in the state of nature. Marx used the phrase to describe competitive bourgeois society.

In *Imperialism and the World-Economy,* Bukharin observed that in the contemporary Leviathan state, parliament becomes a merely decorative institution. Workers become bondsmen attached to the plant, "white slaves" of the predatory imperialist state, which has absorbed all productive life into its body.[25] He also alluded to Jack London's nightmare of "the iron heel of the militarist state." (London was a Marxist and a Nietzschean.) Around the same time, Bukharin published an article titled "The New Slavery," in a journal he and Trotsky edited in New York. By 1917, the German Leviathan state was even more powerful. It set prices, controlled competition, nation-

---

23. Excerpt in Daniels, *Documentary History*, 39–41. I changed "bandit" to "predator."
24. Ibid., 41.
25. Nikolai Bukharin, *Imperialism and the World Economy* (New York, 1966), 128, 160.

alized certain industries, determined wage and labor policy, and so on, thereby overcoming what Marxists called the anarchy of capitalist production.

Kautsky had suggested, in 1914 and 1915, that a peaceful division of the world by international cartels was possible, an "ultra-imperialism." Bukharin disagreed. He assumed a national will to power—a nonrational, extra-economic force that recognizes no limits. The state, therefore, must be exploded entirely. The war would make this possible, because it had created new men. The masses, "originally tame and docile" but aroused to political life, "steeled in battle forced on them from above, accustomed to look into the face of death every minute," with the very same fearlessness, would turn the imperialist war into a civil war. The armed proletariat would smash the Leviathan state. Nietzsche wrote: "Only there, where the state ceases" does the man who is not superfluous begin: does the song of the "necessary man," the unique and irreplaceable melody begin (*Z,* 77). For Bukharin, that was where communism would begin. Adapting Luxemburg's idea that imperialist expansion cannot go on indefinitely, Bukharin predicted that capitalism would break at its weakest link. Lenin wrote the preface to *Imperialism and the World Economy.* "Peaceful" capitalism is gone for good," he said. "Finance capital took over as the typical 'lord' of the world" (*LCW,* 24:104–5). And even the "peaceful" period of capitalism meant oppression, suffering, and horror, for all but a tiny minority of the world's population.

Bukharin's book spurred Lenin to formulate his own position on the state (in *State and Revolution*) and to write *Imperialism: The Highest Stage of Capitalism* (1916). In the introduction to the latter, Lenin praised Hobson's and Hilferding's books and said that he would try to show briefly and as simply as possible "the connection and relationships between the *principal* economic features of imperialism. I shall not be able to deal with the noneconomic aspects of the question, *however much as they deserve to be dealt with*" (*LA,* 211, emphasis added). That Lenin was aware of the psychological features of imperialism, such as, for example, the "will to power," is obvious in his cryptic note on Louis Esteves's book *Une nouvelle psychologie de l'imperialisme, Ernest Seilliere,* 1913), "a psychological interpretation of imperialism a la Nietzsche, deals only with psychology" (*LCW,* 39:205). Seilliere was the author of *Philosophie de la Imperialisme* (2 vols., 1903, 1905). Volume 2 was subtitled *Apollon ou Dionysus, Etude critique sur Frederik Nietzsche et l'utilitarisme imperialiste.* According to Seilliere, imperialism stemmed from human nature, from the "will to power," either in its "rational Apollonian" or "mystical Dionysian" form.

Bukharin came perilously close to saying that the state was the dominant economic force and that monopolists could end the anarchy of production. Lenin considered Bukharin's treatment of imperialism insufficiently dialectical; decadent monopoly capitalism was rife with profound, unresolvable contradictions. In *Imperialism: The Highest Stage of Capitalism,* Lenin defined exploitation in national and class terms and advocated what would later be called national liberation movements. Painting a picture of overwhelming oppression and suffering inflicted on the masses by a monstrous few, he described a different kind of cold monster—"capitalist threads in thousands of different intercrossings" form the web of an enormous spider that is strangling the overwhelming majority of the world's population. (A spider was one of Dostoevsky's favorite metaphors.) Two or three "plunderers armed to the teeth" (America, Great Britain, Japan) have drawn the whole world into "*their*" war over the question of "their" booty (*LA*, 207–9). The financial oligarchy uses its "*superprofits*" to bribe labor leaders and the upper strata of the labor aristocracy (209). Hilferding was right; finance capital "does not want liberty, it wants domination" (240). Kautsky's definition of imperialism as a "striving for annexations" was correct but incomplete; it was "a striving toward violence and reaction." Accusing Kautsky of confusing the form of the imperialist struggle with its substance, Lenin claimed that "ultra-imperialism" is "super-imperialism," the parasitical exploitation of the small nations of the world (*LA*, 245–47). (Actually, Kautsky did not advocate "ultra-imperialism," he suggested it as one of several possibilities.) But deliverance was at hand. Imperialism was the last stage of decadent monopoly capitalism. A revolution of oppressed peoples was imminent, and it would engulf the entire world. Borrowing Bukharin's "weakest link" theory, Lenin predicted that world revolution would begin in Russia. When he founded the Comintern, in March 1919, he linked the survival of the socialist fatherland to world revolution, but he may also have believed that an organism must "expand or die." In an uncanny parallel to the Asian orientation of the futurists and the Scythians (see Chapter 6), the Comintern paid special attention to Asia.

In *The Economics of the Transition Period* (1920), Bukharin reversed himself. Rather than smash the Leviathan state, the proletariat must construct its own. Force was the midwife of the new society; the greater the force, the shorter the transition period. The dictatorship of the proletariat and the collapse of the economy were historically necessary. Bukharin's term for the collapse, "expanded negative reproduction," presumably to be followed by expanded positive reproduction, could be interpreted as a dialectical version of Nietzsche's concept of creative destruction. In this book, Bukharin talked about "forging" communist mankind out of the "human material" left from capitalism, called the proletariat the "Promethean class," and referred to the "proletarian avant-garde" (the usual Marxist term is vanguard). He cited Marx's description of the "brutality" of the transition from feudalism to capitalism to support his own view that a period of "primitive socialist accumulation" was necessary. Bukharin's view was compatible with, and probably colored by, Nietzsche's belief that "we should reconsider cruelty and open our eyes. . . . Almost everything we call 'higher culture' is based on the spiritualization of cruelty" (*BGE,* 158). Communism was going to lead to a "higher culture," not in the rarefied sense but as something superior to "bourgeois culture."

According to Bukharin, Russia was now going through the "cruel" process predicted by Marx. Only the proletarian state could bring order out of chaos. Justifying the same policies he had decried in Imperial Germany—control of every aspect of the economy and all social relations; state concentration of all the coercive and administrative energies of society—Bukharin maintained that it was not the policies but their class essence that mattered. When used by the Dictatorship of the Proletariat, these policies were progressive. *The Economics of the Transition Period,* says Neil Harding, "remains the fullest and most sophisticated account of the dictatorship of the proletariat. It was a vindication of total power that rejoiced in the unchallengeable monism of its structure—a hierarchy of centralized authority patterns . . . [a] 'would-be triumph of the will.'"[26]

The ABC of Communism (1919), which Bukharin coauthored with Evgeny Preobrazhensky (1886–1937) and addressed to the masses, conveys the same ideas in simplified form. The contemporary world faced two alternatives: chaos or communism. Peace between social classes was as impossible as peace between wolves and sheep. Unlike hypocritical "bourgeois democracy," "Soviet power" (*vlast'*) did not pretend to be above politics. *Vlast'* also means authority. The word was used by the tsarist government too, but Bukharin and Preobrazhensky really hammered it in, alluding to "Soviet power" throughout and making it the title of the sixth chapter. They defended "new forms of compulsion" such as the abolition of "so-called freedom of labor" and the disarming of formerly middle- and upper-class individuals. The penalty for illegal possession of a weapon was death. As for the "rich peasants," they would inevitably prove to be irreconcilable enemies of the proletarian state; it might eventually be necessary "to undertake a deliberately planned expropriation" of them (317). The authors included a list of books recommended for further reading, one of them being Jack London's *The Iron Heel.*

Bogdanov's influence is obvious in Bukharin's emphasis on the role of ideological workers—teachers, authors, journalists, and so on—in achieving and maintaining proletarian hegemony. "The bourgeoisie is well aware that it cannot control the working masses by the use of force alone. It is necessary that the workers' brains be completely enmeshed as if in a spider's web. The bourgeois State looks upon the workers as working cattle; these beasts must labor, but they must not bite . . . they must be trained and tamed, just

26. Neil Harding, "Bukharin and the State," in *The Ideas of Nikolai Bukharin* (Oxford, 1992), 108–9.

as wild beasts in a menagerie" (44). Such training was the function of school, church, and press in the bourgeois state. The Soviet state would train the masses its own way. The leitmotif of *The ABC of Communism* was organization—of industry, army, distribution, banks, and so forth. The section on industry advocated a union of production and science (292), a clear echo of Bogdanov's view. In *Tektology*, Bogdanov emphasized equilibrium, proportionality, and freely moving parts. The integral vision of Bukharin and Preobrazhensky featured coercion in a communist version of the "military state."

In *Historical Materialism, A System of Sociology* (1921), written for use in the Higher Party Schools, Bukharin argued that historical materialism was based on the premise that there is no difference between the social and natural sciences in methods of investigation or approach to causality. Dialectical materialism teaches that there is nothing permanent in the universe; all things are interconnected and affect one another. Changes arise from internal conflicts and struggles, for in society, as everywhere else, all equilibrium is unstable and is eventually overthrown. The new equilibrium must be based on new principles and situated in a complex web of institutions, rituals, popular ideas, and psychology, given coherence by Marxist ideology and supported by state power. Much like Bogdanov, Bukharin thought that in the last analysis all aspects of human culture could be explained by technological change. Ethics were a product of the fetishism of class society and would vanish when class society vanished. The proletariat needed only technical norms, norms of construction, as when a carpenter follows certain rules when making a chair. In *Historical Materialism* Bukharin acknowledged his debt to Bogdanov on the origin of religion and the separation of body and spirit, and argued for the class nature of the social sciences, but in deference to Lenin he denied the class nature of the physical sciences.

Bukharin referred to "the fullness of life," but unlike the Nietzschean Marxists, he related it to wealth. Like all Bolsheviks, he extolled activism and will. "Marxism *does not deny the will but explains it*. When Marxists organize the Communist Party and lead it into battle, this action is also an expression of historical necessity, which finds its forms precisely through the will and actions of men . . . social *determinism* must not be confused with fatalism" (*HM*, 51). The understanding of necessity is empowering. Moreover, "animals adapt to nature passively, biologically; human society adapts itself to nature, not biologically, but technologically, actively" (116). Apropos of contemporary literature and art, Bukharin called Merezhkovsky talented, but objected to his "religious mania." Futurism was "the poetry of the brazen blare," a product of the "noise and racket" of contemporary cities, of "nervous exhaustion"; it expressed the "militaristic turmoil of a dissolving bourgeois civilization" (131).

As a "Left Communist" (the Party changed its name in 1918, we recall) Bukharin opposed the institution of NEP, but in 1924–25 he modified his views and advocated a pro-peasant policy that was based, in part, on Bogdanov's idea of equilibrium and proportionality and, possibly, on Bazarov's theories of economic planning, which distinguished between forecasting and target-setting, "genetics" and "teleology."[27] "War communism," Bukharin said in 1924, was necessary at the time; the error was that "we thought that our peacetime policy would be a continuation of the centralized planning system of that period."[28]

Leon Trotsky's Nietzschean Unconscious

Trotsky was not part of Bogdanov's circle, but he was certainly a romantic revolutionary. Well before he became head of the Red Army and second only to Lenin in the government, he saw himself as the actor in a great historical drama. Trotsky's debt to Nietzsche is obvious in his speeches to the Red Army, in his defense of terror, and in his autobiography. His favorite passage from Nietzsche was "I tell you: one must have chaos in one, to give birth to a dancing star" (*Z*, 46). A "dancing star" can denote a distant ideal; Trotsky never explained what he meant.

In "Something about the Superman" (1900), Trotsky emphasized the authoritarian elements of Nietzsche's thought, giving Nietzsche's "will of the legislator" as an example, and called the Superman a "rapacious beast-aristocrat," an allusion to D'Annunzio's admiring essay on Nietzsche, "The Beast Who Wills" (1892). Two decades before D'Annunzio's "March on Fiume" (1919), Trotsky noted the Italian poet's desire for a Roman Caesar, "beautiful, strong, cruel, passionate." Trotsky explained Nietzsche's philosophy by the social soil that engendered him—the rapacity of bourgeois society.[29]

During the 1905–7 Revolution, Trotsky opposed a worker-peasant alliance and broke with Lenin on this point. The basic issue was not a Dictatorship of the Proletariat and some other class, peasants, middle, or whatever, Trotsky argued, but "who has the hegemony in the government and through it in the country? *When we speak of a labor government, we meant that the hegemony belongs to the working class.*" The proletariat's first measures would be reformist; then it would proceed to a class policy. Collectivism will become

---

27. For Bazarov's economic theories, see King, "Political and Economic Thought," 206–28.
28. "O likvidatorstve nashikh dnei," *Bolshevik*, 2 (1924): 3–9.
29. L. Trotsky, "Koe-chto o filosofii 'sverkhcheloveka,'" in *Sochineniia* (Moscow, 1926), 20:147–62, especially, 160–61.

the order of the day.[30] Trotsky's "hegemony" fused Nietzsche's "will of the legislator" with Rousseauian and Jacobin conceptions of the general will and Marx's idea of proletarian rule. Trotsky wanted the proletariat to seize power and turn its temporary supremacy into a permanent socialist dictatorship. In 1906, he praised the heroism and "proletarian character" of the Paris Commune (despite the fact that very few Communards were proletarians) and said that the Commune showed that a Dictatorship of the Proletariat could be achieved without an advanced industrial economy.[31] The Russian proletariat, however, was too weak to retain power without direct aid from the European proletariat, hence Trotsky's life-long emphasis on world revolution. Trotsky viewed the Great War as the crucible for a great experiment, even though he realized that the experiment might fail, that the Revolution might be drowned in blood. In the summer of 1917, he reconciled with Lenin and was elected to the Bolshevik Central Committee. In September he became head of the Petrograd Soviet.

Trotsky later said that he disbanded the Constituent Assembly in January 1918, because it was useless for "revolutionary creative work." "We are not about to share power with anyone. If we were to stop halfway, then it wouldn't be a revolution, it would be an abortion . . . a false historical delivery." A few months later, he declared: "Yes, we are weak, and that is our greatest historical crime, because one cannot be weak in history. The weak become the prey of the strong." The proletariat gets power by the right of revolutionary force. And if some confused Marxist theorist starts getting under their feet, then the working class will step over that theorist, as over much else."[32]

One of Trotsky's first measures as head of the Red Army was to institute the death penalty for deserters, cowards, and looters. Later on, he instituted severe discipline for all infractions. No crime or misdemeanor, even the most petty, was to be left unpunished. Repression, Trotsky wrote, "is not an end in itself but is directed towards didactic, military aims."[33] In speech after speech, he urged soldiers to show their will to power, to be brutal, violent, merciless, because the Revolution required it.

> History is no indulgent soft mother who will protect the working class; she is a wicked stepmother who will teach the workers through bloody experience how they must attain their aims. . . . The possessing classes never give up the struggle. . . . The working class needs not the universal forgiveness that Tolstoy preached, but hard tempering, intransigence, profound conviction that without struggle for every step, every

30. Excerpt in Daniels, *Documentary History*, 23–25.

31. "Thirty Years After: 1871–1906," in Leon Trotsky, *Writings on the Paris Commune*, ed. Douglas Jennes (New York, 1970).

32. Quoted in Dmitri Volkogonov, *Trotsky* (New York, 1996), 121–22.

33. Quoted in ibid., 175.

inch of the road leading to betterment of life, without constant, irreconcilable harsh struggle, and without organization of this struggle, there can be no salvation and liberation.[34]

A "merciful" release of prisoners, he told the soldiers, allowed those prisoners to rejoin the enemy and return to inflict heavy casualties on the Reds (*Military Writings*, 1:337). Such incidents had occurred. As for looting, Trotsky taught that it is acceptable, indeed desirable, for the state to expropriate property but not for individuals to steal. Everything is morally permitted that serves the Revolution.

Military necessity led Trotsky to seek a "new word" and a "new myth." "What a revolutionary army needs is not a multitude of learned *words* but a clear and scientific *word,* reducing to a system the rich experience of the epoch" (2:219). Trotsky's "new word" was "solidarity." He expected it to "become the new religion—though of course, without any mysticism. As I see it, a new religious bond between men will arise in our epoch, in the form of solidarity—and it is with this idea that we must imbue the army, the people, the school, the factory, and the village." "Solidarity" will inform all areas of Soviet society. "We shall unite education and work with the army. We shall link with it all the various forms of sport" (2:188).

Like Lenin, Trotsky stressed "Apollonian" qualities—authority, discipline, order, carefulness, attention to details (a battle was lost because of a typing error in the orders), cleanliness, and personal responsibility. Socialist solidarity did not mean the "herd instinct," the "disease of our Russian peasant." The socialist economy is founded on the "thinking worker, endowed with initiative." It is necessary to develop personal initiative in the worker.[35] He advocated one-man-management (rather than collegial responsibility) in all areas of Soviet life, stressed the importance of good commanders, and asserted that one well-tempered soldier was preferable to ten half-hearted ones.

Trotsky wrote *In Defense of Terror: A Reply to Karl Kautsky* (published in 1920) on a military train at the height of the Civil War. Outraged at Kautsky's *Terrorism and Communism* (1919), which condemned the Dictatorship of the Proletariat and the Red Terror, Trotsky declared:

> Who aims at the end cannot reject the means[36]. . . . The bourgeoisie, hurled from power, must be forced to obey. In what way? The priests used to terrify the people with future penalties. We have no such

---

34. *The Military Writings and Speeches of Leon Trotsky: How the Revolution Armed,* trans. and annotated by Brian Pearce, 5 vols. (London, 1979), 1:58.

35. *Terrorism and Communism* (Ann Arbor, 1969), 165–66; first published as *In Defense of Terror: A Reply to Karl Kautsky* (1920).

36. This is a Machiavellian *and* a Nietzschean idea. Nietzsche said that "if one wills an end, one must also will the means to it" (*TI,* 95).

resources at our disposal. But even the priests' hell never stood alone, but was always bracketed with the material fire of the Holy Inquisition and with the scorpions of the democratic state. . . . The man who repudiates terrorism in principle . . . repudiates the dictatorship of the proletariat, repudiates the Socialist revolution, and digs the grave of socialism. (22–23)

The "fierce" measures of the Soviet republic were forced upon it by the needs of "revolutionary self-defense" (96).

In response to Kautsky's praise of the nonviolent general strike of October 1905, Trotsky claimed that the strike was just the prelude to revolution and armed conflict. "Only by breaking the will of the armies thrown against it can the revolutionary class solve the problem of power—the root problem of every revolution." That the proletariat "will have to pay with blood, that in the struggle for the conquest of power and for its consolidation, the proletariat will not have only to be killed, but also to kill—of this no serious revolutionary ever had any doubt" (25). Similarly: "The enemy must be made harmless and in wartime this meant that he must be destroyed. The problem of revolution, as of war, consists in breaking the will of the foe" (54). Moreover, Kautsky falsely equated the White and the Red terror—the first was reactionary, the second, progressive—and failed to distinguish between the Whites, who claimed to be Christian and to regard "individuality (their own)" as an end in itself, and Bolsheviks who have never indulged in "Kantian-priestly and vegetarian-Quaker prattle about the 'sacredness of human life.' To make the individual sacred we must destroy the social order which crucifies him. And this problem can only be solved by blood and iron" (Bismarck's slogan) (63). For his part, Kautsky called Bolshevism "Tartar socialism." Minimizing the violence of the Paris Commune, Kautsky contrasted self-sacrificing, idealist Communards with egoistic, ruthless Bolsheviks. Trotsky countered that the Commune was "drowned in blood" while the "international proletariat put before itself as its problem the conquest of power (88–89). The Bolsheviks were not renouncing the Commune, but its helplessness.

Recognizing that the Russian republic faced a daunting task of economic reconstruction after the Civil War, Trotsky recommended that forced labor be continued and, rather than demobilize the troops, he organized them into labor armies performing their duties under military discipline (the *Arakcheevshchina* Bogdanov had feared). Women were drafted too. Trotsky's labor armies were in line with Marx and Engels's recommendation: "Equal liability of all to labor. Establishment of industrial armies, especially for agriculture" (CM, 490; see also CM, 474). They were also in line with Nietzsche's description of a "military state," Fedorov's idea of labor armies directed by a tsar-autocrat, and Peter the Great's drafting peasants to build St. Petersburg.

In Trotsky's version, "labor deserters" were shot. To him, militarizing the economy signified, "in the concrete conditions of Soviet Russia, that economic questions must be equated . . . with military questions" (*Military Writings*, 3:67). He believed it was folly to antagonize the peasants, however, and wanted to end forced requisitions of grain. The labor armies were disbanded as part of the New Economic Policy. In mid-1921, Trotsky justified previous Bolshevik policies. "Every class society (serf, feudal, capitalist), having exhausted its vitality does not simply leave the arena, but is violently swept off by an intensive struggle which immediately brings to its participants even greater privations and sufferings than those against which they rose."[37]

Trotsky's recollection of his experiences as an orator resembles God-builders' paeans to enthusiasm and Ivanov's invocations of ecstasy. "No speaker, no matter how exhausted, could resist the electric tension of that impassioned human throng . . . which had become merged into a single whole. . . . "On such occasions, I felt as if I were listening to the speaker from the outside." The arena "had its own contours, fiery, tender, and frenzied."[38] A passage in the chapter titled "On Power" celebrates the union of (Dionysian) masses and (Apollonian) intellectuals, articulated in the language of Marx and Freud (Trotsky popularized Freud in the 1920s).

> The creative union of the conscious with the unconscious is what one usually calls "inspiration." Revolution is the inspired frenzy of history. . . . the unconscious rises from its deep well and bends the conscious mind to its will, merging it with itself in some greater synthesis. . . . The hidden strength of the organism, its most deeply rooted instincts, its power of scent inherited from animal forebears— all these rose and broke through the psychic routine to join forces with the higher historico-philosophical abstractions in the service of the revolution. Both these processes, affecting the individual and the mass, were based on the union of the conscious with the unconscious: the union of instinct—the mainspring of the will—with the higher theories of thought.[39]

According to Philip Pomper, for Trotsky, "revolution signified those moments of wholeness, when both the fittest individual leaders and the masses joined in the creative act," a breakthrough to revolutionary creativity. Trotsky believed that he and Lenin had inborn qualities of leadership that could not

---

37. Quoted in Abbott Gleason, *Totalitarianism* (Oxford, 1995), 221.
38. Trotsky, *My Life* (New York, 1970), 295–96.
39. Ibid., 334–35.

be taught and that "that the leaders play the role of ego to the masses' id."
He saw himself as an "artist of revolution."[40]

A few words about "Iron Felix," Feliks Dzerzhinsky (1877–1926), director
of the Cheka (the secret police) and a personification of "instrumental" cruelty, as distinct from sadism. Chekists were not supposed to enjoy their work.
Dzerzhinsky hailed from an aristocratic Polish family, had a Catholic upbring-
ing, started out to be a priest, and became a revolutionary at the age of eighteen. The ruthlessness and asceticism of this Bolshevik Torquemada stemmed
from his seminary training, his revolutionary immoralism, and a twisted version of "self-overcoming." "Life rules out sentiment, and woe to the man
who lacks the strength to overcome his feelings."[41] A "left Marxist" in
1905–6, Dzerzhinsky tried to subject terrorists in Warsaw to strict discipline
under social democratic leadership and participated in a multiparty conference in Finland on joint terrorist ventures.

Dzerzhinsky was an ardent admirer of Juliusz Slowacki, a Polish poet of
the 1840s, who was later considered a precursor of Nietzsche and his most
famous poem "King-Spirits," an equivalent of *Zarathustra*. Dzerzhinsky
could recite stanza after stanza of "King-Spirits" by heart. For "King-
Spirits," everything was permitted. Slowacki described them performing
cruel and monstrous crimes and sadistically enjoying them. But these crimes
"were hardening and strengthening the spirit, thus furthering the cause of
progressive evolution." In this way, the love for the most distant, for the
superhuman individuals of the future, "justified cruel sufferings of the
really existing, non-perfect individuals of the present."[42] The Chekists were
supposed to be the most honest, just, and disciplined of people, no matter how lethal or revolting their work. Instead the Cheka became a mag-
net for sadists and a law unto itself, notorious for gross abuse of power
and outright corruption.

By 1921, Nietzsche was a vital element of Bolshevism. The "hard" aspects
of his thought fused with and reinforced the Bolsheviks' activist, heroic, voluntaristic, mercilessly cruel, and future-oriented interpretation of Marxism.
The prerevolutionary intelligentsia had its iron men too, Chernyshevsky's
Rakhmetov, for example, but he was not cruel. Militarization of society went
along with an exaltation of sheer power, of the warrior virtues of daring,

---

40. Pomper, *Lenin, Trotsky and Stalin*, 266–67.
41. Quoted in L. D. Gerson, *The Secret Police in Lenin's Russia* (Philadelphia, 1976),
14. For Dzerzhinsky's support of terror, see Geifman, *Thou Shalt Kill*, 110, 195–96; for terrorists in the employ of the Cheka and its successor, the GPU, see Geifman, 254.
42. Andrzej Walicki, "Nietzsche in Poland," in Freifeld, Bergmann, and Rosenthal, *East
Europe Reads Nietzsche*, 57.

heroism, and will, and with a Spartan standard of living. The values and attitudes of the Bolsheviks discussed in this chapter were imprinted in the Soviet psyche in its formative period and became part of the new society's foundational myth.

Beyond Bolshevism:
Visions of a Revolution of the Spirit

Yes, my friends, believe with me in Dionysian life and
in the rebirth of tragedy. The age of the Socratic man
is over.

. . . Prepare yourselves for hard strife, but believe in
the miracles of your god.   —*BT,* 124

Advocates of a "revolution of the spirit" accepted the
Bolshevik Revolution, believing that a non-egoistic, non-
materialistic, new man was being forged in the furnace of
war and revolution, and that socialism would liberate creativity. Scythians recycled symbolist myths of the 1905–8
period in a new tragic ideology. Futurists called for a "third
revolution," a spiritual or cultural revolution. Proletkult
was inspired by Bogdanov's ideas. Nietzschean Christians
who rejected the Bolshevik Revolution (not all of them did)
had their own versions of a "revolution of the spirit," which
featured rejection of godless humanism. I include them
because they were still part of the dialogue. All the above
viewed the unprecedented suffering of the Russian people
as part of an eschatological transition and, in a land devastated by shortages of food and fuel, disdained concern
with material well-being as philistinism. None of them

defended individual rights, not just because defense would have been futile, even dangerous, but also because they were indifferent or hostile to the very idea of individual rights.

The Scythians

Scythianism was an ideology formulated mainly by the literary critic Ivanov-Razumnik (1891–1981), organizer of two miscellanies of poetry and prose, each called *Scythians* (*Skify* 1917, 1918), and with Bely, Blok, and others, of *Vol'fila* (*Vol'naia filosofskiaia assotsiatsii*, The Free Philosophical Association, Petrograd 1918–24), a successor to the St. Petersburg Religious-Philosophical Society and a haven for followers of the occult doctrine of Anthroposophy, the brainchild of Rudolf Steiner (1861–1925), a former Theosophist and an admirer of Goethe and Nietzsche.[1] The dates of the miscellanies are misleading; the first one was largely a response to World War I, which Ivanov-Razumnik blamed on philistinism, "the eternal enemy," and the second one, a response to the February Revolution. The contributors included Bely, Briusov; Remizov; Shestov; the "peasant poets" Sergei Esenin (1895–1925) and Nikolai Kliuev (1887–1937); Evgeny Zamiatin (1884–1937), future author of the antitotalitarian novel *We*; Vera Figner (1852–1943), formerly a leader of the People's Will; and the future Soviet writers Mikhail Prishvin (1873–1954) and Olga Forsh (1873–1961) under a pseudonym, A. Terek. Not every single contributor was a Scythian ideologically, but Bely, the "peasant poets," and Zamiatin definitely were. Blok published with the Scythians elsewhere, upheld Scythian ideals, and gave *Vol'fila*'s inaugural lecture, "The Collapse of Humanism" (November 1919). Politically, the Scythians were closest to the left SRs, who accepted the Bolshevik Revolution and were part of the government until March 1918, when they resigned to protest the Treaty of Brest-Litovsk.

Scythian ideology distinguished between "revolutionary socialism" (anarchism), typified by Herzen and Nietzsche, and "philistine socialism" (Marxism). The Revolution was creating a new type, a man-artist who, like the original Scythians (from whom the new movement took it name), would never settle down into some sort of bourgeois order, as had occurred in France. Ivanov-Razumnik compared Russians who complained of hunger and cold to Israelites yearning for the fleshpots of Egypt. Russia was experiencing its Golgotha, so Resurrection would follow. The fall of the Roman

---

1. The Scythians also had a newspaper, *Znamia truda (Banner of Labor)*, and a journal, *Nash put'* (*Our Path*). See also Stefani Hoffman, "Scythian Theory and Literature, 1917–24," in *Art, Society, Revolution: Russia 1917–21*, ed. Nils Nilsson (Stockholm, 1979), 138–64, and Renata von Maydell, "Anthroposophy in Russia," in Rosenthal, *Occult*, 153–67.

Empire and the birth of Christianity were being replicated by the collapse of Imperial Russia and the rise of the "new faith" of socialism. The Scythians' "new type" (the Scythian) had Nietzschean traits. He (it was always a he), was bold, daring, and free; his soul was untamed and untamable, and he rejected materialist ontologies, acquisitiveness, dogma (especially political dogma), metahistorical systems, and determinism.[2] A spiritual maximalist, he had his own vision of justice, truth, and beauty. The Scythian imagined by Ivanov-Razumnik and Blok was part of a horde; Zamiatin's Scythian gallops alone over the steppes.[3] The "peasant poets" emphasized the dominance of the countryside over the city and were adamantly anti-intellectual.

The Scythians praised the barbaric potential of the people (*narod*). By "barbarian" they meant the "uncivilized" peoples of the ancient world who accepted Christianity and brought down the "civilized" Roman Empire in which people were thrown to the lions. They expected the Revolution to accomplish an eschatological reconciliation of opposites by exploding the confines of ordinary consciousness, restoring harmony, and resurrecting "eternal Hellenic values." Among the opposites to be reconciled were city and country, intelligentsia and people, mind and heart, Europe and Asia, civilization and culture, the first item in each dyad representing arid rationalism (broadly speaking) and the second, instinct and creative freedom—in other words, Apollo and Dionysus. The Scythians welcomed proletarian involvement in culture, but they insisted that culture was national, hence beyond class. They did not exalt cruelty, but they accepted it as part of a process of spiritual purification and cultural renewal. Their writings are studded with "will to" formulations, such as the "will to cross the abyss."

Scythianism is perhaps best expressed in Blok's poem "The Scythians" (January 1918). The ancient Scythians were Caucasians, but Blok took Soloviev's lines for his epigram: "'Pan-Mongolism'! Though it sounds queer / It falls like a caress upon my ear." Blok's poem opens with the lines: "Yea, we are Scythians! Yea, Asia gave us birth— / Gave us our slanted and greed-filled eyes!"[4] He described the blood-curdling savagery of the East (Asiatic Dionysianism), noted Russia's role in shielding Europe from the Mongols, and invited Europeans to a brotherly feast, threatening them with destruction, should they decline. In "The Twelve" (also January 1918), Blok expressed Scythianism differently. This poem follows twelve Red Guards on patrol in storm-swept Petrograd (the snow storm is Blok's image for Dionysian chaos). Holy Russia and bourgeois Russia have been swept away. In their place are

2. The cover illustration of both volumes of *Skify* depicts a Scythian couple; the woman is behind the man and clinging to him. Both look very sad.

3. For Zamiatin and Nietzsche, see Clowes, "From Beyond the Abyss," in *NSC*, 313–37.

4. "The Scythians," in *Anthology of Russian Literature in the Soviet Period*, ed. and trans. Bernard Guilbert Guerney (New York, 1960), 27. "The Twelve" is on pages 16–27.

looting, random murder, and the crack of gunfire. Callousness, licentiousness and rancor prevail. Nevertheless, Jesus is leading the twelve guards, though they do not know it. Invisible in the storm, He is wearing a garland of white roses instead of a crown of thorns.

Blok perceived revolution as the revenge of the elements (not just the Dionysian folk but the physical universe) breaking through the encrusted lava of rational civilization, sweeping away legal niceties, persons, and property. He had been obsessing about such a revolution since 1908, linking it with cultural renewal and the "spirit of music."[5] In January 1918, he told intellectuals to "listen to the [music of] Revolution."[6] In "The Collapse of Humanism" he proclaimed that bourgeois civilization is dead, that the rationalism and individualism that dominated Europe since the Renaissance are doomed. Already, only isolated islands remained of the once great continent of civilization and they too would be engulfed by the rising flood. Where others heard a "wild chorus, an unstructured howl," Blok heard the musical preparation of a new cultural movement, those elemental primordial rhythms that would form the overture to the new era. "The bell of anti-humanism resounds," "a new man is being formed" (*BSS*, 6:93–115, esp. 112–15). He will be an artist, for only an artist can survive in a Dionysian world.

Bely's new man-artist would unite the Dionysian elements of ecstasy and fire with the Apollonian elements of thought and lyricism in a union of the intelligentsia and the people (*narod*). The "new I" will be complete only as part of the collective. "Heroic anarchy" would be replaced by synarchy ("you in me and I in you"). Each person would become a creative being, but the transformation of the masses into heroes would be difficult, indeed tragic. A Nietzschean Christian in his own way, Bely "compared the new heroes to Christ; each faced a tragic fate and each had to prepare himself to receive the new creative word or Logos within himself."[7]

The Futurists

Mayakovsky, Kamensky, and Burliuk preached a "third revolution," a bloodless but cruel "revolution of the spirit" that would accompany and complete the political revolution and implement their ideas on art.[8] Mayakovsky proclaimed "the streets are our brushes / the squares are our palettes" (in "Order No. 1 to the Army of the Arts," 1918). In another poem, "It's Too Early to

5. "Stikhiia i kul'tura" and "Na pole kulikovom," in *BSS*, 3:350–59 and 249–53.

6. Blok, "The Intelligentsia and the Revolution," in *Russian Intellectual History, an Anthology*, ed. Marc Raeff (New York, 1966), 371.

7. Hoffman, "Scythian Theory and Literature," 157.

8. Details in Bengt Jangfeldt, *Majakovskij and Futurism*, 1917–1921 (Stockholm, 1977), 51–94.

Rejoice" (1918), he asked: "Why has Pushkin not been stood against the wall" (and shot). "Have you forgotten Raphael? / Have you forgotten Rastrelli?" (Rastrelli was the architect of classical St. Petersburg and good for a pun with *rasstreliat'*—to shoot.) "It is time / to pepper museum walls with bullets" and to dynamite the Cathedral at Ascension Square. Mayakovsky was speaking metaphorically; he wanted to prevent the new culture from being dominated by the classics, but his cultural iconoclasm antagonized Lenin, partly because it coincided with an orgy of real vandalism. Nevertheless, Bolsheviks needed futurists for agitation and propaganda, and futurists needed government commissions, so the two avant-gardes joined forces (for a time).[9] The futurists' Marxism was superficial, however, a set of "new words" grafted onto personal mythologies.

Some of Mayakovsky's propaganda pieces featured proletarian supermen. In *Mystery Bouffe* (1918, 1921), a revolutionary mystery play based on the flood, A Simple Man, a composite superman/Christ, leads the Unclean (the proletariat) to the Promised Land of socialism. The protagonist of Mayakovsky's long poem "150,000,000" (1919–20) is an allegorical Ivan/Superman who represents the Soviet population and defeats Woodrow Wilson, representative of capitalism, in a match for world domination. The poem includes the lines: "Clearing away the old / in wild destruction / we will thunder a new myth / over the world." And: "the old people—kill them / Use their skulls for ashtrays." Mayakovsky was still promoting a cult of youth.[10] Lenin called the poem trash.

Khlebnikov wrote agitational pieces for the Red Army and Navy, but his ultimate vision was apolitical and his Marxism highly unconventional. "I announced to the Marxists that I represented Marx squared" (*KhCW*, 1:27). In 1920 he claimed to have discovered the numerical Tables of Destiny. "I wanted to discover the reason for all those deaths" (1:418). In his long poem "Lightland" ("*Ladomir*," 1920), cosmic upheaval generates a new world order, a "creatocracy" in place of an "aristocracy," and a marriage of nature and science brings forth universal happiness, peace, freedom, and (Christian) love. "Run to the rabid watchdog / and kiss his slavering mouth / then go kiss your enemy / kiss him until he dissolves" (3:169). In "Russia and Me" (1921), the poet-liberator grants "freedom to my people" and "suntans to the masses" (3:94). Khlebnikov imagined Mont Blanc decorated with the head of Zarathustra (2:144). At other times, he imagined a universal being, a world body, "a tree of Mr. People" that could be divided into a multitude of I's. In some of his poems the lyrical "I" perishes in the cosmic struggle,

---

9.   For the attraction and repulsion of the political and the artistic avant-gardes from the French Revolution to the 1930s, see Matvei Calinescu, *Five Faces of Modernity* (Durham, N.C., 1987), 100–110.

10.   Maiakovsky, *Sobranie sochinenii v dvukh tomakh* (Leningrad, 1950), 1:284.

but returns to life fortified for future battles—the Nietzschean *agon* coupled with "eternal recurrence." In 1921–22, Khlebnikov wrote several pieces on Stenka Razin, his long-time hero. In "Two Trinities" he pictured the "greatest firebrand of several centuries" as a boy hermit, an anchorite, on the shores of the Arctic Ocean (*KhCW*, 2:146–49).

Malevich regarded the Revolution as the beginning of a new era of spirituality and continuous creativity. "Clear the squares of the remains of the past, for temples of our image are going to be erected. Clean yourselves of the accumulation of forms belonging to past ages." "Let us tear ourselves away from earth-bound shackles. . . . Let tall steeples and flying houses prepare for flight" (from "Architecture as a Slap in the Face of Ferro-concrete"). Note the Nietzschean/Fedorovian idea of overcoming gravity. "I have torn through the blue lampshade of color limitations and come out into the white: after me comrade aviators sail into the chasm." "We are entering a new paradise and creating our new image, throwing off the mask of the old deity. We will no longer build in our own likeness, but according to the perfection marking off our likeness. The new man and our new world are dispersed and our consciousness cannot yet see them as a whole."[11] Malevich also represented this dispersion in his paintings.

Still believing in the occult tenet of a fourth dimension, a realm beyond death, Malevich added a fifth dimension—the economy—in which a united humanity builds a new world, according to a "new single plan of action," his version of a Nietzschean "great project" or a Fedorovian "common task," except that Malevich imagined an objectless universe of pure spirit or energy. He was obsessed with purity. In Malevich's thought, Dionysian dissolution becomes dematerialization and meshes with the occult tenet that the individual is but a microcosm of the macrocosm.

> This is why nowadays no individual person is allowed to have the freedom of isolation or to live as it pleases, arranging a personal economic program for its own vegetable garden, since it must be included in the system of sharing and of common freedom and rights; hence the individual has no rights, for the rights are common to all, and the individual personality itself is simply a fragment from a united being; all of whose fragments must be joined together in one, since they originated from one.[12]

The "united being" expands to "super" magnitude. "Man is also a Cosmos or a Hercules around which rotate suns and their systems. . . . Thus unity after unity joining one-another strives toward the endless path of the non-

---

11. *Malevich: Essays in Art*, 51, 64, 122, 171–72.
12. Ibid., 167–68 (slightly amended).
13. Ibid., 196.

objective."[13] After the Revolution, he founded UNOVIS (Union for the New Art) as a collective; members signed their works UNOVIS to express their desire for anonymity.

Many futurist posters had geometric figures, but no people. Posters that did portray people often blurred or omitted their facial features. The impersonality was deliberate. As the sculptor Natan Altman explained:

> A futurist picture lives a *collectivist life.*
> This is the exact same principle on which all creativity of the proletariat is constructed.
> Try to distinguish an individual face in a proletarian procession.
> Try to understand it as individual persons—madness.
> Only together do they acquire all their strength, all their meaning . . .
> Only futurist art is constructed on collectivist foundations.
> Only futurist art is right now the art of the proletariat.[14]

The latter contention brought the futurists into conflict with Proletkult, which made the same claim.

Proletkult

Originally a loose coalition of workers' clubs, factory committees, worker theaters, and educational societies, Proletkult grew into a national institution. At its peak in 1920, it numbered over half a million workers, mostly young men.[15] Bogdanov was the unofficial theoretician. The first president was Lebedev-Poliansky, a former *Vperedist,* a Party member (he rejoined the Party in August 1917), and a personal friend of Lunacharsky. Bogdanov and Lebedev-Poliansky wrote the resolutions for the first Proletkult Congress (September 1918), except for those on education, which Nadezhda Krupskaia (Lenin's wife) wrote. Art was called the "organizer of social experience," the "organizer of the collective will," and "the strongest means for the organization of the feelings and will of the masses."[16] Artists and writers were urged to draw on folklore in order to make their work comprehensible to the people and to shun abstract forms that the people did not understand (a swipe at futurism).

Tensions in Party-Proletkult relations existed to be sure, but during the Civil War they cooperated. Krupskaia sat on Proletkult's Central Committee.

14. "'Futurism' and Proletarian Art" (1918), in Rosenberg, *Bolshevik Visions,* 401.

15. For a history of Proletkult, see Lynn Mally, *Culture of the Future* (Berkeley and Los Angeles, 1990).

16. P. I. Lebedev-Poliansky, ed., *Protokoly pervoi vse-rossiiskoi konferentsii proletarskikh kulturno-prosvetitel'nykh organizatsii* (Moscow, 1918), passim.

Kerzhentsev, author of *Creative Theater,* headed ROSTA (the state telegraph agency) as well as the state publishing house. Over half the delegates to the first Proletkult conference were Party members; by the second conference (1920) this had risen to two-thirds. Nevertheless, officially, Proletkult remained a non-Party organization.

Proletkult's mission was to create a new man and a new culture. The term "culture" was used rather loosely to encompass literacy and other basic skills; familiarity with the cultural legacy; personal behavior (activism, hard work, self-discipline, sobriety, comradely cooperation); and a new way of life distinguished by collectivism, egalitarianism, productivity, and reason. Proletkult leaders frequently invoked "mastery," "autonomy," "self-activity," and "collective creativity." "Autonomy" pertained to Proletkult as an organization and to the proletariat as a class, not to individual proletarians.

Kerzhentsev defined the "task of the proletkults [as] the development of an independent proletarian spiritual culture, including all areas of the human spirit—science, art, and everyday life." This task entailed "*giving* the proletariat a comprehensive and complete worldview, permeated with a combative socialist spirit and [rearing] strong tireless fighters for the future socialism" (emphasis added).[17] "Giving" also included distributing questions and answers to classes in political education and presenting "living newspapers" and agitational scenarios to workers' theaters and clubs. The top-down approach contradicted Proletkult's declared goal, a new culture to be created by the proletariat itself. To resolve this contradiction, some leaders distinguished between educational and culture-creating activities, and between not-yet-conscious workers and the advanced minority, and advocated concentrating scarce resources on the latter, or on worker-writers and worker-artists who had already demonstrated their talent. To underscore the scientific nature of Marxism, and also to indicate that participants must be qualified, Proletkult studios and theaters were called laboratories.

The Bolsheviks vaunted industrialization as Russia's way out of poverty and backwardness. Proletkult gave equal weight to spiritual transformation. "Proletkult is a spiritual revolution," said the writer Il'ia Sadofeev (1889–1965). "For the old, dark, capitalist world, it is more terrifying, more dangerous than any bomb. They know very well that a physical revolution is only a quarter of the Bolshevik-Soviet victory. But a spiritual revolution— that is the whole victory!"[18] At a time of great financial stringency, Proletkult leaders insisted that "art is not a luxury" and demanded adequate funding for a wide range of educational and cultural activities, including newspapers, journals, and workers' clubs. The clubs were not just for relaxation;

17. Kerzhentsev, "Out of School Education and the Proletkults," in Rosenberg, *Bolshevik Visions,* 343–46.
18. Quoted in Mally, *Culture of the Future,* xxix.

they were intended to be incubators of a collectivist consciousness and loci of a new way of life—functions that Ivanov ascribed to the theater. Most clubs were male enclaves.

Proletkult leaders feared that just as Greece had conquered Rome spiritually, the bourgeoisie might conquer the workers. To prevent this, Proletkult had to be class-exclusive. Lebedev-Poliansky insisted on barring the old intelligentsia. Other leaders wanted to restrict all activities to "advanced" workers. On the local level admission policies varied. Some Proletkults considered white-collar workers part of the "toiling" intelligentsia. Other Proletkults made special attempts to draw in women. There were even attempts to develop peasant Proletkults, which Bogdanov strenuously opposed, lest they impede development of a proletarian consciousness.

What would proletarian art be like? First of all, said Bogdanov, it would extol collectivism. If an individual was at the center, it was not proletarian art. In addition, it would be distinguished by simplicity, clarity, and purity of form, as in the works of Goethe and Pushkin, but with a socialist spirit and an "unheard-of harmony." Militarism, destructiveness, and symbolist "refinement" had no place in it.[19] Neither did hatred, lynch law, and sadism; militancy did not mean militarism. Proletarian art was optimistic as befits a victorious class. Melancholy was a sign of decadence or defeatism. Bogdanov's model proletarian was inspired by positive values and goals; he was not to act like a mutinous slave or indulge in swaggering and bullying.

Bogdanov wanted to revalue the cultural legacy, not discard it, but young, half-educated zealots misinterpreted his ideas, or confused them with futurism, as mandating a total break. The poet-activist Vladimir Kirillov (1890–1943) proclaimed: "In the name of our Tomorrow—today we will burn Raphael / Destroy museums—tear apart the flower of art." Bogdanov rebuked Kirillov; bombs and bullets were soldiers' weapons, he said, not tools for workers building a new life. In factories and plants, class exclusiveness translated into class chauvinism. Workers used egalitarian rhetoric to justify harassing managers and engineers, the so-called bourgeois specialists.

Ultimately, the entire proletariat would become culture-creators, Bogdanov believed, but since this could not be achieved overnight, he advocated nurturing a proletarian intelligentsia and concentrating scarce resources on them.[20] Other Proletkult leaders objected to his "elitism" and denied the need for any intelligentsia at all.

Proletkult writers and artists thought of themselves as Marxists, but Nietzsche endowed their work with some of its most distinctive images, most notably

---

19. Bogdanov, *Elementy proletarskoi kul'tury* (1918; Moscow, 1920); idem, "Iskusstvo i rabochii klass," in *A. A. Bogdanov*, 411–60.

20. Bogdanov, "Nauka i rabochii klass" (1918), in *A. A. Bogdanov*, 360–75.

a proletarian Superman. Taking the word "super" literally, they portrayed workers as giants or titans capable of enormous feats, even miracles, frequently conflating the Superman with folkloric heroes or the risen Christ. A character in a play by Pavel Bessalko (1887–1920) proclaimed that workers do not fear God, because "we are our own God, judge, and law." The hero of Petr Kozlov's play *Legend of the Communard* was a handsome Superman/Savior, clad in a Greek tunic. His iron will saves the workers from languishing in the desert, and he leads them to the Promised Land of socialism. The poet Aleksei Kraisky proclaimed: "Love to you, superman / Lord of the mountains, seas and rivers / Of earth and air. Creator / of both God and miracles." Kirillov described factories as cathedrals to the new deity—man: "Thrusting into the heavens/huge smokestacks exhale incense of the new god-man."[21] Mikhail Gerasimov's poem "Song of Iron" combined industrial imagery with Nietzschean, Christian, and futurist themes. Kirillov's "The Iron Messiah" (Jesus as an industrial worker) did the same.[22] Many Proletkult writers and artists made the collective proletariat their cult figure and icon. Popular Proletkult poems were set to music and became revolutionary hymns. Bessalko, Gerasimov, and Fedor Kalinin (1882–1920) had been in Lunacharsky's circle in Paris. Kalinin, a founder of the Petrograd Proletkult and a government official, had studied at the Capri and Bologna Schools as well. His brother, Mikhail Kalinin (1875–1946), a Party member since 1898, was president of the Supreme Soviet from 1938 to 1946.

Aleksei Gastev (1882–1938) poeticized factory work and called for a robotic iron man—"an iron demon of the age with a human soul / with nerves like steel, with muscles like rails." Industrial, accidents were inevitable, Gastev observed; he had no compassion for the casualties. "So what if there are disasters ahead . . . many more graves, many more fall . . . so what." And

> Thirteen armies to the digging of Graves!
> Take the millions of corpses on the cranes, toss them in the graves!
> Four battalions of madmen.
> Laughing to the sea.[23]

Note the futurist motifs of madness and laughter. Ultimately, the entire universe would be transformed, and all humanity would participate in the process. Gastev's own role, says Rolf Hellebust, "was not as a member of these expendable millions, but the individualist engineer-inventor, the mod-

---

21. Quoted in Mark Steinberg, "Workers on the Cross: Religious Imagination in the Writings of Russian Workers, 1910–24," *Russian Review* 53 (April 1994): 233–34.

22. Full text in David Rowley, *Millenarian Bolshevism* (New York, 1977), 345–46.

23. Quoted in Kurt Johansson, *Aleksey Gastev, Bard of the Machine Age* (Stockholm, 1983), 69, 79, 87.

ern alchemist, the Faustian (or rather Nietzschean) rebel who can be as great a misanthrope in practice as he is a lover of humanity in theory."[24] Not surprisingly, Gastev admired military organization and discipline. In the 1920s, he became interested in the ideas of the American efficiency expert F. W. Taylor and tried to implement them on the factory floor. Gastev's attempt to make man into a machine was so depersonalizing that even the ultra-collectivist Bogdanov objected.

Gastev also advocated the "technicalization of the word"—a precise, super-laconic language devoid of nuances and emotional connotations— which he considered superior to the futurist concept of "word-creation." Other Proletkult poets spoke of a "special language . . . many-sounded, many-colored, many-formed." They interpreted egalitarianism as standardization or synchronization and tended to view workers as interchangeable parts of an industrial mechanism, a mechanism they sometimes described in terms of *sobornost'*.[25]

Proletkult was supported by Lunacharsky and, in a limited way, by Bukharin, and opposed by Gorky and Lenin. Initially, Lunacharsky envisioned a modest culture-carrier role for the organization, but by 1919, he was extolling Proletkult as a new incarnation of the "Church militant," as distinct from the "Church triumphant," a classless society.[26] Bukharin supported the idea of proletarian culture more than Proletkult as an institution. As drama critic for *Pravda,* he proclaimed that the old theater must be smashed and attacked Lunacharsky for his "slavish" respect for bourgeois culture. *The ABC of Communism* is replete with references to "spiritual slavery" and "spiritual subjugation." Liberation entailed (among other things) abolishing the separation of mental and physical labor. Every Soviet citizen was to be acquainted with at least the elements of all the crafts. Even the "most brilliant man of science must also be skilled in manual labor" (237). There would be specialist training, but no petrified specialist groups. What form specialist training would take was not specified, but universities in their present form were unsuitable. "For the time being [they] can be reformed by leavening the professorial staffs" with persons who may not perhaps attain the standard of the "learned specialists of bourgeois society," but who will be competent enough, and who will be able to "expel bourgeois culture from its last refuge" (239). As late as 1922, Bukharin considered educational and cultural construction more important than economic recovery. He never abandoned the ideal of cultural revolution, but developed his own theories on how to go

24. Rolf Hellebust, "Aleksi Gastev and the Metallization of the Revolutionary Body," *Slavic Review* 56, no. 3 (Fall 1997): 509–10.

25. *Literaturnyi manifesty* (Moscow, 1929), 152, 155, 159, 164, 165.

26. A. Lunatscharski, "Die Kultur Aufgaben der Arbeiterklasse" (Berlin, 1919; reprint, Nendeln, Liechtenstein, 1973), 18–19.

about it (see Chapter 9).

Gorky lamented the collapse of humanism, in which he included humaneness, and objected to Proletkult's anti-intellectualism and class chauvinism. He regarded the rioting masses as Dionysus run amok—savage, mindlessly destructive, and cruel—hence more in need of intelligentsia guidance than ever. Only two weeks after the Bolshevik Revolution, Gorky claimed that Lenin and Trotsky had been "poisoned by the corrupting poison of power."[27] In June 1918, he accused Bolsheviks of pandering to the masses' worst instincts and Lenin of acting like a Nietzschean lord of the earth.

> [Lenin] possesses all the qualities of a "leader" and also the lack of morality necessary for this role, as well as an utterly pitiless attitude, worthy of a nobleman, towards the lives of the popular masses.
>
> Lenin is a "leader" and a Russian nobleman, not without certain psychological traits of this extinct class, and therefore he considers himself justified in performing with the Russian people a cruel experiment which is doomed to failure beforehand.[28]

This appeared in Gorky's column "Untimely Meditations" (the title is borrowed from Nietzsche), a regular feature of his newspaper *New Life* (*Novaia zhizn'*, 1917–18), a center of socialist opposition to Bolshevism. Bazarov, a regular contributor, became a Menshevik in September 1917. Volsky was a correspondent.

After the Civil War broke out, Gorky sided with the Bolsheviks. He used his friendship with Lenin to organize projects to conserve the cultural heritage that employed writers, artists, and scientists (which entitled them to food rations), and he intervened with the censor on their behalf. In 1921, Gorky, Lenin, and Krupskaia founded the first Soviet "thick journal," *Red Virgin Soil* (*Krasnaia nov'*). One of their purposes was to prevent either Proletkult or the futurists from dominating the culture. Gorky emigrated later that year. In emigration, he was obsessed with Russian cruelty as a prominent feature of the national character, particularly marked in the peasantry, and associated cruelty with Russia's Asiatic heritage.

Lenin's attitude to Proletkult shifted from grudging acceptance in 1917 to extreme hostility in 1919–20. Not only was the burgeoning non-Party movement permeated with Bogdanov's ideas, Lenin suspected a link between Proletkult and the "Workers' Opposition," a faction in the Party that demanded labor union autonomy, worker control of industry, and an end

---

27. Quoted in Bertram Wolfe, *The Bridge and the Abyss: The Troubled Friendship of Maxim Gorky and V. I. Lenin* (New York, 1967), 67.

28. Gorky, *Untimely Meditations*, trans. Herman Ermolaev (New York, 1968), 88. For Gorky's distinction between a "revolutionary pro-tem" (Lenin) and an "eternal revolutionary" (presumably himself), see 228–29.

to hierarchy and privilege. On December 1, 1920, *Pravda* published a decree by the Party's Central Committee that denounced Proletkult as a petit bourgeois attempt to establish an institutional base outside "Soviet power" and a haven for "socially alien elements" such as futurists and Machists. Soon after that, Proletkult lost its autonomy, Lebedev-Poliansky resigned as president, and the membership plummeted. The next president, Valerin Pletnev (1886–1942), a worker turned playwright, was appointed by the Central Committee. Apparently, Bukharin was his mentor; he had praised Pletnev's play *The Avenger,* about the Paris Commune, in *Pravda* in 1919.[29] An advocate of *partiinost'* (party-mindedness), Pletnev acceded to most Party demands while also trying to fulfill Proletkult's mission, a virtually impossible task. Proletkult faded away and was formally abolished in 1932.[30]

Pressure from Lenin and the Central Committee resulted in Bogdanov being dropped from the Central Committee of Proletkult in December 1920. In 1921–22 he resigned from Proletkult, so as not to jeopardize its existence, and abandoned political activity. Even so, in 1923 he was arrested on charges of conspiring against the Soviet power, interrogated for several weeks, and then released. Dzerzhinsky was one of his interrogators. In the NEP period, Bogdanov concentrated on founding an institute of blood transfusion, a longstanding interest. He considered blood transfusion a scientific way of making people into "blood brothers." In his novel *Red Star,* mutual blood exchanges are systematically practiced as a means of renewing life.[31] He believed that "the broadening of life depends on going beyond the limits of individuality."[32] Surprisingly, Bogdanov got Lenin's support for an institute of blood transfusion, but only in principle. Already ailing, and preoccupied with other matters, Lenin did not provide funds. After Lenin died, Stalin funded it. Douglas Huestis says that Bogdanov's "physiological collectivism" might have appealed to Stalin, and he might have appreciated the importance of transfusion in military medicine, which Bogdanov told him about at length.[33] The Institute of Blood Transfusion opened in 1926, the first of its kind in the world. In 1927, Bogdanov died from an experiment in blood exchange with a young student who was suffering from both malaria and tuberculosis.[34]

29. Sheila Fitzpatrick, *The Commissariat of Enlightenment* (Cambridge, 1970), 147–48, 239.

30. Details in Zenovia Sochor, *Revolution and Culture: The Bogdanov-Lenin Controversy* (Ithaca, 1988), 148–57 and Mally, *Culture of the Future,* 193–228.

31. *Red Star,* 85–86. Bogdanov referred to "younger blood brothers" in a poem titled "A Martian Stranded on Earth" (1924), in *Red Star,* 238.

32. Bogdanov, *Essays in Tektology,* 155.

33. Douglas Heustis, letter to author, May 1, 2001. Details in Heustis's forthcoming book, which will include his translation of Bogdanov's "Struggle for Viability" and "First Year of the Institute of Blood Transfusion."

34. Loren Graham believes that Bogdanov's death was a suicide. "Bogdanov's Inner Message," in *Red Star,* 252. Douglas Heustis does not. He claims that Bogdanov's death

Kollontai was not involved with Proletkult, but she supported the "Workers' Opposition." Championing "worker creativity" and "self-activity," she decried the use of "bourgeois specialists" and complained that "bureaucracy" (a code word for authoritarianism) "binds the wings of worker self-activity, the creativeness of the working class," thereby hindering the creation of "new forms" of economic life.[35] At the Tenth Party Congress (1921), she opposed NEP as a concession to the peasants (which it was). Soon after that, she was removed as head of Zhenotdel (the woman's section of the Party). At the next party congress (in 1922), there were demands that she be expelled from the Party. Instead, a few months later, on Stalin's recommendation, she was appointed ambassador to Norway, thereby removing her from domestic politics and giving the Soviet Union a propaganda coup at the same time. She was the first woman ambassador in the world.

Still highlighting the psychological aspects of woman's liberation, Kollontai argued that during the Civil War, people had time only for the "wingless Eros," for hasty, purely physical unions; but now it was time to move to a higher stage, the "winged Eros": spiritual union and sexual fulfillment in a partnership of equals.[36] Vehemently attacked for this and other writings, Kollontai became more circumspect.[37] She was one of the few Old Bolsheviks (people who joined the Party before 1917) to survive Stalin's purges.

The visions of spiritual revolution discussed above became part of the general culture. *Vol'fila* sponsored poetry readings and lectures that attracted capacity audiences of sailors, soldiers, and workers. Blok's "The Twelve" and "The Scythians" became part of the Soviet canon. Mayakovsky declaimed to huge, enthusiastic audiences. Kerzhentsev's *Creative Theater* went through five editions. Over the course of its existence, Proletkult issued ten million copies of literary works and three million copies of musical scores.[38] Out of Proletkult workshops, theaters, studios, and clubs came future Soviet writers, artists, and theatrical figures. The iron man celebrated by Proletkult poets became a trope of Soviet fiction. The popularity of Proletkult was a factor in the Party's decision to open a "culture front" in 1920–21. Militant organizations of writers and artists who claimed to speak for the proletariat

---

was caused by incompatibility of blood types, a subject not well understood at the time. See Heustis, "The Life and Death of Alexander Bogdanov, Physician," *Journal of Medical Biography*, 1996, no. 4:141–47, and "Death in the Blood," *The World and I*, April 1999, pp. 184–91.

35. Alexandra Kollontai, "The Worker's Opposition," in *Kollontai: Selected Writings*, 184, 199–200.

36. "Make Way for the Winged Eros," in *Kollontai: Selected Writings*, 291.

37. See Polina Vinogradskaya, "The 'Winged Eros' of Comrade Kollontai," in Rosenberg, *Bolshevik Visions*, 127–38, and Barbara Clement, *Bolshevik Feminist* (Bloomington, 1979), 232–34.

38. Gabriele Gorzka, *A. Bogdanov und der russische Proletkult* (Frankfurt, 1980), 27.

were formed in 1922–23 (see Chapter 8). "Bourgeois individualism" was attacked in all these venues, and personal concerns were trivialized or condemned. The individual was supposed to devote himself or herself to the Revolution and "building socialism."

Some of Bogdanov's former associates held, or moved into, leadership positions in the cultural and educational apparatus. Lunacharsky, of course, was the Commissar of Enlightenment; Pokrovsky, a former *Vperedist,* was his deputy. Lebedev-Poliansky became head of the censorship bureau only three days after he resigned as president of Proletkult. In addition, he edited the *Soviet Encyclopedia* (first volume, 1926), was the chief editor of the journal *Literature and Marxism* from 1928 to 1930, coeditor of the *Literary Encyclopedia* (1934), was on the editorial board of the first edition of the *Great Soviet Encyclopedia,* and editor of *Literary Heritage* from 1934 to 1948. Ilia Trainin (1876–1949), another former *Vperedist,* and a personal friend of Bogdanov, headed the Soviet film trust from 1924 to 1930. Kerzhentsev became a promoter of Stalin's cultural revolution.

The Higher Party Schools established between 1920 and 1922—the Socialist Academy (renamed the Communist Academy in 1924), Sverdlovsk Communist University, and the Institute of Red Professors—grew out of Bogdanov's idea of a workers' university.[39] Bogdanov, Lebedev-Poliansky, and Pokrovsky cofounded the Socialist Academy; another former *Vperedist,* Martin Liadov (1878–1947), was the rector. Bogdanov taught there until 1923. The Communist Academy brought out the above-mentioned encyclopedias, which grew out Bogdanov's idea of a proletarian encyclopedia and his emphasis on collective scholarship. The Higher Party Schools trained Party and government officials and Marxist teachers and scholars, raising a privileged "new nobility," which was contrary to Bogdanov's intention. Pokrovsky was instrumental in the Bolshevization of scholarship in the late 1920s.

The Nietzschean Christians

The Nietzschean Christians regarded the Bolshevik Revolution as the culmination of godless humanism. In their eagerness to "overcome" Bolshevism spiritually, they developed integral visions of their own. Ivanov and Florensky reacted to a truly Hobbesian situation by seeking ever tighter bonds of cultic unity. Berdiaev became even more elitist and antibourgeois, and turned his hand to writing history, treating history as myth. Merezhkovsky had always exalted heroes; after the Bolshevik Revolution he sought a "new

---

39. For a history of these schools, see Michael David-Fox, *Revolution of the Mind: Higher Learning Among the Bolsheviks, 1918–1929* (Ithaca, 1997).

Napoleon" to save Russia from the Red Terror. In 1918, Berdiaev, Ivanov, Frank, and Mikhail Gershenzon (1869–1925), organizer of *Landmarks,* founded the Free Academy of Spiritual Culture (*Vol'naia akademiia dukhovnoi kul'tury*) in Moscow. Surprisingly, Kamenev, who headed the Moscow Soviet, helped Berdiaev find a building in which to house the Academy. It was a successor to the Moscow Religious-Philosophical Society and a counterpart to *Vol'fila.* Lectures at the Free Academy attracted hundreds, even thousands, of people. Florensky was one of the lecturers.

Ivanov

Ivanov maintained that contemporary humanity was moving "beyond humanism" to the Hellas of the pre-Socratic thinkers and Dionysus, to a different kind of humanism for which he coined a new word, "monanthropism," literally a "movement toward one-man-ness" or a "feeling of one-man-ness."[40] This sort of humanism, he explained, entailed the development of new feelings, new values, and the fostering of a mythological consciousness that would enable man to overcome egoism and achieve *sobornost',* redefining *sobornost'* to mean an integral humanity, a "single Adam," Adam Kadmon, the primordial man of the Kabbala, reborn, according to Christian Kabbalists in Jesus Christ. He perceived the Revolution in Christian terms of death and resurrection and expected it (the Revolution) to be a seedbed of new cultural and artistic forms.

Positing an "original sin of 'individuation' that has poisoned the whole historical existence of man—all of culture," Ivanov claimed that cults of all kinds were manifestations of humanity's longing for unity, which is constantly defeated by the "many-headed hydra of our culture . . . unable to become one harmonious cult." He predicted that culture would become a cult of God and the Earth, insisting that the cult be internal and voluntary. But he rejected external forced unions. "The craving for unity must not seduce us into concessions and compromises, that is, into establishing outward, apparent bonds where the very roots of consciousness, the blood vessels, as it were, of our spiritual selves, are not interwoven into a single web. In the ultimate depths, where we cannot reach, we all form a single universal circulatory system, feeding the single heart of humanity."[41] The Nietzschean aspects of Ivanov's Christianity are obvious in his exchange of letters with Gershenzon, written when they were roommates in a sanitarium. In the ninth letter, Ivanov wrote:

40. Ivanov, in "O krizise gumanizma i k morfologii sovremennoi kul'tury i o psikhologii sovremennosti," in *ISS,* 3:368–82, especially 373, 377–80.
41. Ivanov, in "A Corner to Corner Correspondence," in *Russian Intellectual History, an Anthology,* ed. Marc Raeff, trans. Gertrude Vakar (New York, 1966), 396.

If at any time you had been in any degree a Nietzschean, you would feel in yourself how it is when lion's claws cut through on man, on that camel-pack animal of culture . . . you would sense how the furious desert hunger of a beast of prey rises in him, compelling him to tear to pieces some living creature he used to fear and to taste its blood. . . . But Nietzsche is not only a tearer-to-pieces, a drinker of blood, and a psychophage—he is a lawgiver as well. Not yet having become the "child" into which, as he predicts, the lion must change, he smashes the tables of the old values, to engrave on new ones *ungue leonis* [with the lion's claw] other signs. . . . He is one of the great creators of ideals; from an iconoclast, he turns into an ikon painter. (389–90)

In the same letter, Ivanov talked about "each unique and irreplaceable human personality" and posited a "human-divine . . . striving for death in order to live. Truth, love, and beauty want to be eucharistic." A value must be crucified and entombed; the "heart will see it resurrected on the third day" (392). Gershenzon was horrified at Ivanov's aestheticization of cruelty and his acceptance of human sacrifice.

Ivanov emigrated in 1924 (Lunacharsky helped him get permission). He settled in Rome, converted to Roman Catholicism, and was sympathetic to Mussolini's attempt to create an alternative to capitalism and communism (as many people were at the time, to their later embarrassment). But he never joined the Fascist Party, which cost him a university professorship in 1934.

Florensky

In the revolutionary period, "cult" replaced "ecclesiality" as the central concept of Florensky's theology.[42] He even called Christianity a cult and asserted: "To a cult [presumably Bolshevism] one can oppose only a cult" ("Iz naslediia," 123). Convinced that cults have metaphysical importance, he interpreted Church art and rituals in cultic terms and attempted to revalue all aspects of culture, including mathematics and science, in the light of Orthodoxy. The cult of Dionysus was Florensky's model, but he also drew on archaeological and anthropological studies of cults. He described them as living organisms, centered on real persons, and united by powerful emotional bonds. Every cult has *its own* way of organizing the world, *its own* conception of space and time, and *its own* rituals. Rituals sanctify reality; they are the core of religion. Aristotle called man a political animal; Ivanov called him an ecstatic animal; Florensky referred to "liturgical man," "*homo liturgus*" (107). In the ancient world, he maintained, the cult was the cen-

---

42. Florenskii, in "Iz naslediia," 87–248. See especially "Filosofiia kul'ta," 195–248; "Tainstva i obriady," 135–42; "Deduktsiia semi tainstv," 143–47; and "Osviashchenie real'nosti," 147–55. These essays were first given as a series of lectures at the Free Academy.

ter of life and not an interpretation. Everything was more or less symbolic and emanated from religious experience. The Dionysian ritual centered on the real body and real blood of Dionysus; "only wine" did not exist for ancient man, or for Christians either (221). The Greeks drunk the real blood of Dionysus (221). He wanted Christianity to return to its cultic origins, to the worship of Jesus as a living person, to His real body, His real blood, a real cross (131). In hindsight, Florensky's emphasis on blood is reminiscent of the Nazi mystique of blood and soil, the defining elements of the German (Aryan) *Volksgemeinschaft,* especially since Florensky was a visceral anti-Semite. During the Beilis case, the tsarist government's frame-up of a Jew, Mendel Beilis, on charges of ritually murdering a Christian boy, Florensky claimed (in private letters to Rozanov) that "real Jews" murder Christian children in order to use their blood in religious rituals.[43] Rozanov agreed and published a good deal on the subject.[44] The Beilis case became a cause célèbre, like the Dreyfus Case in France, from the time of Beilis's arrest in 1911 to his trial in 1913. (He was acquitted.) Merezhkovsky was one of his most vociferous defenders. Rozanov was expelled from the Religious-Philosophical Society for his open anti-Semitism. Merezhkovsky and Ivanov contributed to an anthology called *The Shield* (*Shchit,* 1916), which condemned anti-Semitism and pogroms.

Florensky was a member of the Commission for the Preservation of the Monuments of Art and Antiquity of the Trinity-Sergeev Monastery (1918–20). In that capacity, he tried (unsuccessfully) to dissuade the Bolsheviks from closing the monastery and making it into a "dead" museum.[45] Using language intended to appeal to cultured Bolsheviks, he extolled the monastery as a "living museum," a "Russian Athens," and a "laboratory of creativity." The synthesis of the arts (the *Gesamtkunstwerk*) that contemporary aesthetes seek has been achieved long ago in church rituals that address all the senses in a unique theatricality. Icons cannot be isolated from church ritual, the only artistic environment in which they have true artistic meaning. Moreover, the icons, architecture, music, embroidery of the monastery constitute a creative deed (*podvig*) of the Russian people (*narod*), hence they are "democratic" in the broad sense of the word.[46] The futurists wanted to bring art out of the theaters and museums and into the streets. Florensky

43. Details in Michael Hagemeister, "Wiederverzauberung der Welt: Pavel Florenskijs neues Mittelalter, " in *Pavel Florenskij,* 33–41 ("Von Antijudaismus zum Antisemitismus").

44. See, for example, Rozanov, *Oboniatel'noe i osiazatel'noe otnoshenia evreev k krovi* (The Olfactory and Sensory Attitude of Jews to Blood) (St. Petersburg, 1914).

45. In February 1918, the Bolshevik government separated church and state and prohibited religious instruction in the schools, but it proclaimed freedom of religion and freedom of antireligious propaganda. The Trinity-Sergeev Monastery was nationalized in November 1918 and put under the jurisdiction of Narkompros. In April 1920, Lenin signed a decree that made it into a museum.

46. "Khramovoe deistvo kak sintez iskusstv," in *Sviashchennik Pavel Florenskii:*

had an analogous concept: "Decentralizing the museums . . . creating a living museum that would educate the masses on a daily basis," instead of collecting rarities for art gourmets, the "worst facet" of the culture of the past that truly deserved the epithet "bourgeois" (46).

To Florensky, a church is the sacred space of the Orthodox Cult, the place where the visible and invisible worlds meet. Ivanov thought of a cultic theater as a church; Florensky thought of a church as a cultic theater. He frequently contrasted the "rich organic wholeness of Church culture" to "eclectic and contradictory" Renaissance culture; his ideal was a society in which religion permeated every aspect of life (*Iconostatis,* 147). All culture is essentially religious, he insisted; there is no culture without God ("Iz naslediia," 126–27). Christian culture is "the sanctification of nature, of all areas of life. Art, philosophy, science, politics, economics, and so forth, cannot be seen as self-contained entities" separate and apart from Christ."[47] Christianity must not be passive with respect to this world. For Florensky, as for Lenin, there are no neutral zones.

After the Bolshevik Revolution, Florensky maintained that until the old was "liquefied in total chaos and reduced to dust" it would be impossible to speak of new and stable values."[48] During the NEP period, he thought that the worst was yet to come, and he was right. In May 1928, he was arrested and released. In February 1933, he was arrested again and imprisoned. He was executed in 1937. An essay, penned in 1933, "The Hypothetical State Structure of the Future" was found in the KGB archive. In this essay, he claimed that only a charismatic figure, a "true autocrat," could bring humankind out of its present impasse. "Mussolini, Hitler, and others" (Stalin) were but surrogates for such a person, phenomena of a transition period. They served to "wean the masses away from democratic forms of thought, from parties, parliaments, and similar prejudices," but had no real creativity.[49] Florensky's "true autocrat" was impelled by a divine force. A kind of Christian "artist-tyrant" (*WP,* 504), he would create the structures of the new era.

Sochineniia v chetyrekh tomakh, ed. Igumen Andronik (A. S. Trubachev), P.V. Florenskii, and M. S. Trubacheva (Moscow, 1992), 2: 370–82. Henceforth cited as *FSS.* In *FSS,* also see "Troitse Sergeeva Lavra i Rossii," 352–69, and "Ikonostas" (1918–20), 419–526.

47. P. Florenskii, "Khristianstvo i kul'tura," *Zhurnal moskovskoi patriarkhi,* 1983, no. 4:54.

48. "P. A. Florenskii po vospominaniiam Alekseia Loseva," *P. A. Florenskii: pro et contra* (Moscow, 1996), 178.

49. "Predpolagaemoe gosudarstvennoe ustroistvo v budushchem," *Literaturnana ucheba,* 1991, no. 3:98. Details in Rosenthal, "Florensky's Russifications," 256–58.

Berdaiev

Berdiaev hailed the February Revolution. The Bolshevik Revolution he regarded as a purely negative phenomenon, a poison that must be expelled, a Dionysian eruption of irrational instinct, a terrible soulless Leviathan. When he began *The Philosophy of Inequality: Letters to a Foe in Social Philosophy* in the summer of 1918, he expected the Bolshevik government to fall.[50] In this book, Berdiaev exalted aristocracy and attacked the "bourgeois" ideals of equality and peace, alluding to Leontiev (the "Russian Nietzsche") and the French reactionary Joseph de Maistre (1753–1821), among others, but not to Nietzsche, perhaps regretting the hubris he had expressed in *The Meaning of the Creative Act*. The elitist views were certainly compatible with Nietzsche's distaste for democracy, liberalism, and socialism. According to Berdiaev, the masses neither value freedom nor connect it with their vital interests; contemporary liberalism is a synonym for moderation and compromise that no longer inspires anyone, and constitutions are abstract and formal arrangements, in which it is "senseless to believe" (417–21). Freedom is an aristocratic principle that means "first of all the right to inequality." The Great War was a terrible blow to philistinism, which was to its credit! Spiritually, war is its own goal because the terrible sacrifices it mandates cannot be justified by self-interest. Moreover, there is an instinct for self-sacrifice. The army is a mystical organism, as are the state, the nation, and the economy, which are all part of a cosmic hierarchy; therefore, anarchism is demonic. Almost as an afterthought, Berdiaev mentioned that the Great War was a catastrophe for Russia and nothing positive came out of it (533). In an afterword, added in 1923, he said that rather than try to restore the old world, people must understand the spiritual significance of the Bolshevik Revolution, its meaning for the realization of Christian truth in this world (592).

He had already come to that conclusion when he wrote *The Meaning of History* (*Smysl istorii*) in the winter of 1919–20, which was not about the Bolshevik Revolution, per se, but a metahistorical view of the historical period that began with the Renaissance and was now ending, Berdiaev believed.[51] Marx and Nietzsche marked the transformation of Renaissance humanism into antihumanism because each one denied the soul. After Nietzsche, humanism was no longer possible; he laid bare all its contradictions (155–60). Implicitly justifying his own metahistorical approach, Berdiaev said that "history is not an objective empirical datum; it is a myth. Myth is no fiction, but a reality; it is a reality of a different order from that of the

50. Berdiaev, *Filosofiia neravenstva: Pis'ma k nedrugam po sotsial'noi filosofii* (Paris, 1990), 258–60, 305, 454.
51. Berdiaev, *The Meaning of History*, trans. George Reavy (London, 1936).

so-called objective empirical fact" (21). All great historical epochs give birth to myths. They are a way of understanding the hidden meaning of history, its "mystery." The Pyramids are a "great monument to the human spirit [because they refute] the materialistic conception of history and interpretation of life" (101). That they were built by slave labor (this was not disputed at the time) did not disturb him. It was not the torment and suffering of these years to which Berdiaev objected, but Bolshevism's lack of a tragic component and a religious justification. The greatest evil was human self-affirmation, man's presumption and rebellion against God.

In 1922, in response to Oswald Spengler's *The Decline of the West,* which was indebted to Goethe and Nietzsche, Berdiaev added an appendix titled "The Will to Life [Civilization] and the Will to Culture." Spengler regarded Russia as fundamentally different from Europe. By contrast, Berdiaev considered the Bolshevik Revolution the culmination of a pan-European crisis—the "tragic antimony" of civilization and culture. According to Berdiaev, culture originated in cult, in religion, and matured into a new way of life, losing its soul in the process of objectification. Civilization is impelled by the "will to power" and crude physicality; it create things. Culture is intangible. It creates new values; its achievements are symbolic. This "tragic antithesis" need not be permanent, however; it can be resolved by the "religious transfiguration of life," by the Christian "will to a miracle" (222–23), which has weakened and died in modern (Western) man, but still lives in the Russian soul. Russians must repent and purify themselves before they can embark on their mission.

Despite his hostility to "materialistic" Bolshevism, Berdiaev was allowed to keep his books and his apartment, to write, and to hold a regular open house. In addition, he was allotted a double ration of food as one of twelve well-known writers protected by the Bolsheviks and nicknamed the "immortals."[52] This was at a time when other intellectuals were starving to death and the anarchist Kropotkin was banned from Petrograd and Moscow. Berdiaev was even appointed Professor of Philosophy at Moscow University in 1920, but in 1921 the Faculty of History and Philology, which housed philosophy, was shut down. In the spring of 1922, Berdiaev and Frank began organizing a philosophical humanities faculty under the auspices of the Free Academy. By then, however, Bolsheviks feared that NEP might bring about a revival of "bourgeois ideology." In late 1922, Berdiaev and Frank were expelled from Russia along with over 160 non-Marxist intellectuals and the Free Academy was shut down. Lenin himself decreed the expulsions, which were preceded by denunciations in the Communist press and interrogations by Dzerzhinski, who reported to Lenin. In emigration, Berdiaev opposed

---

52. Jane Burbank, *Intelligentsia and Revolution* (Oxford, 1986), 204. She doesn't name the other eleven.

capitalism and communism as equally un-Christian. In *Une nouveau moyen age* (1924) (translated into English under the title *The End Of Our Time*, 1933), he looked forward to a "new Middle Ages" and praised Mussolini as the only original contemporary statesman.[53]

Merezhkovsky

The great hopes that Merezhkovsky invested in Kerensky and the provisional government were quickly dashed.[54] He never "accepted" the Bolshevik Revolution. To him, it was a "new barbarism," a "metaphysical will to savagery," the realm of the Antichrist. He supported the Whites in the Civil War and fled Russia in December 1919, when it was clear they would lose. In emigration, he sought a "new Napoleon" to topple the Soviet regime, placing his hopes on Pilsudski (ruler of newly independent Poland, which attacked Russia in 1920), then on Mussolini, and then on Hitler. Having long considered Bolshevism a secular religion, Merezhkovsky argued that its messianic zeal would impel it toward world conquest. Our age will witness the "mortal combat of a great religious truth with a great religious lie."[55] He considered Napoleon a synthesis of the human and the superhuman (as Nietzsche did, see *GM,* 54) and described him as not just an Apollonian figure, but as "Napoleon-Dionysus," and called Dionysus one of the "baptized gods," the others being Osiris, Tammuz, and Quetzalcoatl. Conflating "eternal recurrence" with the occult doctrine of Anthroposophy, Merezhkovsky considered Napoleon a reincarnation of past warriors. In his studies of saints and mystics, Merezhkovsky alluded to a "divine ecstasy," a special mystical ecstasy that connects people to God and enables individuals and entire nations to break the chains of necessity.[56]

The views of the Nietzschean Christians seeped into early Soviet culture. Berdiaev's lectures at the Free Academy were standing-room only; Ivanov's and Florensky's were well attended. In the NEP period, their ideas were discussed under other rubrics in academies devoted to the study of aesthetics or classics, and in private study circles such as the one to which Bakhtin belonged. Merezhkovsky's books remained popular. The Nietzschean Christians' alternative to Bolshevism was not liberal democracy, which had

53. Berdiaev, *The End of Our Time* (New York, 1933), 142.

54. For Kerensky's relationship with the Merezhkovskys, see Michael J. Fontenot, "Symbolism in Persuasion: The Influence of the Merezhkovskii Circle on the Rhetoric of Aleksandr Fedorich Kerenskii," *Canadian-American Slavic Studies* 26 (1992): sec. 2, pp. 241–66.

55. D. S. Merezhkovskii, *Taina trekh* (Prague, 1925), 9.

56. Details in B. G. Rosenthal, "Merezhkovskii i Nitsshe (k istorii zaimstvovanii)," in *D. S. Merezhkovskii, mysl' i slovo,* ed. V. A. Keldysh et al. (Moscow, 1999), 130–35.

indeed failed in Russia, but the other side of the Bolshevik coin, a spiritual monolith just as hostile to individual rights and potentially just as brutal. Berdiaev idealized inequality and war. Ivanov aestheticized the blood-thirsty lion. Florensky was fixated on blood (and not in the brotherly way that Bogdanov was). Ivanov, Berdiaev, and Merezhkovsky were drawn to the new myth of fascism. Florensky ended up yearning for a "true autocrat."

Taken together, the visions of the "revolution of the spirit" discussed in this chapter exemplify the spiritual maximalism and utopianism evoked by the turmoil of war, revolution, and civil war. Featuring collectivism (in various degrees), desire to create a new man and a new culture, and in some cases, a will to cult, this type of utopianism remained a current of Soviet culture in the NEP period, both complementing and contradicting the political and economic emphasis of Bolshevism.

Nietzschean Ideas in the Period of the New Economic Policy (NEP), 1921–1927

Under the New Economic Policy (NEP), the government controlled the "commanding heights" (large factories and plants, credit, and foreign trade), but peasants could sell any after-tax surplus and small private businesses were allowed. Incentives worked. By the end of 1927, production had regained 1913 levels in most categories. The workers' standard of living remained abysmally low, however; and the peasants' willingness to sell grain was contingent on the price they got for it, relative to the price of consumer goods.

In the summer of 1921, Lenin's health began to fail. He died on January 21, 1924. The struggle to succeed him began in March 1923, after his fourth stroke, which left him incapacitated. Stalin allied with Grigory Zinoviev (Radomysky, 1883–1936) and Lev Kamenev (Rozenfeld, 1883–1936) to isolate Trotsky. In mid-1924, Stalin changed course and teamed up with Bukharin, Aleksei Rykov (1881–1938), and Mikhail Tomsky (1880–1936). Stalin and Bukharin were corulers from 1924 to 1928. At the Fifth Party Congress (December 1927), Stalin got full control of the Politburo, Trotsky was expelled from the Party, and Stalin began to move against NEP. How long NEP would have lasted if Lenin had lived is impossible to determine; his statements on the subject were contradictory.[1]

The NEP period was liberal only in comparison with what came before and after. Private printing presses and theaters opened (or reopened). The censorship was relaxed, but not eliminated, and dangerous books, including books by Nietzsche, were removed from the People's Libraries beginning in 1920. The Agitprop (agitation and propaganda) section of the Party was expanded; the Cheka was replaced by the GPU, and a show trial of SR leaders and their "collaborators" was staged in 1922. Ivanov-Razumnik was one

---

1. See Alan Ball, *Russia's Last Capitalists* (Berkeley and Los Angeles, 1987), 10–12, 16–37.

of the defendants. By then, an extensive cultural apparatus was in place, staffed by "party entrepreneurs of culture" (Christopher Read's term), persons whose primary loyalty was to the Revolution, even if they appreciated literature and art. Their mission was to mold the masses' consciousness.[2]

Bolshevik leaders were feeling their way in an unprecedented situation. Not surprisingly, their policies sometimes worked at cross-purposes. Encouraging production entailed promoting class reconciliation at the workplace and material incentives for peasants and "bourgeois specialists," but class-based hiring and promotion militated against optimum utilization of personnel; NEPmen (small businessmen) were pariahs, and government-funded organizations of artists and writers preached a proletarian militancy that shaded into class hatred. In 1925, Bukharin encouraged peasants to enrich themselves and advocated "dampening down" the class struggle, but he assured Communists that the class war had not ended, it had just changed its forms.

On the "culture front," Bolshevik leaders were also feeling their way. Marx and Engels offered no guidance on what socialist culture would be like or how to go about creating it. Nietzschean ideas helped fill the gap. Lenin, Trotsky, and Bukharin agreed that a "cultural revolution" was necessary but they differed on what "culture" entailed and how "cultural revolution" should proceed. Stalin was silent on these issues. In 1928–29, he adopted and radicalized Bukharin's strategy (see Chapter 9).

Marx and Engels assumed that culture would change more or less automatically in accord with changes in the economic base. Therefore, Bolshevik leaders feared, the partial restoration of capitalism meant that "bourgeois ideology" would return with it and could even lead to a "bourgeois restoration." Literature and art produced by a hostile class could undermine Soviet power, just as the intelligentsia had undermined tsarism. Fueling Bolshevik worries, the proletariat was an island in a peasant sea; the number of "conscious" workers was miniscule, and new Party recruits were mostly unsophisticated workers and peasants.[3] In addition to all that, the economy depended on "bourgeois specialists," the Soviet Union was encircled by capitalist powers, and there was the contaminating influence of NEP commercial culture. Eisenstein's film *The Battleship Potemkin* (1925) received worldwide acclaim, but Russian audiences preferred Mary Pickford and Douglas Fairbanks.

At first, Bolshevik leaders concentrated on combating "ideological infection" from SRs and Mensheviks. The show trial of the SRs (who were arrested

2. Christopher Read, *Culture and Power in Revolutionary Russia* (New York 1990), 143 and 162.

3. For their low educational and moral level (many abused their authority), see Vladimir Brovkin, *Russia After Lenin* (London, 1998).

in the summer of 1921) lasted several months and was accompanied by an orchestrated hate campaign with full press coverage. Lunacharsky was one of the prosecutors. He called the defendants "germs" (that could infect the entire population) and "vermin" (*vrediteli*, that had to be exterminated), using the latter term extensively in his pamphlet about them, "Former People" (*byvshie liudi*).[4] The term comes from Gorky's short story, "*Byvshie liudi*" (1903), which was translated into English as "Creatures That Once Were Men." The courtroom was packed with hostile spectators and periodically invaded by a preselected mob that jeered at the defendants and demanded their deaths—a new kind of "chorus" in a highly theatricalized trial that was intended to "educate" the public and intimidate critics, actual or potential.[5] The defendants were found guilty and sentenced to death, but in response to protests from abroad, including Gorky's, several of them were allowed to leave the country instead.

Bolshevik leaders soon realized that to prevent "bourgeois" ideas and values from "infecting" the population, they had to be proactive. (The idea of "infection" comes from Tolstoy. He thought that art should "infect" people with Christian ideals, using the term "infect" in an inspirational sense, not as spreading some disease.) They had to combat "spontaneity" by inculcating a socialist consciousness and constructing a socialist culture, despite the partly capitalistic economic base. In other words, they were trying to accomplish a "revaluation of all [bourgeois] values." In an unacknowledged vindication of Bogdanov's views, *Pravda* reopened debate on proletarian culture in August 1922. The heightened emphasis on culture led Bukharin to write *The Proletarian Revolution and Culture* (1922) and Trotsky, *Problems of Everyday Life* (serialized in *Pravda* in 1923) and *Literature and Revolution* (1924).

Religion, one of the most dangerous "ideological infections" was indeed making a comeback, hence the expulsion from Russia of Berdiaev, Frank, and the other non-Marxist intellectuals in late 1922. Also in 1922, the Old Bolshevik Emilian Iaroslavsky (Gubelman, 1878–1943) founded a journal called *The Godless* (*Bezbozhnik*). In 1923 he "unmasked" the mysteries of religion and culture and "exposed" the earthly roots of all cults including Christianity, a cult like any other, in his book *How the Gods are Born, Live, and Die*. The title is a play on Merezhkovsky's still popular trilogy of historical novels. It also connotes, less directly, the idea that the latest god, the Christian god, is dead. In 1925, Iaroslavsky founded the League of Atheists ("Militant" was added later). Members harassed priests, disrupted church services, organized Communist festivals on Christmas and Easter, and (to be proactive), promoted "Red Weddings," "Octoberings" (instead of baptisms), and "Red Funerals." Designers of "Red" rituals included Kerzhentsev,

---

4. Lunacharskii, *Byvshie liudi* (Moscow, 1922).
5. Burbank, *Intelligentsia and Revolution*, 108–9; Cassiday, *The Enemy on Trial*, 42–47.

Iaroslavsky, and Vikenty Veresaev (Smidovich, 1867–1945), author of *Apollo and Dionysus* (1915, reissued 1924) and "On Ritual, Old and New" (1926).[6]

Other proactive measures included subsidizing organizations of "left" writers and artists such as LEF (Left Front of the Arts, a coalition of the avant-garde), and VAPP (All-Russian Association of Proletarian Writers) and their journals. In 1924, the head of Agitprop advocated a literature created according to Party specifications and suitable for the "ideological education of the broad masses in the spirit of socialism."[7] In a related move, the Party encouraged adventure stories with Bolshevik heroes and "Red Pinkertons," after a Nat Pinkerton, the superhero of prerevolutionary detective stories. *Mess-Mend* (1924), a novel by Marietta Shaginian (1888–1982, a former associate of the Merezhkovskys), tapped into the popular fascination with the occult; the "white magic" of the proletarians defeats the "black magic" of the capitalist conspirators.[8] The Party did not mandate a particular art form or language, indeed it declined to do so, but it was widely assumed that sooner or later a single socialist art form would prevail. Rival organizations of writers and artists wanted to make sure it was theirs.

The Party also had to make sure that the neither the masses nor rank-and-file Communists construed the New Economic Policy as the abandonment of socialism, or as a slackening of will or a loss of direction on the part of the Bolshevik elite. The most frequently used metaphors in *Pravda*—"the task," "the path," and "building," as in "building socialism"—signaled control, purposefulness, and leadership from above. *Pravda*'s metaphors were echoed in other newspapers down the line. "Tasks" are usually assigned by a higher authority. "The path" reinforced the meaning of "the task." Lenin used the word "path" to express his conviction that there was only one way to do things, "one strategy, one ideology, and one direction." By the mid-1920s, phrases such as "on the Leninist path" and "the path to socialism" were ubiquitous, and "the path" narrowed to "the line," as in Stalin's "general line." Sometimes "path" and "line" were used together, as when in 1926 one editor equated the "general line" with the "highway" to socialism.[9]

The "path" metaphor did not stem from Marx and Engels. They assumed linear historical movement but used vaguer metaphors. The Bolsheviks may have picked up "the path" metaphor from Merezhkovsky. "The path" is the central symbol of Christian mysticism. Whether or not the Bolsheviks knew

6. V. V. Veresaev, *Apollon i Dionis*, 2d edition (Moscow, 1924). See also J. S. Durrant, "V. V. Veresaev's Reaction to Nietzsche," *Germano-Slavica*, no. 5–6 (1987): 231–41; Irina Paperno, "Nietzscheanism and the Return of Pushkin," in *NSC*, 216–18, 220–22, 224, 230; and Mikhail Agursky, "Nietzschean Roots of Stalinist Culture," in *NSC*, 270–71, 277.

7. Robert Maguire, *Red Virgin Soil* (Princeton, 1968), 422–26.

8. Anthony Vanchu, "Technology as Esoteric Cosmology," in Rosenthal, *Occult*, 205, 212–22.

9. Jeffrey Brooks, *Thank You Comrade Stalin!* (Princeton, 2000), 48–51.

that, and Lunacharsky and the former seminarian Stalin probably did, the "path" metaphor conveyed the religious quality of Bolshevism, an ideology of secular salvation. The "path" metaphor also conveyed a sense of assurance; it said, in effect, that Party leaders had not lost their way, even if the masses were confused. On another level, the "path" metaphor reflected the Party's future-orientation; a communist society was still a long way off.

The Higher Party Schools inculcated party-mindedness (*partiinost'*), proletarianization, and practicality. Knowledge for the sake of knowledge was denigrated as "scholasticism" or "bourgeois academicism." Sverdlovsk University had the atmosphere of a seminary; zealotry and an ultra-collectivist lifestyle were associated with political loyalty. The Socialist Academy, which defined itself against the "bourgeois" Soviet Academy of Sciences, advocated academic planning (organizing and controlling higher learning) and collective scholarship. Scholars affiliated with it brought out encyclopedias, textbooks, and compilations accessible to a broad audience and reworked (revalued) the social sciences from a Marxist perspective. In 1923, the Party authorized the Academy to include the physical sciences. The Institute of Red Professors trained young Party politicians, scholars, and publicists in Marxism. Rivalries between the Higher Party Schools, and within each one, were exacerbated by intra-Party struggles as faculty and students took sides.

The change from "Socialist" to "Communist" Academy in 1924 presaged a broader shift around 1925, when the battles between rival organizations of writers and artists escalated and restrictions were tightened on the import of foreign publications and travel abroad. The Fourteenth Party Congress (1925) resolved to turn the Soviet Union into a self-sufficient, industrialized nation ("socialism in one country") and instructed GOSPLAN (State Planning Agency) to compile control figures (projections) for a comprehensive economic plan. The first versions emphasized balanced development and were informed by Bogdanov's and Bazarov's views.[10]

Despite the situation just described, NEP was the golden age of Soviet culture. The Party's lack of an all-embracing cultural policy left space for the experimentation that made the Soviet avant-garde world famous. A distinctive feature of NEP culture was the coexistence of functional rationality with millenarian enthusiasm as components of an overarching Prometheanism. The latter term implies rebelliousness, struggle with God, the subjugation

---

10. Biggart, "Rehabilitation of Bogdanov," 15–16; Francis King, "The Russian Revolution and the Idea of a Single Economic Plan, 1917–28," *Revolutionary Russia* 12, no. 1 (June 1999): 69–83; *Alexander Bogdanov and the Origins of Systems Theory*, ed. John Biggart, Peter Dudley, and Francis King (Brookfield, Vt., 1998), especially the essays in part 3, "Applications to Economics," 131–220.

of nature by science and technology, and "the deep penetration of reality by *nous* [intellect or mind]."[11] The Prometheanism inherent in Marxism bonded with Nietzschean, Fedorovian, and occult ideas (Soloviev was not Promethean enough for Bolshevik taste). Propagandists tried to replace faith in magic and religion with faith in the wonder-working powers of science and technology. Cosmists, adherents of a quasi-occult doctrine at the margins of science, envisioned the abolition of death, space travel, and an immortal Superman capable of anything.[12] The dominant psychological schools were reflexology and Freudianism. Ivan Pavlov (1849–1936) stressed conditioned reflexes, while Vladimir Bekhterev (1857–1927) emphasized associative reflexes; he was particularly interested in "psychic contagion" and the role of suggestion (*vnushenie*) in social life. Trotsky considered Freudianism a kind of materialism because it was grounded in bodily needs, not in some ineffable soul or psyche. A number of Freudians had been, and perhaps still were, interested in Nietzsche.[13] I suspect that Freud gave them a cover for "scientific" discussions of the (Dionysian) unconscious and the "will to power."

Soviet Marxism was not yet codified. Intellectuals applied Marxism to a wide range of problems and issues, utilizing non-Marxist ideas, including ideas derived from Nietzsche, that they deemed relevant. By and large, intellectuals emphasized construction rather than demolition, rationality rather than ecstasy, science and technology rather than art, and neurophysiological or psychophysiological sensations rather than passion, and they valorized the traits needed to "build socialism"—self-discipline, purposefulness, and sublimation—in addition, of course, to party-mindedness. This reorientation involved Apollonian appropriations of Nietzsche. Bogdanov's tenet that art "organizes" society and strengthens the "class will" was taken for granted. *Red Star* (1907) was reprinted in 1918, 1922, and 1928; *Engineer Menni* (1912) was reprinted at least seven times. *Tektology* had a special appeal to engineers, technicians, and the avant-garde. As before the Revolution, individuals picked up (and reworked) those aspects of Nietzsche's thought, and of his popularizers, which struck them as relevant or useful and ignored the rest.

---

11. George L. Kline, "Reply to Commentators" ("Hegel and the Marxist-Leninist Critique of Religion"), in *Hegel and the Philosophy of Religion*, ed. D. E. Christensen (The Hague, 1970), 213.

12. Michael Hagemeister, "Russian Cosmism in the 1920s and Today: Its Connections with Occult and Mystical Tendencies," in Rosenthal, *Occult*, 185–202.

13. On Freud, see Martin Miller, *Freud and the Bolsheviks* (New Haven, 1988); Etkind *Eros of the Impossible*, 179–257; and V. N. Voloshinov, *Freudianism: A Critical Sketch*, trans. I. R. Titunik, ed. in collaboration with Neal H. Bruss (Bloomington, 1987). Voloshinov refers to Nietzsche on pages 31, 32 (note), 67, and 76.

Nietzschean ideas entered NEP culture through several conduits. Old Bolsheviks such as Lunacharsky, Trotsky, Bukharin, Kerzhentsev, and Iaroslavsky (a Left Communist in 1918) drew on Nietzschean ideas for their cultural strategies. Lunacharsky's power as Commissar of Enlightenment was reduced in 1920–21, but it was still significant. Gorky's writings remained popular, and he kept in touch with Soviet colleagues. Mayakovsky's poetry readings drew huge audiences. Proponents of new aesthetic doctrines responded to prerevolutionary "isms" with Nietzschean components, and to one another, as they sought fresh solutions to the issues of the still-extant Nietzschean agenda. For the generation that came to maturity after 1917, it is often difficult to tell who read Nietzsche, who got his thought second- or third-hand, and who simply picked up a Nietzschean idea that was in the air. Nietzsche's books were being removed from the Peoples' Libraries, but not from all libraries, and individually owned copies passed from hand to hand. Books about Nietzsche, some new, some reissued, were brought out by private publishers.

Literature was a major conduit for Nietzschean ideas. Merezhkovsky's historical novels, Artsybashev's *Sanin,* and Verbitskaia's *Keys to Happiness* interested a new generation of readers. Merezhkovsky's *Peter and Aleksis* was made into a film in 1919. The film version (1913) of Verbitskaia's *Keys to Happiness* was re-released in the mid-1920s and became a box-office hit. Symbolism was a formative influence on young writers and an inspiration for utopian mythologies.[14] Skits produced in workers' theaters incorporated texts from symbolist works. The protagonist of Ilia Ehrenberg's novel *Julio Jurenito* (1922) was modeled loosely on Zarathustra and included characters modeled after Merezhkovsky and Berdiaev. The writer Iury Olesha (1899–1960) depicted Supermen, gravity-defying aviators, and tightrope walkers (Z, 41, 43, 48).[15] Historical novelists portrayed Stenka Razin and other Cossack leaders as deindividuated mythic types, stepping out of the chorus while remaining of it, so to speak, and guided by instinct rather than reason. Scenes of drunken revelry and chorus-like dialogues between the leader and the masses underscore the Dionysian nature of their revolt. Stenka Razin was the favorite subject of the futurist poet Kamensky.

The Civil War, the favorite subject of early Soviet writers, lent itself to a vulgar Nietzschean or Nietzschean/Darwinian approach that accentuated animalistic behavior, brutality, and amoralism. A character in Boris Pilniak's *The Naked Year* (1922, but set in 1919), declares, "Let only the strong survive . . . the devil with humanism and ethics." To literary critics who picked

14. Anthony Vanchu, "Jurij Olesha's Artistic Prose and the Utopian Mythologies of the 1920s" (Ph.D. diss., University of California, 1990).
15. Agursky, "Nietzschean Roots," in *NSC*, 264; Vanchu, "Jurij Olesha's Artistic Prose," passim.

up the Nietzschean subtext, Isaac Babel's *Red Cavalry* (1926) celebrated the beauty of power, even though Babel himself was ambivalent about power and stopped short of endorsing it without reservation.[16] The book contains scenes of horrible cruelty, for example, a former swineherd stomping on the face of his former master to avenge past wrongs. Vsevolod Ivanov's *The Armored Train (14–69)* (1922) became a Soviet classic. Contemporaries regarded Ivanov as "Revolution plus Gorky," and Gorky endorsed Ivanov's portrait of "elemental man." The words used to praise Ivanov—"joyful," "vital," "fresh creative energy"—hint at the Nietzschean thread linking author and critics. Ivanov read all of Nietzsche's major works and owned copies of most of them.[17] Other Civil War novels, such as Iury Libedinsky's *One Week* (1923) and Ilia Selvinsky's *The Iron Flood* (1924), to name a few, portray (Dionysian) upheaval, or iron men, or both.

Katerina Clark sees a spontaneity/consciousness dialectic as the structuring focus of the "master plot" of Soviet novels.[18] This dialectic can also be described as Apollonian and Dionysian, and not just because Lenin's polarities correspond to them. "Apollonian" and "Dionysian" were ensconced in the lexicon, and new publications explained them to Soviet readers. In *Nietzsche, Philosopher and Musician* (1922), Evgeny Braudo wrote that Nietzsche's "tragedy" was his failure to balance his scientific interests (Apollo) with his artistic soul (Dionysus) and stressed Dionysus' capacity for suffering, an oblique reference to the latest ordeal of the long-suffering Russian people.[19] Braudo's book went through several editions. Evreinov (the theatrical director) subtly associated Dionysus with Jesus in his book *Azazel and Dionysus* (*Azazel i Dionis*, 1924), when he argued that tragedy originated among the Semites and that Dionysus was of Semitic origin. In *Apollo and Dionysus,* Veresaev equated Dionysianism with pessimism and decadence and set forth his own philosophy of "living life" (Dostoevsky's phrase). The symbolists and Nietzsche forgot about Apollo, Veresaev asserted, and "so did we." Homer represented the summit of Greek culture, symbolized by Apollo.

In Dmitry Furmanov's novel *Chapaev* (1923), his "diary" about the legendary peasant commander of the Civil War, "consciousness" (Apollo) is represented by the political commissar (Klychkov in the novel, Furmanov in real life). To Klychkov, Chapaev "represents all that is irrepressible and spontaneous . . . all the wrath and protest that has accumulated within the peasantry. But the devil knows how such spontaneous elements may manifest themselves." So Klychkov resolves to "take [Chapaev] captive in an

16. On critical response to Babel, see Gregory Freiden, "Revolution as an Esthetic Phenomenon: Motifs in the Critical Reception of Isaac Babel," in *NSC*, 149–73.
17. I am indebted to his son, Vyacheslav Vsevolodovich Ivanov, for this information.
18. Katerina Clark, *The Soviet Novel* (Chicago, 1981), 15.
19. Evgenii Braudo, *Nitsshe, Filosof-muzykant* (Petrograd, 1922).

intellectual sense . . . to enlighten him."[20] Furmanov mingled fact and fiction in his "diary" to create the impression of objective reporting that was really myth-creation (another Nietzschean idea that was in the air). He demythologized Chapaev in order to create the countermyth of the Bolshevik commissar.

Western art and thought constituted another conduit for Nietzschean ideas. Political and cultural ties were especially close with Weimar Germany, the first nation to recognize the Soviet Union. Expressionism, a Nietzsche-imbued aesthetic movement, was at the peak of its influence.[21] German expressionists politicized by war, revolution (1918–19), and economic collapse had much in common with Soviet futurists. The dramatists Bertolt Brecht (1898–1956) and Sergei Tretiakov (1892–1939) were linked by friendship and professional interests. Meyerhold staged Ernst Toller's *Mass Man* (*Masse Mensch*) as an "urban agitational spectacle," adding crowd scenes and other changes he deemed appropriate for Soviet audiences. Directors of the Soviet amateur theater TRAM were in contact with the German directors Erwin Piscator (1896–1966) and Max Reinhardt (1873–1943). Lissitzky (Lazar Markovich, 1891–1941) and the Nietzsche-influenced architect Bruno Taut (1880–1938) were good friends. Émigrés who returned in 1921–23 were conversant with the latest European ideas. Political and cultural ties were also close with Fascist Italy, the second nation to recognize the Soviet Union. The Italian cultural elite included persons influenced by Nietzsche. Jack London (a Nietzschean and a Marxist, we recall) was extremely popular. Russians could easily identify with the experience of his heroes in the frozen north.

Oswald Spengler's *The Decline of The West,* translated into Russian as *Zakat Evropy* (The Decline of Europe), in 1922, reinforced the Goethe/Nietzsche archetype. Spengler described "Faustian culture" as a "culture of will" and "Apollonian culture" as "classical culture"—two separate periods. Although Spengler's book was banned in the Soviet Union, there were articles about it in the Soviet press, and its contents were known to intellectuals before the Russian translation appeared. Berdiaev and Frank contributed (before their expulsion from Russia) to a symposium titled *Oswald Spengler and the Decline of Europe* (1921), to which Bazarov and other Marxists replied in the journals *Red Virgin Soil* (*Krasnaia nov'*), *Under the Banner of Marxism* (*Pod znamenem marksizma*), and *Press and Revolution*

20. Dmitri Furmanov, *Chapaev* (Moscow, 1955), 71, 118–19.
21. Seth Nayler, *Left-Wing Nietzscheans: The Politics of German Expressionism* (Berlin, 1990); John H. Zammito, *The Great Debates: Nietzsche and the Literary Left in Germany, 1917–30* (New York, 1984). See also Richard Hinton Thomas, *Nietzsche in German Politics and Society, 1890–1918* (Manchester, 1983); Aschheim, *Nietzsche Legacy in Germany*; and R. F. Krummel, *Nietzsche und der deutsche Geist*, Berlin, 2 vols. (Berlin, 1974, 1983).

(*Pechat' i revoliutsiia*).

Spengler interpreted the Bolshevik Revolution as a Dionysian upheaval and predicted that the myth of the future would originate in Russia. "For what this townless people yearns for is its own life form, its own religion, its own history. Tolstoy's Christianity was a misunderstanding. He spoke of Christ and meant Marx. But to Tolstoy's Christianity the next thousand years will belong."[22] Although Spengler's prediction contradicted the Bolsheviks' image of their revolution, it enhanced their self-confidence vis-à-vis "rotting Europe" and reinforced their conviction that they were building a new civilization. They compared themselves to the first Christians and predicted that their reign would last a thousand years, using the phrase "thousand-year reign" routinely until Hitler came to power.[23]

The cumulative effect of Nietzschean ideas entering Soviet society through all these conduits was enormous. They sensitized the Party elite to the importance of "culture" and helped foster extravagant hopes of remaking man, a brutal class-based morality, Bolshevik myth-creation, and a will to cult that crystallized in the Lenin Cult. Incorporated into new aesthetic doctrines, Nietzschean ideas inspired fresh art forms and linguistic experimentation. The new doctrines were politicized from the beginning, or became politicized, as rival groups competed to script the state-sponsored culture. The following two chapters do not treat the full range of Nietzsche's influence in the NEP period. That would require a separate book. This book, it bears repeating, treats only the Nietzschean ideas that became part of Stalinism.

22. Oswald Spengler, *The Decline of the West*, 2 vols. in 1 (New York, 1928), 2:196.

23. Nadezhda Mandelstam, *Hope Against Hope* (New York, 1970), 164; idem, *Hope Abandoned*, 409; M. G. Leiteizen, *Nitsshe i Finansovyi kapital* (Moscow and Leningrad, 1928), 62 and 66.

Concretizing the Myth: New Cult, New Man, New Morality

The content of the tragic myth is, first of all, an epic
event and the glorification of the fighting hero.

—*BT,* 140

The Bolsheviks treated the October Revolution and the Civil
War as a single "epic event," which they mythologized and
invested with eschatological significance. Hell was in the
past, a realm of poverty and oppression; heaven on earth
was still in the future but it was being created. The new
man was also being created, but his qualities were disputed.
The proposed models had Nietzschean traits—which traits
depended on the model. The new proletarian morality
demanded ruthlessness, hard work, struggle for socialism,
and contempt for "bourgeois" comforts and conveniences.
The Lenin Cult provided the Bolshevik myth with a "fighting hero," new rituals, and a temple—Lenin's Tomb.[1]

1. On the importance of ritual in generating a sense of unity and
controlling behavior, see Olga Velikanova, *Making of an Idol: On Uses
of Lenin* (Göttingen, 1996), 46.

The Lenin Cult

The history of the Lenin Cult, from its origin in 1918 (after an attempt to assassinate him) to its elaboration and systematization after his death, has been written by Nina Tumarkin and will not be repeated here.[2] Its Orthodox roots are well known and so is its function: to rally the masses around the Party as Lenin's rightful heir by hammering in the message that Lenin is dead but his cause lives on; the Party and Lenin are one. My purpose is to lay bare its Nietzschean roots, some of which are intertwined with the Orthodox ones. The Lenin Cult marked a new stage in Bolshevik myth-creation. For one thing, God-building lacked an Apollonian image, an icon in Christian terms. Lenin's persona filled this gap.

Casting Lenin as the Superman inspired all sorts of hyperbole about him. Grigory Evdokimov, deputy chair of the Leningrad Soviet, said, in his eulogy: "The world's greatest genius has left us. This giant of thought, of will, of work, has died. Hundreds of millions of workers, peasants, and colonial slaves mourn the death of the mighty leader. . . . From his grave, Lenin stands before the world in his full gigantic stature."[3] Autopsy reports emphasized Lenin's enormous brain, as if to provide tangible proof of his superhuman status. In Lunacharsky's words, the "sage of the Communist world . . . its creator, its champion, its martyr . . . totally destroyed his gigantic brain by his excessive, superhuman, enormous work." In Lenin, "we have seen Man with a capital letter" (a reference to Gorky's 1903 essay); in him "are concentrated rays of heat and light."[4] Lenin was the sun of the Communist universe.

The funeral was a theatricalized ritual. The quasi-Orthodox tone of Stalin's eulogy couched the Bolshevik myth in familiar liturgical forms. In a different speech, Stalin attributed qualities to Lenin (modesty, force of logic) that were later attributed to him (*SW*, 6:54–56). Zinoviev, chief mourner at the funeral and immediately after, asserted that "the genius of Lenin" flew "with wings" over his own funeral; moreover, "the common people, inspired by the ideas of Lenin, improvised this funeral together with us."[5] In other words, the funeral was the product of collective creativity. Similar rituals were conducted all over the country. Trotsky missed the funeral, but his articles about Lenin "often approached the hagiographic tone of a later, more obedient generation." In praising Lenin, says Dmitri Volkogonov, Trotsky was praising himself.[6]

2. Nina Tumarkin, *Lenin Lives!* (Cambridge, Mass., 1983).
3. Quoted in ibid., 161.
4. Quoted in ibid., 200. For the autopsy reports, see pages 169–73.
5. *Pravda*, January 30, 1924; Tumarkin, *Lenin Lives!* 160; Jay Bergman, "The Image of Jesus in the Revolutionary Movement," *International Review of Social History* 35 (1990): pt. 2, p. 241.
6. Volkogonov, *Trotsky*, 238.

Gorky's encomium to Lenin, written and published abroad, opened with the words "Vladimir Lenin is Dead," as if to announce that "God is dead." Gorky described Lenin as

> an amazingly complete incarnation of will striving for a goal that no one before him had put for himself in practice. And more than that, he was for me one of those just men, one of those monsters, semi-legendary and unexpected in the history of Russia, men of will and talent such as Peter the Great, Mikhail Lomonosov, Lev Tolstoi and the like . . . for me Lenin is a hero of legend, a man who tore out of his breast his burning heart in order to light by this fire the way for people out of the shameful chaos of our time, out of the rotting, bloody swamp of corrupting "statism."[7]

Gorky had used the "burning heart" and "swamp" metaphors in "The Old Woman Izergil" (1895), the short story that marked the beginning of his search for a Russian Superman. Peter the Great was widely regarded as a Nietzschean figure (in the twentieth century), and, by some people, as a monster. By calling Lenin a "monster," Gorky was also associating him with Napoleon as Nietzsche described him, a "synthesis of the inhuman and the superhuman" (*GM*, 54). In Gorky's collected works (*GSS*, 17:5–46), the word "monster" was omitted as was Gorky's justification of Lenin's cruelty. "Probably more people were killed under Lenin than under [Wat] Tyler, Thomas Müntzer, Garibaldi . . . but the resistance to Lenin was more widely and more powerfully organized." Also omitted was Lenin's apologia: "Our generation has accomplished a task astounding in its historical importance. The cruelty of our life, imposed by circumstances, will be understood and pardoned. All will be understood. All!"[8] Gorky's unqualified hero-worship was a far cry from his position in 1917–18 (see Chapter 6) and even from the 1920 article in which Gorky praised Lenin as an exemplar of the "sacred madness of the brave." And among the brave, "Vladimir Lenin is the first, and the maddest."[9] Lenin did not regard this as a compliment.

Mayakovsky extolled Lenin as "the most human of men" in terms that connoted an immortal Superman/Christ in his long poem "Vladimir Ilich Lenin" (1924), The lines "Lenin is more alive than the living" and "Lenin—lived! Lenin—lives! / Lenin—will live!" became the Cult's mantras (Fig. 2). The triadic formulation echoes the liturgy: "Christ died. Christ is risen. Christ will come again." Mayakovsky dedicated the poem to the Russian Communist Party, because the Party and Lenin are "brother-twins." "When we say one,

7. Quoted in Wolfe, *The Bridge and the Abyss*, 156.
8. Quoted in ibid., 158.
9. Quoted in ibid., 154.

we mean the other."[10] In the same poem, Mayakovsky gave the violent language of the futurists a collectivist spin. "Woe to the individualist! / Explode united! / Pound with Party / The workers forged into one great fist" (272). And, the Party is "a million-fingered hand / clenched / into one / gigantic fist. / The single—is nonsense, / the single—is nil" (283). Mayakovsky wanted to lead great masses of people as he once did the smaller dithyrambic choruses. The Lenin Cult was the perfect venue. The avant-garde journal *Lef* devoted an entire issue to Lenin's language (see Chapter 8).

Lenin was the favorite subject of the photographer Gustav Klutsis (1895–1938). As early as 1920, when the avant-garde was painting geometrical forms, Klutsis was arguing that propaganda requires representation. His photomontages were dominated by gigantic figures that depicted in stark, visually compelling images the new world being created by socialism. "The Electrification of the Entire Country" (1920) features an enormous Lenin astride the globe, carrying an electric tower in his hands.[11] In 1924, Klutsis produced a series of photomontages dedicated to Lenin (one was in the published version of Mayakovsky's "Vladimir Ilich Lenin"), and an illustrated book titled *Lenin and Children*. To demonstrate that "Lenin Lives!" Klutsis inserted photos of Lenin into crowd scenes, among the athletes at the Moscow All-Union Olympic games in 1927, for example. Reputedly, only under pressure did he shift to collective subjects in the early stages of the First Five-Year Plan, but even then Lenin and/or Stalin were usually present in some form.

The decision to preserve Lenin's body played into the Russian belief that saints do not decompose and, on a different level, into Nietzschean/Fedorovian visions of an immortal Superman. When the body began to decompose, the Immortalization Committee decided to embalm it. Stalin and Krasin, a former *Vperedist* and an admirer of Fedorov, were on the Committee. When the embalmed body was put on display in August 1924, the Party press vaunted the expertise of Soviet science, making clear that there was nothing miraculous about the process or the body; it was not a wonder-working relic. Implicitly, Soviet science would accomplish what Christianity could only promise—personal immortality. Nothing was said about Krasin's belief that only great men should be resurrected.

Krasin, an engineer by profession, had manufactured explosives and engaged in gun-running and "expropriations" in 1905–7, working closely with Bogdanov and Stalin.[12] In his autobiographical essay for the *Granat*

10. "Vladimir Ilyich Lenin," in *Mayakovsky*, trans. and ed. Herbert Marshall (New York, 1965), 249, 255, 256. 284.
11. Illustration in Rita Tupitsyn, "From the Politics of Montage to the Montage of Modern Life," in *Montage and Modern Life, 1919–1942*, ed. Matthew Teitelbaum (Cambridge, Mass., 1993), 85.
12. Timothy O'Conner, *The Engineer of the Revolution: L. B. Krasin and the Bolsheviks*

Fig. 2 "Lenin Lived! Lenin Lives! Lenin Will Live!" In *The Russian Political Poster* (St. Petersburg, 2000). Russian State Library, Moscow.

Encyclopedia, Krasin neglected to mention *Vpered* or his disagreements with Lenin. He did say that he learned German in prison, read almost all the works of Goethe and Schiller in the original, "discovered Schopenhauer and Kant, and made a thorough study of Mill's logic and Wundt's psychology" (which included the idea of mythic archetypes).[13] To mention Nietzsche would have been impolitic, but surely the well-read Krasin was familiar with Nietzsche's thought.

In 1920, Krasin predicted "that the time will come when science will become all-powerful, that it will be able to recreate a deceased organism." He was equally certain that "the time will come when the liberation of mankind, using all the might of science and technology, will be able to resurrect great historical figures."[14] Lenin was an obvious choice. In February 1924, Krasin claimed that the world significance of Lenin's grave would surpass that of Mecca and Jerusalem and urged discussion of a mausoleum in the press and at worker and Party gatherings as part of a monumental propaganda campaign. He had already announced a competition for the mausoleum's designer as the beginning of a campaign to mobilize the popular imagination around the celebration of Lenin's memory.

Krasin wanted the mausoleum to have a platform for speakers, which would have made it a theater temple (Ivanov's idea). The winning design did not include one, but the mausoleum functioned as a temple all the same; it became the central shrine of world communism. The constructivist artist Vladimir Tatlin (1885–1953) wanted the mausoleum to be a triumph of engineering with a huge auditorium, an information bureau with a radio station, and two or three hundred telephones. Malevich proposed that Lenin's body be housed in a cube (symbol of the fourth dimension), and said that "every working Leninist should have a cube at home to establish a symbolic, material basis for a cult."[15] He envisioned a complete cult with music and poetry, and Lenin corners instead of icon corners in Russian homes. The cube would be the Soviet equivalent of "pyramid power," a popular fad based on the mystique of the Great Pyramid at Giza.

The winning architect Aleksei Shchusev (1873–1941) also proposed that the mausoleum be constructed in the form of a cube. In fact, one of his early sketches had three cubes, a modernist rendition of the Holy Trinity. Before the Revolution, he had designed churches and was associated with the World of Art movement. In 1905, Shchusev urged church architects to "creatively imitate" the "beauty and sincerity" of medieval Russian art and architec-

(Boulder, Colo., 1992), 51, 75, 86–87, 107–8; Roy Medvedev, *Let History Judge* (New York, 1989), 32.

13. Georges Haupt and Jean Jacques Marie, *Makers of the Russian Revolution* (Ithaca, 1974), 299.

14. Quoted in Tumarkin, *Lenin Lives!* 181.

15. Quoted in Robert Williams, *Artists in Revolution* (Bloomington, 1977), 124–25.

ture, "not in the copying out and correcting—that is distorting—of old forms, but in the creation of new forms that express, just as sincerely and beautifully as of old, the idea of a place of communion between the people and God."[16] In Soviet architectural politics, Shchusev usually sided with neoclassicists, but he also proclaimed that architecture must express "a new romanticism, a romanticism of revolutionary enthusiasm."[17] The stark simplicity of Shchusev's design for the Mausoleum was modernist in spirit. It was, after all, a cube. The first mausoleum was made of wood. Soon after it was opened, plans were announced for a mausoleum of stone. Another round of competitions for the designer was held, and once again, Shchusev won. The architect Konstantin Melnikov (1890–1974) won the right to design the sarcophagus. Construction began in July 1929 and was completed in October 1930, almost four years ahead of schedule, thanks to Stalin's interest in the project.

The Lenin Cult had a major impact on scholarship. The year 1923 saw the establishment of a Lenin Institute, to study his writings, and a Lenin Museum. Seminars on Leninism at Moscow University, and chairs in the history of the Party and of Leninism, were instituted in 1924–25. Before long Bolshevik and non-Bolshevik scholars, and Party activists, were defending their views with appropriate quotations from Lenin, making his chance remarks into dogma.

The New Soviet Man

The idea that man can be remade, that human perfection is possible, has inspired generations of radicals, not only in Russia, but certain features of the new Soviet man—boundless energy, daring, hardness, physical vitality—derived from Nietzsche. The "new woman" (not a major propaganda theme in the 1920s) had such "male" virtues as independence, activism, courage, and hardness, rather than the "female" virtues of motherliness or compassion. Bolshevik women had to be hard (*tverdaia*), like men. In Barbara Clements's words: "A *tverdaia* revolutionary woman was tough, durable, and if need be merciless. She was also understood to be diligent, rational, and unsentimental."[18] In addition, she was expected to suppress any identification with other women and not to think critically about the gender discrimination that occurred within the Party.

Artists and writers offered two basic models of the new man—the superfunctional machine-model of the avant-garde and the human or superhu-

16. Quoted in William Brumfield, *The Origins of Modernism in Russian Architecture* (Berkeley and Los Angeles, 1991), 104.
17. "Slovo o Shchuseve," *Arkhitektura SSSR* 9 (1973): 12.
18. Barbara Clements, *Bolshevik Women* (Cambridge, 1997), 19.

man model of the realists—and some hybrid versions. An example of the latter is the Stenberg Brothers poster (Fig. 3), which symbolically represents the enhancement of human power by tools. Another example is Lissitzky's montage of a man with calipers coming out of his eyes.[19] The machine-model expressed the early Soviet mystique of the machine as the way out of poverty and backwardness. On different levels it also expressed a materialist philosophy (man is only a machine) and Prometheanism. The human species would create itself, according to its own specifications. Realists portrayed a folkloric adaptation of Nietzsche's superman—big, strong, courageous, and super-energetic—a shock worker (the civilian counterpart to a shock trooper in the army). The shock worker did not merely overcome Oblomovitis; his work was a heroic deed (*podvig*), and he accomplished miracles.

The super-functional model combined the Apollonian principle of form with a secular version of the Christian contempt for the corruptible flesh. Form was the immortal soul of the machine, so to speak, and the human body was a machine made for work, not pleasure. The journalist Fülop-Miller likened the Soviet "imitation of the machine" to the "imitation of Christ" and attributed the skeletal structure of the new man to the Bolshevik intent to rebuild him entirely.[20] In some cases, the difference between man and machine got lost. In other cases the machine was humanized, as in references to its "beating heart" or in the interactive furniture of constructivist stage design (constructivism will be discussed in Chapter 8).

Tatlin envisioned a man who could fly and designed a machine for that purpose, a huge winged glider which he called the Letatlin, after himself, Le Tatlin, or after the Russian word "to fly" (*letat'*), or both. Tatlin asserted that "man can fly with the help of his muscles, the flexibility of his body, and the oscillating movement of [Letatlin's] wings," which were modeled on a bird's. Flying would be like swimming in the air and would be learned in childhood, beginning at age eight.[21] Letatlin required its user to be active (a proletarian and a Nietzschean virtue) and carried no passengers. The society using Letatlin would have to consist of strong, physically well developed individuals, that is, of Supermen. Tatlin's invention linked man with the machine, but did not turn him into one, and it was nonpolluting, evidence of an ecological consciousness rare at the time. Tatlin worked on Letatlin all through the 1920s. It was unveiled in 1931 but never put into production.

Like symbolists and prerevolutionary futurists, avant-garde writers and artists believed that art could transform the psyche, but they couched their

---

19. Illustration in Margarita Tupitsyn, *El Lissitzky: Beyond the Abstract Cabinet: Photography, Design Collaboration* (New Haven, 1999), 69. Above this montage, and isolated from it, is a woman whose mouth is taped shut, possibly an allusion to the marginalization of women in Bolshevik political culture.

20. Fülop-Miller, *Mind and Face of Bolshevism*, 24.

21. Zhadova et al., *Tatlin*, 310.

Fig. 3 Stenberg Brothers, "Symphony of a Great City" (1928). The Museum of Modern Art, New York.

views in "scientific" physiological terms—stimuli, sensations, energy flows—to be consciously selected and applied by themselves to produce the desired reflexes in a new form of social engineering that manipulated the autonomic nervous system. Reflexology did not derive from Nietzsche, Marx, or Engels, but it could be combined with Nietzsche's physiologism and Marxist materialism.

Lissitzky's "The New One" (Fig. 4), drawn for a planned German production of *Victory over the Sun,* in 1923, illustrates his conception of the relation of the director and the "actors." An electro-mechanical puppet, the "New One" was lithe, lean, poised for movement, already air-borne and moving higher, striding across space, a striking change from the slow-moving, massive, super-peasants of the 1913 production (Fig. 5). The puppet had a red square for a heart and two stars, one of them red, for eyes. Its gender was not immediately obvious, if indeed it had one, and it was light-footed, like Nietzsche's "higher man" (*Z,* 305). Had the production materialized, it would have been an agitprop version of the "conditional theater" (discussed in Chapter 1) that was simultaneously a political theater, a *Gesamtkunstwerk,* and a "theater of one will." For Lissitzky, as for Meyerhold, the "one will" was to be the director's. In Lissitzky's words: "Every energy is employed for a specific purpose. . . . All energies must be organized into a unity, crystallized and put on show. . . . All the parts of the stage and all the bodies are set in motion by means of electromechanical forces and devices, and the control center is in the hands of a single individual. . . . His place is in the center of the stage, at the switchboard controlling all the energies. He directs the movements, the sound and the light."[22] If the theater was a microcosm of society, a "microenvironment," as constructivists put it, the puppet was a model for the new Soviet man, and the director, for the ruling elite.

In the early 1920s, Meyerhold developed biomechanics, a psycho-physiological method for training actors that eliminated random movements in order to make the actor's body as expressive as possible. The opposite of the free-flowing dithyrambs beloved by symbolists, and of Zarathustra's "dancing mad feet" (*Z,* 241), biomechanics had a didactic purpose: to present the ideal worker—well-organized, self-disciplined, purposeful, and class-conscious—whose inner communist psyche is reflected in his actions and gestures. The vogue of Taylorism gave Meyerhold's long-held interest in gesture, rhythm, and movement a new thrust.

Taylorism inspired Gastev (the former Proletkult poet) to found an Institute of Labor that featured use of production gymnastics to train workers in precision, punctuality, and self-discipline. As described by Richard Stites: the

22. *Lissitzky. Life, Letters, Texts,* ed. Sophia Lissitzky-Kueppers (Greenwich, Conn., 1968), 347–48.

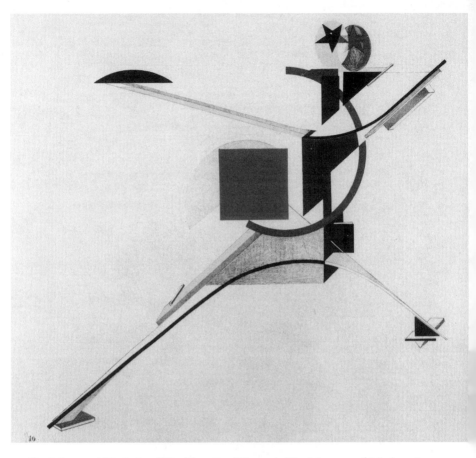

Fig. 4 Lazar el Lissitzky, "The New One" (1923). The Museum of Modern Art, New York.

worker "enters the factory as though it were a battlefield with commander-like briskness, regimental routine, and a martial strut. For him, no romance, no heroic individual deeds, only a relentless battle waged scientifically for production."[23] Kerzhentsev (former Proletkult leader and the author of *Creative Theater*) organized a League of Time (1923–26) that emphasized "social performance"—punctuality, efficiency, and elimination of needless meetings. As Stites noted, Kerzhentsev "really wanted to theatricalize life."[24]

Dziga Vetgov's (1896–1954) cinematic vision of the "new man" was light-footed, like "the New One," and constantly in motion. He loved his tools and enjoyed his work.

23. Richard Stites, *Revolutionary Dreams* (New York, 1989), 153–54.
24. Ibid., 158.

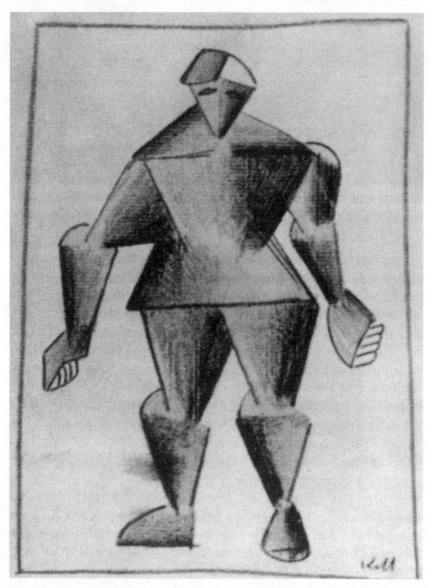

Fig. 5 Kazimir Malevich, "Futurist Strongman." In *The Drama Review* 15, no.4 (1971) 92. Billy Rose Theatre Collection, The New York Public Library for the Performing Arts, Astor, Lenox and Tilden Foundations.

Our path leads through the poetry of the machine, from the bungling citizen to the perfect electric man. In revealing the machine's soul, in causing the worker to love his workbench, the peasant his tractor, and the engineer his engine—we introduce creative joy into mechanical labor. We bring people into closer kinship with machines, we foster new people. The new man, free from unwieldiness and clumsiness, will have the light, precise movements of the machine and he will be the gratifying subject of films.[25]

Vertov's "Kino-Eye" (the camera) was an agent of superhuman perfection and an instrument of perspectivism:

> I am kino eye, I create a new man more perfect than Adam. . . .
> From one person I take—hands, the strongest and most dexterous; from another I take—legs, the swiftest and most shapely; from a third, the most beautiful and expressive head—and through montage I create a new, perfect man. . . .
> Now and forever I free myself from human immobility, I am in constant motion. . . .
> My path leads to the creation of a new perspective of the world.
> I decipher in a new way, a new world unknown to you.[26]

Walter Benjamin noted that the expanded perception of Vertov's camera-eye (close-ups, slow motions, enlargements, etc.) "reveals entirely new structural formations of the subject and hitherto invisible forms of movement."[27] In other words, a new perspective discloses a new reality.

Some Bolsheviks wanted to breed the new man by means of eugenics. A flourishing discipline in the 1920s, eugenics fit in with the utopian and Promethean currents of the time, including Bolshevik scientism. Trotsky predicted that the human species would determine the characteristics of its offspring. "The human race will not have ceased to crawl on all fours before God, kings, and capital, in order later to submit humbly before the dark laws of heredity and a blind sexual selection!" (*Literature,* 255). Soviet eugenicists, mostly biologists or geneticists by profession, claimed their field had tremendous potential importance in human biological improvement as well as in agriculture. They assumed that their discipline was compatible with Marxism, a view also held by the British scientist J.B.S. Haldane, the

---

25. Dziga Vertov, "We," in *Dziga Vertov, Kino Eye,* ed. Annette Michelson (Berkeley and Los Angeles, 1971), 8.

26. Ibid., 17–18.

27. Walter Benjamin, "The Work of Art in the Age of Mechanical Reproduction," in *Illuminations* (New York, 1969), 213, 236.

American geneticist Herman J. Muller, and the Austrian biologist Paul Kammerer, who were sympathetic to the Soviet Union. Eugenicists also called their discipline "race hygiene" until the Nazis appropriated the term, at which point "left" eugenicists dropped it.

The Russian eugenics movement included Lamarckians as well as Mendelian geneticists. The latter assumed an inborn biological makeup, relatively untouched by environmental influences. Lamarckians emphasized the direct influence of the physical environment on the transformation of animals and plants and made the inheritance of acquired characteristics the main mechanism of evolution. Political radicals emphasized the social environment, which affects the physical environment. Some Lamarckians were also Darwinians, strange as that might seem; the combination dates back to the 1870s.[28] Bogdanov accepted Darwin's theory in general, but he believed that acquired characteristics were inherited.[29] Stalin claimed (in 1906–7) that neo-Darwinism was "yielding place" to neo-Lamarckianism. The latter, he thought, was compatible with the Bolshevik emphasis on planning; Darwinism was anarchistic because mutations occur spontaneously (*SW*, 1:304, 380–81). Nietzsche was a Lamarckian for a similar reason; Darwinian evolution was beyond man's control.[30] He envisioned breeding a pan-European master race. Lunacharsky lionized Kammerer, who called for a "Lamarckian socialist eugenics" because genetics makes us "slaves of the past," while Lamarckianism makes us "captains of the future."[31]

The leading Russian eugenicists, Nikolai Kol'tsov (1892–1940) and Iuri Filipchenko (1881–1930), were familiar with the latest trends in European thought (including Nietzsche) and the views of the Nietzschean Marxists. Kol'tsov and Gorky were personal friends. The Bolshevik eugenicist, Aleksandr Serebrovsky (1892–1948), a protégé of Kol'tsov's, came from the family of a leftist architect who knew Bogdanov and Lunacharsky. Serebrovsky believed that genetics was an objective science, but the use of scientific data was a matter of values. Each class must create its own eugenics. A Bolshevik eugenics could help build socialism by raising the quality of the population.[32]

The Russian Eugenics Society and the Bureau of Eugenics of the Academy of Science were created in 1921. Each of them published a journal. Among the issues treated were whether the loss of intellectuals and aristocrats in 1917–21 had lowered the quality of the genetic pool, the impact of enor-

28. Alexander Vucinich, *Darwin in Russian Thought* (Berkeley and Los Angeles, 1988), 6, 82–83, 104.
29. Bogdanov, *Essays in Tektology*, 156.
30. For Nietzsche's Lamarckianism, "to which he remained faithful," see Walter Kaufmann, *Nietzsche* (New York, 1968), 294–95; 132, 192, 294.
31. Quoted in Mark Adams, "Eugenics in Russia," in *The Wellborn Science: Eugenics in Germany, France, Brazil, and Russia*, ed. Adams (Oxford, 1990), 177.
32. Ibid., 173–74, 178.

mous population losses in World War I, the Civil War, and the famine, and the ramifications of the high birthrate of the peasants and the low birthrate of Party members. Kol'tsov compared the later to a stockbreeder castrating his most valuable bulls. Some eugenicists wanted society to prevent "defective" individuals from breeding and to improve the human race through scientific sexual selection.[33] The Old Bolshevik Preobrazhensky did too.[34] Other eugenicists advocated artificial insemination to increase the number of people with desirable heritable traits and claimed that the disintegration of the "bourgeois family" made this possible; women could be educated to desire babies from selected sperm.

Eugenics was discussed at the Higher Party Schools, in major intellectual journals such as *Under the Banner of Marxism* and *Science and Marxism* (*Estestvoznanie i Marksizm*), and in the popular press. The Communist Academy invited Kammerer to head a laboratory in Moscow, and he accepted, but a week before he was scheduled to depart for Moscow, he committed suicide, apparently because his experiments with midwife toads had been exposed as frauds. Immediately after Kammerer's death (September 23, 1926), Lunacharsky wrote the scenario for a film, *Salamander,* which blamed the fraud on enemies of socialism and presented Kammerer as a hero and martyr. The film, which starred Lunacharsky's wife, was shown all over the Soviet Union.[35]

Lamarckian eugenicists objected to genetics, because if the aristocracy or the bourgeoisie were genetically privileged (smarter or more energetic), then the proletariat was genetically deprived and would never be able to rule. Genetics was incompatible with Marxism, Lamarckians claimed, because Marxism posits the innate equality of all human beings and it views man not just as a biological entity but as a social being, subject to environmental influences and guided by social consciousness. Filipchenko countered that "good" genes were distributed among the lower classes as well; all individuals would reach their potential in a beneficent socialist environment.

Most Soviet eugenicists came to advocate positive eugenics, "the direct introduction of desirable heritable changes, whether by the control of mutation or by some Lamarckian mechanism" (as yet undiscovered) or by encouraging people with desirable traits to have more children, rather than negative eugenics, namely, sterilizing the "unfit."[36] The "optimistic" solution was

33. Loren R. Graham, "Science and Values: The Eugenics Movement in Germany and Russia in the 1920s," *American Historical Review* 82, no. 5 (December 1977): 1133–64 (the discussion of Russia starts on page 1144); Diane Paul, "Eugenics and the Left," *Journal of the History of Ideas* 45, no. 4 (October–December 1984): 567–90.

34. Preobrazhenskii, *O morali i klassovykh normakh* (Moscow, 1923), 101–2.

35. A synopsis of the scenario is in Arthur Koestler, *The Case of the Midwife Toad* (London, 1971), 144–46.

36. Adams, "Eugenics in Russia," 174.

more suited to Soviet political realities and in accord with the utopianism and Prometheanism mentioned above. On the popular level, however, genetics was seen as a "bourgeois" science. Radical students were particularly opposed to it because the idea of an unchangeable genotype set iron limits to human improvement and had conservative social implications—at best a meritocracy rather than complete social equality. The controversy over biology versus society, and genetics versus environment, came to a head during the Cultural Revolution and was an important element in later Soviet attitudes to genetics.

Eugenics appealed to the Soviet futurist Sergei Tretiakov (1892–1939), author of a pro-eugenics play, titled *I Want a Child!* (1927). The protagonist, Milda, a biologist by training, currently a Red Commissar on a ship, decides to have a baby according to rational principles; the father must be healthy and "100 percent proletarian." Using genetic criteria, she selects a strong young worker to impregnate her but refuses romantic involvement with him and remains unmarried. The eugenicism of the ship's-doctor, "Doctor Discipline," is even more emphatic. He complains about the low quality of children in the orphanages and wants procreation to be controlled according to health, talent, and class position. Milda ignores talent.[37] In this play, Tretiakov once said, he laid love on the operating table and studied its social consequences. He wanted to rationalize every area of life and render the individual's physiological and psychological state transparent to all. "So-called private life" should be controlled by the collective and leisure time eliminated altogether. Instead of squandering their sexual energy, people should redirect it to industrial production. Tretiakov's separation of procreation from sexual pleasure paralleled Marinetti's progression from a phallocentric to a degenitalized sexuality. Viewed in terms of the controlling figure of the machine, their views celebrate "industrialized fecundity," the body as a deeroticized machine for (re)production.[38]

Realist writers depicted a human or a superhuman model of the "fighting hero." Whether a soldier or a civilian, he was a warrior for socialism. Gleb Chumalov, protagonist of Fedor Gladkov's novel *Cement* (1925), is an epic hero, a *bogatyr*/superman. Gleb returns from the front (in the Civil War) to find his wife Dasha changed, the cement factory closed, the workers idle, and the town in a state of disarray. The plot revolves around his campaign to reopen the factory and begin building socialism. The subplot is the rev-

---

37. This is the second version of the play. In the first, much shorter, version (1926), Milda is a cultural functionary, isolated on an island of petit bourgeois views. A German translation of the 1927 version is in Fritz Mierau's *Tretjakow: Erfindung und Korrektor Tretjakows Asthetik der Operativität* (Berlin, 1976).

38. Andrew Hewitt, *Fascist Modernization* (Stanford, 1993), 151–53.

olution in personal relations. Having become economically and emotionally independent in Gleb's absence, Dasha refuses to resume her wifely role. Their daughter is neglected and miserable in a children's home, but Dasha refuses to take her out because, as a Zhenotdel activist, she must set an example. Ultimately the child dies. The moral is that building socialism is more important than any individual. Allusions to "avalanches of people," "human torrents," "the resurrected music of the machine," "the blood and suffering of our struggle," and "future immortality" shout God-building (Gorky was Gladkov's mentor and read the manuscript), but the purple prose is from symbolism. When *Cement* was published, Gladkov (1883–1958) sent an autographed copy to Bely, his former teacher in a Proletkult school.[39] One of Stalin's favorite novels, *Cement* was made into a film in 1929 and became a canonical work of Socialist Realism. As such it went through numerous revisions.

The formalist critic Osip Brik (1888–1945) called *Cement* a cheap piece of proletarian mythology and found Gladkov's conflation of Nietzsche's Superman and folk heroes backward-looking. Instead of "a *Soviet* Gleb Chumalov," Brik complained, we have a "Gleb-Hercules," or a "Gleb-Achilles, Gleb-Roland, and Gleb Ilia-Muromets" (a hero of Russian folklore). The "construction of Soviet life" does not require "proletarian Athenians" and making Dasha into a "Joan of Arc" does not solve the complex problems facing the new woman.[40] Brik wanted a new, specifically Soviet, image of the Superman.

Levinson, leader of the partisan detachment depicted in Fadeev's novel *The Nineteen* (1927, Russian title *Razgrom*, the Rout), is a Nietzschean "new man" in several respects: he has an iron will, is self-created, and "almost the only man in the company who had not yet forgotten how to laugh."[41] Like many "fighting heroes," Levinson doesn't need sleep, a quality that combines overcoming Oblomovitis with Nietzsche's contempt for inactivity (only slaves need a sabbath) and Fedorov's belief that sleep is a waste of time. Cruel when necessary, Levinson poisons a fatally wounded comrade to prevent him from falling into the hands of the enemy, an act that suggests Nietzsche's concept of "holy cruelty." "But is it not crueler to let it live?" (*GS,* 129). Levinson's solitude is another Nietzschean quality; he is alienated from his family and has no affectional ties with his unit. To retain their confidence he conceals his weaknesses with a facade of invulnerability, ultimately cracking under the strain, but he recovers and fights on in the spirit of *amor fati*. Levinson's solitude is metaphysical and existential, not just situational or tactical. That Fadeev was aware of Nietzsche, at least superfi-

39. I am indebted to Maria Carlson for this information.
40. Vahan Barooshian, *Mayakovsky and Brik* (The Hague, 1978), 87–88.
41. A. Fadeyev, *The Nineteen*, trans. R. D. Charques (Westport, Conn., 1973), 152.

cially, is indicated by his announcement: "We will orient ourselves . . . not upon the Superman, but upon those colossal layers of the populace which are rising to the tasks of literature and whom no one can ever take away from us."[42] Fadeev was extolling the Soviet writer's "humble task" of educating "backward" workers and peasants. Levinson and similar heroes of popular fiction lack an essential attribute of an Nietzschean hero. They are not autonomous agents, but agents of the Party, or the state, which were euphemistically hailed as "the Revolution" or "the proletariat," which were in turn agents of impersonal historical laws.[43] The truly Nietzschean hero makes his own laws.

Robert Maguire describes the "new man" of Aleksandr Voronsky (1884–1943), editor of Red Virgin Soil, as strong, healthy, a fighter for social justice, and "a sort of Russian American who performs prodigies of economic and social construction, solves the riddles of the cosmos with science, and displaces the superfluous heroes of traditional Russian literature."[44] In other words, he is a Superman in the Soviet sense. Voronsky himself wrote:

> [The hero] is always a warrior, always on watch. He is never demobilized, he never rests long or easily. He is always in the masses, with the masses. He is with them in the trenches, in the dugouts. He must develop in himself a scorn for death. His intimate, personal life should be so merged with the social that it is no hindrance at all in the camp life he must lead. He must carry only the minimum of personal belongings, but full military equipment . . . in the old society he ought to feel as if he were in an enemy camp, like a scout. He ought to be able to hate the old world as his personal enemy. He has no "home."[45]

This type of "fighting hero" appears in many of the works published in Red Virgin Soil. The authors were the luminaries of early Soviet literature—Babel, Gorky, Gladkov, Ilia Ehrenberg (1891–1967), Boris Pilniak (Vogau, 1894–1938), Valentin Kataev (1879–1986), Olesha, Leonid Leonov (1899–1931), Nikolai Tikhonov (1896–1979), Vsevolod Ivanov (1895–1963), and Aleksei Tolstoi (1882–1955). The first version of Cement was serialized in Voronsky's journal, Red Virgin Soil. The "proletarian" writers Aleksandr Bezymensky (1898–1973) and Iury Libedensky (1898–1958) got their start in Red Virgin Soil.

N. Gredeskul, a former Kadet turned Nietzschean Marxist, thought that the new man should be called a "co-man" rather than a Superman, to exemplify the collective ideal. In Gredeskul's writings. fundamental Marxist key-

42. A. Fadeev, "Na kogo my orientiruemsia?" Na literaturnom postu 14 (July 1927): 14.
43. Brooks, "Russian Popular Fiction" (forthcoming), p. 33 of typescript.
44. Maguire, Red Virgin Soil, 272–73.
45. Quoted in ibid., 273.

words, slogans, phrases, and terms take on a "Nietzschean surcharge."[46] Glorification of the "fighting hero" went along with contempt for intellectuals as "soft," "weak," "vacillating," "conciliating," and therefore undependable and untrustworthy—traits that were also imputed to women. The highly gendered language used to describe the intelligentsia (a feminine noun in Russian) included metaphors for rape. Implicitly, the intelligentsia must succumb to the proletariat (a masculine noun).[47] In Lissitzky's poster "Beat the Whites with the Red Wedge" the red wedge can be interpreted as a phallic symbol penetrating the white circle, a woman's womb.

Some models of the new man included a cult of the body that vulgarized Nietzsche's physiologism. Veresaev idolized the "radiant muscular Apollo" and contrasted the "Apollonian Goethe" with Dionysus' "holy sickness," associating the latter with decadence.[48] *Apollo and Dionysus* is replete with quotations from *Zarathustra:* "the body is the great reason," "the weapon of the body," the "wisdom of the body," "the first persuader is the body" "create [for yourself] a higher body!" Also quoted were Nietzsche's statements, "there are no facts, only interpretations" and "truth is created, not discovered"—ideas that became important in the 1930s. Each chapter of *Tempering the Body Through Sun, Air, and Water* (1927) a manual used in Red Army Schools, begins with an epigram from Nietzsche, Gorky, Lessing, Byron, or Homer.[49] Instructors used it to promote personal hygiene, athletics, and the martial virtues of daring, self-discipline, and hardness.

Trotsky expected socialism to produce a "higher social-biologic type, *or if you please, a Superman*" (*Literature,* 256, emphasis added). This is on the last page of the last chapter; the entire chapter is a response to "the Nietzscheans" (Trotsky's words) who fear that an "excess of solidarity, threaten[s] to degenerate man into a sentimental, passive, herd animal" (230). Quite the contrary, Trotsky maintained. Emancipated man (species-man) "will reconstruct society and himself in accord with his own plan" (244). He "will learn to move rivers and mountains, to build people's palaces on the peaks of Mont Blanc and on the bottom of the Atlantic. . . . Life in the future will not be monotonous" (254).

> The human species . . . will once more enter into a state of radical transformation, and, in his own hands, will become an object of the most complicated methods of artificial selection and psycho-physical training. . . . Emancipated man will want to attain a greater equilib-

46. Igal Halfin, "The Rape of the Intelligentsia: A Proletarian Foundational Myth," *Russian Review* 56 (January 1997): 92 and 102.

47. Ibid., 94–99.

48. Veresaev, *Apollon i Dionis,* 119–21, 130, 135.

49. Mark von Hagen, "School of the Revolution: Workers and Peasants in the Red Army, 1918–1928" (Ph.D. diss., Stanford University, 1984), 372.

rium in the work of his organs and a more proportional developing and wearing out of tissues in order to reduce the fear of death. . . . Man will become immeasurably stronger, wise, and subtler; his body will become more harmonized, his movements more rhythmic, his voice more musical. The forms of life will become dynamically dramatic. The average human type will rise to the heights of an Aristotle, a Goethe, or a Marx. And above this ridge, new peaks will arise. (254–56)

As for woman, she "will at last free herself from her semi-servile condition." (253). That was all that Trotsky said about women.

Proletarian Morality

Marx and Engels assumed that after a harsh transition period a humane socialist morality would prevail, and then wither away along with the state and law. Most Bolsheviks agreed. In the interim, a ruthless proletarian morality was in force which devalued the individual, sanctioned brutality against class enemies, and mandated hard work, self-discipline, and a Spartan lifestyle for leaders and masses alike. The true communist was supposed to scorn the comforts of home and material things, not only because the masses lacked them, but also as part of a Party-directed onslaught against the bourgeois way of life (*byt*). The onslaught had an aesthetic component, encapsulated in the slogan "Down with domestic trash!" (clutter, unnecessary objects). The scorn for comfort and material things was a residue of the self-denying kenotic ideal, and was also in the spirit of Zarathustra's contempt for the "soft bed and what is pleasant" (*Z*, 101). A crude utilitarianism excluded human warmth, romance, love, tenderness, and compassion. Students at Sverdlovsk University were told that "Nepification" did not relieve them of their mission as fighters. Personal life could not be separated from Party life; Communists had to set behavioral standards for the masses. Their mission precluded a disorderly sex life, drunkenness, fancy dress, jewelry, taking wives from hostile classes, and participating in religious rituals.[50]

Proletarian morality provided a rationale for all sorts of conduct, including denouncing a rival to the secret police. One critic attacked Babel's *Red Cavalry* as an attempt to justify revolutionary violence with such "petit bourgeois" concepts as right and wrong. "This alone is bad enough. Morality has no jurisdiction over the revolution. On the contrary, revolution has jurisdiction over ethics."[51] Mayakovsky and the "proletarian" writer Ilia Vardin

---

50. A. A. Solts, "Communist Ethics," in Rosenberg, *Bolshevik Visions*, 42–54.
51. Quoted in Freiden, "Revolution as an Esthetic Phenomenon," in *NSC*, 161.

(1890–1943) belonged to rival organizations but they agreed on the need for a "literary Cheka" (to be controlled by their organization, of course). Brik reminded his contemporaries of Briusov's opposition to Lenin's "Party Organization and Party Literature" in 1905 and supported Lenin's position that literature must be integrated with Party work.

People were supposed to turn their backs on "bourgeois morality," "abstract humanism," and family ties if they impeded socialist goals. In his eulogy to the populist writer Vladimir Korolenko (1853–1921), who died of starvation, Lunacharsky said: "Righteous men are appalled by the blood on our hands. Righteous men are in despair over our cruelty. The righteous man will never understand that love 'demands expiatory victims,' that it is not only a question of self-sacrifice (this he understands), but also of the sacrifice of others." Korolenko was "too much of a humanitarian to be a good revolutionary."[52]

Dzerzhinsky became the exemplar of dispassionate, selfless cruelty, of "holy cruelty" in the Nietzschean sense. If class enemies were allowed to live, they could destroy the Revolution. After his death Dzerzhinsky became a cult figure. Mayakovsky and the poet Eduard Bagritsky (Dziubin, 1897–1934) wrote poems to "iron Felix." His admirers compared him to Christ because both gave themselves to redeem man's sins. But Dzerzhinsky, it was said, took the sins of mass murder and torture upon himself, committing them "in the name of the creation of a Heavenly Kingdom on earth. So that in Soviet iconography, the Crucified Lord is replaced by a Holy Executioner."[53]

"Iron Felix" was appalled by the plight of homeless children (the *besprizorniki*) and organized a committee to save them. To demonstrate that anyone could be rehabilitated, he founded a children's colony in 1924. The GPU soon had several children's colonies under its jurisdiction. Some Chekists (the term was used for employees of the Cheka in its successive incarnations—GPU, NKVD, MVD, KGB) believed that homeless children were "splendid material for breeding the new Soviet man," because they were untainted by their parents' values. Other Chekists referred disparagingly to their boss's "baby farm." Outside the GPU there was also disagreement. A Komsomol activist held that street life nurtured Soviet virtues—boldness, resourcefulness, perceptiveness, and a collectivist spirit. The educational theorist Viktor Shulgin (1894–1965) viewed the *besprizorniki* as allies in the fight for socialism because they lived in constant struggle with bourgeois notions of property and order. "They are objectively interested in the destruction of bourgeois society and they are destroying and undermining it." Other educators believed that the *besprizorniki* were "morally defec-

---

52. Quoted in Maurice Friedberg, *Russian Classics in Soviet Jackets* (New York, 1962), 98.
53. Andrei Sinyavsky, *Soviet Civilization* (New York, 1990), 126; see also 129–30.

tive," because they were born that way or had been irrevocably damaged by their experiences.[54]

A stock figure of literature and theater was a person who either lacked human feelings or suppressed them for the sake of the Revolution. A character in Libedinsky's novel about an episode on the Civil War, *One Week* (1924), advocated the transformation of "great pity into great hatred." The ideal was a man of iron. A frequently performed play, *Liubov Iarovaia,* depicted a schoolteacher who "heroically" betrays her SR husband. Around 1925, some writers began to depict human solidarity across class lines, but "left" writers denounced them.

The term *burzhui* (feminine *burzhuika*), stemming from "bourgeois," was used very loosely, often in a context that connoted poisonous weeds that had to be removed. The chilling term "former people" (*byvshie liudi*), usually softened in translation to "people of the past" or "has beens," became a commonplace in literature and theater, subliminally disseminating the idea that some people are not quite human. *Lishentsy* pertained to a legal category, a subclass without civil rights. Etymologically, the term is related to the superfluous man (*lishnii chelovek*) of nineteenth-century Russian literature. *Lishentsy* were people whose income did not come from their own labor; the category encompassed peasants who hired temporary labor, clergymen, NEPmen, and petty traders, including the impoverished Jewish peddlars of the old Pale of Settlement. These people paid a special tax, could not vote, could not bear arms in defense of the Republic, and were denied equal access to food rations, housing, medical care, employment, and higher education. Periodic "social purges" removed teachers and students of the wrong class origin from the schools. Concealment of social origins was grounds for expulsion. Like the Nazi definition of a Jew, *lishenets* status was hereditary. Children of *lishentsy* were barred from Soviet youth organizations and higher educational institutions. Exceptions were made, however, and enforcement was uneven. Some people managed to conceal their class origin and "pass." Persons involved in "socially useful labor" for at least five years could shed their *lishentsy* status. Unemployment was a problem all during the NEP period, however, and *lishentsy* were last hired, first fired. *Kulaks* (so-called rich peasants) were not categorized as *lishentsy;* they could vote and be elected to village soviets, but after the Party decided to "revive the soviets" (in 1924), it manipulated elections to produce the proper socioeconomic mix of poor and middle peasants, Party members, and demobilized war veterans.[55] Periodic

---

54. Alan Ball, *And Now My Soul is Hardened: Abandoned Children in Soviet Russia* (Berkeley and Los Angeles, 1994), 129, 192; Mikhail Heller, *Cogs in a Wheel: The Formation of Soviet Man* (New York, 1988), 173.

55. Glennys Young, *Power and the Sacred in Revolutionary Russia* (University Park, Pa, 1997), 142–46.

roundups of *lishentsy* for "rehabilitation through labor" (forced labor) occurred through the 1920s and became routine after 1928–29, when kulaks were targeted as well. Also rounded up were women who resorted to prostitution to feed themselves and their children. The category of *lishentsy* was eliminated in the Stalin Constitution of 1936, but by then so were most *lishentsy*. Those that remained were retargeted in 1937–38.

In the mid-1920s, the Bolsheviks began to worry that the collapse of bourgeois morality was leading to amoralism and ideological confusion. One reason that Tretiakov's *I Want a Child!* was not produced was Milda's refusal to marry. Social service agencies were swamped with destitute women and children seeking support. Open interest in the occult, religion, symbolism, and pornography was growing. To the Bolsheviks all this smacked of pre-revolutionary decadence. Communists who fought in the Civil War complained that their sacrifices were in vain, while younger Communists regretted missing out on their chance for heroism. Condemnations of sexual promiscuity, mistreatment of women, abandonment of children, alcoholism, drug abuse, idleness, and hooliganism appeared regularly in the Party press, and government-sponsored films warned against the dangers of syphilis and abortion. Freud was attacked for his "mechanical" theories on sex. The avantgarde journal *New Lef* bewailed the waste of sexual energy (*RF,* 266).

The Bolsheviks regarded the cult of Esenin that developed after the poet's suicide in 1925, and included a vulgarized "Nietzschean" amoralism and aspects of Scythianism, as symptomatic of a deeper ailment. Bukharin attacked the *Eseninshchina* as the idealization of backwardness, of the "slavish past," and associated greatness with sobriety and hard work. Anyone who "reveled in his own slavery was a boor" (*kham*), a term popularized by Merezhkovsky in *Griadushchii Kham.*[56] Bukharin advocated regulating the everyday life of young people and Communist education; the latter included intensifying the struggle against populism, liberal Marxism, and God-seeking—still considered dangerous.[57]

In 1926, the Komsomol set about "colonizing" everyday life. Books addressed to young people attacked religion, alcoholism, sexual promiscuity, pleasure-seeking, desire for consumer goods, and personal irresponsibility as bourgeois philistinism. One example is *The Old and The New Way of Life (Byt),* (1927), written by two Komsomol activists, with an introduction by Lunacharsky. Denouncing the *Eseninshchina,* the authors called for a socialist morality and praised the "complete 'revaluation of values'" exemplified by a village lad who served in the Red Army and returned to

---

56. *Pravda,* January 12, 1927; reprinted in N. Bukharin, *Zlye zametki* (Letchworth, 1979), 14–15, 20, 24.

57. Nikolai Bukharin, *K novomu pokoleniiu* (Moscow, 1990), 68–70, 217–18, 307–10.

his village transformed, propagating socialism in word and deed.[58] Kant's moral imperatives were unsuited to the new order. The authors called him a bourgeois moralist accepted only by opportunists who have betrayed their class (115–16). A socialist morality was based on expediency (an unacknowledged adaptation of Bogdanov's idea of expediency norms).

> The Communist Party will not throw out of its moral lexicon such conceptions as "truth" [istina], "justice," "good," "evil," and so on. But all these conceptions will be filled with other content. . . . We speak of truth from the point of view of the interests of the working class. A "just" or "unjust" deed we examine from the side of its revolutionary expediency: "Good" and "evil" also preserve their meaning insofar as these conceptions are connected in our representations with class expediency. (126)

Another book, M. Rafael's For the New Man (1927, 1928), also written by a Komsomol activist, trumpeted Soviet progress. Despite difficult conditions, a "real cultural Olympus" was being created in Soviet factories and plants. Every newspaper displays the "authentic creativity of the people [narod]. . . . Every newspaper reflects the greatest effort, "the will to labor," "the will to overcome old bad habits," the "will to create a new man."[59] (Note the Nietzschean formulations.) Nevertheless, obstacles remain in the path to the new man. Among them were Sanin and The Keys to Happiness (still popular among young people), the Eseninshchina, "cults of madmen," suicide clubs, Schopenhauer's pessimistic philosophy, "unhealthy circumstances," and miscreants and malefactors, whose names Rafael made into negative symbols (15–16, 46, 55–57). "Iurovshchina," after an Andrei Iurov, referred to students who "succumbed to pessimism" and sought a "philistine super-existence" (sverkhbytie) (51–52). Semenovshchina, after a factory worker whose prank resulted in the death of another worker, meant hooliganism, "militant philistinism," and "anarcho-individualism," falsely regarded as "heroic." Such types were particularly "harmful and dangerous" (65). Young workers must combat "slavish" attitudes toward labor and "boorish" (khamskii) attitudes to other people, by creating their own clubs, theaters, and cinemas. They must also "liquidate illiteracy" for in addition to a "culture of labor" (hard work and sobriety), a "culture of rest" (proper use of leisure time) was also needed (98–99). Cultural revolution could not be accomplished without pain and sacrifice. After all, "we are not living in the times of Vladimir Soloviev" (105).

---

58. V. Grigorev and S. Shkotov, Staryi i novyi byt (Moscow, 1927), 92. Thanks to Anne Gorsuch for lending me her copy.
59. M. Rafail, Za novogo cheloveka (Moscow, 1928), 22–26.

A different myth was propounded by a group of émigrés known as the *Smenovekhovtsy,* after their manifesto, *Smena vekh* (Change of Landmarks, 1921).[60] Ardent Russian nationalists, they exalted powerful rulers, perceived the Bolshevik Revolution as an organic outgrowth of Russian history, and accepted brutality on national grounds, rather than class grounds. Welcoming NEP as Russia's Thermidor, they advocated reconciliation with the Soviet government, and encouraged émigrés to return. Nikolai Ustrialov (1890–1938), a resident of Harbin, Manchuria, and the movement's most prominent advocate, called himself a National Bolshevik and Struve's disciple (to Struve's dismay) and claimed to be continuing the dialogue that *Landmarks* initiated. Ustrialov's writings are pervaded with ideas taken from Nietzsche, Pushkin, Leontiev, Spengler, Hegel, and the Slavophiles. Bolshevism was "a quintessentially Russian 'blind revolt, senseless and merciless' " (Pushkin's description of the Pugachev Revolt), but it was also an invigorating and renewing force, a "new barbarism." The Bolsheviks were the perfect embodiment of an "aristocracy of the will." The outcome of their Revolution would be a "superdemocracy (*sverkhdemokratiia*) that was truly popular (*narodnyi*), as distinct from the "arithmetic democracy" of the West that failed Russia in 1917. The "odd dialectic of history" had cast the internationally minded Bolsheviks in the role of national unifiers.[61] Lenin and Trotsky welcomed *Smenavekhovtsvo* and subsidized the movement's publications, but Bukharin considered it a "bourgeois ideology." Lenin's incapacitation emboldened the movement's critics, who made it into a symbol of "bourgeois ideology," "Caesarism," or "Great Russian nationalism." Another émigré ideology, Eurasianism, also had Nietzschean components.[62]

Psychologically, the 1920s were a softening-up period for Stalinism. Party leaders fostered a mythic/cultic orientation that contradicted the reason and science they frequently invoked. People were conditioned to regard the individual as nothing, to acquiesce in, and even participate in, the victimization of "subhumans." Pursuit of personal agendas continued under the cloak of

60. *Smena vekh. Sbornik statei: Iu. V. Kliuchnikova, N. V. Ustrialova, S. S. Luk'vianova, A. B. Bobrishcheva-Pushkina, S. S. Chakhotina, i. Iu. N. Potrokhina* (Prague, 1921). See also Ustrialov, *Pod znakom revoliutsii* (Harbin, 1925), and idem, *Na novoi etape* (Shanghai, 1930).

61. Hilde Hardeman, *Coming to Terms with the Soviet Regime: The "Changing Signposts" Movement among Russian Emigres in the Early 1920s* (DeKalb, Ill., 1994), 41, 51, 84–85.

62. For Eurasianism, see *Exodus to the East: Forebodings and Events. An Affirmation of the Eurasians,* trans. Ilya Vinkovetsky, ed. Ilya Vinkovetsky and Charles Schlacks, Jr., afterword by Nicholas Riasanovsky (Marina del Rey, Calif., 1996). *Exodus to the East* was first published as *Iskhod k vostoku: predchyvstiia i sversheniia. Utverzhdenie evrasiistsev* (Sofia, Bulgaria, 1921). See also Nikolai Trubetzkoi, "The Legacy of Genghis Khan," and "Europe and Mankind," trans. Kenneth Brostrom, in *The Legacy of Genghis Khan and Other Essays on Russia's Identity* (Ann Arbor, 1991).

proletarian militancy. A new generation, liberated from traditional moral constraints, proceeded to construct the new order, using "human material" as bricks, and turning literature and the arts into instruments of socialist construction.

New Forms, New Language, New Politics

While we dawdle and quarrel
In search of fundamental answers
All things yell:
"Give us new forms!"
There are no fools today
to crowd open-mouthed round a maestro
and await his pronouncement.
Comrades
give us a new form of art—
an art
that will pull the republic out of the mud!

—Mayakovsky,
"Order No. 2 to the Army of the Arts"

The issues of art form and language became combat zones
as rival schools contended for Party patronage and hegemony in their fields. Neither the avant-garde nor its realist
opponents were monolithic; fissures and personal rivalries
existed in every camp. Alliances shifted frequently because
of political and economic pressures and also because political and aesthetic positions did not always match. On aesthetics, even the Bolsheviks spoke with many voices. Both
camps depended on government subsidies, because the private market for serious art was very small. The literature
wars are the best known, but there were counterparts in
almost every field. The Party was drawn into the literature
wars in 1925, creating a precedent for future interference
and ultimately for direct control of all the arts.

The avant-garde represented the Soviet experiment in the
eyes of the world, but within the Soviet Union, the realists

had a wider following. Each camp recycled the Nietzschean ideas embedded in symbolism, futurism, and Proletkult in its own way, and echoed Bogdanov on the nature and organizational functions of art, typically without mentioning either Bogdanov or Nietzsche by name. The bulk of this chapter is devoted to the avant-garde, because it was the driving force in the search for a new art form and language, and because of its novel applications of Nietzsche.

The Avant-Garde

The most prominent avant-garde movements—constructivism, futurism, and formalism—were primarily interested in form. Allied in the Left Front of the Arts (LEF), which published the journals *Lef* (1923–25) and *New Lef* (*Novyi lef*, 1927–28), their bailiwicks (which were government-funded) included VKhUTEMAS (Higher State Art Technical Institute), INKhUK (Institute of Artistic Culture), and UNOVIS. The avant-garde's rational-analytic and functional approach to art seems remote from Nietzsche because it reformulated the modernist tenet—that art could transform the psyche and shape life—in a way that obscured the tenet's prerevolutionary provenance.

Trying to carve out a place for themselves in the new order, avant-gardists emphasized the practical importance of art and translated Nietzschean ideas into the lexicon of Marxism, industry, and the physical sciences. They talked about political or economic utility, the rationalization of life, and the "culture of materials" and claimed to be reworking "human material" or "producing" the psyche of the new man. A text was a "product"; the artist was a "worker" or a "craftsman"; the studio was a "laboratory"; and the word was "material" to be used in "constructions" or "assaults." To underscore the union of art with industry and science, the word "artist" was hyphenated, as in "artist-engineer," "artist-psychologist," or "artist-constructor." Society was a "language laboratory"; language was a "weapon" in the class war; and the poet was a "verbal engineer," a "psycho-engineer," and a "sensitive barometer" that registered changes in the nation's subconscious and organized them aesthetically. The emphasis on practicality is alien to Nietzsche: "The highest virtue is uncommon and useless" (*Z*, 101).

The word "constructivism" encapsulates the new mood crystallizing in Russia in 1919–20: enough of upheaval and turmoil, enough of theorizing, it is time to build. Visionaries who thought they were realists, constructivists extolled the aesthetic aspect of labor and its transformation into the "exultant work" of communism. The photographer Aleksandr Rodchenko (1891–1956) proclaimed that a "revolution of the spirit" was imminent. "We have thrown away the age-old chains of the photographic, banality, subjectivity. We are the Russian doves of painting, discoverers of new paths of creation."[1] Art is "the will to construction"; artists must work "for life," not for "palaces, cathedrals, cemeteries, and museums."[2] He used Nietzschean language in articles in published in *Anarkhiia* (Anarchy, 1917–18), and he belonged to *Zhivskulptarkh* (1919–20, a collective devoted to synthesizing art, sculpture, and architecture); the members discussed a wide range of subjects, including Nietzsche.[3] Lissitzky proclaimed that the World War "requires us to reassess [= revalue] all values." Architects are "actively participating in the organizing of a new consciousness." Separating art and work is "counterrevolutionary."[4] The Stenberg brothers, Vladimir (1899–1982) and Georgy (1900–1933), regarded the factory as the quickest way to the "development of the earth's one and only organism," the place where a "gigantic trampoline is created being for the leap into universal human culture."[5] The avant-garde was internationally minded.

The constructivists' goal was the complete integration of art and industry (which meant jobs for artists). Seeking new art forms based on the machine, they declaimed such slogans as "Not the old, not the new, but the necessary," "From art into life," and "Death to Art!" by which they meant death to old art forms. Tatlin declared, "our material" is metal, the material of the technological age.[6] Constructivist poets emphasized accuracy and precision (*tochnost'*)—qualities needed in industry.

Constructivist art and architecture has a distinctive "look." Geometric shapes, the forms of industry—squares, rectangles, pyramids, triangles, circles, parallelepipeds—were carefully interspersed with industrial products and tools (hammers, calibrators, wheels, telephones) and revolutionary symbols. Everything was stark, clear, and purposeful. Bold primary colors and sharply defined objects conveyed an impression of order and control, which was further reinforced by straight lines, sharp angles, and economic use of materials (a socialist virtue)—all very different from futurist spontaneity, or the mystical haze of symbolism, or the sensuous curves of *art nouveau,* and deliberately so.

1. Caption and text of untitled poster (1919), in *Alexander Rodchenko*, exhibition catalogue, Museum of Modern Art (New York, 1998), 160.
2. Selim Khan Magomedov, *Rodchenko: The Complete Work* (Cambridge, Mass., 1987), 97.
3. I am indebted to Nina Gurianova for the information on *Anarkhiia* and to Gail Harrison Roman for the information on *Zhivskulptarkh*.
4. *Lissitzky. Life, Letters, Texts*, 329–30, 337, 371.
5. Quoted in *The Stenberg Brothers: Constructing a Revolution in Soviet Design*, exhibition catalogue, Museum of Modern Art (New York, 1997), 12, from their manifesto (with Konstantin Medunetsky), "The Constructivists Address the World" (1922).
6. *Art Into Life: Russian Constructivism, 1914–32*, exhibition catalogue, Henry Art Gallery, University of Washington, Seattle (New York, 1990), 150, 225–26; Zhadova et al., *Tatlin*, 18, 133–34.

The constructivist aesthetic featured lightness (= overcoming gravity), "transparency," "dynamism" (sometimes called "kineticism"), and perspectivism. "Kineticism" meant continuous movement, sometimes in rhythmic form. A mechanized version of the force lines of Dionysus and of Bogdanov's emphasis on energy, "kineticism" incorporated the hope that electrical energy would propel the entire country into the modern era. Architects designed flying buildings, or colonies in space, or houses made of glass and asbestos, for transparency and lightness. "Transparency" expressed the Apollonian impulse to clarity—the opposite of symbolist mystery. In architecture "transparency" meant visible structural skeletons. In theater, it meant conspicuous stage machinery, new versions of "conditional theater," and unmasking villains. In some contexts, "transparency" meant no dissimulation, that is to say, truthfulness (a Nietzschean virtue, see Chapter 9).

Perspectivism, a signature device of constructivist theater, film, and photography, was informed by Nietzsche, Bergson, and contemporary scientific studies of perception, spatial orientation, and optics. Perspective was debated extensively at VKhUTEMAS, where Florensky taught spatial theory. To him and to the avant-garde, linear perspective and the Euclidean geometry on which it was based, expressed the values and worldview that had dominated Europe since the Renaissance, something which the avant-garde regarded as obsolete and Florensky, as never valid at all. Rejection of linear perspective was an intrinsic aspect of their revaluation of all values. To the avant-garde, linear perspective epitomized "bourgeois individualism" and stasis, so they experimented with a variety of perspectives. To Florensky, linear perspective epitomized self-centered subjectivism and the mechanical universe of Copernicus and Newton. He extolled the reverse perspective of the Russian icons as the expression of an "objective and supra-personal metaphysics" and argued that from the perspective of relativity theory, the Ptolemaic system was just as valid as the Copernican system.[7] Lissitzky differentiated between planimetric space, perspectival space, and irrational space in his essay "A [Art] and Pan-Geometry" (1925), which was informed by Nietzsche, Florensky, Malevich, and the non-Euclidean geometry of Nikolai Lobachevsky (1792–1856). Inspired by Malevich's experiments in form, for a time Lissitzky regarded suprematism as the "Third Testament." Communism was the second.[8]

Constructivists worked in a variety of fields, but they privileged architecture as the "organizer of life," attributing to architecture the transformative

7. Florenskii, "Obratnaia perspektiva," in *FSS*, vol. 3, bk. 1, pp. 46–103, esp. 48–54; idem, *Mnimosti v geometrii*, ed. Michael Hagemeister (1922; reprint, Munich, 1985); idem, *Analiz prostvanstvennost' i vremeni v khudozhestvenno-izobrazitel'nykh proizvedeniiakh* (1924, Moscow, 1993). See also Rosenthal, "Florensky's Russifications," 255–56.
8. *Lissitzky. Life, Letters, Texts,* 330.

power that Ivanov attributed to the theater, except that they thought in terms of psycho-physiological responses and energy flows. By architecture, they meant all aspects of the built environment, not just buildings, but furniture, city planning, and great works of engineering, such as hydroelectric plants. Marx used architecture as a paradigm for specifically human productive work. To Nietzsche, the architect represented

> neither a Dionysian nor an Apollonian condition: here it is the mighty act of will, the will which moves mountains, the intoxication of the strong will, which demands artistic expression. The most powerful men have always inspired the architects: the architects has always been influenced by power. Pride, victory over weight and gravity, the will to power, seek to render themselves visible in a building; architecture is a kind of rhetoric of power, now persuasive, even cajoling in form, now bluntly imperious The highest feeling of power and security finds expression in that which possesses *grand style*. Power which no longer requires proving; which disdains to please . . . which reposes in itself, fatalistic, a law among laws: that is what speaks of itself in the form of grand style. (*TI*, 74)

For Nietzsche-influenced architects in the 1920s, the key words were "victory over weight and gravity." In the 1930s, they were "power" and "grand style" (see Chapter 14).

In Western Europe, Le Corbusier, Peter Behrens, Henry Van de Velde, Bruno Taut, Ludwig Mies van der Rohe, and Walter Gropius, applied Nietzsche's thought to architecture, each in his own way. All of them regarded architecture as a dynamic life-shaping force and sought a symbiosis of art and life. Some of them designed habitats conducive to what they considered a Nietzschean lifestyle, such as, for example, Taut's "alpine architecture." Others envisioned temples as energy structures that would produce the man of the future. Still others designed streamlined skyscrapers that maximized light and air and decent housing for workers.[9] Some Nietzsche-influenced architects "stressed the plurality of the open-ended montage process, together with relativity and the temporal process of change." Then, soon overlapping with the "Dionysian tendency toward montage," a contrary principle emerged, "the Apollonian machine aesthetic," which strengthened the relation between art and science."[10] Russian architects followed the work of their Western counterparts and vice-versa.

---

9.   Details in *Nietzsche and "An Architecture of Our Minds,"* ed. Alexander Kostka and Irving Wohlfarth (Los Angeles, 1999).

10.   Hanne Bergius, "Architecture as the Dionysian-Apollonian Process of Dada," in Kostka and Wohlfarth, *Nietzsche*, 133 and 135.

In Soviet Russia, Nietzschean ideas on architecture were refracted through the prism of socialism, utopian as well as Marxist. Also very important were Bogdanov's depiction of the built environment in his novel *Red Star,* Enlightenment ideas on city planning, and Spengler's privileging of architecture as the quintessential expression and foundational art of every culture. Avant-garde architects emphasized neurophysiological or psychophysiological stimuli and reflexes. By designing (or controlling) the environment in which people lived and worked, architects believed, they could mold behavior and produce a socialist psyche. To foster (or mandate) a socialist lifestyle, they designed communal housing, public buildings, and entire towns and cities. Most of their designs remained on the drawing board because they were too expensive or too impractical, or both.[11]

Tatlin's Tower, an early example of the search for new architectural forms, was tilted to conform to the earth's axis, as befit the headquarters of the Third International. As stated above, it was a functional monument, not just something to look at. Made of iron and glass (transparency), and built in the form of a spiral (a Theosophist symbol), it had three levels that revolved at different speeds (kineticism). Lissitzky's PROUNs (Project for the Affirmation of the New), intended as an intermediate form between painting and architecture, were enormous painted three-dimensional entities that could be hung in different ways, upside down for example. Reversibility was an aspect of Lissitzky's perspectivism. The PROUNs flew into a void, signifying an infinite horizon, and they moved. He related "dynamism" to the fourth dimension.

In city-planning, Lissitzky rejected "archaic horizontals," "classical spheres," and "gothic verticals" for "economy and spatial diagonals."

> we left to the old world the idea of individual house individual barracks individual castle individual church. we have set ourselves the task of creating the town The center of collective effort is the radio transmitting mast which sends out bursts of creative energy into the world. By means of it we are able to throw off the shackles that bind us to the earth and rise above it. . . .
>
> this dynamic architecture provides us with the new theater of life and because we are capable of grasping the idea of a whole town at any moment . . . the task of architecture—the rhythmic arrangement of space and time—is perfectly and simply fulfilled for the new town will not be as chaotically laid out as the modern towns of north and south america but clearly and logically like a beehive.[12]

---

11. For Nietzsche and the Soviet architectural avant-garde, see Milka Bliznakov, "Nietzschean Implications and Superhuman Aspirations in the Architectural Avant-Garde," in *NSC*, 174–210.

12. *Lissitzky. Life, Letters, Texts,* 328. Idiosyncratic punctuation in original.

According to Lissitzky, the "new man" would be fully in tune with his social-ist environment, but he would not be tied down. "The Egyptian pyramid is obsolete. The flying human being is at the frontier. . . . A new energy must be released, which provides us with a new system of movement. . . . Even for revolutions, new forms must be invented."[13]

In mid-decade, the architectural avant-garde split into rival schools—rationalism and constructivism—championed by ASNOVA (Association for the New Architecture, founded 1923) and OSA (Organization of Contemporary Architects, founded 1925) respectively. Their vitriolic competition for commissions and students poisoned the atmosphere at VKhUTEMAS, the institute in which they were housed. Lissitzky joined ASNOVA. Melnikov remained unaffiliated but he was closer to ASNOVA. Both schools held that form follows function and argued for a machine-based aesthetic. Rationalists maintained that architecture should be ideologically expressive as well. Nikolai Ladovsky (1881–1941), their leader, advocated a "psychoanalytic method of design," by which he meant measuring perceptions and other psycho-physiological processes and functions so that the architect could organize space to elicit the desired response. One of his slogans was "space not stone is the material of architecture."[14] The polemics of rationalists and constructivists with one another, and with architects of other schools, revolved around issues that would have to be resolved when funds became available—architecture and the reconstruction of the psyche, the degree of privacy (if any) in communal housing, and functionalism (sometimes called the international style) versus Russian or neoclassical style.[15] Meanwhile, government commissions went to traditionalists and eclecticists as well as to the avant-garde. Some architects worked in a variety of genres, according to the wishes of the client.

Constructivism had a profound impact on theater, photography, and film. Meyerhold applied constructivist principles in his productions and employed constructivists as set and costume designers, as did other avant-garde directors such as Aleksandr Tairov (Kornblit, 1885–1950), founder of the internationally renowned *Kamernyi* (Chamber) Theater.[16] In 1921, Meyerhold announced a "theatrical October" and declared war on "obsolete" theatrical forms, attacking the academic theaters (the nationalized Bolshoi, Maly,

13. Ibid., 345.

14. Bliznakov, "Nietzschean Implications," in *NSC*, 179–82.

15. Elizabeth English argues that Rationalism was a uniquely Russian movement. "Arkhitektura i mnimosti: The Origins of Soviet Avant-Garde Rationalist Architecture in the Russian Mystical-Philosophical and Mathematical Intellectual Tradition" (Ph.D. diss., University of Pennsylvania, 2000).

16. For Tairov, see Nick Warrall, *Modernism to Realism on the Soviet Stage: Tairov-Vakhtangov-Okhlopkov* (Cambridge, 1989).

and Moscow Art Theaters) for their classical repertory, and Tairov's theater for its apoliticism. The function of art was not to embellish life, but to organize it, Meyerhold insisted. To demonstrate his militancy, he wore a pistol to rehearsals, a holdover from his days in the Red Army Theater.

Meyerhold sought to induce a new revolutionary perspective in the spectator by demystifying the theater and "making strange" and "baring the device" (formalist concepts). His productions have been compared to distorting mirrors, magnifying glasses, and lenses held at oblique angles. By drawing attention to the artificiality of what he was doing, to the theatricality of his theater, he enhanced the effect of the "new angle."[17] He used psycho-physiological stimuli to "energize" the audience and kept track of its responses. "We don't need *ecstasy*," he said, "we need *arousal*, based on a firm physical foundation."[18] Marked by continuous action, his productions were entertaining as well as ideologically instructive. His "montage of attractions" incorporated circus and vaudeville elements, slapstick, farce, jazz, specially designed machines, and interactive furniture that did not always work as planned. In *The Death of Tarelkin* (1922), prisoners were put through a giant meat-grinder.[19] The term was later used to describe the Gulag, a possible example of "art into life." Meyerhold described a performance as a series of "passes" intended to evoke new associations in the spectator, some premeditated, others outside the director's control. The "imagination is activated," the "fantasy stimulated, and a whole chorus of associations is set forth. A multitude of accumulated associations gives birth to new worlds."[20] Note Meyerhold's recycling of the symbolist concept of the generative word.

In his "theater of social masks," Meyerhold politicized the conditional theater"; this time the actors' masks depicted "the concept of 'former people' literally. A man who was and no longer exists, from whom remains only the external, or more exactly, the 'appearance'—a unique dead soul." Grotesque caricatures of Nepmen or compromisers, these masks signified an "ossified social type devoid of individual characteristics."[21] A segment of the population had been dehumanized, if only in the theater.

In the new art forms of photography and cinema, man "mastered" the machine and created a new reality, or the illusion of one. Photomontage, a favorite device of the avant-garde, was pioneered in Germany by the "left" artists Hannah Höch and John Heartfield, who used it to mock Junkers and

17. Robert Leach, *Vsevolod Meyerhold* (Cambridge, 1989), 127.
18. Quoted in Alma Law and Mel Gordon, *Meyerhold, Eisenstein, and Biomechanics* (Jefferson, N.C., 1961), 143.
19. Illustration in ibid., 46.
20. Quoted in Leach, *Vsevolod Meyerhold*, 136.
21. B. Alpers, *Teatral'nye ocherki v dvukh tomakh*, vol. 1 (Moscow, 1977), 89, 102.

the bourgeoisie. Early Soviet photomontages were apolitical (Klutsis was an exception). Some were collections of snapshots on a common theme or snapshots combined with graphics. Rodchenko's photomontages portrayed a complex multilayered world with private references. The illustrator of Mayakovsky's *About That* (*Pro Eto*, 1923), Rodchenko rearranged "things" in an surrealist manner, externalizing (= making transparent) the poet's inner world. One photomontage combines a huge building, crowded streets, Lily Brik (Mayakovsky's beloved), an automobile tire, an airplane, and Mayakovsky atop a church steeple in his crucifixion pose (Fig. 6). When reading poetry, Mayakovsky would sometimes suddenly stand up very straight with his arms at right angles, a pose intended to remind audiences of the crucifixion. The airplane and the steeple also make a cross. Rodchenko's signature "devices" were sharp diagonals, slanting compositions, extreme close-ups, and bird's eye and worm's eye views.

Nietzsche said: "There is *only* a perspective seeing, *only* a perspective 'knowing': and the *more* affects we allow to speak about one thing, the *more* eyes, different eyes, we can use to observed one thing, the more complete will our 'concept' of this thing, our 'objectivity,' be" (*GM*, 119). Rodchenko used double or triple exposures to illustrate the possibility of multiple perspectives. Lissitzky used multiple exposures to depict body movements and the passage of time.[22] They were striving for a kind of surreal objectivity, not for verisimilitude. There was a play element in their photography; they experimented with the camera like a child with a new toy. The Stenberg Brothers invented a film projector that was "capable of not only enlarging and reducing, but also distorted the projected image; we could distorted a vertically organized image, for example, to make it look like a diagonally organized image."[23] Vladimir Stenberg said: "Ours are eye-catching posters which, one might say, are designed to shock. We deal with the material in a free manner . . . disregarding actual proportions . . . turning figures upside down; in short, we employ everything that can make a busy passerby stop in their tracks [*sic*]."[24] The avant-garde's enemies accused them of "aestheticism," because their work lacked obvious political content. Moreover, multiple perspectives confused the viewer and blurred the message, if any.

Cinematic montages disaggregated reality but, unlike cubism, they reassembled the components to create an illusion that was compelling because it looked real. Vertov believed that art should reveal (= unmask) the naked truth, so he concentrated on filming "life caught unaware." The director's role was to overcome the weakness of the human eye by his "super-eye" (the camera), to plunge into the chaos of reality and create a new order. A pio-

22. Tupitsyn, *El Lissitzky*, plates 15 and 39.
23. Vladimir Stenberg, quoted in *The Stenberg Brothers*, 16.
24. Vladimir Stenberg, quoted on the title page of *The Stenberg Brothers*.

Fig. 6 Aleksandr Rodchenko, "I catch my balance / waving terribly."
In Mayakovsky, *Pro eto* (Moscow, 1924). Slavic and Baltic Division,
New York Public Library, Astor, Lenox and Tilden Foundations.

neer of the documentary, Vertov opposed theatricality and denigrated Eisenstein's film-drama as the opium of the masses.[25]

Eisenstein was a mythmaker intent on creating a new collective hero, the proletariat (though he also portrayed exemplary individuals), so he sacrificed strict realism and historical accuracy to perceptual and emotional impact. The sequence on the Odessa steps in *The Battleship Potemkin* (1925) fuses the Odessa massacre with the one in Baku and the triumphal ending omits the exile of the mutineers. "We stop the event at this point where it had become an 'asset' to the revolution."[26] This sequence, which contains horrifying violence, became the most famous one in silent cinema. Joseph Goebbels extolled *Battleship Potemkin* as "a marvelous film without equal in the cinema. The reason is its power of conviction. Anyone who had no firm political convictions would become a Bolshevik after seeing the film."[27] The Nazis picketed the movie-houses where it was shown and banned it after they came to power.

Before the Revolution, Eisenstein wrote: "It is worth taking the 'fanaticism' out of religion; it can later be separated from the original object of worship and be 'displaced' to other passions."[28] After 1917, he "displaced" fanaticism to politics. Eisenstein started out in Proletkult as Meyerhold's protégé (Meyerhold's alliance with Proletkult was short-lived because of irreconcilable differences on issues such as the role of the director). From observing his mentor, Eisenstein concluded that Meyerhold's "basic material" was the audience, which he activated by "the aggressive moments of theater" drawn from popular sources (music halls, circus, etc.). These "moments" administered a series of jolts that shocked the audience into a revolutionary perspective. Eisenstein's cinematic montage did the same. His "collision montage" polarized reality into enemies / people, tsars and ministers / Bolshevik Party, clowns / heroes, Winter Palace / Lenin's headquarter), languid inertia / purposeful activity, grotesque satire / streamlined functionality, and to a lesser extent, effeminacy / masculinity.[29] In *Strike* (1924), he used montage to subliminally associate capitalists and animals. In *October* (1928), he preceded or followed shots of Kerensky by shots of a mechanical peacock (reputedly Kerensky was very vain). Women are either absent from Eisenstein's silent films or they play a secondary role. Each film begins with a quotation from Lenin. Brutality, violence, and theatricalized death abound. *Strike* (1924) includes a sacrificial ritual, the bloody slaughter of a bull (the sacrificial object in some Dionysian rites). The cruelty was

25. Vertov, *Kino-Eye*, 63, 71.

26. Quoted in David Bordwell, *The Cinema of Eisenstein* (Cambridge, Mass., 1993), 62.

27. Quoted in David Welch, *Propaganda in the German Cinema* (Oxford, 1983), 17.

28. Quoted in Hakan Lovgren, "Sergei Eisenstein's Gnostic Circle," in Rosenthal, *Occult*, 280.

29. Bordwell, *Cinema of Eisenstein*, 83, 92.

deliberate.[30] As militant as Meyerhold, Eisenstein proclaimed: "It is not cine eye that we need but a cine fist!" He advocated "a fully armed cinematic October." His characters were depersonalized symbols (mythic types) or pawns in the tides of history.

Eisenstein considered the driving force of aesthetic creativity the conflict between Dionysus and Apollo, between pre-logic and logic, the diffuse and the distinct, the dim and the clear, the "animal-elemental" and the "sunny-wise."[31] Nietzsche's chorus of satyrs underlies the director's approving remarks on the "ancient 'animal' element" in Japanese Kabuki theater.[32] All his life, Eisenstein tried to depict the "ecstatic" and the "dynamic" (the Dionysian). He defined "ecstasy" as a state of transport, in which the self fuses with the other, in some cases with a transcendental other, creating a feeling of unison. Unlike Ivanov, Eisenstein specifically rejected the connotation of sexual ecstasy and "egoistic" pleasure. In David Bordwell's words, "religious ecstasy more closely approximates what he was aiming at."[33] Eisenstein perceived the Civil War hero Chapaev (film version, 1934) as a tragic hero stepping out of the chorus, "not only leading [his class] but also listening to it, a genuine people's hero. This could be the 'ecstatic' image of an ordinary soldier who breaks forward from his place in the ranks [= chorus] to become a hero. In such a hero we can feel that he is—us."[34] The director referred to the "passion" of Chapaev in terms that recall Ivanov's Christ/Dionysus archetype; as a result he was rebuked for his debt to symbolism. "Behind the constructivist exterior of a materialistically conceived *October,* there lurk the vestiges of a decadent and outmoded style of our art," Piotrovsky charged (the same Piotrovsky who organized Red Army Theaters).[35]

Futurists and formalists emphasized the psychopolitical importance of language and the functional uses of poetry. Using the journal *Lef* as their podium, they claimed to be carrying out the class war in culture and fulfilling the "social demand" (*sotsial'nyi zakaz*)—Brik's reformation of Viacheslav Ivanov's idea of a "commission" from the people (*narodnyi zakaz*).[36] Ivanov wanted the poet to write for the people (*narod*). In Brik's version, the proletariat (its representatives, not individual proletarians) places the order and the artist decides how to execute it.

The first issue of *Lef* announced its program: "Sweeping away the old

30. *Eisenstein, Writings,* ed. and trans. Richard Taylor (Bloomington, 1988), 2:43–44, 176.
31. Quoted in Lovgren, "Sergei Eisenstein's Gnostic Circle," 283.
32. *Eisenstein, Writings,* 2:117.
33. Bordwell, *Cinema of Eisenstein,* 194.
34. *Eisenstein, Film Essays and a Lecture,* ed. Jay Leyda (New York, 1970), 43, 67, 102.
35. Quoted in Richard Taylor, ed., *The Film Factory: Russian and Soviet Cinema in Documents* (Cambridge, 1988), 216.
36. *Zakaz* means commission, order, command, or demand, depending on the context.

junk with the revolution, we have cleared the ground for the construction of art. No more earthquakes. Cemented by blood, the USSR stands firm. It's time to undertake *big projects*" (*RF,* 199), projects that would unify art, technology, and politics.[37] Brik and Mayakovsky declared that their "linguistic work" was modeled on the "precise language of science" and refused to distinguish between poetry and prose. "We recognize only a single linguistic material and we will process it according to today's methods. . . . We are not priest-creators but master-executors of the social demand" (*RF,* 202–3). Note the jabs at symbolism.

To underscore its claim of a link between language and revolution, in 1924, *Lef* devoted an entire issue to analysis of "Lenin's language."[38] The contributors, all formalists, viewed Lenin "as someone who not only makes a new world, but does so, precisely by speaking a new word," as Dragon Kujundžić puts it. "It is indeed by his ability to produce a new word that Lenin is able to produce new politics."[39] Treating Lenin as a literary classic as well as an innovator, they highlighted the effectiveness of Lenin's language, attributing it to Lenin's debunking of worn-out words and empty phrases ("old words" as Nietzsche put it) and to his trenchant "slogan-formulas," graphically violent language, and authoritative style. Viktor Shklovsky (1893–1984) called Lenin a decanonizer, who changed the meaning of words and coined new ones, pointedly giving *Komchvanstvo* (Communist arrogance) as an example. Boris Eikhenbaum (1886–1959) contrasted Lenin's direct style with the "splendid" (obsolete) style of Soloviev, Merezhkovsky, and Berdiaev. Lev Iakubinsky described Lenin's "lowering of high style" (= his linguistic descent to the people). Iury Tynianov (1894–1943) described Lenin's "linguistic politics" (*iazykovaia politika*), emphasizing his dissuasive speech, his struggle against such "smooth words" as "liberty," "equality," and "fraternity." To expose such words as "empty chatter," Lenin put them in quotation marks, Tynianov noted. And when words became stale, Lenin discarded them, changing the Party's name from Bolshevik to Communist, for example, in order to signify the Party's transition from opposition to rule and to distinguish Communists from "bourgeois" Social Democrats. Tynianov also pointed out the "thing-like concreteness" of Lenin's speech, and credited the terseness and lexical unity of Lenin's slogan "expropriate the expropriators" for making Marx's idea ("the expropriators are expropriated") into a true command. B. Kazansky called Lenin's word an "an act of will" and his discourse "a heroic deed" (111–12) and underscored

---

37. For a history of *Lef,* see Halina Stephen, *Lef and the Left Front of the Arts* (Munich, 1981).

38. "Iazyk Lenina," *Lef* 1, no. 5 (1924): 53–148.

39. Dragan Kujundžić, *The Returns of History* (Albany, 1997), 130. In *Der Russische Formalismus* (Vienna, 1978), Aage Hansen-Löwe pointed out the formalists' use of Nietzschean concepts, but did not suggest that the formalists were influenced by Nietzsche.

Lenin's use of words as weapons: "'Don't move. Hands up. Surrender.' This is the character of Lenin's speech" (136). Boris Tomashevsky described Lenin as the inventor of a "new rhetoric" that turns the word into the deed (political action) and enables culture to penetrate life (142, 148). A year later, Kruchenykh analyzed Lenin's language from a futurist perspective in a booklet titled *Lenin's Language*."[40]

Other *Lef* authors concentrated on reconciling avant-garde aesthetics with Marxism. Nikolai Chuzhak (1896–1937) had been advocating a new dialectical art, "ultra-realism," since 1912, an art that would express the collision between "what is" and "what will be" and help move society forward. In 1919, he suggested that futurism was the needed "ultra-realism," because it was the closest artistically to the emotions and psychology of the proletariat. Futurist linguistic experimentation could develop the new "iron language required for a new Sermon on the Mount."[41] Clearly, Chuzhak's "new word" would not be mutable like *zaum*. He repeated these arguments in *Lef*, substituting "collective creativity" for the individual "artist-genius," and made "life-building" (*zhiznestroenie*) the basis of "ultra-realism." "Life-building" reformulated the symbolist concept of life-creation (*zhiznetvorchestvo*) in the spirit of "building socialism."

Tretiakov listed new practical tasks for futurism, among them: "action on mass psychology," "organization of the class will," "propaganda about forging the new human being," and "production of a new human being through art." Futurism is "alloyed [note the industrial metaphor] to a new world sense . . . the living driving force which determines all actions of the human being, his everyday physiognomy." The futurist was an "instigator-agitator" who breaks down "art's self-sufficient posture," throws the "energy of art" into serving reality, and colors "every human production movement with the mastery and joy of art" (*RF,* 212). For Tretiakov, art was a battlefield and writers were soldiers of the class war. Not only enthusiasm, but discipline, organization, planning, and will were essential.

> This new type of worker must feel a fundamental hatred toward all things unorganized, inert, chaotic, sedentary, and provincially backward. . . . He is repelled by thick pine forests, untilled steppes, unutilized waterfalls which tumble not according to our order. . . . He finds beauty in those things upon which one can see the mark of the organizing human hand; he finds greatness in every object of human production designed to overcome, subject, and master the elements and inert matter. (*RF,* 214)

40. Kruchenykh, *Iazyk Lenina; Odinnadtsat' preemov leninskoi rechi* (Moscow, 1925).
41. Irina Gutkin, "The Legacy of the Symbolist Aesthetic Utopia: From Futurism to Socialist Realism," in *Creating Life,* ed. Irina Paperno and Joan Grossman (Stanford, Calif., 1994), 187–88.

The worker's "emotional training" requires a new language, consciously reorganized "according to the new forms of life" (*RF*, 215). The poet must produce a living, concretely useful language that is precise and psychologically compelling.

Another *Lef* author, Boris Arvatov (1896–1940)—formerly a Proletkult activist, a cultural bureaucrat and an Agitprop specialist in 1922—argued that the proletariat had to be educated to understand nonrepresentational art, just as it had been educated to understand Marxism.[42] Socialist art would "build and shape life," ending the separation of art and life, and of content and form. Arvatov also argued for "organized language creation" (*rechetvorchestvo*), a variant of life-creation, maintaining that "the engineering culture of language is the practical task of our epoch." The futurists were only the "partial individualistic heralds" of the new language, because their methodology was "anarcho-emotional, 'intuitive,' and 'inspirational.'" The conscious proletariat would complete the process. A fusion of poetic and practical language was imminent (*RF*, 230–31).

The psychopolitical approach to language of futurists and formalists could be useful to Bolsheviks who wanted to hone their agitprop skills, to learn to do what Lenin did naturally. The violent language used by futurists (and Bolsheviks) and analyzed by formalists became an ever more prominent aspect of cultural politics. Chuzhak's "ultra-realism" was a stepping-stone to Socialist Realism and, ultimately, to a mandated "iron language." In their "linguistic laboratories," avant-gardists were forging weapons that would later be used against them.

Nietzsche was part of the ambiance in which formalism, a new type of literary criticism, emerged in 1914. Shklovsky, Tynianov, Eikhenbaum, and Brik read Nietzsche, and they referred to formalism as a "Gay Science."[43] Sidney Monas alludes to Shklovsky's "Nietzschean affirmation, in all areas of life, of the primacy of the aesthetic."[44] "Dioneo," a pseudonym Shklovsky sometimes used, suggests Dionysus. Shklovsky's concept of framing can be considered a transposition to literature of Nietzsche's concept of the horizon.

Formalist critics analyzed the structure of a text and the "devices" that made it effective, treating the author as merely a locus of the literary processes of his time. They rejected sociological and metaphysical approaches to literature, played down inspiration, talent, and genius, and did not delve into content, meaning, or truth-function. Their concept of "making strange" or

---

42. Boris Arvatov, "The Proletariat and Leftist Art," in Bowlt, *Russian Art of the Avant-Garde*, 226–30, first published in *Vestnik iskusstv*, no. 1 (1922). The cover illustration (reproduced on 227) is a winged muscular man aloft in space, carrying a torch.

43. Kujundžić, *Returns of History*, 9–10.

44. Sidney Monas, "Historical Introduction," in *Viktor Shklovsky: A Sentimental Journey, Memoirs, 1917–22*, trans. Richard Sheldon (Ithaca, 1970), xliii, xli; see also xvi.

"defamiliarization" (*ostranenie*) was intended to deautomatize perception in order to revive the freshness of the original sensation. Sources of defamiliarization include Tolstoy (who used it to ridicule, not to refresh), Nietzsche's perspectivism, and Bely's concept of the "death of the word," which Shklovsky drew on in his essay, "The Resurrection of the Word" (1914). In another essay, "Art as Device" (1917), Shklovsky explained "making strange" as the device whereby the artist separates his art from everyday life (the raw material) and forms it into an aesthetic whole. In their early writings, formalists maintained the separation of art and life. The impersonality of formalist criticism stemmed from a desire to be scientific and from the structural linguistics of Ferdinand Saussure, author of *A Course on General Linguistics* (1916).

Formalists who remained in Russia after the Revolution, or returned in 1921–22, affiliated with state institutes. These formalists interpreted changes in literary and artistic forms as a process of struggles, breaks, shifts, changes, and reactions that were in turn part of a struggle for ascendancy in the renewal of perceptive modes. Each age "canonized" its own forms, a process that entailed the "decanonization" of previous forms which had become stale. "Decanonization" was a literary equivalent of smashing the old "tables of values," because literature, especially in Russia, expresses the values of a society (even though formalists avoided questions of value). By the same token, "canonization" represented the inscription of new values on new tables, which would someday be smashed in turn. Shklovsky introduced the concept of "decanonization" in his essay on Rozanov (1921), conjoining it with the possibility of "eternal recurrence." "A younger school bursts into the place of an older one. . . . However, the defeated school is not destroyed, does not cease to exist. It is only displaced from the top to the bottom . . . and can rise again."[45] If interpreted politically, this thought is counterrevolutionary. (Indeed, Shklovsky sympathized with the SRs in 1917–18.) Shklovsky's disjuncture of art and life paralleled the futurist sense of a disjuncture in history, which world war and revolution confirmed. Russians had moved beyond history and were constructing a new world.

Shklovsky and Tynianov analyzed the music and rhythm of a text in functional terms and its verbal or structural components in terms of dominance and subordination. Every literary construction was a struggle to destroy old forms and construct new ones from the same elements in an endless cycle of "archaists and innovators" (Tynianov's terms). Tynianov compared the evolution of literature to "a factory where things are incessantly reforged; tractors are assembled from tank parts and tanks from tractor parts."[46] Note

45. Shklovsky, *Rozanov* (Petrograd, 1921), 5–7.
46. Yuri Tynyanov, Preface (1925), in *Russian Prose*, ed. B. Eikhenbaum and Yu. Tynyanov (Ann Arbor, 1985).

the reversibility and the updated version of swords and plowshares. Tynianov viewed the literary word as a dynamic entity. "Flow and dynamics may be taken as such, outside of time, as pure movement. Art lives by means of interaction and struggle. Without this sensation of subordination and deformation of all factors by the one factor playing the constructive role, there is no fact of art."[47] Bergsonian notions of time are obvious here, but the *agon* is from Nietzsche and the backdrop is the literature wars of the 1920s. Tynianov's concept of a "dynamic" word paralleled the constructivists' transformation of Dionysianism into kineticism. Shklovsky's central metaphor was the machine.

The formalists' emphasis on process, structure, and function married an essentially Dionysian ontology to the Apollonian industrial-scientific-constructivist orientation typical of the decade. They described combinations and recombinations of words in terms of chemical elements or processes such as crystallization, in effect transposing to chemistry the couplings and uncouplings of Apollo and Dionysus. Chemistry, the privileged science of the 1920s, was one of the sciences from which Nietzsche took his metaphors. Later in the decade, formalists extended their purview to cinema, analyzing techniques (or devices) of light, music, and gesture and their effects on the viewer.[48] Formalism can be made compatible with Marxism if literary processes are interpreted in sociological terms. Toward the end of the 1920s, formalists did just that, abandoning the idea of a disjuncture between art and life and viewing the writer as a locus of social processes.

As if to demonstrate that a new myth needs a new word, intellectuals and politicians alike were preoccupied with language. V. N. Voloshinov (1895–1936) approved of "the Freudians'" emphasis on language, even though he found "Freudianism" itself animalistic. The characters of Zamiatin's *We* speak a special language, Russian but not quite Russian, and the government decides what the words mean. Pilniak depicted the masses' misperceptions and manglings of the government's language. Furmanov used language to underscore the different mentalities of Chapaev and Klychkov and to contrast "disciplined" workers and "anarchic" peasants. Linguists experimented with *zaum* as a new, more "rational" medium for public communication or as the prototype for a new, truly popular, language.[49] There were proposals to simplify Russian grammar and further simplify the spelling (which had been already simplified in 1918) in order to speed the eradica-

47. Yuri Tynianov, *The Problem of Verse Language*, ed. and trans. Michael Sosa and Brent Harvey (Ann Arbor, 1981), 32–33.
48. Herbert Eagle, *Russian Formalist Film Theory* (Ann Arbor, 1981). Piotrovsky contributed an essay in which he talked about space as being "dynamized," "exploded," and "set in motion" by film.
49. Smith, *Language and Power*, 76.

tion of illiteracy. There were also proposals to standardize or to rationalize the language (in addition to those made by futurists) that were intended to enhance communication or to foster a rational mind-set. There was great interest in Esperanto (supposedly an international language) and in adopting the Latin alphabet throughout the Soviet Union. Latinization would end the "script separation" between Russia and Europe, cut Moslems off from their co-religionists outside the Soviet Union, and foster an eventual merger (*sblizhenie*) of the languages within it. These and other language-related issues were discussed under the aegis of the Commissariat of Enlightenment and the Commissariat of Nationalities (Stalin's bailiwick), and by the Orgburo of the Party's Central Committee.

Bolsheviks also addressed the language issue publicly. In March 1923, responding to its critics of its prose, *Pravda* declared:

> Our press is always setting forth, in an especially striking way, the main slogans, key issues, and main campaigns, and it keeps hammering away at them stubbornly and systematically—"boringly" our enemies say. Yes our brochures, newspapers, and leaflets do indeed drum into the heads of the masses a certain number of the main "key" formulas and slogans . . . "hammer into" . . . 'drum into' . . . [with] exceptional clarity and precision of style. . . . It is harsh and coarse, elementary and vulgar, our enemies say. It is truthful, sincere, bold, and merciless.[50]

Bukharin advocated a "living language" in tune with "practical life" that would be as pithy as the street language of the proletariat.

Trotsky included discussions on language in his books on culture. He considered the philological work of the futurists "vital and progressive." Despite their "utopian sectarianism" and "almost monstrous bias for sound as against sense," their "fundamentally purifying and truly revolutionizing work [in] poetic language will remain." Futurism is "a necessary link" to the poetry of the future (*Literature*, 142–43, 161). Formalism, however, "represents an abortive idealism applied to the questions of art" because it emphasizes "the word" rather than "the deed" (182–83). He also discussed other Soviet authors. Pilniak, he said, erred in having the archbishop Sylvester (a character in *The Naked Year*) pronounce the acronyms of Soviet agencies as if they were sounds made by witches, or demons, or the elements. "Gviu, Glavbum are not simply correlations of sound," but "purposeful working words, thought out and consciously put together . . . for a conscious, purposeful, planful construction, such as has never been in the world before" (84–86).

---

50. Quoted in Heller, *Cogs in a Wheel*, 235.

In *Problems of Everyday Life,* Trotsky equated the "struggle against bad language" in intellectual culture with "the fight against filth and vermin in physical culture" and said that while the Revolution had enriched the language with "new descriptive forms" and "new, much more precise and dynamic expressions," it had also created "useless words and expressions" that must be "cast out" along with words "not in keeping with the spirit of the time." Also to be "cast out" were swearing and abusive language, which demean personal dignity, incorrect grammar, misspelling, and "faulty words and expressions." Now that the proletariat is in power, it needs the "instrument" of a clear, precise, incisive language to build a new life. Rudeness and deferential speech, for example, using the polite form (*vy,* "you") to officers, and familiar form (*ty,* "thou") to soldiers, were relics of feudalism.[51]

Realist Writers and Painters

Realist writers and painters emphasized political content, rather than a work's formal qualities. Nevertheless, finding nineteenth-century realism inadequate to describe the "epic events" of their time, they too advocated new forms: "neorealism" and "monumental realism" in literature and "heroic realism" and "monumental forms" in painting.

The All-Russian Association of Proletarian Writers (VAPP, 1921–28) claimed to represent the proletariat, even though its leaders, Leopold Averbach (1903–39) and others, were of bourgeois origin. Appropriating Proletkult's ideology but accepting Party discipline (they were all Party members), they pushed for a position of leadership in literature comparable to that of the Communist Party in politics. Literature serves one class at a time, they argued; its function is to organize the psyche and consciousness of that class. Therefore, nonproletarian writers should be limited to a certain percentage of journal space and a "communist cell," appointed to supervise literature. VAPP journals regularly announced enemies to be attacked.[52] In 1926, because of disagreements within VAPP, Averbakh founded a new journal *On Literary Guard (Na literaturnom postu),* which the Party supported.

VAPP's first target was *Red Virgin Soil,* a target of LEF as well. Both organizations advocated a class-conscious art policy and denounced Voronsky (editor of *Red Virgin Soil*) for publishing "fellow travelers" (Trotsky's term for non-Communists who accepted the Revolution). Voronsky judged a literary work by aesthetic, as well as political criteria, and contended that to fulfill its "educational" (= ideological) function, literature must depict real

---

51. Trotsky, *Problems of Everyday Life* (New York, 1973), 48–51, 52–56, 77–78.
52. Maguire, *Red Virgin Soil,* 160–62; Edward Brown, *The Proletarian Episode in Russian Literature, 1928–1932* (New York, 1953), 19.

human beings in real-life situations, including their confused or conflicted psychological states. Voronsky's "neo-realist" aesthetic mingled Tolstoy, romanticism, and "vitalistic doctrines of the early 20th century" (which would include Nietzsche, Bergson, and Freud).[53] He believed that the old intelligentsia was living through a harsh collapse and revaluation of its spiritual and cultural values. *Red Virgin Soil* would diagnose that process, hasten (as in Nietzsche's dictum, "what is falling should also be pushed") and guide it, making "fellow travelers" into Communists, for example. The journal's mandate required him to be a polemicist, so for the first few years of its existence, Voronsky attacked authors "deemed to be 'typical' of the class enemy," often in crudest and most reductionist way.[54] When he dropped the aggressive manner around 1923, "proletarian" zealots accused him of softness, even while appropriating his aesthetic. VAPP's slogan, "for the living man," stemmed from Voronsky's psychologism. Voronsky told young writers to master their craft by studying Pushkin and Tolstoy. VAPP told them to "study the classics" and called for a Red Tolstoy.

The "fellow traveler" Aleksei Tolstoi (1883–1945), an émigré who returned in 1923, proposed a new type of epic novel—"monumental realism." Tracing the "degradation" of the European novel from the great epic hero to the will-less intellectual and the "faceless" everyman, he asked: "Where are the authors who have gathered into great epics millions of wills, passions, and deeds? . . . To aestheticism I oppose the literature of *monumental realism*. Its task is the *creation of man*. . . . Its path leads straight to the highest goal: to create, with passion and grandiosity, a type of new Great Man. . . . From this point on, the paths of Russian and European literature must part. . . . Hero! We need a hero of our time. A heroic novel."[55] For Tolstoi, the principal goal of the new monumental realism is "the emotional cognition (*chuvstvennoie poznanie*) of the Great Man (*Bol'shogo cheloveka*)," the creation of a perfect human being. Tolstoi did not allude to class struggle or to the Marxist scheme of history but, as Irina Gutkin observes, only these absences separate Tolstoi's "monumental realism" from Socialist Realism.[56]

Marxist critics associated "monumental" forms, such as the epic novel, with periods of cultural vigor and short forms with periods of decadence— yet another example of the association of "super" with size. To fulfill its "educational" function, a novel had to hold the reader's attention. This required a linear plot and a hero with whom the masses could identify. In a 1921 discussion of such issues, Lunacharsky argued that the true hero is a revolutionary, a representative of the masses, a condensed expression of their

53. Maguire, *Red Virgin Soil*, 253.
54. Read, *Culture and Power*, 166–68.
55. Quoted in Irina Gutkin, *The Cultural Origins of the Socialist Realism Aesthetic* (Evanston, Ill., 1999), 77.
56. Ibid.

consciousness, giving Oliver Cromwell as an example (he wrote a play about Cromwell), while Kerzhentsev wanted Soviet theater to depict "those unknown to history, the Johns, Jeans, and Ivans, who were the flesh and blood of the oppressed mass."[57] By 1923, the former Proletkult leader had abandoned the ideals he had championed in *Creative Theater* and was advocating a state cinema that instructed the masses in class struggle.

The Proletkult ideal was kept alive by amateur groups, such as TRAM (Theater of Young Workers), founded in Leningrad in 1925 by Mikhail Sokolovsky, a young railroad worker and Komsomol activist, who wanted to develop a theater of "meetings, manifestos, and barricades" that would not only describe the worker's life but change it. Only full-time workers could belong. The plays, which the TRAM collective wrote, treated problems that young workers faced in their personal lives and on the job. The worker-actors were playing themselves and were more agitators than actors. Although TRAM stressed political content, its productions used such modernist "devices" as distortion, fragmentation, and actor-audience interchange to sustain interest. "Social masks" and "the revolutionary laugh" ridiculed and vilified such class enemies as hooligans, shirkers, dissipaters, and malingerers.[58] Piotrovsky, TRAM's patron in the Party, believed that an amateur (*samodeiatel'nyi*) theater emerged from the rituals and festivals of the lower classes and then rose to challenge the dominant modes of expression in the professional theater. In his eyes, TRAM was laying the groundwork of the theater of the future. To accelerate that process, TRAM tried to shut down the academic theaters and attacked Lunacharsky for subsidizing them.

The Association of Artists of Revolutionary Russia (AKhRR, 1922–32) denigrated the "abstract concoctions" and "fractured forms" of the avant-garde. "Revolutionary" pertained to subject matter—Red Army, workers and peasants, and Bolshevik leaders—not style. The artist's "civic duty" was to document artistically "the revolutionary impulse of this great moment in history," and this required "monumental forms." Even though AKhRR placed itself in the realistic tradition of the Wanderers (*Peredvizhniki,* a school that dominated Russian painting in the 1870s and 1880s), it advocated a new style, "heroic realism," "a strong, precise, invigorating style that organizes thought and feeling. AKhRR manifestos constantly extolled the "organizing" and "will-strengthening" functions of art and proclaimed its members' "will to express the revolution creatively."[59] The most prominent AKhRR

57. Robert A. Maguire, "Literary Conflicts in the 1920s," *Survey* 18, no. 1–2 (Winter 1972): 112–13.

58. V. Mironov, *TRAM: Agitatsionnyi molodezhnyi teatr, 1920–30x godov* (Leningrad, 1977), 13; Lynn Mally, "The Rise and Fall of the Soviet Youth Theater TRAM," *Slavic Review* 51, no. 3 (Fall 1992): 411–30.

59. Bowlt, *Russian Art of the Avant-Garde,* 266, 268–69, 270; Brandon Taylor, *Art and Revolution under the Bolsheviks* (London, 1992), 1:163–71, 2:21–22.

painters were Isaak Brodsky (1884–1939), Evgeny Katsman (1898–1976), and Aleksandr Gerasimov (1881–1963).

AKhRR's 1925 exhibition, "The Peoples of the Soviet Union," was truly monumental in scope. Lunacharsky gave the opening speech. By then AKhRR was the most influential single body of artists in Russia, with affiliates throughout the land, a young artists' section, a direct relationship with the Army and the Trade Unions that enabled it bypass the cultural bureaucracy, and powerful Bolshevik patrons—Iaroslavsky, Kamenev, Klement Voroshilov (1881–1969, Commissar of War), Sergei Kirov (1886–1934, head of the Leningrad Party), and Karl Radek (1885–1939, Comintern leader).

The Culture Wars Escalate

The peak of experimentation, cultural pluralism, and Bolshevik tolerance was reached in 1925. From then on, the culture wars escalated in scope, intensity, and viciousness. Lunacharsky was excoriated for his relative tolerance. VAPP and LEF each claimed to be the exclusive voice of the proletariat and called on the Party to enforce its claim. In 1925, thirty-seven writers, including Aleksei Tolstoi, Babel, and Esenin asked the Party for protection. The Central Committee of the Party responded with a resolution titled, "On the Policy of the Party in the Area of Artistic Literature," June 18, 1925, published in *Pravda* on July 1. Such was the importance attributed to literature. The Resolution affirmed diversity of form and style but it also said that the Soviet Union has "entered the zone of cultural revolution" and that "neutral" literature was impossible in a class society.[60] This resolution set the stage for the final battle between LEF and VAPP. The journal *Lef,* which many Bolsheviks perceived as destabilizing and nihilistic, lost its subsidy. UNOVIS was closed down after a critic condemned objectless art for its lack of utility.

The culture wars escalated again in 1927. Criticism by vilification became the norm. The journal *Lef* reappeared as *New Lef* (1928–28) and claimed to renounce futurism in favor of the "literature of fact," a style comparable to the *Neue Sachlichkeit* in Germany. Brik reminded readers of Marinetti's cold reception in Moscow (in 1914) and then said that while the Russian futurists never accepted Marinetti, they did make use of his slogans and "remain true to them to this very day." Among these slogans, which Brik quoted, were: "Beauty does not exist outside of battle. There are no masterpieces without aggressiveness. Poetry should be a cruel attack against unknown forces, demanding that they bow down before man" (*RF,* 252).

60. English translation in C. Vaughn James, *Soviet Socialist Realism: Origins and Theory* (New York, 1973), 116–19.

Furthermore, rather than "infect" people, or arouse an "unnecessary waste of emotions," or quarantine "dangerous" works, literature should incite people to a specific direction, "to the one we need." *New Lef* was not only for facts, but "also for distortion, for falsehood, for caricature, for the grotesque. We are against verisimilitude, against all art and literature that gives neither fact nor falsehood, nor truth nor invention with which one does not know what to do."[61] Tretiakov maintained that socialist construction does not need conflict-ridden neurotics, but "standardized activists," "robot-bureaucrats," and "communoid businessmen."[62]

At the end of 1927, Voronsky was removed as editor of *Red Virgin Soil* and expelled from the Party (he had supported Trotsky), a new censorship bureau was instituted, and the end of NEP was taken for granted. In 1927–28, VAPP and LEF engaged in a war to the death. VAAP won. Renamed RAPP, the Russian Association of Proletarian Writers (1928–32), it became the *de facto* ruler of Russian literature. RAPP's slogan "tear off the masks!" brutally summarized one of the key themes of the decade: "unmasking," "transparency," demystification," "baring the device," "tearing off the veils," Voronsky's phrase, which he took from Tolstoy. Indeed, Lenin himself had credited Tolstoy with "the most ruthless, sober realism, the tearing away of all and sundry masks" in a 1908 essay "Lev Tolstoy as the Mirror of the Russian Revolution" (*LCW*, 15:205).

"Unmasking" and its variants stemmed from, or were compatible with, Nietzsche's concept, which was in turn compatible with Marxism-Leninism. Nietzsche's hermeneutics of suspicion was directed against the "lies of millennia." Marx and Engels used the term "illusion" as a kind of mask and exposed the tawdry economic motivations of persons who professed lofty ideals. In "Party Organization and Party Literature" (1905) Lenin declared: "The freedom of the bourgeois writer, artist, or actress is simply masked (or hypocritically masked) dependence on the moneybag, on corruption, on prostitution. And we socialists expose this hypocrisy [and] rip off the false labels"; socialist literature is "*openly* linked to the proletariat" (*LA,* 151).

Trotsky predicted that in a socialist society, the powerful force of competition would not disappear, but "will be sublimated" into "struggle for one's opinion, for one's project, for one's taste." Political struggles will have vanished, because there will be no more classes:

> The liberated passions will be channeled into technique, into construction, which also includes art. . . . People will divide into "parties" over the question of a new gigantic canal, or the distribution of

61. Quoted in Barooshian, *Mayakovsky and Brik*, 101.
62. Mierau, *Tretjakow*, 65–66; *RF*, 267.

oases in the Sahara (such a question will exist too), over the regula-
tion of the weather and the climate, over a new theater, over chemical hypotheses, over two competing tendencies in music, and over a
best system of sports. . . . All will be equally interested in the success
of the whole. The struggle will have a purely ideologic character. It
will have no running after profits, it will have nothing mean, no betray-
als, no bribery, none of the things that form the soul of "competition"
in a society divided into classes. (*Literature*, 230–31)

According to classical Marxism, class struggle stems from scarcity, so the
final stage of communism is contingent on a fully developed industrial base.
But a Marxist or even a Marxist-Darwinist explanation does not fully explain
the extraordinary viciousness of the culture wars, which exceeded the viciousness that may have been necessary to survive as artists. The excess viciousness stemmed from fanaticism, sheer aggressiveness, and a push for hegemony.
Amazingly, for the statement just quoted was part of Trotsky's response to
"the Nietzscheans," he forgot about the "will to power."

By 1927–28, realism was changing into something "heroic" and "monumental," and the avant-garde was using representational forms. Even though
the avant-garde ultimately lost out to the realists, it had a profound impact
on Soviet political culture. Avant-garde polemicists sensitized Bolshevik pol-
icymakers to the psychopolitical importance of art form and language in
establishing the myth and imprinting it on the psyche. The avant-garde's
recognition of the power of the camera to create an alternate reality, and its
experiments with perspectivism, helped make photography and film into
some of the most effective instruments of Soviet propaganda. The vicious
cultural politics of the NEP period accelerated the search for a single socialist art form and language that became even more vicious during the Cultural
Revolution and culminated in the formulation of an official aesthetic in the
mid-1930s.

Echoes of Nietzsche in Stalin's Time, 1928–1953

In Stalin's time, ideas moved "from art to life," but not as symbolists, futurists, or the Soviet avant-garde had intended. The issues of the Nietzschean agenda were resolved by the Party; show trials theatricalized life, and coercion was ever present. The new myth, a happy and prosperous Soviet Union (thanks to Stalin), was propagated (after 1932–34) in a new art form, Socialist Realism. The qualities and morality of the new Soviet man and woman varied according to the needs of society, as the Party defined them. The new politics was "great politics," Stalin-style. A series of "new words" transmitted the Party line to the masses. To quote Vladislav Todorov:

> There was in fact a permanent usurpation of power by new words. Every single moment communist power was reconfirmed through newer and newer names: at one time to modernize society, at another to smash the enemy, at another still to collectivize the population, then to expose the conspiracy of the traitors, later to build the first "stage of socialism," then to build another stage that denied the previous one ... and so on. Somewhere in the conspiratorial spaces of Party power the ideology was worked out together with the plot for the next seizure of power. A new Party plenum comes, the course is changed, a new ideological strategy is formulated, the worn-out metaphors are replaced by recently fabricated ones.[1]

Previously used metaphors acquired new connotations. "The path" connoted a movement from one planned period of activity to another, thereby creating, in Jeffrey Brooks's words, "an imagined historical continuum in which every effort constituted a step toward further goals" and projecting the image of a community of activists "who were on the path, completing tasks, fol-

---

1. Vladislav Todorov, *Red Square / Black Square* (Albany, 1995), 160.

lowing the line, and moving forward" on various "fronts." "The line" was the Party line from which no "deviation" was allowed. "The task" subordinated current measures to a greater goal and "reduced the temporal and moral significance of atrocities."[2] "Building socialism" and "socialist construction" pertained to Party policy in general and to specific projects; the workers were "human material." Military metaphors mobilized the masses to fulfill their tasks and identified enemies to be attacked. Religious metaphors reinforced the military ones in the mid-1930s, conjuring up images of a Final Conflict. Systematic attempts to create a "proletarian" or a "socialist" science began during the Cultural Revolution and continued, on and off, for the next three decades. Victory in the Great Patriotic War (World War II) became the basis of postwar myths on the superiority of the Soviet system, the unity of the Soviet people, and the wisdom of Stalin, the "organizer of victory."

Stalin's tenure is usually subdivided into the periods of the First Five-Year Plan and Cultural Revolution (1928–32), the "great retreat" from communist principles (from 1932 or 1936 to 1939), World War II (1939–45), and the postwar period (1945–53).[3] I concentrate on the first two periods because the system established by 1939 remained intact, with variations to be sure, until after Stalin's death. Ronald Suny and Lewis Siegelbaum call the second period "building Stalinism."[4] Donald Treadgold calls it "the consolidation of totalitarianism."[5] Scholars who reject the "totalitarian" model point out the fissures and messiness beneath the facade of monolithic unity and pay great attention to voices "from below."[6] The goal, however, of the Party elite (and eventually Stalin) was indeed totalitarian, a society in which every aspect of life is controlled "from above." Even though the Party never attained this degree of control, as Robert Service observes, the project itself was "so ambitious that even its half-completion was a dreadful achievement."[7]

---

2. Brooks, *Thank You*, 136–37
3. Nicholas Timasheff, *The Great Retreat: The Growth and Decline of Communism in Russia* (New York, 1946). Note that scholars disagree on exactly when the "great retreat" began.
4. Ronald Suny, *The Soviet Experiment* (Oxford, 1998), chap. 11, "Building Stalinism," 252–68; Lewis Siegelbaum, "Building Stalinism, 1929–41," in *Russia: A History*, ed. Gregory Freeze (Oxford, 1997), 291–319.
5. Donald Treadgold, *Twentieth Century Russia* (Boulder, Colo., 1990), 255–76.
6. For details, see Abbott Gleason, "Totalitarianism Among the Sovietologists," in *Totalitarianism*, 121–48. See also Sheila Fitzpatrick, ed., *Cultural Revolution in Russia, 1928–31* (Bloomington, 1978); Arch Getty, *Origins of the Great Purges: The Soviet Communist Party Reconsidered* (New York, 1985); and "From the Editor: Controversy" and "Discussion," in *Russian Review* 45, no. 4 (October 1986): v–vi, 357–414; "From the Editor: More Controversy" and "Discussion," in *Russian Review* 46, no. 4 (October 1987): 375–78, 379–431. There are six articles in the first discussion and eleven in the second. See also, Ronald Suny, "Revision and Retreat in the Historiography of 1917: Social History and Its Critics," *Russian Review* 53, no. 2 (April 1994): 165–82.
7. Robert Service, *A History of Twentieth Century Russia* (Cambridge, Mass., 1997), 253.

Nietzschean ideas infused Stalin's projects, operating as currents within Marxism-Leninism and mingling with other currents in the Russian political and cultural legacy. Transmitters of Nietzschean ideas include both figures familiar to us (such as Gorky, Lunacharsky, Bukharin, and Kerzhentsev) and younger figures who developed an idea already present in the culture or picked up from Fascist or Nazi propaganda. (I do not follow the Soviet practice of conflating Fascism and Nazism because it obliterates major differences between the two, such as anti-Semitism, which was originally alien to Italian Fascism, but was always the major tenet of Nazism.) In most cases, whether or not the younger figures themselves read Nietzsche cannot be ascertained.

Propagandists in the dictatorships kept an eye on one another's techniques and adapted them to their particular ideological requirements. None of them were interested in the subtleties and complexities of Nietzsche's *oeuvre*, but only in compelling images and slogans. Soviet propagandists dubbed Nietzsche the "philosopher of fascism," but they constructed a Soviet Superman to counter the Nazi model. Both models vulgarized Nietzsche's concept. Incidentally, the American comic-strip hero made his debut in 1938 as a champion of "truth, justice, and the American way."

In Stalin's time, government publishing houses brought out two books on Nietzsche, M. G. Leiteizen's *Nietzsche and Finance Capital* (1928) and B. M. Bernadiner's *The Philosophy of Nietzsche and Fascism* (1934). The dates are significant. Leiteizen's book coincided with the beginning of the First Five-Year Plan and Cultural Revolution, and Bernadiner's with the inception of policies that had Nietzschean components: Socialist Realism, the full-blown Stalin Cult, and complementary cults. Both books can be read on two levels: the exoteric (the obvious meaning) and the esoteric. which elliptically explained current or anticipated Soviet policies that contradicted Marxist ideals or were otherwise embarrassing.

After 1928, and especially after 1932–34, the trail we have been following narrows, and conflicting appropriations of Nietzsche and Nietzschean ideas disappear. One Party-approved appropriation (never acknowledged as such) was a function of larger domestic and foreign policy considerations. During the First Five-Year Plan, propagandists extolled "iron will," "great politics," "mad" enthusiasm, and "collective creativity." Later on, they mythologized individual heroes. Socialist Realism was informed by Nietzsche's idea of art as a lie and defined against "bourgeois realism" on the one hand and aesthetic doctrines with Nietzschean components on the other. Anti-Nietzscheanism became a trope of Soviet "antifascist" propaganda in 1934. Stalin's will to power operated throughout. It was a factor in his desire to make "his" country into an industrialized superstate, to institute a command economy, to control intellectual and cultural life, to rehabilitate strong tsars, and to make himself the object of a new cult.

Much about the inner workings of Stalinism remains obscure. The Bolshevik elite did not oblige us by leaving written records of their experiences or their private thoughts and feelings. (Khrushchev wrote his memoirs years later, and they are mostly about the postwar period.) As far as we know, neither Stalin nor any member of Stalin's inner circle kept a diary. Recently opened archives often offer only clues about major policy decisions and debates because the Bolshevik elite continued to use underground methods, conducting much of its business by word of mouth, or giving instructions in documents that recipients were ordered to destroy after reading. Other archives are still off-limits to researchers.

I draw on Nietzsche's thought for hypotheses that might fill in some of these gaps and help us interpret aspects of Stalinism. In hindsight, his insights, observations, and predictions seem amazingly relevant. Was this because Nietzsche was already the political unconscious of Bolshevism? Or because, having internalized aspects of Nietzsche's thought, Soviet leaders extrapolated from them? Or because literal-minded Communists took Nietzsche's observations as recommendations? I suggest that beneath the surface of events all these factors were in play. In addition, I view Stalinism through a Nietzschean prism that centers on the "will to power." A nonrational drive, it helps explain policies that were economically counterproductive and gratuitously cruel.

Dionysus Unleashed: The Cultural Revolution and the First Five-Year Plan, 1928–1932

The First Five-Year Plan unleashed the primeval energies of destructiveness and creativity (the Dionysian impulse) to demolish the old world and build the new. Marx considered capitalism tremendously creative and tremendously destructive. Could communism be any less? By means of sheer human energy and iron will, a backward nation would be transformed into a prosperous, industrialized super-state, populated by new men and women building an "advanced" civilization. In Stalin's words: "When we have put the U.S.S.R. in an automobile, and the peasant on a tractor, let the worthy capitalists, who boast so much of their 'civilization,' try to overtake us! We shall yet see which countries may then be 'classified' as backward and which as 'advanced'" (*SW*, 12:141). Mayakovsky declaimed: "in aeroplanes, in tractors, at whatever task / your world-famous streamlined America . . . / we shall overtake and surpass."[1] "Overtake and surpass America!" became a slogan of the Plan. The egalitarianism and collectivism exalted for most of this period stemmed from Marxism, of course, and was reinforced by Dionysian appropriations of Nietzsche (deindividuation, self-forgetting) and a long-standing mystique of the commune. Propagandists recreated the secularized apocalypticism of the revolutionary period and stimulated the passion of fanaticism (Merezhkovsky's term) even while vaunting "reason" and "science." Merezhkovsky once referred to "the most abstract, insatiable, and destructive of the passions—fanaticism, the passion of ideas" (*MPSS*, 18:14). This passion inspired stupendous efforts to fulfill and overfulfill the plan, on the one hand, and fostered brutality toward individuals and entire categories of the population, on the other, because they were accused of obstructing the path to socialism, Some zealots expected a Final Conflict to precede the entry into the New World.

---

1. "Americans are Astounded" (1929), in *The Bedbug and Selected Poetry*, ed. Patricia Blake, trans. Max Haywood and George Reavey (Bloomington, 1975), 395.

The idea of "unleashing," and the word itself, was used by proponents, critics, and observers of Stalin's policies.[2] The American reporter, Eugene Lyons, wrote: "The tides are in leash and the leash is in the grip of a small group in Red Square."[3] The "super" scale of the Plan, directing the economy of a nation that occupies one-sixth of the earth's landmass, while simultaneously transforming human nature, constituted a distillation and a bonding of the Promethean elements in Marxism, Leninism, and Nietzscheanism. The success of the Plan depended on "unleashing" the (Dionysian) enthusiasm and energy of the masses. The extra-economic aspects, the fixation on psychological and cultural transformation, made the Plan "great politics" in the Nietzschean sense.

The same Fifteenth Party Congress that expelled Trotsky in December 1927 tacitly adopted the Trotsky/Preobrazhensky industrialization strategy of concentrating on heavy industry and getting the capital by squeezing the peasants financially. The First Five-Year Plan featured rapid industrialization and collectivization of agriculture. Pictured as getting the Revolution back on course at last, it was formally approved by the Sixteenth Party Congress in April 1929 (which backdated the official starting point to October 1928), and scheduled to end in October 1933. In the summer of 1929, production targets were raised, the pace accelerated, and the Party resolved to complete the Plan in four years—in slogan form "2 + 2 = 5." The expression was first used by Dostoevsky's underground man to signify the triumph of individual will over the constraints of reality; the Soviet slogan pertained to the triumph of collective will. In November, Stalin proclaimed 1929 the "year of the great break" ("*god velikogo pereloma*"). This phrase connotes the Marxist leap from "necessity" to "freedom," the futurist sense of disjuncture, and a secularized apocalypticism, a complete rupture with the accursed old world. Under Stalin's leadership, the masses were building an earthly paradise.

The Stalin Cult emerged in December 1929; its functions were to rally everyone around "the leader" (*vozhd'*) and to obscure the gap between promise and fulfillment. The gap expanded in the next few years as the Plan turned into a series of crash programs that allocated resources to heavy industry, epitomized by iron and steel, to the neglect of consumer goods. Failure to coordinate production schedules with deliveries of raw materials and parts left factory managers scrambling to fulfill their production norms. Illegal deals for needed materials and parts, "shock work," "socialist competition," and "storming" (working at a breakneck pace) became routine.[4] In this frenetic atmosphere, Stalin was pictured as a helmsman calmly steering the ship

2. Moshe Lewin, *Political Undercurrents of Soviet Economic Debates* (Princeton, 1974), 103–4; Fitzpatrick, *Cultural Revolution*, 30.
3. Eugene Lyons, *Assignment in Utopia* (New York, 1937), 103.
4. Details in Hiroyoke Kuromiya, *Stalin's Industrial Revolution* (Cambridge, 1988); Moshe Lewin, *Russian Peasants and Soviet Power* (New York, 1968); Anne Rasweiller, *The*

of state through stormy seas, or as the driver of a train. Implicitly, without "the boss," the ship would sink or the train would derail. The stock market crash of October 1929, followed by the Great Depression, confirmed Soviet leaders' belief that they were on the right course. The sharp drop in the Soviet standard of living (bread rationing began in 1929) was considered temporary. Meanwhile, unemployment had been eliminated, and women were entering the work force in large numbers, making gender equality feasible at last.

For the peasants, the Plan was a disaster. In December 1929, Stalin called for the "elimination of the kulaks as a class." Brutality against the "kulaks" was followed by a reign of terror against the peasantry as a whole.[5] The peasants resisted collectivization by demonstrating, rising up in armed rebellion, slaughtering their livestock, and planting less.[6] In March 1930, Stalin called off forced collectivization, lest the spring sowing be jeopardized and blamed "excesses" on Communists "dizzy with success." Once the harvest was in, forced collectivization resumed, leading once again, to massive resistance. The government retaliated by expropriating the grain. During the "terror-famine" (Robert Conquest's term) of 1932–33, which followed collectivization, millions of peasants were deliberately starved to death.[7] When internal passports, an artifact of the tsarist era, were reintroduced at the end of 1932, peasants did not receive them, tying them to the land in what they bitterly called a "second serfdom." Selective recruitment for industry continued, however, and it was mostly young men who left. As early as 1933, the majority of collective farmers were women.

Lenin once said that "politics cannot fail to take priority over economics. Not to understand this is to forget the ABC of Marxism."[8] Note that here, Lenin had reversed the base-superstructure model of classical Marxism. Politics, of course, is about power. Like just about all Marxists, however, Lenin considered private property a form of power. He assumed that abolishing private property would liberate humanity. Instead, the "command economy" became the cornerstone of Stalinism. Elimination of the private sector made the state the sole employer and enabled it to determine what was produced, how it was distributed, and what was reported by the state-owned newspapers,

Generation of Power: History of Dneprostroi (Oxford, 1988); and Stephen Kotkin, *Magnetic Mountain* (Berkeley and Los Angeles, 1995).

5. For the sheer brutality of dekulakization, see Merle Fainsod, *Smolensk Under Soviet Rule* (New York, 1963), 242–51; the semi-autobiographical account in Vasily Grossman's *Forever Flowing* (New York, 1972), 140–66; and Sheila Fitzpatrick, *Stalin's Peasants* (Oxford, 1994), 54–55.

6. Details in Lynn Viola, *Peasant Rebels Under Stalin* (Oxford, 1996).

7. Robert Conquest, *The Harvest of Sorrow: Soviet Collectivization and the Terror Famine* (New York, 1986).

8. *Quotations from Chairman Mao*, ed. Stuart Schram (New York, 1967), 181 n. 9.

journals, and radio-stations. To avoid arousing sympathy for the kulaks, pictures of the actual process of dekulakization (e.g., a kulak family being driven out of its home) were forbidden. All private publishing was banned in 1930, after Kaganovich denounced "deviant intellectuals."

Forced collectivization was not just a way to finance industrialization by a "super-tax" or "tribute" (the terms used) exacted from the peasants. "Tribute" implies inequality, even conquest, as when Russians paid tribute to the Mongols. The fundamental purpose of collectivization, and that of the "terror-famine" as well, was to extend "Soviet power" to the countryside and break the will of the peasantry once and for all. Subjugating the peasants cost the country its best farmers, millions of peasant lives, and a permanently impaired agricultural sector—a scandalous waste in economic terms, necessary costs in power/political ones. On the "industrial front," political considerations overrode economic efficiency. At a time when managerial and technical expertise were desperately needed, "bourgeois specialists" were fired and demonstrations against them took workers out of production for hours at a time.

Despite enormous waste and unprecedented brutality, the First and Second (1933–38) Five-Year Plans created the infrastructure of an industrialized society. Martin Malia considers industrialization "the supreme feat of Bolshevik voluntarism."[9] Industrialization made possible the Soviet Union's other main achievement, victory in World War II.

Bukharin preferred financial coercion to physical coercion and indoctrination to violence, but he was entranced by visions of "great politics," and he wanted to remain among the Party's "higher men"—one of its two Himalayas as Stalin put it, Stalin being the other. In "The Great Reconstruction" (February 19, 1930), Bukharin lauded the ongoing economic, technological, and psychological revolution as "gigantic," "stupendous," "colossal," and "enormous." Denying that Stalin had returned to "war communism" (which of course he had), Bukharin supported "extreme measures" against the peasantry, even while noting their significant costs.[10] Stephen Cohen considers this article an Aesopian protest against collectivization.[11] But the protest, if such it was, was very subtle. The article can also be read as an olive-branch to Stalin, offered in vain, it turned out.

Some two weeks later, Bukharin published another article titled "Finance Capital in the Mantle of the Pope," in which he used the pope as a surrogate for Stalin and the Jesuit order as a surrogate for what the Party had

---

9.   Malia, *Soviet Tragedy*, 201.
10.   "Velikaia rekonstruktsiia," in *N. I. Bukharin, Izbrannye proizvedeniia*, ed. L. I. Abalkin et al. (Moscow, 1990), 491–95.
11.   Stephen Cohen, *Bukharin and the Bolshevik Revolution* (New York, 1975), 349.

become.[12] This was definitely Aesopian language and Stalin retaliated. The details of the "right opposition's" confrontations, recantations, and reconciliations with Stalin, and their ultimate defeat are well known and will not be repeated here.[13] By the end of 1930 the highest echelons of the government and the Party were staffed by "Stalin's men," namely, Molotov, Voroshilov, Lazar Kaganovich (1893–1991), and Andrei Zhdanov (1896–1948). All had been commissars during the Civil War and were accustomed to command.

Questioning the feasibility of any aspect of the Plan was considered disloyal and called "creeping empiricism," a phrase that unintentionally encapsulated the Plan's utopian nature. Bazarov and other GOSPLAN economists were arraigned for "criminally" trying to undermine industrialization by proposing low (= realistic) planning targets. Managers of food trusts were charged with destroying food supplies or poisoning workers. To gauge the level of popular enthusiasm for the Plan in such an atmosphere is impossible, because expressions of doubt or dissatisfaction could be construed as "wrecking." Hardly any workers were so accused, however, because the target was "bourgeois specialists," such as the engineers of the Shakhty mines. Their show trial was the first of a series of trials that scapegoated engineers and managers as "saboteurs" of the Plan.

Sheila Fitzpatrick dates the Cultural Revolution from the announcement of the Shakhty trial (March 1928) to Stalin's "New Conditions" speech (June 1931), which attacked "specialist-baiting" and denounced the "leftist" policy of equal wages.[14] The Cultural Revolution went beyond war on the "bourgeois specialists," however. It was intended to "smelt" or "recast" workers and peasants into new men and women, remove all "bourgeois" influences from Soviet life, and create a distinctively proletarian art and science. The Cultural Revolution was not completely over until April 1932, when the Central Committee ordered RAPP and all other literary and artistic factions (organizations), including the remnants of Proletkult, to dissolve.

The Cultural Revolution was set in motion "from above," but it was also propelled "from below" by Communists who considered NEP a betrayal of their ideals and by workers resentful of the high salaries and perquisites of "bourgeois specialists." Other forces "from below" were artists, writers, scholars, and scientists pushing for hegemony in their fields; young people motivated by ambition, or idealism, or fanaticism, or combinations thereof;

12. Ibid., 349. Full text in Bukharin, *Etiudy*, 335–53.
13. Robert Daniels, *The Conscience of the Revolution* (Cambridge, Mass., 1960); Cohen, *Bukharin;* Leonard Schapiro, *The History of the Communist Party* (New York, 1971).
14. Sheila Fitzpatrick, *The Cultural Front: Power and Revolution in Revolutionary Russia* (Ithaca, 1992), especially 91–114 and 115–48. Stalin's speech "New Conditions—New Tasks of Economic Construction" is excerpted in Daniels, *Documentary History,* 183–85.

and assorted visionaries. Shulgin preached the "withering away of the school." Evgeny Pashukanis (1891–1937) advocated the "withering away" of law. Perceiving that it was safe to do so, zealots and opportunists attacked "bourgeois" engineers, factory managers, scholars, and teachers. Like "aristo" during the French Revolution, "bourgeois" was an attack-word, not a designation of actual class origin or belief. Intellectuals and professionals were automatically "bourgeois." Crash programs were instituted to produce more "Red specialists," and *rabfak* schools were expanded. Workers and peasants known as *vydvizhentsi,* from the Russian word "to push forward," were promoted to white-collar, managerial, and professional positions in a Soviet version of affirmative action. The power of the Soviet Academy of Science was reduced, and it was forced to accept Communist members. In every academic field, militants attacked "apoliticism" and "neutralism."[15]

Institutions of cultural control were strengthened and new ones established. Some officials wore several hats. Kerzhentsev (the former proletarian culture theorist), was deputy chair of *Kul'tprop* (founded in January 1930), deputy chair of the Communist Academy, head of the All-Union radio from 1930 to 1933, and on the editorial board of *Press and Revolution.* A. I. Stetsky (1896–1938), *Kul'tprop's* founder and chair, also chaired the Communist Academy's Institute of Literature, Art, and Linguistics and edited *Press and Revolution,* after the original editor was removed for being too liberal. The Communist Academy was one of the prime movers of cultural revolution in the arts and in the sciences.

Like so much else in these years, cultural policy was confused and contradictory. Top Bolsheviks disagreed with one another; there were fights between various government agencies (the Commissariat of Enlightenment versus the Supreme Economic Council on training engineers, for example), and between local and central officials. Personnel changes in cultural institutions were frequent, as were feuds within the victorious "proletarian" groups. In every sector of Soviet society, parallel hierarchies of officials and overlapping jurisdictions led to intrigues, infighting, and provocations. People were confused and nervous and waited for instructions "from above." Sometimes multiple authorities had to be satisfied. Leaders operated by indirect orders, signals, and innuendoes. Around 1930–31, a new type of intellectual emerged, the Party-approved specialist whose role was to transmit the Party line in his field.

The Party had always considered itself the embodiment of reason and will directing the (Dionysian) energies of the masses. As the elemental forces "unleashed" by the Cultural Revolution gained momentum, they jeopard-

15. David Joravsky, *Marxism and Natural Science, 1917–32* (New York, 1961), 234–39; Alexander Vucinich, *Empire of Knowledge: The Academy of Sciences of the U.S.S.R.* (Berkeley and Los Angeles, 1984), 188–94.

ized fulfillment of the Plan. After Stalin's "New Conditions" speech (June 1931) the adjective *stikhiinyi,* "elemental," took on the connotation of willful or out of control. The April 1932 resolution that ended the dictatorship of RAPP showed that what the Party had "unleashed," it could rein in. The Cultural Revolution was over. Organizations of scientists, considered interest groups, were ordered to dissolve just as literary and artistic organizations were. In December 1932, the First Five-Year Plan was officially declared complete, ten months ahead of schedule.

Complete nationalization, centralized planning, and the elimination of market forces are vintage Marxism, but the emphasis on psychological transformation and cultural construction (*stroitel'stvo*) came from Nietzsche and his Russian appropriators. Bukharin drew on Bogdanov for his strategy of cultural revolution. As for Stalin, in 1907–10, he was closer to Krasin and Bogdanov than to Lenin. The future dictator found good sides to "Machism" and liked the idea of making Marxism into a religion.[16]

16. Williams, *Other Bolsheviks,* 120–21, 142.

"Great Politics" Stalin-Style

The concept of politics will have merged entirely with
a war of spirits; all power structures of the old society will have been exploded—all of them are based
on lies: there will be wars the like of which have never
yet been seen on earth. It is only beginning with me
that the earth knows great politics.   —*EH,* 327

The First Five-Year Plan merged politics, economics, and
culture in a war against anyone or anything labeled "bourgeois." Stalin radicalized Bukharin's strategy of cultural revolution "from above" and "unleashed" proletarian zealots
"from below." Leiteizen's book *Nietzsche and Finance
Capital* (1928) endorsed Nietzsche's concept of "great politics" and proclaimed that communists, not fascists, were
Nietzsche's true heirs![1] Bolshevik zealots followed the
Machiavellian (and Leninist) principle that the end justifies
the means. Machiavelli, however, was not trying to change
human nature or to create a new kind of society or a new
culture. His horizon was the limited and pragmatic politics
of the Italian city-states. Nietzsche's "great politics" was
consonant with the millennial enthusiasm and global visions

1. Leiteizen, *Nitsshe i finansovyi kapital.*

of Bolshevism and early Stalinism. The Five-Year Plan can also be considered a "great cultural project" (Nietzsche's term) because Bolsheviks regarded material edifices as part of culture. Nietzsche's appropriators did not make the Plan (they were not number-crunching types), but they helped create the atmosphere that made its grandiose targets seem feasible. By the end of 1927, "genetic" planning (extrapolations from empirical data) was a derogatory term, and "teleological" planning (setting targets), a term of praise, because it implied that Soviet economic growth need not be constrained by "objective" economic laws.[2]

The Nietzschean Substratum of the First Five-Year Plan

Nietzsche's "great cultural projects" would take thousands of years to complete. Stalin, however, promised paradise on earth in a few years. With passionate belief and indefatigable will, people could do anything. What had taken the English one hundred years to achieve, the Soviet Union would accomplish in ten. An Old Bolshevik, Georgy Piatikov (1890–1937), asserted: "The essential feature of the Bolshevik Communist party is the limitless extension of the possible. . . . This feature distinguishes it from all other parties and makes it a party of miracles."[3] GOSPLAN economist Stanislav Strumilin (1877–1974) declared that objective economic laws were obsolete, because the leap from necessity to freedom was already taking place.[4] Eugene Lyons recalled: "Socialism in one mad leap! I saw its daring, but disregarded the madness."[5] Factories were exhorted to exceed their production norms, even if overfulfillment disrupted the schedules of other factories or resulted in bottlenecks and shortages down the line. In Sheila Fitzpatrick's words, this Plan "was not meant to allocate resources or balance demands but to drive the economy forward pell-mell."[6]

The masses were regarded as objects to be reworked and transformed. Radek called the Soviet Union a "workshop for the mass production of heroes."[7] The writer Olesha said (perhaps ironically), "If I cannot be an engineer of the elements [stikhii], I can be an engineer of human material."[8] A shock worker asserted: we are living in a "colossal period of reconstruc-

---

2. King, "Russian Revolution," 79. "Genetic" and "teleological" are Bazarov's terms. He helped draw up the original Plan, which emphasized balanced development. Subsequent versions were markedly unbalanced.

3. Quoted in Walicki, *Marxism*, 460.

4. Quoted in Lewin, *Political Undercurrents*, 99.

5. Lyons, *Assignment in Utopia*, 197.

6. Fitzpatrick, *Russian Revolution*, 132.

7. Karl Radek, "Shock Brigadiers" (1931), in *Portraits and Pamphlets* (Freeport, N.Y., 1935; reprint, 1966), 293–94.

8. Iuri Olesha, *Izbrannye* (Moscow, 1974), 229.

tion of human material. Socialist competition puts each of us under fire. . . . Competition recasts and reeducates us."[9] In the fiery furnaces of the steel mills, human nature would be smelted and recast.

Trotsky predicted that when the economy developed a surplus, "the Soviet state will take up the problem of gigantic constructions that will suitably express the monumental spirit of our epoch." There would be a "gigantic expansion of the scope and artistic quality of industry." Architecture would perform "monumental tasks," including the "titanic construction of city-villages" (*Literature,* 246, 249). Such grandiose predictions were reflected in the Plan, but there was no surplus when it began and none when it ended.

The task of rapid industrialization was so daunting that without "mad" Dionysian enthusiasm it might not have been undertaken at all. Three decades later, the economist Naum Jasny labeled the years 1928–31 the "era of bac-chanalian planning," intuitively recognizing its substratum.[10] People worked at a frenetic pace, for the slogan was "Tempo decides everything!" In February 1931, Stalin warned that the tempo could not be slackened. The "socialist fatherland" was "fifty or a hundred years behind the advanced countries. We must make good this distance in ten years. Either we do it or we shall be crushed."[11] Stalin wanted Communists to master technology, so he replaced the "Tempo" slogan with a new one, "Technology [*tekhnika,* sometimes translated as "technique"] decides everything!"

The Party adapted the warrior ethos of the Civil War to "socialist con-struction," giving the Plan the aura of a military campaign and the pace of a forced march. Factories operated around the clock; loudspeakers blared forth statistics on production battles won, ambushes carried out, fortresses to be stormed, mobilizations to be completed, and targets to be destroyed. The press reported on "campaigns" and "fronts." "Brigades" and "shock troops" of workers stormed "narrow passes." "Iron battalions" took "com-bat sectors under heavy fire." The "light cavalry," a Komsomol organiza-tion established in 1927, took possession of "commando outposts" in dangerous "raids" or "attacks." "Deserters" were shamed or ridiculed. Writers and artists became "writer-fighters" battling on theatrical or literary "fronts." The already mythologized "heroic period" of Soviet history (the Revolution and the Civil War) was ritually reenacted in literature, theater, and film. The war climate fostered zealotry and brutality and made it possible to deploy the masses in a way that might have been unacceptable in peacetime. In addi-tion, war sanctioned the creation of an all-powerful state and an economy which disregarded civilian needs (consumer goods). "Primitive socialist accu-mulation" mandated a Spartan lifestyle for the masses.

9. Quoted in Kuromiya, *Stalin's Industrial Revolution,* 126.
10. Naum Jasny, *Soviet Industrialization, 1928–52* (Chicago, 1961), 73–80.
11. Stalin, "The Tasks of Business Executives," in Daniels, *Documentary History,* 181–82.

The war included the conquest of nature, an aspect of the Plan that melded Nietzschean, Fedorovian, and Marxist tenets with a Nietzschean apotheosis of will. The conquest of nature is a classically American idea too—"taming" the wilderness—but the Soviet version was more drastic. Trotsky predicted that man would rebuild the earth, "if not in his own image, at least according to his own taste. . . . He will point out places for mountains and for passes. He will change the course of the rivers, and he will lay down rules for the oceans" (*Literature,* 251–52). Mountains were dynamited, primeval forests cleared, rivers straightened, and canals built, not just for economic reasons but as expressions of man's triumph over "the elements," his subjection of the world to reason. Mayakovsky declaimed: "Siberia will blaze with furnaces like a hundred suns . . . the taiga, defeated, will retreat beyond [Lake] Baikal."[12]

The gigantic construction projects were functional monuments as Tatlin's Tower would have been. Foreign critics compared them to the Pyramids and Party leaders to Pharoah. Bukharin replied: "The pyramids of the Pharoahs are the materialization of unproductive labor, symbol of gods and tsars, ancient Bastilles of the soul, like the Gothic cathedrals of the middle ages. . . . Our colossi are the great tools of productive labor."[13] In *Historical Materialism,* Bukharin had asked why a vast quantity of labor had been expended on the Pyramids and answered: to constantly impress upon slaves and peasants, the sublimity and divine power of their rulers. In the absence of newspapers and telegraph agencies, art served as the ideological bond (*HM,* 220). Soviet functional monuments did the same.

Propagandists associated Stalin with Peter the Great. Stalin identified with Peter and thought of himself as continuing Peter's modernization of Russia. The Moscow-Volga Canal (built 1931–37) was a step toward fulfilling Peter the Great's plan of making Moscow into a port that served five seas. Built entirely by forced labor, this canal gave Moscow access to the Baltic, White, and Caspian Seas; the completion of the Volga-Don Canal in 1952 brought the Black and Azov seas into range. The word "*zek,*" slang for convict, is an acronym for the Russian words "prisoners of the canal-building directorate"[14]

The Plan's Nietzschean substratrum appealed to foreign supporters of the "Soviet experiment." An American woman who emigrated to Russia, Margaret Weitlin, "chose to see socialism as a complete and immediate transvaluation of values marking the end of one era and the beginning of the

---

12. "The Construction Sites and the Men of Kuznetsk" (1927), quoted in Anatole Kopp, *Town and Revolution* (New York, 1970), vi.

13. Quoted in Loren Graham, *The Soviet Academy of Sciences and the Communist Party* (Princeton, 1967), 154.

14. For details on the canal, including its magnitude, see Timothy Colton, *Moscow: Governing the Socialist Metropolis* (Cambridge, Mass., 1995), 257–58.

next." Invoking Spengler's conception of Faustian culture, she declared that the sun was setting in the West.[15] Anna Louise Strong hailed collectivization as a most "spectacular act of ruthlessness" made by a political machine in defiance of the majority opinion in its own ranks and praised the Soviet Union's "daring leadership." Sidney and Beatrice Webb wrote: "Strong must have been the faith and resolute the will of men who, in the interest of what seemed to them the public good, could take so momentous a decision." They were lauding the elimination of the kulaks. George Bernard Shaw—a socialist, a Nietzschean, and an admirer of Mussolini and Stalin—made light of the hunger of the Soviet people and denied the very existence of a famine.[16] André Gide declared: "The notion of liberty such as it is taught us . . . seems to me false and pernicious in the extreme. And if I approve of Soviet constraint, I must also approve of Fascist discipline. . man does nothing valid without constraint, and those capable of finding this constraint within themselves are very rare." "We should side with the men who made Socrates drink the hemlock."[17]

In the mass rallies, parades, and show trials that accompanied the First Five-Year Plan, a sinister form of Dionysian theater arose, one that demanded human sacrifice. The Shakhty engineers and other "bourgeois" scapegoats were called "former people" and "vermin" (*vrediteli*), Lunacharsky's epithets for the SRs in the 1922 show trial. *Vrediteli* acquired a new meaning in the 1928–30 trials, "wreckers" or "saboteurs," which it retained thereafter. Andrei Vyshinsky (1883–1955), the prosecutor in the trial of the so-called Industrial Party (1930), said that he was inspired by Lunacharsky's performance in 1922.[18] Half a million workers marched against the "wreckers" and "saboteurs" of that "party" in 1930. As described by Eugene Lyons:

> Hour after hour as night engulfed the city, the gigantic parade rolled past the Nobles Club and its shouts of Death! Death! Death! could be heard in the columned ballroom where the trial was underway. . . . It was a synthetic delirium, its very phrases prescribed, a litany of blood thirst. At the proper moment it would be shut off as artificially as it

---

15. Margaret Weitlin, *Fifty Russian Winters* (New York, 1992), 37.

16. Lyons, *Assignment in Utopia*, 283–84, 428–31; A. L. Tait, "George Bernard Shaw and the USSR," *Irish Slavonic Papers*, no. 5 (1984): 83–113.

17. Quoted in Alistair Hamilton, *The Appeal of Fascism* (New York, 1971), xxi–xxiii. Hamilton emphasizes the appeal to intellectuals of Nietzsche's idea of the "artist-tyrant."

On other occasions, however, Gide advocated a "communist individualism" and he protested the criminalization of male homosexuality in 1934. After touring the Soviet Union in 1936, he concluded that it was a Dictatorship of the Bureaucracy that exploited workers and peasants, and became one of its most vehement critics. See Gide's contribution to *The God That Failed* (New York, 1959, 157–76, and Enid Starkie's introduction, 147–56.

18. A. B. Khalatov, ed., *Pamiati A. V. Lunacharskogo* (Moscow, 1935), 41.

had been loosed upon the country. Only the bitterness and hatred were real, because they sprang from real pain and real anger.[19]

He found Soviet parades imposing and ominous because of their organization. "They are demonstrations of government-organized and disciplined strength . . . reviews of fighting forces, counting of heads. The slogans are in no sense a spontaneous expression of public opinion. They have been carefully selected and announced by the 'ruling group' in formal edicts. Not simply the subject matter but the precise wording has been officially prescribed."[20] Lyons regarded the "demonstration trial" (show trial) as the unique Bolshevik contribution to the art of propaganda. "Every actor from the judges down to the 'extras,' knows his assigned role" (371). Indeed, the actors in the show trials were engaging in myth-creation, though not all of them knew it. The playful, let's pretend elements of the "conditional theater" were dropped and the illusion on the "stage" was passed off as truth. Mood-creating techniques honed by symbolists and others were adapted to political liturgies in which the "single will" was neither the director's nor the actor's, but the Party's. The prerevolutionary "conditional theater" separated art and life. Stalin's theatricalization of life fused the two, producing millions of real victims.

Bukharin's Strategy of Cultural Revolution

To Bukharin, culture was a function of power, an extra-economic phenomenon like the state which affects the economic base, rather than merely reflects it. "Bourgeois culture" would have to be destroyed, just as the "bourgeois state" had been destroyed, and the psyche of the masses totally reconstructed—ideas derived from Bogdanov, crudely applied and set in a Leninist framework. John Biggart showed that Bukharin's strategy represented a link in official thinking between late Leninism and Stalinism.[21] Bukharin proposed a "hard" strategy of cultural revolution in 1922–23, softened it in the mid-1920s, and returned to the "hard" strategy in 1928. Sheila Fitzpatrick says that stylistic evidence points to Bukharin as the author of *Pravda*'s first editorial statement on the cultural implications of the Shakhty trial, which was in the spirit of "militant proletarian purism."[22]

19. Lyons, *Assignment in Utopia*, 372.
20. Ibid., 103.
21. John Biggart, "Bukharin's Theory of Cultural Revolution," in *The Ideas of Nikolai Bukharin*, ed. Anthony Kemp-Welch (Oxford, 1992), 131. See also idem, "Bukharin and the Origins of the 'Proletarian Culture' Debate," *Soviet Studies* 39, no. 2 (April 1987): 234.
22. Fitzpatrick, *Cultural Front*, 121.

In 1922–23, Bukharin advocated a cultural revolution to be conducted by iron-willed cohorts or cadres (*kogorta*), whose low educational level mandated simplification and codification of Marxist ideology—the very dogmatism that Bogdanov had opposed. Bogdanov had worried about the subjugation of the proletariat to a new social stratum. Bukharin feared a technocracy ruled by "bourgeois specialists," but he came to accept specialization. "We have to put out of our mind the idea that everybody can do everything. Now we need specialists who perhaps know nothing about other disciplines but who are expert in their own discipline, as the bourgeois specialist used to be."[23] Even the Russian saints had their specialties (*HM*, 171). Bogdanov had argued that cultural revolution had to precede political revolution, as it had for the French bourgeoisie. Bukharin contended that for the proletariat the situation was different. Excluded from the temples and laboratories of bourgeois culture and exhausted by incessant labor, the proletariat had to seize political power *before* it could develop its own culture. The process had begun, but it had to be accelerated lest the masses be seduced by the temptations of NEP.

The iron-willed cadres would be "a unique revolutionary order" composed of zealots who disdained all "liberal and reformist groups, everything 'scattered-brained,' 'soft,' 'broad,' 'tolerant.'" This "order" would be "a steel instrument for processing [*obrabatyvaioshchii*] the brain of the *masses*, for uniting the masses, for leading the masses." Assuming leadership roles in mass organizations and workers clubs, the "iron cohorts" would be a "real ideologically moving force which adjusts the gigantic wheel of the mechanism of all classes and the entire mass of workers."[24] (Note the mechanical metaphor and who adjusts whom.) The cadres would have the same traits that enabled the Bolsheviks to seize and retain power—daring, decisiveness, consciousness, activism, will, hardness, and Marxist steadfastness—because "the gargantuan task" of cultural revolution "demands the greatest concentration of forces, not from the entire mass but from its class avantgarde." Their activist Marxism was not "scholasticism or talmudism, but a brilliant understanding of Marxist dialectic as a weapon of *practical* struggle." We have "a splendid instrument [*orudie*] which *we* possess; it doesn't possess us. And this living revolutionary Marxism will actually help create a miracle!" (*HM*, 37–38). In Gorky's novel *Confession*, the people (*narod*) create miracles; Bukharin was transferring the wonder-working power to Party cadres armed with the "new word" and backed by state power. His emphasis on "iron cohorts" was also a response to Fascist "methods of combat" in Italy. After Mussolini came to power, Bukharin said: "If one regards

23. Quoted in Biggart, "Bukharin's Theory," 143.
24. Bukharin, "Zheleznaia kogorta revoliutsii" (1922), in *N. I. Bukharin, Izbrannye proizvedeniia*, ed. G. L. Smirnov et al. (Moscow, 1988), 35–36.

them [Fascists] from the formal point of view . . . then one discovers in them a complete application of Bolshevik tactics, and especially those of Russian Bolshevism, in the sense of the rapid concentration of forces [and] energetic action of a tightly structured military organization in the sense of committing one's forces . . . mobilization, etc., and the pitiless destruction of the enemy whenever this is necessary."[25]

To counter the non-Marxists, who dominated the "commanding heights" of Soviet academia, Bukharin advocated a "command staff" of the Dictatorship of the Proletariat to be composed of "generals of Marxist ideology," "*Marxist* historians, *Marxist* mathematicians" who would rework [= revalue] their subjects in the light of dialectical materialism. Together with other Marxist scientists and scholars, they would produce the "officers" and "noncommissioned officers" of the Dictatorship of the Proletariat, who would in turn train lower-level soldier-educators in the "reworking" (*pererabotka*) of the masses. Only such measures could prevent the retrogression of the working class to capitalism.[26]

Only two years later, however, Bukharin told "proletarian" zealots that no directive had told Pushkin how to write poetry and noted the difficulty of distinguishing between "all-human" and specifically proletarian traits. Achieving cultural hegemony was not the same as achieving political hegemony. "Proletarian" writers must "first build and then receive," produce quality literature and not just polemicize.[27] Bukharin was the primary author of "On Party Policy in the Field of Literature" (June 1925), the resolution mentioned in Chapter 8. Although that resolution rebuffed VAPP's bid for hegemony, it also said that proletarian leadership must continue in a "series of new sectors of the ideological front. The process of the penetration of dialectical materialism into quite new fields (biology, psychology, the natural sciences in general) has clearly begun." The "conquest" of literature by dialectical materialism was "infinitely more complicated," because the Party did not yet have definite answers to questions of artistic form. Proletarian writers had the historic right to hegemony, but have not yet earned it. First, they had to attain the technical level of the "old masters." Only then would the "proletarian avant-garde" be able to create a literature "intelligible *to the millions,*" thereby fulfilling its "*historical cultural mission.*"[28]

This was at the height of Bukharin's support for NEP, when he told peasants to enrich themselves and expected them to "grow into" socialism. Even then, he would brook no challenge to proletarian hegemony in the worker-

25. Quoted in Richard Pipes, *Russia Under the Bolshevik Regime* (New York, 1993), 253.
26. *Proletarskaia revoliutsiia i kul'tura* (Petrograd, 1923), 53.
27. "Stenogramma rechi N. I. Bukharina 'Proletariat i voprosy khudozhestvennoi politiki' proiznesennoi na literaturnom soveshchanii pri TsK VKPb," in *Kul'turnoe stroitel'stvo v SSSR 1917–25* (Moscow, 1989), 202–14.
28. English translation in James, *Soviet Socialist Realism*, 116–19.

peasant alliance (*smychka*) or to the power of the Party. In reply to the philologist A. Sakulin, who claimed that Soviet power had infringed on the freedom of research and would ultimately harm science, Bukharin asserted there cannot be freedom to "promote monarchism," or preach "vitalism in biology," or give "Kantian idealists free reign." Indeed, "Given this kind of freedom, our universities would produce cultural workers who would do just as well in Prague as in Moscow. But we want workers who do well only in Moscow. . . . It is vital that our intellectual cadres be ideologically trained in a specific way. Yes we will stamp our intellectuals, we will process [*vyrabatyvat'*] them just like in a factory."[29] In 1927–28, Bukharin revised his views on economic policy to sanction a greater role for the state.

The key word of his speech "Leninism and the Problem of Cultural Revolution" (January 1928) was "remaking," *peredel'ka,* which appears as "remaking," "re-formation," "re-modeling," and "transformation" in the Inprecor (International Press Correspondence) translation. The goal of the cultural revolution, Bukharin announced, is "*a transformation in the entire predominant class, the working class*" [*peredel'ki samogo rukovodiashchego klassa, rabochego klassa*]. Its focus is not on "isolated priests" (*otdel'nye zhretsy*) or "exotic hothouse plants" (allusions to symbolism and to apolitical art). "The enormous historical-cultural process may be considered from the vantage point of the *remodeling of the masses,* the reformation of their nature, and in particular the re-formation of the entire proletariat" [*peredel'ki mass, izmeneniia ikh prirody, i v pervuiu ochered', s tochki zreniia peredel'ki samogo proletariata*].[30] In other words, the cultural revolution would accomplish a massive and total "revaluation of all [bourgeois] values."

Expounding at length on Soviet achievements in literacy, education, and health, Bukharin also claimed that culturally, the Soviet Union had arrived. Writers who greeted "our Party" as the "Coming Huns" (an allusion to a 1905 Briusov poem, which was not about the Bolsheviks) had been proven wrong. Talented proletarian writers and artists have emerged. "In the natural sciences also, a far-reaching re-formation [*peredel'ka*] is taking place." Marxism is "carefully feeling its way." In biology, physics, chemistry, physiology, reflexology, psychology, pedagogy, and mathematics, the application of Marxist dialectics is being discussed. Indeed, Marxism is "now extending its work to the entire cultural front." "Such are our achievements and successes in regard to the *remodeling of the masses,* in regard to the *remodeling and training of the cadres* and in regard to the *revolution in science*

29. *Sud'by sovremennoi intelligentsii* (Moscow, 1925), 27.

30. Bukharin, "Leninizm i problema kul'turnoi revoliutsii," in *N. I. Bukharin, Izbrannye proizvedeniia,* ed. Smirnov et al., 374–75; idem, "Leninism and the Problem of Cultural Revolution," *Inprecor,* 1928, no. 7:158–59.

and art" [*po linii peredel'ki mass, peredel'ki i vyrabotki kadrov, po linii revoliutsii nauki i iskusstva*].[31]

Even though the "iron laws of history" guaranteed Soviet dominance, the Party could not rest on its laurels, Bukharin warned. Alcoholism, syphilis, lack of labor discipline, and uncultured use of leisure time were still problem areas. More schools, libraries, public baths, and laundries (personal hygiene was considered part of culture) were needed. The Party had to use cinema, clubs, and radio more effectively in order to steadfastly combat "all signs of decline, decay, and dissolution" in literature, politics, and everyday life. Self-confidence and an "optimistic psychology" characterize a rising class.

Throughout, Bukharin lauded Lenin's "iron will" and "iron logic." Lenin was the model of the "new man-warrior" (*novogo cheloveka-bortsa,* "new type of men and fighters" in the Inprecor translation). He "revealed the new forms of our social existence."

> We can clearly see what tremendous historical perspectives are opened before us. The world is already trembling with the distant rumble of the great revolution, which will surpass all that has ever been experienced or imagined. Gigantic masses will be put into motion and in our country the way will be opened up for further stupendous creative efforts. If we read the stupid references to "savage Huns" and if the "civilized" hangmen of the international bourgeoisie accuse us, the creators of a new life, of "barbarity," we can answer with quiet consciences: "We are creating and shall continue to create a new civilization, in comparison with which the civilization of capitalism will appear like circus dogs dancing [*sobachii val's,* "caterwauling" in the Inprecor translation] compared with the heroic symphonies of Beethoven.[32]

Before the Revolution, the symbolists, the futurists, and Lunacharsky himself had called the masses the "new barbarians." Bukharin was now claiming that the workers were the civilized ones, distinguishing communism from fascism, which openly proclaimed its "barbarism." The Soviet Union was creating a great civilization that would be a model for humankind.

Two months later, in a eulogy to Bogdanov, Bukharin praised the "rock-hard nature of our party . . . a party of warriors . . . not distinguished by slackness of will or sweet sentimentality" and said that Bogdanov's "daring flights of fantasy," his unusually consistent intellect, and the harmony and internal elegance of his theoretical constructions, made him "one of the most

31. *Inprecor,* 1928, no. 8:184; "Leninizm," 383.
32. *Inprecor,* 1928, no. 9:211; "Leninizm," 390.

powerful and most original thinkers of our time," despite the undialectical and abstract nature of his thought (criticisms Lenin had made of Bukharin, *LA, 727*). Bogdanov fought like a fanatic for his ideas. "To philistines 'fanatic' is a bad word. For us a 'fanatic' is a person who unbendingly and sternly" fights for the goals that he sets for himself. "Bogdanov died a *beautiful death*. . . . He was a martyr for science." To philistines, his death (from an experiment in blood transfusion) seems "mad," because it was unnecessary. "But this 'madness' is the summit of the human heart and mind. Bogdanov died at his post."[33] Note Bukharin's positive reference to "madness," hardly a quality of "scientific socialism."

Bukharin's subsequent pronouncements on science and technology indicate his continuing debt to Bogdanov, except that Bukharin often replaced Bogdanov's term "proletarian" with "socialist." In mid-1929, he became the head of the Scientific and Technical Administrative Council of the Supreme Economic Council. In that capacity, he advocated coordinating research with economic development and insisted that the "utility" of science did not entail its degradation. Quite the contrary. "Great practice requires great theory. The building of science in the U.S.S.R. is proceeding as the conscious construction of the scientific 'superstructures' . . . we are arriving *not only at a synthesis of science, but at a social synthesis of science and practice*. The relative disconnection between theory and practice characteristic of capitalism is being eliminated. The fetishism of science is being abolished."[34] By "fetishism," Bukharin meant science for science's sake. Like Bogdanov, he denigrated "pure" science as parasitical and scholastic. Bukharin wanted Marxist scientists to develop new theories and methodologies by way of the "unity of scientific method" that dialectical materialism represented. Bogdanov wanted a unified scientific method, but not a dogmatic straitjacket.

In the capitalist world, Bukharin claimed, the ruling class and their "chosen" specialists speak in mysterious symbols inaccessible to the crowd (*chern*). They have cut off the process of knowledge from the labor process and the class struggle and turned all society into one centralized and powerful technological combine that subjugates human goals to itself. By contrast, in the Soviet Union, science is conducted in "closest ties to the economic and class struggle" and the socialist unification of theory and practice is their "most *radical* unification." It is "gradually destroying the division between intel-

33. Bukharin, "Pamiati Bogdanova," addendum to *Tektologiia* (reprint, Moscow, 1989), 2:345–47.
34. "Theory and Practice from the Standpoint of Dialectical Materialism," in *Science at the Crossroads* (n.p., 1971), 31. This volume is comprised of the papers presented by the Soviet delegation, which Bukharin headed, to the International Conference of the History of Science and Technology, in London, June 29–July 3, 1931. Bukharin's speech included references to Mach, not all of them negative. Boris Hessen gave a talk on the social and political roots of Newton's *Principia* that echoed Bogdanov's idea of the class nature of science.

lectual and physical labor, extending so-called 'higher education' to the *whole* mass of workers [and fusing] theory and practice in the *heads of millions*."[35] As the Great Depression deepened, Bukharin boasted that in the Soviet Union technology was not a threat, while in the capitalist world production and research were restricted to maximize profit and engineers and scientists could not find jobs.

In his review of Spengler's new book *Man and Technics* (1931), Bukharin called it a document of dying capitalism and Spengler, an ideologue of the imperialistic German bourgeoisie. He contrasted Spengler's condemnation of "cursed technology" with Stalin's slogan "Technology decides everything" and claimed that while Spengler divides animals, including man, into herbivores and carnivores, rational Marxism inspires people to rise above animalistic behavior.[36] Bukharin did not exaggerate Spengler's antitechnologism. Spengler believed that modern technology was leading inexorably to man's doom because it divided society into leaders and masses. His scenario of doom inverted Marxist theories of imperialism, including Lenin's and Bukharin's, which were well known in Germany. According to Spengler, soon the masses would mutiny, plunging all humanity into chaos and poverty. To "Faustian Western man," constant improvements in technology expressed a spiritual need, but to colonized peoples in Asia and Africa, technology was merely a weapon, which they would learn to use in order to destroy the West and then discard. This development was inevitable. Western leaders could only battle to the end in the tragic spirit of *amor fati*.

To Bukharin, antitechnology, and more broadly antimaterialism, reflected the polarization of the world into two economic and cultural-historic systems, one in its death throes, the other just being born. The culture of the dying world was characterized by a return to religion, calls for a return to preindustrial methods of production ("back to the hoe and the spade"), and the substitution of intuition and idealism for rational cognition. In this context, Bukharin quoted the Austrian economist Othmar Spann, author of *The New Zarathustra*, who warned of the dangerous consequences of a materialism that features "knowledge without God" and "knowledge without virtue."[37] Bukharin also pointed to a "*new medievalism*," giving Berdiaev's *Le nouveau Moyen Age* (1924) as an example. The new world was, of course, "young socialism." "It is not only a new economic system which has been born. A new culture has been born. A new science has been born. A new style of life has been born. This is the greatest antithesis in human history . . . the forces of the proletariat—the last class aspiring to power in the long run to put an end to all power whatsoever."[38] Note the similarity to Bukharin's 1915 vision of "great politics."

35. Ibid., 31.
36. "Retsenzii," in *Izbrannye trudy*, ed. E. P. Velikov (Moscow, 1988), 400–405.
37. "Theory and Practice," 32–33.
38. Ibid., 33.

A Communist Endorsement of Nietzsche

Nietzsche and Finance Capital (1928) by Moris Gavrilovich Leiteizen (1897–1939) was not just any book; it was published by the state press in Moscow and Leningrad, and crowned with an introduction by Lunacharsky, who was, at the time, still Commissar of Enlightenment. Only two thousand copies were printed, presumably because it was addressed to an elite. (Nietzsche remained off-limits to the masses.) Little is known about the author. Lunacharsky identified him as "a young researcher." Leiteizen himself said that he had lived in Weimar in 1922 and used the Nietzsche archive there. He dedicated the book to his father, G. Lindov (pseudonym of Gavril D. Leiteizen), a Party member, who worked with Gorky on *New Life* and was killed in the Civil War.[39] The son joined the Party in March 1917, took part in the October Revolution, and worked in the Soviet missions in Stockholm and in Munich in 1918 and 1919. Exactly what he did in Munich or whether *Nietzsche and Finance Capital* was commissioned, and if so by whom, is not known. The book could have been a sally in an intra-Party debate, the details of which are lost to us. We do know that Lunacharsky was under attack for "rightist tendencies." A reviewer in *Bolshevik* called Leiteizen's book pretentious, politically illiterate, ignorant of Marxist theory on imperialism, and not dialectical.[40] *Nietzsche and Finance Capital* ended up in the closed section of research libraries—even Lunacharsky's daughter was not allowed to read it[41]—and Leiteizen confined his future efforts to books on the technical aspects of aviation. In view of the date of his death, he was probably purged. The first and last open Soviet co-optation of Nietzsche, this little-known book is an example of the shift from libertarian to authoritarian appropriations of Nietzsche going on throughout Europe after World War I.

In his introduction, Lunacharsky praised Leiteizen for providing a specifically Marxist explanation of Nietzsche's thought, but he disagreed with Leiteizen's contention that Nietzsche spoke for the ruthless, hypocritical financial oligarchy that controlled the League of Nations, even though the oligarchy appropriated his ideas. Nietzsche was not a financial "big-shot" (*tuz*), nor was he close to the financial oligarchy materially or morally (15). Rather, he spoke for the sensitive, cultured, petit bourgeois German intelligentsia; the tastes of the "new oligarchy" are crude, almost anticulture. That Lunacharsky also had the new Stalinist oligarchy in mind is indicated by the next sentence: "Anatole France, an intellectual no less sensitive and cultured than Nietzsche was repelled by the hostility to culturedness that has penetrated the ranks of the Communist Party." For Nietzsche, Lunacharsky con-

---

39. King, "Political and Economic Thought," 16.
40. V. K., "Kritika i bibliografiia," *Bolshevik*, no. 17–18 (1928): 138–43.
41. Elena Kuzminichna Deich, letter to author, March 31, 1993. I am indebted to her for the biographical information about Moris Leiteizen.

tinued, "evil and integral force was a brilliant-self-affirming manifestation of life," which he tried to reconcile with the coarse and simple culture of "large-scale-capitalist Americanism." But Nietzsche was uncertain of the Superman's characteristics; hence "the most tender culture of music, so often heard in his sermons [*propovedi*] must be related to the most culturally refined parts of the German intelligentsia from which Nietzsche emerged." Hating its melancholy and sentimentality, he "wanted to raise himself to the cold summits of the self-affirming power of the strongest people" (18).

Nietzsche, "proclaimer and precursor of the principles of financial super-humanity (*sverkhchelovechestva*)," did not himself conduct secret diplomacy. His Superman was devoid of guile. "With childish joy, with purely intellectual pride, he shouted the most terrible secrets of the heights, the inhuman cruelty and in the last analysis the complete aimlessness [*bestsel'nost'*] and cynicism of these supermen" (19). Lunacharsky might have had in mind Nietzsche's paean to truthfulness:

> [Zarathustra's] doctrine and his alone posits truthfulness as the highest virtue; this means the opposite of the cowardice of the "idealist" who flees from reality. Zarathustra has more intestinal fortitude than all other thinkers taken together . . . the self-overcoming of morality out of truthfulness; the self-overcoming of the moralist, into his opposite—into me—that is what the name of Zarathustra means in my mouth. (*EH*, 328)

Lunacharsky credited Nietzsche with inspiring Bolsheviks such as himself and Gorky with enthusiasm for the "struggle with Christianity, petit bourgeois morality with its tiresome monotony, with toothless pacifism, and with all kinds of Tolstoyans, semi-Tolstoyans, and with Tolstoy-tinged humanists and sentimentalists" (20).

Leiteizen's text is studded with quotations from *The Antichrist, Twilight of the Idols, Beyond Good and Evil,* and *The Will to Power.* He ignored aesthetics, slighted *The Birth of Tragedy,* and affirmed Nietzsche's apotheosis of the will to power. "Nietzsche taught us . . . that only naked force is right . . . and that the power and force of the capitalists who rule society need no other justification than the fact that they have the power and force and the will to power. Really have we not taken up this doctrine? Really, do we not say: yes, we agree. The relation between you [fascism] and us is a question of force. But we are stronger than you and therefore we will come to power" (73). One revaluation evokes another and is the forerunner of yet another, Leiteizen continued. Both the bourgeoisie and the proletariat are disenchanted with parliamentary democracy. "This dual process is going on before our very eyes. The entire capitalist world is the arena of that struggle and of the unity of the revaluation. And if one revaluation is going on under the banner of Lenin, under the victorious banner of Lenin, then the best exemplar of that revaluation is Nietzsche" (74). Communists, not fascists, are Nietzsche's true heirs!

Throughout, Leiteizen emphasized the aspects of Nietzsche's thought that led to fascism and the cruelty needed to maintain a fascist society. His book reads very much like appropriations of Nietzsche made by Nazis a few years later—selective quotations taken out of context, with no reference to contradictory statements. Following is a summary of the main points, some of them borrowed from Bukharin's *Imperialism and the World Economy* (1915).

1. The militarization of life, the distinguishing feature of fascist ideology, can be traced to Nietzsche's militarism. Nietzsche realized that military service creates a new consciousness; it accustoms people to rank-order, subordination, and obedience and schools them in the cruelty and hardness needed to crush revolts and keep the masses enslaved. Hence, Nietzsche's assertion that "a long war is better than a short war." Finance capitalism uses militarism on the one hand and trusts and syndicates on the other to achieve its goal—" 'a universal trust, one world state—an ideal of which the most fervent minds of preceding epochs did not dream.' Bukharin's words characterize Nietzsche's ideal" (23).

2. Nietzsche was not an anarchist as bourgeois thinkers mistakenly believe, but an advocate of an all-powerful state. The fascist super-state makes men into machines, ensures that not one drop of their energy is wasted. "The gigantic energy of humanity—up to now pitilessly fragmented—will be concentrated, will be entirely directed into one channel" (46). Fascism strengthens the state, makes it into a monstrous machine, one worldwide factory "organized from the top down" for the "maximum exploitation of man" (88). Everyone would be a wheel in a huge mechanism working for the new "lords of the earth." In support of his argument, Leiteizen quoted Nietzsche's recommendation that the workforce should be militarized: "The workers should learn to feel like soldiers. An honorarium, an income, but no pay. No relation between payment and achievement! But the individual, each according to his kind, should be so placed that he can achieve the highest that lies in his power" (90; *WP*, 399). (The first number in parenthesis refers to Leiteizen's book, the second to the English translation of *Will to Power*.) Only in the distant future when the slaves become reconciled to their lot, will the state no longer be necessary.

3. Nietzsche recognized that a new ruling class was emerging, that under the cloak of liberal democracy a "new tyranny and a new slavery" was being prepared. He was the "prophet of hierarchy." His ideal was a strictly organized society, a definite structure in which each person knows his place, a strict "rank order" with distance between each rank, a social pyramid with a brutal new ruling class at the top. In Nietzsche's "revaluation of all values" compassion was forbidden and equality disappeared. He advocated "the

diminishment [*izmel'chanie*] of man" as the basis for the Superman of the future (92) and rejected equal rights for women. In such a society, personal development was a luxury. Nietzsche opposed individualism, except for the few who rule. And individualism as a primary and fundamental right for every person, "this is neither in Nietzsche nor in us" (79). Marxists shared Nietzsche's ideal of personal development and a harmonious healthy individual, but only as part of a collective and only as the culmination of a long process of social transformation when personal development is possible for everyone.

4. Nietzsche observed that wealth inevitably creates a racial aristocracy because it permits a rich man to "select the fairest women, pay the best teachers, grants to a man cleanliness, time for physical exercises, and above all, freedom from deadening physical labor" (52; *HH,* 177). Indeed, said Leiteizen, the bourgeoisie has become a caste and is turning into a race. Nietzsche opposed "coincidental marriage" (marriage for love) in favor of "higher goals," and he had an "almost religious attitude toward the infant" as a potential Superman. Nietzsche's cosmopolitanism (his desire to breed a pan-European master race) was a response to finance capital's outgrowing of narrow nationalism. Nietzsche's statement "I am no man . . . I am dynamite" expressed the impatience of an emerging new class struggling to burst asunder the bonds of the old order. (Note the combination of Nietzschean and Marxist imagery.) To illustrate the cruelty of the new lords of the earth, Leiteizen quoted Nietzsche's statement "'barbarous' means are not arbitrary and capricious [when needed to keep] control over barbarians, in the Congo or elsewhere" (27; *WP,* 487).

5. The bourgeoisie has always ruled by force and guile, following one morality for itself and preaching another to the people. For them, the bourgeoisie cynically creates illusions such as pacifism, Menshevik socialism, and Christianity. But Nietzsche was not a hypocrite. Contemptuous of eternal ideas, absolute truth, religion, pity, or the state, he openly proclaimed a master morality, including deliberate cruelty, as part of the master's self-affirmation and as an expression of his unlimited "will to power." For the master, "the Artsybashevian idea that 'all is permitted'" (a reference to *Sanin*), for the slave, obedience. Nietzsche's truthfulness illustrates the confidence of finance capital, a force so powerful that it could dispense with persuasion and the creation of illusions.

6. Nietzsche noted that Christianity makes people subservient and recognized the usefulness of religion to rulers who wished to imbue the masses with "one mood and one will." Despite their initial anticlericalism, Italian fascists were making themselves into a church. "We find in Nietzsche many pointed words, aphorisms, thoughts, which can be used for our antireligious propaganda" (109). Nietzsche's physiologism places him in the materialist camp, but his materialism reflects industrial rather than finance capitalism (because industrial capitalism created tangible goods).

7. By "great politics" Nietzsche meant "serious politics, the politics of a firm and resolute government" that is not subject to public scrutiny, "the politics of the fundamental reorganization of Europe and of the organization of humanity, the politics of the thousand year realm" (61). Nietzsche scorned the "petty politics" of bourgeois parliaments. He considered the Russian Autocracy the best example of "great politics," the only nation in Europe where the will to power survives. This is a reference to Nietzsche's statement:

> I do not say this because I want it to happen: the opposite would be rather more after my heart—I mean such an increase in the menace of Russia that Europe would have to resolve to become menacing too, namely *to acquire one will* by means of a new caste that would rule Europe, a long, terrible will of its own that would be able to cast its goals millennia hence—so that the long-drawn-out comedy of errors of its many splinter states as well as its dynastic and democratic splinter wills would come to an end. The time for petty politics is over: the very next century will bring the fight for domination of the earth— the *compulsion* to large-scale politics. (*BGE*, 131)

Soviet Russia was even more dangerous, Leiteizen boasted. Nietzsche was the unintentional prophet of an approaching Final Conflict between fascism and communism that will culminate in a Soviet universe. Mussolini will not create his world empire. "Only one state in the world—The Soviet Union— can conduct genuine great politics with the establishment of a thousand year realm" (64). One can regard Nietzsche as the thinker most sympathetic to the bourgeoisie or as the most cynical bourgeois thinker; "it's a matter of taste" (143). Either way communists and fascists are closer to each other than either is to social democracy.

> Nietzsche's struggle against the "swindles" of democracy places him closer to us than the ideology of petit bourgeois social democracy— sincere in its worship of the "little gods" [Lenin's term] of democracy, freedom, truth, morality, even god.
>
> We are one with Nietzsche in his struggle against individualism, the anarchy of capitalist society, his passionate dream of the union of the earthly globe, his struggle with nationalism.
>
> We are one with Nietzsche because he, like many of the best minds of the bourgeoisie, of necessity, against their own will, often reach our truth. . . .
>
> And all that is sunny and joyous in him, his "Yes to life," his super-human happiness, his exultation of lords of the earth and rulers of the world—this will also be close and comprehensible to us, when the lords of the earth are not the small circle intended by Nietzsche but the millions. (144)

Lunacharsky concluded his introduction in the same combative tone: "But we also . . . are full of fighting spirit. We are equally for dictatorship; we are equally for mercilessness in combat; we are equally for force, because we and they are actual forces. . . . [Those who believe] that social problems can be solved by words alone, who struggle against struggle, will soon fall on their knees before reality . . . [the inevitable] terrible and annihilating struggle to the death and the final victory of the proletariat" (21).

Despite his martial rhetoric (which might have been an attempt to prove his militancy), Lunacharsky was too "soft" for the time. Narkompros had never been a "heavy hitter" in disputes with other commissariats and government agencies, and its standing plummeted in the winter of 1928–29, as Stalin moved against the leaders of the "right opposition" (Bukharin, Rykov, and Tomsky). Lunacharsky was himself the target of ever-more slanderous rumors and petty harassment. In March 1929, Gorky attacked him in *Pravda,* implying that "on questions of 'science and labor" Lunacharsky's views were not in accord with Stalin's.[42] Shortly afterwards, Lunacharsky resigned as Commissar of Enlightenment, a victim of the zealotry he preached but, with notable exceptions, did not practice. From 1929 to 1930 he headed a committee in charge of reorganizing the Soviet Academy of Sciences. Elected a member of the Academy in 1930, he became director of its Institute of Literature, Art, and Language in 1931. In 1932–33, he was instrumental in the formulation of Socialist Realism. He died in December 1933.

Aspects of what Leiteizen called the fascist appropriation of Nietzsche existed in the Soviet Union as well. Was Leiteizen unaware of Soviet reality? I suggest that he was not, that *Nietzsche and Finance Capital* was meant to be read on two levels. On the first (exoteric) level, it promoted the Soviet myth. On the second (esoteric) level, it "explained," in highly coded language, the divergence between Soviet myth and Soviet reality, and argued that if Communists want to accomplish their goals, they must do what fascists are doing, even if such practices contradict Marxist ideals.

This reading is not as far-fetched as it might seem. The Bolsheviks were accomplished practitioners of Aesopian language; they used it before the Bolshevik Revolution, and they continued to do so. According to Stephen Cohen, contemporary Soviet power struggles were conducted in Aesopian language whose meaning was clear "to every literate member of the Party."[43] Robert Tucker says that under Stalin one could deduce actual practice or future plans from what was being attacked.[44] Vladislav Todorov posited an

42. Sheila Fitzpatrick, *Education and Social Mobility* (Cambridge, 1979), 132.

43. Cohen, *Bukharin,* 277.

44. Robert Tucker, in speech to the Mid-Atlantic AAASS at Princeton University in the mid 1980s, confirmed in letter to author, 23 January 1990.

"integral coded system of communication and government."[45] Sheila Fitzpatrick noted that instead of reporting the 1932–33 famine, Soviet newspapers "told readers about the disastrous famines and harvest failures that were [allegedly] occurring throughout the rest of the world and accused the starving peasants who thronged city streets and railroad stations of "trying to *stage a famine*," in order to evade their procurement obligations.[46] Of course the Soviet Union in 1932–33 was not the same country it had been in 1928. Even so, state control of the economy and the militarization of labor and of life characterized the Soviet Union in 1928, and other aspects of the "fascist" appropriation of Nietzsche would soon apply. In fact, Ernst Jünger, author of *Der Arbeiter* (The Worker, 1932), and a long-time admirer of Nietzsche, viewed Stalin's militarization of labor as a model for Germany, except that Jünger substituted "nation" for "class."[47]

"Barbarous means to control barbarians," or in the Soviet case, the peasants—long considered "dark forces" by Marxists—became de facto Soviet policy in 1929–30. "Rank order" and hierarchy were instituted after Stalin's "new conditions" speech (June 1931); pay differentials were increased, and the nomenklatura system was expanded. Marx and Engels predicted that the state would wither away; Leiteizen "explained" why the Soviet state was getting stronger and more brutal. Reduction or elimination of pay differentials in the first stage of the Plan was consistent with Nietzsche's recommendation: "no relation between payment and achievement" and with Lenin's vision (in *State and Revolution*) of socialism "as one big office and one big factory with equality of work and equality of pay." "Socialist competition" spurred workers to ever greater efforts, which did not necessarily bring greater rewards. Workers received subsistence rations but little or no discretionary income. In Nietzsche's words, "an honorarium, income, but no pay." The Nazis often quoted that phrase.

Elimination of the "kulaks as a class" (December 1929), forced collectivization of agriculture (1929–31), and the "terror famine" (1932–33) illustrate the new rulers' use of "barbarous means" to control peasant "barbarians." Writers who participated in dekulakization and collectivization campaigns bore witness to their sheer brutality and unwittingly testify to the impact of Nietzsche on the new morality. Lev Kopelev recalled perceiving collectivization as "heroic high tragedy." Convinced of his ideological superiority to the peasants, he was "ashamed of feeling pity while we

45. Todorov, *Red Square / Black Square*, 168.
46. Fitzpatrick, *Stalin's Peasants*, 74–75.
47. Louis Dupeux, *National bolschewismus in Deutschland, 1919–30* (Munich, 1985), 271. Abbott Gleason emphasizes the similarity bewteen Jünger's views and Trotsky's labor armies, *Totalitarianism*, 23–25. Jünger's novel *In Stahlgewittern* (1929), published in English under the title *The Storm of Steel*, was a best-seller. In that work, Jünger romanticized the front-line experience in World War I. He believed that a new world order would be achieved through violent struggle that would give birth to a new man, heroic and brutal.

robbed them."[48] A character in Vasily Grossman's semi-autobiographical novel *Forever Flowing* says: "To speak in terms of the Gospels: push those who are falling."[49] No Gospel says that. Grossman did not know that this most un-Christian sentiment derived from Zarathustra's dictum, "that which is falling should also be pushed." This character is a prosecutor in the 1936–38 trials, but Bolsheviks engaged in dekulakization and the plunder of the peasantry could have said the same thing. The revaluation of values had succeeded. Good and evil, humaneness and inhumanity, were "old words"; what mattered was the good of the Revolution, as defined by a pitiless elite.

Militarization of labor, and of life, was rapidly becoming the norm in the Soviet Union. Marx's description of capitalist factories applied to conditions in Soviet factories too. "Masses of laborers crowded into the factory are organized like soldiers. As privates of the industrial army, they are placed under the command of a perfect hierarchy of officers" (*CM*, 479). Rather than quote Marx on the subject—and he could not, of course, allude to Trotsky's Labor Armies—Leiteizen quoted Nietzsche's militaristic statements and ignored the antimilitarist ones, presumably because, having decided on the "higher tasks" of the First Five-Year Plan, the Party used a rhetoric of combat to mobilize the masses. Gorky's favorite Nietzsche text, "Of War and Warriors" (*Z*, 73–75), contains the lines: "I do not exhort you to work but to battle. I do not exhort you to peace but to victory. May your work be a battle, may your peace be a victory."[50] Zarathustra recommended a life of "obedience and war." For obvious reasons, Leiteizen also ignored Nietzsche's statement: "The state is the coldest of all cold monsters. Coldly it lies, too; and this lie creeps from its mouth: 'I, the state, am the people' . . . and whatever it says it lies—and whatever it has it has stolen" ("On the New Idol," *Z*, 75–76).

Leiteizen's attacks on Nietzsche's "racism" can be read as a hidden polemic against Soviet geneticists. Lunacharsky favored a Lamarckian eugenics; probably Leiteizen did too. The dispute about eugenics came to a head in 1929–30. In 1929, Serebrovsky complained that the Plan ignored the issue of the biological quality of the population. After extolling the practical advantages of "cleansing the country's population of various forms of hereditary ailments" (exactly how the "cleansing" would be conducted is not clear), he proposed a concrete Bolshevik form of eugenics that would fit with centralized planning, namely "the widespread use of "artificial insemination, not necessarily from a beloved spouse."

---

48. Lev Kopelev, *To be Preserved Forever* (Philadelphia, 1977), 256–61.
49. Grossman, *Forever Flowing*, 78.
50. Similarly, Fascist Italy told the masses to "believe, obey, fight" and waged a "battle for wheat" and a "battle for births."

[Given the] tremendous sperm-making capacity of men and the current state of artificial insemination technology (now widely used in horse and cattle breeding), one talented and valuable producer could have up to 1,000 children. . . . In these conditions, human selection would make gigantic steps forward. And various women and whole communes would then be proud of their successes and achievements in this undoubtedly most astonishing field—the production of human beings.[51]

On June 4, 1930, *Izvestiia* published a long poem, "Eugenics" (*"Evgenika,"* 4) by the proletarian poet Demian Bednyi (Iefim Pridvorov, 1883–1945), which associated genetics with aristocratism and ridiculed the very idea of a genetic pool. Soon after that, the major eugenics research institutes and laboratories were suddenly disbanded and the *Russian Journal of Eugenics* ceased publication. Bednyi did not oppose eugenics per se, however, just the elitist eugenics of the "bourgeois specialists." "Our eugenics is class eugenics—proletarian—and it comes from the masses not from an armchair in a stuffy room" (4). In 1931, attempts to posit theoretical links between the biological and the social were prohibited, a new pejorative entered the language—*biologizirovat'* (literally "to biologize")—and eugenics was officially banned. The turnabout in official policy can be attributed to several factors. Serebrovsky's unabashed elitism contradicted the militant egalitarianism of the time. Also, Bolsheviks were worried about a technocracy, rule by "bourgeois" experts who regarded social problems merely as technical problems with technical solutions. Some Bolsheviks were truly horrified at Serebrovsky's depersonalization of reproduction and claimed that he was turning women into baby-making machines. At the time, women were being encouraged to enter the workforce. Parts of eugenics survived as "medical genetics," however, and there is evidence of joint Russian-German eugenics research projects.[52] Research in agricultural genetics continued, but progress was impeded by the political situation.

The First Five-Year Plan and the Cultural Revolution were conducted under the banner of Marxism-Leninism, but ideas derived from Nietzsche informed these projects, inspiring Soviet visions of Great Politics, fueling the "mad" drive for industrialization and the pitiless repression of the peasants, and contributing to a theatricalization of life that demanded real victims. Bukharin revised Bogdanov's theory of cultural revolution along Leninist lines. Leiteizen's description of the fascist appropriation of Nietzsche fit Soviet practice too. As far as we know, Stalin did not create the conflicts to be described in the following chapter, but he used them in his drive for power.

51. Quoted in Adams, "Eugenics in Russia," 180–81.
52. Ibid., 184, 186–92.

Cultural Revolution in the Arts and Sciences

And it is not for nothing that Gorky constantly repeats:
Write the history of factories and plants. Write the
history of the Red Army. Create the history of the great
Russian proletarian revolution which is a thousand
times greater and more splendid than the "great"
French Revolution.
May not a single trifle, not even the smallest detail of
our inimitable, heroic days of the first Five Year Plan
be forgotten!   —Valentin Kataev, *Time Forward!*

Just as Stalin took over and radicalized Trotsky's industrialization strategy, so he took over and radicalized Bogdanov's
and Bukharin's ideas on cultural revolution. Stalin's cultural revolution was militarized, as well as militant, and it
included a large dose of class hatred. He could not admit being
indebted to the "anti-Leninist" heresy of "Bogdanovism,"
lest it undermine his claim to be Lenin's legitimate heir.

Cultural revolution in the arts entailed integrating art
and life by mobilizing writers and artists for socialist construction, which included "the task of constructing a proletarian culture," and for class war.[1] The myth had a new
"epic event" (the Five-Year Plan) and new "fighting heroes."
Brigades of artists and writers visited construction sites and
depicted the feats of labor being performed there. Other

1. David-Fox, *Revolution of the Mind*, 270.

brigades went to the countryside to recite poems, sing songs, or perform plays that would inspire the peasants to work harder. The Party conveyed the "social demand," but it did not always speak with one voice. Neither did the victorious "proletarian" organizations. In some cases, a faction transmitted the Party's views. In other cases, the faction and the leadership each had Party supporters, so the outcome depended on whose supporters had the most clout. Issues in the struggle included "unmasking" versus "varnishing reality," individualized heroes (the "living man") versus depersonalized protagonists or the collective as a whole, and montage versus unified composition. These issues (inherited from the NEP period), involved conflicting appropriations of Nietzschean ideas, subordinated to Marxism-Leninism and reworked, along with tropes taken from Russian folklore and the Russian classics, in the light of the great tasks of the day.

Cultural Revolution in the sciences entailed integrating science with life, that is, with production and politics; having scientists work on practical projects, "reworking" (= revaluing) each discipline in the light of dialectical materialism; formulating a "proletarian" or a "socialist" science with its own methodology and goals; and launching crash programs to train, hire, and promote "Red specialists" of proletarian or peasant origin. The Marxist tenet that perception of truth depends on class melded with Bogdanov's view of science as a function of myth. Centralization of research, a feature of the "command economy," enabled the Party to determine what subjects were to be investigated and what constituted "materialism" and "idealism" in each field. Radek popularized the idea of a total reconstruction of the sciences in the light of materialist dialectics and proclaimed that "to master science is the duty of the generation now going into battle," and "the slogan 'overtake and surpass the world in applied science' is the slogan of the coming ten years."[2] The Communist Academy was designated as the national center for research and graduate teaching in the summer of 1929. Increasingly, the simplification and codification of Marxism-Leninism meant that there was one correct interpretation of dialectical materialism and a single reigning authority in each field.

Cultural Revolution in the Arts

Scholars have emphasized the links between the nineteenth-century "positive hero" and the new Soviet man but have ignored the latter's Nietzschean traits until recently.[3] There is no mystique of energy, no frenzied activity, no

2. Karl Radek, "A New Stage in Civilization," in *Portraits and Pamphlets*, 287–92.
3. The classic study is Rufus W. Mathewson, Jr., *The Positive Hero in Russian Literature* (1958), 2d ed. (Stanford, 1975). For the exceptions, see Agursky, "Nietzschean Roots," and

brutality, in Chernyshevsky's *What Is to Be Done?* The "new people" depicted therein are rational egoists who proceed calmly and carefully, demonstrating the viability of their approach rather than forcing it on others. Vera's workshop was a cooperative, not a collective; unlike the situation on the new collective farms, entry was voluntary and exit was permitted. Most nineteenth-century Russian intellectuals assumed that once the authority of government and church were removed, the natural harmony of the universe would reassert itself; human relations would then be characterized by voluntary cooperation and love. By contrast, the new Soviet man of this period is in perpetual struggle—the Nietzschean *agon,* conflated with Marxist and Fedorovian motifs. A bundle of enthusiasm and energy, he has no ego (a kenotic and a Dionysian quality). The *Literary Encyclopedia* condemned Verbitskaia for having advocated "personal happiness" and "personal freedom" (2:157).

The crescendo of the culture wars in the arts was reached in 1930, in line with a December 1929 Party resolution that declared war on "any backsliding from a class position, eclecticism, or benign attitude toward an alien ideology." Literature, theater, cinema, painting, music, and radio were to assume an active role in the struggle against "bourgeois and petit bourgeois ideology, against vodka and philistinism" and against "the revival of bourgeois ideology under new labels and the servile imitation of bourgeois culture."[4] Around the midpoint of the Cultural Revolution (exactly when depends on the field), emphasis shifted from "little men" to Supermen and from enthusiasm to self-discipline and mastery of technology (or technique).

Literature

The slogans of the Organization of Proletarian Writers (RAPP) were "Ally or Enemy!" "Down with Plekhanov!" and "For the Bolshevization of Proletarian Literature!" Their journals attacked independent writers, including Gorky, and rival organizations such as LEF. In December 1929, a Central Committee resolution urged all writers to unite around RAPP. Mayakovsky joined his old enemies in January 1930 and committed suicide the following April.[5] After achieving hegemony in literature, RAPP tried to extend its domain to theater.

Despite their zealotry, RAPP writers refused to "lacquer" or "varnish" reality.[6] In Fadeev's words: "The new style of proletarian literature is a

---

Margarita Tupitsyn, "Superman Imagery in Soviet Photography and Photomontage," in *NSC,* 256–86 and 287–310, and Günther, *Der sozialistische Übermensch,* especially 104–54.

4. Quoted in Heller and Nekrich, *Utopia in Power,* 269.

5. Mayakovsky opted for ideology and may have regretted his decision later. The following April he committed suicide, apparently for personal as well as professional reasons. He gave no explanation in his suicide note.

6. For a history of RAPP, see Brown, *Proletarian Episode.*

stranger to any and all adornment of the truth; it is a stranger to all 'illusions which exalt us'; it must and will be a style involving the most resolute, consistent, and merciless removal of all masks."[7] The communist and the class enemy had to be shown in their "full living reality," including the psychological conflicts that beset people living in an era of transition. Grigory Melekhov, protagonist of Mikhail Sholokhov's *The Quiet Don* (4 vols., 1928–40) is an example of the "living man." Torn between conflicting loyalties, personal and political, Melekhov sides with the Whites, then the Reds, then with the Whites again, and ends up lost and defeated. The novel has communist heroes too, but Melekhov upstages them. Another "living man," Kiril Zhdarkin, hero of Fedor Panferov's four-volume novel *Bruski* (Ingots, 1928–37), is torn between his peasant individualism and his attraction to the collective, which ultimately prevails. A peasant Superman, he carries out prodigious feats of daring and will. Mikhail Agursky described him as a "Dionysian blond beast who know no restraints in his quest for power and in his passions."[8] Both writers were rebuked for their "Nietzscheanism"; Sholokhov because he treated Melekhov's "willful individualism" too sympathetically and Panferov because his Superman was too elemental, among other reasons.

Within RAPP, a faction called Litfront challenged the leadership for not being "left" enough. Litfront and its supporters in the Communist Academy advocated party-mindedness in literature and claimed that RAPP's slogans "Tear off the Masks!" and "For a Living Man!" undermined party-mindedness by fostering "indiscriminate" unmasking and preoccupation with personal problems. Kerzhentsev supported Litfront. He wanted a clear Party line in literature and a proper deployment of literary forces in a single Party-controlled organization, but not RAPP. "Fellow travelers" had to choose between being revolutionary writers or class enemies, he declared; "there is no third way."[9] Joining Kerzhentsev's attack on RAPP were two younger members of the Communist Academy, Pavel Iudin (1899–1968) and Mark Mitin (1901–87), who would play a prominent role in the cultural politics of the 1930s.

In 1930, new slogans appeared in the literary press: "for a great art of Bolshevism" and "Show the Country Its Heroes." In 1931, Stalin's lieutenant Kaganovich coined another slogan, "For a Magnitogorsk of Literature," by which he meant not just great works, but literature about industrialization and collectivization. The so-called production novels, which were printed in enormous quantities, depicted strong leaders bringing order out of chaos and imposing their will on the elemental forces of nature, including their

7. Quoted in Aleksandr Selivanovskii, "Korni tvorcheskikh raznoglasii," *Oktiabr* 5 (May 1929): 187.

8. Agursky, "Nietzschean Roots," in *NSC*, 276–77

9. Anthony Kemp-Welch, *Stalin and the Literary Intelligentsia* (New York, 1991), 72

own instincts. *Peter the First* (1929), a novel by Aleksei Tolstoi, illustrates the shift from collective to individual heroes and, deliberately or not, was in accord with Stalin's image of himself as the new Peter. Tolstoi's novel ignored the father-son conflict and the love episodes that Merezhkovsky foregrounded. Tolstoi's Peter is a ruthless modernizer. "In Russia," he says, "everything must be smashed and built anew."[10] The "chaotic" Russian nature must be transformed; the lazy must be put to work. The novel became a canonical work of Socialist Realism and was made into a film in two parts. Part 1 was released in 1937, and part 2 in 1939.

Gorky became the chief bard of the First Five-Year Plan, and some younger writers took up his song. The boldness and scale of the Five-Year Plan appealed to him as a Nietzschean "great project" and reactivated his God-building hopes. He made several extended visits to Russia and returned to stay in 1931. Revamping the God-building myth to suit industrialization, Gorky extolled the heroic deeds of "little men" acting collectively. In "Ten Years" (1927), he proclaimed his pride and joy in the "new Russian man, the builder of the new state," "a small but great man," and praised the masses' outgrowing of their "individualistic, slavish" psychology as "a real dithyramb!" (*"Da, difiramb!"*). All his life, Gorky claimed, his heroes were people who love to work and know how to work; in the era of "gloomy reaction" he had called them God-builders to convey the idea that human reason can and will work miracles. He predicted the advent of "a man whom the world still has not seen," who will take upon himself the "grandiose task of educating the masses in his own image and likeness," implicitly, a god-like leader.[11] In "The Old and the New" (1927), Gorky lauded the new woman. No longer confined to domestic tasks, she is the "proprietress" (*khoziaika*) of the Soviet state.[12] In "On Little People and Their Great Tasks" (1928) he praised the "little people's" collective accomplishments and denounced the ideal of the great man, the Superman.[13] In "Conversations about my Trade" (1929), Gorky denied his debt to Nietzsche and claimed that only his villains had Nietzschean traits.[14]

Nevertheless, Gorky continued to invoke the Nietzschean concepts of his youth, especially the "madness of the brave," and urged people to go "forward and higher," to defy all limits, even if they perish in the attempt. In "On Philistinism" (1929), he associated Nietzsche and Spengler with declining bourgeois civilization and claimed that the real heroes, "the heroes of

10. Aleksey Tolstoi, *Peter the First*, trans. Tatiania Shebunin (New York, 1959), 298.
11. "Desiat let'," in *GSS*, 24:289, 292–93.
12. "O novom i o starom," in *GSS*, 24:294.
13. "O 'malenkikh' liudakh i o velikikh rabotakh," in *GSS*, 25:8–17.
14. "Besede o remesle," in *GSS*, 25:319–25.

our day," arise from the masses and are "men of the masses."[15] In "On Little Old Men" (1929), written against foreign critics of the Soviet Union, he praised the epic deeds performed by the masses, maintained that "our concentrated energy can create a miracle," and described Russians as a passionate people, passionate in their hate and passionate on behalf of their beliefs.[16] Hate was a new theme for Gorky. The falcon and the snake, or the woodpecker and the finch (figures in his early short stories), were polar opposites not mortal enemies. In "On Our Attainments" (1928), Gorky mingled Nietzschean, Christian, and folkloric images in a new mythic vision:

> Our reality is difficult, contradictory, confused—all this it is. . . . But all reality must be rendered heroic and our reality already fully deserves this. How to render reality heroic? Only by great feats of labor [*trudovym podvigom*], only by work that cleanses life of its abominations, only by struggle against evil, against slavery, and for freedom. Only on this principle, on great feats of labor, were all the beautiful legends and tales of Hercules, the *bogatyri* [epic heroes] of all people and epochs constructed. Even the saints, so much as they are "living"—entered into the domain of folk legends and tales—the "saints" whom the people honored with their love [were] not those who withdrew from the world, from life, "for the sake of their own salvation," but only those who struggled against the evil in life, in the world, among people.[17]

He wrote this before the intensification of the antireligious campaign.

Gorky had long attributed Dionysian qualities to the masses and Apollonian qualities to their leaders, men of reason and will, who channeled the masses' energy and enthusiasm. In the early 1930s, he reverted to this position, constantly proclaiming that passion must be rationally controlled. Still preaching man-made miracles to be achieved by daring and will, he substituted purposeful striving for undirected, hence wasteful, expenditures of energy. Through reason, science, mastery of technique, and willpower, Man will master "Asiatic chaos," conquer the elemental forces of nature, and vanquish death. Linking the conquest of nature to the class struggle, Gorky wrote: "The elemental forces of nature create masses of parasites; our rational will forbids us to make peace with them—rats, mice, gophers do the economy of the country a great deal of harm."[18] Implicitly, the kulaks were a mass of rodents to be exterminated; he also called them "yet-unthrottled snakes." It was Gorky who coined the slogan "if the enemy [the kulak] does not surrender he must be destroyed!"

15. "O meshchanstve," in *GSS*, 25:18–28.
16. "O starichakh," in *GSS*, 25:280, 281, 292.
17. "O nashikh dostizheniiakh," in *GSS*, 24:386–87.
18. "O bor'be s prirodoi," in *GSS*, 26:198.

Asserting that Soviet workers were on a par with Homer's heroes, Gorky urged Soviet writers to depict worker-heroes as part of the epic of industrialization. Valentin Kataev (1897–1986) and Leonid Leonov (b. 1899) were among the young writers who heeded his call. Kataev took the title of his novel, *Time Forward!* (*Vremia vpered!* 1932), from Mayakovsky's *Mystery Buffe* (1919), where it connoted breaking out of the endless cycles of nature, creating paradise on earth, and vanquishing death. Kataev's title implied these too, but his main point was speeding up industrialization.

Time Forward! describes the attempt of a shock-worker brigade at Magnitogorsk to establish a world record in the pouring of concrete, thereby defeating a rival brigade in the city of Kharkov. Gorky's influence is obvious in lines such as "Little men and their tremendous songs ran back and forth. But they were the songs of giants."[19] The novel contains references to "creeping empiricism" and "right opportunism," but the spotlight is on heroism and self-sacrifice. The line "frozen fingers, people falling from fatigue and cold, the mad duel of man with God" (183) combines Gorky's "madness of the brave" with Viacheslav Ivanov's "struggle with God" (*Bogoborchestvo*). Frozen fingers became wounds of honor; industrial accidents were combat casualties. Inspired workers performed feats previously thought to be beyond human power, and aspired to still others such as changing the climate, a Fedorovian theme. "We shall surround the continents with warm streams. We shall compel the Arctic Oceans to produce billions of kilowatts of electricity. And we shall grow pine trees there—a kilometer in height" (193). Allusions to the "wondrous light" of the blast furnace that illuminates the night and to "electric blue stars that burst forth" from acetylene torches (309) seem to echo *Victory over the Sun*, except that the futurist opera did not promise paradise. The shock-worker brigades were building it.

The hero, Margulies, is an engineer whose "daring" (a Nietzschean virtue) to violate tradition by using a new technique of pouring concrete enables the workers in his section to win, showing up an unimaginative "bourgeois specialist" and personifying Stalin's slogan, "technique [*tekhnika*] decides everything!" Margulies believes that enthusiasm is as essential as technique. He expresses his willingness to put a piano at the work site if that would increase productivity, but does not do so, because he realizes that the music of socialist construction (an update of Blok's "music of the revolution") is more than sufficient. At the beginning of the novel and twice at the end, Margulies repeats the key passage of Stalin's February 1931 speech on why the tempo cannot be slackened and swears: "Never again shall we be Asia!" (11, 334–35). Margulies hardly sleeps, works all day, ignores personal comfort, is not distracted by love, and does not dissipate his energy in sex. Toward

---

19. Valentin Kataev, *Time Forward!* trans. Charles Malamuth (Bloomington, 1976), 309.

the end of the novel, he accepts a proposal of marriage from a fellow worker, Shura Soldatova. Note the reversal of gender roles and that his bride's name means soldier (*soldat*). In Nietzschean terms, Margulies is a "higher man" but not a Superman. In Katerina Clark's typology (big, bigger, biggest), Margulies is big.[20] Like Levinson, hero of *The Nineteen*, Margulies is Jewish, which makes him different. Showing Jews in a positive light was a way of combating anti-Semitism. Another character observes that Magnitogorsk is very noisy but it lacks the "noise of time," because here history is only beginning (157). One of the slogans of the Plan was "We are building a new world!" The same character says that the laws of nature are immutable, but "human genius is limitless." "We shall attain the speed of light and we shall become immortal!" (159).

Leonov's novel *Soviet River* (*Sot*, 1930) is set in Asiatic Russia. The heroes are building a gigantic industrial combine at the confluence of two rivers, subjugating the elements to reason and science while simultaneously transforming human beings. The chief engineer says: ""Everything's possible in this country, down to the resurrection of the dead! . . . The new Adam comes and gives out names to creatures that existed long before he did. And rejoices at it. I don't know how to write poetry. My job is to build."[21] At the end of the novel we learn that the chief engineer will marry Suzanne, also an engineer and formerly a Red partisan. She proposed to him.

Another character, Vissarion, a runaway monk, presently secretary of the workers' club, preaches a "crazy faith" that is a melange of futurism and Scythianism. His ravings remind Suzanne of "the ravings of that Greek who was named the Dark" (245). "Our task," Vissarion says, "is to burn out this poisoned inheritance . . . of all these Homers and Shakespeares." Humanity must "learn how to forget its past and begin afresh . . . youth will come back again. Hellas will return, but we won't turn back to it. The Hellas of the future will develop individuality, for it will repose on steel serfs, the machines. . . . There shall arise a new friendship—based on equality, not on subordination. There shall be a collective soul." "A man must be summoned to being, who shall save." "You speak of a Bonaparte?" Suzanne interrupts. No, he replies indignantly, "I spoke of an Attila" (248–50). A new Attila is being born in Russia. "He will come riding on a steed, clad in a rag the color of burnt ashes . . . the weak will die in a year, but he shall seat the strong on horseback and lead them back once more to Thesis. The hand of the clock will flow backward over the dark days; it will have to swim across rivers of blood, swarm over Himalayas of new things with the meaning fresh

---

20. Katerina Clark, "Utopian Anthropology as a Context for Stalinist Literature," in *Stalinism*, ed. Robert C. Tucker (New York, 1977), 183.

21. Leonov, *Soviet River*, trans. Ivor Montagu and Sergei Nalbondov, foreword by Maxim Gorky (Westport, 1973), 350.

torn out of them" (251). Suzanne interjects, "and break into the cellars and drink all the vodka." (She doesn't drink.) But Vissarion goes on: "In this last pilgrimage will be born the members of a new generation, void of memory. . . . The boundaries of the regions shall be effaced, the whole planet shall become the Fatherland of Man, the words Love and Sun shall recover their original significance. Not all but *each* shall be happy. Through the wilderness shall gallop free and naked men" (251). Vissarion's prophecy represents the unchanneled Dionysianism that Gorky considered dangerous. "And is it necessary to blow up the Soviet factories and works or is it not necessary?" Suzanne asks. Vissarion claims that she does not understand him, but clearly he cannot be trusted. We later learn that he fought for the Whites and is a wrecker.

Mass Festivals and Theater

A new type of mass festival incorporated technological elements in an updated rendition of the Nietzsche/Wagner/Ivanov syndrome designed to stimulate enthusiasm for the Plan. The amateur theater TRAM received funds that enabled it to become professional and expand all over the Soviet Union. Within RAPP, playwrights argued over a monumental theater (with anonymous heroes) versus a theater of the "living man."

Agitprop decided to revive mass festivals in May 1927. The following November, Piotrovsky and others staged a mass festival, "Ten Years" (the tenth anniversary of the Revolution), as an industrial sound-and-light show, using the city of Leningrad as the stage. People could neither be seen nor heard across such vast distances, so the "actors" were things—boats, smoke stacks, sirens (to warn people of danger), and fire (signifying the destruction of the old order). Another mass festival of the new type celebrated "Industrialization Day," which replaced a religious holiday, "The Transfiguration of Our Lord." Gorky wrote an article for the occasion.[22] The mechanical metaphors and gigantic scale of the new festivals incorporated the spirit of constructivism and symbolically diminished man individually and as a species. All festivals should be on a gigantic scale, one activist wrote, with "super-powerful musical instruments, super-powerful cinema, super-sized sculptures and painting . . . huge posters . . . three-dimensional charts" and "monumental propaganda pavilions" in the city squares.[23]

The festival that celebrated the completion of the First Five-Year Plan in 1932 was a combination sound-and-light show and carnival, with carnival

22. "Den' industrializatsii," in *GSS*, 25:50–52.
23. L. Roshchin, "Raising Enthusiasm to the nth Degree," quoted in *Street Art of the Revolution: Festivals and Celebrations*, ed. Vladimir Tolstoy, Irina Bibikova, and Catherine Cooke (London, 1990), 192.

floats, cascades of light spilling over dams, figures telling how much electricity these dams would produce, and eruptions of light pouring out of blast furnaces. Shop windows became exhibition stands that displayed sketches and drawings for the next Five-Year Plan. Leading actors performed on temporary stages. Puppet shows and slapdash political skits showed bloated capitalists downed by worker champions. All the city was a stage for the enjoyment and edification of the populace. Special rations ensured that everyone had flour and enough vodka for a toast.[24]

TRAM's speciality was dialectical plays that revealed the contradictions inherent in Soviet life even while promoting the Plan and carrying on the class struggle. To underscore the conflicting pressures on young workers, and also because TRAM assumed a (Dionysian) reality of perpetual flux, the plays lacked linear plots and unambiguous endings, and no one voice prevailed.[25] The audience drew its own conclusions, a practice that neither RAPP nor the Party appreciated. A permanently unstable reality could be construed as "Machism" or worse, as ideological "contraband" for Trotsky's theory of permanent revolution.

As the Cultural Revolution escalated, TRAM began to organize other left theatrical groups, entering into direct competition with RAPP. When TRAM incorporated Litfront, the tensions between TRAM and RAPP exploded into open warfare. The Komsomol newspaper supported TRAM, and *Literary Gazette* supported RAPP. TRAM's campaigns against "formalism" pitted Meyerhold against Piotrovsky, its patron, and led TRAM to denounce him in 1931. Nevertheless, Piotrovsky continued to work with TRAM, and he retained his position as artistic director of the Leningrad Film Studio (a position he had held since 1928). In 1932, Piotrovsky confessed that his ideas on theater were fundamentally flawed because they were based on "reactionary" notions inspired by Viacheslav Ivanov and Nietzsche. That year TRAM dropped the avant-garde elements that made its performances effective and presented entirely positive heroes, losing its audience as a result.

The leading advocates of a monumental theater were Nikolai Pogodin (1900–1962) and Vsevolod Vyshnevsky (1900–1952), both members of RAPP. Pogodin's first play, *Tempo* (1929), celebrated the building of the Stalingrad tractor plant. According to Pogodin, the key issue was not whether or not the protagonist was getting married, but whether the Communist was keeping up the struggle. Vyshnevsky's *Komandarm 2* (1929) dramatized the transformation of ignorant peasants into "conscious" Red Army men in the Civil War. The play opens with "a meeting on the steppe," features choral scenes, espouses a kind of primitivism, and includes quasi-symbolist and

24. Weitlin, *Fifty Russian Winters*, 12–13.
25. Mally, "Soviet Youth Theater," 217.

liturgical forms.[26] By contrast, Vladimir Kirshon (1902–38), also a member of RAPP, spotlighted the "living man" and human relations. *Bread* (1931) features a kulak conspiracy, but it also has a love triangle and probes the issue of the individual and the collective. The Communist in charge of collectivization does not want to be like everyone else, but he is even more horrified at the thought of the parade passing on without him. Moreover, he realizes that he needs Party discipline to "weld together" the disparate elements of his personality.

Cinema

In cinema, the issue was documentaries versus myth-creation (though the boundaries were becoming blurred) and the related issue of anonymous masses or exemplary individuals. *Turk-Sib* (1929), a documentary of the building of the Turkestan-Siberia railroad, honored anonymous workers and purveyed a mystique of the machine using constructivist composition and imagery. Shklovsky coauthored the screenplay. Motion (= kineticism) was the leitmotif of Dziga Vertov's documentary *Man with a Movie Camera* (also 1929), which featured shots of people working and playing or machines in operation, shot from above, from below, and from different angles (perspectivism). Toward the end of the film, a giant man with a movie camera towers above the crowd, as if in anticipation of the magnification of the hero that would soon become official policy. A shot of a banner hung across a street saying "Maksim Gorky" appears at least four times. Another Vertov documentary, *Enthusiasm,* subtitled *Symphony on the Don* (1930), opens with peasants removing the crosses from a church.

Eisenstein's *The General Line,* subsequently retitled *The Old and the New* (1929), celebrated the machines that will "transform this conquered land" and the "new breed of man" being produced by "cross[ing] the peasant with science. Collectivist man. Collectivizing man. A man who feels an unprecedented enthusiasm for this unheard-of kind of factory."[27] The protagonist, a determined peasant woman, convinces her peers to form a cooperative, and then to acquire a cream separator, a breeding bull, and a tractor, struggling against kulaks, suspicious peasants, and bureaucrats all the while. In addition to mythologizing collectivization and the "profound" collaboration of town and countryside, Eisenstein wanted to show what ordinary people can achieve. The triumphant last scene is the "wedding" of the new breeding bull and a cow decked out for the occasion. The fireworks that mark their union illustrate a new "device," overtonal montage, associations

---

26. Details in D. Zolotitskii, *Budni i prazdniki teatral'nogo oktiabria* (Leningrad, 1978), 218–23.

27. Taylor, *Film Factory,* 256, 257.

that reinforce or undercut the main line of imagery.[28] Some critics objected to the "erotic" motif. RAPP accused Eisenstein of regarding content as raw material for formal experiments. Eisenstein claimed that his was an "experiment intelligible to the millions" (which is what the Party wanted). Opposed to RAPP's "living man," he declared that his hero was the sun.

Name-calling and threats became regular features of film criticism. Aleksandr Dovzhenko's *Earth* (1930) was labeled a kulak film because of its (symbolist) lyricism. RAPP attacked ARRK (Association of Workers of Revolutionary Cinematography) for lacking a clear ideological platform and compromising with "formalism."[29] *The New Babylon* (1929), a film about the Paris Commune, directed by Grigory Kozintsev and Leonid Trauberg with music by Dmitri Shostakovich (1906–75), received hostile reviews for its avant-garde elements and failed to draw an audience. The directors were formerly associated with FEKS (Factory of the Eccentric Actor), which featured a kind of dadaist constructivism. In the 1930s, they shifted to simple propaganda films, such as *The Youth of Maksim* (1935), the first of a trilogy, using modernist devices to underscore the message.

Direct Party intervention was greater in cinema than in any other area.[30] Stalin personally screened all films before they were released. Party officials were de facto codirectors. Film directors were given contradictory instructions or accused of "formalism" or "mechanical materialism," a jab at the avant-garde. Many films were started but never finished, because of the resulting confusion as to the correct line. Abrupt transitions from one scene to another fell out of favor, because the Party wanted easy-to-follow plots that reflected the logical unfolding of historical laws.

Painting and Photography

Painters and photographers depicted construction projects and collective farms; workers, peasants, and soldiers; and Lenin and Stalin. Muscular, proletarian Supermen replaced ordinary workers, but there was a countertrend: human beings dwarfed by the mammoth edifices they were building. The Association of Artists of the Russian Revolution (AKhRR), renamed itself the Association of Artists of the Revolution (AKhR) in 1928. Still championing "heroic realism," AKhR expanded its purview beyond "the past and present of our struggle" to "the prospects created by the Proletarian Revolution" (the radiant future).[31] In addition to portraits, members of

28. Bordwell, *Cinema of Eisenstein*, 14–15.

29. "RAPP Resolution on Cinema," in Taylor, *Film Factory*, 278.

30. Details in Peter Kenez, "The Cultural Revolution in Cinema," *Slavic Review* 47, no. 2 (Fall 1988): 414–33.

31. Bowlt, *Russian Art of the Avant-Garde*, 271–72.

AKhR painted gigantic banners and street signs for mass festivals, decorated workers' clubs, and designed articles of mass consumption. Isaak Brodsky's "Lenin at Smolny" and Aleksandr Gerasimov's "Lenin On the Tribune" (both 1930), contributed to the burgeoning Lenin Cult. Brodsky depicted a seated Lenin absorbed in his writing. Gerasimov portrayed an animated Lenin speaking to the masses (who are not in the painting). Most of the bottom half is a red banner; its diagonal sweep, a device of the avant-garde conveys a sense of dynamism.[32] Enthusiasts, or rivals, reproached Brodsky for merely copying reality.

In May 1928 Lissitzky, Eisenstein, Klutsis, Dmitri Moor (Orolov, 1883–1946), and Aleksandr Deineka (1899–1969) founded an organization called October; Rodchenko joined in 1929. Committed to "organiz[ing] the consciousness, will, and emotions of the proletariat and of the working masses with maximum force," October promoted its own new art form— "proletarian realism"—an art that "expresses the will of the active revolutionary class, a dynamic realism that reveals life in movement and action . . . that rebuilds rationally the old way of life." October rejected "aesthetic, abstract industrialism," unadulterated technicism," and "philistine realism" and opposed a single Party line in art and architecture and any view that treated reality as a continuous organic entity. They preferred obviously constructed montages.[33] In Rodchenko's photographs, sharply tilted angles signify the radical instability of the Great Break.

Geometric forms yielded to representational images. The cube metamorphosed into stylized depictions of "square-built" powerful workers. Deineka usually did not delineate his subjects' facial features. Sometimes their heads are in the shadows; at other times only the side or back of the head is visible. In "Demonstration" (1928), he depicts enthusiasts on a series of balconies which seem suspended in mid-air. Banners floating in the wind suggest flight, reinforcing the impression of gravity overcome (a Nietzschean and Fedorovian theme). Klutsis photographed miners as giants of the earth (= titans of the new age). His photographs illustrate the transition from a collective to an individual hero. First he depicts shock brigades or other groups, then one or two super-sized workers towering over the others, or Stalin leading columns of marching workers.

Portraits of athletes and gymnasts featured exemplary individuals (male and female), sports parades, and human pyramids (two or more tiers of individuals), in other words, orderly collectives rather than random crowds. The Party encouraged sports because they fostered self-discipline and a collective spirit plus increasing agility and muscular strength. Deineka's "The Race" (1930), which portrays two muscular sportsmen, was a reminder that

32. Illustrations in Igor Golomstock, *Totalitarian Art* (London, 1990), 180 and plate 5.
33. "October—Association of Artistic Labor Declaration," in Bowlt, *Russian Art of the Avant-Garde,* 273–79.

"tempo decides everything." Klutsis's "Spartakiada" (1928) shows male and female sharpshooters (perhaps honing their skills for a successful Spartacus Revolt that would liberate the wage slaves of the world).[34] The human pyramids can be interpreted as pictorial renditions of Nietzsche's dictum, "man has value and meaning only insofar as he *is a stone in a great edifice* and to that end he must be *solid* first of all, a 'stone'—and above all not an actor!" (*GS*, 303). He stays where he is put. Bukharin alluded to this passage a few years later.

Supermen and Superwomen in action dominate other Five-Year Plan posters, their faces and postures expressing either extreme determination or enthusiasm to the point of ecstasy. The typical Superwoman is a collective farmer; sometimes she is shown driving a tractor to show her "mastery of technology," formerly a male preserve. Valentina Kulagina's poster for International Woman's Day (1930) depicts a Superwoman at her spinning machine towering over other women spinners,[35] a reflection (intentionally or not) of the gender-composition of the textile industry. Natalia Pinus's poster "Woman Delegate, Worker, Shock-Worker" had no men in it either. In posters that depict both men and women, the women are smaller or helping the men, except when the men are class enemies, in which case the women tower over them.[36] All posters had topical captions, such as "We Are Building Socialism!" "Let Us Mechanize the Donbass!" "Proletarian Cadres to the Urals-Kuzbass!"

Architecture

For architects, the First Five-Year Plan was an opportunity to design buildings, gigantic industrial complexes, enormous dams, complete towns such as Magnitogorsk, and monumental projects such as the Palace of Soviets and the Moscow Metro. VOPRA (All-Russian Association of Proletarian

34. Illustration in Margarita Tupitsyn, *The Soviet Photograph, 1924–1937* (New Haven, 1996), plate 50.

35. Illustration in Tupitsyn, "Superman Imagery," in *NSC*, 293. For the Pinus poster, see *The Great Utopia: The Russian and Soviet Avant-Garde, 1915–1932*, Guggenheim Museum (New York, 1992). For male Supermen, see Klutsis, "The Struggle for Heat and Metal," in Tupitsyn, "Superman Imagery," in *NSC*, 295; Iury Pimenov, "We Are Building Socialism," in *Great Utopia*, plate 391; Kulagina, "We Are Building," in ibid., plate 438; and Nikolai Dolgurukov, "Transportation Worker! Armed with a Knowledge of Technology," in ibid., plate 444.

36. Nikolai Mikhailov, "There Is No Room in Our Collective Farm for Priests and Kulaks!" (plate 3); "Come, Comrade, Join Us in the Collective Farm!" (figure 3.3); and "Peasant Woman, Join the Collective Farm! (figure 3.5), in Victoria Bonnell, *Iconography of Power: Soviet Political Posters Under Lenin and Stalin* (Berkeley and Los Angeles, 1997), plates 3, 3.5, 3.7.

Architects, founded 1929) set out to destroy OSA and ASNOVA but concentrated most of its fire on OSA, taking some of its intellectual ammunition from ASNOVA. Lunacharsky worked closely with VOPRA, for in architecture, his taste ran to the monumental, by which he meant the architecture of ancient Greece, Rome, and the Renaissance. The announcement, in July 1931, of a competition to select the architect of the Palace of Soviets was the start of a second monumental propaganda campaign. (The Palace and the Metro will be discussed in Chapter 14.)

VOPRA accused OSA architects of "technocratism," "mechanism," practicing "architecture for architecture's sake," and promoting the "capitalist principles" of economy, utility, and comfort. These were serious charges; "bourgeois specialists" were being purged on account of them. OSA architects used the language of science and engineering while ASNOVA architects spoke more and more in the language of symbolism or of the psychology of art. Ladovsky (their leader) advocated an architecture of awe—a monumental architecture that peasant masses flooding into the towns could understand viscerally and that would imbue them with enthusiasm and awe for the great tasks of socialist construction.[37] All camps expected housing to play a leading role in the transformation of life. Increasingly, architectural debates were conducted in the language of raw political power.

In May 1930, *Pravda* rebuked the "super-collectivizers" who wanted to surmount the obstacles to socialism "in one leap." Actually, most OSA architects had already abandoned the idea of gigantic communes in favor of separate dwellings for each individual as the most appropriate environment to "liberate the personality and create optimum conditions for its full development." Their theorist, Mikhail (or Moisei) Okhitovich (1896–1937), a member of GOSPLAN and the leading advocate of deurbanization, defended "individuality" in Marxist terms; socialism made self-development possible for all.[38] Marx had expected the difference between town and country to disappear under socialism. Okhitovich went farther; the city was a product of capitalism which severed peasants from the land. Forced collectivization was a regression to capitalism. He opposed monumental architecture on aesthetic grounds and because it diverted resources needed for housing the masses. In June 1931, Kaganovich cut short the debate on the nature of the socialist city, by declaring that all Soviet cities and towns had become socialist "from the very moment of the October Revolution." The "challenge was to devise an architectual formulation of the Soviet city that will give [them] the necessary *beauty*" (emphasis added).[39] Implicitly, he was downgrading functional qualities.

37. Hugh D. Hudson, *Blueprints and Blood* (Princeton, 1994), 78.
38. Bliznakov, "Nietzschean Implications," in *NSC*, 193–94.
39. L. M. Kaganovich, *Socialist Reconstruction of Moscow and Other Cities in the U.S.S.R.* (New York, [1931]), 83–85.

Cultural Revolution in the Sciences

Debates on the relevance of Marxism to a particular discipline went on throughout the NEP period, partly as a way of legitimating that discipline. In some disciplines, debates were amiable and non-Marxists and even open anti-Marxists, such as Pavlov, participated. In other disciplines, rival schools struggled for dominance. Debates about what Marxism meant for each discipline became intense in 1927–28, escalated further in 1929–30, and were resolved "from above" in 1931 and after (depending on the field).

In philosophy, physics, and psychology, mechanists and dialecticians (also called "Deborinites" after their leader Abram Deborin, 1881–1963) had been battling one another for years. The philosophical and scientific issues that they fought over need not detain us.[40] The important thing is that their disputes were politicized and that the Party decreed the solution(s). First it favored the Deborinites. Then, in June 1930, Mitin, Iudin, and Vasily Ralchevich (also of the Communist Academy) attacked the Deborinites in a *Pravda* article that the Party endorsed.[41] The following December, Stalin denounced Deborin for "Menshevizing idealism" (= separating intellectual endeavor from the Party line). No discipline was autonomous. In 1931, mechanists and Deborinites were both repudiated. The new line stressed the importance of Hegel for Marxism (Lenin steeped himself in Hegel in 1914), but emphasized the contradiction between Hegel's reactionary philosophical system and his progressive methodology (the dialectic).

The physical sciences were targeted in 1929–30. The Komsomol's "Light Cavalry" called on all graduate students and assistants to intensify the class struggle. In June 1929, the Central Committee instructed research institutes to increase the number of scientists of proletarian origin and to induce scientists to become Party members. Physicists working in quantum mechanics were accused of "Machism" and Einstein's theory of relativity was condemned as "bourgeois subjectivism." Deborin's lecture on "Lenin and the Crisis of Contemporary Physics" (1930) reveals the lowered level of debate. Lenin never claimed expertise in physics.

The Marxist historian Mikhail Pokrovsky (1868–1932), a key figure in politicizing scholarship, was a former *Vperedist,* a Left Communist during the Civil War, a founding member of the Socialist Academy, and Deputy Commissar of Enlightenment from 1918 until his death in 1932. Known as

---

40. It is worth noting that Bogdanov was labeled a "mechanist" and that after Lenin's *Materialism and Empriocriticism* was republished in 1922, the "mechanists" distanced themselves from him.

41. "Stat'ia trekh," *Pravda*, June 7, 1930. The Deborinites replied with an "article of ten" ("statia desiati") warning against the dissolution of philosophy in the political slogans of the day. Details in Ewert Van der Zweerde, *Soviet Philosophy: The Handmaid and the Ideology* (Nijmegen, 1994), 96–97.

the "organizer of scholarship," he promoted training Marxist historians and was one of the troika of Party scholars on the commission that masterminded the Bolshevization of the Academy of Sciences.[42] The other two were Liadov, head of the Communist Academy, and Otto Schmidt (1891–1956), its leading authority in the physical sciences and editor-in-chief of the first edition of the *Great Soviet Encyclopedia.*

The impact of the Cultural Revolution varied from one discipline to another. History, biology, and linguistics were the most affected. These disciplines were relevant to the Nietzschean agenda—history, to the new myth; biology, to the new man; and linguistics, to the new word.

History

Pokrovsky's activities on the "historical front" amounted to a Marxist revaluation of Russian history that combined Lenin's "party-mindedness" with Bogdanov's idea of a proletarian science. Pokrovsky had taught Russian history at the Capri School, and his *Outline History of Russia* (1910–13) was based on the Capri School courses.[43] Reminiscent of Bogdanov are Pokrovsky's belief that history is an ideology (= myth) and his neglect of political structures and "great men." As for "party-mindedness," Pokrovsky declared that "the Leninist History of the Party is alien to bourgeois 'objectivity' torn from contemporary concerns."[44] Historiography is part of the class struggle, so the historian must take sides. He was openly disdainful of facts presented by "bourgeois historians," but he urged Marxist historians to master their technique, and he did not advocate fabricating evidence. Pokrovsky's slogan "history is present-day politics projected into the past" expresses the truism that history is written by the victors, but it also suggests Nietzsche's conception of a history that "serves life" (*H,* 14). By "life" Nietzsche had meant cultural life or cultural vitality. Pokrovsky wanted history to serve the proletariat by critically "revaluing" bourgeois historiography, using different sources, and developing a collectivist methodology. He treated impersonal socioeconomic forces as the agents of history.

In *On the Advantage and Disadvantage of History for Life,* Nietzsche described three types of history—antiquarian, critical, and monumental. Pokrovsky's approach was closest to critical history, for he debunked con-

---

42. He helped found the Higher Party Schools, established the first *rabfak* to train new cadres of Party historians, and organized the Society of Marxist Historians as part of the Communist Academy. In addition, he headed RANION, a network of research institutes (and helped engineer its demise in 1929–30).

43. Utechin, "Bolsheviks and Their Allies After 1917," 16; Biggart et al., *Bogdanov and His Work,* 68 and 265.

44. Quoted in George Enteen, *The Soviet Scholar Bureaucrat: M. N. Pokrovsky and the Society of Marxist Historians* (University Park, 1978), 129.

ventional Russian historiography and was hostile to antiquarian history (history for history's sake). His abstract, schematic approach was the opposite of monumental history, which isolates and exalts heroes and great events. Pokrovsky diminished the role of the tsars, did not treat the Bolshevik Revolution as an epic, and paid little attention to events in general. Lenin once remarked that one of Pokrovsky's books needed a second volume to tell the reader what had happened in the first.

Pokrovsky did not initiate the campaign against "bourgeois historiography" launched by radical students in late 1927, but he joined it. In April 1929 he declared that peaceful collaboration between Marxists and non-Marxists must end, denied that objective history is possible, and attacked non-Marxist scholars. A few months later, the Communist Academy was designated the national center for research and graduate teaching. Around this time, Pokrovsky shifted from claiming that prerevolutionary Russia was not behind Europe socioeconomically (so the October Revolution was a natural development) to contrasting the backwardness of the Russian past with the progress being made under socialism, and to emphasizing the importance of mass will and enthusiasm. In Robert Daniels's words: "Voluntarist Marxism superceded determinist Marxism."[45]

Pokrovsky was not involved in the historical dispute, conducted in the journal *Proletarian Revolution,* that triggered Stalin's intervention. That dispute was between Iaroslavsky (the same Iaroslavsky who combated religion) and A. G. Slutsky on Lenin's relation with German Marxists, especially Kautsky, before World War I. In October 1931, in a letter to *Proletarian Revolution* that was published simultaneously in *Bolshevik,* Stalin denounced "archive rats," "rotten liberalism," and "Trotskyist contraband" and demanded that political correctness take precedence over historical accuracy.[46]

Pokrovsky used his clout with the Central Committee and Kul'tprop to destroy other historians.[47] As his power grew, opposition to him increased. At a plenum of the Communist Academy in June 1930, Pokrovsky's leadership was severely criticized by his old enemies (Iaroslavsky was among them), and by a new member, Stalin's lieutenant Kaganovich.[48] Working against Pokrovsky were his inattention to Peter the Great at the very time that Stalin was being associated with him and his downplaying of the state when its "progressive" role in Soviet society was growing. Also working against him were the return of Russian nationalism in Soviet guise, the Party's desire for

45. Robert Daniels, "Social Thought in the 1930s," in idem, *Trotsky, Stalin, and Socialism* (Boulder, Colo., 1991), 145.

46. Details in Robert Tucker, *Stalin in Power* (New York, 1990), 151–60. See also Biggart, "Anti-Leninist Bolshevism," 151–53.

47. Graham, *Soviet Academy of Sciences,* 129.

48. George Enteen, "Marxist Historians During the Cultural Revolution: A Case Study of Professional In-Fighting," in Fitzpatrick, *Cultural Revolution,* 162–63.

a monumental history (see Chapter 13), and the winding down of the (Dionysian) Cultural Revolution. Dionysianism obliterates memory. In February 1933, the Party decreed that regular textbooks be prepared for all basic subjects, including history. In May 1934, the Party praised narrative history and condemned schematism, implicitly declaring Pokrovsky's school to be mistaken, without mentioning him by name. In the Soviet Union it was said that Pokrovsky died twice; biological death came in 1932 and ideological or political death in 1934. In 1936 he was attacked by name and Kaganovich led the assault. History remained "present-day politics projected onto the past," in other words myth-creation, but the specifics of the myth had changed and it had a new epic hero—Stalin.

Biology

The charlatan Trofim Lysenko (1898–1976) emerged from obscurity during the Cultural Revolution and was challenging genetic theory by 1936. David Joravsky attributes Lysenko's rise to the Cultural Revolution, "which launched a quarrelsome search for an appropriate theory for the red specialists in biology."[49] There was more to it than that. The Prometheanism that fueled the drive for a "conquest of nature" fostered a receptivity to schemes that promised to subject evolution to human will. Lysenko claimed that by manipulating the (physical) environment, man can induce heritable changes in plants. He used the politicization of science and the widespread hostility to theoretical science ("science for the sake of science") to promote himself and his theories.

Bukharin, a formulator of Party policy in science, inadvertently helped pave the way for Lysenko by insisting on subordinating the physical sciences (as well as the social sciences) to dialectical materialism (his version of Bogdanov's "proletarian science") and by calling for a post-Darwinian biology. In debates of the 1920s on environment versus heredity, Bukharin sided with the Lamarckians, who maintained that radical environmental changes such as those produced by social revolution could produce behavioral changes that would subsequently become permanent characteristics of the [human] species. "If not," he said in 1928, "if we took the view that racial or national peculiarities are so persistent that it would take thousands of years to change them, then of course our whole work would be absurd because it would be built on sand."[50]

Four years later, Bukharin supported genetics, because new research on mutations had demonstrated that they could be deliberately induced. In a speech titled "Darwinism and Marxism" (1932), he argued that the "dis-

49. Joravsky, *Soviet Marxism and Natural Science*, 310.
50. Quoted in Fitzpatrick, *Education and Social Mobility*, 141.

coveries of genetics (the doctrine of combinational variability on the basis of Mendel's laws, Johannssen's 'pure lines' and the generalizations of the American school headed by Morgan) in no way undermines the basis of Darwinism," but could be considered "a further development of Darwinism." He praised the work of Nikolai Vavilov (1887–1942) and urged Soviet biologists to apply genetics to the "process of production." A botanist and geneticist, Vavilov believed that man can create new biological species and forms at will. He meant plants and lower forms of animal life, but if they could be created, eventually, so could a new human being. The main point of Bukharin's speech, however, was that Marxism was "higher" than Darwinism. Darwin revealed the fact of biological evolution, but man is not just an animal; he is a product of social conditions and is guided by social consciousness. Moreover, Darwinism mirrors conditions in capitalist society. For all these reasons, Darwin's theory must be reworked in the light of "*our* worldview which lays on us the obligation to further develop biology by a conscious (and not a spontaneous) application of the methods of dialectical materialism."[51]

In a different speech, "Goethe and His Historical Significance" (also 1932), Bukharin quoted an unpublished fragment by Nietzsche "in defense" of Goethe against Darwin. " 'Germans, have you taken as philosophy the mediocre understandings of these [upright] Englishmen. To put Darwin next to Goethe is *to do violence to majesty*, the majesty of genius' " (*KSA*, 11:317). Bukharin omitted the word "upright" as well as the title of the fragment, "To the German Jackasses." Bukharin continued:

> These evaluations on the part of Nietzsche, a philosopher-artist, a master of the aphoristic style, a biologizing aesthete, and at the same time the creator of the bestial-predatory ideology of the openly aggressive and openly plundering capitalist-Junker bloc, reveal a great deal. The issue here is not Nietzsche's attack on the relative and traditional narrowness of English empiricism, traits of which appear even in the most brilliant biologists, but that Nietzsche saw the essence of genius in the irrational, in intuition, in "organic reaction," which he opposed to rational cognition; such treatment of the whole leads beyond the gates of intellect and reason to a metaphysical-mystical "first cause" interpreted on the model of Platonic ideas.[52]

Here, too, the implication is the need for a post-Darwinism biology developed along the lines of a specifically Marxist philosophy. To "biologize" was a pejorative, but Bukharin was not using the term in a pejorative sense here. He may have liked Nietzsche's physiological orientation.

51. "Darvinizm i marksizm," in Bukharin, *Etiudy*, 122, 135–36.
52. "Gete i ego istoricheskoie znachenie," in Bukharin, *Etiudy*, 165.

To a charlatan like Lysenko, treating science as a function of myth (which is what Bogdanov and Bukharin did) was not just a matter of a "proletarian" or a "socialist" perspective, which could indeed reveal new truths, but a license to misrepresent data, manipulate experiments, and engage in outright fraud. Bogdanov and Bukharin never advocated such practices, nor did they claim that bourgeois scientists engaged in them. Stalin's backing enabled Lysenko to silence criticism and destroy his critics, including Vavilov, who was one of his first backers.[53] (We will return to Lysenko in Chapter 14.)

Linguistics

The injunction to apply dialectical materialism to all areas of scholarship fostered a search for a Marxist linguistics that did not treat "the word" in isolation, but in its historical, socioeconomic, and cultural settings. The victor was Nikolai Marr (1864–1934), a native of Georgia, formulator of the Japhetic theory of linguistics, professor at Saint Petersburg University since 1901, member of the Russian Academy of Sciences since 1912, an academic entrepreneur, and like Lysenko, an astute politician. Marr named his theory after Japheth, the third son of Noah, whose descendants settled on the shores of the Black and the Caspian seas.[54] Georgian nationalism was the original impetus for the Japhetic theory, which Marr began to formulate in St. Petersburg around 1908, when the intellectual atmosphere was saturated with Nietzsche and Nietzschean ideas.

Aspects of Marr's theory intersected with Nietzsche's archaeological approach to language (Marr used the term "paleontological"), with Nietzsche's emphasis on myth, which linked word and myth, and with futurism, Scythianism, and Eurasianism. Marr's writings are studded with references to ancient myths, especially myths of the Caucasus unknown to Western scholars. He opposed looking down on "primitive peoples," did not call them "barbarians," and came close to exalting folk creativity. The Japhetic theory appealed to Lunacharsky and Pokrovsky, so in the 1920s, they helped him reformulate it along Marxist lines.[55]

53. For the early stages of Lysenko's career, see Valery N. Soyfer, *Lysenko and the Tragedy of Soviet Science*, trans. Leo Gruliow and Rebecca Gruliow (New Brunswick, 1994), chaps. 1–4, pp. 8–59.
54. The following is not intended as a full treatment of Marr's theories. For that, see Smith, *Language and Power*, 81–102; Lawrence Thomas, *The Linguistic Theories of Na. Ia Marr* (Berkeley and Los Angeles, 1957); Thomas Samuelian, "The Search for a Marxist Linguistics in the Soviet Union, 1917–1950" (Ph.D. diss., University of Pennsylvania, 1981); Katerina Clark, *Petersburg, Crucible of Cultural Revolution* (Cambridge, Mass., 1995), 212–23; Yuri Slezkine, "N. Ia. Marr and the National Origins of Soviet Ethnogenetics," *Slavic Review* 55, no. 4 (Winter 1996): 826–62; and Marr's own writings, especially N. Ia. Marr, *Izbrannye raboty*, 5 vols. (Moscow, 1933–37), henceforth cited parenthetically as *IR*.
55. Slezkine, "N. Ia. Marr," 841.

A practitioner of myth-creation on a grand scale, Marr debunked existing myths, manipulated others, and invented new ones. Challenging the myth of an Aryan proto-language propagated by the Indo-European school of linguistics, which he associated with imperialism and racism (much as the émigré Eurasian linguist N. S. Trubetzkoi did) Marr offered a countermyth of origins based on the "Japhetic" languages. Beginning with a Georgian-Hebrew connection, "Japhetic" ultimately encompassed the other Semitic languages (living and dead), Armenian, Basque, the languages of the ancient Scythians, Sarmatians, and Khazars, the Dravidians of India, and the tribes of the Pamir region. The great migration of peoples was the "great spread of the Japhetic tribe" from its Caucasian homeland to the Atlantic coast and possibly to Central Asia, the Far East, and Africa. Mount Ararat was a Japhetic mountain; the goddess Athena hailed from the Caucasus, and so did Homer's epics and legends of the birth of Moses, Romulus, Sargon (king of Assyria), and Prometheus.

Marr foregrounded the ancient Scythians and was oriented to Asia (aspects of his theory that paralleled early futurism), and like the futurists, he was interested in the (nonrational) language of shamans and priests, mimicry and gesture, and he emphasized the spoken word. Soviet futurists were fascinated, for a time, with Marr's linguistics as something akin to *zaum*. Marr's statement "Down with Venus de Milo!" (1924) has the iconoclastic ring of a futurist slogan. In the 1920s, he belonged to a study circle that discussed linguistics, psychology, and aesthetics, including the aesthetics of Nietzsche, Wagner, symbolists, and the Soviet avant-garde. Eisenstein was a member.

After the Bolshevik Revolution, Marr declared himself to be a Marxist, which made him the only Marxist in the Academy of Sciences. Steadily expanding his domain, he founded and/or headed the State Academy for the History of Material Culture; the Japhetic Institute; its successor, the Institute of Language and Thought; and the Section of Materialist Linguistics of the Communist Academy (this is a partial list). Marr's championing of the linguistic and cultural rights of the non-Russian nationalities, his opposition to racism and Great Russian chauvinism, and his prediction that the other languages of the Soviet Union would eventually splice with Russian fit in with the Party's nationality policy and Stalin's myth of the Great Soviet Family.

Marr's Japhetic theory appealed to Lunacharsky, partly because he wanted to replace the "agnostic pluralism" (his term) of formalist theory with a materialist analysis that encompassed all aspects of social life, including class struggle.[56] Impressed by the boldness and sweep of Marr's linguistics (or myth-creation), which incorporated archaeology, ethnology, and anthropology, Lunacharsky gave him institutional support and publicized his work.

56. Lunacharskii, "Formalizm v nauki ob iskusstve," in *LSS*, 7:420.

In an article about Marr titled "Materialism and Philology," published in *Izvestiia* on April 12, 1925, Lunacharsky noted the questions that Marr "titanically posed and often turned upside down" and called him the "greatest living philologist of our Union, and perhaps the greatest living philologist of our day" (2). This tribute did not stop Marr from treating Lunacharsky shabbily a few years later.[57]

By 1923–24, Marr's Marxist revision of his theory was more or less complete (he tinkered with it until his death). He contended that the chief organ of speech was not the mouth but the hand, the agent of production, and that humankind's transition to sound speech was connected to its acquisition of tools. His slogan "Long live the hoe and hoe culture" encapsulates his contention that all culture is based on material artifacts, but the slogan also suggests a preference for rural "culture" over urban "civilization," and in that sense favored the nationalities of Soviet Asia. The tribe or ethnos was not a racial but a socioeconomic category. Language and thought were determined by economic processes that corresponded to Marx's three stages (feudalism, capitalism, communism). Each language had to be studied in its "paleontological section," layer after layer, the "material-real soil" in which language develops" (*IR*, 1:218). Since language was part of the superstructure, any major changes in language reflected changes in the socioeconomic base. All languages were tending toward unification by a process of crossing or hybridization (*skreshchenie*) that occurs when people with different languages are thrown together by economic need. In a classless society, a "single and unified language" much more precise than present languages would develop. Within the Soviet Union the national languages would splice with Russian naturally (not out of pressure from Great Russian chauvinists), because Russian was the language of the most advanced class, the revolutionary proletariat.

To tighten the fit of his theory with Marxism, Marr claimed that "Japhetic" was a scientific term, "far from biblical ideology," indeed opposed to it. The Tower of Babel was a "tale for children." Using a mythical term for linguistics was "just as legitimate" as naming planets after Venus, Saturn, and Mars. On this mythical basis, Marr coined another new term, "Promethean" (*prometeidskii*), to denote the Indo-European languages, including Russian. "Promethean" had a positive connotation to Marxists, Lunacharsky especially. Marr contended that "Promethean" was "a proper totemic name," known to the Greeks from the hero of the Caucasian Scythians, who invented (!) fire and various form of light. In the Greek legend, Prometheus stole fire from the gods and, as punishment, was chained to a rock in the Caucasus: the edge of the known world to the Greeks, the cradle of civilization to Marr. Over the centuries, according to Marr, Prometheus's name was replaced by

---

57. Details in Fitzpatrick, *Education and Social Mobility*, 85.

the geographic term "'Indo-European', remaining only to signify the old doctrine, its disciples, and their opinion" (*IR*, 1:291). Why the name was replaced, Marr didn't explain. Marr connected the emergence of the "Promethean" languages to the discovery of metal and its widespread use in the economy. Just as Prometheus invented fire, the "Promethean" peoples invented the great technology of the modern era, the industrial machine. The non-Russian nationalities would forge ahead under Russian leadership. Marr's theory was replete with ambiguities and inconsistencies. In a different essay, Marr said the "legend" of the Tower of Babel stemmed from the collective memory of a Japhetic protolanguage (*IR*, 1:120–21), which made it much more than a "tale for children."

Marr's revised theory included a sociolinguistic millennialism that dissolved ethnic peculiarities and kinship-based groups and transcended national boundaries. Linguistic and cultural changes stemmed not from tribal migrations but from "revolutionary shifts that resulted from qualitatively different conditions of material life, qualitatively new technologies, and a qualitatively new social system" (*IR*, 4:61). All languages are class languages. A new world language would follow the unification of the world economy made possible by the triumph of socialism. This new language would not be "mechanical" like Esperanto, which Marr once supported, but would express the linguistic experience of all humankind, its "emotional word," and would free humankind from "the narrow, closed circle that hinders its psychological growth" (*IR*, 1:176). In 1927, Marr published *The Japhetic Theory: The Program of a General Course on Linguistics* (1927). It was intended to supersede Saussure's *Course in General Linguistics,* published in Russian in 1922, which was a major influence on "bourgeois" linguistics.

During the Cultural Revolution, Marr's sociolinguistic millennialism became even more pronounced.

> [The proletariat's] greatest accomplishment . . . is the fusion of science and its ideological technology with art and its formal technology, as well as the unity of beauty and intellect . . . dialectical materialist thought has outgrown linear speech, no longer fits within sound speech, and as it outgrows sound speech, it is preparing to mold—to create—a new unified language based on the final accomplishments of both manual [written] and sound languages—a language wherein supreme beauty will merge with the highest development of the mind" Where? Only in a classless communist society, comrades. (*IR*, 3:111–12)

This would occur in the foreseeable future. The First Five-Year Plan will be the last and decisive battle against all tyranny in general and against the dictates of biological descent in particular.

On May 23, 1928, *Izvestiia* marked the fortieth anniversary of Marr's scholarship.[58] Pokrovsky wrote, "Marr's theory is far from ruling supreme, but it is already known everywhere. Already it is hated everywhere. This is a very good sign. Marxism has been hated everywhere for three-quarters of a century and under this mark of hatred it conquers more and more of the world." The "organizer of scholarship" predicted an "equally glorious future" for Marr's theory. "If Engels were still living among us, every student at an institution of higher education would be studying Marr's theories: they are mandatory for a Marxist understanding of human culture" (Pokrovsky, "Ia. Marr," 2). Marr's dissolution of ethnic peculiarities and national boundaries complemented Pokrovsky's heroless history, and Marr's inclusion of technology probably had a special appeal to the former *Vperedist*.

Not all Marxist linguists accepted Marr's theory. E. D. Polivanov, a Party member since 1919 (Marr didn't join until 1930) and a founding member of OPOIAZ, advocated a linguistics of fact, not fantasy, that built on Western scholarship. The "Language Front," a clone of RAPP formed in 1930, attacked Marr for his inconsistencies and his "divorce from practice" (language reform). The Language Front truly believed that language is power; the words of the ruling Marxist-Leninist ideology could change the world.[59]

As the struggle between Marrists and anti-Marrists intensified, it became clear that the central issue was not the criteria for a Marxist linguistics, but who would control the language used in schools, universities, and editorial boards.[60] Polivanov was exiled to Samarkand in 1930, and the Language Front had to disband in April 1932. As in other fields there could be only one correct application of Marxism. Marr's reductive dialectical materialism prevailed. Marr died in December 1934. By that time, according to Yuri Slezkine, "most ethnological disciplines had been proclaimed to be Marrist; Marrism had been proclaimed to be a subset of Marrism," and Marr himself was buried alongside the famed scientist and poet Mikhail Lomonosov (1711–65) and "immortalized" by various decrees.[61] The "great retreat" that resulted in Pokrovsky's dethroning affected Marrism too. The more fanciful aspects of Marr's theory disappeared from public discourse soon after his death. Marr was not dethroned, but his disciples exercised only a partial hegemony. "Marrists" retained primary institutional power, but structural linguists held important positions in linguistic studies and language reform projects. Both Marrists and anti-Marrists were caught up in the Great Purge.

58. In 1888, Marr's first article was published in the leading Georgian journal *Iveria*. Stalin might have read it; he published poetry in that journal in 1894.
59. Smith, *Language and Power*, 98.
60. Samuelian, "Search for a Marxist Linguistics," 334.
61. Slezkine, "N. Ia. Marr," 832.

The winding down of the Cultural Revolution implied a shift from egalitarianism to hierarchy, from chorus to hero, from madness to rationality, and from chaos to structure. In field after field, luminaries of the Cultural Revolution were repudiated, "socialist" replaced "proletarian," and many "bourgeois specialists" regained their positions. The Communist Academy was abolished in 1936.

The Cultural Revolution can be compared to an explosion that changed the landscape for years to come. Nietzsche wrote, "Where the Dionysian powers rise up as impetuously as we experience them now, Apollo, too, must already have descended among us . . . and the next generation will probably behold his most ample beautiful effects" (*BT,* 143–44). The "unleashing" of Dionysus set the stage for the construction of a rigid Apollonian order, which was not, however, beautiful. Stalin's post-1932 policies played into a wide-spread desire for stability and an end to conflict and turmoil. The Soviet Union acquired a single official aesthetic (Socialist Realism), a cult of heroes, and a new god (Stalin). Socialist Realism featured the deliberate creation of illusions to "mask" a disappointing and then a terrifying reality, and the new aesthetic included control of language.

Art as a Lie: Nietzsche and Socialist Realism

When the First Five-Year Plan was declared complete in October 1932, the promised paradise was still in the distant future. Bread was rationed; there were severe shortages of other necessities, and the peasants forcibly herded into collective farms were sullen and angry. In the cities, smoldering resentment flared into open resistance in demonstrations and strikes. Stalin's wife committed suicide. Within the Party, the opinion was widespread that Stalin had to go.[1] Hundreds of thousands of people were arrested, deported, and executed in 1932–33 alone, and millions of peasants perished in the "terror famine" (also 1932–33). But force alone could not bolster morale or, by itself, prevent slackening of effort at the workplace, or cover up the Party's mistakes.

The Party elite realized that they needed inspiring visions that would controvert experienced reality and keep hope alive. Socialist Realism entailed the creation of such visions. Its mandate was to depict reality not as it is, but as it *would be* under socialism, and treat that future *as if* it were the present. This collapsing of linear time distinguishes Socialist Realism from present-centered critical realism and Norman Rockwell's sentimental portrayals of everyday life. There is definitely idealization in Rockwell, but it is of a simpler past rather than a glorious future. Socialist Realism was a political aesthetic from the start. The Party was the moving force in its formulation and implementation, which were governed by what Evgeny Dobrenko calls the "logic of self-preservation, the logic of keeping power."[2] The Union of Soviet Writers unanimously adopted Socialist Realism at the end of its first Congress (August 17–September 2, 1934). The Union was supervised by Kul'tprop. Its bailiwick included Party propaganda and education,

---

1. Cohen, *Bukharin*, 344–45; Lars Lih, ed., *Stalin's Letters to Molotov* (New Haven, 1995), 225; Jeffrey Rossman, "The Teikovo Cotton Workers' Strike of April 1932: Class, Gender and Identity Politics in Stalin's Russia," *Russian Review* 56 (January 1997): 44–59; Brooks, *Thank You*, 55.

2. Evgeny Dobrenko, "The Disaster of Middlebrown Taste," in *Socialist Realism Without Shores*, ed. Thomas Lahusen and Evgeny Dobrenko (Durham, 1997), 158.

press and publishing, schools, and "cultural-enlightening work" (libraries and clubs; cultural work in the countryside; cinema, radio, and drama; unions of writers, artists, and architects; and science and technology).[3]

Preparation for the Congress began in April 1932. The resolution that ordered all literary and artistic factions to dissolve announced that writers who wanted to "participate in socialist construction" would be united in a single Union of Writers, which would have a Communist faction; analogous unions would be formed in all the arts. In September 1932, the Organizing Committee decided to promote Gorky as a symbol of Soviet literature. The next month, at an impromptu meeting held in Gorky's home, Stalin explained the nature and purpose of the Writers' Union and its Communist faction; the Communists would guide non-Party writers. It was at this meeting that Stalin called writers "engineers of human souls" and used the term "socialist realism."[4]

At the Congress, Zhdanov, supervisor of the "ideological front," said that Socialist Realism was openly "tendentious" and called for a "romanticism of a new type, revolutionary romanticism," which depicts reality, not in a "in a dead, scholastic way, not simply as 'objective reality,'" but as "reality in its revolutionary development." Soviet literature "must be able to portray our heroes; it should be able to glimpse our tomorrow. This will be no utopian dream, because our tomorrow is being prepared today by dint of conscious planned work" (*PSL*, 21–22).[5] He called Socialist Realism a "method," implying that a variety of applications would be permitted, and emphasized the role of literary criticism in guiding readers to the correct conclusions. Going well beyond creating a passive culture of consent, Socialist Realism was a mobilizing myth. Its purpose was to energize the masses for the tasks that lay ahead and to imbue them with "love of the most distant," so to speak, without telling them that full socialism was still in the distant future. What may have begun as a short-term strategy, until after the Second or Third Five Year Plan, say, became a permanent feature of the Soviet system. The radiant socialist future was always in the distance, but the masses had to keep on building it. The official aesthetic shaped every area of Soviet culture, including political culture, until well after Stalin's death.

Gorky chaired the Congress. There were twenty-six sessions, almost three hundred speeches, and close to six hundred delegates. A supplement to the stenographic report identified them as Party or non-Party (Gorky was non-

3. A. Kemp-Welch, *Stalin and the Literary Intelligentsia*, 242–43.
4. Ibid., 126–31.
5. H. Scott's *Problems of Soviet Literature* (*PSL*) contains the speeches by Gorky, Zhdanov, Radek, Bukharin, and Stetsky (the head of Kul'tprop). The stenographic transcript was published as *Pervyi Vsesoiznyi s"ezd sovetskikh pisateli, 1934. Stenograficheskii otchet*, ed. Ivan Luppol et al. (Moscow, 1934; reprint, 1990). Henceforth cited parenthetically as *Pervyi*.

Party), and by nationality (in Soviet usage, this meant ethnicity, not citizenship). The Union's Charter postulated "a close and direct link of the Party's policies and the Soviet regime" and announced that the "new creative principles" that would guide its members were formulated on the basis of the "critical assimilation of the literary heritage of the past" (= revaluation) and contemporary experience. "Socialist realism as the basic method of Soviet artistic and literary criticism demands from the artist a true, historically concrete depiction of reality in its Revolutionary development. In this respect, the truth and historical concreteness of the artistic depiction of reality must be combined with the task of the ideological remolding and education of the workers in the spirit of socialism" (*Pervyi*, 712). Writers were assured "of exceptional prospects for manifesting creative initiative" and a choice of diverse forms, styles, and genres (712). The new aesthetic was held to be applicable to all literature, not just Party literature, and to all the arts.

Socialist Realism cannot be regarded solely as a doctrine imposed from above on a recalcitrant membership. Many writers truly believed in the glorious future of Communism (the West was still in the grip of the Great Depression) and were willing, even eager, to do their part, especially since membership in the Union would provide them with regular employment and a stable income. Liberalizing measures preceded the Congress and led many Soviet citizens to assume that the worst was over. By September 1934, Hitler was securely in power (many Communists had not expected his regime to last), and Germany was conducting an unremitting propaganda war against the Soviet Union. No one could doubt the need for an effective response.

The Congress met in a festive atmosphere. An orchestra opened the proceedings. Constant interruptions by enthusiastic delegations of workers and peasants illustrated the union of the writer and the people (the dream of the old intelligentsia) and underscored the importance of the writers' work. Exactly how the writers were to implement the "method" (which delegates also called a "style" or a "doctrine") was left open. The straitjacket that Socialist Realism turned into was a product of developments the writers could not have foreseen—the Great Purge and the Great Terror.

As formulated between 1932 and 1934, elaborated between 1934 and 1939, and codified after the war, the principles of Socialist Realism were the following: party-mindedness (enthusiastic support of Party doctrine); reflection (art and literature must "reflect" the underlying socioeconomic circumstances and must avoid "scholasticism," "abstractness," and detachment from reality); typicality of characters and situations; "revolutionary romanticism"; the positive hero; and *narodnost'* (nationality or popular appeal, depending on the context). "Revolutionary romanticism" entailed depicting Soviet men and women, who combined "the highest practical labor with the highest heroism and a grand perspective," as idealized but credible characters living and working in "epic yet real life settings." The positive hero was

to be an "incarnation of will" and a model of self-discipline, political consciousness, and sobriety. A role model for the masses, he or she (more often
a he) was to be depicted in objectively real situations ("typicality") along
with his or her "inner development" ("consciousness") toward the communist ideal. *Narodnost'* required a language and form that appealed to and
was easily understood by the masses, the development of a national style,
veneration of the Russian classics, and promotion of the "Soviet classics,"
Gorky in prose and Mayakovsky in poetry, as the equals of any in world literature.[6] Stalin himself canonized Mayakovsky in 1935. A mobilizing myth
had to appeal to the masses; surveys were taken to see what kind of literature and art they liked. The writings of Marx, Engels, and Lenin were combed
for pronouncements on literature and the arts, and their personal tastes
gained canonical force. Stalin's taste had the force of law.

By 1939, Socialist Realism meant a homogenized and regulated language,
standardized plots, one-dimensional heroes and villains, representational
forms, and monumentalism. The method also entailed degradation of the
text to a "half-manufactured article" (Gorky's phrase) to be improved or
corrected by other writers, or cultural bureaucrats, or Stalin. Survival mandated conformity to a canon of classics, but conformity was no guarantee
of survival. The Party line shifted without warning, leaving a paper trail of
"errors" which the writer had to renounce. During the Great Terror, and
not only then, humiliating confessions were often in vain.

Presented as heir to, and culmination of, the humanist tradition in Russian
and world literature, Socialist Realism was an eclectic doctrine that included
a variety of elements. Socialist Realist novels had a "master plot" (Katerina
Clark's term)[7] that replicated the morphology of Russian epics, folktales,
and hagiography. From nineteenth-century Russia came realism, the positive hero, the ideal of an organic aesthetic (unity of form and content), and
moral and social didacticism, especially as articulated by Tolstoy in *What
Is Art?*[8] Communist didacticism replaced his Christian didacticism. Recent
scholarship has added Nietzschean elements. Boris Groys claims that under
Stalin, the avant-garde's dream (its will to power) "was in fact fulfilled and

---

6. This follows Hans Günther, *Die Verstaatlichung der Literatur; Entstehung und
Funktionsweise des sozialistisch-realistischen Kanons in der sowetischen Literatur der 30er
Jahre* (Stuttgart, 1984), chap. 2, pp. 18–54. For the visual arts, see John Bowlt, "The Stalin
Style: The First Phase of Socialist Realism," in *Catalogue to Sotsart Exhibition* (New York,
1986), 17, and Matthew Cullerne Bown, *Socialist Realist Painting* (New Haven, 1988). See
also *Sotsrealisticheskii kanon*, ed. Hans Günther and Evgeny Dobrenko (St. Petersburg,
2000).
7. Clark, *Soviet Novel*.
8. On the "positive hero" in Soviet literature, see Mathewson, *Positive Hero*, 179–253.
On the organic aesthetic, see Victor Terras, "Phenomenological Observations on the Aesthetics
of Socialist Realism," *Slavic and East European Journal* 23, no. 4 (1979): 450.

the life of society was organized in monolithic artistic forms, though of course not those that the avant-garde itself had favored."[9] Hans Günther traces the "Socialist Superman" to the early writings of Gorky and Lunacharsky.[10] Irina Gutkin argues that Socialist Realism grew out of the theurgic projects of symbolism.[11]

Groys, Günther, and Gutkin each touched on a piece of a larger phenomenon, the Nietzschean subtext of Socialist Realism, which was defined, in large part, against Nietzsche and the Nietzsche-influenced doctrines discussed in this book, and also against Fascism and Nazism. The official aesthetic incorporated and reworked aspects of these doctrines, most importantly, Ivanov's idea of myth-creation and Soviet adaptations of it. At all points, the purpose of myth-creation was to rally the people around a new myth and transform them psychologically.

Socialist Realism was the Stalinist "method" of myth-creation. Ivanov's myth-creation was based on Platonic epistemology, a higher reality already exists. In Stalin's version, the masses are building an entirely new reality and the Platonic elements (working toward an ideal) were overwhelmed by Nietzsche's idea of art as a lie. That idea grew out of his Dionysian epistemology, which was anti-Platonic and which contradicted the rationalism and the materialist epistemology that Communists professed. For this reason, and also because Nietzsche was central to Fascist and Nazi ideology, Stalin's myth-creators appropriated Nietzsche's idea of art as a lie covertly, denouncing him all the while.

Regine Robin called Socialist Realism an "impossible aesthetic" because "it unconsciously aims at blocking all indeterminacy, the unspeakable of language; because it tends to designate for all time the historical vector with full certainty, blocking the future since it is already known, as well as the past, which is always reinterpreted in function of the origin time of October."[12] These features were not unconscious at all, I submit, but part and parcel of a conscious strategy of myth-creation. Indeterminacy is the enemy of a mobilizing myth.

Official pronouncements on Nietzsche were uniformly negative. The entry "Nietzsche" in the *Literary Encyclopedia* (1934) was written by the Hungarian philosopher György Lukács (1875–1971), who lived in Moscow from 1933 to 1944. Lukács maintained that Nietzsche's irrationalist epistemology *must* result in illusions, lies, and "myth-creation" (the term he used),

9. Groys, *Total Art*, 9.
10. Günther, *Der sozialistische Übermensch*. See also Tupitsyn, "Superman Imagery," in *NSC*, 287–310, and Agursky, "Nietzschean Roots," in *NSC*, 272–83.
11. Gutkin, *Cultural Origins*.
12. Regine Robin, *Socialist Realism: The Impossible Aesthetic*, trans. Catherine Porter (Stanford, 1992), 74.

and postulated an inevitable progression from Nietzsche, to expressionism, to fascism.[13] Lukács participated in discussions on Socialist Realism (though he did not attend the Congress of Writers), insisting on realism and opposing modernism of any kind. His views on the consequences of irrationalism may have influenced Bernadiner (author of *The Philosophy of Nietzsche and Fascism,* 1934). A Nietzschean in his youth, Lukács had his own myth, a kind of Hegelianized Marxism, but he didn't think of it as a myth.

The next entry, "Nietzsche in Russia," associated Nietzsche with "decadent" fin de siècle writers and the "bourgeois aristocratic bloc" in the "period of intensified class struggle," and claimed that bourgeois literary critics "created the legend of the Nietzscheanism of the young Gorky" because they misunderstood Gorky's struggle for the rights of the human person, being trampled on by capitalism.[14]

The establishment of Socialist Realism marked a cultural shift from (Dionysian) chaos to (Apollonian) order, and was so perceived at the time. An article on theater was even titled "Without Dionysus."[15] At the Congress, speaker after speaker announced the start of a new era, extolling wholeness (*tsel'nost'*), organic unity, and cultural coherence, and associating modern art with nihilism, decadence, and disintegration. This brought into play another set of polarities found in Nietzsche's writings (though not only therein)—sickliness/health, decadence/vitality, old-age/youth—that Lunacharsky, Gorky, Bukharin, and Radek emphasized. Lunacharsky was deeply involved in formulating the official aesthetic.[16] He did not attend the Congress because he died before it met. (He died in December 1933, en route to Spain where he was to be the Soviet ambassador.)

At the Congress, Gorky, Bukharin, Radek, and countless other speakers contrasted the decline and decay of bourgeois literature to the youth and vitality of Soviet literature. Nietzsche said that nihilism represented a "pathological transition period" (*WP,* 14). The Soviet Union claimed to have overcome nihilism and decadence.

Marx and Engels did not discuss artistic decadence, per se, but Tolstoy and fin de siècle writers and critics certainly did. Marxist critics picked up the idea of decadence from Max Nordau's book *Degeneration* (1893), which connected artistic, societal, and class decadence and lambasted Nietzsche, Wagner, and modern art. Plekhanov attacked "decadent" literature and

13. For Lukacs's use of the term "myth-creation," see Ieorz Lukach, "Nitsshe," *Literaturnaia Entsiklopediia* (Moscow, 1934), 8:104.
14. V. M. Mikhailovskii, "Nitsche v Rossii," *Literaturnaia Entsiklopediia,* 8:104–8.
15. "Bez Dionis," *Krasnaia nov',* 1936, no. 6:227–33.
16. See his essays, "Sotsiologicheskie i patologicheskie faktory v istorii iskusstva," in *LSS,* 8:67–116; "Sotsialisticheskii realizm," in *LSS,* 8:491–523; and "O sotsialisticheskom realizme," in *LSS,* 8:524–30.

Nietzsche in *Art and Social Life* (1912). Distinguishing between "art for art's sake" and "utilitarian art," Plekhanov favored the latter because it indicated the artist's commitment to a social ideal. "Art for art's sake" was mere escapism. Modern artists attacked the bourgeoisie, but they were part of it. Their work could not possibly be positive because they spoke for a doomed class. Nietzsche's admirers were ultrareactionaries, dreaming of some "superman of genius at the head of the State, who by force of his iron will can strengthen the now tattering edifice of class domination." Plekhanov contrasted French Revolutionaries in 1793, who "temporarily placed themselves 'beyond good and evil' in their struggle against despotism," with neo-Romantics (including symbolists) who opposed the contemporary emancipation movement. "Decadents" interested in politics were often admirers of Napoleon, Plekhanov observed.[17] Having polemicized at length against the "so-called new religious consciousness," he probably had Merezhkovsky in mind.

Socialist Realism assimilated Plekhanov's distinction between "art for art's sake" and "utilitarian" art, and his association of modern art with decadence, but ignored the Kantian aspects of his aesthetic, which allowed a degree of autonomy for art and assumed an inborn instinct for beauty. Lunacharsky contended that Nietzsche's "pathology" (syphilis and madness) had a social aspect; as a "cultured philistine," he suffered from the coarseness and crudeness of Imperial German society.[18] Gorky regarded Dostoevsky's characters as the embodiment of the "unhealthy principle." Before the Revolution he tried to prevent the Moscow Art Theater from staging Dostoevsky's novels because the neurotic protagonists were poor role models. Lenin followed the controversy, apparently sharing Gorky's views. As a result, Dostoevsky was viewed with disfavor for much of the Soviet period

Socialist Realism established the new myth to be celebrated in all the arts—a happy and prosperous "land of socialism"—and it mandated a new art form, a distinctive language, and a mythologized new man. The new woman was problematic because of her dual role as worker and mother. When Soviet policy changed, details of implementation changed accordingly. During the Great Patriotic War, propagandists emphasized Soviet patriotism and celebrated a new set of heroes and martyrs. Their heroism was not a myth, however, and the enemy was real and truly evil. Postwar propaganda featured Stalin leading a united and heroic Soviet people to victory over fascism, an image that contained truths and lies—outright lies and lies of omission such as the Hitler-Stalin Pact, the Holocaust, and the casualties and deaths that resulted directly and indirectly from Stalin's decisions. To prevent discordant notes, memoir literature was prohibited.[19] Postwar litera-

17. Plekhanov, "Art and Social Life," in *Art and Social Life*, 3:6–14, 18, 30, 39, 40–41, 58.
18. Lunacharskii, "Sotsiologicheskie," in *LSS*, 8: 74, 113, 114.
19. Nina Tumarkin, *The Living and the Dead: The Rise and Fall of the Cult of World*

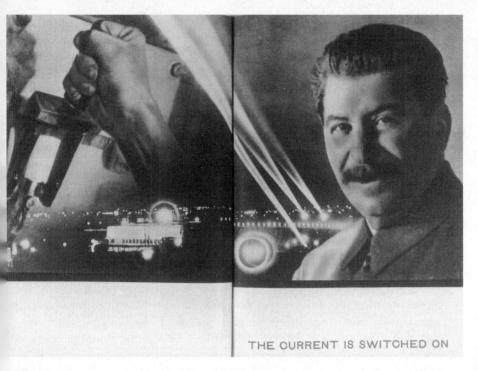

THE CURRENT IS SWITCHED ON

Fig. 7 "The Current is Switched On." *USSR in Construction*, 1932, no.10. Avery Architectural and Fine Arts Library, Columbia University in the City of New York.

ture about Soviet life placed less emphasis on struggle and sacrifice, and more emphasis on material rewards and a satisfying personal life.

Socialist Realism was the first step in a Soviet version of *Gleichschaltung,* the Nazi term for synchronization of all areas of life from a central point. The term originally referred to turning on an electric current and regulating its flow throughout the system. A two-page photomontage in *USSR in Construction* captioned "The Current Is Turned On" (Fig. 7) (1932) conveys that idea. On the first page is a gigantic hand pulling down an enormous lever at the Dneprostroi Dam and lighting up the night sky; on the second page is Stalin's head. He is looking into the future, but the two pages are symbolically connected by diagonal beams of light. Note that this is a constructivist composition; the seams are obvious and the diagonals convey a sense of dynamism. The transition from modernism to realism took several years. The visual arts had a different "look" after 1936.

War II in Russia (New York, 1994); Rosalinde Sartori, "On the Making of Heroes, Heroines, and Saints," in *Culture and Entertainment in Wartime Russia,* ed. Richard Stites (Bloomington, 1995), 176–93.

Nietzsche's Contributions to the Theory of Socialist Realism

The origin of the holy lie is the *will to power*. . . .
Establishment of rule: to this end the rule of those
concepts that place a *non plus ultra* of power with
the priesthood. . . . Power through the lie . . . the lie
as a supplement to power, a new concept of "truth."
                                                  —*WP,* 92

As the Stalinist "method" of myth-creation, Socialist Realism
was imbued with Nietzsche's idea of art as a lie and a future-
oriented optimism that glossed over the negative features
of present-day Soviet reality. Absent from the official aesthetic were Nietzsche's antiromanticism and his concept of
a pessimism of strength. Debates at the first Congress of
Soviet Writers revolved around issues of the Nietzschean
agenda—new myth, new word, new form, new man—which
were resolved in rather general terms at the Congress and
codified over the next few years. The delegates included
older writers steeped in the culture of the Silver Age and
former members of RAPP and LEF. Nietzsche's name was
used only as a negative symbol, but a negative symbol can
be a powerful influence because it channels the search for
alternatives.

Art as a Lie

Nietzsche did not invent the idea of art as a lie—art has always been used for propaganda—but he articulated it very forcefully and provided a philosophical justification. In *The Birth of Tragedy,* he called art a beautiful illusion that veils the horror of the abyss. The line between "lie" and "illusion" is blurry, but "illusion" is the gentler term; unlike "lie," it does not connote willful or malicious deception. "Lie" encompasses harmless "white lies" and hurtful lies. Russians distinguish between "*vran'e*," bluster or loose talk, as in the size of the fish one caught, and "*lozh'*," a manipulative or malevolent lie. In any language, there are lies of omission and lies of commission, the invention of "facts" that are nothing of the kind. "Myth" can refer to the "ruling idea" of a society, or it can be the antonym of "truth." For Nietzsche, of course, there was no absolute truth. Like everything else, "truth" is a matter of perspective and also of power. The ruler decides what is "true."

According to Nietzsche, people need lies in order to live. "Truth is ugly. We possess *art* lest we *perish of the truth*" (*WP,* 435). And: "Truth does not count as the supreme value, even less as the supreme power. The will to appearance, to illusion, to deception, to becoming and change (to objectified deception) here counts as more profound, primeval, 'metaphysical' than the will to truth, to reality, to mere appearance:—the last is itself merely a form of the will to illusion. . . . art is *worth more* than truth" (*WP,* 453). Nietzsche was speaking primarily of ultimate truth as revealed by religion or discovered by philosophers or scientists and only secondarily about truth and lie in politics. He did note, however, that "without the assistance of the priests even now no power can become legitimate: as Napoleon grasped" (*HH,* 171), a reference to Napoleon's Concordat with the pope.

Paradoxically, Nietzsche considered "truthfulness" Zarathustra's highest virtue, the "opposite of the cowardice of the 'idealist' who flees from reality; Zarathustra has more intestinal fortitude than all other thinkers taken together" (*EH,* 328). For Nietzsche, "'faith' means not *wanting* to know what it true" (*AC,* 169). Nietzsche's critique of the "holy lies" told by priests and philosophers can be regarded as a call for truthfulness. "But philosophers, too, as soon as with priestly ulterior motives, they form the intention of taking in hand the direction of mankind, at once also arrogate to themselves the right to tell lies; Plato above all" (*WP,* 89). It is a mistake to suppose an "*unconscious and naive* development here, a kind of self-deception —Fanatics do not invent such carefully thought out systems of oppression— The most cold-blooded reflection was at work here; the same kind of reflection as Plato applied when he imagined his *Republic*" (*WP,* 92). Nietzsche meant the "necessary lie" that justified the social order of Plato's Republic. "Observe the hatred of the herd for the truthful," Nietzsche once said (*WP,* 162). This statement can be taken to mean that truthfulness is "noble," or that it is folly to be truthful with "the herd." In 1928, Lunacharsky praised Nietzsche's honesty; in 1933, he accepted the need for guile and rationalized deception in terms of the Hegelian-Marxist concept of becoming. What is false today will be true tomorrow. Illusion will become reality.

In 1932–34, many Soviet writers and artists truly believed in the radiant future of socialism. Some of them became disillusioned later on; others believed to the end of their days. But the formulators of the official aesthetic knew exactly what they were doing. They were creating a mirage to sustain morale. Lunacharsky explained that socialism was constructing a splendid palace for the workers, but that it was not yet complete. The "bourgeois realist" sees that the palace has no roof and gloats, "Here's your socialism!" Such a person "does not understand that truth [*pravda*] does not sit in one place; truth flies, truth is development, truth is struggle, truth is the day after tomorrow. He who does not understand this is a pessimist, a whiner, a swindler, and a falsifier . . . voluntarily or involuntarily, a counterrevolutionary and a wrecker." "From the point of view of socialist realism," his observation "is not the truth—it is unreality, a lie, a substitution of carrion for life." The socialist realist understands that reality is development, movement, that a "static truth" does not exist, so he depicts the palace in its finished form with the roof already on.[1] Similarly: "The Socialist Realist does not accept reality as it is. He accepts it as it will be." "The Communist dream is not a flight from the earthly but a flight into the future." And: "In his struggle with negative phenomena, the Socialist Realist may of course resort to all sorts of hyperbole, caricature, and utterly improbable comparisons—not to conceal reality but, through stylization, to reveal it."[2]

Gorky announced that "critical realism" is the work of "superfluous people" who no longer exist in the Soviet Union, where the negative aspects of life were rapidly disappearing, but it was appropriate for the capitalist world. Apparently, Gorky regarded "the lie" as a holding action until Soviet reality matched the myth. In the course of the 1930s, inspiring illusions turned into outright lies. Nietzsche considered "truth" and "lie" extramoral concepts. Communists considered lying for the Party a moral imperative. Piatikov declared that he would call "black" "white" if the Party required it, because "outside the party, there is no life for me."[3] Of course, if Piatikov truly believed that black was white, he was not lying.

Bernadiner's *The Philosophy of Nietzsche and Fascism* (1934) was part of a propaganda war with Nazi Germany, which Communists hardly ever called

1. Lunacharskii, "Sotsialisticheskii realizm," in *LSS*, 8:497.
2. Ibid., 8:615–16.
3. Quoted in Walicki, *Marxism*, 461. A former Trotsky supporter, Piatikov was expelled from the Party, recanted, and was readmitted.

Nazi Germany, because Stalin said (in January 1934), that the term "National Socialism" was incorrect and referred to "fascism of the German type" (*SW*, 13:299). Ten thousand copies were printed (a small printing by Soviet standards), presumably for use by trusted cadres.[4] It was only 140 pages long. The epigraph, bordered in black like an obituary, was as follows:

> The specifically reactionary views of Nietzsche are exceptionally popular in contemporary fascist Germany. The philosophy of Nietzsche is being popularized by the national socialists almost as the official philosophy of "The Third Reich." This book is dedicated to explaining the cause of that phenomenon; it is a social-political analysis and critique of the most important Nietzschean propositions in the work of his fascist restorers and successors, mainly in Germany.

The format symbolically buried the "revolutionary" Nietzsche. The text was a compilation of quotations, mostly from Nietzsche's late works, strung together by commentary. Unlike the Nazis, who used a bowdlerized version of *Zarathustra* as a surrogate bible, Bernadiner rarely quoted it. *The Birth of Tragedy,* he did not even mention, though he referred to "Dionysianism" in a passage attacking the "legend" of Nietzsche as an individualist. Frequently quoted were Nietzsche's late works, Mussolini, Spengler, and the Nazi ideologues H. F. K. Günther, Alfred Bäumler, Alfred Rosenberg, and Gottfried Feder.

Like Leiteizen's book, Bernadiner's can be read on two levels: a straightforward description of fascist (really Nazi) appropriations of Nietzsche's thought and as an Aesopian guide to Soviet policy. (See my discussion of Soviet Aesopian language in Chapter 9.) When Leiteizen wrote, multiple voices contended in the Party. When Bernadiner wrote, the Party spoke with one voice and the government press was the only press. His book articulated the Party line on Nietzsche: "the philosopher of fascism." The section on epistemology is relevant to Socialist Realism. The rest of the book will be discussed in the introduction to Part III.

On the straightforward level, Bernadiner attacked Nietzschean irrationalism and argued that it actually required the creation of illusions and lies. If people could not know reality, if there was no connection between cause and effect, then "things" (and "facts") could be ignored. Indeed, they did not exist (52). Nietzsche himself said: "The world, so much as it has any significance for us, is false [Bernadiner uses *lozhen*], that is to say, there is nothing factual in it, only interpretation surrounded by a barren sum of observations; it flows as something always becoming, as a constantly changing lie, which never approaches truth, because there is no truth (52; *WP*,

---

4. B[er] M[oisevich] Bernadiner, *Filosofiia Nitsshe i Fashizm* (Moscow and Leningrad, 1934).

330). (Slight differences in the Kaufmann/Hollingdale translation do not change the meaning.) According to Bernadiner, Nietzsche advocated an "art, in which precisely *the lie* is sanctified and the *will to deception,* underlined by Nietzsche, the creation of illusions, has a clean conscience" (53, *GM,* 153). Giving the impression that Nietzsche advocated outright lying, Bernadiner ignored Nietzsche's praise of truthfulness, Zarathustra's complaint (which repeats Aristotle) that "poets lie too much" (*Z,* 149), and the "*compulsion to lie*" which Nietzsche detected "in every predestined theologian" (*AC,* 169). Bernadiner considered fascist irrationalism the ideological expression of the bourgeoisie's inability to posit a logical, coherent worldview, because it was unwilling to face the reality of its inevitable doom. A rising class does not need illusions and lies. Reason characterized the bourgeoisie in its progressive period, and it characterizes the proletariat today.

On the Aesopian level, Bernadiner was explaining why rational, scientific communists were turning to revolutionary romanticism and, more importantly, why they needed illusions and lies. The exploiting class "has never ruled by physical force alone" (11); it manufactures illusions to keep the masses in thrall. Elliptically addressing widespread skepticism about Stalin's leadership, Bernadiner quotes Nietzsche a bit less accurately than he might have: "Skepticism is the intellectual [*razymno*] expression of weak nerves and sickliness—it is the result of the crossing of races and estates [*soslovie*], which for a long time have been separate" (52–53; *BGE,* 130). The Kaufmann translation follows the German (*KSA,* 5:138): "For skepticism is the most spiritual [*geistige*] expression of a certain complex physiological condition that in ordinary language is called nervous exhaustion and sickliness." Why did Bernadiner omit the phrase "a certain complex physiological condition"? I believe it was because Bernadiner was addressing communists from worker and peasant backgrounds who were "exhausted" by the stress of collectivization. The coded message was that skepticism resulted from weakness and lack of faith. Moreover, Bernadiner declared, Nietzsche was not an absolute skeptic; a philosopher who demanded the greatest activism could not be satisfied with skepticism. Activism demanded firm convictions, which could stem from instinct alone. "Yes, reason deceives us—says Nietzsche—but instinct does not lie. To separate the real world from the apparent one—is an idle occupation, but it is necessary to create for oneself a picture of the world which will fortify life" (53). That, of course, was the task of Socialist Realism. Bernadiner ignored Nietzsche's statement: "It does indeed make a difference for what purpose one lies: whether one preserves with a lie or *destroys* with it" (*AC,* 179). Preservation could justify Socialist Realism as the art form of the Soviet civil religion, but then the Party would have to admit not only to lying but to making Marxism into a religion.

"It is necessary to understand the essence of events not as was done up to now," Bernadiner continued. "Ordinarily, newspaper readers say that the party made some sort of mistake that will be its undoing. Nietzsche does not agree with this. [My *higher* politics says] the party that makes a mistake is already on the brink of ruin; it no longer has confidence in instinct. 'Every error, of whatever kind, is a consequence of degeneration of instinct' [of disgregation of will]" (53; *TI,* 48; *KSA,* 6:90). (Bernadiner omitted the phrases in brackets.) His subliminal point was the Party could not admit that it had made a mistake. Having affirmed a new truth, it had to live by it. "Life requires illusions." The illogical is necessary; it "springs up [*sozdaetsia*] 'in speech, in feelings [*chuvstvakh*], in art, in religion, and generally in *everything that gives value to life*'" (53; *HH,* 28). Hollingdale's translation—"the illogical . . . is implanted so firmly in the passions"—is closer to the German: the illogical "is firmly rooted"; *es steckt so fest* (*KSA,* 2:51). "Springs up" (or arises) can suggest something unpredictable or erratic that must be contained, a twinge of doubt, for example.

"In the name of what are illusions created?" Bernadiner asked rhetorically; "what criteria show they are needed?" The answer lies in Nietzsche's theory of knowledge. "Knowledge works as a tool of power. Hence it is plain that it increases with every increase of power" (53–54; *WP,* 266). Knowledge has a definite biological meaning, Bernadiner continued. Every species strives to preserve itself. The coded message was that the Party (some members considered themselves a new species) needed illusions to stay in power and to increase its power. "The measure of the desire for knowledge depends upon the measure to which the will to power grows in a species: a species seizes as much reality as it can conquer and forces it to serve itself (54; *WP,* 267). The Kaufmann/Hollingdale translation of the last sentence is softer and more accurate: "A species grasps a certain amount of reality in order to become master of it, to press it into service."[5] Nietzsche's statement that "the criterion of truth [*istina*] lies in the enhancement of the feeling of power" (54; *WP,* 290) expressed the "unique pragmatism" that is the essence of Nietzsche's theory of knowledge. Socialist Realism was pragmatic; "truth" was what worked to accomplish the Party's goals.

Gorky had long questioned the value of truth and praised the beautiful lies that give mankind success. His mythologizing of Soviet reality was the latest expression of his belief in the "salutary lie," Bertram Wolfe's term for a lie that inspires people to perform great deeds, thereby making "the lie" become "truth." Wolfe considered truthfulness and lying the central theme of Gorky's play *The Lower Depths* (1902), giving as an example an exchange that Wolfe did not realize was a Nietzschean dialogue.[6] One character,

---

5. For the German, see *Nachgelassene Werke von Friedrich Nietzsche. Die Wille zu Macht, Drittes und Viertes Buch* (Leipzig, 1911), 11.

6. Wolfe, *The Bridge and the Abyss,* 55. In a footnote, Wolfe pointed to Pushkin's concept of an "elevating lie."

Bubnov, says, "give 'em the whole truth, just as it is." To which Klestch replies: "What truth? Where's the truth? No work, no strength, not even a place to live. The only thing left is to die like a dog! This is the truth. . . . What do I want the truth for? I want to breathe more freely—that's all I ask. What have I done wrong? Why should I have been given the truth?" Still another character, Luka, says, "You've been saying we need the truth. But it isn't always truth that is good for what ails a man—you can't always cure the soul with truth." To prove his point, Luka tells about a simple man who believed in the existence of a "true and just land" until a learned man showed him that it did not exist. Unable to bear this bitter truth, the simple man "went home—and hung himself."[7] In the same act, Luka advises Natasha to marry Peppel, also known as Vassya, saying: "He's all right, he's a good fellow. Only you have to remind him as often as you can that he's a good fellow—so that he doesn't forget it. He'll believe you. Just keep telling him—you're a good man Vassya, remember that! And besides, my dear, where else can you go?" (51). Throughout the play, Luka purveys comforting lies. The character Satin, arguably Gorky's voice, says, "Lies are the religion of slaves and bosses. Truth is the god of the free man" (64).

Socialist Realism represents the victory of Luka over Satin. To paraphrase Luka: "Just keep telling" the people that the future is at hand, that they are heroic, energetic, creative, hard-working, self-disciplined, and rational. Telling them might make it come true, and besides "where else can they go?" To return to capitalism was unthinkable, but if the people knew that the socialist paradise would not be reached in their lifetime, they might loose confidence in the Party and succumb to despair. Then who would build socialism?

Gorky wanted a constructed truth that would serve as an mobilizing myth. In 1929, he broke with an old friend, Ekaterina Kuskova, because she told the truth about Soviet Russia. In a letter to her he wrote: "What is important to me is the rapid all-round development of human personality, the birth of a new man of culture, of workmen in a sugar refinery who read Shelley in the original. . . . Such men do not need a petty accursed truth in the midst of which they are struggling. They need the truth they create for themselves. . . . I am now one-sided."[8] The full human cost of the Plan was not yet evident and confidence was high. Gorky regarded hardship and suffering as obstacles to be overcome by reason and will. In December 1931, when the costs were all too evident, Gorky warned of the dangers of skepticism.[9] In 1932, he wrote:

> In the Soviet Union a new man is developing and it is already possible to define his qualities unmistakably.

---

7. *The Lower Depths and Other Plays by Maxim Gorky*, trans. Alexander Bashky (New Haven, 1971), 47–49.

8. Quoted in Wolfe, *The Bridge and the Abyss*, 60.

9. Gorkii, "O bor'be s prirodoi," in *GSS*, 26:186–87.

He has faith in the organizing force of reason. . . . He feels himself the creator of a new world and although he still lives in difficult conditions, he knows that he is creating different conditions. That is his goal and the deed of his rational will, therefore, he has no basis for pessimism.[10]

Despite his praise of reason, Gorky did not want people to think for themselves. The "salutary lie" helps explain Gorky's reaction to Aleksandr Afinogenov's play, *The Lie* (1933), which depicted Party leaders who lie as a matter of policy. A long monologue by the protagonist (a woman communist) bemoans the collision between word and deed in contemporary Soviet society. Another character says that people lie and cheat because they are being lied to and cheated. Afinogenov sent the manuscript to Gorky, who replied that such a play could have been extremely useful if it were performed in a closed theater, before a thousand educated Leninists who were unshakably persuaded of the validity of the general line. But it could never be shown to an audience in which there were not socialists, but sons of bitches from the past, "in exile from the shambles of their bourgeois life."[11] In Regine Robin's words, "not all truths are fit to tell, especially negative truths concerning the present," because truth is dialectical. "A bad Bolshevik will become good; that is the law of history, the emergence of the new."[12] Afinogenov revised the play and sent it to Stalin, who disliked it intensely. Although the play had gone into rehearsal in over three hundred theaters in the Soviet Union, it was taken out of production in all but one.

In his opening remarks to the Congress, Gorky called on Soviet Writers to "create a new socialist reality" in the land "illuminated by Lenin's genius, in the land where Joseph Stalin's iron will works tirelessly and miraculously" (*Pervyi*, 1). Praise of Stalin was *de rigueur* by then, but it is also explained by Gorky's admiration for iron-willed leaders. He believed that Russians have a "passive nature" and therefore require such leaders. "It is impossible to have a leader who is not to one degree or another a tyrant."[13] Gorky managed to avoid writing a biography of Stalin, however; the French writer Henri Barbusse took on that task.

Gorky's talk on Soviet literature took up most of the first day. Describing myth as "invention," he said that romantic myths engender attitudes that change the world in practical ways, and he exalted folk heroes such as Hercules, Prometheus, Don Quixote, and Faust, whose deeds or "mad" dreams had benefited humanity (*PSL*, 44). Gorky wanted Socialist Realism

10. Gorkii, "O starom i novom cheloveke," in *GSS*, 26:289.
11. Quoted in Kemp-Welch, *Stalin and the Literary Intelligentsia*, 248–49.
12. Robin, *Socialist Realism*, 61.
13. Quoted in Wolfe, *The Bridge and the Abyss*, 157.

to be modeled partly on folklore, which has "created the most profound, vivid, and artistically perfect types of heroes" (*PSL*, 35). "Pessimism is entirely alien to folklore," because the collective "knows" that it will ultimately triumph over all hostile forces. "The hero of folklore, the 'simpleton' always turned out to be wiser" than those who despised him (*PSL*, 36, 44). Tragedy, suffering, and neurosis have no place in Soviet literature.

Soviet writers had to be leaders, Gorky declared. Distinguishing between "leaderism" and "leadership," he called "leaderism" a "contagious philistine disease . . . the fruit of effete, impotent and impoverished individualism," epitomized by such "festering sores" of the capitalist world as Friedrich Ebert, Gustav Noske, and Hitler (*PSL*, 62).[14] "Leadership" requires energy, reason, and science. "Leadership" in literature entails choosing worker-heroes, treating labor as creativity, portraying the new woman, improving literary quality, inculcating a socialist morality, and curbing artistic individualism. It also entails purging the "toxic weed" or "microbe" of philistinism from Soviet literature and eliminating parasitic characters and superfluous people.

Lambasting Nietzsche, Dostoevsky, and the Silver Age, Gorky claimed that Nietzsche's "ideas form the basis of the fanatical creed and practice of fascism" and called Dostoevsky's heroes egocentrists and degenerates. Alluding to Merezhkovsky, Mystical Anarchism, Rozanov, Andreev, and Artsybashev, Gorky claimed that when "Russian writers enjoyed full freedom of creation," the results were deplorable. The decade 1907–17 "deserves to be branded the most shameful and shameless decade in the history of the Russian intelligentsia" (*PSL*, 45, 48–49).

Gorky's mythologizing of Soviet reality included glorifying forced labor and the secret police. He coedited a collective history of the construction of Belomor, the Stalin White Sea–Baltic Canal, that was built entirely by forced labor—even the engineers were prisoners—who worked in appalling conditions. Over 200,000 prisoners died, mainly from hypothermia and starvation. The canal turned out to be too shallow for oceangoing ships. Loren Graham claims that it was a supremely irrational project from the start.[15] The book, which the GPU (successor to the Cheka) commissioned, was comprised of articles by 36 authors (out of over 120) who toured the canal in August 1933. Published in time for the Congress of Soviet Writers, it served as a model text because it represented a collective effort and exalted building socialism.[16] The authors participated out of ideological commitment,

---

14. Ebert and Noske were German social democrats, but Gorky associated them with Hitler, in accord with the Party line, which called social democrats "social fascists."

15. Loren Graham, *The Ghost of the Executed Engineer: Technology and the Fall of the Soviet Union* (Cambridge, Mass., 1993), 61–65.

16. Greg Carleton, "The Problem of Genre in Socialist Realism," *Slavic Review* 53, no.

fear, opportunism, self-deception, or combinations thereof. Shklovsky's brother was a convict and he wanted to get him released (he was). The key word, "reforging" (*perekovka*), pertains to the rehabilitation of so-called criminals by "corrective" labor. The overwhelming majority of the prisoners were not criminals but "class enemies." One of the slogans of Belomor was "Man, in changing nature, changes himself." To demonstrate that "reforging" had occurred, 12,484 prisoners were paroled, 59,516 received reduced terms, and 15 were decorated with the Order of the Red Banner.

Gorky titled his chapter "The Truth of Socialism."[17] He was not being ironic. In another article, "From 'Enemies of Society' to 'Heroes of Labor,'" he predicted that "in fifty years, when life will be a little calmer . . . and the first half of the century will seem like a splendid tragedy, a proletarian epic, it is likely that art as well as history will be able to do justice to the wonderful cultural work of the rank-and-file Chekists in the camps."[18] Although Gorky knew about the appalling conditions in the Solovky prison camp, he praised its directors for being "bold creators of culture." Several prison camps were named after him,[19] which is ironic, for *gorkii* means bitter in Russian, and life in the camps was bitter indeed.

How to explain Gorky's transition from a defender of human rights in the early Soviet period, and again during the Cultural Revolution (he interceded on behalf of Pilniak and Zamiatin), to a concealer of Stalinist brutality? One reason was his future-orientation. Dazzled by visions of the radiant future of socialism, he blinded himself to suffering in the present. If building socialism required enslaving the herd, so be it. He considered the peasants an inferior race and associated kulaks with capitalism, capitalism with philistinism, and philistinism with his brutal grandfather, so his hatred of them had a personal edge. Another reason was the honors and material benefits that were heaped on him. He was awarded the Order of Lenin; the city of Nizhni Novgorod was renamed Gorky; and a film titled *Our Gorky* was made. *Izvestiia* devoted most its September 25, 1932, issue to him as well. Bukharin's encomium appeared on October 17. A certain amount of self-deception is natural for a person faced with such acclaim. Solzhenitsyn claims that Gorky's return to the Soviet Union was motivated solely by material factors; his fame was fading in the West and his royalties along with it. In Moscow, he lived in the nationalized Riabushinsky mansion.[20] Irwin Weil

---

4 (Winter 1994): 993–94; Cynthia Ruder, *Making History for Stalin: The Story of the Belomor Canal* (Gainesville, 1998).

17. Gorkii, "Pravda sotsializma," in *GSS*, 27:127.

18. Gorkii, "Ot 'vragov obshchestva'—k 'geroiam truda'," in GSS, 27:509; see also "O vospitanii pravdy," in *GSS*, 27:58–66.

19. Aleksandr Solzhenitsyn, *The Gulag Archipelago*, trans. Thomas P. Whitney, vol. 1 (New York, 1973), 512; vol. 2 (New York, 1975), 60–63.

20. Ibid., 2:63n.

believes that Gorky hoped to influence Stalin, as he had influenced Lenin, and realized too late that he could not.[21] In his last years he was under a de facto house arrest.

The Nietzschean Agenda at the First Congress of Soviet Writers

Gorky dominated the Congress. Virtually every major speaker paid tribute to him, and he vetted some speeches beforehand, forcing revisions on the authors.[22] Literature was taken to include theater and by extension cinema. The painter Igor Grabar (1871–1960), a former *Miriskusnik,* proclaimed his fellow artists' commitment to Socialist Realism and seconded Gorky's condemnation of the "distant" and "dismal" past.

In the official aesthetic, mythologized individual heroes replaced anonymous masses; discipline, rationality, and consciousness channeled passion and enthusiasm; classicism and monumentalism overcame cultural iconoclasm, and experimentation gave way to new norms and canons. The speakers emphasized the need to raise the quality of Soviet literature; derided "abstract," "mechanical," or "naturalistic" works; attacked "aesthetic anarchy"; and invoked coherence, organic union, and harmony. Calling for a new art form that expressed the new Soviet reality and for "mastery" of language and technique, they frequently used words that had Nietzschean associations to their audience—"tragic," "tragism" (*tragizm*), "self-will," "enthusiasm," "passion," "colossal," and "summits." To "fascist barbarism," the speakers opposed civilization and culture; to "fascist irrationalism," reason and science; to the criminals, prostitutes, neurotics, and degenerates of bourgeois literature, the heroes of the proletariat; to the fragmented productions of the avant-garde, socialist integration and wholeness (*tsel'nost'*); to linguistic experimentation, a language that was simple and clear.

Formalism was said to reflect the inner turmoil and confusion of hyperindividualistic authors. Naturalism was conflated with "bourgeois" realism and denigrated as backward and reactionary because it stressed the unsavory aspects of life. "Socialist individuality" was counterposed to "bourgeois individualism." Gorky talked about a new form of collective creativity, writers "reeducating each other," making clear that the writer did not own his "product"; it would be reworked and reassembled by other writers (*Pervyi,* 225–26). Tretiakov expressed a similar idea during the Cultural Revolution: "literary workers" would practice their craft in workshops to which some would bring materials, others would rearrange them, and still others would recast then in simple language.

21. Conversation with author, December 28, 1992.
22. Kemp-Welch, *Stalin and the Literary Intelligentsia,* 172.

Several speakers invoked a "new socialist humanism," as distinct from obsolete "bourgeois humanism," and predicted a Soviet Renaissance that would overtake and surpass the Italian Renaissance and dwarf the achievements of the capitalist world. The Italian Renaissance, they kept repeating, was the work of a privileged elite; the Soviet Renaissance was being created by workers and peasants.

The New Myth

Neither Gorky nor anyone else at the Congress called the radiant Soviet future a myth. Rather, the speakers used terms such as "epic," "monumental," "titanic," and "living truth," as distinct from "abstract truth" or mere facts. "Monumental" connoted "big" or "super." Lunacharsky had envisioned a "proletarian Prometheus," not as an illusion, but as a representation of "the gigantic collective forces of his class in a monumental form that does not exist in a single human person."[23] Radek attacked bourgeois writers' belief that "there is nothing big in life—no big events, no big people, no big ideas" (*PSL,* 153). To be treated in epic terms were the building of factories and plants, the conquest of nature, the revolutionary period, the new village, the worldwide struggle for the victory of socialism, and the dramatic rescue, by air, of the explorers of the Cheliuskin expedition marooned on an ice floe near the North Pole.

Radek stressed the decadence of contemporary Western literature, the impossibility of great literature under fascism, and the Soviet writer's duty to fight for socialism. Apropos of duty, Radek quoted Goebbels's assertion that apoliticism "'might have been permissible in the past, when politics reduced themselves to parliamentary squabbles,' but when fascism came to power, when politics became a national drama in which whole worlds tumbled to the ground, the artist cannot say 'This does not concern me.'" Neither can Soviet artists say "leave us alone"; the international proletariat is engaged in a fight to the death with fascism. There can be no neutrals (*PSL,* 114–15). Radek's quotation of an Italian literary critic (Telesio Interlandi) had a double message. "'We need a writer who will see our villages gay, our peasants joyful, our workers calm, trustful and reconciled to the fatherland, who will see how our roads, radiating out from Rome, stretch to all corners of the world, who will hear the metallic voice of Mussolini filling the public squares.' And the unfortunate fascist writers battle with the task assigned them: they depict Italy as she is not" (*PSL,* 118). Implicitly, Soviet writers were to do the same. Meanwhile, Italian leaders were studying Soviet literature and film for their own ventures in myth-creation.[24]

23. Lunacharskii, "Sotsialisticheskii realizm," in *LSS,* 8:499, 615–16.
24. Ruth Ben Ghiat, "The Formation of a Fascist Culture: The Realist Movement in Italy, 1930–43" (Ph.D. diss, Brandeis University, 1991), 53–60, 78–83.

The New Man (and Woman)

That the new man and woman would be heroic, rational, energetic, optimistic, strong-willed, resolute, and totally committed to socialism was taken for granted. Otto Schmidt, leader of the famed Cheliuskin expedition and a living exemplar of the Soviet hero (he was well over six feet tall and looked the part), addressed the Congress on the third day. Gorky noted that neither literature nor drama have portrayed the "new woman" adequately, but no consensus about her image was reached.

Shaginian (a former associate of the Merezhkovskys) argued that just as Nazi literature depicts the love of blond German men and women for one another and hatred for other "biological types," Soviet literature must stress the loving atmosphere of "our culture," and new forms of Eros and humanism. "Only we in the entire universe of literature possess the 'keys of love,' an 'absolutely new path'" (*Pervyi*, 208–9). The implicit comparison was to Verbitskaia's novel *The Keys of Happiness* and Merezhkovsky's *New Path*, still resonating after all these years. Radek spoke of a literature of love and of hate and praised Sholokhov for demonstrating (in *Virgin Soil Upturned*, 1931) why "severe, firm, drastic" measures against the kulaks were necessary (*PSL*, 124).

Several writers defined the "new man" by the absence of "Nietzschean" qualities. Valeriia Gerasimova (1903–70) alluded to the "free man-beast of the old world" and named Nietzsche, Tolstoy, and Dostoevsky as its "highest Himalayas" (*Pervyi*, 262). Aleksandr Tarasov-Rodianov (1885–1938) decried the "cult of force, racism, and Nietzscheanism of the Hitlerites" (*Pervyi*, 325). The playwright Vyshnevsky announced: "To the cult of the superman which is developing in Germany, to the cult of the 'sons of heaven' which is developing in Japan, we oppose the image of the authentic proletarian leader [*vozhd'*], of a simple, calm, human-leader [*vozhdia-cheloveka*]. . . . To the blindly following fanatical masses in fascist books, we oppose the consciously proceeding masses. We establish the [proper] correlation of the leader and the masses" (*Pervyi*, 284). The playwright Kirshon asserted that Soviet writers do not depict "unusual people in unusual circumstances," or a "Superman," or "the struggle between good and evil forces as a collision of gods" or as some "fantastic struggle of giants." Soviet heroes were simple and unaffected like the explorers of the Cheliuskin expedition. He denied that socialism turns humanity into a herd (*Pervyi*, 406, 408).

The New Form

The delegates' calls for a socialist literature and drama included a good deal of definition by negation. Radek claimed that contemporary Western literature mirrored the decadence, corruption, and madness of the bourgeois world, using James Joyce's novel *Ulysses* as an example. "A heap of dung

crawling with worms, photographed by a cinema apparatus through a micro-
scope," the novel depicts in minute detail, one day in the life of a "vile" hero
and "petty, trivial, insignificant people," encircling them with an "intricate
cobweb of allegories and mythological allusions," hallucinations, and "phan-
tasmagoria of madness," all of which are extraneous to the plot. Joyce's
"method" is worthless in depicting the "great events of the class struggle,
the titanic clashes of the modern world" (*PSL,* 153–55). Moreover, the novel
is incomprehensible to the masses (*PSL,* 180–81). Implicitly, the Soviet novel
would be an epic, with a linear plot and simple language. Surveys had shown
that the masses liked epics.

V. A. Kirpotin (b. 1898), secretary of the Organizing Committee, rejected
the individualistic themes of bourgeois drama and the "old realism" as part
of an alien (*inoi*) social practice and an alien worldview (*Pervyi,* 376, 380)
and faulted plays that lacked an "logical iron route of development." Socialist
drama must have a linear plot, emphasize the unity of the person with his
class-collective, and exude empathy for the masses' struggle for a just new
world. Optimistic, eventful, full of "socialist tendentiousness," socialist
drama must portray the heroes of our time and the new look of city and
countryside without kulaks and superfluous people. Socialist audiences did
not want to see the indecisive intellectuals of the old world but the shores
of a new world. Unacceptable were Stanislavsky's psychological realism
(which emphasized personal life), symbolist theater, Andreev's naturalism,
Meyerhold's "theater of immobility," and the bourgeois theater of pure spectacle. The new man and woman must be portrayed as activists and masters
of their fate, by contrast to Greek tragic drama where fate rules them. Socialist
plays must tell the masses that "*we* today are the masters of life, *we* are the
victors in the class struggle; power belongs to us. *We* created the economy
and the culture of the land, *we* are its nobility [*znatnie liudi*]. . . . We want
to see *ourselves* in art, in the images of *our* men, *our* women, *our* children"
(*Pervyi,* 382). Kirpotin did not mean that the masses should play themselves,
as Proletkult had advocated, but that Soviet plays give them the feeling (or
illusion) of power and provide role models. Other speakers predicted that
tragedy would disappear entirely, and still others warned against plays that
fostered defeatism or passivity.

Kirshon, a former RAPPist, objected to the absence of plot, the "mechanical word-combinations," and the "abstract theatricality" of the avant-garde.
The new theatrical forms will not be as "our innovators" say—irregular,
undefined, indistinct—but distinct, harmonious, and regular, because "all
that is going on in our country is not chaos nor a conglomeration of accidental events—no, it is the expression of inner laws of historical development . . . the laws of scientific Marxism" (*Pervyi,* 405). Soviet tragedy has
special qualities; it "mobilizes, calls for future struggle, fortifies will and
courage." In the play *Intervention,* for example, Communists die, which is

"indeed a tragedy," but the foreigners are expelled from Soviet soil (*Pervyi,* 403). He saw nothing optimistic in Vyshnevsky's *An Optimistic Tragedy,* a play in which every single sailor on a ship dies battling the Whites during the Civil War. For his part, Vyshnevsky maintained that Communists had gone through a cruel class struggle that should be reflected in their art.

Turning to literature and theater in Nazi Germany, Kirshon quoted Goebbels's demand for a "steely romanticism" as well as his contention that "language and literature must have roots in the people" in order to inspire them to "struggle for the national idea" and build "confidence in their strength and their mission." Implicitly, Socialist Realism must do the same. Kirshon alluded to plays and films with storm trooper heroes such as *Schlageter* (a youth martyred in German resistance to the French occupation of the Ruhr), *The Hitler-Youth Quex,* and *SS Man Tönnies* (*Pervyi,* 397–99), but did not go into detail. (Hans Jöhst, author of *Schlageter,* believed, much as Ivanov did, that the purpose of theater was to create a community of faith.) Kirshon mentioned Goebbels's novel, *Michael* (1929), but did not expound on his conflation of Nietzsche, Marx, anarchism, apocalyptic Christianity, and anti-Semitism in the Nazi version of a "revolution of the spirit," one of the Nazis' favorite phrases. The protagonist (Michael) prophesies a new Leader, a poet-politician who will demand total sacrifice— Goebbels's rendition of Nietzsche's artist-tyrant. The novel ends with Nietzsche's dictum "Die at the right time."

Aleksei Tolstoi said that all modernist theatrical experiments have failed. In theater, as in the other arts, there are canons and laws that cannot be violated. The architectonics of a play must be carefully constructed to convey a unified impression (*Pervyi,* 416–18). Tolstoi's truism that dialogue is the heart of a play and must be "crystal clear" was a barb against the avant-garde. Dialogue was relatively unimportant in Meyerhold's plays.

In the last few years of his life, Lunacharsky became interested in laughter, a subject treated by Nietzsche, Bergson, and Freud (among others). He intended to write a book about the role of laughter "in the social process" and its great role "even in our struggle, the last struggle for the liberation of humanity."[25] The subject of laughter was discussed at the Congress. Kirshon advocated a new Soviet form of comedy that featured positive heroes and alluded to the "laughter of the victors."[26] Pantaleimon Romanov (1895–1958), playwright, critic, and future winner of the Stalin prize, claimed that satire will be replaced by merry laughter.

"Formalism" was used as an epithet to harass or destroy writers by calling their work "mechanical" rather than "organic," or their characters insuf-

---

25. Lunacharskii, "Sotsialisticheskii realizm," in *LSS,* 8:538, 622.
26. See also I. Eventov, "Smekh pobeditelei. Dvadtsat' let sovetskoi satiry," *Literaturnyi sovremennik,* 1937, no. 7:223–42.

ficiently positive, or accusing them of purveying contraband "Trotskyism." Particularly unwelcome were techniques that delegitimized, demystified, defamiliarized, bared the device, undermined the old canon, or unmasked illusions, for they were indeed subversive. Gorky linked "formalism" to fascism, Plato, and Hegel, but neither defined it, nor explained why it was fascist.[27]

The New Word

The issue of language was the point at which larger issues that could not be openly debated converged: authorial autonomy and its limits; the link between word and myth; the relationship between language and power; the conflict between truthfulness and illusion; the conflict between self-discipline and spontaneity; and the question of whether an elite or the masses were language creators. "The word" was treated as a generator of myth, an organizer of reality, and an instrument of power, much as three generations of Nietzsche's appropriators had treated it, and as poststructuralists treat it today.

Gorky's input was as crucial on "the word" as it was on myth. From May 1931 on, he demanded linguistic clarity and correctness (no spelling or grammatical mistakes) as part of the Soviet writer's mission, and attacked dialect and slang as linguistic pollution. In his essay "On Socialist Realism" (1933, not to be confused with his report to the Congress), he said that "the authentic beauty of the language, acting as a force, is created by the precision, clarity, and sonority of the words that form the pictures, the characters, the idea of the book."[28] Effective writing required hard work and self-discipline; the author could not simply put down anything that came into his or her head. Writers must struggle against the "verbal chaos" and "verbal nonsense" of Bely and Khlebnikov.

Gorky's goal was a Homeric language, a language of epic and myth, as distinct from the trenchant utilitarian or scientific language advocated by Trotsky and others in the 1920s. Again and again, Gorky declared that complex, clumsy, or convoluted language obscured the meaning and concealed "the lie." Priests deceived the populace by speaking in an alien language. Truth demanded simplicity and clarity. George Orwell claimed that insincerity is "the great enemy of clear language."[29] Having in mind the convoluted language used by Westerners who wanted to conceal Stalinist brutality, Orwell forgot that lies can also be expressed clearly and simply. Concealment

27. Gorkii, "O formalizme" (1936), in *GSS*, 27:521–31.
28. Gorkii, "O sotialisticheskom realizme," in *GSS*, 27:5. Gorky's first major article on language, "O rabote nad iazykom" appeared in *Literaturnaia gazeta* on May 15, 1931. See also "O boikosti" and "Nash iazyk" in *GSS*, 26:154–60 and 164–70.
29. George Orwell, "Politics and the English language," in *A Collection of Essays by George Orwell*, ed. Sonia Brown Orwell (New York, 1954), 173.

was not Gorky's only goal, however; he believed that dialect and incorrect speech pandered to, and reinforced, the masses' crudeness and primitivism. He wanted the Soviet writer to be a Pygmalion to the masses.

In January 1934, Gorky initiated a vitriolic debate on the language of Socialist Realism that was conducted mainly in *Literary Gazette*. Initially couched in the rhetoric of a campaign for literary quality, the debate quickly assumed a political dimension. Gorky attacked Panferov's *Bruski* for its dialect, colloquialisms, and incorrect speech and accused the author of pseudo-folklorism and of polluting the Russian language. A few days later, the writer A. S. Serafimovich came to Panferov's defense; *Bruski* lacked refinement, but it incarnated a great "peasant power" and articulated instinctual elemental forces in a very powerful way. Panferov's novel had undeniable popular appeal.

To Gorky, Panferov's "peasant power" was precisely the problem. It was "kulak power," a socially unhealthy force, animal in nature, "the instinct of the small property-owners who express themselves, as we know, with bestial ferocity." Panferov captured this class instinct quite well, but one cannot always tell whether it was Panferov speaking or one of his characters. Gorky wanted a cultured and rational hero, even if the reality were different. "Linguistic and lexicological ignorance always appears as the sign of a lower cultural level and is always accompanied by a lack of ideological formation. It is finally time to recognize this." Workers who make defective products are blamed, but writers get away with it. This must not continue. Literature must be purged of its linguistic weaknesses. Writers must struggle for the simplicity and lucidity that ideological clarity requires. Cultural-political Party work must be devoted to rooting out primitivism. Siding with Gorky, the writer Mark Serebriansky (1900–1941) charged that Panferov portrayed the hero of *Bruski* as a "kind of Superman" above the masses, a strong man, an elemental force who is at the center of everything. As a result, the other characters did not emerge clearly, and the Communists were unconvincing and one-dimensional. Moreover, Panferov's depiction of peasant dialogue was dated; the peasants were learning to speak correctly.[30]

On March 18, *Pravda* entered the fray, so important had the issue of language become. "The Party, government, and whole country demands the resolution of all cultural questions from Gorky's standpoint of the struggle for quality," an editorial declared. *Pravda* was assumed to speak for Stalin. Even so, the debate continued, presumably because authorial autonomy was at stake. Tolstoi agreed that clarity was important, but he wanted some room for experimentation. Shaginian rejected the idea of linguistic pollution and spoke of an enriching cross-fertilization of languages. Olga Forsh

30. This follows Robin, *Socialist Realism*, 166–77.

(1873–1961), another former associate of the Merezhkovskys, and a contributor to *Scythians,* opposed linguistic restrictions of any sort.

On April 18, 1934, *Literary Gazette* endorsed Gorky's position in an editorial that said that to accomplish its purpose, Socialist Realism required language that was precise, lucid, and clear. Clumsiness and spontaneity blurred the ideological message and lowered literary quality. While not opposing linguistic experimentation per se, the editorial accused Gorky's opponents of lacking a historical sense. Khlebnikov's and Bely's experiments were very useful before the Revolution, when poetic clichés stifled the development of poetry, but today the artist has to "experiment" by continually raising his cultural level, by assimilating the classical heritage, and "by organizing the language proper to socialist culture. We need to develop our language scientifically, so to speak; this means that we have to introduce artificial elements, planned choices, into spontaneous processes."[31] In other words, the literary vocabulary must be regulated (a new version of "speech-creation"). Establishing a direct relationship between Socialist Realism and a particular kind of language for the first time, this editorial illustrates what Nietzsche meant when he linked language, truth, and power.

The debate about language continued at the Congress in muted form. Exponents of experimentation (authorial autonomy) tried to justify it in the light of *Literary Gazette*'s editorial. Dialect, slang, and grammatical errors were called vestiges of class or regional inequality that would soon vanish. Panferov pointed out that before the French Revolution, there were two languages, that of the masses and that of the nobility. Radical intellectuals such as Marat spoke the language of the masses. After the Revolution, the language of the masses prevailed, but it had changed because of the equalizing impact of the Revolution. Language is an aspect of the class struggle: "This is what the menders-schemers do not understand." In the Soviet Union one language was being created. The language of the city was penetrating the countryside. Literature should reflect that process, rather than "correct" the peasants' grammatical errors or expunge dialect, swear words, and slang (*Pervyi,* 272–75). Tretiakov defended Panferov (and his own interest in linguistic innovation) by granting him parity with Gorky; the language of both writers was revolutionary.

For the other side, Gladkov upheld the simple language of Gorky and Stalin as a models and maintained that the language of people living in a socialist country was different from that of people living under the yoke of capitalism—richer, more dynamic, more cultured. Socialist literature must reflect this. Soviet writers must perform "serious and stubborn work on themselves" (*Pervyi,* 155). His own novel, *Cement,* went through several editions to remove dialect and slang. One writer echoed Gorky's assertion

31. Quoted in ibid., 175.

(in 1909) that priests use an alien language to dominate the people. Another one noted Lenin's belief (in *Two Tactics*) that anarchistic ideas are reflected in anarchistic speech.

Bukharin talked about poetry. Thanks to the uplifting effects of the Cultural Revolution, he said, the masses demand "higher quality and a more subtle approach to all kinds of literary production, poetry included" (*PSL*, 187). Poetic language has special qualities; it does not "reflect" reality the same way that science does. His talk ranged from Russian poetry from the seventeenth century to his own time, and from Chinese and Indian conceptions of language to the theories of Humboldt, Potebnia, symbolism, acmeism, and futurism, which he conflated with formalism. One of his points was that Potebnia had underestimated the social character of language. "Examine a word, and you discover the paleontology of language. Words are the depository of the whole previous life of mankind, which has passed through various social-economic structures. Within the microcosm of the word is embedded the microcosm of history. The word, like the concept, is abridged history. . . . It is a product of this life, not a Demiurge of history, nor a Logos creating a world out of nothing" (*PSL*, 195–96). Bukharin's approach resembles Nietzsche's in *Genealogy of Morals*. If the word is abridged history, it contains and inevitably activates all sorts of associations. For Bukharin, as for Nietzsche, "the word" was creative because the poet and the reader can use it in a new way while still taking advantage of all its baggage, for that is the nature of language. Nonrational language (*zaum*) was unacceptable, however. It is "individualism bordering on solipsism, where sound almost ceases to be a form possessing any 'content.'" If content is extraneous, then "poetry's main line of development can be expressed in the slogan, 'Down with *Faust* and long live [Kruchenykh's poem] '*Dyr bull shirr*'!" (*PSL*, 204–5). In painting and architecture only dots and lines would remain.

Urging Socialist poets not to imitate Blok, Esenin, or Mayakovsky, but to keep moving forward, Bukharin wanted socialist poetry to present all the contradictions, conflicts, and tragedies of "our remarkable era," and their culmination in the triumph of the proletariat (*PSL*, 248). He envisioned a "synthetic" and "monumental" poetry (*PSL*, 244), a socialist equivalent of Goethe's *Faust,* which portrayed the struggle of the human spirit and offered a philosophic-poetic conception of the bourgeois era establishing itself.

Praise of Goethe was politically correct, because Marx and Lenin had praised him. Moreover, Faust ended up directing a social project, reclaiming land from the sea, and Goethe himself had outgrown his storm and stress period, as the Soviets were now doing.

Socialist poetry would be based on dialectical materialism and have a different content and consequently a different form, Bukharin explained (*PSL*, 256). Interpreting "synthetic" and "monumental" broadly, he allowed for a variety of themes, stylistic innovation, authorial diversity, and the full range of human emotions (*PSL*, 246–47). Anything supernatural, mystical, or idealistic, would be excluded, however. There was no place in socialist poetry "for the fog of mysticism," "the poetry of the blind," "the tragic loneliness of a lost personality," "the inconsolable grief of individualism, nor its aimless anarchistic mutiny." This is not the restful repose of well-fed respectability . . . nor the unbridled passions of a zoological chauvinism, rabid hymns or subjugation or odes to the golden calf" (*PSL*, 223). Note the definition by negation. "Our Soviet poetry has its own heroes, its own themes . . . it is the ideological reflex of a different world, which is marching forward" (ibid.).

Bukharin's talk elicited vehement protests from "left" writers who accused him of denigrating Mayakovsky (and themselves) and trying to "remove poetry from the battle-stations of life." Semen Kirsanov (1906–72, formerly of LEF) praised Khlebnikov. Aleksei Surkov (1899–1983, formerly of RAPP) castigated Bukharin's invocation of "'humanism' . . . a word which we used to treat with mistrust and even enmity." Surkov's ideal was not "a brown-haired girl in a white dress . . . gazing into the Future," but a battle-hardened Chekist, as described in a poem by the late Eduard Bagritsky, which Surkov quoted:

> You are alone; the age be your guide.
> Stretch out your hand; your friends fly!
> Glance all around you; enemies still.
> And if he tells you to lie, you lie!
> And if he tells you to kill, you kill!

"Humanism," Surkov continued, expresses love, joy, and pride, but it also has a fourth side, "that is expressed in the stern and beautiful conception of *hatred*" (*Pervyi*, 514–15). He objected to the sugary "lemonade ideology" of a recent Soviet film *The Jolly Fellows* (1934). Surkov's speech was met with prolonged applause, but whether it was motivated by his revolutionary morality or his truthfulness cannot be determined from the transcript.

Socialist Realism implied an authoritative word and an impersonal truth delivered in a such a way that no misunderstanding was possible and no questions were raised. In 1909, Gorky considered language and myth products of collective creativity. Now he wanted them to be defined "from above." The requirement of simple language that unsophisticated workers and peasants could understand precluded the expression of subtle or complex thoughts and shrunk the permissible vocabulary. In official pronouncements, the editorial "we" became the norm, along with phrases such as "the people want" or "the people demand." Jeffrey Brooks observed that anonymous commentators in *Pravda* "often affected a bullying tone and wrote as if they had a monopoly on truth, which, in their eyes, they did."[32]

The official aesthetic mandated an Apollonian language. For Nietzsche, "Apollonian" denoted:

> all that simplifies, distinguishes, makes strong, clear, unambiguous, typical: freedom under the law
> . . . Plenitude of power and moderation the highest form of self-affirmation in a cool, noble, severe beauty: the Apollonianism of the Hellenic will. . . . the Dionysian Greek had to become Apollonian to break his will to the terrible, multifarious, uncertain, frightful, upon a will to measure, to simplicity, to submission to rule and concept. (*WP*, 539–40)[33]

Nietzsche conceived of the Apollonian as a dream state. For him, it bears repeating, there is no "true world." Simplification is itself falsification. The Apollonian language of Socialist Realism exalted Soviet power and described a mirage. Like all Apollonian languages, it was simple, clear, precise, and concrete. But the "concreteness" was an illusion. The "new word" of the futurists and of the Soviet avant-garde referred to a real entity. The entity that Socialist Realism described did not yet exist and perhaps never would.

Symbolists and futurists thought of "the word" as mutable. Socialist Realism turned into a "frozen" Apollonian language, the vehicle of the eternal truth proclaimed by the Party. Compare Nietzsche: "*Apollo's* deception: the *eternity* of beautiful form; the aristocratic legislation: '*thus shall it be forever!*'" (*WP*, 539). In Chapter 4, I argued that *zaum* was a Dionysian language; as such, it privileged sound over sight. Socialist Realism featured the Apollonian image, "word-pictures" as Gorky put it, the opposite of *zaum*, the other side of the Nietzschean coin. Theodor Adorno's observation is relevant here: "The eye is always the organ of effort, work, concentration: it apprehends something in an unambiguous way. The ear, in contrast, is unconcentrated and passive."[34] A picture can *seem* objective; sound (and not just the spoken word) leaves more space for subjectivity.

The trenchant style that Nietzsche admired—"the language of Sophocles' heroes . . . Apollonian precision and lucidity" (*BT*, 67), required self-discipline and consciousness on the part of the writer and was conducive to the self-discipline that the Party wished to inculcate in everyone. Nietzsche noted

---

32. Jeffrey Brooks, "Socialist Realism in *Pravda*," *Slavic Review* 53, no. 4 (Winter 1994): 984.

33. I changed "Apollinian" to "Apollonian."

34. Theodor Adorno, *In Search of Wagner* (Manchester, 1981), 99–100.

approvingly that French dramatists imposed stern constraints on themselves (*HH*, 102) and advocated "profound obedience to law in language" (*WP*, 441). In the Soviet Union, this came to mean fidelity to the canon (the Russian classics and a new Soviet canon) and obedience to authority generally.

Apollo is the god of beauty, but Sovietese was not beautiful, replete as it was with bureaucratic jargon and high-flown tributes to the toiling masses. Apollo is also the god of individuation but, beginning in the mid-1930s, distinctive authorial styles were edited out. Multiple layers of editorial control assured that the language was clear, correct, and unambiguous. Writers had to avoid words with multiple connotations, lest they invite personal interpretation. Standardization of the language would prevent subversion of the Soviet civil religion. Nietzsche's observation turned out to be prescient: "Another mark of the theologian is his incapacity for philology" (*AC*, 169).

If breaking the old tables of values meant breaking linguistic norms, writing new values on new tables denoted establishing new norms. If the death of God invalidated "old words," old concepts of truth, the "new word" of Socialist Realism entailed a new truth and new values. It was an "authoritative dogmatism," to borrow Voloshinov's term. In "Discourse and the Novel" (written 1930–34), Mikhail Bakhtin (1895–1975) described authoritative speech as that which imposes itself on us without regard for its degree of internal persuasiveness. In the Soviet Union, loudspeakers and radios blared the latest production statistics; a few years later, they broadcast the 1936 purge trials throughout the land.

For Nietzsche, language is the embodiment of a particular moral system; it controls what can and cannot be said and done. He related literary style to morality: "What is essential and inestimable in every morality is that it constitutes a long compulsion. . . . Every artist knows how far from any feeling of letting himself go his 'most natural' state is—the free ordering, placing, disposing, giving form in the moment of 'inspiration'—and how strictly and subtly he obeys thousandfold laws precisely then" (*BGE*, 100). He wanted a "stronger species" to arise out of contemporary Europeans, "A species with a *classical* taste?" (*WP*, 464). Note the question mark.

> Classical taste; this means will to simplification, strengthening, to visible happiness, to the terrible, the courage of psychological nakedness (—simplification is a consequence of the will to strengthening . . . a consequence of the will to be terrible—). To fight upward out of that chaos to this form—requires a compulsion: one must be faced with the choice of perishing or prevailing. A dominating race can grow up only out of terrible and violent beginnings. Problem: where are the *barbarians* of the twentieth century? Obviously they will come into view and consolidate themselves only after tremendous

socialist crises—they will be the elements capable of the greatest severity toward themselves and able to guarantee the most enduring will." (*WP,* 464–65)

The first Congress of Soviet Writers met after just such a "tremendous socialist crisis"—forced collectivization.

Socialist Realism reconstituted the horizon broken by futurism on a new basis, pulled together a new world, and restored ontological wholeness, partly by means of language. Nietzsche implied that since no objective reality exists, language *is* the world, a concept taken up by contemporary poststructuralists. "What things *are called* is incomparably more important than what they are. . . . What at first was appearance becomes in the end, almost invariably, the essence and is effective as such. . . . it is enough to create new names and estimations and probabilities in order to create in the long run new 'things'" (*GS,* 121–22). The new "things" to be created were a new Soviet man (and woman), a new culture, and a new society. Nietzsche also noted the power of the rulers to "name" the enemy, a power Stalin frequently exercised.

Soviet leaders believed that they were building a distinctive civilization that would have its own style, its own voice. Their ultimate goal was a seamless web—the interpenetration of culture, politics, and economics, all directed from the center—"a single socialist literature . . . united by singleness of aspiration, singleness of ideas, singleness of aim" (*PSL,* 9). To accomplish its didactic mission, Socialist Realism required uniformity, repetition, a master plot, canonical works to be imitated by younger writers, and a circumscribed vocabulary. Nietzsche observed: "What do the common people take for knowledge? . . . Something strange is to be reduced to something familiar" (*GS,* 300). Soviet literature was addressed to an unsophisticated mass audience that did not, for the most part, appreciate experimentation. Like mass audiences everywhere, Soviet audiences wanted novels which were a "good read," catchy tunes they could sing, and pictures they could recognize. It was not only Communists who were outraged by Joyce (and not all of them were). It took a federal court decision to clear *Ulysses* for publication in the United States in 1933. And one should not forget the stranglehold on Hollywood exerted by the Legion of Decency, which threatened a boycott of offensive films. That said, there are important differences. In the Soviet Union, the Party was directly involved in the creative process. Linguistic and other stylistic constraints in literature and the arts interacted with programmatic political content.

The government's monopoly on the means of communication, which Marx and Engels recommended (*CM,* 490), meant that artist and writers had to work for the government, or not work in their profession at all, and enabled the government to bombard the masses with the same words and slogans, orchestrate their delivery, and screen out cognitive dissonance. Forceful and constant repetition of the message in *Pravda, Izvestiia,* and all other newspapers, as well as in journals, novels, poetry, paintings, posters, theater, photographs, radio and films imprinted it on the psyche. We now know that internal resistance did exist and that the message was sometimes subverted, deliberately or unconsciously. My point is the Party's intention.

T W E L V E

The Theory Implemented

For the chorus, the Greeks built up the scaffolding of
a fictitious *natural* state and on it placed fictitious
natural beings.   —*BT,* 58

Artists in the Soviet Union have created an art founded
on "yes," on the conception: I uplift, I inspire,
I educate.   —Aleksandr Dovzhenko,
                                   Za bol'shoe kinoiskusstvo

The implementation of Socialist Realism varied according
to the genre, the cultural bureaucrat(s) in charge, the style
of the artist, the topic, and the Party line, but in all cases,
the purpose was to turn passive readers or spectators into
active performers, to inculcate behavioral norms, and to
make the masses into visceral socialists. Generally speaking, Socialist Realism meant individuated, but uncompli-
cated heroes in literature, theater, and film and inspirational
plots with political themes. In painting, photography, and
sculpture, the official aesthetic meant monumentalism, unified composition, and pictorial applications of the idea of
art as a lie. The new Soviet man (or woman) was represented as "conscious," rational, and self-disciplined (Apollonian qualities). Paeans to energy and enthusiasm were
accompanied by cautions on the need for purposefulness,
in addition to iron will. Rebelliousness and the "madness

of the brave" were channeled into "daring" to set new records, to surpass production norms, to brave the elements, but not to defy political authority. "Expressiveness" and "sincerity" became artistic desiderata and figures of "classic" harmony and beauty replaced super-muscular types. Among the favorite subjects in all genres were the Cheliuskin Expedition and the White Sea–Baltic Canal. Around the middle of the decade, Soviet patriotism was emphasized, and a new set of villains appeared—spies and traitors in league with Hitler, Trotsky, Wall Street, and other enemies of the Soviet people, for the Great Purge was under way. Hundreds of artists, writers, and cultural bureaucrats were purged, including Klutsis, Meyerhold, Piotrovsky, Stetsky (head of Kul'tprop), and Shumiatsky (head of the Soviet film industry).

Scholars have noted the similarity of Fascist, Nazi, and Stalinist art, but not their common roots in Nietzsche, Wagner, and socialism.[1] Mussolini started out as a Marxist. He admired Nietzsche, Sorel, and Lenin and called Lenin "an artist" who works with human beings "as other artists worked with marble or metals." Reputedly, Trotsky, Gorky, and Lenin regretted "losing" Mussolini for socialism.[2] Fascists and Nazis insisted that theirs was the "only 'true' socialism," a spiritual collectivism.[3] Communists did not allude to "a revolution of the spirit" in Stalin's time, but Fascists and Nazis did, in order to distinguish their form of socialism from "materialistic" and "impersonal" communism. Communists did use the word "spiritual" (*dukhovnyi*) in discussions of Socialist Realism, presumably to set it off from the art of materialistic capitalism.

A second phase of Soviet *Gleichschaltung* began in January 1936, with an unsigned *Pravda* editorial titled "Muddle Instead of Music," that denounced Shostakovich's opera *Lady Macbeth of the Mtsensk District* for "formalism" and "naturalism." Kerzhentsev was the probable author.[4] Later that year, he became the head of a new supervisory body for the arts—the Committee for Art Affairs attached to the Council of Ministers of the U.S.S.R. (*Komitet po delam iskusstv pri sovete ministrov SSSR*), which resembled, and may have been modeled on, the Reichskulturkammer (Reich Chamber of Culture), established in 1933, which in turn had resemblances to Kul'tprop.

For Mussolini, Stalin, and Hitler, cultural policy was part of a strategy of "great politics," a vehicle of their will to power, and a way to overcome (or conceal) regional and class divisions. The dictators did not initiate the "nationalization of the masses" (George Mosse's term), but they pursued it very sys-

---

1. Martin Damus, *Sozialistischer Realismus und Kunst im Nationalsozialismus* (Frankfurt, 1981); Golomstock, *Totalitarian Art*.
2. Quoted in Simonetta Falasca-Zamponi, *Fascist Spectacle* (Berkeley and Los Angeles, 1997), 21, 51, 207 n. 52, 224 n. 61.
3. Roger Griffin, *Fascism* (Oxford, 1995), 6.
4. Brooks, *Thank You*, 122.

tematically.[5] Going beyond patriotism, they claimed to be creating a new civilization (or culture) and expended vast sums to project an image of national greatness, often at the expense of the material needs of ordinary people (the herd). All of them spoke of a "new man," a "new life," and "new forms" of art," and adapted Christian and national symbols, rituals, and myths to their doctrinal requirements. Communists, Fascists, and Nazis learned from one another. Mussolini asked for and obtained from Stalin a stage plan for the May Day celebrations.[6] Soviet unionization of writers and artists may have been influenced by Fascist syndicalization (1925–30).[7] Kerzhentsev was Soviet ambassador to Italy in 1925–26, and Gorky lived there for most of the 1920s. Propagandists in the dictatorships also learned from American advertising, with its slogans and jingles, and American films with their happy endings and their semiotics of marking heroes and villains.

Italian Fascists considered themselves the heirs of Imperial Rome, the Renaissance, and the Risorgimento, but they also claimed to be creating "a new art for our times, a Fascist art."[8] Nazis idealized medieval Germany and the Holy Roman Empire, but they regarded technology as uniquely German (Aryan) and as an extension of the will to power indispensable for the new Caesarism.[9] The Nazi pantheon included Frederick Barbarossa, Martin Luther, Schiller, and Goethe—presented as precursors of Nazism— and romantic, nationalist, volkisch, and racist intellectuals. The Soviet Union developed its own pantheon, comprised mostly of Russians. Igor Golomstock maintains that "in totalitarian societies the function of art is to mask the social deficit."[10] In each society, art became more dream-like as the gap between ideal and reality increased.

Mussolini began talking about a distinctive Fascist culture after the Socialist deputy Giacomo Matteotti was murdered in June 1924 by a Fascist thug to prevent a Socialist victory in the upcoming elections. In 1925, Mussolini had the philosopher Giovanni Gentile (1875–1944), a Hegelian, organize a Congress of Fascist Intellectuals to show that Fascists were not just a gang of toughs. In a series of related moves, the Fascist Academy was founded in 1926, the National Syndicate of Fascist Art in 1927, and the Exhibition of the Fascist Revolution (Mostra della rivoluzione fascista) was staged in

5.   For Germany, see George Mosse, *The Nationalization of the Masses: Political Symbolism and Mass Movements in Germany from the Napoleonic Wars to the Third Reich* (New York, 1975).

6.   Emilio Gentile, *The Sacralization of Politics in Fascist Italy*, trans. Keith Botsford (Cambridge, 1996), 86.

7.   For syndicalization, see Marla Stone, *The Patron State* (Princeton, 1998), 25–28.

8.   Quoted in Philip Cannistraro and Brian Sullivan, *Il Duce's Other Woman: The Untold Story of Margherita Sarfatti, Benito Mussolini's Jewish Mistress, and How She Helped Him Come to Power* (New York, 1993), 371.

9.   Jeffrey Herf, *Reactionary Modernism* (Cambridge, 1984), passim.

10.   Golomstock, *Totalitarian Art*, 259.

1932–34. The word "totalitarianism" was coined to describe Fascist Italy and used by friend and foe alike from 1924–25 on.[11] Mussolini did not go as far as Hitler or Stalin in controlling culture, however, and he resisted calls to establish an official art of Fascism.

Attacks on "decadent" Weimar culture and "cultural Bolshevism" were staples of Nazi propaganda, even though Goebbels wanted expressionism (a Nietzsche-imbued aesthetic) to be the official art of Germany. He and like-minded Nazis contended that the expressionist "revolution of the spirit" paved the way for the Nazi revolution by discrediting the bourgeoisie. But Hitler preferred the *volkish* kitsch championed by Alfred Rosenberg, head of the Fighters for German Culture, and author of the anti-Semitic tract, *The Myth of the Twentieth Century* (1930). In September 1934, Hitler referred to the "shameful last decade" of Weimar Culture. Some three years later, the Nazis staged an exhibition of "Degenerate Art" in Munich. To Hitler, both art and politics were products of the authoritarian will and the political power of creating forms. The Reichskulturkammer was intended to synchronize and aryanize the culture and was closely linked to the Nazi Ministry of Propaganda, headed by Goebbels, who advocated a "union of book and sword" and called writers "soldiers" in the "battle for art."[12] In Germany, control of literature was achieved by censorship, the outright banning of specific books and authors, the ritual burning of proscribed works, and the prohibition of literary criticism, the last because "to think is to begin to doubt," as Goebbels put it. In the Soviet Union, "dangerous" books were placed in closed stacks in libraries or quietly pulped, and literary critics guided the reader to the correct interpretation. Introductions to Soviet editions of the Russian classics identified what was "progressive" and what was "reactionary" in the author's work and life.

Literature

Most of the canonical novels of Socialist Realism were written before the "method" was officially adopted: Gorky's *Mother* and *Klim Samgin,* Furmanov's *Chapaev,* Serafimovich's *The Iron Flood,* Gladkov's *Cement,* Tolstoi's *Peter the First;* Fadeev's *The Nineteen,* Sholokhov's *The Quiet Don* and *Virgin Soil Upturned* (2 vols., 1931 and 1959), and Nikolai Ostrovsky's *How the Steel Was Tempered* (1934, written 1932–34).[13] The positive heroes

11. For origin of the term, see Gleason, *Totalitarianism,* 15–17, 157.
12. Von Dietrich Strothmann, *Nationalsozialistische Literaturpolitik* (Bonn, 1968), 1–14, 162–63. See also J. M. Ritchie, *German Literature Under National Socialism* (Totowa, N.J., 1983).
13. Clark, *Soviet Novel,* 4.

of these novels, and of hundreds of other novels written according to the specifications of the official aesthetic, are "iron men" (or "iron women") with iron wills. Totally committed to the "Revolution," or "building socialism," or in Peter's case, modernizing Russia, they battle class enemies, be they reactionaries, White Guards, kulaks, saboteurs, traitors, or the insidious forces of inertia. These heroes are Apollonian types: conscious, self-disciplined, and psychologically integrated, as distinct from the "elemental" heroes of the 1920s and RAPP's conflicted "living man." Some of them lack full mastery and resolution, but gain them in the course of the novel; other heroes are masterful and resolute from the start.

Pavel Korchagin, hero of *How the Steel was Tempered,* is a prototype of the new hero. Except for his communist passion, there is nothing Dionysian about him. He scorns the "infantile disease of leftism" and subjugates his personal feelings to his will. Although he can work harder than anyone else, he does not squander his energy and advises young communists that to disregard their health is not heroic. To accomplish his self-imposed task, writing an inspirational novel, Pavel overcomes blindness, physical paralysis, and pain (the result of wounds incurred during the Civil War) by sheer force of will. At one point he almost commits suicide, but then says to himself: "Paper heroics my boy! Any fool at any time can kill himself. That is the most cowardly and the easiest way out. Put that revolver away and never let anybody know you thought of it. Find out how to live even when life has become unbearable. Make your life useful."[14] His decision is, in effect, a rejection of Nietzsche's dictum "Die at the right time." Or perhaps the time simply wasn't right, since Pavel could still be useful.

Korchagin's "inner development" is a rational process, but it is described in hagiographic terms. Paralysis and blindness are his ordeal or religious trial, and his accomplishment is a *podvig* (a feat or heroic deed). Korchagin truly believes Stalin's dictum "there are no fortresses Bolsheviks cannot storm." He struggles to master Russian grammar and to write correctly, for he has not had the benefit of a formal education. His tiny library consists of *The Iron Heel, Capital, Spartacus,* and books by Gorky. Although Pavel cannot participate personally, he exults in the conquest of "the elements" in pitched "battles" won by the builders of the Dneprostroi Dam (432). When he is no longer able to see the pencil, Pavel invents a writing board with slots to keep the lines straight, and studies by means of the radio, occasionally venting his fury about being blind. When his book is almost complete, "forbidden feelings would break through his ever watchful will more easily . . . sorrow and a whole string of simple human ones, burning and tender, which in nearly every other man or woman had a right to exist, but

14. Nikolai Ostrovsky, *How the Steel was Tempered;* quotations from the English translation, *The Making of a Hero* (New York, 1937), 418.

not in him. Were he to give in to but one of those feelings, things would have ended in tragedy" (438–39). *How the Steel Was Tempered* has a happy ending; Korchagin's novel is accepted for publication.

Like Chernyshevsky's hero Rakhmetov, Korchagin follows an ascetic lifestyle, but not as drastically, for he is married. Taia Klutsam, his wife, pupil, and comrade, is not a memorable character like Chernyshevsky's Vera or Gladkov's Dasha; the heroine of *Cement* "educates" her husband. There was a Nazi counterpart to *How the Steel Was Tempered,* Karl Aloys Schenzinger's *The Hitler Youth Quex* (1932), modeled on Herbert Korkus, who was killed in 1932 in a street fight between Communist and Nazi gangs. Hans Günther argues that both characters descend from Marinetti's Mafarka, the metallic man.[15] Each novel was widely disseminated and made into a film.

Babel's short story "In the Town of Berdichev" features an "iron woman," a commissar in the Red Army who becomes pregnant and is lodged with a Jewish family until she gives birth. Tearfully, for she is not all iron, she leaves the child with them and returns to her post. Babel's inspiration was a real-life woman commissar, Larissa Reisner (1896–1926), a passionate Nietzschean, by the way.[16] The film version, *Commissar* (1968), was not released until 1988 because it depicted Jews positively. Reisner was also the inspiration for the iron-willed woman commissar in Vyshnevsky's *An Optimistic Tragedy* (1933), who makes the anarchic sailors of her ship accept discipline. Two choral leaders tie the episodes of the play together and act as the author's voice. The "optimism" is voiced by the second choral leader; even though all the sailors died, he says, their wives remarried, their children grew up and carried on their work, and their descendants (literal and ideological) are in the audience. "Life does not die. Why, men can laugh and eat their dinners over the graves of their fellow men. And this is beautiful! When our boys lay dying, they'd say, "Keep smiling! Look lively, Revolution."[17] In the Soviet Union, heroes died for their cause, but there was no counterpart to the Nazi cult of death. The focus was on the hero's immortality.

Regine Robin considers Socialist Realism a failure aesthetically, partly because of its iron-willed, one-dimensional heroes. "Realism, the great realism [nineteenth-century realism] is sustained by the problematic individual, just as the problematic individual sustains it in turn. But the new man cannot be a problematic individual."[18] True, but this is because Socialist Realism was a political aesthetic; its function was myth-creation. Mythic heroes can-

---

15. Hans Günther, "Education and Conversion: The Road to the New Man in the Totalitarian Bildungsroman," in *The Culture of the Stalin Period,* ed. Hans Günther (New York, 1990), 195. For the Nazi cult of death, see Jay Baird, *To Die for Germany* (Bloomington, 1990).

16. Agursky, "Nietzschean Roots," in *NSC,* 257.

17. V. Vyshnevsky, "An Optimistic Tragedy," in *Four Soviet Plays,* ed. Ben Blake (New York, 1937), 84–85.

18. Robin, *Socialist Realism,* 242.

not be "problematic" individuals nor can they be psychologically complex. Hence the poor characterization that Robin rightly points out.

Theater

New plays had political messages. Pogodin's *Aristocrats* (1934) depicts the "reforging" of the prisoners of *Belomor*. Tairov staged *An Optimistic Tragedy* in 1933 and 1935, and a play about the Cheliuskin expedition, titled *No Surrender*, in 1935. Pogodin's *Man with a Gun* (1937) depicts a soldier who comes to Petrograd in 1917, fights in the October Revolution, and meets Lenin and Stalin, who are in close communication with each other. Consonant with the new emphasis on patriotism, Tairov staged *Bogatyri* in 1936. Kerzhentsev denounced the production in an article titled "On the Falsification of Our National Past" (*Izvestiia*, November 15, 1936), in which he accused Tairov of depicting Russian history as putrid, old Russian culture as foolish, and the people as idlers, and of distorting the epics (*byliny*) by portraying the *bogatyri* as feudal aristocrats in conflict with the toiling masses. The Aesopian message was that writers and artists were to promote idealized versions of the Russian past, even if that meant glossing over class conflict.

Meyerhold might have been the hidden target of "Muddle Instead of Music," for that *Pravda* editorial lambasted Shostakovich's opera as a musical version of "the most negative traits of 'Meyerholdism' multiplied to the nth degree," namely "formalism" and "naturalism." In March 1936, Kerzhentsev singled out Meyerhold as the "big leader [*vozhd'*] of formalism," and convoked a series of meetings for artists in various fields.[19] Soon after, Meyerhold was attacked again, but he did not bend. On December 17, 1937, in a *Pravda* article titled "An Alien Theater," Kerzhentsev accused Meyerhold of "systematic deviation from Soviet reality" and bringing Soviet theater to "total ideological and artistic ruin, to shameful bankruptcy." During the Cultural Revolution, Kerzhentsev had praised Meyerhold as the one who delivered the heaviest blow to the old theater. Now he questioned whether "Soviet Art and the Soviet public really need such a theater?" The answer was obvious. The Meyerhold State Theater was closed in January 1938. Meyerhold was arrested the following June, a few days after the Congress of Theater Producers, presided over by Vyshinsky, prosecutor at the 1936–38 show trials.[20] Meyerhold was executed in February 1940.

---

19. Sheila Fitzpatrick, "The Lady Macbeth Affair: Shostakovich and the Soviet Puritans," in *Cultural Front*, 187, 200–201.

20. For conflicting reports about Meyerhold's speech, see Iurii Zhelagin, *Temnyi genii* (London, 1982), 406–10, and Law and Gordon, *Meyerhold, Eisenstein, and Biomechanics*, 71–73.

Eisenstein's production of Wagner's *Die Walküre,* at the Bolshoi Theater in 1940, was not Socialist Realism, of course, but it had a political purpose—a good-will gesture to Germany after the Nazi-Soviet Pact (1939), which Eisenstein may have intended to subvert. A contemporary described the production as a "wild parody of Wagner's opera, the view-halloo of the Valkyries like ululations of Heil Hitler." Some Nazi diplomats wanted to lodge an official protest against Eisenstein's "desecration" of Wagner.[21]

In "The Embodiment of Myth," Eisenstein's essay about the production, he posited Greek prototypes for the Wagnerian gods and imagined Wotan as a tragic figure comparable to Prometheus.[22] In his notes, he said that the tragedy of Siegmund and Sieglinde gave birth to two powerful forces: the "limitless anarchism of Wotan" and the "super-legality" (*superzakonnost'*) of Fricka and specified that "both these forces provided the ground [*pochva*] of the rise of 'petit bourgeois revolt [*bunta*] that is to say fascism.' On one side, the superanarchism [*sverkhanarkhizm*] of the old god, the god of the primordial hordes of Wotan, convinced that to them, 'all is permitted.' On the other side, the formal law and order [*pravoporiadok*] of Fricka, who controls this horde and thus fastens them to the 'superstate' [*sverkhgosudarstvo*]."[23] While this clearly applies to the Fascist and Nazi "superstates," Eisenstein may also have had the Soviet "superstate" in mind. In either case, the "two forces" can certainly be described as Dionysus and Apollo; Eisenstein had deployed these concepts before. "All is permitted" is Dostoevsky's phrase, of course. Nietzsche had an equivalent phrase: "Nothing is true. All is permitted" (*Z,* 285).

Eisenstein perceived Wagner's music pictorially and asserted that to be realistic the myth had to be embodied in tangible forms (Apollonian images). "This music wants to be visible, to be seen. And its visibility must be sharply defined, palpable, frequently changing, material. . . . Exploding at its climax with the whirlwind of the 'Flight of the Valkyries,' this first day of the Ring dictates . . . visualization, objectivization, material tangibility, dynamism [*aktivnost'*]. Dynamism resolved scenically vertically upward" (24). According to Rosamund Bartlett, the word "vertical" is crucial. "The vertical as a stylistic co-ordinate recurs almost like a Wagnerian *leitmotif*" in Eisenstein's writings and productions from his earliest theatrical experiments to his last project, the third part of *Ivan Groznyi* (Ivan the Terrible).[24] She attributes Eisenstein's emphasis on the vertical to James Frazer's *The Golden Bough* (1890), which Eisenstein quoted in "The Embodiment of Myth." Verticality

21. David Fisher, *The Deadly Embrace* (New York, 1988), 535.

22. "Voploshchenie mifa," *Teatr,* 1940, no. 10:17–18, 37.

23. M. Nestiev and N. Kleiman, "K izucheniiu naslediia S. M. Eisenshteina: Vydaiushchiisia khudozhnik-gumanist," *Sovetskaia muzyka,* 1979, no. 9:77.

24. Rosamund Bartlett, "The Embodiment of Myth: Eizenshtein's Production of Die Walkure," *Slavonic and East European Review* 70, no. 1 (January 1992): 62–63.

can also be regarded as Eisenstein's version of Nietzsche's imagery of height, as interpreted by prerevolutionary futurists and the Soviet avant-garde. Eisenstein's interest in the cross-cultural aspects of myth cannot be reduced to Nietzsche, but Nietzsche and his popularizers helped inspire it. The same applies to Eisenstein's interest in "devices" that activate the archaic layers of the psyche, drums for example, and in "dynamism" (kineticism). Eisenstein's production of *Die Walküre* featured movement: "the movement of people and scenery, the expressiveness of fluent staging, the play of light and fire" (24). He counterposed the movement and physicality of the Ring with the 1909 production of *Tristan und Isolde,* in which reality "dissolves into illusion" (23), but dared not name Meyerhold as the producer. In *Die Walküre,* mountain cliffs move, like the moving walls of Meyerhold's constructivist productions, and tall trees rise and fall in accord with the activities of the gods.

Wagner rejected the chorus. Eisenstein used a mimetic chorus to "materialize" various thoughts and represent man "in the epoch of the birth of the epic," when man was one with nature and the collective (32). Fricka's chariot is drawn by a "chorus" of figures that are "half-sheep, half men, not quite domesticated animals, not quite people, who have betrayed their own passions and have voluntarily put on the yoke of the tamed instead" (33). The implicit comparison is to the Greek satyr, half-goat, half-man rather than half-sheep, half-man. Nietzsche described the satyr as the "archetype of man," not at all a "contrived shepherd" (like Jesus), but "something sublime and divine" (*BT,* 61).

Cinema

Lenin considered cinema "for us [Bolsheviks] the most important of the arts."[25] Stalin observed that "cinema is an art of illusion, yet it dictates its laws to life itself."[26] Soviet films were supposed to be entertaining as well as ideologically instructive for, as Lunacharsky once said, boring propaganda is bad propaganda. Soviet films were geared to present role models for the masses, direct their passions to designated love and hate objects, arouse enthusiasm for Party policy, and create a "community of faith" that encompassed millions.

Dovzhenko's *Ivan* (1932) depicts a young peasant who leaves the fields to build the Dneprostroi Dam and has problems adjusting to his new life. By the end of the film, Ivan is a productive worker conscious of his social responsibility. The Italian equivalent, a wayward youth who learns disci-

---

25. Lunacharsky, quoted in Taylor, *Film Factory,* 57.
26. Quoted in Svetlana Boym, *Commonplaces* (Cambridge, Mass., 1994), 238.

pline in Fascist sponsored activities, was a direct response to *Ivan*. Fascist propagandists studied Soviet cinema very carefully, even having Vsevolod Pudovkin's theoretical works translated into Italian.[27] *The Youth of Maksim* (1935) was lyrical in tone and portrayed Maksim's "inner development" from an exploited worker (before the Revolution) to a committed Bolshevik. The directors, Kozintsev and Trauberg (formerly of the avant-garde theater FEKS), wanted to make the audience love Maksim, because he represented the best of his class. Natasha, his future wife, belongs to a Marxist study circle. Sensitive to the psychological effect of "devices," the directors applied touches of avant-garde grotesquerie to create a film that was both "Red and entertaining." The same team produced *The Return of Maksim* (1937), which depicts the hero as a fully formed worker-revolutionary, and *The Vyborg Side* (1939), which follows Maksim's activities in the workers' suburb of Petrograd from the storming of the Winter Palace to the dissolution of the Constituent Assembly. After the Bolsheviks take power, Maksim becomes a political commissar in charge of the State Bank, and Natasha, now his wife, becomes a judge. *The Maksim Trilogy, Chapaev,* and *Peter the First* were produced by Leningrad Film Studio when Piotrovsky was artistic director. He succeeded in combining entertainment and ideology.

In the film version of *Chapaev* (1934), the Party hit upon the "lucky find of a genre formula," a Soviet counterpart to a foolproof Western.[28] The partisan-hero is depicted as embarrassed about his ignorance, but eager to learn from the political commissar and to teach others. In an editorial titled "The Whole Country Is Watching Chapaev" (November 21, 1934), *Pravda* proclaimed:

> The Party has been given a new and powerful means of educating the class consciousness of the young. . . . Hatred of the enemy combined with a rapturous admiration for the heroic memory of warriors who fell for the Revolution acquires the same strength as a passionate love for the socialist motherland. . . . The old warriors recalling the past help us to evaluate the present more clearly and more fully. "We created a new world. Now we are rich and powerful."[29]

The Soviet Union was far from "rich" and was not yet a great power. Shumiatsky pointed out that alongside Chapaev's "brave folly" was an exceptional strategic talent.[30] In the patriotic film *Minin and Pozharsky* (1939; screenplay by Shklovsky), which exalted the butcher and the prince who ral-

27. Ben Ghiat, "Formation of a Fascist Culture," 116–29.

28. Maya Turovskaya, "The Taste of Soviet Moviegoers," in *Late Soviet Culture*, ed. Thomas Lahusen (Durham, 1993), 101.

29. Quoted in Taylor, *Film Factory*, 335.

30. Boris Shumiatsky, "A Cinema for the Millions," in Taylor, *Film Factory*, 359.

lied the population against the foreign invaders, thereby ending the Time of Troubles (1698–1713), Minin (the butcher) is depicted as a Chapaev-like figure. This was not inaccurate; Minin combined the ability to inspire people with level-headedness and organizational and other practical talents.

In *Pilots* (1935), two pilots love the same woman, Galia, also a pilot. The hero, Rogachov, is restrained and disciplined; he combines American efficiency with Russian revolutionary zeal and is described as a Stalinist as well as an Old Bolshevik. His rival, Beliaev, has not overcome the "contradictions" of an earlier (Dionysian) epoch. Unruly, impulsive, and brave, he defies an order not to make a test flight, crashes his plane and almost gets killed. Rogachov then declares war on "Beliaevism" (indiscipline and irresponsibility) and expels Beliaev from the flying school but, mindful of Beliaev's heroism in the Civil War, finds him another job. Rogachov seems to win Galia, whose role is passive; the action is between the two men.

Dziga Vertov's *Three Songs of Lenin* (1934), which won the prize at the Venice Film Festival, treated documentary material lyrically and used religious symbolism, both departures from his previous style. The first two songs were about Soviet Central Asia. The first one opens with the words "My face was in a black prison," and shows women liberated by Lenin reading, writing, and operating machines. The second one is about the death of Lenin, whose spirit lives on, and the people's love for him. "To us Lenin was a father and more than a father," for no father ever did for his children "what Lenin did for us." He made darkness into light (electricity), the desert into a garden (irrigation), and death into life (Lenin lives!). The third song opens in "a great stone city" (Moscow) and shows what the Soviet Union has accomplished since his death. The last scene is a paean to Lenin's global import—in the polar regions, in the air, under the earth, and beyond the borders of the Soviet Union to Germany, China, and Spain. Shumiatsky praised the film for overcoming "documentarism" but noted vestiges of "formalism."

The Jolly Fellows (*Veselaia rebiata*, 1934), a series of song and dance numbers set in comic situations, had no real plot, but it did have a message: "cheerful and joyful spectacles" were appropriate for the new times. Some critics disparaged the film, not unjustly as "Soviet Hollywood." Surkov attacked its "lemonade ideology" at the Congress of Writers. Shumiatsky replied: "Why does Surkov think that in the epoch of proletarian revolution the proletariat does not need poetry, laughter, and love? Neither the Revolution nor the defence of our socialist fatherland are a tragedy for the proletariat. We have always gone into battle, and we shall go into battle again in the future singing and, at times, laughing." Furthermore, *The Jolly Fellows*

> is first step on the path toward mastering the comic genre and in particular, that most difficult genre, the eccentric musical comedy film.
> Tsarist and capitalist Russia were not acquainted with happy joyful laughter. . . . The laughter in Gogol, Shchedrin, and Chekhov is

accusing laughter, laughter derived from bitterness and hatred. . . . If [they] were alive today, their actual laughter would in the Soviet Union acquire *joie de vivre*, optimism, and cheerfulness. . . . The victorious class wants to laugh with joy. . . . Soviet cinema must provide the audience with this joyful Soviet laughter.[31]

In Nietzschean terms, the new Soviet man could "learn to laugh."

The Jolly Fellows had no dance routines in field or factory, but the work was choreographed (a new version of Meyerhold's biomechanics). One song, "The March of the Jolly Fellows," became very popular. Shumiatsky praised the film for its effective use of song and maintained that every film should have a song that typifies a character and has a dramatic role in the film— in other words a *leitmotif*. In 1935, Stalin announced, "Life is getting better comrades; life is getting more merry."

The Jolly Fellows was produced by Grigory Aleksandrov and starred his wife Liubov Orlova. The same couple collaborated on *Circus* (1936), a jolly *Gesamtkunstwerk* with a serious theme, racism; *Volga-Volga* (1938), a spoof on bureaucracy with an underlying threat, for the Great Purge was under way; and *Radiant Road* (1940), about a female superworker/Cinderella who marries a worker-engineer (her prince), and is decorated by Mikhail Kalinin in Moscow. "Song of the Motherland," written for *Circus*, became the broadcast signal for Radio Moscow in the 1930s. The lyric resembles an old religious song.[32] "March of Enthusiasts," from *Radiant Road,* includes the line, "In a few years the work of centuries has been accomplished." Choruses and choirs usually stand still. In Soviet films, the "chorus" resolutely marches forward. "March of the Aviators" includes the lines: "We were born to make fairy tales come true / To conquer distances and space / Reason gave us steel wings for arms / And a flaming motor for a heart" (a new conflation of man and machine). That simple Soviet people create miracles, was a common theme of "song-posters," catchy tunes with a topical message.

Eisenstein was a militant defender of the Party line, but he was criticized for "formalism" nevertheless. In 1935, he began shooting *Bezhin Meadow,* about Pavlik Morozov, the martyred youth who turned in his kulak father for hiding grain during collectivization and was killed by his father's relatives, or so the myth goes. Actually, Pavlik's father was not a kulak but a collective farm chairman, who deserted his wife and children for another woman. Apparently, his mother and uncle put the not very bright Pavlik up to denouncing his father, the mother for revenge, the uncle because he cov-

---

31. Ibid., 368–69. *Veselaia rebiata* is translated *The Happy Guys.*
32. James von Geldern and Richard Stites, *Mass Culture in Soviet Russia* (Bloomington, 1995), 271.
33. Iurii Druzhnikov, *Informer 001: The Myth of Pavlik Morozov* (New Brunswick, 1997).

eted the chairmanship.[33] The filming of *Bezhin Meadow* was stopped in 1936, resumed in 1937, and then stopped for good. Shumiatsky attacked Eisenstein for depicting collectivization as a "veritable bacchanalia of destruction" and portraying some of the characters as biblical and mythological types. He was particularly incensed at Eisenstein giving a kulak, a clear class enemy, the "features of a mythological Pan who has descended from the canvasses of the symbolist painter Vrubel." Note the Nietzschean associations: Bacchus is the Roman equivalent of Dionysus; Pan was a satyr, and Vrubel was an admirer of Nietzsche. Shumiatsky also objected to Eisenstein's portrayal of Pavlik as a "saintly youth"; in some scenes, Shumiatsky complained, "this fair-haired boy in a white shirt is depicted as radiating light."[34] Uncomfortable with the film's Christian/symbolist subtext, Shumiatsky wanted a "conscious" hero.

Eisenstein apologized for *Bezhin Meadow*. To make his work "heroic in spirit, militant in content, and popular in its style," he chose Prince Aleksandr Nevsky (1220–63) as his next hero.[35] *Aleksandr Nevsky* (1938) depicts a flawless Russian patriot leading the masses against the German invaders. The film was modeled on the exaggerated simplicity of a folk epic. Visual motifs demarcate good and evil, friend and foe. The Germans are faceless creatures peering through narrow cross-like slits in their bucket-shaped helmets; the Russians' open-visored helmets resemble onion-domed churches. Prokofiev wrote the score, collaborating with Eisenstein to achieve an unusually tight symbiosis of music and image. The film was shelved in late 1939 because of the Nazi-Soviet pact and re-released and widely circulated during World War II.

The filming of *Counterplan* (1932) was supervised by Sergei Kirov, head of the Leningrad Party. The codirectors were Sergei Iutkevich, a founder of the (now defunct) avant-garde theater FEKS, and Fridrikh Ermler (1896–1967), a Party member and a Chekist. Depicting the efforts of Leningrad factory workers to build a powerful turbine before the deadline, this film was the first to depict the saboteur-engineer as a full-blown villain—hence the title *Counterplan*.[36] Ermler was the sole director of *Peasants* (1935), a film that presented the Communist rationale for collectivization and the "elimination of the kulaks as a class." According to Jay Leyda, "the brutality of style harmonizes with the violent story and its milieu. One needs a "strong stomach" to watch it.[37]

Ermler's film *The Great Citizen* (Part 1, 1938; Part 2, 1939) justified the Great Terror and was shot while it was going on. Using cinematic techniques pioneered by the Soviet and German avant-garde—dramatic contrasts of

---

34. "The Film *Bezhin Meadow*" (1937), in Taylor, *Film Factory*, 379.
35. Quoted in Bordwell, *Cinema of Eisenstein*, 210.
36. Solomon Volkov, *St. Petersburg: A Cultural History* (New York, 1995), 457.
37. Jay Leyda, *Kino* (New York, 1960), 325–26.

light and darkness, magnification to the point of repulsiveness, multiple exposures, overlayering, and visual leitmotifs—to activate ancient archetypes of good and evil, Ermler portrayed the villains as devils, gangsters, and vermin, exactly as they were being described in the press. So loathsome was the arch-villain, that the actor who played him was reluctant to take the role on for fear of being lynched on the street after its release.[38] To the end of his life, Ermler considered this film his greatest achievement. *The Great Citizen* is sometimes compared to Leni Riefenstahl's *Triumph of the Will* (1935) which Hitler commissioned for the mammoth September 1934 Party meeting at Nuremberg. But there is nothing loathsome in Riefenstahl's film. She conceals the brutal essence of Nazism with a veil of beauty. A closer Nazi equivalent is *The Eternal Jew* (1940), which uses modernist techniques of distortion to associate Jews with rats and lice, and was intended to prepare Germans for the Final Solution (the Holocaust).

Painting, Photography, and Sculpture

Painters, photographers, and sculptors also became myth-creators, omitting the uglier parts of Soviet reality, rendering everyday reality heroic, and exalting healthy and happy "new men" and "new women." Two journals *Art* (*Iskusstvo*) and *Creativity* (*Tvorchestvo*), both founded in 1933, guided artists on how to fulfill their tasks, sometimes using coded language. Both journals were published by the Moscow section of the Union of Artists, the most significant union in terms of size, the eminence of its members, and the role it played in implementing Socialist Realism. To insure a single ideological line, the critic Osip Beskin (1892–1969) edited both. *Creativity* was addressed to a popular readership. The more high-brow *Art* aspired to international status, so the illustrations were captioned in French and Russian. Because of space limitations, I will discuss only *Art*.

The first issue opened with an editorial titled "Our Tasks," which called Socialist Realism "an openly tendentious art form" (Zhdanov's words at the Congress of Writers) and told artists to portray the new man and woman in a manner "comprehensible to the millions." Illustrated articles "revalued" a variety of painters—Russian and European, prerevolutionary and Soviet—from the perspective of Socialist Realism and its "agitational tasks." Subsequent issues provided additional guidance for gleaning what was useful and what to avoid in the art of the past. The art and architecture of classical antiquity, the Italian Renaissance, Jacques Louis David (1748–1825), Valentin Serov (1865–1911), and Vrubel were vaunted as part of the "rich cultural legacy" that culminated in Socialist Realism. Some issues were devoted to one theme, "the Art of the Revolution of 1905," for example

38. Richard Stites, *Soviet Popular Culture* (Cambridge, 1992), 93.

(1935, no. 6), which included painters of the World of Art movement.

Monumentality was stressed from the very first issue. In an article titled "Problems of Monumental Painting" (1933, no. 1) N. M. Chernyshev explains that monumental painting is about memory, not decoration, and praises the art of Ancient Greece, Rome, the Renaissance, and David. Another article titled "Louis David: The Classicism of the Third Estate" (1933, no. 3) by D. E. Arkin describes David's rendering contemporary bourgeois reality heroic" an allusion to his portrayals of the virtuous citizens of the Roman Republic as role models for the French. Arkin ignored David's paintings of Napoleon, which conveyed the power and grandeur of the Roman Empire.

In his article on a "positivist aesthetic" (1904), Lunacharsky said that "realistic idealism" (classicism) is the art of a successful revolution, having the French Revolution in mind. By the early 1930s, Soviet artists and architects had another model, the monumental art of Italy, described by B. Nikolaev in "Italian Fascism and Art" (*Art*, 1933, no. 3), and by Iuri Kolpinsky in "Fascism and Monumental Art," (1934, no. 4). Both articles conveyed a double message—criticism of Fascist monumental art and coded instructions to Soviet monumentalizers.[39]

Nikolaev labeled futurism the artistic expression of fascist irrationalism and claimed that futurism was alien to the masses. The turn of certain futurists to neoclassicism in the mid-1920s (the *novecento* movement) reflected the Italian bourgeoisie's recoil from the "horrors of revolution" (184) and search for comfort in a glorified past. To stay in power, the fascists[40] needed a nationalist art that the masses could understand.

> Having come to power, Italian fascism strives to utilize the chauvinistic and nationalistic mood of the Italian bourgeoisie and to infect the higher strata of the workers with it. It brings to the forefront the ideal of "Great Italy" by using art to propagate the idea of nationalism, by undertaking grandiose constructions, planning entire quarters of cities, building new highways (Rome), erecting triumphal arches, fountains, colossal monuments to those who fell in the war, statues of the "Duce." All this artistic propaganda is calculated in order, with the effect of the grandiose, to create the impression of "power," of the "greatness" of the epoch of fascism, to connect it with the epoch of the greatness of Rome. (180)

The stark, huge, and powerful human figures and imposing monuments of Italian art expressed the aggressive, militaristic, expansionist, character of

39. B. Nikolaev, "Italianskii fashizm i iskusstvo," *Iskusstvo*, 1933, no. 3:177–86; Yuri Kolpinskii, "Fashizm i monumental'noe iskusstvo, *Iskusstvo*, 1934, no. 4:186–98.

40. I do not capitalize "fascist" when quoting Soviet sources directly or indirectly here to reflect standard Soviet practice of denying "fascism" the status of a proper noun.

futurism, and its function—"rendering fascist everyday life heroic" (184) (much as Gorky wanted to render Soviet everyday life heroic). The hybrid futurist/Christian compositions that began to appear in Italian art around 1929/30 reflected the fascists' realization that the Catholic Church was a powerful support for their state (185), a reference to the Lateran Accords of 1929. Nikolaev noted that fascist art was optimistic on principle and closed its eyes to the poverty of the masses. His observations also applied to Soviets recoiling from the horrors of collectivization and to the compulsory optimism of Socialist Realism, which treated the poverty of the Soviet masses as a "negative truth" that did not exist. Nikolaev's allusion to a hybrid futurist-Christian art anticipated the mystical aura that would pervade Socialist Realism in a few years.

Kolpinsky's article appeared in an issue entirely devoted to monumental art. His first lines were:

> Italian fascism, in its system of political demagoguery, always attached and attaches great significance to art as a powerful means of influencing the will and consciousness of the masses toward the goals that its reactionary politics justifies and glorifies, toward the goal of fixing to false illusions in the consciousness of the laboring masses.
>
> Mussolini said: "What is the task of those who create? It is essential that writers (and artists) . . . [ellipsis in text] be carriers of a new type of Italian civilization. Artists must conduct what could be called spiritual imperialism.
>
> "Art must serve the fascist dictatorship. Art must be popular in the fascist sense of the word. It must obtain the broad popular spirit which it lacks.
>
> "This task which stands before fascist art induces it to incline to monumentality as the means for its solution." (186)

That is why, Kolpinsky continued, fascism turned to the art of Imperial Rome. "This is not the first time the bourgeoisie has turned its gaze to antiquity." The French Revolution depicted its heroes—Desmoulins, Danton, Robespierre, St. Just, and Napoleon—in Roman costumes and used Roman phrases that embodied their "deed," the liberation of society from feudalism. Fascist neoclassicism gives only the illusion of heroes, however, because it is based on an antirealistic aesthetic. It is "a means to conceal the irrational-mystical content of fascist art in the rational form of regular classical beauty" (187). The art of classical Greece expressed the ideal of a democratic collective. The art of Imperial Rome

> had as its goal the creation of a monumentality estranged from and opposed to the living individual, suppressing him with its dispropor-

tionality. The art, and first of all the architecture and monumental sculpture of imperial Rome, was the art of the spiritual suppression of the rightless masses of the population. It was the artistic exaltation of the alienation of the people [*narod*] from state power, represented by a superhuman personage [*sverkhchelovecheskoi osobe*], the emperor. (187)

Stalin was not yet presented as a Superman but these lines foreshadow that trope. The grandiose edifices of Nazi Germany had not yet been built, but Kolpinsky's statement would apply to them too.

Kolpinsky explained the emergence of fascist neoclassicism as a reflection of the stabilization of capitalism. To stay in power after capitalism collapsed, fascism required a more expressive art. "One of the first, most powerful, and in the opinion of the fascists, the most successful attempt to mobilize artists to create monumental synthetic portraits of the 'fascist revolution' was the Mostra" (192), the Exhibition of the Fascist Revolution.

The Mostra opened on October 18, 1932, the tenth anniversary of the Fascists' March on Rome, and closed two years later. Its popular and critical success surprised even the organizers. Attracted by discounts on railroad tickets, package tours, and other inducements, over 2,800,000 visitors attended, including Jean Paul Sartre, Simone de Beauvoir, Le Corbusier, André Gide, and Paul Valéry. There were special tours for schoolchildren, workers, and peasants. Dino Alfieri, organizer of the Mostra, Minister of Propaganda, and director of the Milanese Institute of Fascist Culture, engaged prominent artists from a cross-section of schools. The exhibition combined modernist forms, such as repeated geometrical motifs, blown-up photographs and photomontages, with Fascist content to create a Fascist Modernism. Painting, sculpture, documents, memorabilia, and historical simulations were coordinated to present a mythologized history of the origins and development of Fascism from 1914 to 1922. Twenty-three rooms, each one designed by a team of historians and artists, symbolized crisis, revolution, and deliverance from Marxist-induced chaos. Alternation of the spatial configurations of the rooms conveyed a sense of perpetual movement and instability, except for the last two, the Room of the Duce and the Chapel of the Martyrs, which betokened salvation and eternity. Mussolini's image was omnipresent as a trinitarian icon of Il Duce, Fascism, and Italy, much as "Red icons" conflated Lenin and Stalin with Communism and the Soviet Union. The stark neoclassical building that housed the Mostra made it a monument to Fascist power. Enhancing the building's monumentality were four enormous metal *fasci* on the front and two enormous metal Xs (for the Roman number ten), on each side. One visitor called the Mostra a "terrorist" composition, thoroughly Bolshevik in spirit.[41] This was not a coincidence. The Italians had

---

41. Quoted in Jeffrey T. Schnapp, "Epic Demonstrations: Fascist Modernity and the

studied Soviet mass spectacles, rationalist architecture, and photography, paying special attention to Lissitzky and Klutsis.

To return to Kolpinsky. He quoted a fascist critic who claimed that the Mostra embodied "collectivity" (*kollektivnost'*) and "populism" (*narodnost'*), as opposed to capricious bourgeois individualism, which leads to anarchy in art and in politics. But fascist "collectivity" was really "reactionary neoclassicism" and "reactionary anti-individualism"; the latter theme was closely interwoven "with its antipode, the "super-individualism of the leader" and, as such, directly opposed to the real interests of the laboring masses, especially the proletariat (188). Fascist "anti-individualism" is an attempt to subjugate the masses to a "super-real and super-individual monumental 'collectivity.'" Kolpinsky also quoted Alfieri's instructions to the artists working on the Mostra: "throughout the entire exhibition the pulsation of some sort of higher will must be felt, that it is inspired by the creative will of the leader [*vozhd'*] in whom is found the mysterious force of the race" (192). The Mostra was an "apologia for the leader" that instills the "poisons of mysticism and racism" into the masses. The facial expression on a bust of Mussolini (194), was intended to express Roman sternness, but it actually expressed the will of the *condottieri* (Renaissance mercenaries). The antireality and falseness of fascism impel it to appeal to the passions and turns fascism into "evil theatricalization" (196). The phrase eerily anticipates the show trials of 1936–38. The Aesopian message of Kolpinsky's article was that Communists should not replicate fascist monumental art, but develop a monumental art of their own. In a different article, Dmitri Moor (1883–1946), a former *Miriskusnik*, declared that the "uncritical adoption of form from old style is contraband." In other words, Soviet monumental art must be something new.

After 1934, Hitler eclipsed Mussolini, and Germany and the Soviet Union responded mostly to each other. Their pavilions at the International Exhibition (Paris, 1937) were remarkably similar. Tall, stark monuments to power, they had a common ancestor in the building that housed the Mostra. Boris Iofan, designer of the Soviet pavilion, said that it "bears the definite imprint of the artistic method we call Socialist Realism."[42] Atop the Soviet Pavilion was Vera Mukhina's stainless steel sculpture, "Worker and Collective Farm Woman." Two enormous figures stride serenely, yet purposefully, "forward and higher." Positioned to overwhelm the Nazi pavilion, they personify the "invincible movement of the Soviet Union along the paths of conquest and

---

1932 Exhibition of the Fascist Revolution," in *Fascism, Aesthetics, and Culture*, ed. Richard J. Golsan (Hanover, N.H., 1992), 26. See also Marla Stone, "Staging Fascism: The Exhibition of the Fascist Revolution," *Journal of Contemporary History* 18 (1993): 215–43; an illustration of the building is on p. 219.

42. Golomstock, *Totalitarian Art*, 133.

victory." The man is slightly ahead of the woman and slightly taller; his arm is raised in a gesture of triumph, and he holds a hammer in his hand. Her arm is also raised and she is holding a sickle. Their faces express optimism and joy.[43] Atop the Nazi pavilion was an enormous eagle holding a swastika in its claws. At ground level, Josef Thorak's sculpture "Comradeship" depicted two huge, super-muscular men holding hands, a homoerotic element absent in Soviet art. Their bodies convey a sense of solid immobility; their facial expressions are stoic, even brutal.

The young, happy, and healthy "new men" and "new women" of Soviet, Fascist, and Nazi art were perfect physical specimens, living incarnations of the cult of the body championed by some of Nietzsche's admirers, who distorted his physiologism. For Nietzsche, physiologism meant first of all the "wisdom of the body," as opposed to abstract intellectuality. For the Nazis, the nude represented the perfect Aryan body and was a further development of the cult of nudity that originated in the back-to-nature movement of early-twentieth-century Germany. This was an essentially romantic movement but Nietzsche's physiologism was a factor in it too. A 1907 painting depicts him sitting naked in the mountains.[44] Nudity was rare in Soviet painting after the mid-1930s, partly to set it off from Nazi biologism. Soviet ideology was grounded in reason, history, and science, for which bodily beauty and even physical strength were theoretically irrelevant. Nevertheless, participants in Soviet physical culture parades were selected by their physical appearance and fitness. Weaker or less attractive persons were excluded, much to their dismay. Another criterion was ethnicity; the parades displayed the racial diversity of the Soviet Union, partly as a challenge to Nazi racism.[45]

Soviet and Nazi artists alike depicted labor as a heroic struggle or joyful festival and monumentalized "the miner," "the steel worker," "the farmer," and so on, struggling for his class or his *Volk*.[46] The portraits of men were almost interchangeable, even though the quintessential Nazi "new man" was a soldier and the new Soviet man, a worker. The representations of women were quite different. Nazi artists depicted young girls and "mother and child." The iconic Soviet "new woman" was an industrial worker or collective farmer. In Germany, women were pushed out of the labor force so that unemployed men could take their jobs; in the Soviet Union, women's

43. Illustrations in Golomstock, *Totalitarian Art*, 360–61, enlargements pp. 362–63, 74.

44. Plate 10 in Aschheim, *Nietzsche Legacy in Germany*.

45. Karen Petrone, *Life Has Become More Joyous, Comrades: Celebrations in the Time of Stalin* (Bloomington, 2000), 30–35.

46. For Nazi art, see Berthold Hinz, *Art in the Third Reich* (Oxford, 1980); Brandon Taylor and Wilfried van der Vill, *The Nazification of Art: Art, Design, Music, Architecture, and Film in the Third Reich* (Winchester, 1990); and Peter Adam, *Art of the Third Reich* (New York, 1992). For Soviet art, see *Agitation zum Gluck: Sowjetische Kunst der Stalinzeit* (Bremen, 1994) and *The Aesthetic Arsenal*, ed. Miranda Banks (New York, 1993).

labor was essential to the Plan. Posters of the First Five-Year Plan feature women with slim, athletic bodies. After 1936, reflecting the new emphasis on marriage and motherhood, their figures fill out. A poster depicting two giant milkmaids is captioned with Stalin's statement "Women are a great force on the collective farms!" (*Art*, 1938, no. 5:71). Another poster (5:70), captioned "More women in the soviets," depicts a woman speaker in profile, positioned as if following Lenin and Stalin. Photomontages portray women performing their tasks under Stalin's patriarchal gaze and female super-workers being rewarded by male officials. Even though *Pravda* and *Izvestiia* portrayed female super-workers, athletes, and pilots, to document the opportunities open to women, overall the message was decidedly mixed, especially since heroism and comradeship were described as masculine traits.

The "look" of Soviet photography and photomontage changed from factographic to mythographic representations, from fragmenting and deframing to synthesizing and totalizing, and from unusual angles or other signs of radical instability to a fixed perspective. The new "look" used the camera to convey a false verisimilitude. "Maximum expressiveness" replaced "documentary impartiality" or "mechanical" facticity, and soothing pastels supplanted bold colors, especially red. To make sure that only the official picture of reality could be shown, at-large photography was prohibited in 1933.

The showcase of Soviet photography, the magazine *The USSR in Construction*, featured works by Lissitzky, Rodchenko, and other leading photographers. Gorky was on the editorial board. Founded in 1930 to popularize industrialization domestically and trumpet the Soviet system abroad, *The USSR in Construction* was published in Russian, French, English, German, and for a few years, Spanish, in a new form of image-oriented journalism. The text was minimal. The leading Soviet photography critic, L. Mezhericher, praised the magazine as "an ecstatic artistic reflection of socialist reality." At first, its documentarism "inspired a just criticism . . . then in an attempt to have more expression and to relate the grand scale and tense tempo of construction, the snapshot began to grow and acquire a compositional force." The magazine now offered a style of "monumental artistic photography."[47] A typical issue was devoted to a single theme, for example, Magnitogorsk, civil aviation, collective farms, railroads, undersea explorations. Roughly 20 to 40 percent of the articles demonstrated the transformation of an autonomous republic or region in Soviet Asia (the percentage varied from issue to issue).

The December 1933 issue exalted *Belomor*. The cover illustration is Stalin's head superimposed on a quiet sea. On the last page, we see Stalin and his encourage going through the canal (which he never actually visited).[48] The

47. Quoted in Tupitsyn, "From Factography to Mythography: The Final Phase of the Soviet Photographic Avant-Garde," in Banks, *Aesthetic Arsenal*, 102.

48. *Aesthetic Arsenal*, plates 53 and 60.

entire issue bears the imprint of Rodchenko, the chief photographer. Familiar modernist devices remain—oblique angles and the genre of photomontage itself—but a "sense of overarching narrative" replaces his former aggregate structure and its potentially multiple meanings to reinforce a particular reading and a single perspective. The constructed nature of the photograph is much less obvious; the "seams" are muted, making their juxtapositions seem natural.[49] Under attack for "formalism," Rodchenko may have wanted to redeem himself. Besides, he had to accept government commissions or not work as a photographer at all. In an article titled, "The Reconstruction of an Artist" (1936) he lauded the "gigantic will" that had brought the "former people" to the canal, praised the "sensitivity and wisdom" of their "reeducation," and disingenuously claimed that he didn't even think of form.[50]

All of the issues celebrate Soviet achievements, often putting Stalin and/or Lenin in the picture. For example, the issue devoted to the Dnieper-conglomerate (the new industries made possible by the Dneprostroi Dam) had a two-page spread of a beaming Stalin with "his" creation (Fig. 8) while also treating the Dam as the fulfillment of Lenin's plan to electrify the whole country (Fig. 9).

Soviet painters filled fields with tractors and factories with the most up-to-date industrial technology, as if they were the norm. Conversely, German painters were instructed to depict "simple German types in their social and natural surroundings," for example, "the farmer on his land," the "reaper in the field," and persons who "follow the callings of nature" such as hunters and fisherman, implicitly denying preparations for war. The slogan "to make all collective farmers prosperous" was coined at the height of the "terror famine." Sergei Gerasimov's painting "Collective Farm Festival" (1937), a vision of plenty in a land where peasants barely survived, exemplifies the inverse relationship between image and truth typical of Stalinist culture. Retitled "New People of the Socialist Village" (Fig. 10), it was included in "Painting in the Land of Socialism" (*Art,* 1937, no. 6), along with a similar painting, Arkady Plastov's "Kolkhoz Festival," and portraits of Kirov, Stakhanov (the super-worker, see Chapter 13), an NKVD border guard, a woman collective farmer, and a miner (the mythic types of Soviet society). Purged Communists were expunged from photographs and paintings.[51]

The Gerasimov and Plastov paintings were displayed, along with two portraits of Stalin and his disciples, in the last room of the *Industry of Socialism* Art Exhibition, which opened in March 1939. The focal point of Plastov's painting is a picture of Stalin above a banner that says "Life has gotten better. Life has gotten jollier!" The preceding sixteen rooms depicted the hor-

---

49. Leah Dickerman, "The Propagandizing of Things," in *Rodchenko* (New York, 1998), 89–90.

50. Quoted in Tupitsyn, "From Factography," 105.

51. Illustrations in David King, *The Commissar Vanishes* (New York, 1997).

Fig. 8 "Dnepr-Kombinat." *USSR in Construction,* 1934, no.3. Avery Architectural and Fine Arts Library, Columbia University in the City of New York.

rors of capitalism in prerevolutionary Russia and the laborious process of building socialism. This room focused on the rewards. "Suddenly all around was light, bright color, and rich, sensuous painterly facture. Here [visitors] could glimpse the radiant future."[52]

The darker the reality, the brighter the picture. Outdoors, bright sunshine; indoors, sun imagery in decor, elaborate light fixtures, chandeliers in the subway, all sorts of "electric suns." Images of the sun were prevalent in the art of the 1930s, and had multiple connotations: Apollo the Sun God, the religion of the pagan Slavs, the account of creation in *Genesis,* the uncreated light of Mount Tabor, the Fedorovian hope of changing the climate, and the universal symbol of the sun as the herald of a new day. Water imagery was also prominent. Depictions of fountains, rivers, and canals connoted the taming of the elements, the cooling of the passions of revolution, the calm flow of eternity, and the second day of creation.

The more instability and unpredictability existed in life, the more the arts depicted an ordered and stable world. The more overcrowding in commu-

---

52. Susan E. Reid, "Socialist Realism in the Stalinist Terror: The *Industry of Socialism* Art Exhibition, 1935–41," *Russian Review* 60 (April 2001) 172. An illustration of Plastov's painting is on the same page. For critical responses to Gerasimov's painting, see ibid., 176–77.

THE DNIEPER POWER STATION—A MAGNIFICIENT MONUMENT TO LENIN.
AN EMBODIMENT OF THE LENINIST ELECTRIFICATION SCHEME

Fig. 9 "The Dnieper Power Station. A Monument to Lenin." *USSR in Construction*, 1934, no.3. Avery Architectural and Fine Arts Library, Columbia University in the City of New York.

Fig. 10 Sergei V. Gerasimov, "New People of the Socialist Village." *Iskusstvo*, 1937, no.6. Slavic and Baltic Division, New York Public Library, Astor, Lenox and Tilden Foundations.

nal apartments, the more space in the photo; the more sacrifice demanded of the individual, the more talk of individuality; the greater the terror, the more people had to smile (pessimism was equated with disloyalty); the more tragedy in real life, the more comedy in film; the more fear and distrust pervaded life, the greater the emphasis on intimacy and love. Intimacy was a bad word in the 1920s; its return in the mid-1930s denied the lack of private living space. The cult of love was part of an attempt to humanize the heroes and to provide spiritual/emotional compensations for material deprivation. The situation was not unique to the Soviet Union. Americans flocked to lighthearted musicals and slapstick comedies during the Great Depression. But in the Soviet Union their production was government policy. The introductory text to the Soviet Pavilion at the 1939 World Fair proclaimed that Soviet painting was distinguished by its truthfulness, its democratic and humanitarian nature, and its simplicity and clarity.[53] The Nazis expected writers and artist to cast off the "dogma of the truth of reality" and demanded clarity, which they considered a racial trait. Goebbels proclaimed that "to be German means to be clear."[54]

53. "The Introductory Text to Soviet Pavilion at the World's Fair, 1939," in *Aesthetic Arsenal*, 8.
54. Hinz, *Art in the Third Reich*, 77, 173–74; Damus, *Sozialistischer Realismus*, 253.

The establishment of a new myth requires an explanation of origins, a new sacred text, and restoration of the severed links between the present generation and its ancestors. In Nietzsche's words:

> At a certain point in the evolution of a people its most enlightened . . . class declares the experience in accordance with which the people is to live—that is, *can* live—to be fixed and settled. Their objective is to bring home the richest and completest harvest from the ages of experimentation and *bad* experience. What consequently is to be prevented above all is the continuation of experimenting, the perpetuation *in infinitum* of the fluid condition of values, tests, choices, criticizing of values. A two-fold wall is erected against this: firstly *revelation*. . . . Then *tradition*. (*AC*, 176–77)

Revelation was accomplished by fixing the writings of Marx, Engels, Lenin, and Stalin into a dogma that admitted no interpretation but Stalin's. Socialist Realism proclaimed itself the heir to the Russian classics—named as Pushkin, Turgenev, Tolstoy, Chekhov, Gorky, and Mayakovsky in literature; Repin and the Wanderers in painting; and Stanislavsky and Nemirovich-Danchenko in theater. The importance of Hegel for Marxism was downplayed, and greater emphasis was placed on the Russian materialist tradition (Belinsky, Chernyshevsky, etc.). Nietzsche's observation on the misuse of the "classics" by philistines who believed that "all seeking is at an end" (*UT*, 9), is relevant here. By the end of the 1930s, experimentation had just about ceased. Bakhtin observed (in "Discourse and the Novel") that authoritative speech is organically connected with the historical past; it is the speech of the fathers.

The return to a narrative history with great events and heroes reflected a mythologizing impulse. Gorky proclaimed, "A People Must Know Its History," and called for histories of the Civil War, of Young People, of the Five-Year Plan, and so on.[55] In addition, he edited a series titled *Lives of Great Men* and several histories of the Soviet era, and proposed that the people themselves write the history of their plants, factories, and villages in order to testify to the great events in which they were participating. This proposal adapted the "literature of fact" to the "collective creation" of his-

---

55. Gorky, "Narod dolzhen znat' svoiu istoriiu!"in *GSS*, 25: 272–76; first published in Pokrovsky's journal *Bor'ba klassov* (Class Struggle). According to L. Spiridonova, Gorky's interest in history can be traced back to 1913, when he began to study the role of nations in history and to read the major Russian historians. Actually, it can be traced back to the Capri School, when he and Lunacharsky proposed an encyclopedia of Russian history written from a proletarian point of view. Spiritonova claims that the key issue for Gorky was less class struggle than the struggle with Asiatic Russia, represented (to him) by the peasantry; he regarded the civil war as a fight between the proletariat and the peasantry who defended "holy private property." L. Spiridonova, *M. Gorkii. Dialog s Istoriei* (Moscow, 1994), 24, 36, 252, 260–62.

tory and was intended to psychologically engage the masses in "building socialism." Stalin was associated with Peter the Great modernizing Russia and, after 1934, with Ivan the Terrible saving Russia from foreign invaders and domestic traitors. *The History of the Communist Party of the Soviet Union (Bolsheviks), Short Course* (1938), became the new sacred text.

Apollo draws boundaries (*BT*, 72). The new history reconstituted, on a new basis, the horizon that the futurists wanted to destroy. Nietzsche's remark is relevant here: "What such a [strong] nature cannot master it knows how to forget; it no longer exists, the horizon is closed and whole. . . . And this is a general law: every living thing can become healthy, strong, and fruitful only within a horizon; if it is incapable of drawing a horizon around itself . . . it will wither away" (*H*, 10). The Pushkin Centennial (1937) consolidated the repudiation of modernist iconoclasm and ahistoricism. Conducted with great fanfare, it celebrated a "fighter for freedom," Soviet cultural attainments, and Soviet humanism in the worst year of the Great Terror.

The Lie Triumphant: Nietzsche and Stalinist Political Culture

Stalinism entailed purge and terror, brazen lies, the Stalin Cult, a new rank order, and Stalin-approved models in the arts and sciences. The murder of Sergei Kirov (December 1, 1934) was the pretext for a new round of purges that escalated into the Great Purge and Great Terror, also known as the *Yezhovshchina*, after Nikolai Yezhov (1895–1940), head of the NKVD from September 1936 to December 1938. Under Lenin, being purged meant expulsion from the Party. During the Great Purge, it usually meant expulsion from the Party followed by imprisonment or execution. In a series of show trials held between 1936 and 1938, Old Bolsheviks confessed to traitorous conspiracies and monstrous crimes. All of them were sentenced to death.[1] Also executed were over half the delegates to the Congress of Victors (the Seventeenth Party Congress, 1934), two-thirds of all Party members and candidate members, and one-third of the officer corps. Entire local, regional, and republican committees disappeared into the Gulag (forced labor camps run by the NKVD). So did trade union officials, factory and collective farm managers, schoolteachers, scientists, engineers, technicians, artists, and writers. The leadership strata was disproportionately affected, but no one was safe. NKVD operatives had quotas to fill, and they strove to exceed them. Individuals denounced other individuals to save themselves or their families, or to satisfy personal ambitions, or to settle old scores. Arrestees "confessed" under torture and implicated others.[2] The Great Terror abated after Lavrenty Beria (1899–1953) replaced Yezhov on December 8, 1938. Yezhov was arrested in April 1939 and executed the following year. Most of his NKVD subordinates were arrested as well. Terror on a lesser scale continued, however, and the Gulag remained. Economically, the Great Terror was

1. Zinoviev, Kamenev, and others were tried in August 1936; Radek, Piatikov, and fifteen others in January and February 1937; and Bukharin, Rykov, Henrikh Yagoda (1891–1938), Yezhov's predecessor), and eighteen other members of the "rightist-Trotskyite bloc" in March 1938. All were executed. Trotsky was condemned to death in absentia three times and murdered in Mexico City in August 1940.

2. Details in Robert Conqest, *The Great Terror* (Oxford, 1990).

disastrous. Production dropped as experienced managers, engineers, scientists, and technicians were lost to the Gulag. Work routines were disrupted and fear resulted in sycophancy and avoidance of responsibility. The purge of the officer corps almost cost the Soviet Union the war. After the war the Gulag population swelled with former prisoners-of-war and other persons considered disloyal or potentially disloyal. The postwar Gulag operated at a financial loss; forced labor was cheap, but maintaining the security apparatus was expensive.[3] Nevertheless, on the eve of his death, Stalin was preparing a new purge.

The masses resisted policies they considered unjust with the usual weapons of the weak—foot-dragging, "misunderstanding" of orders, and lack of initiative—and managed to extract concessions from the authorities. These concessions were not the product of negotiation between equals, however; the authorities held the power of imprisonment and death. Open pursuit of self-interest was unacceptable; people had to couch their wishes in politically correct language, to learn to "speak Bolshevik."[4]

Outside the Soviet Union, the most important event was Hitler's installation as chancellor of Germany on January 20, 1933. Stalin did not want war, and Hitler was not ready for one, so their relations were confused and contradictory until mid-1934, when Hitler stepped up his propaganda war against the Soviet Union, which responded in kind.[5] Claims of cultural superiority were part of the propaganda war. The Nazis attacked "cultural Bolshevism" and preached anti-Semitism, contempt for intellectuals, and a mystique of blood and soil. The Soviets condemned "fascist barbarism" and claimed that their country was guided by reason and science, painting a picture of ethnic and class harmony and of constantly rising economic, educational, and cultural levels. *Pravda* declared that the mysticism and paganism comprising the "arsenal of fascist ideology" were rooted in "Hegel's reactionary idealism," "Nietzsche's chauvinism," and "Bergson's anti-scientism" (September 19, 1935). Nazis called Nietzsche the prophet of the Third Reich, and Soviet propagandists agreed.

The Nazis endorsed the most authoritarian and brutal aspects of Nietzsche's thought and suppressed the others. Stalinists, on the other hand, concealed their appropriations of Nietzsche behind a veil of socialist-humanist rheto-

3. Elena Zubkova, *Russia After the War*, ed. and trans. Hugh Ragsdale (Armonk, N.Y., 1998), 165.

4. Stephen Kotkin, "Coercion and Identity: Workers Lives in Stalin's Showcase City," in Siegelbaum and Suny, *Making Workers Soviet*, 302–5; Nikolai Krementsev, *Stalinist Science* (Princeton, 1997), 81–83.

5. Walter Laqueur, *Russia and Germany* (New Brunswick, 1990), 172–80, 236–38; Aleksandr Nekrich, *Pariahs, Partners, Predators: German-Soviet Relations, 1922–41* (New York, 1997), 66–86.

ric. Ideologues in both societies read Nietzsche as the philosopher of the "will to power," the divider of humanity into masters and slaves. They interpreted the will to power politically, regarded culture as a part of politics, and had no illusions about Nietzsche's humanitarianism and no qualms about the instrumental use of "human material." Ignoring Nietzsche's championing of personal integrity, generosity (the "bestowing virtue," *Z*, 99–101), fidelity to one's own values, magnanimity, truthfulness, a gracious ruling class, and his antimilitarist, anti-German, and pro-Jewish statements, Nazis and Stalinists alike took literally brutal and authoritarian statements that exponents of a "gentle," or a liberationist, Nietzsche perceive as symbolic or metaphoric.

Nietzsche's late works are replete with statements that invite appropriation by dictators. He called Julius Caesar the "finest type of tyrant" (*TI*, 93), idealized the Roman Empire, and described its "grand style" as "no longer merely art but art become reality, truth, *life*" (*AC*, 182), all parts integrated into a whole. The very idea of a "labor question" was ridiculous: "If one wills an end, one must also will the means to it; if one wants slaves, one is a fool if one educates them to be masters" (*TI*, 95). The Russian Autocracy was the one place in Europe where the "will to power" endured. "The nations which were worth something, which became worth something, never became so under liberal institutions" (*TI*, 93). Time and again, Nietzsche invoked discipline, obedience, and compulsion. "'You shall obey'—someone and for a long time: *else* you will perish and lose respect for yourself—this appears to me to be the moral imperative of nature which, to be sure, is neither 'categorical' as the old Kant would have it . . . nor addressed to the individual (what do individuals matter to her?), but to peoples, races, ages, classes—but above all to the whole human animal, to *man*" (*BGE*, 102). Walicki argues that because the Marxist idea of freedom pertained to the species man, it "provided an excellent justification for the totalitarian strivings of Lenin and Stalin."[6] Nietzsche emphasized the species man too.

> We have a different faith; to us the democratic movement is not only a form of the decay of political organization but a form of the decay, namely the diminution of man, making him mediocre and lowering his value. Where then, must *we* reach with our hopes?
>
> Toward new *new philosophers,* there is no choice; toward spirits strong and original enough to provide the stimuli for opposite valuations . . . toward men of the future who in the present tie the knot and constraint that forces the will of millennia upon *new* tracks. To teach man the future of man as his *will,* as dependent on a human will, and to prepare great ventures and over-all attempt of discipline and cultivation by way of putting an end to that gruesome dominion of non-

6. Walicki, *Marxism*, 399.

sense and accident that has been called "history"—the nonsense of the "greatest number" is merely its ultimate form. (*BGE,* 117)

Similarly: "We count ourselves among conquerors; we think about the necessity for new orders, also for a new slavery—for every strengthening and enhancement of the human type also involves a new kind of slavery" (*GS,* 338). For Hitler personally, Wagner and Schopenhauer were more important than Nietzsche. The Führer was enthralled with Wagnerian theatricality and could quote pages of Schopenhauer's *The World as Will and Idea* by heart. But Schopenhauer's pessimism and his Christian/Buddhist ethic contradicted Nazi doctrine. With some adjustments, Nietzsche's yea-saying and warrior ethos were more suitable. Excerpts from Nietzsche's writings were an integral part of Nazi indoctrination.[7] To connect himself symbolically with Nietzsche, Hitler had a well-publicized meeting with Nietzsche's sister, an ardent Nazi, and had a photograph taken of himself at the Nietzsche Archive, contemplating Max Klinger's bust of Nietzsche, "sober, resolute, sane, and self-controlled—subjecting the world to his will through the power of his eyes."[8] Otto Dix's very different bust of Nietzsche—an introverted, mad visionary—was confiscated and destroyed. At their 1936 meeting, Hitler presented Mussolini was a complete edition of Nietzsche's works. Whether Hitler read Nietzsche is unclear, but Mussolini read a great deal of Nietzsche as a young man. He even wrote an article about him, titled "The Philosophy of Force" ("La filosofi della forza," 1908).

There is no direct evidence that Stalin read Nietzsche, but he certainly knew about him from Nazi propaganda and, very likely, from Bukharin, Lunacharsky, and Gorky. In 1925, Stalin began a systematic reading of philosophy and political theory. Bukharin and Trotsky were on his list. "The Boss" had no patience for the intricacies of the Hegelian dialectic, but anything concerned with struggle seems to have caught his attention.[9] Nietzsche's trenchant aphorisms might well have appealed to him. Stalin also read Machiavelli and Nechaev (he kept Nechaev's archive in his office where it was discovered after his death), and historical literature. Especially fond of biographies of emperors and tsars, Stalin was fascinated by Genghis Khan and attributed the following adage to him: "The death of the vanquished are necessary for the tranquility of the victor."[10] Mikhail Agursky claims that no tyrant could afford to ignore the opportunity for philosophical legitimation that Nietzsche provided.[11]

7. Aschheim, *Nietzsche Legacy in Germany,* 232–53.
8. Hans Sluga, *Heidegger's Crisis: Philosophy and Politics in Nazi Germany* (Berkeley and Los Angeles, 1993), 182.
9. Dmitri Volkogonov, *Stalin: Triumph and Tragedy* (New York, 1991), 226–30.
10. Service, *History,* 226.
11. Agursky, "Nietzschean Roots," in *NSC,* 281.

Reviving aspects of the tsarist legacy, Stalin's propagandists associated him with Peter the Great and Ivan the Terrible, and they exalted heroes of old Muscovy and the Time of Troubles. Orthodox pageantry and tsarist "scenarios of power" (Richard Wortman's term) returned in Soviet guise. An aura of invincibility and inevitability surrounded the dignitaries who presided over Stalin's triumphal processions and parades and testified to the Party's monopoly on truth. By image, word, gesture, and music, they conveyed the message: "There is no one in the world like us." Nietzsche's observation about the Caesars applies to the Caesars of the 1930s as well. "And one employed festivals and arts for no other purpose than to feel oneself *dominant,* to *show* oneself dominant; they are means to making oneself feared" (*AC,* 108). *Pravda*'s articles on the appropriate slogans for May Day were articulated in authoritative language, or as Nietzsche put it, "an imperative tone, the 'thou shalt,' the precondition of being obeyed" (*AC,* 176).

Official pronouncements on Nietzsche traced the gratuitous cruelty of fascism to his master morality, even though Nietzsche disapproved of sadism; his cruelty was instrumental. Zarathustra's observation, "man is the cruelest animal" (*Z,* 235), is tinged with sadness, even disgust. Nietzsche did regard cruelty as necessary, however. "Almost everything we call 'higher culture' is based on the spiritualization of *cruelty,* on its becoming more profound" (*BGE,* 158). "Who will attain anything great if he does not find in himself the strength and the will to *inflict* great suffering? Being able to suffer is the least thing: weak women and even slaves often achieve virtuosity in that. But not to perish of internal distress and uncertainty when one inflicts great suffering and hears the cry of this suffering—that is great, that belongs to greatness" (*GS,* 255). Such passages could be used by Stalinists (and Nazis) who wanted to demonstrate their "greatness," or to justify the "necessity" of cruelty, or to rationalize their sadism. Of course, cruelty could also be justified in terms of the Hegelian-Marxist conception of "historical necessity" and the future-orientation found in Marxism and in Nietzsche. The "passion of fanaticism" can make sadism into a "good," as it was for Christians who tortured heretics in the Middle Ages.

The Great Purge and Great Terror were in no way related to modernization, or to the number of critics who "had" to be silenced, or to the number of corrupt or incompetent officials who deserved to be fired. Stalin's paranoia was a factor, to be sure, but his love of power was more important. Trotsky claimed that a "desire to exert his power as an athlete exerts his muscles" was the mainspring of Stalin's personality. Milovan Djilas regarded Stalin as a believer in power for its own sake.[12] Nikita Khrushchev (1894–1971)

12. Trotsky and Djilas quoted in Daniel Rancour-Laferriere, *The Mind of Stalin* (Ann Arbor, 1988), 24. Also quoted is a childhood friend of Stalin's, Iosef Iremashvili, who recalled the young Stalin's "love for might" and "striving for power."

asserted that "to stay in power," Stalin and Mao Zedong considered it indispensable . . . not only to make the people obedient to them, but to make the people afraid of them as well."[13] Andrei Sinyavsky declared that Stalin loved to test "the force and magic of his power" and was "forever toying with his victims, as if power gave him a kind of aesthetic satisfaction."[14]

Power can be used constructively or destructively; to help people or to ruin them. And what better way to "exercise" power than to condemn millions of people to terrible suffering and premature death? Or to terrorize people into blind obedience? Or to move them around like pawns on a chessboard? I do not argue that Nietzsche "caused" this type of behavior, but that his concept helps explain it. Power can also be "exercised" by granting favors and gifts, a posture Stalin liked to assume. Soviet citizens had to thank him for just about everything, most famously for giving them a "happy childhood."

The Soviet hierarchy was a pecking order, characterized by obsequiousness toward those above and browbeating and bullying of those below. Political prisoners, the lowest of the low, were tortured to extract confessions and then tormented by criminals and sadistic guards in the Gulag. Varlam Shalamov, a prisoner for seventeen years, says that NKVD operatives were intoxicated by power. Solzhenitsyn says they were motivated by greed as well as by power, but mostly by power.[15]

Socialist Realism set the tone for Stalinist political culture and its ever more brazen lies. Assertions of Stalin's absolute genius were the perfect cover for disregarding facts; changing basic precepts of Marxism-Leninism; imposing Stalin's personal preferences in literature, art, and science; and sudden reversals of policy such as the Hitler-Stalin Pact (August 1939). At the Congress of Victors, Stalin described the Soviet Union as a land where poverty, exploitation, and unemployment had been abolished, the antithesis between town and country was disappearing, the cultural gap between the intelligentsia and the people was closing, and the material conditions of life were far above those of workers and peasants in the bourgeois democracies. This was after the horrors of collectivization and the terror-famine, and despite continuing and severe shortages of food, housing, and other necessities. Reports on economic achievements manipulated statistics to create the impression of success. Alan Bullock's observation about Nazi Germany applies to the Soviet Union too: "Not only was the message of success drummed home by every

---

13. *Khrushchev Remembers*, trans. and ed. Strobe Talbott; introduction, commentary, and annotation by Edward Crankshaw (Boston, 1970), 7.

14. Sinyavsky, *Soviet Civilization*, 98–99.

15. Varlam Shalamov, *Kolyma Tales*, trans. John Glad (Harmondsworth, 1994), 447; Solzhenitsyn, *Gulag Archipelago*, 1:147.

means, day in and day out, but its effect was doubled by the fact that any note of skepticism or criticism was suppressed. Success thus exercised a coercive as well an attractive force, making it almost impossible to resist."[16]

After bread rationing ended in the cities in 1935, Stalin set up one campaign of mass propaganda after another to make people forget the hungry years and believe that the glorious future had arrived. Magnificent all-Union congresses and elaborate receptions were continually being arranged: for collective farm shock workers, leading stockbreeders, Stakhanovites, metalworkers, and wives of engineers, executives, and army officers. A solemn ceremony in the Kremlin would be followed by the setting of tables for thousands of people, with Stalin officiating like a master of ceremonies.

Stalinist carnivals, a new type of mass festival, were characterized by a "holiday mood which knows nothing of scarcity, tension, or necessity, but quite the contrary, a world of overabundance, amusement, and forgetting," a true fairy-tale world.[17] The first carnival that did not celebrate an explicitly political event took place in July 1935. Another such carnival was organized in Gorky Park in the summer of 1937. Sports, entertainment, and dance were described as the "self-activity" of the masses, even though carnival activities were carefully scripted from above. Details arranged beforehand included the time and place of participants' arrival in the park to join their collective, the masks and costumes to be worn, the route to be followed in the park, and the songs to be sung (and learned in advance). Stalinist carnivals continued until 1939. They perverted the traditional peasant carnival, with its boisterous and unrestrained conduct, including drunkenness, into a state show of what the Party considered the appropriate artistic expression of joy and happiness in an allegedly classless society. Rosalinde Sartori concludes: "In this respect, Stalinist carnival was just another form of Socialist Realism: showing what there is of the future in the present." A later study by Karen Petrone tells us that participants were ordered "to leave [their] sadness outside," that there was some space for purely diversionary entertainment, and that a limited mocking of the "heroic" language was allowed. The celebratory rhetoric created problems for the cadres; they had to mobilize people for goals that Socialist Realist rhetoric told them had already been achieved.[18]

Bakhtin's dissertation, "Rabelais and His Time" (1936) set forth an inverted, grotesque image of the official carnival culture. Revelers gorged themselves on food, wine, and sex; subjected people to ritual thrashings; beat them to a pulp; threw excrement at them; and tore them limb from limb

16. Alan Bullock, *Hitler and Stalin* (New York, 1992), 452.

17. This follows Rosalinde Sartori, "Stalinism and Carnival," in Günther, *Culture of the Stalin Period*, 64–72.

18. Petrone, *Life Has Become More Joyous*, 101–3, 174.

(as was done to Dionysus) as if to illustrate Nietzsche's dictum: "Without cruelty there is no festival" (*GM*, 67). Bakhtin's (Dionysian) account of popular culture linked destruction and creativity, death and rebirth.

The show trials were ritualized charades with a facade of concocted evidence, an illustration of the "will to deception" that Bernadiner attributed to Nietzsche (see Chapter 11). These trials can be regarded as the culmination of the theatricalization of life, the supreme tragedy of heroes "unmasked" as traitors and receiving their just deserts. Witnesses and defendants were given their scripts and rehearsed beforehand. The media functioned as a Greek chorus and reported the trials just that way, extolling the proceedings as evidence of the superiority of Soviet justice over exploitative, obsolete bourgeois law. In another kind of chorus, carefully controlled mass meetings expressed their outrage at the "reptiles," "vermin," "vipers," and "mad dogs" in the dock and "voted" to execute them by a show of hands. Ivanov regarded the chorus as the authentic voice of the people, but this is not what he had in mind. The epithets were a further step in the dehumanization of the villain, a staple of the political theater of the 1920s. The slogan "to see through and expose the masked enemy" perpetuated the theme of "unmasking." The defendants were not just "vermin," however. They were mythic incarnations of the forces of evil—"deformed," "monstrous," and "repulsive." In Russian Orthodoxy, ugliness (*bezobraznost'*), literally formlessness, is associated with the devil, and beauty or perfect form, with God. They were "Judases," "traitors," "fiends," "double-dealers" (*dvurushniki*) who had betrayed the Soviet Union. The accused were ritual sacrifices in the Dionysian sense—a Soviet counterpart to the autos-da-fé of the Inquisition, the witch hunts of early modern Europe, the public executions of Jacobin France, and Nazi violence against Jews. The Manichaean rhetoric, typical of this period, was the expression of a secularized apocalypticism that perceived the Final Conflict as imminent and that divided the world into the forces of good and the forces of evil,

Nadezhda Mandelstam called the first Chekists the avant-garde of the new people: "They had completely revised, in the manner of Supermen, all ordinary human values. They were later replaced by people of a completely different physical type who had no values at all—revised or otherwise."[19] This is not entirely accurate. In some cases, the unscrupulousness stemmed from zealotry. Nietzsche's discussion of the "psychology of conviction" (*AC*, 172–74), applies to these cases: "The 'believer' . . . does not belong to *himself*, he can be only a means, he has to be *used*, he needs someone who will use him (*AC*, 172). Implicitly, he will not question orders; he will simply obey. "Zarathustra is a skeptic" (ibid.). Nietzsche considered fanaticism a trait of the convinced, giving Savanarola, Luther, Rousseau, Robespierre,

19. Mandelstam, *Hope Against Hope*, 79–80.

and Saint-Just as examples. "Now this desiring not to see what one sees, this desiring *not* to see as one sees, is virtually the primary condition for all who are in any sense party: the party man necessarily becomes a liar" (*AC*, 173). His observation applies to Communists who did not "see" what was going on.

Advance publicity for the Stalin Constitution began in June 1936, six months before its formal adoption the following December. Billed as the "most democratic constitution in the world," its guarantees of civil liberties were hedged with qualifications, and the document itself was only for show. It was called the "the sunny Stalin Constitution" (and Stalin was routinely called "our sun," *nashe solntse*), even though the author was not Stalin but a team of writers, including soon-to-be-purged Bukharin and Radek. Described as a life-transforming document (another example of the magic of words), the Constitution was the Apollonian illusion *par excellence,* a veil of legal rights and guarantees that concealed the truly terrifying reality of the Gulag. The media presented the Constitution as Stalin's gift to the Soviet people. In Nietzschean terms, Stalin was the lawgiver who inscribed "new values on new tablets." The new values included a strict moral code. A moral person had to obey the laws of the Soviet state and despise and denounce violators of these laws.

The more purge and terror wracked Soviet society, the more Stalin was portrayed as the loving father of his people. The more extravagant the Stalin Cult became, the more Stalin affected a pose of exceptional modesty; he loved to be described as a person totally devoid of vanity. The press exalted the strong Soviet family, but the cult of Pavlik Morozov taught children to spy on their parents, and spouses and children of purged individuals were pressured to denounce them. The misleadingly titled Protection of Motherhood Act (June 1936) prohibited all but medically necessary abortions and restricted divorce in order to raise the birthrate. To justify the about-face (abortion was legalized in 1920), *Pravda* and *Izvestiia* claimed that the conditions that drove women to abortion in the capitalist countries (hunger, unemployment, hopelessness, unavailability of child care) no longer existed "in the land of socialism, in the land of Stalin's concern for women, of continuous improvement in the material and cultural conditions of life." Actually, child-care facilities were woefully inadequate there too. The press called abortion a dangerous operation, invoked a woman's "right" to a family and her "duty to bear children," and criticized women who "treat the issue of childbearing as if it were a personal matter." "We must take care of our family," *Pravda* intoned, "bear and raise healthy Soviet *bogatyri.*" A few weeks later, Stalin announced that since women are now equal (another lie), special measures to insure their hiring, training, and promotion were no longer necessary. Factory managers did not want to train and promote women who would be pregnant most of the time (contraceptives were unavailable), so the overwhelming majority of Soviet women ended up in low-skill, poorly paid jobs. For them, "equality" meant heavy manual labor, not considered dangerous to their health, plus keeping house in extremely difficult conditions. In 1937, following Italian and German practice, a new title was introduced—"Heroine Mother"—for women who bore and raised seven or more children.

In his speech to the Eighteenth Party Congress (1939), Stalin spoke of the abolition of hostile classes. Soviet workers, peasants, and intellectuals were living and working in friendly collaboration; their community of interest formed the basis of the moral and political unity of Soviet society, the mutual friendship of the nationalities, and Soviet patriotism. His words hid the purges that had decimated the leadership cadres of the national minorities (who were accused of "bourgeois nationalism"), the mass arrests of foreign communists living in Moscow, and the *Yezhovshchina*. As in previous speeches, he used statistics to create a smoke screen of "facts" that concealed shortfalls of the Plan and the low standard of living.

Robert Tucker's observation (quoted in Chapter 9), that in Stalin's time one could tell what the Soviets were doing or about to do by what they were attacking, was especially true during the period of "building Stalinism." According to Volkogonov, "Saying one thing and doing another became the norm for Stalin: condemning the leadership cult while reinforcing it, criticizing Jesuit practices while encouraging them in Soviet life, talking about collective leadership while reducing it to one man rule."[20] Soviet antireligious propaganda denounced the cruelties committed by Christianity, but Chekists began their careers by studying the Inquisition. In 1933–34, some Chekists were sent to Germany to study the Gestapo.[21] Barbara Kiteme, author of a dissertation on the Stalin Cult, says that "while the Cult remained a highly public phenomenon, it couched its messages in Aesopian language, that appeared vague or befuddled to the outsider while communicating critical directions to the Party throughout the Union in order to overcome problems and build this system of power."[22] Bernadiner's *The Philosophy of Nietzsche and Fascism* is another example of a two-level communication. On the obvious level, Nietzsche personifies everything detestable in "fascism of the German type." On the esoteric or Aesopian level, we find coded explanations of the Stalin cult, Soviet brutality, and the emerging rank order of Soviet society.

Bernadiner presented Nietzsche as a specifically German phenomenon, saying that he spoke for the Junkers, the most reactionary sector of the

20. Volkogonov, *Stalin*, 189.
21. Anthony Antonov-Ovseyenko, *The Time of Stalin* (New York, 1983), 257.
22. Barbara Kiteme, "The Cult of Stalin: National Power and the Soviet Party-State" (Ph.D. diss., Columbia University, 1989), 5.

The Lie Triumphant   361

German bourgeoisie, and not for international finance capital, as Leiteizen claimed. Diverging from Leiteizen in other ways too, Bernadiner ignored early Bolshevism's debt to Nietzsche and declared that rank order pertained to groups—castes, races, peoples—but not to individuals. This was in line with Stalin's assertion that "equalization in the sphere of requirements and personal, everyday life is a reactionary petit-bourgeois absurdity worthy of some primitive sect of ascetics, but not of a socialist society organized on Marxist lines" (*SW*, 13:361).

Going beyond Leiteizen's contention that Nietzsche did not advocate "individualism," Bernadiner associated a desire for personal freedom with political disloyalty. "Every petit bourgeois hero protesting against the compulsion of the state and the existence of the police and going beyond good and evil in his relations with others declares himself a Nietzschean" (61). That such people must be crushed, that the entire population must be regimented, was the double message of the following statements: "terror is the basic form" of fascist rule; Mussolini is merciless to his enemies (he "openly demands their blood"); Rosenberg dreams of turning Germany into a "colossal barracks"; the fascist "cult of war" demonstrates the indifference of fascist leaders to the ruin of millions of people (8, 116, 114, 129). Bernadiner was silent on the millions of Soviet citizens dead as a result of collectivization, the "terror-famine," and slave labor, and on the barracks-like accommodations and worse for Soviet workers. His reference to the "necessity" of a "cruel class struggle" (137) and his claim that Spengler hoped to base fascism on the rich peasantry (*kulachestvo*) (90) obliquely justified dekulakization, the collectivization of agriculture, and the "terror-famine." The fascist subordination of women, Bernadiner traced to Nietzsche's opposition to gender equality, his "cynicism" about marriage for love, and his belief that woman's main purpose was to bear healthy children (55–58), as if Nietzsche were the only source of fascist misogyny.[23] Bernadiner's quotations from a Nazi questionnaire to women: "Why have you not married?" "Why have you no children?" (120–21), anticipated mandatory motherhood for Soviet women.

To substantiate his contention that Nietzsche regarded the people as a herd, as useful animals, Bernadiner noted Nietzsche's view that the slaves who built the Pyramids did not protest (39) and quoted Nietzsche's dictum: "He who cannot command; let him obey" (50). Nietzsche's basic division was between strong and weak, masters and slaves. The strong did not need

---

23. Actually, Nietzsche's disapproval of marriage for love stemmed not from his "cynicism" but from his elitism. "In marriage in the aristocratic, old aristocratic, sense of the word it was a question of the breeding of a race (is there still an aristocracy today? [one asks]—thus of the maintenance of a fixed, definite type of ruling man: man and woman were sacrificed to this point of view" (*WP*, 388).

principles or norms. For them, there was no law, no conscience, just the "truth of cruelty" (38) practiced by "blond beasts" who live by plunder. Nietzsche's ideal was a society in which a privileged minority represented happiness, beauty, and goodness on earth. All humanity existed for "the chosen," a "higher caste"; any sacrifices that the people had to make on its behalf were justified. Nietzsche did not even try to disguise his cruelty, Bernadiner asserted, quoting him once again.

> Let us say without mercy, how every *higher* culture on earth so far has *begun*. People of a primordial nature, barbarians in every terrible sense of the word, still in possession of unbroken strength of will and striving for power, hurled themselves upon weaker, well-behaved, peaceful races, perhaps traders [or cattle raisers] or upon older decrepit [*mürbe*] cultures whose last vitality was even then flaring up in splendid fireworks of spirit and corruption. (34; *BGE,* 201–2)

The foregoing is from the section titled "What is Noble." Compare Kaufmann's translation: "Let us admit to ourselves without being considerate" (*ohne Schönung,* literally "without prettifying, *KSA,* 5:205), and he translates *mürbe* as "mellow," its primary meaning (*KSA,* 5:206). I put "or cattle raisers" in brackets because Bernadiner omitted it. Perhaps he did not want to remind his readers that meat was scarce; peasants resisting collectivization had slaughtered their livestock. He also omitted the last sentence— "In the beginning the noble class was always the barbarian caste; their predominance did not lie mainly in physical strength but in strength of the soul—they were more *whole* human beings (which also means, at every level, 'more whole beasts')" (*BGE,* 202), presumably because it contradicted the cultured image of themselves that the Soviet elite wanted to project.

To reinforce his association of Nietzsche with Nazi elitism and brutality, Bernadiner quoted the following passage:

> The essential characteristic of a genuine [*guten*] and healthy aristocracy is that it feels itself *not* as a function of royal power or society, but as their "meaning" and highest justification—and therefore it accepts with a good conscience, the sacrifice of innumerable multitudes of people [*Unzahl Menschen*] who, for its sake, must be reduced and lowered to incomplete human beings, to slaves, to instruments . . . as the foundation and scaffolding on which a chosen being [*gesuchte Art Wesen*] is able to raise itself to its higher task and especially to a higher state of being. (36; *BGE,* 202, *KSA,* 3:206–7)

In Kaufmann's translation, which follows the German, "*guten*" is "good," "*Unzahl Menschen*" is "untold human beings," and *gesuchte Art Wesen* is "choice type of being," but "especially" is ommitted. The above passage could also be read as an Aesopian justification for the cruelty of the Soviet elite. The "chosen being" was, of course, the Superman. He would embody the force, power, and beauty of countless generations who existed only for the purpose of creating him. "He is the entire hope and glory of humanity" (38). "Chosen," one of Bernadiner's favorite words, played into Russian and Soviet messianism.

Bernadiner's discussion of the leader (Führer) contained a powerful double-message.

> The sickness of the era is that there are no leaders [*vozhdei*]. Nietzsche grieved about the absence of sovereigns [*povelitelei*], people with strong and proud wills, who dared to compel subordination. Strong, impassive, accustomed to rule . . . "Such leader-guides [*vozhaki*] are necessary," he writes—"The danger that threatens us is that they might fail to appear, or that they might turn out badly, or not develop fully, ruined [or crushed] by external circumstances." (41; *BGE*, 117–18)

"External circumstances" is Bernadiner's addition; Kaufmann's translation follows the German (*KSA*, 5:127): "the frightening danger that they might fail to appear or that they might turn out badly or degenerate these are *our* real worries and gloom." Bernadiner omitted the line "It is the image of such leaders that *we* envisage," but his subliminal message was that the people needed Stalin, who could not, of course, degenerate. "Such leader-guides are necessary," Bernadiner repeated, " 'before whom whatever has existed on earth of [concealed] terrible and benevolent spirits will look pale and dwarfed by comparison' " (41; *BGE*, 117). I put "concealed" in brackets because Bernadiner omitted it, perhaps to avoid implying that Stalin was concealing a terrible spirit.

"Humanity yearns for people of strong will," Bernadiner declared, ostensibly summarizing Nietzsche. "The greatest crime is not to give them the opportunity to develop, not to create the circumstances in which they can grow. These people must come from the highest estate" (*soslovie*) (41). Nietzsche dreamed of a leader who is "the chosen of the chosen, the strongest of the strong," directing all his thought and hope to him. This leader is the Superman for whom humanity is only a "bridge," only "rungs on a ladder." Generations of slaves "had to be expended [*zatracheny*] so that he could be created" (42).

Such leaders existed in history, Bernadiner asserted, "and they shine to *us* [emphasis added] as beacons of the future. They are extremely strong because they embody in themselves long-accumulated strength, they concentrate in themselves all the energy of the high estates of preceding generations. And the best example of such a leader was Napoleon." Nietzsche

deeply esteemed him as the negation of the French Revolution, "the negation of its nihilism, [its] preachments of equality and brotherhood" (42).
(Note Bernadiner's juxtaposition of nihilism, equality, and brotherhood.)
"Napoleon as the problem of the *noble ideal as such* made flesh. One might
well ponder what kind of problem it is: the synthesis of the *inhuman* and
the *superhuman*" (42; *GM,* 54). The next year, *Art* published a portrait of
Stalin in a Napoleonic pose (1935, no. 1:6). The fully elaborated Stalin Cult
(see Chapter 13) presented him as a synthesis of human and divine qualities.

Contemporary capitalism needs strong centralized power, Bernadiner
asserted, a cruel hand to suppress the Revolution; liberty and equality no
longer serve as bourgeois ideals. The openly amoral fascist elite rules by
naked exploitation and force. But it also erects a cult of heroes to reinforce
its leadership and provide the masses with models of courage and military
prowess. "In typical Nietzschean form," the fascist elite exalts "separate
chosen individuals, setting them off from the majority, the entire remaining
mass" (94), surrounding them with a mystical halo and depicting them as
demigods and saviors. Fascist irrationalism encourages the masses to expect
miracles from the hero. He can accomplish what ordinary people cannot.
Only through his power and will can the people (*narod*) be reborn. But such
heroes alone cannot save capitalism (95). Faced with the threat of proletarian revolution, the bourgeoisie needs a dictator, "one man in whose hands
the threads of the entire country can be concentrated." "In every country
where a fascist dictatorship has been established there arises the figure of
some kind of 'leader' [*vozhd'*] who is destined to lead the people to the
'promised land.' He embodies all the traits of the Messiah, in his hands are
concentrated all the threads of providence. Only he knows where and how
to steer the ship of political life" (96). The people are told that only a strong
leader can save them. His name is surrounded by scores of legends.
"Superhuman qualities and the capacity of genius are attributed to [him]."
He is depicted as the Superman. "A halo of glory and power conceals his
bloody deeds." In this context, Bernadiner quoted Hitler's statement that
the mass is like a woman, passive and weak, who wants to be ruled (94–97).
(Stalin considered Russians a feminine people.)[24] The Aesopian message was
that chosen heroes alone could not save communism; a strong leader was
far more important. The mention of "bloody deeds" can be read as an allusion to the suppression of Soviet peasantry and as a hint of unspecified "bloody
deeds" to come. On May Day 1939, *Pravda* announced that the Soviet Union
had arrived at the "promised land of socialism," led there by Stalin.

Also relevant to the Stalin Cult were Bernadiner's remarks on religion.
He traced the fascists' cynical use of religion to Nietzsche's statement on its
usefulness in training the people in virtues their rulers desired (63; *BGE,*

---

24. Günther, *Der sozialistische Übermensch,* 161. Berdiaev did too; see Chapter 6.

72–74). Religion makes slaves content with their lot and teaches them non-resistance to evil, forgiveness of injury, Bernadiner claimed. Nietzsche's atheism had an "aristocratic cast" (62); slaves need religion but nobles do not. Here, Nietzsche is a stand-in for Robespierre, who declared that atheism is aristocratic. "The idea of a superior being [*grand être*] who watches over oppressed innocence and who punishes triumphant crime is completely popular. The people, the unfortunates, applaud me. If I have critics, they will be from the rich and the guilty."[25] Robespierre tried to establish a civil religion, as advocated by Rousseau (and Machiavelli). Bernadiner knew about Rousseau and Robespierre; eighteenth-century thought was one of his specialties. Although he counterposed Marx and Lenin's "scientific atheism" to Nietzsche's "irrational atheism," the Aesopian message was that the Soviets needed a more elaborate civil religion. Bernadiner ignored Marx's dictum that "religion is the opium of the people" and the statement that precedes it: "the abolition of religion as the *illusory* happiness of men is a demand for their *real* happiness. The call to abandon their illusions about their condition is a *call to abandon a condition which requires illusions*" (MER, 54). Stalinism required illusions.

Bernadiner held that Soviet and fascist leaders are fundamentally different. Each one reflects the qualities of his society: rationalism in one, irrationalism in the other.

> To create a communist society, the proletariat conducts a cruel class struggle guided by the Communist Party and its leaders [*vozhdei*]. But the leader of the ComParty [*sic*] is not a person surrounded by a mystical divine halo.
>
> The leader of the proletariat is he who embodies in himself the force and power of the rising class, who enjoys the confidence and love of this class. The will of the leader of the proletariat—this is the will of millions of workers who have pushed him forward, who are struggling to build a new communist society. . . .
>
> The fascist doctrine of the stupidity of the proletarian mass contradicts the slogan of our great teacher that "every cook must learn to rule the state." (137)

The slogan was Lenin's but it is presented as if it were Stalin's.

The rank order that Bernadiner attributed to Nietzsche, and associated with fascism, also pertained to the Soviet Union in Stalin's time. Bernadiner claimed that Nietzsche wanted to limit the "right to philosophy" to the hereditary aristocracy. "'All higher education belongs to exceptions alone;

25. Quoted in David P. Jordan, *The Revolutionary Career of Maximilian Robespierre* (New York, 1985), 196–97.

one must be privileged in order to have this right [*pravo*]" (55: *TI*, 64). The Kaufmann/Hollingdale translation follows the German (*KSA*, 6:107): "One must be privileged to have a right to so high a privilege." Nietzsche was referring to the "privilege" of innate intelligence or talent. His elitism is indisputable, but he envisioned a "new nobility" rather than the hereditary aristocracy of his day. Bernadiner was comparing the unprivileged masses of the capitalist world with Soviet workers and peasants who had the "right" to a higher education, while at the same time indicating that higher education was not for everyone.

Visible symbols of authority and rank, such as uniforms, epaulettes, medals, ribbons, returned in 1934, and wage differentials were steepened. The emerging social pyramid was an updated version of Peter the Great's Table of Ranks. Peasants and workers were at the bottom (they were not on Peter's table), the new tsar at the top, and gradations of Party bosses, bureaucrats, specialists, and managers in between. Promotion did not necessarily depend on achievement, and there were overlapping hierarchies. The top echelons were remote, aloof, solemn, and inscrutable. The new Soviet elite had special privileges that money could not buy. The bureaucratization of all areas of Soviet life, each with its own pecking order, and Stalin above all, exemplifies Nietzsche's observation, which Bernadiner did not quote (Bukharin referred to it, see p. 369) on the enhancing of power by the creation of distance.

> Every enhancement of the type "man" has so far been the work of an aristocratic society . . . a society that believes in the long ladder of an order of rank and differences in value between man and man, and that needs slavery in some sense or other. Without that *pathos of distance* which grows out of the ingrained difference between strata—when the ruling class constantly looks afar and looks down upon its subjects as instruments and just as constantly practices obedience and command, keeping down and keeping at a distance—that other more mysterious *pathos* could not have grown up either. (*BGE*, 201)

Leiteizen opposed rank order as a step toward breeding a new ruling caste. The new Soviet elite may have hoped to become one. If so, its hopes were dashed in 1936–38. The third generation of Communists who stepped into positions vacated by the *Yezhovshchina* was closer to a caste.

The association of Nietzsche and "German fascism" was reinforced by articles in *Under the Banner of Marxism*, the Party's theoretical journal. I. Vainshtein, author of "The Philosophy of Nietzsche and fascism" (1935, no. 6), described fascism as the "openly terroristic dictatorship of the imperial-

---

26. I. Vainshtein, "Filosofiia Nitsshe i fashism," *Pod znamenem marksizma*, no. 6 (1935): 80–89.

ist bourgeoisie" and called Nietzsche its major ideological source.[26] This article included double messages on lying and terror as government policy, and on the increasingly religious and mystical cast of government language, and hammered in the tenet that because Nietzsche's antimaterialism rendered him incapable of knowing reality, he denied objective truth and preached the "value of artifice, the utility of falsification," concealing his "will to exploitation of the mob [*chern'*], the worker and peasant masses" with a mantle of "tragic" phraseology. Moreover, Nietzsche was not an enemy of Christianity; he admired the illusory order that Christianity created as a way to reconcile the oppressed classes with reality. His was the morality of a plunderer who openly and cynically recognized the "higher truth" of suppressing the masses for the sake of a chosen few. Nazi ideologues based their stress on rank order, racism, and "cult of personality rising above the mob" on Nietzsche's teaching. The "mysticism," "obscurantism," and outright falsification in German science also stemmed from Nietzsche. This statement would soon apply to Soviet biology.

L. Kait, author of "Nietzscheanism and fascism" (*Under the Banner of Marxism*, 1938, no. 5), contended that even though fascism calls itself National Socialism, it has nothing in common with socialism; fascism is animalism, chauvinism, and "political banditry." Nazi ideologues preach the value of suffering, but only for the workers, not for the parasitical, untalented fascist elite.[27] To a degree, Kait's observation also applied to the Soviet elite, for although it did not preach suffering, it certainly caused it, and there were mediocrities and opportunists in its ranks.[28] Bernadiner's book and the articles just mentioned were addressed to the leadership strata. Newspapers and journals for the masses hammered in the association of Nietzsche and fascism, usually in pieces about other subjects. For example, an article on the Stalin Constitution alluded to Nietzsche's "open enmity" to a workers' state.

Bukharin used Nietzsche as a symbolic of fascism, but his Marxist eschatology was still colored by Nietzsche's "great politics," and he occasionally used Nietzsche to make Aesopian criticisms of Stalinism. In "The Crisis of Capitalist Culture and Problems of Culture in the USSR" (*Izvestiia*, March

---

27. L. Kait, "Nitssheanstvo i fashism," *Pod znamenem marksizma*, 1938, no. 5:94–101.

28. Mention should be made of "The Case of Nietzsche," by Hans Günther, a German communist living in Moscow, published in the German edition of *Under the Banner of Marxism* (1935, no. 11), which argued that Nietzsche's brutal thought reflected Germany's economic and political retardation. In another work, *Die Herren eigner Geist: des Ideologie des National Sozialismus* (Moscow-Leningrad, 1935), published by the Association of Foreign Workers in the U.S.S.R, Günther emphasized Nietzsche's irrationalism. So many German communists fled to Moscow after Hitler took power that a special section of the Union of Writers was established to accommodate them. Many were arrested during the Great Terror; others were handed over to Germany after the Hitler-Stalin Pact.

6, 18, 30, 1934), published in English as *Culture in Two Worlds,* Bukharin claimed that "two class camps—two doctrines, two cultures . . . are forming in military array for coming battles—for the battles that will be really final (in the world-historical sense) and really decisive."[29] The cover illustration counterposes Russians at a bookstall to Nazi book burners, the "two worlds" separated by two diagonal lines. According to Bukharin:

> Communism is struggling for the *fullest life* for all. But the struggle itself has certain costs, and the heroism of this struggle, which unties and uplifts the masses, demands standards which develop a *contempt for death* and the greatest liberality in spending lives, if necessary, for the attainment of its basic aims. Communism is not characterized by Philistine niggardliness and cowardice. Great aims assume the existence of operative heroism, which becomes manifest as a "natural" social characteristic of a great class and a great Party. (28)

Note that Bukharin transferred heroism, a romantic and a Nietzschean idea, from an individual to the proletariat and the Party, and he was willing to expend countless lives for communism.

His acknowledgment of the resemblance of fascist and Soviet practices was unique for a Communist at the time.

> The petty bourgeois Philistines of the "center" will say: "But you Communists also do many of these things." Or, as the Social-Democratic petty-bourgeois phrase it: "There is dictatorship here and dictatorship there, both equally abominable." Or: "There is 'Left' Bolshevism and there is "'Right' Bolshevism; and there is no difference in principle between them."
>
> These miserable people who receive blows from the left and from the right do not understand that the *formal* side of the matter alone ("dictatorship" in general), which they understand incorrectly at that, does not decide anything. *The important thing is its class meaning: its content—material and ideological, the dynamics of its development, its relationship to the general current of world historical development.* Only imbeciles can fail to understand that the dictatorship of the *proletariat* and the dictatorship of the *capitalists* are polar opposites, and that their content and historical significance are entirely different. (4)

The difference was that fascism was reactionary and communism, progressive. And yet, in his discussion of the "paradoxes of fascism," Bukharin contended that fascism was "creating something new, (reactionarily new) in the

---

29. Nikolai Bukharin, *Culture in Two Worlds* (New York, 1934), 2.

capitalist ways of living and thinking" (4). As examples he gave back-to-the-earth sloganeering, Spengler's antitechnologism, and the vogue of "semi-feudal romanticists and philosophers of reaction . . . Nietzsche, first of all," the "chief underminer of Christian and liberal humanism" (9) and an open enemy of socialist humanism, quoting Nietzsche several times. "Whom do I detest most among the modern scoundrels, the socialist scoundrels . . . who make the workers envious and teach them revenge (F. Nietzsche, *The Will to Power)*" (10). And "Socialism is for the most part a symptom of the fact that we are treating the lower class too humanely, so that they get a taste of the happiness that is forbidden to them. . . . It is not hunger that causes revolution, it is the fact that when people begin to eat they acquire larger appetites" (ibid.).

Decrying the "animal hatred" of other nations and the "nationalist fury" sweeping Germany (10–12), Bukharin highlighted the fascist slogan "back to barbarism" and quoted Spengler's view of man as a beast of prey, who "throbs with emotion when his knife cuts into the flesh of an enemy. . . . Every real man, even in modern cultural cities, sometimes feels within him the smouldering fire of this primitive soul" (10). Bukharin also quoted Hans Jöhst's call for a priest "who will spill blood, more blood and still more blood." By contrast, Bukharin declared, life in the Soviet Union was shaped by "rational perception and perceptional optimism" (28), "a creative perceptional optimism," though not the Encyclopedists' "abstractly schematic rationalism," with its antihistoricism and its theory of the immobility of the rational truth that had been given once and for all" (29). Implicitly, there is no such thing as a natural right.

According to Bukharin, hierarchy, not racism or statism, was the "central unifying idea" (= myth) of fascism. In this context, he mentioned Berdiaev's *The Philosophy of Inequality* (11) and pointed out that "Nietzsche wrote long ago, in his *Antichrist,* that *Hierarchy and the caste system* are simply a formulation of the highest law of life" (22). By contrast, the communist vision of the future "*involves the elimination of all social and political hierarchy in general* . . . a path of development directly opposite to the one which the fascists have in mind when they repeat phrases after Nietzsche about the necessity of the 'fervor [*pafos*] of distance where the common mortal is only a dumb stone, obligated to stick always in the same place'" (23). These lines can also be read as an Aesopian critique of Stalin's reinstitution of internal passports, which were denied to peasants.

Bureaucracy was a problem in the Soviet Union, Bukharin admitted, but the Communist Party was conducting a "sharp struggle" against it. In this context, he alluded to Max Weber's prediction (which was influenced by

30. For Nietzsche's influence on Weber, see Robert Eden, *Political Leadership and Nihilism: A Study of Weber and Nietzsche* (Tampa, 1983), and John Patrick Diggins, *Max Weber: Politics and the Spirit of Tragedy* (New York, 1966).

Nietzsche)[30] of a "bureaucratic-monocratic method of rule" in which the masses would be reduced to the condition of fellaheen (23). This prediction applied only to *state capitalism* (23) Bukharin asserted. (Authentic) communism would eliminate class oppression, foster "individuality," but not "individualism," and create complete human beings. Bukharin's assertion, "We destroyed exploitation as the basis of culture" (30), was not true but he hoped it would become so.

Bukharin's essay, "The Philosophy of a Cultured Philistine" (*Izvestiia*, December 8 and 10, 1935) was a lengthy review of Berdiaev's book, *The Fate of Man in the Modern World* (*Sud'ba cheloveka v sovremennom mire*, 1934). Berdiaev called Nazi Germany and the Soviet Union the "two Leviathans" and charged that both societies dehumanized people, attributing that dehumanization to the influence of Nietzsche and Marx. "How can one unite Nietzsche and Marx?" Bukharin asked rhetorically. His answer was: by positing naturalism and technologism as their link. By "naturalism," Bukharin explained, Berdiaev meant an emphasis on the physiological aspects of human existence, on food and sex. But communism was not gross naturalism; it addressed spiritual as well as physiological needs. Berdiaev failed to distinguish between "soulless" capitalist technology and liberating socialist technology; instead he blamed "all powerful technology" for dehumanization. The evil, however, was neither in technology, nor in large-scale organizations, but in "the idea of violence, of coercion as a permanent method of exercising power" and in the "real gulf between . . . a small group of ruling exploiters and the exploited masses." In the fascist total state, the dehumanization of the masses was in direct proportion to the glorification of the Leader, and three ethical norms prevailed: "devotion to the 'nation' or to the 'state,' 'loyalty to the Leader,' and the 'spirit of the barracks'" (arguably, he meant Stalinism as well as fascism).

Bukharin's last published article, "The Routes of History, Thoughts Aloud" (*Izvestiia,* July 6, 1936), warned of an approaching conflict with Germany and urged Soviet citizens to remain loyal to their ideals and believe in the eventual victory of socialism. "Fascist regimes" (in which he seemed to include Stalinism), were doomed by a "paradox of history." For them the masses were "untermenschen," "subhumans," "inferior." But the masses had already entered the historical arena; there was no way they could be driven completely underground. The illusion of mass participation would be exposed, to be followed by real mass participation. Already ordinary people were ceasing to be "mere *instrumenta vocalia,*" instruments with voices as slaves in ancient Rome were called, and were becoming conscious, self-governing personalities. In other words, the Leviathan state was a nightmare from which people would soon awake. The Nazi (and Stalinist) appropriation of Nietzsche so horrified Bukharin that he associated Nietzsche solely with elitism, racism, militarism, and brutality. He expressed similar views in his *Prison Notebooks*. The lines from his poem "The Mad Prophet (Nietzsche)" bear repeating.

> All Zarathustra's aphorisms
> And the virgin soil of paradoxes
> Elegantly-subtle sophistries,—
> All turned into blood.[31]

Apparently, Bukharin regretted having been captivated by Nietzsche's eloquence. But he never openly challenged Stalinism, nor did he ever question his Hegelian-Marxist historicism and its tenet that sacrifice is necessary for progress.

After 1936 the usefulness of Nietzsche as an Aesopian guide to Soviet policy diminished, perhaps because the parallels between Stalinism and Nazism were too obvious. References to Nietzsche petered out in 1937–38 and disappeared while the Nazi-Soviet pact was in force (1939–41). During the Great Patriotic War, Nietzsche was once again coupled with fascism (really Nazism). For example: "The philosophy of Nietzsche is first of all a philosophy of inequality, exploitation, aggression. In the realization of Nietzsche's precepts, fascist Germany beheld its historical mission."[32] If not for the war, Nietzsche might have become a nonperson like purged Old Bolsheviks. Nazi and Soviet propaganda led many people, inside and outside the Soviet Union to associate Nietzsche only with Nazism. That Nietzsche was a source of the Stalin Cult and its complements never occurred to them.

---

31. Nikolai Bukharin, "Bezymnyi prorok (F. Nitsshe)," *Tiuremnye rukopisi* (Prison notebooks), ed. Genadii Bordiugov and Stephen Cohen (Moscow, 1996), 365.

32. B. Bykhovskii, "Nitsshe i fashizm," *Pod znamenem marksizma*, nos. 8–9 (1942): 115. This article might have been intended to cut short attempts to distinguish between Nietzsche's philosophy and fascism. In the previous issue, D. Zaslavskii (in "Razboinynych'ia moral': Fashistskih rabovladel'tsem") had said that Germans repeat Nietzsche's aphorisms, but few have read him because their educational level is too low; they cannot understand his complex and paradoxical ideas. Moreover, Nietzsche was not a fascist. He liked classical French literature and culture, considerd French culture superior to German, esteemed the Russian *narod* and opposed anti-Semitism.

THIRTEEN

The Stalin Cult and Its Complements

And how many new gods are still possible!
—*WP,* 534

We have seen the man-god (alias the superman) in
action.   —Nadezhda
                    Mandelstam, *Hope Abandoned*

The Stalin Cult emerged in late 1929 and became the apex of an elaborate civil religion between 1934 and 1939, with lesser cult figures and a sacred text: *The History of the Communist Party of the Soviet Union (Bolsheviks): Short Course* (1938, English edition 1939). Stalin's image was everywhere. He was routinely described as all-knowing, all-powerful, and the object of his people's boundless veneration and love. Theatricalized mass meetings expressed the extent and enthusiasm of Stalin's popular support. Trappings of the Cult itself included Nietzschean, Christian, Russian, and Marxist motifs. Stalin was an Apollonian image (the visual representation of the myth) and a Superman. He was also an icon and a savior, a new Autocrat, the vehicle of a great historical force, and the expression of the people's will.

That the Stalin Cult built on the Lenin Cult is well known. Stalin's cult-builders also followed the progression of the

Mussolini and Hitler Cults, which the elaborated Stalin Cult was to intended to counter. The cult of Soviet heroes, instituted in 1934, set them off against the Nazi version of a Nietzschean hero. *The Short Course* glorified Stalin; it also served to justify the purges and, in a limited way, as a counterpart to *Mein Kampf.* Also nourishing the Stalin Cult (and the Hitler Cult) were residues of the turn of the century occult revival.[1] Propagandists in both societies invested the Leader with magical powers.

When the Stalin Cult emerged, the cult of Il Duce was already in full bloom and the Lenin Cult was one of its models. Propagandist inflation of Mussolini's actions and speeches began in 1925 and was continuous and pervasive. Gorky admired Mussolini's energy and said (claiming to quote Trotsky), "Mussolini has made a revolution; he is our best student."[2] Radek witnessed, and learned from, the construction of the Hitler Cult in Germany. Cult-builders in all three societies used iconography, the printed word, and the new medium of radio. To reach the many Italians who did not have radios, Mussolini had loudspeakers installed in the piazzas, a practice D'Annunzio initiated while dictator of Fiume. Goebbels had inexpensive radios manufactured so that each German home could own one. Relatively few Soviet citizens had their own radios but radios (or loudspeakers) were standard equipment at the workplace.

Symbols and rituals celebrated the Leader and his heroic disciples in ways that fit the particular society's historical, cultural, and religious legacy, its doctrinal requirements, and the dictator's personal style. Hitler was presented as the savior of Germany and the epitome of the Aryan Superman. Mussolini was the restorer of Roman greatness, heir to the Caesars, and a Hegelian "world-historical individual." Soviet propagandists described Stalin in superhuman terms, even while emphasizing his modesty. "It is people who make history," Stalin told the journalist Emil Ludwig, "but they do so only to the extent that they correctly understand the conditions that they have found ready-made and only to the extent that they understand how to change these conditions. . . . Marxism has never denied the role of heroes. On the contrary, it admits that they play a considerable role, but with the reservations I have just made" (*SW,* 13:107–8). Implicitly, Stalin was an example.

Stalin's calm, impassive public image; his rare, stage-managed public appearances; and his orderly speeches—question and answer, each point carefully laid out—were notably different than Hitler's hysterical ravings and Mussolini's gesticulating bombast. Stalin and Hitler were secretive about their private lives. Mussolini's amorous exploits were public knowledge. He had himself photographed bare-chested in a Herculean pose to demonstrate his physical strength and his affinity with manual laborers. It is difficult to

---

1. See Rosenthal, "Political Implications," in Rosenthal, *Occult.*
2. Quoted in Falasca-Zamponi, *Fascist Spectacle,* 51.

even imagine Hitler or Stalin in that pose. Hitler once said that he never married, because if he did German women would cease to fantasize about him as their lover. Soviet propagandists extolled Stalin as a loving father, the head of the "great Soviet family." The kinship model underscores the return of hierarchy and the taming of the futurist cult of youth, for these sons will never displace this father. The emphasis on sons infantilized the population vis-à-vis the government and was intended to retard individuation.[3]

The Stalin Cult

The Stalin cult developed in stages. In the 1920s, streets, factories, collective farms, and entire cities were named after Politburo members. Tsaritsyn became Stalingrad in 1925. As Stalin packed the Party with his supporters, tributes to him became ever more effusive; the "leader" (*vozhd'*) was genuinely popular among the rank and file; they thought of him as one of them, partly because of his "toughness" and his plain, even crude, speech. Robert Tucker has shown how Stalin used the Lenin Cult to position himself as Lenin's rightful heir.[4] That goal accomplished, between 1933 and 1936 Stalin elevated himself above the Party. Only in the third stage, 1936–53, was he described in superhuman terms. I do not argue that Stalin set out to be the new god. Rather, as the French say, appetite comes with eating. But even gourmands can eat only so much; the "will to power" is insatiable. At all stages, propagandists aroused passionate love for the Great Leader and passionate hatred for designated enemies, using techniques gleaned from three decades of experience in bypassing the rational intellect.

Initially, the Stalin Cult was a way to mobilize the masses around the Party and its Great Leader at a time of extreme confusion and chaos, conceal differences of opinion within the Party, and solidify Stalin's victory over the Party's "right." Proselytizers of the new Cult included true believers and opportunists eager to rise by flattering "the boss" or use his already considerable power to remove competitors. Stalin was viewed as first among equals and as a tough but effective taskmaster, not as a god. In the first half of 1929, photos of Stalin became front-page items. Throughout the year, the press trumpeted his "wise and firm" leadership of the struggle to build socialism.

On December 21, 1929, *Pravda* and *Izvestiia* commemorated Stalin's birthday with articles praising him as "Lenin's most reliable aide," Lenin's successor as "leader and boss of the party," and the warrior-hero who defended Petrograd during the Civil War (erasing Trotsky's role), master-

3. Günther, *Der sozialistische Übermensch*, 181–83.
4. Robert Tucker, *Stalin as Revolutionary* (New York, 1973), 462–87.

mind of the victory over the White army general Denikin, and originator of the idea for the celebrated First Cavalry Army. These tributes played into Stalin's image of himself as the heroic leader of a band of faithful warriors, which derived from Georgian concepts of leadership—yet another example of the bonding of Nietzschean and indigenous ideas. In addition to being a warrior-hero, Stalin was the "blazing champion of the idea of industrialization," the leader of the international proletariat, and the greatest living Marxist theoretician. He was "rock-hard," "iron-willed," "determined," "steadfast," "unbending," "strong," "brave," and "ruthless toward enemies." Soon after, a special birthday anthology, *Stalin,* was issued with articles by Kalinin, Kuibyshev, Kaganovich, Voroshilov, and Ordzhonikidze. Whether Stalin himself decided on the birthday articles, their subjects, and who would write them is not known.

Between 1929 and 1933 official listings of the Politburo placed Stalin's name first but maintained the standard practice of alphabetical order for the others. Initially, Stalin appeared alongside Lenin, but by 1933 he had upstaged Lenin through a campaign of conscious diminishment and standardization of the Lenin Cult. References to the "classical works of Marx, Engels, Lenin, and Stalin" became commonplace that year. Deviations from Stalin's interpretation of Marxism became treason to socialism, which he personified. Steadily, Stalin became the arbiter of virtually all areas of intellectual and cultural life.

Cult-building activities were stepped up in 1934. Their function at this point was not just to mobilize the masses but to conceal the gap between the promise and the results of the First Five-Year Plan, to raise Stalin to unattainable heights, thereby protecting him from criticism, to counter the Hitler Cult, and according to Roy Medvedev, "from the need to cover up the miscalculations, the mistakes, and the crimes that Stalin had committed, was committing, and was preparing to commit."[5] In a similar pattern, the full-blown Cult of Mao Zedong followed the debacle of the "Great Leap Forward" (1958–59) in which thirty million Chinese died of starvation.

Karl Radek's article, "Stalin, Architect of Soviet Society," published in *Pravda* on January 1, 1934, and reissued as a pamphlet in 225,000 copies, heaped extravagant praise on Stalin and set the stage for the grotesquely hyperinflated tributes that followed.[6] According to Georges Haupt, Radek's autobiography "gives the measure of his character: loquacious, extremely intelligent and sharp, unstable, clever and opportunist, leaving in the shade without a scruple that which does not flatter, and choosing the events in his

5. Medvedev, *Let History Judge,* 316–17.
6. Radek, "Stalin: Architect of Soviet Society," in *Portraits and Pamphlets,* 3–34. This volume contains selections from the two-volume Russian edition, *Portrety i pamfleti* (Moscow, 1933).

life which show him off to advantage."[7] Trotsky said that Radek was "indisputably one of the best Marxist journalists in the world," but his journalistic strength was his political weakness. "Radek exaggerates and goes too far. He measures in yards where he should be looking at inches."[8] These were ideal traits for a cult-builder. Radek moved in circles that were suffused with Nietzsche. Lunacharsky and Bukharin were his personal friends, and Larissa Reisner (who was on the board of Proletkult, by the way) was his lover.

Radek had been honing his cult-building skills for some time. In 1923, in a speech commemorating the twentieth anniversary of the Party, Radek extolled Lenin as "the personification of the will to revolution" (note the Nietzschean formulation) and "the Moses of the international proletariat."[9] In "Lev Trotsky, Organizer of Victory" (*Pravda,* March 14, 1923), he exalted Trotsky's exploits as head of the Red Army. For supporting Trotsky, Radek was expelled from the Party in 1927, but he publicly recanted and was reinstated in 1930. In "Feliks Dzerzhinsky" (1926), Radek eulogized the head Chekist for realizing that "any soft-heartedness" towards enemies of the revolution would only bring distress and suffering to millions. "If we can say that the masses will always think of Lenin as the brain of the revolution, Radek declared, "we can say that Dzerzhinsky will be remembered as its heart."[10] Privately, he told Victor Serge, "Felix died just in time. He was a dogmatist. He would not have shrunk from reddening his hands in our blood."[11] In "Larissa Reisner" he described his recently deceased lover as a prototype of the new woman—beautiful, intelligent, a Renaissance person and a "woman-warrior."[12]

Radek also wrote defamatory articles. The "wrecker" Leonid Ramzin, Radek said in 1930, was not just a "hireling" of the French Secret Service, his personal goal was to make the "engineer class" into a new dynasty of pharoahs, to be worshiped as gods. But these "pitiful" figures (Ramzin and his codefendants) were "not strong enough to struggle with us face to face. They could strike at us only by hiding in our institutions, and, like the reptiles they are, striking from behind . . . their behavior in court is that of crushed and squirming creatures of a lower order."[13]

7.   Haupt and Marie, *Makers of the Russian Revolution*, 379.

8.   Quoted in ibid., 383

9.   Radek, "Lenin," in *Portrety i pamfleti*, 1:29, 36.

10.   "Felix Dzerzhinski," in *Portraits and Pamphlets*, 107 and 110.

11.   Victor Serge, *Memoirs of a Revolutionary*, trans. Peter Sedgwick (Oxford, 1967), 221.

12.   "Larissa Reisner," in *Portraits and Pamphlets*, 260–74. For an equally laudatory portrait of Reisner, see Trotsky, *My Life*, 408–9. Radek dedicated the first volume of the Russian edition to her: "warrior and songbird of the proletarian revolution."

13.   "A Wrecker: Leonid Konstantinovitch Ramzin," in *Portraits and Pamphlets*, 217, 228–29. See also "The Struggle Between Two Worlds," 230–42, about the "wrecker" A. Fedotov. In the Russian edition, these articles are in the section titled "Demons" (*Besy*), 2:215–25 and 226–38.

As the Party expert on Germany, Radek accompanied Lenin to Brest-Litovsk, co-founded the Spartakus League and the German Communist Party, and was the Comintern representative there. In addition, Radek was the Communist architect of National Bolshevism, a movement that advocated socialism on the Soviet model, German-Russian cooperation, and an anti-Western orientation generally. The most prominent National Bolsheviks were Ernst Niekisch, Moeller von der Bruck (author of *The Third Reich* [1923], admirer of Merezhkovsky, and translator of Dostoevsky), Count Ernst Reventlow (a popularizer of the *Protocols of the Elders of Zion*), and Radek, despite his Jewish origin. Left-wing Nazis, such as Goebbels and the Strasser brothers (Otto and Gregor), were sympathetic to National Bolshevism.

German nationalists of various stripes fused the Nietzschean "mythos" with images of historical and folkloric German heroes in a mystique of transcendence and creative "becoming" that promised national regeneration through political power and will. One of their inspirations was Ernst Bertram's *Nietzsche, An Attempt at a Mythology* (*Nietzsche, Versuch einer Mythologie,* 1918), reprinted seven times between 1918 and 1929, which transmuted Nietzsche's life and thought into a nation-saving prophetic myth. Bertram was in turn influenced by his Jewish teacher Friedrich Gundolf (born Gundolffinger, 1880–1931), a practitioner of Nietzsche's "monumental history" and a member of the Nietzsche-worshiping Stefan George circle. Composed of writers with a variety of political views, the circle had an enormous impact on twentieth-century German historiography, poetry, and literary criticism. The mission of history writing, the members believed, was legend-making (= myth-creation), and only great men were worth writing about. Gundolf is best known for his monumental biographies of the Caesars, whom he exalted as symbols of a unifying force in a fragmented world. Gundolf's most famous student was Goebbels, the primary creator of the Hitler Cult and a co-creator of the Schlageter Cult.

Radek was not a member of the George circle, of course, but his propaganda was informed by its mythic/cultic orientation. In 1923, Radek latched onto the Schlageter cult in the hope of appealing to "everyone who is suffering in Germany," the middle class as well as the proletariat, and thereby trigger the longed-for "German October" (a communist revolution). On June 21, at an open session of the executive committee of the Comintern, Radek said that in 1920 National Bolshevism was an alliance to save the generals (he had invited them to join the communists in battling the Treaty of Versailles), but now the movement was striving for the salvation of the German people from the Entente; therefore, "the strong emphasis on the nation in Germany is a revolutionary act." Two days later, Clara Zetkin urged the working class to organize for self-defense against fascism. Taking her speech as his cue, Radek declared that he could not follow her all the way, because he had before his eyes, "the corpse of a German fascist, our class enemy, condemned and shot . . . by French imperialism." Schlageter was a "courageous and brave soldier of the counterrevolution [who] deserves recognition from us who are soldiers of the revolution," because he sincerely believed that he was serving the German people. Schlageter's admirers should take up his struggle against the capitalist powers who are striving to enslave the German and the Russian people alike. Instead being "wanderers in the void" (the title of a best-selling novel), Schlageter's admirers would be "wanderers into a better future for all mankind."[14] The executive committee endorsed Radek's strategy and the German communist newspaper *Rote Fahne* praised it. Goebbels appreciated Radek's speech; Rosenberg denigrated it as a "Jewish swindle."

Radek's "Schlageter strategy" produced mass meetings organized by the German Communist Party that were publicized by political broadsides bearing a red star and a swastika. A pamphlet on Schlageter included Radek's speech, articles by Moeller and Reventlow, and a postscript by Fröhlich, the communist leader. When Reventlow wanted to comment on Fröhlich's article, he was given space in *Rote Fahne*. Goebbels did not participate in the third attempt to popularize National Bolshevism in 1930 because Hitler opposed it. Apparently Radek was not involved in that attempt, but one cannot be sure; the full story of his relations with German nationalists, including left-wing Nazis, is yet to be told. He followed developments in National Bolshevism and mentioned the travails of the Strasser brothers (both were purged from the Nazi Party) in his reports from Germany, which parroted the Party line that social democracy is social fascism. In 1933, Radek was involved in secret diplomacy between the Soviet Union and Nazi Germany, reporting directly to Stalin.[15]

Radek's article "Hitler" (1932) was notable, not for its class analysis, which was boilerplate Marxism (Hitler was the "hero of the petite bourgeoisie" and "the hireling of monopoly capital"), but for going beyond socioeconomic categories to stress the effectiveness of Nazi propaganda. His Aesopian message was that the Soviet Union must match it. Describing the mass appeal of "the idea of a hero savior," the "electric" atmosphere of Nazi mass meetings, and the substitution of "magical formulas" for concrete proposals, Radek noted that the Nazis had "their own agitprop," formulated by a "cadre of propaganda specialists." The Nazis did not promise that the

---

14. Karl Radek, "Leo Shlageter; bredushchii v nichto," in *Portrety i pamfleti*, 1:137–42. See also *Schlageter, Eine Auseinandersetzung*, ed. Count Reventlov, Moeller von den Bruck, and Paul Froelich; Klemens von Klemperer, "Towards a Fourth Reich? The History of National Bolshevism in Germany," *Review of Politics* 13, no. 2 (April 1951): 191–210; Marie Louise Goldbach, *Karl Radek und die deutsch-sowjetischen Bezeihungen 1918–1923* (Bonn, 1973); E. Gnedin, *Iz istorii otnoshenii mezhdu SSSR i fashistskoi Germanii* (New York, 1977); Nekrich, *Pariahs*, 67–85; Louis Dupeux, "National Bolschewismus in Deutschland 1919–33," 193–98; and Laqueur, *Russia and Germany*, passim.

15. Tucker, *Stalin in Power*, 236; Nekrich, *Pariahs*, 69, 76.

masses would direct state policy, Radek noted. Quite the contrary, "they put into the head of the masses, that it must be decided by a savior, a hero, a boss, selected by God and by fate. The masses must blindly follow his will, because only he can know the final goals of the movement and the necessary path." Nazi propaganda promised the masses the revolution they needed and wanted even though, as the "hireling of monopoly capital," Hitler would betray them later on. Once in power, he would embark on a course of international expansion, for such is the nature of monopoly capital. The Social Democrats and the Catholic Center Party were incapable of defeating Hitler; they were too conservative.[16] Like Bukharin, Radek realized that "German fascism" contained new elements and that Hitler had to be taken seriously.

Radek's magnification of Stalin served a counterpoint to the burgeoning Hitler cult. The title of Radek's article echoed Hitler's description of himself as the architect of Nazi Germany. Whether the idea for the article was Radek's or Stalin's is not known. Extolling Stalin as Lenin's best pupil, the model of the Leninist Party, "bone of its bone, blood of its blood" (13), Radek lauded Stalin's leadership of the revolutionary movement, his "creative Marxism" (19), his solution of ethnic conflicts that had divided workers in Transcaucasia, and his successful campaign to build socialism.[17] Radek ridiculed Bukharin's idea that peasants would "grow into" socialism and affirmed that Stalin was a better leader than Trotsky. Stalin translates "thought into deed" by his tremendous will, determination, power, and imagination, and in the light of his extensive personal experience. Stalin "knew that a great human ant-hill [note Radek's inversion of Dostoevsky's metaphor for socialism in *Notes From Underground*] would arise and that its labors would change the face of the mountains and the valleys, of the rivers and the seas of the Soviet Union." Stalin inspired the "great march forward of the peoples to socialism" (25). He accomplished fifty years work in five years of heroic effort. "But the pace, the intensity of the Five-Year-Plan were not arbitrarily selected by Stalin. The stern commands from the bridge, the orders to keep a full head of steam, the strict orders that no one was to leave his post, the sleepless nights at General Headquarters—all this was the result of the far-sightedness of the leader of the revolution and of his immediate comrades in arms" (32). Although the warrior-hero image was dominant, Radek introduced a cosmic note when he asserted that during the First Five-Year Plan "socialism acquired wings . . . when on May Day of 1932, hundreds of aeroplanes soared over Red Square and blotted out the sun; the roar of their engines seemed to be singing the chorus of Lenin's favorite song:

16. Radek, "Gitler," in *Portrety i pamflety*, 2: 353–76, especially 364–68.

17. Jim Tuck says that Radek meant the article to be a satire, told Stalin so, and was purged for that reason. *Engine of Mischief* (Greenwood, Conn., 1988), 67–71, 110, 121, 128. Even if Tuck is correct (which I doubt) Radek's article was taken literally.

'Never, no never, shall communists be slaves'" (33). Put differently, the aeroplanes achieved a "victory over the sun."

Stalin scheduled his speech to the Congress of Victors for January 27, 1934—the same time as his oath to Lenin ten years before. On January 26, *Izvestiia* published Radek's article "An Oath Fulfilled." This Congress set a new high point in the adulation of Stalin. Nearly every speaker dwelled on Stalin's greatness and genius. Bukharin praised him as the field marshal of the proletarian forces, the best of the best. Kamenev predicted that the era in which we live will be known to history as the era of Stalin, just as the preceding era entered history as the era of Lenin. Even more extravagant encomiums to Stalin followed and became the norm. *Literary Gazette* claimed that "Stalin is a direct successor to Goethe and to all the great spirits in history."[18] Stalin was the most profound critic of Hegel, and he spoke the best Russian (despite his Georgian accent). In a subsequent article on the Stalin Constitution (*Izvestiia,* July 7, 1936) Radek proclaimed, "the architect of socialist society has become the builder of socialist democracy."

Illustrated articles in *Art* guided painters on how to portray Lenin and Stalin. "On Portraits of Leaders" (1935, no. 1) featured a full-page portrait of Lenin (ibid., 5), followed by a full-page portrait of Stalin (6) in a Napoleonic pose, which became a trope after the war. "Lenin in Portraits, 1933–37" (1937, no. 6), "New Portraits of Comrade Stalin" (ibid., 59–68), and "Characteristics of the Art of the Epoch of Stalin" (ibid., 69–79) provided further guidance. Stalin's sixtieth birthday was the occasion for similar articles (*Art,* 1939, no. 6). Over half the 1947 winners of the Stalin prize were portraits of the Soviet leadership; in 1949, thirteen of the winning portraits were of Stalin.[19]

Soviet photomontage provides a capsule history of the Stalin Cult. In the first stage, Stalin or a portrait of Stalin was in the background, for the subject was the collective—groups of workers or peasants or political activists. In Nietzschean terms, Stalin was part of a chorus. Soon after, he moved to front and center, still the same height as the rest of the actors, or only slightly taller, but wearing distinctive clothes. Then he was portrayed as a Superman towering over an industrial landscape or presiding over tiny workers arrayed in military columns with airplanes and dirigibles flying overhead.[20] In a parallel development, Stalin was depicted next to Lenin, sometimes even in his shadow, then as Lenin's equal, and finally as the dominant figure in the montage. Bogus documentation "showed" Stalin alongside Lenin at key episodes

18. Quoted in Gerd Koenen, *Die grossen Gesänge—Lenin, Stalin, Mao Tse-tung: Führer Kulte und Heldenmythen des 20. Jahrhunderts* (Frankfurt am Main, 1991), 114.

19. Golomstock, "Problems in the Study of Stalinist Culture," in Günther, *Culture of the Stalin Period,* 114.

20. Illustration in Tupitsyn, "Superman Imagery," in *NSC,* 304.

of Bolshevik history, or supervising a construction project he may never have visited, or inspiring soldiers at the front even though he spent the most of the war in Moscow. Photographs were retouched to eliminate Trotsky and other purged Bolsheviks. Photomontage was an ideal vehicle for such "corrections." Painters "corrected" history too. "The History of the Red Army in Artistic Images" (*Art,* 1933, no. 4) "documented" Stalin's inspirational role. Other paintings portrayed workers and peasants reverently listening to him. Photographs of new industrial sites put Stalin in the picture.

The second stage of the Stalin cult shaded into the third. Soviet propagandists turned Stalin into a Superman (or man-god) sometime in 1936, the year that the threshold to the full-blown Hitler Cult was crossed. According to Ian Kershaw, the function of the constructed Hitler myth was to counter the centrifugal forces within the Hitler movement and establish a consensus among the German people. The greater the gap between promise and fulfillment, the greater was the functional necessity for the reification and ritualization of the myth of Hitler as Germany's savior.[21] This applies to the Stalin Cult as well.

Cult-builders in both societies depicted the Leader as a Superman-Savior who would take care of "his" people and lead them to an earthly paradise, a far cry from Nietzsche's values. He did envision an "artist-tyrant," however. Hitler saw himself in that role; Stalin probably did too. In both societies, the Leader was the star in a new theatricalization of life. In Ivanov's vision of a cultic theater, strong passional bonds connected the performers to one another and to a mystical beyond. In Stalin's version, the passional bonds went primarily from citizens to the Leader, though they also served to inculcate a sense of "we" and "they." The "we" could be a factory, a village, an organization, or the entire Soviet people; the "they" were outsiders and designated enemies.

The purge of the Sturmabteilung (SA, "Brownshirts") preceded the full-blown Hitler Cult. The elaborated Stalin cult preceded and accompanied the Great Purge. To justify his decision to eliminate the Old Bolsheviks, purge the leadership strata of the Party, and subject the entire Soviet Union to a reign of terror, Stalin had to invent conspiracies that were so sophisticated, so clever, and so insidious that only an omniscient Superman could see them. In addition to inventing conspiracies, Stalin imagined countless others, and his paranoia grew over time. The more people he purged, the more enemies he thought he had. Some of Stalin's cronies fed his paranoia to increase their own power and to eliminate rivals. On July 20, 1936, two months before Yezhov replaced Yagoda as head of the NKVD, *Pravda* and *Izvestiia* commemorated the tenth anniversary of Dzerzhinsky's death, an ominous portent. Radek's contribution, in *Izvestiia,* was titled "A True Son of the Party."

21. Ian Kershaw, *The Hitler Myth* (Oxford, 1987), 80–83; also see 4 and 69.

Bukharin was still the editor but how much control, if any, he exercised is not known. By then Stalin was managing his own cult-building activities. He did not do all the work himself, of course, but he laid out the themes and supervised their implementation. In 1938, a competition for the designer of a statue of Dzerzhinsky was announced.

Stalin's name achieved god-like status in 1936. The writer Vera Inber was not the first to surround it with a mystical aura or invest it with magical powers, but her article "The Name of Stalin" (*Literary Gazette,* August 10, 1936) institutionalized the practice. Stalin's name was bestowed on towns, villages, industrial plants, and collective farms. Heroes in all areas of Soviet life claimed that Stalin's name inspired their feats. Valery Chkalov, first Russian aviator to fly over the North Pole, asserted that his crew flew the entire route "with Stalin's name in our hearts"; where Stalin is "there is no darkness, there is only bright sunshine."[22] Earlier panegyrics had been Stalin-centered, but not in the same way. Now Stalin's countenance, his voice, his word, his look, were held to have magical and miraculous powers. Religious terms such as "sacred" and "sin," new for Soviet culture, entered the vocabulary. Empirical reality was covered over by a mystical haze. In painting, the beatific effect was achieved by using pastels rather than red and other bold colors, and depicting Stalin in a white uniform gazing out into eternity in an immobile pose against a light blue sky. The iconographic conflation was Stalin = socialism = Soviet Union, a new holy trinity.

In July 1938, *Under the Banner of Marxism* published an article titled "Lenin's Struggle Against God-building," yet another example of denouncing an idea while covertly appropriating it.[23] The author, A. Tsaritsyn, mythologized Lenin's "struggle" against Lunacharsky, "the machist Bogdanov," and Bazarov, and quoted Lenin's letters to Gorky, but not Gorky's letters to Lenin. Tsaritsyn said only that Gorky, "that great author of the working class, a clear enemy of liberalism, philistinism, and mysticism . . . fell under" Bogdanov's and Lunacharsky's influence for a short time, but Lenin "with great tact" convinced him that Bogdanov's philosophy was reactionary (40). (Bogdanov and Gorky did have a falling-out but it was mainly for personal reasons.) The same issue had two articles about Marx's friend Dietzgen, another influence on God-building. The following December, in an article titled "The Atheism of Marxist-Leninist Teaching," Iaroslavsky recounted Lenin's battle against the God-builders (9–12), not just Bogdanov and Lunacharsky, but Gorky as well; Gorky, however, "admitted his mistake." Another article (November 1938) discussed the "reactionary philosophy of Machism" and the influence of Bogdanov's Tektology on the "fascist hireling" Bukharin.[24]

22. "Rech' tovarishcha Chkalova," *Pravda,* August 13, 1938, p. 1.
23. A. Tsaritsyn, "Bor'ba Lenina s bogostroitel'stvom," *Pod znamenem marksizma,* 1938, no. 7:27–46.
24. A. Shcheglov, "Reaktsionnaia filosofiia makhizm i ee korni," *Pod znamenem marksizma* 1938, no. 11:118, 130.

Stalin's dictums were endlessly repeated: first "tempo decides everything," then, "technology decides everything"; then "cadres decide everything." There were slogans and formulas for all areas of Soviet life. "They provided a definite solution for *everything*, determining what was the *most* valuable, the *most* important."[25] Drumming out independent thought, they became mantras casting a spell over those who shouted them, a living example of "the magic of words." Stalin delivered his speeches in a monotone, using repetition to hammer in the message in a manner akin to hypnotic suggestion.

Stalin's status as the new god was indicated by his position vis-à-vis other people. Stalin looks down, but they look up. Sometimes serious, sometimes smiling, he never laughs. Apollo is serene. Moreover, as Merezhkovsky frequently noted, Jesus never laughed; He only smiled. Nietzsche observed that "in Germany higher men . . . do not laugh" (*GS*, 202), meaning this as a criticism, but his observation can also be taken prescriptively: a would-be "higher man" must not laugh. No photograph of Stalin could be published without prior approval by him or his secretary. He liked to be shown in his soldier's uniform as the personification of "proletarian sternness" (a counterpart to Roman sternness) with a child on his lap. After the war, Stalin posed in his generalissimo's uniform as the great military leader.

Bakhtin's carnival laughter challenged this pontificating solemnity. His study of Rabelais reflects the tormenting times in which it was written. Although Rabelais was not a stand-in for Nietzsche, Bakhtin was utilizing the Nietzschean weapon of laughter: "One kills, not by anger but by laughter" (*Z*, 324). For Bakhtin, "terror is conquered by laughter"; "fear is defeated by laughter"; "laughter defeats power"; "laughter purifies from dogmatism"; and "only equals laugh."[26] In "Epic and Hero" (1940), Bakhtin said that there is "nothing for memory and tradition to do. One ridicules in order to forget."[27]

Monumental History, Stalin-Style

In *The Advantage and Disadvantage of History for Life,* a key text for futurists and formalists, Nietzsche observed: "Whenever the monumental vision of the past *rules* over the other ways of looking at the past, I mean the antiquarian and the critical, the past itself suffers *damage:* very great portions of the past are forgotten and despised, and flow away like a grey uninterrupted flood and only single embellished facts stand out as islands: there

---

25. Heller, *Cogs in a Wheel,* 237.
26. Bakhtin, *Rabelais and His World* (Cambridge, Mass., 1968), 59, 68, 91, 92, 94, 123, 336, 394.
27. Quoted in Gary Saul Morson and Caryl Emerson, *Mikhail Bakhtin* (Stanford, 1990), 442.

seems to be something unnatural and wondrous about the rare persons who become visible at all" (*H*, 17). Monumental history is a form of myth-creation. As such, it was a useful device for glorifying Stalin, despite important differences in Marxist and Nietzschean conceptions of time.

Soon after Stalin made himself the arbiter of Party history in 1931, Party publications began printing early Staliniana, and historians embarked on the creation of a "hyphenate cult of an infallible Lenin-Stalin" that highlighted the Stalin-related aspects of Lenin's life and work and cast others in the shadows.[28] Having falsely established Stalin's role in the Bolshevik Revolution and Civil War, the glorifiers created an equally false legend of Stalin as the Lenin of the Caucasus. As the Party chief of Transcaucasia, Beria played a key role in this process.[29] Working on the basis of a speech that Beria gave in January 1934, a group of Georgian historians produced a book called *On the History of the Bolshevik Organizations in Transcaucasia*. Soon after, they were shot, and Beria claimed authorship. The work, which contained outright fabrications, was published in installments in *Pravda* from July 29 to August 5, 1935, and simultaneously, as a book in 100,000 copies. Subsequent editions further embellished Stalin's role, for with the Old Bolsheviks out of the way, Beria was free to distort history even more. The 1949 edition, which was published in English and other foreign languages, was quite different from the 1935 one, even more fanciful. Another book, Voroshilov's *Stalin and the Red Army* (1937), depicted Stalin as its creator.

The Short Course was written according to Stalin's instructions, and he supervised the project from start to finish.[30] Almost forty-three million copies in sixty-seven languages were published in Stalin's lifetime. Treating the history of Communist Party as a great and glorious epic, it showed that the Party "gained strength and became tempered" in revolutionary struggle. Study of Bolshevism's "heroic history . . . strengthens our certainty of the ultimate victory of the great cause of the Party of Lenin-Stalin, the victory of Communism throughout the world" (1–2).

Transforming futurist ideas on "forgetting" history altogether to "forgetting" particular events or persons and misreporting or inventing other events in a new "created legend," to borrow Sologub's term, the *Short Course* demonized purged Bolsheviks and featured an infallible Lenin fighting alone, then with Stalin, and then Stalin alone fighting opportunists, left and right deviationists, and traitors in his victorious struggle to build socialism. Those who could have contradicted Stalin's version of Party history were dead. Passages such as the following are typical: "An effective contribution to the ideological defeat of Trotskyism and to the defense of Leninism was Comrade Stalin's theoretical work *The Foundations of Leninism,* published in 1924.

---

28. Tucker, *Stalin in Power*, 160.
29. Ibid., 333; Amy Knight, *Beria* (Princeton, 1993), 54–64.
30. Tucker, *Stalin in Power*, 532–36; Volkogonov, *Stalin*, 221.

This book is a masterly exposition and a weighty theoretical substantiation of Leninism. It was, and is today, a trenchant weapon of Marxist-Leninist theory in the hands of Bolsheviks all over the world" (267). Purged Bolsheviks were called "Trotsky-Bukharin fiends," "Whiteguard pygmies," "Whiteguard insects," "useless rubbish," "traitors," and "Judases" master-minding a vast, decades-long, conspiracy against Lenin, the Party, and the Soviet state in league with the espionage services of bourgeois states. Most recently, they tried to help Germany and Japan "dismember and destroy" the Soviet Union. "These contemptible lackeys of the fascists forget that the Soviet people had only to move a finger, and not a trace of them would be left" (347). The diminutive size and weakness of the purged Bolsheviks was the obverse of the equation of "super" with enormous size and great strength. The unabashedly didactic conclusion (353–63) comprised six points, each one prefaced by the query, "What does the history of the C.P.S.U. (B.) teach us?" The second point emphasized the importance of mastering the substance of Marxist-Leninist theory, applying it to the practical problems of the revolutionary movement, and not being overawed by the letter (355–58). Stalin decided the substance, of course. Earlier histories of the Party, including Iaroslavsky's, were withdrawn from circulation.

The Short Course included a denunciation of Bogdanov, Lunacharsky, and their allies (except Gorky).

> They launched their "criticism" simultaneously against the philosophical foundations of Marxist theory, *i.e.*, against dialectical materialism, and against the fundamental Marxist principles of historical science, *i.e.*, against historical materialism. This criticism differed from the usual criticism in that it was not conducted openly and squarely, but in a veiled and hypocritical form under the guide of "defending" the fundamental positions of Marxism. . . . Some of the intellectuals who had deserted Marxism went so far as to advocate the foundations of a new religion (these were known as "godseekers" and "godbuilders"). (102–3)

The book then exalted Lenin's *Materialism and Empiriocriticism* and explained the difference between dialectical materialism and historical materialism.

Stalin, Molotov, and Zhdanov were the collective editors of *The Short Course,* supervising a brigade of writers, but the press praised only Stalin. To give one example, from an article titled "A Powerful Ideological Weapon of Bolshevism," published in *Science and Life* (*Nauka i zhizn'*) in 1938.

> The Stalinist style, Stalinist dialectical logic—here is what is characteristic of the History of the VKP(b) in particular for its theoretical parts. Only a man knowing completely the works of the classics of

Marxism Leninism, mastering completely the dialectical methods and standing at the top of contemporary advanced science, understanding the depth of all laws of the development of science and seeing further than all the historical fates of humanity, could so deeply and clearly set forth the theoretical bases of the Marxist-Leninist Party, dialectical and historical materialism.[31]

In other words, Stalin was an omniscient, superhuman force. *The Short Course* was the basis of a Union-wide system of political education. Aspirants to Party membership had to learn the entire book by heart, which made it a kind of fundamentalist bible. The English translation comes to over 350 pages.

Writers and artists engaged in monumental history too. A spate of works commemorating the twentieth anniversary of the Revolution (1937) portrayed Stalin as its mastermind. In the film *Lenin in October* (1937), Stalin guides Lenin, and Lenin denounces Trotsky, Zinoviev, and Kamenev as strikebreakers of the Revolution and total traitors. Plays such as Pogodin's *Man with a Gun* (1937), Aleksei Tolstoi's *Bread* (1937), Vsevolod Ivanov's *Parkhomenko* (1938), and Vyshnevsky's *The Unforgettable Year 1919* (1949, film version 1952) "corrected" history in Stalin's favor. In "Lenin in Gorky," a poem about Stalin's visit to the ailing Lenin, Stalin assures Lenin that all is well; the last lines are: "Titans gave birth to the era / Titans create the era." The Titans, of course, were Stalin and Lenin. Paradoxically, in 1938, claiming modesty, Stalin denied permission to publish *Tales About Stalin's Childhood* and suggested that it be burnt.

Celebrations for Stalin's sixtieth birthday (1939) were more extensive and elaborate than the 1929 observances. To guide writers of birthday greetings, a sixteen-page bibliography of suggested references titled *In Commemorating the Sixtieth Anniversary of J. V. Stalin: What to Write About the Life and Activities of Comrade Stalin* was published. The chapter titles indicate this project's monumental function: "The Revolutionary Decades of Comrade Stalin in the Transcaucasus," "Comrade Stalin in the Period of Preparation and Construction of the October Revolution," "The Heroic Struggle of Comrade Stalin on the Front of the Civil War," "Stalin—The Great Organizer of the Victory of Socialism in Our Country," "Stalin—the Great Continuer of the Teachings of Marx, Engels, and Lenin," "The Image of J. V. Stalin in Belles-lettres: Prose," and "The Image of Stalin in Belles-lettres: Poetry." Here, too, he was portrayed as an epic hero. Almost all the entries were written in 1937 or 1938. A pedagogical journal published a similar guide for children's letters to Stalin. The birthday issue of *Pravda,* enlarged from the usual eight pages to twelve, announced that Stalin stipends would be awarded

---

31. Quoted in Kiteme, "Cult of Stalin," 141.

for distinguished contributions in the sciences as well as in the arts.[32] Hitler and Mussolini established similar programs.

The day before Stalin's birthday, *Pravda* published an official biography, *Joseph Vissarionovich Stalin: A Short Biography,* prepared by the Marx-Engels-Lenin Institute. Millions of copies were published separately in Russian, in the major European languages (English edition, 1941), and in the languages of the Union Republics. According to the biography:

> Everybody is familiar with the cogent and invincible force of Stalin's logic, the crystal clarity of his mind, his iron will, his devotion to the Party, his ardent faith in the masses, and his love for the people. Everybody is familiar with his modesty, the simplicity of his manner, his consideration for people, and his merciless severity towards enemies of the people. Everybody is familiar with his intolerance of ostentation, of phrasemongers and windbags, of whiners and alarmists. Stalin is wise and deliberate in solving complex political questions where a thorough weighing of pros and cons is required. At the same time he is a supreme master of bold revolutionary decisions and sharp turns of policy.
>
> Stalin is the Lenin of today.[33]

Students assembled Stalin Museums. Workers attended lectures on Stalin's life and activities. The Red Army chorus gave concerts of songs about Stalin, and the Tretiakov Gallery organized an exhibition of paintings of him. The Comintern imposed the Stalin Cult on foreign Communist Parties, but non-Party intellectuals were also among the acolytes.

Celebrations for Stalin's seventieth birthday (1949) were more extravagant yet. Stalin was called the "sun of all the peoples," for the Soviet Union was now a global force. The original "Sun King," Louis XIV, had ruled only France. Vast tracts of the Soviet Union and Eastern Europe lay in ruins, there had been a terrible famine in 1946–47, and peasants were still underfed, but Stalin expended scarce resources on building monuments, many of them to himself.

The Stalin Cult was the summit of a series of mini-cults. Second-tier leaders such as Beria had cults of their own. There was a cult figure for just about every field of endeavor—Gorky in literature, Makarenko in education, Marr in linguistics, Pavlov in psychology, Stanislavsky in theater, and so on. Films were made about Gorky, Makarenko, and Pavlov.

---

32. Quoted in James Lee Heizer, "The Cult of Stalin, 1929–39" (Ph.D. diss., University of Kentucky, 1977), 150–51.
33. Quoted in ibid., 149–50.

The Cult of Soviet Heroes

Heroes and hero-worship have existed since time immemorial. The Stalinist variant exalted polar explorers, aviators, and super-achievers. The Cult of Soviet Heroes was instituted by the Decree on Heroes, published in *Izvestiia* on April 18, 1934. This cult complemented the Stalin cult by honoring individuals who personified qualities Stalin esteemed and who credited him with inspiring their exploits. In addition, this cult countered the Nazi cult of heroes and trumpeted Soviet achievements abroad. *Izvestiia* explained that Soviet Heroes were neither gods, nor fascist führers, nor blond beasts, "but the best of the Soviet people . . . in our country the hero is a great creative force," and dubbed Nietzsche and the Social Darwinist Herbert Spencer (1820–1903) the "intellectual forebears of the fascist hero" (despite Spencer's critique of the state). Three days later, *Izvestiia* published a list of the heroes awarded the Order of Lenin and the Order of the Red Star and announced plans for a monument to the heroes of the Cheliuskin expedition. These heroes democratized the hero-ideal; they were living proof that in the words of a Soviet popular song, "Here with us anyone can be a hero." Gorky referred to an entire "generation of heroes."[34] Hans Günther distinguished between the hero of the "old romantics," who determines his own path, and the totalitarian hero, who follows the path laid out by the Leader, for this hero's function is to activate and dramatize the myth.[35] Nietzsche probably would have considered the Soviet (and the Nazi) heroes slavish. The Soviet hero had to thank Stalin for everything. Nietzsche's Superman does not say "thank you," neither do his "higher men."

Subsequent newspaper and journal articles contrasted the heroic creators of a new life with the "Nietzschean" heroes of bourgeois society. A *Pravda* editorial (November 13, 1935), titled "A Hero of our Time," after Lermontov's novel, declared that bourgeois heroes are motivated by lust for money, land, and palaces; Soviet heroes are inspired by high ideals. The classic bourgeois hero is a conqueror; "with sword and deception, gold and blood," he affirms himself, glorying in the poverty and unhappiness of the masses. Bourgeois philosophy, science, morality, and literature created a theory of crowds (an allusion to Gustav LeBon), which opposes the hero to the masses, conveying the idea that the masses could serve only as a trampoline for chosen, predestined heroes. "The bourgeois pen of Nietzsche drew the image of the superman, who from his high mountain looks down with contempt on ordinary people, presents them as a gray one-toned, slavish crowd." Bourgeois scientists rehash Nietzsche, Carlyle, and Galton (founder of eugenics), on the select traits of the superhuman hero and the slavishness of the

---

34. Gorkii, "Pokolenie geroev," in *GSS*, 27:162–63.
35. Günther, *Der sozialistische Übermensch*, 108–11.

crowd. Galton openly stated that "the richer the parents, the more valuable the children." In the Soviet Union, by contrast, the hero is one with the masses, first among equals, "a personal example of labor and creativity who summons the masses to new heights of mastery of technique." Heroes in all areas of Soviet life apply their strength, energy, heroism, and technical proficiency to social goals. The superfluous man depicted by Lermontov no longer exists. An article titled "Legendary Champions [*Vitiazi*] of the Third Reich" (*Red Virgin Soil*, May 1935) reported on how Goebbels and Jöhst made Schlageter, Horst Wessel, and others into cult figures, discreetly passing over Radek's "Schlageter strategy."[36]

The German "cult of death," *Pravda* reported on April 25, 1936, exalted irrationalism, nihilism, blood-lust, and fanaticism. "Blood and death are the slogans of expiring capitalism." Soviet propagandists extolled joy, enthusiasm, and the hero's immortality in an unacknowledged or perhaps unwitting appropriation of Nietzsche's "Yes to life" (a favorite theme of his prerevolutionary admirers), as opposed to a Wagnerian *Götterdämmerung*. A cultural difference also comes into play here. Catholic saints had stigmata, the symbols of Christ's suffering; Russian saints were transfigured by the light. Both Nazi and Stalinist propagandists extolled valor, total commitment, selflessness, and discipline. Germans stressed the "beauty of labor" as a physiological or biological concept; Soviets emphasized amazing feats of productivity and talked about the arrival of a "new anthropological type," but not in racial terms.

Typical Soviet heroes came from humble origins, but raised themselves to epic heights by accomplishing some great feat through superhuman endurance, energy, self-discipline, and will. Some overcame the elemental forces of nature. These heroes were enthusiasts, humanized versions of the iron man. Among them were marathon skiers, mountain climbers, the rocket scientist Konstantin Tsiolkovsky, and a "*bogatyr* parachutist." The heroes of the Cheliuskin expedition were depicted as ordinary people whose feats could be duplicated by anyone. According to one account, they kept up their spirits while marooned on the ice by reading Pushkin aloud. Articles celebrating their feat referred to a "great war on the northern ice sea." Subsequent expeditions were either accompanied by reporters or the explorers doubled as reporters, communicating directly with Moscow by telegram and radio. Their reports, and those of the pilot-heroes, were relayed to the public as episodes in an ongoing saga.

"Heroes of the stratosphere" flew higher and longer than anyone else. The cult of pilot-heroes, initiated after the rescue of the Cheliuskin expedi-

---

36. N. Kornev, "Legendarnye vitiazii 'Tret'ei imperii'," *Krasnaia nov'*, 1935, no. 5. In August 1934, *Krasnaia nov* published a series of articles by the same author on Nazi leaders, titled "Germanskie silueti." See also Kornev's article "Fashistskie propovedniki," *Krasnaia Nov'*, 1935, no. 8:171–84.

tion in 1934, was a model for other cults, none of which was as spectacular. The government used the messages of polar explorers and aviators to stimulate patriotic pride, and to give the impression that, in the Soviet Union, state-of-the-art communication technology had conquered distance and time. This was in a period when keeping track of developments in remote areas of the country was a major problem. Front-page illustrations in *Pravda* traced the pilot's progress along the "Stalin Route" (*Po stalinskomu marshrutu*), sometimes putting Stalin in the picture. For example, on July 26, 1936, *Pravda* showed the Stalin route, three pilot-heroes, and a beaming Stalin.

The cult of pilot-heroes had a heaven-storming cosmic dimension.[37] Called "Stalin's Falcons" after Gorky's "Song of the Falcon," they were people of the future, trespassers of forbidden boundaries, hence closer to the Superman than were Stakhanovite *bogatyri* (see below). Poems were written about the pilot-heroes, for there was an element of glamour and adventure in their feats. They personified Gorky's slogan "Forward and Higher!" the Soviet air force slogan, "faster, higher, and farther," and Nietzsche's injunction to live dangerously. Exemplars of revolutionary enthusiasm and will, the pilot-heroes were taking real risks. Not all of them returned. When Chkalov perished on December 15, 1938, newspaper articles proclaimed that the dead hero is immortal. "With us, the falcon will not die" (Gorky's falcon died); "for such names time is powerless"; Chkalov's "name burns in the hearts of Soviet people as the symbol of a creative and victorious life." A film was made about Chkalov in 1941. Descriptions of the pilot-heroes' exploits were couched in stereotypic language, for they were mythic types.

Cults of pilot-heroes existed in other nations as well, for aviation was still new. Americans had Charles Lindbergh and Amelia Earhart. But the Soviet cult was constructed by the government; the pilot-hero possessed characteristics it wished to inculcate in the masses: modesty, selflessness, courage, organization, discipline, technical proficiency, and passionate enthusiasm ("flaming hearts," "hot living blood"), as distinct from the cold calculation and self-interest of man in capitalist society. The pilots' exploits symbolized man's mastery of the machine, the triumph of human will over hostile nature, and the willingness to sacrifice not just comfort but life itself for the Motherland.

Self-sacrifice is a Christian ideal, but it is also the reverse side of Nietzschean self-affirmation. Nietzsche himself conjoined the two when he included readiness "to sacrifice men to one's cause, oneself not excepted" in his definition of freedom (*TI*, 92). The symbolists' Christ/Dionysus archetype made self-sacrifice a good in itself and a prelude to resurrection. Ivanov and Berdiaev

---

37. Details in Hans Günther, "Stalinische Falken: Der mythische Weg des Fliegerhelden," in *Der sozialistische Übermensch*, 155–74. The article appeared in Russian under the title "Stalinskie sokoly" in *Voprosy literatury*, 1991, nos. 11–12:122–41.

considered self-sacrifice morally superior to self-defense; neither had any conception of an ethical pursuit of self-interest. Stalin considered sacrifice an essential attribute of socialism and built the idea into Soviet education. "The personal counts for nothing," he told Central Committee members in charge of textbooks.[38] The Nazis had a comparable slogan, "You are nothing: your Volk is everything."

Actually, many pilot-heroes benefited financially from their exploits; some of them took part in constructing their own myths.[39] There were female Cheliuskinists and pilot-heroes too. Sometimes they were spotlighted, but more often, the media put them in supporting roles, thereby strengthening the male definitions of hero, scientist, and explorer. Pilot-training programs discriminated against women, despite the rhetoric of gender equality.[40] The issue on the Cheliuskin expedition, *USSR in Construction* (1933, no. 9), reported that ten women and two children were rescued, but the picture of a woman shows her nursing her baby. A pregnant woman who embarks on an expedition that, in the best of conditions, would be difficult and gives birth on an ice floe, is indeed heroic, but that was not the message conveyed, which was decidedly mixed. On one hand, pregnancy and motherhood need not impede a woman's career, on the other hand, motherhood is her true vocation.

The Stakhanovite movement, which honored heroes of labor, had the pragmatic aim of increasing production (a Marxist, not a Nietzschean, goal). Launched in August 1935, the movement was named after Aleksei Stakhanov, a coal-miner who exceeded his production quota by an amazing 1,400 percent. His feat was made possible by carefully orchestrated cooperation with other miners, but he got all the credit, yet another example of the use of illusion. Female Stakhanovites were mostly collective farmers. Maria Demchenko worked on a sugar-beet farm in Ukraine. Praskovia (Pasha) Angelina, a tractor driver and a Soviet Cinderella, met and married her "prince," a high Soviet official, as a direct result of her feat. Tretiakov's melodrama *Nine Girls* (1935) told her story.[41]

Previous awards had honored brigades or entire factories, but not individuals. In the Stakhanovite movement the original and still ostensible communist ideal of equality was superseded by a quasi-Nietzschean hero-ideal that undermined worker solidarity by introducing comparisons and material rewards—cash or objects that were deemed part of a cultured lifestyle, such as phonographs or books. Large-scale propaganda campaigns mounted in connection with various political anniversaries culminated in mass awards

---

38. Volkogonov, *Stalin*, 186–87.
39. John McCannon, *Red Arctic* (Oxford, 1998), 134.
40. Petrone, *Life Has Become More Joyous*, 74–75.
41. Stites, *Soviet Popular Culture*, 70.

to leading workers or veterans. Thousands of men and women were decorated in public ceremonies in which they attributed agency to Stalin and
thanked him for giving them a "joyous and happy new life." The honorees
were not part of the new rank order (most were not Party members), but sin-
gling out some individuals, even if only temporarily, indirectly justified it,
especially since honorees were chosen by a higher authority, not by their peers.

During the First Five-Year Plan, shock workers exceeded their targets by
"storming." The Stakhanovite worked calmly, deliberately, rationally. He or
she was not merely *greater* than others, not merely stronger, but represented
"a *qualitative* leap forward in human anthropology," the "new type" produced by Soviet society. His or her feat was a triumph of technology and
skill as well as of strength.[42] To Gorky, the "worker-hero" represented the
new man, creative and productive, the polar opposite of the hobo-protagonists that had made him famous. He described the Stakhanovite movement
in glowing terms that distinguished between energy-draining competition in
capitalist countries, which young Soviet workers "know only from books"
(which was not the case) and socialist emulation, making the latter sound
like a good-natured contest.[43] Actually, their fellow workers resented the
Stakhanovites, because their staged feats were used to raise the production
norms for everyone.

Pravda declared 1936 the year of the Stakhanovite, published lists of
them, and talked about helping shock workers become Stakhanovites. Widely
publicized annual meetings of Stakhanovites served as ritualized celebrations
of the Stalin Cult. The honorees praised Stalin's inspirational leadership in
simple but very effusive speeches, and he praised them for daring to "smash
the conservatism of certain of our engineers and technicians, to smash the
old traditions and standards and allow free scope to the new forces of the
working class."[44] "Daring" and "smashing" have Nietzschean associations;
the Stakhanovites smashed old production norms, not the new Soviet "tables
of values."

Literary Gazette suggested that Stakhanovites be called "Prometheus
Unbound."[45] Lunacharsky had envisioned a proletarian Prometheus for
decades, most recently in his report on Socialist Realism (1933). In *Religion
and Socialism* (1908) he had advocated a "mythology of labor" that encompassed Prometheus, Hercules, and Christ and treated Prometheus as a
Nietzschean and a Luciferan figure (1:96–102). The Stakhanovite was also
called a "Soviet Hercules." The "miraculous records" he or she set were

42. Clark, "Utopian Anthropology," in Tucker, *Stalinism*, 185.
43. Gorkii, "O novom cheloveke," in *GSS*, 27:483–87.
44. Stalin, "Speech at 1st Conference of Stakhanovites," in *Problems of Leninism*
(Moscow, 1976), 788.
45. "Literatura i stakhanovskoe dvizhenie" (editorial), *Literaturnaia gazeta*, October
29, 1935, p. 1.

described in ever more fabulous terms, as evidence of the "age of miracles" in which the Soviets were now living. Nietzsche alluded to myth as a "concentrated image of the world that, as a condensation of phenomena, cannot dispense with miracles" (*BT*, 135). Gorky, a constructor of the Soviet cult of heroes, might have noted the passage and read it prescriptively. The Stakhanovites were also called *bogatyri*, in accord with Gorky's injunction to utilize folk myth. At the height of the purges, the Stakhanovite movement also served to intimidate (and purge) managers, government and Party officials, and technical and scientific personnel in a kind of ritual dethroning that disrupted factory discipline and took time away from production. Dethroning was not a carefree carnival game. For individuals targeted, the result could be a show trial, imprisonment, and death. One cartoon, captioned "The New Gulliver" shows a gigantic Stakhanovite holding lilliputian bureaucrats in his hands.[46] The Stakhanovite movement was intended to increase production, but feverish attempts to set new records increased the number of accidents and led to wear and tear on the machines.[47]

The cult of Pavlik Morozov gave children their own cult figure. Between 1932 and 1934, the name of the "martyred youth" who turned in his "kulak" father for hiding grain appeared in *Pioneer Truth* (*Pionerskaia Pravda*, newspaper of the Soviet youth organization) more often than Stalin's. The function of this cult was not to mobilize young people in support of dekulakization or collectivization (which had already been achieved), but to educate them in hatred, to show them that "not every brother is a brother," and to train the next generation in the ruthless morality required of them.[48] Poems and stories about Pavlik made it clear that in denouncing his father, he had gained a new father, Stalin. Gorky promoted the cult in articles such as "Pavlik Morozov must not be forgotten," and prevailed on the Congress of Soviet Writers to recommend building a monument to the young martyr. During the Great Terror, numerous books about Pavlik and his spiritual descendants, boys and girls, were published, some in print runs as high as 50,000. When the monument to Pavlik was finally completed in 1948, the newspaper *Evening Moscow* (*Vecherniaia Moskva*) announced that "Gorky's Dream has been fulfilled." (Fulfillment took so long because Party members who were fathers did not want their children to inform on them.) The myth of Pavlik Morozov symbolized the undivided loyalty to the state, personified by Stalin, that was demanded of everyone.

46. Lewis Siegelbaum, *Stakhanovism and the Politics of Productivity* (Cambridge, 1988), 96.

47. Stephen Kotkin, "Coercion and Identity: Workers Lives in Stalin's Showcase City," in Siegelbaum and Suny, *Making Workers Soviet*, 292–93; Oleg Khlevniuk, *In Stalin's Shadow: The Career of "Sergo" Ordzhonikidze*, ed. Donald Raleigh (Armonk, N.Y., 1995), 84.

48. Druzhnikov, *Informer 001*, 99, 103, 105; see also chapter 5, "The Family as a Terrorist Organization," 53–64.

The Stalin Cult and complementary phenomena concealed the uglier parts of Soviet reality, and in that sense were applications of Socialist Realism. The image of Stalin as a Superman-Savior struck deep roots in the Soviet psyche. Such is the power of propaganda when directed to the unconscious and conducted in a controlled environment in which contrary voices and images are prohibited.

Cultural Expressions of the Will to Power

And whenever man rejoices, he is always the same
in his rejoicing: he rejoices as an artist, he enjoys
himself as power, he enjoys the lie as his form of
power.   —*WP*, 452

The great man feels his *power* over a people.
                                         —*WP*, 506

As Stalin's power grew, Party control of culture grew accordingly. In the sciences as well as the arts, the Party decided
the subjects to be treated, the lines of research to be pursued, and in some fields, the methodology. Party interventions created additional complements to the Stalin Cult or
furthered Stalin's policies in some other way. Makarenko
became the reigning authority in education because he turned
out the kind of "new men" Stalin wanted. Ivan the Terrible
displaced Peter the Great as a Stalin-surrogate in monumental histories that elliptically justified purge and terror.
Monumentalism was labeled Socialist Realism in architecture. Lysenko's "Michurinist Biology" held out the promise of conquering nature and breeding the "new man." Party
control of culture was relaxed during the war and stringently reinstated after it, in the period known as the
Zhdanovshchina (1946–53).

Unacknowledged Nietzschean ideas informed the phenomena to be discussed in this chapter. Makarenko was a long-time admirer of Gorky, and he benefited from Gorky's patronage. Gorky helped create the cult of Michurin that had preceded the cult of Lysenko. Eisenstein employed Nietzschean and Wagnerian motifs in *Ivan the Terrible*. Monumental structures incarnated Stalin's will to power and put his stamp on the landscape for generations to come. Lysenko purported to enhance the power of species-man. His fraudulent experiments, which the Soviet press trumpeted as successful, can be considered a counterpart in science to Socialist Realism in the arts. All these projects were related to the Nietzschean agenda—the new myth, the new man, the new art form, and the new science—and were part of an over-arching "great project," the construction of a distinctively Soviet and Socialist culture.

The Power to Create New Men: Anton Makarenko's Theory of Education

Anton Makarenko (1888–1939) was not an acolyte of the Stalin Cult—his references to Stalin are amazingly rare—but he would not have become the reigning authority in education without Stalin's approval. As director of colonies for orphans and homeless children (the Gorky Colony, 1917–28, and the Dzerzhinsky Commune, 1928–36), he achieved remarkable success in transforming his unruly charges into the kind of "new men" Stalin wanted—self-disciplined, hard-working, obedient, loyal to the collective, capable of personal initiative, and able to command as well as to obey. Such types accorded with Gorky's vision of the "new man" (Gorky and Makarenko carried on an extensive correspondence) and with Stalin's slogan "cadres decide everything" (1935). To many people inside and outside the Party, Makarenko's methods promised to end the chaos that reigned in the schools and stem the increase in juvenile delinquency that attended the First Five-Year Plan. (Working mothers had no one to mind their children, and dekulakization and collectivization created a second wave of *besprizorniki*.) The Central Committee's decree on "pedagogical distortions" in education (July 1936), which was followed by a purge of the educational bureaucracy, worked to Makarenko's advantage. Much of his support came from former activists in the Cultural Revolution.[1] Like them, he championed a labor-oriented program and opposed knowledge for the sake of knowledge.

The changes in educational policy were closely related to, and in a sense the culmination of, the repudiation of "mechanism" and "biologism" in 1930–31, in favor of a more purposive and voluntaristic approach that emphasized consciousness and molding the personality to make it more amenable to social discipline.

---

1. Fitzpatrick, *Education and Social Mobility*, 251.

Makarenko's methods required a controlled environment and respect for authority. He combined a strict military regimen that included corporal punishment with vocational training, a mystique of the collective, a cult of Gorky, and the "aesthetics of behavior," a term coined by Herzen and used by Struve to mean a realistic morality rather than abstract moralism. Makarenko's version included personal hygiene, good table manners, neatness, punctuality, and saluting, as part of a Communist morality that stressed self-discipline. He demanded firmness and self-control from teachers, as well as from students, and recommended that teachers be trained in control of the voice, facial movements, and posture (note the theatricality). A firm believer in the unlimited power of education, he downplayed inborn characteristics. By "education," he meant not just imparting knowledge and skills, but molding the personality so that the individual identified with the collective.

Makarenko's successes attracted the attention of the GPU, which invited him to run its model orphanage, the Dzerzhinsky Commune. For his part, Makarenko admired the Chekists, especially their group solidarity. "The Cheka experience was rich in the very qualities I had been trying for eight years to instill into the collective of the colony." The Chekists combined "high intellectual standards with education and culture"; they were devoted to principle, but principle was "not a bandage over the eyes." He appreciated their terse speech, their dislike of ready-made formulas, and their "unlimited capacity for work" without a hint of the "nauseating martyr pose." Association with the Cheka confirmed Makarenko's view that his "pedagogical scheme was the true Bolshevik scheme."[2] He discouraged romantic love among his charges (some were of marriageable age), lest it result in divided loyalties. When one teenager committed suicide because Makarenko forbade him to marry his girlfriend, not even one of his peers expressed sorrow or regret. Rather, they criticized him for putting personal desire ahead of collective needs (2:272ff.). They had internalized the Nietzschean virtue of hardness.

To the "Olympians," Makarenko's contemptuous term for educational theorists who disagreed with his harsh methods, he said: "We all know perfectly well what sort of human being we should aim at turning out. . . . The problem therefore is not *what* should be done but *how* it should be done. Techniques must be derived from experience" (3:266). "Ninety percent of the [educational] output is spoiled! You're turning out not Communist personalities but rotten drunkards, shirkers, and self-seekers. Kindly make good this deficit out of your salaries!" (3:269). Makarenko's critics accused him of advocating blind obedience and Pavlovian conditioning, even though Makarenko insisted that the child is a "living person" whose individuality must be respected. He demonstrated real affection and concern for his charges. Despite his emphasis on the collective, Makarenko held individuals responsible for their actions.

2. Anton Makarenko, *The Road to Life*, 3 vols. (Moscow, 1951), 3:383–86.

Gorky helped Makarenko publish his major work, *A Pedagogical Poem: An Epic of Education* (3 vols., 1933–35). The words "poem" and "epic" signal the educator's revolutionary romanticism. The film version, *Road to Life* (1934), was commissioned by the GPU.[3] In 1937, Makarenko moved to Moscow, where he systematized and publicized his theories and was admitted to the Union of Soviet Writers, largely in deference to Gorky's memory. His next major work, *A Book For Parents* (1937), fit in with Stalin's pronatalist, pro-family policy. Makarenko extolled large families as schools of collectivism, attacked parents who produced "shoddy goods," and roundly condemned fathers who abandoned their offspring. He also urged parents to be role models of communist morality and to spend more time with their children (ignoring their physical exhaustion and lack of free time). In the concluding section, he invited parents to write him about their "thoughts, difficulties, and discoveries," which he planned to address in a second volume devoted to "the problems of the spiritual and material culture of the family, and of aesthetic education," but he died before he could write it.[4]

Makarenko's emphasis on discipline, obedience, and loyalty to the collective became the norm in Soviet schools. Loyalty to the collective ended up meaning loyalty to the state. After Makarenko's death in 1939, extensive discussion about his heritage went on in educational and literary journals. His name became a rallying cry for people who thought that Soviet schools had become too rigid. *Pravda* endorsed his theories in August 1940. A seven-volume edition of his collected works (which include short stories, novellas, and plays), was published in 1950–52. A second, seven-volume edition appeared in 1957–58 (during Khrushchev's tenure), and a five-volume edition in 1971.

Ivan the Terrible as a Stalin Surrogate

The mythologizing (or monumentalizing) of Russian history paralleled the mythologizing of Party history in *The Short Course*. Rehabilitation of the tsars helped legitimate Stalin's dominance. Even the radical literary critic Vissarion Belinsky (1811–48) said: "We need a new Peter the Great, a despot of genius, one who would deal with us mercilessly and implacably in the name of human principles. We must go through terror. Before we needed Peter the Great's stick to give us at last a semblance of humanity; now what we need is to go through terror in order to make us human beings in the full and noble meaning of the word." This is quoted by Vadim, the toadying literary critic in Anatoly Rybakov's novel *Children of the Arbat* (1988). When

---

3. Turovskaya, "The Taste of Soviet Moviegoers," 101.
4. Anton Makarenko, *A Book for Parents* (Moscow, n.d.), 412.

challenged, Vadim points out that Ivan Panaev (1816–62) used the same words in his memoirs of Belinsky and so did the historian Konstantin Kavelin (1818–85). Vadim considered Belinsky a "great man who realized that Russia needed a firm leadership. But he was a man of his time . . . he didn't know that there was going to be a dictatorship of the proletariat."[5] The novel is set in 1933–34. And Vadim did not know that Ivan the Terrible was going to displace Peter as a Stalin-surrogate.

In 1934, Stalin instructed historians to extol Ivan the Terrible as a "revolutionary from above." Two years later, *Pravda* and *Izvestiia* attacked Pokrovsky's school (which denied heroes in history and denigrated the tsars) as schematic, abstract, and inaccurate. Bukharin and Radek led the attack.[6] *Art's* publication of a portrait of Ivan in February (1936) portended the *Yezhovshchina.* A two-volume symposium, *Against M. N. Pokrovsky's Conception of History,* appeared in 1938. A new history textbook, *The Short Course of the History of the USSR* (also 1938), treated Soviet history as an organic outgrowth of Russian history, highlighted the positive role of the tsars, and drew implicit parallels between Stalin and Ivan the Terrible.

Until the mid-1930s, Soviet historians distinguished between the "historically progressive" first part of Ivan's reign and his descent into paranoia and madness, much as prerevolutionary historians did. The descent was epitomized by the *oprichnina,* the domain that Ivan carved out for himself from the territory of the Muscovite state in 1565. For seven years, Ivan's personal police force, the *oprichniki,* conducted a reign of terror against the boyars (the hereditary aristocracy) and their servitors. Not a secret police, *oprichniki* wore monk-like hooded black uniforms. Their insignia was a dog's head and a broom—to sniff out traitors and sweep them away.

The Short Course of the History of the USSR and subsequent works explained the *oprichnina* as Ivan's response to boyar treason during the Livonian War, drawing implicit but obvious correspondences between Ivan's time and their own. Ivan corresponded to Stalin; the boyars to the Old Bolsheviks; Kurbsky to Trotsky; the *oprichnina* to the NKVD; Livonia to the Baltic States, which Stalin wished to incorporate (Ivan sought access to the Baltic Sea), and so on. Killings of innocent people were denied, or minimized, or blamed on overzealous or corrupt *oprichniki.* Ivan's execution of leading *oprichniki* elliptically explained the execution of Yezhov and the purge of the NKVD. In March 1941, *Izvestiia* published an article that treated Ivan in solely positive terms and depicted the inhabitants of Livonia as rus-

5. Anatoly Rybakov, *Children of the Arbat* (Boston, 1988), 395.

6. Bukharin's article (*Izvestiia,* January 27, 1935) was titled "Do We Need a Marxist Historical Science? On Certain Important But Unsound Views of Comrade M. N. Pokrovsky." Radek's article, "The Significance of History for the Revolutionary Proletariat" appeared in *Pravda* the same day; another one, "The Shortcomings on the Historical Front and the Mistakes of the School of Pokrovsky," appeared in *Bolshevik* the following March.

sophiles, implicitly justifying the "liberation" of Latvia and Estonia and the Hitler-Stalin Pact.

This is the context in which Eisenstein was commissioned to film *Ivan the Terrible* in January 1941. Using a variety of sources, the director created his own monumental history, selecting facts and episodes of Ivan's biography that he considered "characteristic." In Eisenstein's words: "'characteristic' is not a fact as such, but rather exists in the conception of a historical understanding and an illumination of the facts through a certain historical conviction." In Nietzschean terms, it is a matter of one's perspective. Eisenstein's perspective was dialectical; he emphasized the historically progressive nature of Ivan's reign on the one hand and the cost in human terms on the other, leaving out "not one drop of spilled blood."[7] Again and again in the film, decisive action by Ivan is preceded by wavering and followed by remorse. Ivan emerges as a suffering and tragic hero who had to "become hard!" for Russia's sake.

Filming began in April 1943. Part 1 (1944) portrays the successful early years of Ivan's reign, the deathbed scene, his disillusionment with the boyars, and his "wise and just decision" to crush the boyars with the help of his *oprichniki*. Part 2 (1946), subtitled *The Boyars' Plot,* was a horror story of escalating paranoia, bloodshed, and violence. Ivan emerged as a neurotic despot and the *oprichniki* as sinister and depraved. Part 1 earned Eisenstein the Stalin prize. Part 2 was banned until five years after Stalin's death. Part 3 was never released; to date, only snippets have been found. In Parts 1 and 2, a sun-ray motif is the basis of Ivan's "power-gesture," which is reinforced by icons that intensify the sunburst effect.[8] The sun-ray motif links Ivan symbolically to Apollo, as does the gold in his clothing.

Eisenstein conceived the film as a *Gesamtkunstwerk,* "a coordinated and homologized assemblage of the most diverse means of expression and action . . . welded into a unity. One law regulates all."[9] "We "wished chiefly to convey a sense of majesty and this led us to adopt majestic forms. . . . The principal idea—the formation of a strong state—governs the Tsar's whole conduct."[10] The "majestic forms" were tragedy and grand opera. Action and dialogue were synchronized with Prokofiev's score, which included *leitmotifs* and choral singing. Ivan's speech in the deathbed scene was a spoken aria, and the boyars surrounding him were a kind of chorus. Great attention was paid to the mise-en-scene and to historical accuracy in costumes and settings.

7. "Ivan Groznyi" (editors' commentary), in *Sergei Eizenshtein. Izbrannye proizvedeniia v shesti tomakh*, ed. N. I. Kleiman et al (Moscow, 1971), 548–49. This commentary contains extensive quotations from Eisenstein's notes.
8. Bordwell, *Cinema of Eisenstein,* 235.
9. Eisenstein, "My Drawings" (1943), excerpts included in the introduction to *Ivan the Terrible*, trans. Ivor Montagu and Herbert Marshall (New York, 1962), 301–2.
10. Quoted in introduction to *Ivan the Terrible,* 13.

Eisenstein thought of the film as a "tragedy of autocracy [*edinovlastie*] in all its inner contradictions" (editors' commentary, 548), in other words, a tragedy of power. The film had to emphasize the "historical necessity of a Russian outlet on the sea—the 'supertask' [*sverkhzadachi*] of Ivan's state activity, emphasizing at the same time, in a progressive 'superpersonal' sense [*v progressivnom 'sverkhlichnom'*]—the personal failure [*krakh*] of the first Tsar" (550). At the end of the film, Ivan is all-powerful and all alone, betrayed by everyone except the *oprichnik* Maliuta Skuratov (who has just died). According to the editors of Eisenstein's collected works:

> The loneliness of the Tsar, consumed by remorse of conscience, but already drawn irrevocably into the closed circle of doubt and suspicion, compelled to annihilate the guilty and the innocent around him in order to affirm his own unlimited power—this turned out to be the price of the unacknowledged moral limitation of the thesis: all is permitted "for the sake of the great Russian realm." Ivan's personal failure is at the same time an image of the unavoidable failure of the very idea and system of autocracy, experienced at the time, and that degenerated into a maniacal despotism. (549)

In the film, one of the conspirators quotes Machiavelli without attribution: "A ruler must not swerve from the path of goodness, if this may be, but he must tread even the path of evil, if this be inescapable."[11] Eisenstein has Ivan follow this maxim as well. In Nietzschean terms, Ivan is beyond good and evil.

Ivan had people murdered and then confessed and atoned by awarding pensions to the widows and orphans he had created. Nietzsche's observation (about man in general) may explain this aspect of Ivan's personality—"man finds sensuous pleasure in calling himself a sinner" (*Z*, 235). Dostoevsky said of Ivan: "A criminal enjoyment in breaking every law. A mystical enjoyment (with anxiety at night). An enjoyment of repentance, of the monastery (of the strictest fasts and prayers) . . . an enjoyment of education (and study). An enjoyment of good deeds."[12] Freud said that Ivan reminded him of "one of the barbarians in the great migrations who murdered and did penance for it, until penance became an actual technique for enabling murder to be done."[13] In the film, after murdering his own son in a fit of rage, Ivan is filled with anguish and confesses his murders, and his confessor writes down each victim's name. (Ivan kept such lists, called synodicals.) The confessor's list fills several scrolls (eleven pages of the screenplay), a grisly version of

---

11. *Ivan the Terrible*, 184.
12. Quoted in Koenin, *Die grossen Gesänge*, 184.
13. *Standard Edition of the Complete Psychological Works of Sigmund Freud*, ed. James Strachey (London, 1953–74), 21:17.

Leporello's "Catalogue Aria" in *Don Giovanni*. And even while confessing, Ivan is planning additional murders. By the end of the film, the suffering Ivan is an incarnation of will, for he realizes that "a tsar who hesitates in rewarding the good and punishing the guilty will never make a tsar."[14]

Eisenstein portrayed the *oprichniki* as Dionysian types. In Part 1 they are "the elements," crude and rough but devoted to Ivan and to Russia. In his notes, Eisenstein called them "*vydvizhentsy*, a drawing out from the bottom of *new people* with a particular cast of mind. A replacement." In the film, he portrayed two prominent *oprichniki* (Basmanov, father and son) as *vydvizhentsy*, even though they hailed from a wealthy boyar family (editor's commentary, 550). The "fearful oath" that the *oprichniki* take in Part 1 sets the stage for the bloody sacrifices of Part 2. Among the provisions: "To serve the Sovereign of Russia like a dog / Its towns and villages to sweep with a broom / Villainous scoundrels to tear with my teeth / . . . FOR THE SAKE OF THE GREAT RUSSIAN REALM," and to "forsake kith and kin" for Russia's sake. In "The Tsar's Feast," the foundational scene of Part 2, the *oprichniki* get drunk, sing "shameless songs," and perform wild and frenzied dances (= dithyrambs). The tsar drinks too, but he remains sober. The elder Basmanov thinks of himself as Ivan's kin (since he has sworn to forsake his own), but Ivan rebukes him: "From the dung I raised thee / to trample boyar traitors. Through thee my will to realize. Not to teach—but to serve—is thy bondsman's business. Know thy place!"[15] Ivan will not destroy "boyar oaks" to replace them with "wretched aspens." This correspondence is to the Old Bolsheviks, the "oaks" who were corulers with Lenin and Stalin, as distinct from the *vydvizhentsy*, mere servitors. A 1946 Central Committee resolution accused Eisenstein of representing the "progressive *oprichniki* army as a degenerate band cast in a mold of the American Ku-Klux-Klan and Ivan the Terrible as characterless and weak-willed, a kind of Hamlet."[16]

At a meeting with Eisenstein and Nikolai Cherkasov, the actor who played Ivan, Stalin remarked that if Ivan had liquidated all the boyars, there would not have been a "time of troubles" in Russia. Eisenstein apologized for not using the classic works of Marxism on the questions of history, which "have illustrated and made available to us the historically correct and positive evaluation of Ivan's progressive bodyguards."[17] There were no such works, and Eisenstein knew it. Neither Marx, nor Engels, nor Lenin wrote about the *oprichnina*. After World War II, Stalin no longer needed a surrogate. Films such as *The Fall of Berlin* (1949) and *The Battle of Stalingrad* (1950) glorified him as the organizer of victory.

14. Bordwell, *Cinema of Eisenstein*, 230–31.
15. *Ivan the Terrible* (screenplay), 190.
16. Quoted in Bernd Uhlenbruch, "The Annexation of History: Eisenstein and the Ivan Grozny Cult of the 1940s," in Günther, *Culture of the Stalin Period*, 278.
17. Ibid., 281–83. I changed "life-guards" to "bodyguards."

Power over Space and Time: Monumental Architecture

In the 1930s, because of the Great Depression, most European and American architecture was monumental architecture, financed by the government or a wealthy institution, characterized by attempts to express the national spirit, and motivated, in part, by the need to create jobs. In the Soviet Union unemployment was not a problem. In the dictatorships, monumental architecture expressed the Leader's "will to power" and the official ideology, and was intended to keep the masses in awe. Architecture was a central theme of Hitler's speeches on culture. He believed that architecture embodied the *Gesamtkunstwerk* ideal and that great buildings could create a common will, a feeling of belonging to the great and glorious Aryan community (*Volksgemeinschaft*). Hitler and Stalin repudiated modern architecture in favor of a pseudo-classicism that architectural historian Franco Borsi calls "statist monumentalism."[18] Repudiation of modern architecture took longer in Italy and was never as complete.

Nietzsche admired the "grand style" of Roman architecture. Architects in the dictatorships may have thought they were creating a "grand style," but their structures were grandiose, rather than grand, though they were certainly imposing. Soviet architects favored Roman models as the expression of Imperial power, much as Nietzsche and certain tsars did. When Shchusev asserted, "We alone are the direct heirs of Rome," he was contradicting Italian and German claims.[19] Kaganovich listed beauty and size as desiderata of monumental architecture and instructed architects to "speak in a form in which there is much that is elemental and little that is conscious." Socialist Realism in architecture entailed "not a copying, not a reproduction of forms taken from life, but a creative reworking and artistic formulation of realistic forms" that utilized the Russian historical style.[20] He wanted an architecture that had a visceral appeal to the masses and was imbued with Soviet and socialist content and meaning.

"Statist monumentalism" incorporated the modernists' goal of a life-transforming architecture that would induce a communal spirit, and the specifically rationalist tenet that a structure must be ideologically expressive and inspire awe (Ladovsky's idea). Years before Hitler was on the scene, a German teacher of architecture called for a "Dionysian" architectural style that would express the "might of wholeness, the power of the anonymous mass of the folk spirit" and "echo the heartbeat of the masses."[21] Bruno Taut and Walter

---

18. Franco Borsi, *The Monumental Era: European Architecture and Design* (New York, 1987), 29–34.

19. Quoted in Golomstock, *Totalitarian Art*, 278.

20. Quoted in Hudson, *Blueprints and Blood*, 167–68.

21. Paul Klopfer, "Über Apollinisches und Dionysisches in der Baukunst," quoted in Barbara Miller Lane, *Architecture and Politics in Germany* (Cambridge, Mass., 1968), 234.

Gropius envisioned enormous cathedrals as the sacred spaces of a new organic society. The planned Palace of Soviets in Moscow (begun 1937) and the planned House of the People in Berlin (begun 1939) were to serve similar goals. Each building was to provide a symbolic ideological focus for its country and, in the near future, for the planet earth. The Palace would be the highest building in the world and be topped by an enormous statue of Lenin. The House of the People would be graced by a statue of Apollo, twenty feet high, and have the biggest dome in the world. Each was to have a Great Hall that seated thousands.

Modern technology made it possible to build supersized structures that dwarfed those of antiquity and the Renaissance. "Statist monumentalism" violated the classical norms of harmony, balance, symmetry, and self-containment by using space aggressively. There was no such thing as a structure that was too big or too high. Vertical elongation distorted the proportions, breaking the anthropomorphic equilibrium of Renaissance classicism, and removing any hint of naturalism. Crowds were incorporated in the design. According to Borsi,

> mass rallies provided an opportunity to measure architecture against a new material, namely human material; in a relationship of mutual violence space was to engulf the masses, giving the individual the measure of his annihilation, and the masses were to dominate and fill the space, denoting, in capacity as a mass, the measure of their acquired power.
>
> One man alone placed himself in the equation with the masses as one silhouetted against a great number.[22]

Hitler was the focal point, a fixed object against the moving force of the masses or conversely, the dynamic element confronting the passivity of the masses. Stalin was flanked by Party dignitaries to convey an impression of collective leadership. The dignitaries changed over time as a result of demotions, purges, and executions. Early plans for the Palace of Soviets provided space for mass demonstrations and festival parades; that feature was dropped later on.[23]

"Statist monumentalism" conveyed a spirit of vastness, solidity, immobility, sobriety, and was meant to stand for centuries. Shchusev admired the Pyramids; Stalin was fascinated by them. Speer had a theory of the "value of ruins," which measured the worth of an edifice by what remained after thousands of years, like the Pyramids and Roman ruins. He wanted to build the most grandiose structures since the Pyramids. Stalin followed Speer's

22. Borsi, *Monumental Era*, 34.
23. Catherine Cooke and Igor Kazus, *Soviet Architectural Competitions, 1926–36* (Laren, The Netherlands, 1992), 59.

activities closely, and Hitler followed Stalin's plans for the transformation of Moscow. Mussolini's "E 1942," the colossal exhibit planned for the twentieth anniversary of the Fascist Revolution, was to be a marble city. Soviets architects used a variety of materials that signified durability and strength. Monumental buildings had soaring columns (a symbol of permanence and power in many cultures), gigantic statues, elaborate facades, and ornate lobbies. The buildings were not all alike. Karo Alabian's Red Army Theater was a five-pointed star.[24]

The idea for a Palace of Soviets grew out of 1922–23 plans for a Palace of Labor (public buildings were called palaces to convey the impression that the people were the new ruling class, hence entitled to them). Kirov wanted it to be "an emblem of proletariat might" that would show the bourgeoisie "that we, the 'semi-Asiatics,' are able to adorn the earth with the very finest monuments of art and proletarian inventiveness, with marvellous palaces. And then they will know that we have come to power seriously and forever!"[25] That structure was never built, but the idea was revived in 1931. The Palace of Soviets was intended to celebrate the victory of the First Five-Year-Plan, symbolize and validate that heroic epoch, and challenge the League of Nations headquarters in Geneva as an international center.

The architect was decided by a preliminary competition (spring 1931), an open competition (fall 1931), and two closed competitions (March–June 1932 and August 1932–February 1933). The stipulations for the open competition (announced in July 1931) were that the Palace had to be "monumental" and visible from all parts of Moscow. Foreign architects, including Gropius and Le Corbusier, were among the contestants. Le Corbusier was widely expected to win, but the jury rejected his "factory-like" design, and found fault with all the entries. Rather than name a winner, it awarded thirteen prizes and invited the awardees to revise their projects and resubmit them. The "special prizes" went to Ivan Zholtovsky (1867–1959) for a classic design, Hector Hamilton (an American architect) for a simple structure, and the relatively unknown Boris Iofan (1891–1976), for a complex of circular buildings and a tower.

Kaganovich, Molotov, and Voroshilov were on the jury, which comprised seventy "special experts" in architecture and the arts, including Lunacharsky, Gorky, Stanislavsky, and Meyerhold. The modernist entries enabled the jurists to crystallize their objections to modern architecture, "and to formulate on that, albeit negative basis, the essential characteristics of Soviet architecture."[26] "Tallness" was in accord with the Soviet slogan "Ever Higher" and futur-

24. Illustration in Alexei Tarkhanov and Sergei Kartaradze, *Architecture of the Stalin Era* (New York, 1992), 71.

25. Quoted in Colton, *Moscow*, 218.

26. Antonia Cunliffe, "The Competition for the Palace of Soviets in Moscow, 1931–33," *Architectural Association Quarterly* 11, no. 2 (1979): 41.

ism's exaltation of constructed heights. Architects were warned against "restoration," "eclecticism," "formalism," or "technicism" (= constructivism). Unadorned modern buildings were to be replaced by an architecture that organically incorporated sculpture and painting (the *Gesamtkunstwerk* ideal). Matthew Cullerne Bown maintains that it is "wrong to overemphasize the classical aspect of [Iofan's design]. Its towering circular form is an unmistakable echo of Tatlin's Tower, not a complete break but a transformation."[27] Bown is right about the transformation, but the jury's decision was a defeat for the avant-garde all the same. Not even one of the prizes went to the avant-garde.

The stipulations for the closed competition were that the building had to be "bold," "tall," characterized by "permanence and grandioseness," symmetrical, monolithic (as distinct from "accidental agglomerations"), and incorporate the "class-basis" of Soviet architecture. The architecture and artwork had to be arrived at "by means of the critical assimilation of the architectural heritage" and "mastery" of the techniques and methods of the past, while at the same time fulfilling the "requirements dictated by the present context and meaning of our country," and utilizing the latest advances in construction technology. Roman architecture was declared the best source of inspiration for Soviet needs.[28] The criteria were clearly tilted toward classicism. The Palace was not to be a mere imitation of classical architecture, Lunacharsky explained to a plenum of VOPRA, but something "colossal" and distinctively Soviet. It must "speak of the greatness of the proletariat," its "firmness," "might," "agility," "purposefulness," its "joyous attitude to life," and the "most profound democracy" going on inside the edifice.[29] The personal taste of the jurists was a factor in their decision, of course, but so was their desire for an architecture that "spoke" to the masses. Surveys had shown that the masses did not consider modern architecture beautiful. It was too plain.

In May 1933, Iofan's revised submission—an enormous circular tower, with stepped tiers, each one with a colonnade—was declared the "working basis" of the Palace. Topped by a gigantic statue, "The Liberated Proletarian," Iofan's Palace dwarfed the famous cathedrals of the Europe. Only the Eiffel Tower and the Empire State Building were taller. A few days later, Stalin specified that the Palace must be the tallest building in the world; the statue must be of Lenin (making the entire structure a pedestal for him), and the Great Hall was to have no fewer than 21,000 seats. Soon after that, Vladimir Shchuko (1878–1939, designer of the Lenin Library, 1928) and Professor

27. Matthew Cullerne Bown, *Art Under Stalin* (New York, 1991), 40.
28. Cunliffe, "Competition," 41.
29. Lunacharskii, "Rech' o proletarskom arkhitektury," *Arkhitektura SSSR*, 1935, no. 8:4–7. He gave the speech in January 1932.

Vladimir Gel'freikh (1866–1967) were appointed Iofan's co-architects. Two more tiers were added. With the statue of Lenin, which was to be three times the size of the Statue of Liberty, the Palace would have been the tallest and volumetrically the largest building in the world (Fig. 11). Lenin's outstretched index figure alone was to be twenty feet long. Lunacharsky praised Iofan's design as "grandiose, hospitable, simple and light," in accord with the demands of "our first great architectural monument." "Every great age has a correspondingly great architecture" that is expressed in "great size and great mass."[30] The final design had statues, busts, frescoes, mosaics, bas-reliefs, decorative glass, oil-paintings, a processional staircase, elevators, escalators, and climate control.

Just as the early Christians demolished pagan temples and built churches on the sites, the Palace of Soviets was to be built on the site of the demolished Cathedral of Christ the Savior—in Iofan's words, "a cumbersome edifice which symbolizes the power and the taste of the lords of old Moscow."[31] The Palace of Soviets would reflect the power and taste of the new lords, the people. Stalin personally selected the site. The Palace of Soviets was to last forever. "The centuries will not leave their mark on it. We shall built it so that it stands without aging, eternally [*vechno*]."[32] Construction began in 1937, but was suspended during the war and never resumed. Viacheslav Ivanov's vision of replacing the Church with a theater-temple almost came true, though not in the form he envisioned.

Participants in a symposium on monumental art praised the Palace of Soviets, Magnitogorsk, the Dneprostroi Dam, the Moscow Metro, and the "grandiose reconstruction" (*perestroika*) of central Moscow (*Art,* 1934, no. 4:2–20). Three of the participants were architects—B. N. Blokhin, V. S. Toot, and Shchusev (designer of Lenin's Tomb and chief architect of the Moscow Metro). The other four—Deineka, Moor, Bela Uits, and V. A. Favorsky—were painters. Shchusev emphasized the union of painting, sculpture, and architecture in everyday practice (again, the *Gesamtkunstwerk* ideal) (19–20). Toot specified that Soviet monumental edifices must be visible from a distance, break the monotonous gray of the city, convey great decorative and emotional import, transmit a given content, and incorporate monumental painting (9).

Large sections of Moscow, Rome, and Berlin were reconstructed, for each dictator wanted "his" capital to be the most impressive. Each one looked on "his" capital" as a "Brobdingnagian sandbox in which he could sift, heap, and bore at all."[33] The Plan for the reconstruction of Moscow was formally

---

30. Lunacharskii, "Sotsialistiicheskii arkhitekturnyi monument," *Stroitel'stvo Moskvy* 5–6 (1933): 3–10.

31. Quoted in Volkogonov, *Stalin*, 235.

32. Quoted in Colton, *Moscow*, 333.

33. Ibid., 324.

Fig. 11 "The Palace of Soviets." *Arkhitektura SSSR,* 1937, no.10. Slavic and Baltic Division, New York Public Library, Astor, Lenox and Tilden Foundation.

approved on July 14, 1935, well after work had begun. *Pravda* and *Izvestiia* devoted several articles to it. Bukharin titled his article "Sun-City" (*Izvestiia*, July 14) possibly a reference to Campanella's "City of the Sun" (which, Lenin said, inspired his monumental propaganda campaign) and predicted that Moscow would be a "new mecca to which seekers of human happiness would stream from all ends of the earth." The press referred to "Stalin's Moscow" (*Stalinskaia Mosvka*). This was not just talk. Stalin kept track of everything being built in the city and directed which public works were to be done first, and on what schedule, paying attention to most minute details.[34] A front-page illustration in *Pravda* has him surveying "his" city (Fig. 12). Rank order applied to cities as well as to individuals: Moscow was the first city and Leningrad the second.

The Kitaigorod wall, the Sukharev Tower, and adjoining Sukharevsky market (a "den" of capitalistic activity) were leveled, as were scores of churches, as part of a declared "war on Old Moscow." Entire neighborhoods were razed to make room for monumental buildings and a super-sized stadium, and to remove unsightly slums (a feature of Western city planning too). Curving or crooked streets and alleys (symbolic of the chaotic old order) were straightened or eliminated and Tverskaia Street was renamed Gorky Street. Imposing official buildings and elite residences, all with elaborate facades and ornate lobbies, were erected on the main thoroughfares. A Russian scholar, Vladimir Papernyi, called the preoccupation with externals "facadism" (*fasadnichestvo*) and said, quoting Bruno Taut (who lived in Moscow in 1933), "This is not architecture [but] an art of theatricalized decorativeness," a "lordly" art intended to demonstrate power.[35]

Igor Golomstock refers to a totalitarian hierarchy of space, with the most important buildings in the center and all other buildings planned with reference to them.

> The cults of eternity and of vastness went together. The dimensions of this kind of architecture, rather than being based on the individual were calculated from some super-personal point of view. It would have been impossible, for example, for anyone standing on earth to grasp the harmony of the symmetrical silhouettes, kilometers apart, in the new centres of Berlin and Moscow, just as it was impossible to understand the spatial symbolism behind the construction of certain individual buildings.[36]

34. Ibid., 325.
35. Vladimir Papernyi, *Kul'tura dva* (Ann Arbor, 1985), 69–71, 207–8.
36. Golomstock, *Totalitarian Art*, 281.

Fig. 12 "Stalin's Moscow." *Pravda,* November 25, 1936, p. 1. Slavic and Baltic Division, New York Public Library, Astor, Lenox and Tilden Foundation.

The star-shaped Red Army Theater, best seen from the air, was one of the buildings he had in mind.

The same plan was used, with minor variations, for cities all over the Soviet Union; many were renamed after Stalin or other Soviet luminaries. Discussion of solutions that combined "beauty" and functionalism was forbidden after the Plan for Moscow was published. Either editors censored the articles or architects no longer dared speak out against the official, and therefore compulsory, new form.[37]

Huge squares and broad boulevards dwarfed the individual and symbolized the horizontal conquest of space, the endless plain, which Spengler considered quintessentially Russian. Tall buildings and enormous columns, in effect, refuted Spengler's allegation that Russians are will-less and passive. A formula for an architecture "socialist in form, national in content" emerged in 1939 in connection with the All-Union Agricultural Exhibit in Moscow, which was adorned by Mukhina's statue from the 1937 Paris Exhibition. The designers of pavilions of the Union Republics were encouraged to translate their cultural heritage into the new architectural language of socialist realism.[38]

37. Tarkhanov and Kartaradze, *Architecture of the Stalin Era*, 40.
38. Gregory Castillo, "Peoples at an Exhibition," in Lahusen and Dobrenko, *Socialist Realism Without Shores*, 91–115.

Hugh Hudson described the Stalinization of architecture in *Blueprints and Blood*.[39] In April 1932, all architectural organizations had to dissolve as a prelude to a single Union of Architects. The Party faction in the Union of Architects was led by Karo Alabian, formerly head of the Association of Proletarian Architects (VOPRA), who took his instructions from Kaganovich. Moisei Okhitovich, the leading opponent of monumental architecture, was expelled from the Union of Architects and arrested in 1935. He died in the Gulag. Not satisfied with destroying Okhitovich, Alabian went after anyone else who might oppose him. *Pravda* came to Alabian's aid with an editorial titled "Cacophony in Architecture" (February 20, 1936). By 1937, the Union of Architects had been purged of persons who might spoil its first congress. The others no longer dared to speak out against the official, and therefore compulsory, new aesthetic. The leitmotif of the speeches was that thanks to Stalin's leadership, soon everyone would be living in a palace. Some architects tried to engage in real debate but the Party faction would not allow it. Soon after the Congress, Alabian had Shchusev expelled from the Union, but Nikolai Bulganin, head of the Moscow City Council, ordered him reinstated and reminded Alabian that he did not control architecture; the Party did. The prohibition of private architectural contracts in 1933 forced architects to chose between working for the government or leaving their profession.

The vast amounts of material and labor required for Stalinist monumentalism reduced the amount available for housing ordinary people. The Palace of Soviets alone consumed one quarter of the entire construction budget of Moscow. In Moscow, Leningrad, and other major cities, the masses lived in communal apartments, with an entire family in each room and one sink, washtub, toilet, and stove (usually a primus burner) for all the residents. Outside the major cities, housing conditions were even worse. In the coal-mining centers of Stalino and Makeevka, for example, only the central regions had sewers. Public grandeur concealed private squalor—the mess of communal kitchens, plumbing that didn't work, long lines for toilets, and so on.

After the war, a new general plan for Moscow featured eight "tall buildings" (the so-called wedding cakes). Each one had a steeple topped by a spire. The idea was to create a national architecture and spires were considered a continuation of Old-Russian architecture, as in Kremlin spires and baroque churches. The "skyspires," sometimes called "Stalin's cathedrals," were also a device to distinguish Moscow "tall buildings" from American skyscrapers, while at the same time showing foreign visitors that Moscow was not "backward"; it had skyscrapers too.[40] Classical and Renaissance

39. See especially chapter 10, "The Victory Congress," 185–202.

40. *Khrushchev Remembers: The Last Testament*, trans. Strobe Talbott, foreword by Edward Crankshaw, introduction by Jerrold Schechter (Boston, 1974), 98.

facades were replaced by cartouches, coats of arms, turrets, and other touches such as Babylonian ziggurats to that show that Soviet architecture was the legitimate heir of all the architectural forms of the past. The course of Soviet architecture verifies the theory of the constructivist architect, Moisei Ginzburg (1892–1946), which he articulated in the early 1920s: youth is constructivist; maturity is organic; and decline is decorative.

The conquest of space was both horizontal and vertical, and demonstrated the power of species-man, incarnated in Stalin. A confluence of influences inspired Soviet explorations of the far north, the cult of pilot-heroes, and a mystique of crossing boundaries generally, "trespassing all limits" as Merezhkovsky had put it, of strength so great it could not be contained. Aerial exploits were included in parades and rallies; photomontages frequently included airplanes and dirigibles flying overhead. The completion of the first line of the Moscow Metro in 1935 signaled the conquest of the lower depths as well, the transformation of darkness and dankness into a brightly lit, airy, and warm heaven-on-earth. Richard Stites called the Metro "a monument to power."[41]

The Moscow Metro realized the futurists' ideal of art for the masses, although elaborate chandeliers, bronze statues, and marble columns were not what they had in mind. But this decor symbolized luxury and testified to Stalin's power to transform the lower depths into a worker's palace. The Metro was named after Kaganovich, who supervised its construction. Khrushchev was his deputy. Determined to create in record time the best and the most beautiful subway in the world as a showcase for the superiority of the Soviet system, Kaganovich devised an extraordinarily tight construction schedule. Work went on around the clock in three eight-hour shifts. Wage rates were set to a shock-work tempo, which was drastically accelerated in 1934. Storming techniques and lack of safety precautions resulted in thousands of accidents, some of them fatal. At the opening of the first line, Kaganovich called "the victory of the Metropolitan . . . a victory for socialism" and said that the worker riding the Metro "must feel cheerful and joyous, knowing that he works for himself, knowing that every screw [*gaika*] is a socialist screw . . . this is why, comrades, we have such a display, where a person . . . can feel as if he is in a palace, right in the middle of working Moscow."[42]

The Metro was a splendid forum for promoting state mythology, for millions of riders used it daily. It was also a showcase of Soviet precision, tech-

---

41. Richard Stites, "Stalinism and the Restructuring of Revolutionary Utopianism," in Günther, *Culture of the Stalin Period*, 90.

42. Kaganovich, "Pobeda metropolitena—Pobeda sotsializma," *Pravda*, May 20, 1935, p. 3.

nical excellence, and discipline, and a preview of the good life to come. The opening of a new line was treated as a cultural event. People came just to see the art and architecture, which were reviewed in the press and praised as "sunny," "bright," "festive," and "life-affirming." *Art* (1935, no. 4) celebrated "A Year of Work on the Metro," and the masterpieces of art on display there.

Each station had its own theme ("individuality" applied to architecture) which was carried through in the paintings, sculptures, murals, bas-reliefs, and mosaics (the *Gesamtkunstwerk* ideal). Kaganovich wanted to refute the idea that "socialism is a barracks" peopled by look-alikes. The artwork was a collaborative effort ("collective creativity") in which former *Miriskusniki* and avant-gardists took part. The Kiev station celebrated the fraternal union of the Russian and Ukrainian peoples and the benefits of the Revolution for Ukraine—another example of art as a lie. Ukraine was hardest hit by the "terror-famine," and advocates of nativization (*korenizatsiia*) of the leadership strata had been purged or were about to be.

The first four lines of the Moscow Metro provide a capsule history of aesthetics in Stalin's time. The first one, built 1932–35, was modernist and austere and featured geometric designs. The second line, built 1936–38, was "classical," with some modernist motifs. Huge halls and domed ceilings conveyed an atmosphere of spaciousness, a striking contrast to the crowded apartments in which ordinary Muscovites lived. The critic I. Sosfenov (who also wrote for *Architecture of the USSR*) praised the second line for being "entirely free" of schematism and abstraction; its architectural principle is "expressiveness" and the art is so effective that people forget they are underground. At the Revolution Square station, twelve enormous bronze sculptures monumentalized the mythic types of Soviet society: "Partisan," "Soldier," "Sailor," "Border Guard," "Inventor," "Athlete," "Miner" (holding a pneumatic drill to demonstrate his mastery of technology), "Father," "Mother" (holding her son), "Pioneer," "Woman Athlete," and "Young Girl with a Book." That station, Sosfenov wrote, is a marvelous example of the artistic life of our country. Its creative principles are remote from the "transportation architecture of the past," the synthesis of architecture and art is unique for a metro, and they have ideational content; they are not merely "formal elements."[43]

A few months later, *Art* discussed the artwork of the Gorky Radius—the Mayakovsky Square, Sverdlov Square, and Dynamo stations.[44] The latter

43. I. Sosfenov, "Problema sinteza v metro. Sintez v oformlenii stantsii 'ploshchad' revoliutsii' Moskovskogo metro," *Iskusstvo*, 1938, no. 2:29–42; the list of bronze statues is on page 37.
44. I. Sosfenov, "Problema sinteza v metro. Sintez v oformlenii stantsii gork'ovskogo radiusa moskovskogo metro," *Iskusstvo*, 1938, no. 6:64–74; see also A. Deineka, "Khudozhniki v metro," ibid., 75–80.

was named for an enormous sport stadium nearby, so its artistic theme was sports. Monumental sculptures displayed the perfect body of *homo sovieticus,* male and female, but the basic model was the male athlete of classical Greece. The Mayakovsky Square station celebrated Soviet mastery of the skies. Mayakovsky had written a poem, "The Flying Proletariat" (1925), and futurists were enthralled with aviation. The decor combined assurances of protection (against German invasion) with a quasi-modernist iconography of flight that, in some instances, adapted the avant-garde's perspectivism. Deineka's mosaics replicated aerial views of the earth from different angles as the plane ascended and descended (multiple perspectives), and may have been influenced by *aeropittura,* an Italian genre. He had visited Italy in 1935. The theme of the third line, built 1939–44, was the heroism and endurance of the Soviet people. The lavish gold moldings and marble carvings of the fourth line, built after the war, exemplified Stalinist baroque. The Komsomol Station (built 1952) is generally considered the apogee, or nadir, of Stalinist baroque. An enormous Hall of Victory commemorated Russian and Soviet triumphs over past invaders. Eight gigantic ceiling mosaics, made of lapis lazuli, jasper, malachite and other hard stones set against a gold background, produced a color and sheen reminiscent of Orthodox icons.

The Power to Create New Species: Lysenko's "Michurinist Biology"

Lysenko championed the Lamarckian view that acquired traits are inherited, but he denied being a Lamarckian, because Lamarck did not think dialectically. Rejecting genetics entirely, Lysenko taught that nature was putty to be shaped by human beings, that new varieties of plants could be creating by grafting, or crossing, or controlling the environment (subjecting wheat to extremes of temperature, for example), that sudden transformations from one species to another (wheat into rye, pines into firs, warblers giving birth to cuckoos) were possible. His claim that he could refashion heredity held out the promise of eventually breeding the new man. "In our country, in any area of human activity, one may create miracles" (*Pravda,* May 27, 1937).

The conditions that facilitated Lysenko's rise to power have been described elsewhere—the crisis in agriculture that resulted from forced collectivization, periodic droughts, the search for a cult figure in biology, a tradition of Lamarckianism that stretched back to the 1840s, the government's monopoly on scientific research, which put a premium on having a Party patron, and its monopoly over the means of communication. Orchestrated press campaigns exalted Lysenko and denied his opponents a forum. The Nazis' use of genetics and eugenics to champion racism and inequality gave Lysenko a talking point. From 1936 on, he claimed that fascism, genetics, and eugenics were inseparable. The xenophobia of the late 1930s and the Cold War isolated Soviet scientists from international debate.[45]

An adroit manipulator of Soviet ideology and mythology, and reputedly a mesmerizing speaker, Lysenko hitched on to the cult of Ivan Michurin, utilizing current political catchwords and slogans to get Party support. Lysenko's concept of "two biologies" (Soviet and Western) had antecedents in Bogdanov and Bukharin's desire for a "proletarian" or a "socialist" science that addressed practical tasks, and in Lenin's insistence that there are no politically neutral zones—ideas that came together in the culture wars of the 1920s. Lysenko's claim that he could master nature and create new species fit in with Stalin's slogan, "There are no fortresses Bolsheviks cannot storm." Lysenko was not well-read. Isaak Prezent (b. 1902), a specialist in dialectical materialism and a Party member (Lysenko was not), helped him formulate the "Marxist" aspects of his biology. Lysenko's promoters included Mitin, Iudin, and Kol'man—advocates of Party-mindedness during the Cultural Revolution and members of the Communist Academy until its dissolution. Popularized versions of Marxism undermined the critical standard of the scientific method by proclaiming that traditional distinctions between theory and practice, fact and value, were invalid bourgeois dogmas, and emphasized environment over heredity.

Ivan Michurin (1855–1935), the Russian Luther Burbank, created new varieties and new species of plants, mostly fruits and berries. Michurin had only a grade-school education and no real scientific training but these were assets in the eyes of his promoters. Lenin and Fedor Kalinin (the Proletkult activist) esteemed Michurin's work, but they did not make him into a cult figure. That was largely Gorky's doing. Endorsing Michurin's slogan "man can and must improve nature," Gorky praised the "miracles created by [Michurin's] inexhaustible energy." Michurin was equal to Lomonosov, Faraday, and Edison and superior to Luther Burbank, who worked in sunny California and got financial support for his experiments. Michurin worked in the severe climate of central Russia under conditions of extreme poverty. His entire life was a struggle. Despite tremendous hardships, Michurin *carries the south to the north. . . . to Michurin, belongs the most grandiose revelation.*" He is a "profound elder" (*starets*). Note the religious language. "At the age of seventy-two, he continues to create; he continues to tear off one veil after another of the mysteries of nature" (a new use of the theme of "unmasking").[46] Thanks to Michurin, the human species will be able to make nature serve its needs.

45. David Joravsky, *The Lysenko Affair* (Cambridge, 1970); Zhores Medvedev, *The Rise and Fall of T. Lysenko*, trans. I. Michael Lorne (New York, 1971); Krementsev, *Stalinist Science*; Valerii Soifer, *Vlast' i nauka: Istoriia razgroma genetiki* (Tenafly, N.J., 1987); Soyfer, *Lysenko and the Tragedy of Soviet Science*; Adams, *The Wellborn Science*, 192–201. Douglas Weiner, "The Roots of Michurinism," *Annals of Science* 42 (1985): 234–60; and N. Roll-Hansen, "A New Perspective on Lysenko," ibid., 268–78.

46. Gorkii, in *GSS*, 24:352–54. See also, M. M. Unovich, *Gor'kii—propagandist nauki* (Moscow, 1961).

In 1934, the year that the cult of Soviet heroes was instituted, Michurin's birthday (October 27) was celebrated elaborately for the first time. His death on June 8, 1935, was the occasion for an editorial plus ten articles in *Pravda* and seven in *Izvestiia*. Bukharin's contribution, "Man the Creator," compared plant species to peoples and tribes and contrasted Michurin's hybridization and grafting to Nazi racism. Nikolai Vavilov, the leading Soviet geneticist and a believer in genetic engineering, titled his article "A Heroic Feat" (*Podvig*). Michurin's home town was renamed Michurinsk. The compendium *Ivan Vladimirovich Michurin: His Remarkable Life and Work, 1855–1935* included the *Pravda* editorial, articles from both newspapers, a short biography, and Michurin's description of his life's work, which was guided, he said, by the principle that "we cannot expect favors [*milosti*] from nature; we must seize them from her."[47] Propagandists treated Michurin's "principle" in terms of struggle. When Michurin died, Lysenko claimed to be his successor, perhaps modeling his strategy on Stalin's use of Lenin. Lysenko frequently quoted Michurin's statement: "It is possible, with man's intervention, *to force* any form of animal or plant to *change more quickly and in a direction desirable to man*."[48]

In February 1935, at conference of agricultural shock workers that was attended by prominent scientists and political luminaries, including Stalin, Lysenko denounced his critics as "saboteur-kulaks" in science in a maneuver calculated to get Stalin's attention, which it did. Stalin jumped up, applauding enthusiastically, and shouted "Bravo, Comrade Lysenko, Bravo!" at which point the entire conference broke out in wild applause.[49] *Pravda*'s detailed account of Lysenko's speech omitted the following passage, which came just after Stalin's outburst. "In our Soviet Union, comrades, *people* are not born. Human organisms are born, but *people* are created from organisms in our country—tractor drivers, motorists, mechanics, academicians, scientists, and so on. And I am one of the people created in this way. I was not *born* as a human being. I was *made* as a human being. And to feel myself such, comrades, in such a position—it is to be more than happy."[50] Denying inborn characteristics, Lysenko was also presenting himself as living proof of the opportunities open to a Soviet peasant. Perhaps *Pravda* omitted it because the passage could be read as admitting that some people were being "made" more equal than others.

Lysenko advocated "Michurinist biology" and a "creatively developed Darwinism," taking his cue from Bukharin's 1932 speech, or advised by

47. *Ivan Vladimirovich Michurin. Ego zamechatel'naia zhizn' i rabota, 1855–1935, Sbornik statei* (Voronezh, 1935), 72–76. Bukharin's article is on 29–34, Vavilov's on 21–26.
48. Quoted in Graham, *Science and Philosophy in the Soviet Union*, 235.
49. Soyfer, *Lysenko and the Tragedy of Soviet Science*, 61.
50. Quoted in Soyfer, *Lysenko and the Tragedy of Soviet Science*, 61–62.

Prezent to do so. In Lysenko's version of Darwinism, the struggle for survival is between different species, not within a species. Michurin did not try to monopolize science or destroy his critics. Lysenko did. Demanding that research and teaching of genetics cease, he secured Vavilov's dismissal as director of the Academy of Agricultural Sciences in 1935, after which Lysenko and his allies moved into leadership positions. *Pravda, Izvestiia,* and *Under the Banner of Marxism* praised Lysenko's "Michurinist biology." Michurin was an impoverished nobleman and Lysenko the son of a peasant. The press billed both of them as ordinary people who knew better than the learned professors. One article was titled "Science in the Hands of a Peasant's Son."[51] Playing into Stalin's distrust of theoretical science, Lysenko argued that the geneticists promised only future progress, but had nothing to offer today, or even tomorrow, while he was delivering bumper crops (a lie).

The renowned American geneticist and eugenicist Herman J. Muller, a friend of the Soviet Union and a supporter of forced collectivization, vigorously opposed Lysenko's views. Muller maintained that only in a classless society could eugenics could be properly implemented (he denied that the "lower classes" and the colonized peoples were genetically inferior). In 1932, he accepted Vavilov's invitation to head a new laboratory at the Institute of Genetics of the Soviet Academy of Sciences in Moscow. The following year he was elected a Corresponding Member of the Academy. Throughout his stay in the Soviet Union, Muller argued that eugenics was an intrinsic aspect of a planned society. In *Out of the Night* (1935), he recommended using eugenics to "control the most important form of production, 'reproduction'" by means of artificial insemination (a policy championed by Serebrovsky and Filipchenko in the 1920s). "In the course of a paltry century or two . . . it would be possible for the majority of the population to become of the inner quality of such men as Lenin, Newton, Leonardo, Pasteur, Beethoven, Omar Khayyam, Pushkin, Sun Yat Sen, Marx . . . or even to possess their varied faculties combined."[52] In May 1936, Muller sent a copy of his book to Stalin with a cover letter saying that the results of artificial insemination could be apparent "after only a few years" (as the next generation is born) and urged Stalin to put the technique into practice. By then, some high officials of the Central Committee were worried that an International Genetics Conference, to be held in Moscow in 1937, would provide a forum for Nazi geneticists and eugenicists. Not only was Muller's timing off; bringing human genetics back into the picture was a serious tactical error. Stalin did not reply to Muller's letter, but in the fall of 1936, one of Muller's students was arrested and executed as an "enemy of the people." Warned of his impending arrest, Muller fled the country as a member of the International Brigade headed for

51. Joravsky, *Lysenko Affair*, 189.
52. Quoted in Adams, *The Well-Born Science*, 194–95.

the Spanish Civil War. In the next few months, other Russian geneticists were arrested and shot and the Institute of Medical Genetics was disbanded. Reputedly, even the woman who had translated Muller's book for Stalin was arrested and shot.[53] After Bukharin was arrested, Lysenko linked him with Vavilov, in order to discredit Vavilov, and falsely claimed that Bukharin had "fully accepted the metaphysical aspect of genetics" in his 1932 speech "Darwinism and Marxism."[54]

In their drive for hegemony, Lysenkoites reviled geneticists as "menshevizing idealists," "wreckers," "bandits" in league with Trotsky and "the powers of darkness," supporters of the "Bogdanov-Bukharin theory of equilibrium," and fascists propagating eugenics and racism (even though Soviet geneticists were the first to call attention to Nazi misuse of eugenics) and accused them of "servile grovelling on a world scale." Lambasting "science for the sake of science," Lysenkoites ridiculed experiments with fruit flies as devoid of practical import, called geneticists "fly-lovers and man-haters," refused to conduct rigorous experiments, and forced worthless or even harmful nostrums on peasants and local leaders. Almost all Party patrons of genetics perished in the Great Terror. In 1938, Lysenko was elected to the Soviet Academy of Science. Vavilov was arrested as a "British spy" in 1940 and died in the Gulag in 1943, the year that Lysenko was awarded his second Stalin Prize. His first was in 1941.

In the summer of 1948, Lysenko became the dictator of Soviet biology. His triumph occurred at a week-long meeting of the Academy of Agricultural Sciences that was scripted in advance. Lysenko, the main speaker, claimed that the Central Committee had endorsed his views. Actually, Stalin himself had edited his speech.[55] One of its main points was that among the Morganists (geneticists), "Chance reigns supreme. . . . With such a science it is impossible to plan, to work toward a definite goal. . . . We must firmly remember that science is the enemy of chance."[56] Note the combination of Prometheanism and planning. Implicitly, with proper planning all goals are possible. Genes limit an organism's ability to adapt to new environmental conditions and to transfer these adaptations to its progeny. Lysenko's Promethean biology recognized no such constraints.

After the meeting, the cult-building apparatus, already in operation, was shifted into high gear. *Pravda*'s pro-Lysenko editorials were reprinted in professional journals and local newspapers as part of a campaign "for the complete domination of Michurinist biology." Local party organizations resolved

53. Ibid., 198–99.
54. Soyfer, *Lysenko and the Tragedy of Soviet Science*, 104.
55. Kirill Rossianov, "Stalin as Lysenko's Editor," *Russian History*, 21, no. 1 (1994): 49–63.
56. Quoted in Graham, *Science and Philosophy in the Soviet Union*, 236.

to propagate "Michurinist biology," and biology textbooks were rewritten. Lysenko's fiftieth birthday was celebrated with great fanfare and he was put in charge of the Great Stalin Plan for the Transformation of Nature, a Fedorovian-type scheme of reforestation intended to change the climate and to divert the Siberian rivers to Central Asia, to be used for irrigation. A slogan for this plan was "we will conquer drought too!" A technicolor film, *Michurin,* produced by Dovzhenko with music by Shostakovich, starring a popular actor, was shown throughout the Soviet Union. Lysenko's portrait hung in all scientific institutions. Art stores sold busts and bas-reliefs of him; monuments were erected to him; and the repertory of the State Chorus included a hymn in his honor. Despite all this, genetics was not uprooted entirely; it went underground.

In 1949, Muller denounced Lysenkoism as a "militant mysticism" certain to have "dire repercussions on every branch of intellectual activity in the U.S.S.R. and in countries within its orbit." Moreover, if acquired characteristics are inherited, people living under unfavorable conditions would pass on their disadvantages on to their offspring, and privileged groups would pass on their advantages. "In a word, we should have innate master and subject races and classes."[57] Perhaps this is what Lysenko and Stalin wanted, a Brave New World, to be achieved by controlling the environment, not by genetic engineering.

The Lysenko cult enhanced Stalin's power in various ways. Favoring Lysenko over the geneticists was a way to reassert Party control over all the sciences after the relative autonomy they had enjoyed during the war. The Lysenko Cult also served to invalidate any regional or local Party effort to support a different, non-Stalinist agricultural policy, and ultimately to purge a pro-geneticist faction in the Politburo (the Leningrad affair).[58] Iury Zhdanov (Andrei Zhdanov's son) opposed Lysenko and was forced to recant. The press used the "Great Stalin Plan for the Transformation of Nature" to promote the Stalin Cult: the greater the accomplishment, the more indebted were Soviet citizens to Stalin.

Discarding objective standards of verification made the Party (= Stalin) the arbiter of scientific truth. In the preliminary draft of his speech to the Academy of Agricultural Sciences, Lysenko called Western science "bourgeois." Stalin substituted "reactionary" or "unscientific," and deleted the words "proletarian" and "Soviet," sometimes replacing them with "scientific," which is exactly what Lysenko's biology was not. Once again, Nietzsche is relevant. "It is all over with priests and gods if man becomes scientific!—

57. H. S. [*sic*] Muller, "The Soviet Master Race Theory," *The New Leader*, July 30, 1949, p. 1.

58. Kiteme, "Cult of Stalin," 144.

Moral: science is the forbidden in itself—it alone is forbidden. Science is the *first* sin, the germ of all sins, *original* sin . . . 'Thou shall *not* know'—the rest follows." (*AC,* 164). In *The Antichrist,* Nietzsche referred to "the story of God's mortal terror of science" (*AC,* 163): "Man has become scientific. . . . *He will have to be drowned*" (*AC,* 165). Note that in these statements Nietzsche is pro-science. He extolled the discipline of the scientific method ("Methods, one must repeat ten times *are* the essential, as well as being the most difficult") and counterposed the "*sense for facts* with bad instincts, the Christian instincts" (*AC,* 182).

Lysenko's triumph paved the way for Michurinist meetings in other scientific disciplines. At each meeting there was a speaker whose talk had been edited by Stalin or a high Party official. A Soviet intellectual recalled discussions of the late 1940s and early 1950s "that differed in no way from court trials" in biology and physics as well as philosophy, "that transformed white into black and black into white with astonishing facility . . . people [who expressed] even the most timid doubt about such manipulations" were threatened with severe punishment.[59] Contrarily, Nikolai Krementsev claims that by repenting, performing ritual cleansings, and declaring their obeisance to the Central Committee, the scientists hoped to forestall Party interference.[60] If Krementsev is correct, these practices were a defensive version of the theatricalization of life. Scientists developed a form of "facadism," never calling it that, adorning their publications, especially the introductions, with quotations from Marx, Engels, Lenin, Stalin, and the particular cult figure in their discipline—e.g., Michurin, Mendeleev, Pavlov—and couching their research proposals in politically correct language, "speaking Bolshevik," as Kotkin put it.

The ability to create new life forms implies divinity. Stalin's will to power did the most harm in biology, the science of life. Some physicists perished and others were imprisoned (and later released) in the Great Terror but the discipline was not ruined.[61] It was too remote from the issues that Stalin cared most about—the "new myth," "the new man," and Soviet power—and the atom bomb was essential for the latter. If biological weapons had been crucial, the geneticists might have prevailed.[62] Lysenko's power began to wane in 1956, but Khrushchev revived it in 1958, contradicting his pol-

59. Vladim Sadovskii, "Philosophy in Moscow in the Fifties and Sixties," *Russian Studies in Philosophy* 33, no. 2 (Fall 1994): 49–50.

60. Krementsev, *Stalinist Science,* 51.

61. Six Soviet physicists were awarded the Nobel Prize for work begun in the 1930s and 1940s. Also noteworthy is that special prison camps for scientists were established (apparently by Beria), so that they could continue their work. Solzhenitysyn's novel *The First Circle* (1955–64, English translation 1968) is set in one.

62. David Holloway argues that the most important factor was not the bomb, but that physicists were not divided among themselves. *Stalin and the Bomb* (New Haven, 1994), 186–88, 210.

icy of de-Stalinization in other areas. Never officially dethroned, Lysenko held positions of power as late as his death in 1976.

The *Zhdanovshchina*

During the Great Patriotic War, propagandists stressed patriotism and revenge for Nazi atrocities, and the Party loosened its grip and relaxed cultural controls, allowing scope for personal initiative. After the war, the Party reasserted its control, and in a much more thoroughgoing manner than before the war. Propagandists attributed victory to Stalin's leadership and the superiority of the Communist system, and described the war as a transformative event, which it was for the people who had survived it. The government controlled the official narrative, but individuals had their own memories; many of them wanted the Soviet Union to live up to its professed ideals. To mobilize the war-exhausted masses, the Party proclaimed a new goal, reaching full communism in the near future, twenty or thirty years. In the interim, austerity, hard work, and discipline were necessary, especially since, according to Stalin, as long as capitalism existed there was a danger of war. The Soviet Union had to be prepared. The tropes of propaganda changed. The archetypal Soviet hero was a soldier-liberator (typically a man). Emphasis was on "moral political unity" (harmony), rather than class struggle, and on an intensified Russian-Soviet nationalism that included russification. During the war, entire nationalities suspected of disloyalty or potential disloyalty had been forcibly relocated to Central Asia and Siberia.

In August 1946, Zhdanov launched a campaign against "Western influences," "formalism," and "rootless cosmopolitanism" that included vicious attacks on Zoshchenko and Akhmatova, quotations from *Pravda*'s anti-Shostakovich editorial "Muddle Instead of Music" (1936), and calls for stricter adherence to Socialist Realism. Special meetings were held to guide artists and writers. Impressionism was labeled a virulent strain of formalism and associated with Machism. The reimposition of Party authority over the sciences was part of this process, a resumption of the *Gleichschaltung* interrupted and partly reversed by the war.

"Anti-cosmopolitanism" was a code-word for russification generally and for anti-Semitism specifically. Zhdanov died in 1948, but the *Zhdanovshchina* continued. Quotas limited the number of persons of Jewish origin in high-level positions, research institutes, and universities, and Jewish doctors were accused of plotting to poison Stalin and other Soviet leaders. As in Nazi doctrine, "Jewish" was defined by ancestry, not belief. At the height of the furor over the "Doctor's Plot" (1953), *Pravda* published an article titled "The Jewish Problem Does Not Exist in Soviet Society," which featured Stalin's statement: "National and racial chauvinism is a relic of the cannibalistic period, of man's hatred for man" and distinguished between anti-Semitism (ostensibly forbidden) and anti-Zionism (mandatory).[63]

Russification had repercussions in linguistics. In June 1950, Stalin dethroned Marr in a series of articles published in *Pravda* (reprinted as *Marxism and the Problems of Linguistics*) that declared, among other points, that language was a people's heritage, independent of class, hence not part of the superstructure or the base. The dethroning had a racist component. Marr's term *skreshenie* (interbreeding) was neutral; Stalin's term *skreshchevanie* (mongrelization) was derisive. There were other factors, too. Marr's class-based view of language was not suited to the combative nationalism of the Cold War. These articles enabled Stalin, yet again, to demonstrate his omniscience and to elevate the Russian language, once and for all, to paramount status in the Soviet Union.

Nietzsche's description of the Russian Autocracy as the supreme incarnation of the will to power in nineteenth-century Europe (*TI*, 93) was even more applicable to the Soviet Union in Stalin's time. Rather than trumpet their rejection of humane ideals, Stalinists invoked them while carefully concealing the brutal, oppressive nature of their system. For years, "the lie" was triumphant, for no one within the Soviet Union dared to expose it and few had access to contrary information in any case. Outside the Soviet Union, "the lie" was also widely believed. In the aftermath of Khrushchev's "secret speech," the myth began to fade, along with Party control of culture.

63. Louis Rapoport, *Stalin's War Against the Jews* (New York, 1990), 192.

Epilogue: De-Stalinization and the Reemergence of Nietzsche

Well then, where is *your* Kingdom of God? Show it!
Where is the free personality of the superman you
promised?   —Abram Tertz, *On Socialist Realism*

Stalin died on March 5, 1953. A few days later, Stalin's heir apparent, Georgy Malenkov (1902–88), criticized the "cult of personality" (Marx's term, *MER*, 521) at a Central Committee meeting. In April, the "doctor's plot" was exposed as a hoax and amnesties to prisoners began. *Pravda* started using the term "cult of personality" in June, without mentioning Stalin by name. Beria was arrested and executed in July. Systematic de-Stalinization began with Nikita Khrushchev's (1894–1971) "secret speech" to the Twentieth Party Congress on February 23, 1956. He began by saying that after Stalin's death the Central Committee

> began to implement a policy of explaining concisely and consistently that it is impermissible and foreign to the spirit of Marxism-Leninism to elevate one person, to transform him into a superman possessing

supernatural characteristics akin to those of a god. Such a man supposedly knows everything, sees everything, thinks for everyone, can do anything, is infallible in his behavior.

Such a belief about a man, and specifically about Stalin, was cultivated among us for many years.[1]

For the next four hours, Khrushchev exposed Stalin's crimes against "honest Communists," a few of Stalin's errors and lies, and exalted Lenin.

De-Stalinization progressed in fits and starts, with some retreats along the way. Khrushchev's program entailed "goulash communism" (a higher standard of living for the masses), "a return to Leninist norms," and a much diminished reliance on terror. Vladimir Dudintsev was not punished for his attack on bureaucracy in *Not By Bread Alone* (1957), but Boris Pasternak was forbidden to travel to Sweden to accept the Nobel Prize for *Doctor Zhivago* (published in Italy, in 1957). Stalin's remains were removed from Lenin's Tomb after the Twenty-second Party Congress (October 1961), and Stalingrad was renamed Volgograd. Khrushchev intervened personally to allow publication of Aleksandr Solzhenitsyn's *One Day in the Life of Ivan Denisovich* in 1962, but he lambasted Ernst Neizvestnyi's modernistic sculpture. New "antiparasite" laws exiled offenders to remote areas; ostensibly democratic "comrades courts" were sometimes kangaroo courts, and the death penalty was instituted for vaguely defined "economic crimes." Nevertheless, by the time of Khrushchev's downfall (October 1964), the limits of the permissible had been markedly expanded, and he was not purged. Cultural thaw continued—with some re-Stalinization, during the tenures of Leonid Brezhnev (1964–82), Iury Andropov (1982–83), and Konstantin Chernenko (1983–85)—and reached flood tide under Mikhail Gorbachev (1985–91).

Gorbachev (b. 1931) wanted to humanize Marxism, but his reforms set in motion a process that led to the dissolution of the Soviet Union. In 1988, he announced new policies—*perestroika* (reconstruction), *glasnost'* (openness), and *demokratizatsiia*—and called for "new thinking" and filling in the "blank spaces" in Russian history. The latter led to so much confusion that high school history textbooks were recalled and final examinations in history were canceled. Attacks on Stalin expanded to include the hitherto sacrosanct Lenin. Bukharin was rehabilitated, and Russian translations of George Orwell's *1984*, Arthur Koestler's *Darkness At Noon*, Aldous Huxley's *Brave New World*, and Franz Kafka's *The Castle* and *The Trial*—were published legally for the first time.

Contributors to a compendium on the Stalin Cult used terms such as "beyond good and evil," "demonic Übermensch," "super-Borgia in the

---

1. *Khrushchev Speaks*, ed. and trans. Thomas P. Whitney (Ann Arbor, 1963), 207.

Kremlin." "super-Nero," "superman," "myth-creation," "bloody mystery," "super-values"—to describe it in retrospect but no contributor suggested that Nietzschean ideas had informed its construction.[2] An article in *New World* (*Novyi mir*) by Aleksandr Gangnus, blamed Lunacharsky's positivist aesthetics, but said nothing about Nietzsche's input.[3] A. A. Lebedev traced the Stalin Cult to the Bolshevik Left's "religious interpretation of Marxism," mentioning Nietzsche as one of its sources.[4] Both authors emphasized Lenin's and Plekhanov's opposition to God-building and Proletkult, implying thereby that if "real" Marxism had been followed, all would have been well.

By 1990–91, it was clear that Gorbachev's economic and political reforms were not working. The distribution system broke down, the nationalities expressed anti-Russian sentiments, and the Soviet bloc was unraveling. Nationalist intellectuals resented Gorbachev's reforms (even though they benefited from *glasnost'*) and accused him of "criminally" destroying Russian power. In the aftermath of the failed coup of August 1991, Gorbachev was overshadowed by Boris Yeltsin (b. 1931), and the iconoclasm of 1917–18 was replicated all over the Soviet Union and Eastern Europe. The statue of Dzerzhinsky in front of the Moscow headquarters of the KGB was one of the first to be toppled. In December, Gorbachev resigned; the Union Republics declared their independence (most of them joined the Confederation of Independent States), and Yeltsin emerged as Russia's leader. Inflation, unemployment, rampant corruption, and crime eroded his support and fostered the emergence of authoritarian and anti-Western ideologies. Yeltsin resigned in December 1999, naming Vladimir Putin (b. 1952) as his successor.

Khrushchev truly believed in the "radiant future" of communism, hence the gigantic communes and other utopian schemes that contributed to his downfall. During Brezhnev's tenure, the standard of living rose and ideological fervor waned. The government talked about "realized socialism" or "really existing socialism." Refurbishment of the Lenin Cult and an elaborate Cult of the Great Patriotic War, with rituals and monuments, were attempts to fill the gap left by the demise of the Stalin Cult. E. V. Vuchetich's statue "Motherland" in Volgograd (*Rodina-mat'*, 1967), the largest statue in the world, commemorated the fallen in the Battle of Stalingrad. It was unveiled for the fiftieth anniversary of the October Revolution as part of a memorial ensemble that included extensive statuary, a museum, and a park. Holiday parades displayed the latest military hardware, not only to deter foreign invaders but to keep the Soviet population in awe.

2. *Osmyslit' kul't Stalina* (Moscow, 1989); especially L. Gozman and A. Etkind, "Kul't vlasti," 337–71, and B. Oreshin and A. Rubtsov, "Stalinizm: ideologiia i soznanie," 546–609.

3. Aleksandr Gangnus, "Na ruinakh positivnoi esteteki," *Novyi mir*, no. 9 (1988): 147–63.

4. A. A. Lebedev, "Posledniaia religiia," *Voprosy filosofii*, no. 1 (1989): 35–55.

Some Russian intellectuals sought to revitalize Marxism and/or to "reinvent" the national identity; the Party supported these attempts in order to gain a new basis of political legitimacy.[5] Beginning in the 1960s, government-funded new or revived "thick journals" became the venue for an extended debate on cultural issues that was really a debate on political issues. Liberal journals such as *New World* advocated continued de-Stalinization while *Young Guard* (*Molodaia gvardiia*) and other nationalist journals emphasized the impoverishment and demoralization of the peasantry, ecological devastation, the destruction of Russian culture and monuments, and the infiltration of "corrupt" American values. Such complaints pervaded the novels of the "village prose" school, which were printed in hundreds of thousands of copies. Most nationalist intellectuals were rabidly anti-Semitic as well as anti-Western. Dostoevsky was their favorite author.

The reemergence of interest in Nietzsche was related to de-Stalinization (the fading of the myth). Once again, the Party used him as a negative symbol, first of fascism and capitalist imperialism, then as the personification of traits that it, and nationalist intellectuals, wished to combat—individualism, hedonism, moral nihilism, socially irresponsible behavior, and pursuit of self interest. Intellectuals intent on reclaiming their lost cultural heritage discovered the Godseekers and through them, a different Nietzsche, a mystic and a prophet. They began to circulate illegal typewritten copies (*samizdat*) of *Landmarks* in the late 1960s and of Nietzsche's works in the 1970s. A Russian scholar now living in Israel recalled that "everybody" was reading Nietzsche.[6] Rejection of Stalinist solutions to the Nietzschean agenda stimulated a search for fresh solutions to the same issues.

Nietzsche as a Negative Symbol

S. F. Oduev's *The Reactionary Essence of Nietzscheanism* (1959), published in a press run of 4,400 copies, defined the official position on Nietzsche for the Khrushchev years.[7] Couched in Cold War rhetoric, it was intended to enforce ideological conformity and prevent criticism from getting out of hand. The book was translated into Chinese in 1961 for much the same reason; Mao's "hundred flowers" speech (1957) had inspired too much criticism. Stressing the "genetic tie" between Nietzsche and fascism, Oduev

---

5. Yitzhak M. Brudny, *Reinventing Russia: Russian Natinalists and the Soviet State, 1953–1991* (Cambridge, Mass., 1998), esp. 3, 13, 31, 117.

6. Elana Gomel, conversation with author.

7. S. F. Oduev, *Reaktsionnaia suchnost' nitssheanstva* (Moscow, 1959). For details on this and Oduev's *Tropami Zaratustry* (see note 8), see B. G. Rosenthal, "Current Soviet Thought on Nietzsche," in *Nietzsche Heute: Die Rezeption seines Werkes nach 1968*, ed. Sigrid Bauschinger, Susan L. Cocalis, and Sara Lennox (Berne and Stuttgart, 1988), 196–99.

denounced Nietzsche as a philosopher of spiritual corruption and egocentric subjectivism, an unabashed advocate of a barbaric "will to power," "zoological antihumanism," cruelty, militarism, and racism. Nietzsche's social ideal was at once cosmopolitan and racist, a new world order of masters and slaves. Marxists must struggle against Nietzsche's ideas, because they are dangerous.

Oduev's next book on Nietzsche, *In the Footsteps of Zarathustra: The Influence of Nietzsche on German Bourgeois Philosophy* (1971), appeared during Brezhnev's tenure.[8] Published in a press run of 16,000 copies, it treated authors interested in Nietzsche from the late nineteenth-century to the nineteen sixties, claiming that they were attracted to, and perpetuated, the antidemocratic, antisocialist, and antihumanist aspects of his thought. This book was a response to revisionism in Eastern Europe (at a conference in Yugoslavia interest was expressed in combining Nietzsche with Marx), Nietzsche's appeal to the "new left" in the West, and the "denazification of Nietzsche" (ceasing to blame him for Nazism). Oduev called this interest in Nietzsche a "dangerous diversion" from the revolutionary path. In his words, Nietzsche "attracts radicals dissatisfied with capitalism, but ignorant of the causes of the poverty and horror of the capitalist structure." Marxism never expressed any pretension to a Nietzschean "legacy." The "curious" attempt to "merge" Marxism with Nietzscheanism, or to "open" Marxism to Nietzsche "has nothing in common with the revolutionary-critical method of our philosophy. On the contrary" (414–16). A German translation was published in East Berlin in 1977. Soviet histories, encyclopedias, and dictionaries of philosophy routinely associated Nietzsche with the "will to power," irrationalism, nihilism, and individualism (the prime component of Nietzsche's "moral nihilism").[9]

The first comparisons of Nietzsche and Dostoevsky appeared in the 1970s. Literature specialists compared Nietzsche and Dostoevsky, invariably to Nietzsche's detriment. He was the symbol of the amoral, decadent West while Dostoevsky was the exemplar of Russian morality, a view of Dostoevsky that was itself relatively recent.[10] These comparisons were in accord with the Soviet quest for a specifically socialist morality of everyday life, as part of a larger quest for a humane Marxism. If people internalized socialist val-

---

8. S. F. Oduev, *Tropami Zaratustry (Vlianie nitssheanstva na nemetskiiu burzhuaznuiu filosofiiu)* (Moscow, 1971).

9. A. S. Bogomolov, *Nemetskaia burzhuaznaia filosofiia posle 1865* (Moscow, 1969); T. I. Shvartz, *Ot Shopengaura k Kheideggeru* (Moscow, 1964); *Istoriia filosofii*, vol. 3 (Moscow, 1959), 356–60; I. E. Vertsmen, "Nitsshe i ego nasledniki," *Voprosy literatury*, no. 7 (1962): 49–73; "Nitsshe," in *Filosofskaia entsiklopediia*, vol. 4 (Moscow, 1967), 75–77; and "Nitsshe," in *Entsiklopedicheskii slovar'* (Moscow, 1983), 437.

10. See Vl. Seduro, *Dostoevsky in Russian Literary Criticism* (New York, 1955), and idem, *Dostoevsky's Image in Russia Today* (Belmont, Mass., 1975).

ues, fear could be reduced, or even eliminated, as an instrument of social control. The Twenty-second Party Congress (1961) had adopted a "moral code of the builders of communism" that placed devotion to the communist cause first and emphasized duty to society and self-discipline.[11] The comparisons of Nietzsche and Dostoevsky were also a reaction to Kaufmann's "soft" interpretation of Nietzsche, to existentialism, and to the founding of *Nietzsche Studien* in West Germany, in 1972.[12]

The next round of comparisons drew on the Colli and Montinari *Critical Edition*. The unpublished fragments published in volume 8, parts 2 and 3, show that Dostoevsky's influence on Nietzsche was much greater than previously thought. In addition to *Notes From the House of the Dead* and *Notes From Underground,* to which Nietzsche alluded in his published writings, Nietzsche also read and took copious notes on *The Possessed,* and he knew about *The Idiot* and *Crime and Punishment,* possibly from Lou Salome or Malwida von Meysenbug who read Russian.

Iury Davydov's book *The Ethic of Love and the Metaphysics of Self Will* (1982), published in 50,000 copies by the nationalist journal *Young Guard,* treated Nietzsche and the existentialists as embodiments of the aesthetic nihilism of the bourgeois West, and Tolstoy and Dostoevsky as personifications of the profound moral striving of the Russian people. The heart of Davydov's book is Nietzsche contra Dostoevsky. Using the fragments as evidence, Davydov argued that Nietzsche utilized Dostoevsky's psychological insights to crystallize his own worldview, which was the polar opposite of Dostoevsky's.[13] Nietzsche advocated the amoral Renaissance ideal of self-fulfillment and personal happiness; Dostoevsky stressed duty to others.[14]

Davydov's book was attacked by R. Petropavlovsky, editor of *Kommunist,* the Party's theoretical journal, who objected to Davydov's argument that morality stems from religion, not class interest.[15] Nevertheless, Davydov's

11. James P. Scanlan, "Philosophy of Morality," in *Marxism in the USSR* (Ithaca, 1985), 265–92.

12. See, for example, A. N. Latyna, "Dostoevskii i ekzistentsializm," in *Dostoevskii: khudozhnik i myslitel': sbornik statei,* ed. K. L. Lomunov (Moscow, 1972), 210–59, and V. V. Dudkin and K. M. Azadovskii, "Problema 'Dostoevskii—Nitsshe,'" in *Literaturnoe nasledstvo,* vol. 86, *Dostoevskii: Novye materialy i issledovanie* (Moscow, 1973), 678–88.

13. Iurii Davydov, *Etika liubvi i metafizika svoevolia (Problemy nravstvennoi filosofii)* (Moscow, 1982).

14. Details in Rosenthal, "Current Soviet Thought," 199–204. See also Renata Gal'steva, "Problemy nigilizma v zapadnoi kul'turologii poslednikh let," in *Obshchestvo. Kul'tura. Filosofiia* (Moscow, 1983), 158–200, and V. V. Vivikhin, "Problema nigilizma v zapadnoi kul'turologii poslednikh let," ibid., 222–59. For a later polarization of Dostoevsky and Nietzsche that idealizes Dostoevsky on different grounds, see Assen Ignatov, "Chert i sverkhchelovek: Predchuvstvie totalitarizma Dostoevskim i Nitsshe," *Voprosy filosofii,* no. 4 (1993): 35–46.

15. R. Petropavlovskii, "Po povodu odnoi knigi," *Kommunist,* no. 8 (1983): 102–14. Davydov's statement is on page 7 of the 1982 edition and page 12 of the expanded edition.

treatment of Nietzsche and Dostoevsky, absent the homage to religious ideals and values, resembled that of other Soviet writers whose views achieved quasi-official status, such as Georgy Fridlander, whose *Dostoevsky and World Literature* (1985) won the State Prize in 1983, two years before it was published.[16] An expanded edition of Davydov's book appeared in 1989, in a press run of 65,000 copies. At the conference on Nietzsche and Soviet Culture (Fordham University, June 1988), Davydov claimed that Nietzsche's influence in Russia was totally negative and blamed Nietzsche for creating a "work aesthetic" rather than the "work ethic" Russia needs. In 1989, he called Nietzsche's influence on the Russian literary process a "family secret."[17]

What Davydov and other Soviet scholars did not say about Nietzsche was as important as what they did say, because Nietzsche's works were still unavailable to ordinary people. Their writings helped legitimate academic study of Nietzsche, however, and sparked the interest of a new generation of Russians, partly because of the lure of forbidden fruit.

The Discovery of a Different Nietzsche

By the 1980s, symbolism and God-seeking were in vogue, and a religious revival was under way. Intellectuals read symbolist poetry for its spiritual content and not simply because Bely and Blok "accepted" the Revolution. Symbolist themes are obvious in Tengiz Abuladze's *Repentance* (1984), a film about a hybrid Stalin/Mussolini/Hitler and a victim's daughter who refuses to let the dead dictator rest in peace, and in the films of Andrei Tarkovsky, who approvingly quotes Merezhkovsky, Ivanov, and Florensky in his essays.[18] His film, *The Sacrifice* (1986), includes a discussion about Leonardo da Vinci and Nietzsche. Some authors stressed Nietzsche's influence on God-seeking in order to discredit the contemporary religious revival. Examples include N. S. Semenkin's *The Philosophy of God-seeking (Critique of the Religious-Philosophic Ideas of the Sophiologists)* (1986) and S. N. Saveliev's *The Ideological Bankruptcy of Godseeking in Russia at the Beginning of the 20th Century* (1987).[19] Such attacks had the contrary effect of increasing interest in Nietzsche.

A booklet addressed to academic specialists, *Contemporary Investigations of the Philosophy of Nietzsche Abroad* (1984), published by the Soviet

16. Georgii Fridlander, *Dostoevskii i mirovaia literatura* (Leningrad, 1985).
17. "Dialog nedeli," Nikolai Anastasiev—Iurii Davidov, "Liubov k 'blizhnemu' ili 'dal'nemy'?" *Literaturnaia gazeta*, February 22, 1989.
18. Andrei Tarkovsky, *Sculpting in Time* (New York, 1987), 47, 56, 82.
19. N. S. Semenkin, *Filosofiia bogoiskatel'stva (kritika religiozno-filosofskikh idei sofiologov)* (Moscow, 1986); S. N. Savel'ev, *Ideinoe bankrotstvo bogoiskat'elstva v Rossii, v nachale xx veka* (Leningrad, 1987).

Academy of Sciences, in a press run of 1,000 copies, provided a straightforward review of Nietzsche scholarship in the United States, Western Europe,
and Eastern Europe since the 1970s. The author, I. S. Andreev, summarized
new developments in Nietzsche interpretation, including new understandings of the "will to power" and new perceptions of Nietzsche as a meta-
physician, a "metahumanist," a moralist, and a philosopher of history.
Andreev explained renewed interest in Nietzsche in the West as a product
of the crisis of knowledge in the bourgeois world and existentialism as an
attempt to confront nihilism.[20] Many Western scholars, Marxists or not,
would agree.

In 1988, plans for a forty-volume series, *From the History of National
Philosophic Thought,* were announced for publication as supplements to the
journal *Problems of Philosophy* (*Voprosy filosofii*). Included in this series
were Soloviev, Berdiaev, Frank, Rozanov, Shestov, and Florensky. Neutral
and hagiographical articles about the Godseekers appeared in philosophy
and literature journals. *Doctor Zhivago* was published legally, and Dudintsev's
novel *White Robes* (*Belye odezhdy*), about Lysenkoist persecution of geneticists, won the State Prize. Private publishing cooperatives, legalized in 1990,
brought out works by previously banned authors. Merezhkovsky was rehabilitated in 1991 and the subject of an international conference at the Gorky
Institute.[21] Conferences were also held on Fedorov, Viacheslav Ivanov, the
acmeist poets, and other luminaries of the Silver Age and early Soviet period.

Publication of Nietzsche's writings began in 1989. *The Antichrist* was
included in a compendium titled *Twilight of the Gods* (*Sumerki bogov,* 1989),
along with Sigmund Freud's *The Future of an Illusion,* Erich Fromm's
"Psychoanalysis and Religion," Albert Camus's "The Myth of Sisyphus,"
and Jean Paul Sartre's "Existentialism is a Humanism." Excerpts from *Beyond
Good and Evil* were published in *Problems of Philosophy* (1989) in a printing of over 80,000 copies—almost three times as large as the 35,000 copies
of the Soloviev and Berdiaev supplements.

Nietzsche, Collected Works (2 vols., 1990), published in a press run of
100,000 copies, sold out almost immediately, as did a second press run of
100,000 copies. The editor, K. A. Sviasian, titled his introduction "Friedrich
Nietzsche: A Martyr for Knowledge." Challenging Nazi (and Soviet) readings of Nietzsche, Sviasian disassociated him from pan-Germanism, anti-
Semitism (he quoted Nietzsche's pro-Jewish statements), and slavophobia.
Comparing the search for the real Nietzsche to the search for Ariadne's
thread, Sviasian described the struggle for control of the Nietzsche archive

20. *Sovremennye zarubezhnye issledovaniia filosofii Nitsshe. naucho-analiticheskii obzor*
(Moscow, 1984). See also I. A. Gobozov, "Istoriia filosofii v interpetatsii 'novykh filoso-
fov,'" *Nauch. dokl. vysh. shk. filos. nauki,* no. 6 (1981): 65–73.
21. The conference volume is titled *D. S. Merezhkovskii: Mysl' i slovo,* ed. V. A. Keldysh,
I. V. Koretskaia, and M. A. Nikitina (Moscow, 1999).

and Nietzsche's sister's misuse of her control, an elliptical allusion to the closing of the Nietzsche archive in Weimar, in East Germany. "At last," Sviasian wrote, Russians can read Nietzsche for themselves. He is no longer "doomed to a piratical existence between the closed stacks [*spetskhram*] and the black market."[22] Sviasian also treated Bertram's "biomyth" of Nietzsche, its role in the "cultural canonization of Nietzsche in Germany," and the "deeply symbolic significance" of that canonization. A review in *Problems of Philosophy* hailed Sviasian's work as "an important cultural event," called Nietzsche a great stylist, and referred to the "magic" of his text and the "labyrinth" of his thought (hence the need for Ariadne's thread).[23]

In 1991, a new translation of *Dawn* was published in a press run of 100,000 copies. In his afterword, "What Did Nietzsche Really Say?" the editor, A. V. Pertsev, emphasized Nietzsche's early works and declared that people who never read Nietzsche spread propagandistic clichés about him as the "spiritual father" of Nazism and, more recently, as the corrupter of the *narod*. The Nazis also appropriated Kant, Fichte, and Hegel, Pertsev pointed out, but Soviet historians of philosophy could not "give" them to the fascists, because they would be condemning an important source of Marxism. So they concentrated their fire on Nietzsche.[24]

By 1991 reprints of prerevolutionary translations of *Zarathustra,* some of dubious quality, were widely available, as were Russian translations of Jacques Derrida, Michel Foucault, and Martin Heidegger. On the popular level, the vogue of Nietzsche died down after a year or two, but serious Nietzsche scholarship continued. Valery Podoroga's *The Metaphysics of the Landscape: Kierkegaard, Nietzsche, Heidegger* (1993) is one example. Apropos of the Dionysianism that seems to follow the death of a myth, Podoroga talks about a "Dionysian body," but says nothing about an "Apollonian body."[25] In 1997, the journal *Philosophical Sciences* (*Filosofskie nauki*) brought out "On Truth and Lie in an Extra-Moral Sense." Participants in a conference of "Nietzsche and European Thought," held at the European University in St. Petersburg in June 2001, tried to find common ground for a pan-European discourse on Nietzsche as a possible source for a pan-European identity. Russian scholars' investigations of Nietzsche's influence in their own country have concentrated on the first stage (1890–1917).[26]

22. *Nitsshe: Sochineniia,* 2 vols., ed. K. A. Sviasian (Moscow, 1990), 1:45.
23. A. A. Lavrova, "Kritika i bibliografiia," *Voprosy filosofii,* 1991, no. 3:187–89.
24. A. V. Pertsev, "Chto deistvitel'no govoril Nitsshe?" in *Fridrikh Nitsshe, Utrenniaia zaria* (Moscow, 1991), 291–94.
25. Valentin Podoroga, *Metafizika landshafta* (Moscow, 1993), 173–206
26. See, for example, R. Iu. Danilevskii, "K istorii vospriiatiia F. Nitsshe v Rossii," *Russkaia literatura,* no. 4 (1988): 232–39; idem, "Russkii obraz Fridrikha Nitsshe (Predystoriia i nachalo formirovaniia)," in *Na rubezhe xix i xx vekov* (Moscow, 1991), 5–43; and in the same volume, Marina Koreneva, "Merezhkovskii i nemetskaia kul'tura (Nitsshe i Gete. Pretiazhenie i ottalkivanie)," 44–76. The most important compendiums are *Fridrikh Nitsshe*

The Nietzschean Agenda

In the course of de-Stalinization, the items on the Nietzschean agenda were returned to the table, so to speak. To date, no generally accepted solution to any one of them is in sight.

The New Myth

The myth of the radiant communist future seems dead. A possible replacement is "the Russian Idea," a concept that counterposes Russian spirituality to Western materialism and Russian communalism to Western individualism. There are several variants. The Orthodox one idealizes old Russia and early twentieth-century religious philosophers, especially Berdiaev and Florensky, who have become cult figures. Nationalists emphasize the importance of the Orthodox Church in medieval Russia and the Church's role in ending the Time of Troubles. Gennady Ziuganov (b. 1944), leader of the Communist Party, urged his comrades to resurrect the "Russian idea." James Scanlan contends that Ziuganov and like-minded Communists "are completing the Russification of Marxism."[27]

Neo-Eurasians view religion in terms of a national-cultural "ethnos" that is biological or even racial in character, and contains cosmic energies. A young "ethnos" manifests its spiritual identity in an unprecedented outburst of creative energy that Lev Gumilev (1912–92) called *passionarnost'* (passionateness or innate drive), as opposed to the "sensible" instinct of self-preservation. "Passionateness" is not a synonym for Dionysianism but the concepts have much in common, for the original Eurasians rejected (Western) rationalism and their doctrine had Nietzschean components. Gumilev also held that to overcome its spiritual crisis, Russia needed a "passionary," roughly a charismatic leader, and an ideocratic or theocratic society. His version of the "Russian Idea," which has strong Asian and anti-Semitic elements, became widely known in the late 1980s, thanks to *glasnost'*.

Aleksandr Dugin (b. 1962), author and publisher, became the leading exponent of Eurasianism after Gumilev died. Dugin's occult Eurasianism features Ariosophy (Aryan Theosophy), "sacred geography" (geopolitics), conspiracy theory (*Konspirologiia*), and elitism. He views world history as an eternal struggle between continental and island peoples (the Jews are an island people). In its current phase, the struggle is between Eurasian and Atlantic powers, led by the United States, which is supposedly controlled by

---

i russkaia religioznaia filosofiia, ed. Inna Boiskaia (Minsk, 1993); F. *Nitsshe i filosofiia v Rossii*, ed. N. V. Motroshilova and Iulia V. Sineokaia (St. Petersburg, 1999); and *Nietzsche, Pro et Contra*, ed. Iulia Sineokaia (St. Petersburg, 2001).

27. James P. Scanlan, "The Russian Idea from Dostoevskii to Ziuganov," *Problems of Post-Communism* 43, no. 4 (July–August 1996): 35.

Jews. An admirer of Stalin, Mussolini, and Hitler, Dugin envisions a Eurasian empire dominated by Russia and Germany that stretches from Dublin (!) to Vladivostok and from the Arctic Ocean to the Indian Ocean.[28]

A misquotation from Nietzsche is the epigraph for an article published in Dugin's journal, *Elements: A Eurasian Survey,* about the Hyperboreans, who lived (according to Greek legend) beyond the north wind in a land of perpetual sunshine. Apollo was a Hyperborean. The epigraph, in old German script is "Beyond the north, the ice, today beyond death, out of the way, is our life our happiness. 'Neither by land or by sea will you find the way to the Hyperboreans'—so said a wise mind. F. Nietzsche."[29] The correct quotation is: "Let us look one another in the face. We are Hyperboreans—we know well enough how much out of the way we live. 'Neither by land nor by sea shalt thou find the road to the Hyperboreans': Pindar already knew that of us. Beyond the North, beyond the ice, beyond death—*our* life, *our* happiness" (*AC,* 115; *KSA,* 6:169). For Dugin and his confreres, Russia is not "out of the way" but the heartland of the world.

Dugin calls himself a "conservative revolutionary" and a "national Bolshevik" and praises Spengler, Othmar Spann, Werner Sombart, and Carl Schmitt as the luminaries of the German "conservative revolution." An article about fascist style, also published in *Elements,* emphasized "coldness" (which goes with hardness), aggressiveness, indifference to death, and rejection of liberal humanism, giving Marinetti, Benn, Jünger, D'Annunzio, Gumilev, Mayakovsky, and the painter Pavel Filonov (1883–1941) as examples of fascist style.[30]

The New Art Form

The first major critique of Socialist Realism, Sinyavsky's *On Socialist Realism* (1959), was published in Paris under a pseudonym, Abram Tertz. The author advocated a phantasmogorical literature that will teach people to be truthful with the aid of the fantastic because he feared that realism with its cursed questions, "Who Is to Blame?" (Herzen's novel, 1840) and "What Is To Be Done?" would lead to a new orthodoxy that disregards truth in favor of preaching and subordinates both art and life to some higher purpose (a concept similar to the "future-orientation" George Kline talks about). Sinyavsky wanted fantasy to be recognized as such, not passed off as reality; he insisted on separating art and life.

28. Interview, with Aleksandr Dugin, *Knizhnoe obozrenie*, October 10, 1995, 22–23; Walter Lacquer, *Black Hundred* (New York, 1993), 138–42; Rosenthal, "Political Implications," in Rosenthal, *Occult*, 414–16.

29. Aleksandr Dugin and Evgenii Golovin, conversation, "V poiskakh vechnogo norda," *Elementy*, no. 5 (1994): 48.

30. N. Melentiev, "Fashizm kak 'stil,'" *Elementy*, no. 4 (1993): 55–61.

Jabs against Socialist Realism abound in late Soviet literature. In Fazil Iskander's fable *Rabbits and Boa-Constrictors* (1988), a replica of a large cauliflower, a metaphor for Socialist Realism, hangs over the rabbit-king's throne and becomes ever more colorful as the condition of the rabbits worsens.

For some writers, "truthfulness" (Zarathustra's highest virtue) was the salvific "new word." In Aleksandr Zinoviev's novel *The Yawning Heights* (1976), the character Chatterer (the author's voice) concludes that "truth" is the foundation of any truly human experience. "When people achieve a certain minimum level of truthfulness, they will advance other criteria. But everything begins from there."[31] The hero of Iury Trifonov's novel *The House on the Embankment* (1976) is convinced that the ability to betray is closely linked with the willingness to forget, ignore, or distort the past, so he searches for the "threads of history." Some late Soviet partisans of "truthfulness" stressed the mutability and indeterminacy of language as one element in a pluralistic open-ended worldview that is resolutely antimythological. Aleksandr Solzhenitsyn upheld "truth" in the Christian sense ("You shall know the truth and the truth shall make you free") and urged writers to "VANQUISH LIES! [*POBEDIT' LOZH'!*]. In the struggle against lies, art has always won and will win."[32]

Disenchantment with Socialist Realism led to a reexamination of Gorky that included publication of previously unknown writings and letters, republication of *Untimely Thoughts* (1917–18), and scathing attacks on him.[33] In *Rabbits and Boa-Constrictors,* a Gorky-type character is tempted by fame and wealth. In Vladimir Voinovich's novel *Moscow 2042* (1987) the poet Kartsev (= Gorky) returns from abroad to find himself a cult figure, but he must rewrite his novels to make them politically correct.

Russian postmodernist writers tend to favor horizontal rather than vertical metaphors ("Ever higher!") or nonlinear plots that involve time travel, or multiple perspectives on an event, or issues that remained unresolved, and depict an unreal or an absurd world, a world in chaos. Wary of the very notion of an absolute truth, they treat words and ideas as devices and play with them. They appreciate authors whose works were banned for much of the Soviet period, such as Rozanov, Bakhtin, Mikhail Bulgakov (author of *Heart of a Dog* and *The Master and Margarita*), and Daniil Kharms, an associate of *Oberiu,* the last avant-garde group. Sotsart painters deconstruct, trivialize, or hyperbolize Socialist Realism, which they perceive "not only in its direct meaning as the aesthetic code of the 'ideology in power' but also

---

31. Aleksandr Zinoviev, *The Yawning Heights* (New York, 1979), 828.

32. Alexander Solzhenitsyn, *Nobel Lecture* (New York, 1971), 33. He was not allowed to go to Stockholm to give the lecture in person.

33. Details in Andrew Barratt and Edith Clowes, "Gor'ky, *Glasnost'* and *Perestroika:* The Death of a Cultural Superhero?" *Soviet Studies* 43, no. 6 (1991): 1123–42.

in its delegitimized form, as a special kind of *world of the absurd,* a language of total metaphysical simulation."[34]

The New Word

The demise of Sovietese left a vacuum that was filled, in part, by religious and nationalistic terminology and by Western terms such as "human rights" and "totalitarianism," a word out of fashion in Western scholarship. During Gorbachev's tenure, "left" and "right" were reversed; the "left" wanted market reforms and the "right" wanted a controlled economy. Catchwords and slogans of the Soviet era such as "Man," "stormy" and "storminess" (from Gorky's "Song of the Stormy Petrel"), "the madness of the brave" and "ever higher," were discarded or mocked. In *The Yawning Heights,* the epitaph on the coffin of a cadet who parachuted and died from terror in midair, is "Let us sing the glory of the foolhardiness of the bold."[35] Zinoviev's Chatterer argues that the logical assumptions underlying existing language need to be reexamined, because contemporary language is hackneyed and rigid. Sinyavsky, Liudmila Petroshevskaia, Zinoviev, Venedikt and Vladimir Erofeev, Voinovich, Vasily Aksionov, Iskander, and Solzhenitsyn all pay considerable attention to the issue of language.[36] Solzhenitsyn denounced the use of foreign words and turned to Vladimir Dahl's nineteenth-century dictionary to revitalize contemporary Russian. In *One Day in the Life of Ivan Denisovich,* Solzhenitsyn used prison-camp slang and was criticized for his crudeness.

In some late Soviet fiction, the words "excrement" or "shit" are frequently repeated in a conscious response to the pedantic hyperbole of Socialist Realism and its lofty characters who seem to have no bodily functions. The planners of Zinoviev's utopian city of Ibansk (from the Russian word for "fuck") did not include toilets. The residents must turn in their "secondary product" (excrement) to get food, which is made out of the very same "secondary product." In *Moscow 2042,* excrement is exchanged for a ration card, and the food smells like excrement. This may be an allusion to the "night-soil brigades" of Communist China, which Russians knew about. (Chinese peasants had to save their excrement and spread it on the fields for fertilizer in a cycle of excrement/food/excrement.) Zinoviev and Voinovich simply left out the middle stage. Nietzsche is another possible source: "The world . . . lives on itself. Its excrements are its food" (*WP,* 548).

---

34. Mark Lipovetsky, *Russian Postmodernist Fiction: Dialogue with Chaos,* ed. Eliot Borenstein (Armonk, N.Y., 1999), esp. 182.

35. Zinoviev, *Yawning Heights,* 125. For a spoof of Mayakovsky's "Left March," see 413–14, and 418.

36. For a discussion of the language issue, see Edith Clowes, "The Metautopian Language Problem," in *Russian Experimental Fiction: Resisting Ideology After Utopia* (Princeton, 1993), 94–121.

The New Man (and Woman)

The "new Soviet man" became a joke. Aksionov's novel *The Burn* (1980) includes a spoof on the pilot hero "Airplane Airplanovich Chkalov." In *Moscow 2042,* the chapter titled "Supey" (Supik in Russian) is about an "edited Superman," created by a committee, who is neither male nor female, but not a hermaphrodite either. Originally Supey had a

> perfect physique and his inward development was equally harmonious. He was capable of both physical and intellectual labor. He could perform the most complex mathematical calculations in his head, wrote stunning poetry, composed music of genius and his painting had been snapped up by the best museums in the Third Ring. He performed miracles of athletics, could press over eight hundred pounds, run the hundred meters in 8.8 seconds, and could beat any heavyweight in the world (though he would do it only on points since he was an extremely kind person).

All activities required the approval of a Commission, so Supey's creator presented him to it. "[He] lifted record-breaking weights, repaired the broken watch of one committee member, shot a hundred bull's eyes out of a hundred shots with a pistol, proved Gauss's theorem, played Beethoven's "Appassionata" [one of Lenin's favorite pieces] on the piano, read a passage from the *Iliad* in ancient Greek and the entire *Communist Manifesto* in German." But the Chairperson had nodded off and the committee members began making minor adjustments, in the course of which they castrated Supey![37] Another example of a failed Superman is in *The Yawning Heights:* "The individual who appeared was a head taller than a man, but he had a tiny little head (or none at all) and a heart which was empty (or made of stone)."[38]

In *Strolls with Pushkin* (1975), Sinyavsky dichotomized Pushkin the man and Pushkin the poet, and set up a polarity between the cultic Pushkin and the Pushkin of jokes and popular sayings. The text of "The Bronze Horseman" (Falconet's statue of Peter the Great) belongs to Apollo; Dionysus is his flip side, the "sun-bearing god of Poetry . . . its creative lining." Evgeny (the clerk-victim of "The Bronze Horseman") is an "emanation" or "excretion" of Pushkin's human side.[39] The émigré community denounced *Strolls with Pushkin* as an attack on Pushkin when the book came out, and it provoked a political uproar, for the same reason, when it was published in the Soviet

37. Vladimir Voinovich, *Moscow 2042,* trans. Richard Lourie (New York, 1990), 323–24. For Lenin's response to the "Apassionata," see Bertram Wolfe, *Three Who Made a Revolution* (Boston, 1957), 500.
38. Zinoviev, *Yawning Heights,* 205.
39. Andrei Sinyavsky, *Strolls with Pushkin,* trans. Catherine Nepomiashchy (New Haven, 1993), 126–27. See also idem, *The Poetics of Crime: An Approach to the Writings of Abram Tertz* (New Haven, 1995)

Union in 1989. The "strolling" metaphor contradicts the purposefulness extolled by Socialist Realism.

No generally accepted image of post-Soviet man (or woman) has emerged. Orthodox Christians praise the kenotic virtues and condemn materialism and self-interest. Nationalists uphold a warrior ideal, which includes self-sacrifice and disdain for comfort and material well-being. Nationalist and religious circles extol woman's traditional role as mother and stay-at-home wife and advocate large families. They oppose birth control and want to recriminalize abortion, which was legalized in 1955. Viktor Erofeev's novel *Russian Beauty* (1990) spoofed romantic and Soviet ideals of women; the heroine is sensuous, amoral, bisexual, and ultra-materialistic.

The New Morality

Negative references to Nietzsche recur in discussions of morality. Leonid Soshnin, protagonist of Viktor Astafiev's short story "The Sad Detective" (1986), reads Nietzsche to learn about the evil in human nature, for he must deal with the "lower depths" of Russian society.[40] A reviewer described Soshnin as one "who has even read Nietzsche and a good deal else [and] allows himself the tone of a Slavic Superman."[41] In Zinoviev's novel *The Radiant Future* (1980), the character Anton maintains that "Russian tragedy, and the way in which it is received, lies beyond good and evil, outside the sphere of morality. It is a purely psychological, or indeed physiological reaction to a terrible fact . . . for most of us the moral sense does not exist." Another character, Nameless (a Soviet Everyman), says that he would rather stay among the victims than accept a paradise on earth "built on the blood of victims, on falsehood and oppression." Like Ivan Karamazov, he "returns the ticket." Nameless believes that "a victim is forgiven all his sins. To be a victim means to start becoming a man" (an implicit restoration of the kenotic ideal). This character is sure of only one thing: "Everything that is bestial comes from nature; everything that is human comes from God, that is, it has been invented."[42] Some people yearn for a Christian morality of love, but how to implement it remains elusive.

The New Politics

The collapse of communism was expected to empower the masses, bring prosperity, and make Russia into a "normal society." Instead, Russians got crony capitalism, runaway inflation, and a powerful mafia. Advocates of "the Russian Idea" used these developments to claim that they had been

---

40. Viktor Astafiev, "Pechal'nyi detektiv," *Oktiabr'*, 1986, no. 1:27.

41. Quoted in Kathleen Parthe, *Russian Village Prose: The Radiant Past* (Princeton, 1992), 95.

42. Alexander Zinoviev, *The Radiant Future* (New York, 1980), 95, 110–11.

right all along; Western institutions and values are unsuited to Russia. Some people yearn for an iron hand to restore order and to reinstate Russia's great power status. They may have it in Putin.

The New Science

To date, there is no "new science." Indeed there is very little talk about science at all, even a certain antipathy to it, partly because Communism claimed to be scientific. Serious research has been severely impeded by deep cuts in government funding. Paradoxically, the exposure of the mythological aspects of Stalinism fostered an interest in Orthodox mysticism, in occult doctrines, and in Western philosophers who debunk or deconstruct the Enlightenment, such as Heidegger and the French poststructuralists. Distinctively Russian interpretations of their thought have emerged but to describe them would require another book.

To predict the impact of Nietzsche on the future course of Russian politics and culture would be presumptuous and premature. All we can say is that one phase of Nietzsche reception has ended and another has begun. His thought frames a cultural cycle, from the fading of the dominant myth in the 1890s, to the establishment of a new myth in Stalin's time, to the fading of that myth after Stalin's death. The Dionysian impulse (disintegration, deconstruction, elemental revolt) predominated before and during the Bolshevik Revolution. A shift to the Apollonian—form, structure, reintegration around a new myth—began around 1920, was interrupted and reversed by the Cultural Revolution (1928–31), resumed in 1931, and triumphed in 1934, the date of the first Congress of the Union of Soviet Writers, which marked the establishment of an official aesthetic and the fusion of art and politics. Deconstruction of the Stalinist synthesis began around 1956, accelerated in the 1980s, and culminated in the collapse of the Soviet Union. Sinyavsky's observation still applies:

> After the death of Stalin we entered upon a period of destruction and re-evaluation. It is a slow and inconsistent process, it lacks perspective, and the inertia of both past and future lie heavy on it. Today's children will scarcely be able to produce a new God, capable of inspiring humanity into the next historical cycle. Maybe He will have to be supplemented by other stakes of the Inquisition, by further "personality cults," and by new terrestrial labors, so that after many centuries a new Purpose will rise above the world. But today no one yet knows its name.[43]

43. Abram Tertz [Andrei Sinyavsky], *On Socialist Realism*, intro. Czeslaw Milosz, trans. George Dennis (New York, 1960), 217.

Index